The Cassell
Dictionary of Appropriate
Adjectives

The Cassell Dictionary of Appropriate Adjectives

E. H. Mikhail

CASSELL

Cassell
Villiers House, 41/47 Strand
London WC2N 5JE, England

© E. H. Mikhail 1994

First published 1994

British Library Cataloguing in Publication Data
A catalogue entry for this book is available from the British Library.

ISBN 0-304-34298-X

Printed and bound in Great Britain by Mackays of Chatham PLC

1000144973

CONTENTS

PREFACE

Why a dictionary of adjectives?

It seems surprising that while there are dozens of thesauruses and dictionaries of synonyms, there is not a single dictionary that helps a reader find an appropriate adjective. Not that one wishes by this remark to depreciate the labours of those who have produced such useful works, but simply to assign it as a reason why the time is certainly appropriate to come forward with an attempt to fill up what is obviously and curiously a chasm in reference books. Using this book as a starting point, to be followed up if need be by consulting a conventional dictionary, a writer now does not have to fumble for an appropriate adjective equal to the occasion, and can avoid the use of the same hackneyed, tired adjectives over and over again. Among other uses for this Dictionary:

(a) to find an *exact* adjective that describes a certain noun. For example the user might be looking for the *specific* adjective that describes, say, material which is able to decompose chemically (i.e. *degradable*); an appetite that follows a meal (i.e. *postprandial*); a leader who is the opposite of spiritual (i.e. *secular*); or a cross that is worn on the chest (i.e. *pectoral*). Writers who find themselves in such a situation can easily look for the correct adjective listed under the noun modified.

(b) to find the *technical* adjective that describes something, such as an arch (*rounded, scalloped, corbelled*, etc.); industry (*primary, secondary, tertiary*); consonants (*guttural, cacuminal, palatal*, etc.); herbs (*antispasmodic, aperient, carminative*, etc.); or democracy (*representative, multiparty, pluralistic*, etc.).

(c) to find — at an academically more specialized level — the appropriate *classical* or *mythological* adjective that describes something, e.g. *Pyrrhic* victory; *Daedalian* plot; *Orphic* mystery; *Ciceronian* eloquence; *Spartan* endurance.

(d) to find the appropriate adjective that applies to a certain animal, e.g. *babbling* monkey; *grunting* pig; *cooing* pigeon; *hissing* snake.

About this dictionary

Only words that are listed in standard language dictionaries as adjectives are included in this Dictionary. Thus all other etymological forms, such as participles ending in -ed (*rejected* offer) or -ing (*playing* child), are excluded. However, some words ending in -ed or -ing are legitimate adjectives, e.g. *protected* forest, *money-losing* company. Also included are nouns used idiomatically as adjectives, e.g. *blood* money, *crocodile* tears. These adjectives are usually listed at the end of the entry, together with technical adjectives (e.g. *ecumenical* service, *disepalous* plant, *periodontal* disease). At the very end of some entries, separated by one or more semicolons, come adjectives referring to a specialized sense of the headword (e.g. *military* muscle, *animal* kingdom).

The common adjectives *good* and *bad* are included only when they give precise information, e.g. a *good* share, i.e. fairly great in amount; *good* weather, i.e. appropriate or satisfactory for a specific purpose, such as flying.

All adjectives are listed under headings which are arranged in alphabetical order according to the *singular* form. Thus a reader looking for an adjective to describe teeth should search for it under the entry *tooth*. Likewise, a user looking for an adjective to describe less common nouns should look for it under *more common* ones, e.g. for boutique see *shop*, for boulevard see *street*, for pound see *currency*, for waltz see *dance*, for brooch see *jewel*.

Dictionary of Appropriate Adjectives

abandon all-out, frenzied, ecstatic, hectic, rapturous, zealous, berserk, crazy, reckless, wild, lewd, lubricious, orgiastic, alarming, devil-may-care, total, athletic

abandonment total, utter, complete, absolute, permanent, slow, sudden, wild, overpowering, reckless, careless, undeserved, inevitable, unavoidable

abdomen, abdomens See *belly*

abhorrence, abhorrences See *hate*

ability, abilities deft, consummate, outstanding, exceptional, amazing, striking, astounding, astonishing, extraordinary, unparalleled, unmatched, unequalled, undeniable, unquestionable, undoubted, all-important, impressive, magnificent, superb, remarkable, enduring, prodigious, tireless, enormous, marked, noticeable, conspicuous, distinguished, (un)limited, soaring, legendary, formidable, flawless, informed, (un)canny, marginal, disconcerting, short-term, medium-term, long-term, mediocre, fair, moderate, acquired, new-found, proven, native, natural, innate, inborn, latent, cognitive, spacial, visual, verbal, putative, defective, fictive, creative, histrionic, academic, scholastic, linguistic, descriptive, analytical, communicative, administrative, imagistic, physical, mental, sensory, technical, decision-making

abnormality, abnormalities (un)common, rare, queer, peculiar, bizarre, grotesque, gross, serious, distinctive, characteristic, insidious, fatal, physical, physiological, metabolic, anatomical, mental

abode, abodes See *home*

abolition, abolitions (un)justifiable, (in)excusable, (il)legal, total, partial, immediate, sudden, quick, gradual, (un)expected, (un)warranted, unprecedented

abortion, abortions (il)legal, (il)licit, (un)obtainable, (in)accessible, (un)available, (un)safe, easy, difficult, casual, self-induced, back-alley, backstreet, sleazy, risky, dangerous, spontaneous, painful, commonplace, punishable, sex-selective, compulsory, therapeutic, surgical

abscess, abscesses apical, swollen, painful, painless, acute, chronic, superficial, internal

absence sore, gross, striking, surprising, obvious, noticeable, notable, (in)conspicuous, (un)intentional, (un)accountable, (in)evitable, (un)avoidable, brief, lengthy, long, (in)frequent, total, complete, temporary

abstinence advisable, ascetic, austere, strict, stringent, inflexible, resolute, rigid, rigorous, unbending, unyielding, unrelenting, uncompromising, conscientious, scrupulous, total, complete, thorough, sexual

absurdity, absurdities See *stupidity*

abundance bounteous, excessive, extravagant, inexhaustible, lavish, sumptuous, unending, endless, fantastic, incredible, unbelievable, blessed, heavenly

abuse, abuses (un)justifiable, (in)explicable, (un)warranted, un-called-for, inadvertent, apparent, angry, incredible, unbelievable, shocking, horrible, sharp, flagrant, torrential, rampant, widespread, relentless, unrelenting, ruthless, uncivilized, horrendous, gross, bitter, vehement, wanton, vile, malicious, vindictive, opprobrious, scurrilous, venomous, alleged, repeated, systematic, physical, mental, psychological, sexual, verbal, criminal, political, administrative, ritual, parental

academic, academics erudite, liberal, open-minded, (un)orthodox, (un)conventional, ever-toiling, (in)competent, (un)conscientious, earnest, dedicated, meticulous, systematic, thorough, accomplished, distinguished, eminent, well-known, celebrated, renowned, notable, noted, established, estimable, venerable, reclusive, absent-minded, heavy-handed, stuffy, queer, eccentric, sedentary

accent, accents proper, perfect, flawless, (un)refined, fine, fluent, mellifluous, pleasant, charming, crisp, rich, haughty, soft, high, succinct, slight, low, ordinary, prevailing, dominant, singsong, (un)detectable, discernible, distinctive, decided, mixed, purring, lilting, acute, sharp, strong, grave, funny, heavy, thick, broad, flat, clipped, rough, (un)common, unusual, strange, inexplicable, unintelligible, dreadful, phon(e)y, harsh, vulgar, lingering, marked, rustic, primary, secondary, tonic, dialectal, local, foreign

acceptance, acceptances gracious, graceful, humble, calm, tacit, placid, smug, ready, open, comfortable, genuine, philosophical, (un)conditional, wide(spread), universal, reluctant, grudging, lukewarm, unresisting, meek, cavalier, complacent, permissive, wholehearted, apathetic, patient, unflinching, unqualified, irrevocable, matter-of-fact, implicit, fiducial, racial

access exclusive, privileged, intimate, immediate, ready, constant, gradual, (ir)regular, (in)equitable, (un)equal, (un)fair, (un)easy, (in)direct, (in)effective, clandestine, full, (un)limited, (un)restricted, unsupervised, direct, free, sequential

accident, accidents (1: mishap) devastating, shocking, appalling, fearful, nasty, grisly, atrocious, horrendous, frightful, terrible, dreadful, unfortunate, ghastly, horrible, gruesome, (near-)fatal, sad, terrific, untoward, unlucky, inconvenient, bizarre, freak(ish), singular, unusual, disastrous, bad, regrettable, lamentable, deplorable, spectacular, calamitous, catastrophic, major, minor, unusual, mysterious, survivable, low-impact, unavoidable, inevitable, technological, industrial, natural; genetic

accident, accidents (2: chance) happy, sheer, pure, mere, strange, extraordinary, unusual, rare, exceptional, remarkable, uncommon, phenomenal, singular

acclaim See also *praise* instant, loud, limited, popular, extensive, massive, universal, (world)wide, international, critical

accommodation superb, palatial, luxurious, (in)adequate, (un)comfortable, pricey, (in)expensive, (un)affordable, (un)satisfactory, (un)desirable, (in)secure, decent, low-rent, depressing, substandard, spartan, cramped, cheap, poor, rough, noisy, pestilential, dismal, squalid, shabby, unpretentious, seedy, makeshift, temporary, permanent, rental

accompaniment, accompaniments tasty, pleasing, (un)pleasant, (dis)agreeable, subtle, true, brilliant, percussive, quiet, (in)appropriate, inevitable, harsh, discordant, noisy, loud, aggressive, aimless, alien, syncopated, measured, natural, artificial, traditional, decorative, amateur, professional

accomplice, accomplices (un)witting, (un)willing, ready, demonic, devilish, diabolic, evil, fiendish, ghoulish, malicious, roguish, wicked, vicious, criminal

accomplishment, accomplishments See *achievement*

accord, accords See *agreement*

account, accounts (1: record of business dealings) (in)active, terminal, dormant, endless, dwindling, meagre, straight, (over)due, real, long-standing, outstanding, bogus, false, fictitious, receivable, secret, short, foreign, interest-bearing, final, estimative, individual, joint

account, accounts (2: report) glowing, flourishing, unflattering, sobering, interesting, intriguing, pleasing, gratifying, touching, striking, gripping, absorbing, penetrating, revealing, stirring, compelling, fascinating, unflinching, engaging, amusing, exciting, rollicking, taut, pointed, gallant, spirited, graceful, tell-tale, discrepant, rich, enthusiastic, rose-tinted, funny, invaluable, lucid, incisive, succinct, candid, faithful, rational, meticulous, authoritative, definitive, (un)reliable, (in)adequate, (in)accurate, (in)correct, true, authentic, trustworthy, scrupulous, straightforward, sensational, astute, deft, (un)impassioned, cold-blooded, melodramatic, diverse, ardent, humorous, picturesque, veracious, objective, independent, neutral, (un)fair, one-sided, (im)partial, (un)biased, (un)prejudiced, stark, measured, (un)sympathetic, quirky, breezy, piquant, vivacious, lively, vivid, (un)balanced, (un)favourable, judicious, gritty, exhaustive, comprehensive, full, detailed, blow-by-blow, bland, fluffy, overdrawn, mendacious, lying, colourful, sordid, vulgar, scathing, sleazy, fragmentary, rambling, skimpy, false, phon(e)y, ambiguous, harrowing, chilling, gruesome, spiteful, inconsistent, contradictory, dry, dull, repetitive, repetitious, dreadful, summary, circumstantial, graphic, visual, literal, spoken, written, eyewitness, historical, epic, official, first-person, first-hand, documentary, inside, chronological, day-by-day, factual, journalistic, televisual

accuracy amazing, astounding, startling, astonishing, striking, surprising, uncompromising, unerring, painstaking, conscientious, meticulous, rigorous, superb, magnificent, remarkable, pinpoint, uncanny, baleful, painful, complete, utter, absolute, strict, (near-)perfect, high, utmost, maximum, undisputed, uncontrovertible, incontrovertible, flawless, (un)questionable, minute, photographic, statistical

accusation, accusations flat, grave, serious, (in)substantial, amazing, surprising, sweeping, vexatious, groundless, baseless, (un)true, false, harsh, vague, damaging, venomous, vicious, bitter, reckless, unreasonable, unfair, absurd, ludicrous, wild, monstrous, dreadful, judgmental, all-encompassing, persistent

ache, aches See *pain*

achievement, achievements startling, astounding, striking, amazing, astonishing, staggering, breathtaking, stunning, shining, crowning, thundering, lasting, far-reaching, masterful, solid, noble, lofty, sublime, high, mighty, sturdy, ambitious, proud, laudable, vibrant, positive, hefty, immense, vast, substantial, considerable, colossal, tremendous, remarkable, great, splendid, magnificent, glorious, stupendous, brilliant, illustrious, noteworthy, notable, genuine, true, real, tangible, signal, rare, exceptional, singular, distinguished, unsurpassed, unparalleled, unequalled, unmatched, nonpareil, unprecedented, extraordinary, fine, premier, worthwhile, heroic, memorable, legendary, celebrated, salient, audacious, daunting, prodigious, manifold, admirable, incredible, unbelievable, impressive, (above-)average, mundane, small, modest, sinister, dubious, short-lived, cumulative, personal, scholastic, academic, superhuman

achiever, achievers high, lofty, exalted, towering, ambitious, haughty, imperious, Olympian

acknowledgement, acknowledgements crisp, graceful, warm, generous, glowing, welcome, tacit, implicit, explicit, open, frank, blunt, (in)direct, (un)willing, grudging, reluctant, inadvertent, scrupulous

acquaintance, acquaintances (1: a person whom one knows slightly) new, old, recent, former, fortuitous, casual, passing, nodding, mutual, personal

acquaintance (2: knowledge) See *knowledge*

acquisition, acquisitions important, valuable, new, recent, significant, worthy, welcome, timely, siz(e)able, reckless, unbridled

acquisitiveness callous, stubborn, inflexible, insensible, insensitive, obdurate, obtuse

act, acts (1: division of a play) See also *play* pivotal, climactic, penultimate, final, opening, introductory

act, acts (2: deed; thing done) (un)lawful, (il)legal, (il)legitimate, (un)wise, beneficent, kind, courteous, (im)moral, (un)ethical, righteous, selfless, (un)convincing, (in)credible, unselfish, (dis)honourable, judicious, redemptive, (un)dignified, monumental, creative, valiant, heroic, gracious, charitable, arduous, calculated, (in)comprehensible, unwarrantable, inexcusable, impermissible, thankless, irrevocable, mystifying, frolicsome, capricious, (un)common, (ab)normal, spontaneous, overt, defiant, stupid, purposeless, meaningless, rash, hasty, villainous, vile, outrageous, shameful, maladroit, bloody, selfish, senseless, foolish, disgusting, antisocial, bold, cruel, dishonest, unscrupulous, censurable, unprincipled, sacrilegious, abhorrent, vindictive, criminal, hostile, infamous, evil, wicked, degrading, ignominious, disgraceful, appalling, insensate, unfeeling, brutal, vicious, malicious, mischievous, roguish, disorderly, unimaginable, sinful, lewd, furtive, reprehensible, terrifying, violent, treasonable, unadvised, unchristian, murderous, gruesome, unethical, aggressive, unreasonable, bothersome, troublesome, retaliatory, penal, reprobate, instinctual

acting touching, beguiling, (un)convincing, (in)sensitive, fine, nice, superb, high-profile, intelligent, brilliant, insightful, strong, confident, (un)natural, fervid, hypnotic, mannered, (un)affected, uneven, lax, forced, muddled, heavy, artificial, wooden, ham(my), amateur(ish), melodramatic

action, actions prompt, immediate, urgent, rapid, swift, speedy, thorough, righteous, honest, honourable, scrupulous, well-advised, disinterested, right, noble, selfless, (un)ethical, (il)legitimate, conciliatory, corrective, kind, above-board, independent, direct, (in)effective, deft, commendable, manly, positive, constructive, purposeful, determined, (in)appropriate, meritorious, substantive, concrete, definite, (non-)specific, (un)specified, firm, decisive, strong, drastic, extreme, (im)moderate, (im)modest, ambitious, resolute, vigorous, energetic, significant, momentous, progressive, delaying, aggressive, provocative, boisterous, corrosive, disruptive, base, evasive, hostile, clandestine, covert, timid, mean, cowardly, selfish, tardy, bold, foolish, inept, ill-advised, imprudent, wrong-headed, misguided, unworthy, grim, illogical, impetuous, tough, unthinkable, dishonest, precipitate, precipitous, irascible, hasty, rash, inconsiderate, regrettable, incomprehensible, unacceptable, preposterous, heavy-handed, fraudulent, traitorous, damnatory, dishonourable, offensive, reprehensible, clumsy, malicious, oppressive, radical, violent, half-hearted, draconian, destructive, ambiguous, frantic, retaliatory, inexcusable, blasphemous, sacrilegious, spontaneous, ulterior, unheard-of, unprecedented, unwarranted, (un)necessary, requisite, (un)predictable, concerted, collective, joint, unilateral, massive, full-scale, countervailing, notorious, impulsive, non-stop, would-be, final, reciprocal, defensive, rearguard, corporate, polyphasic, pre-emptive, supervisory, remedial, summary, punitive, retaliatory, disciplinary, reflex, physiological

activism See also *activist* strident, harsh, noisy, blatant, vociferous, clamorous

activist, activists sincere, liberal, vocal, outspoken, strong, tough-minded, hard-headed, determined, strident, militant, fanatical, unrealistic, political, religious, environmental, human-rights, disability-rights, gay-rights, anti-smoking, anti-abortion, anti-pornography, anti-nuclear, anti-apartheid, anti-fur, animal-welfare, nuclear-disarmament, trade-union

activity, activities bustling, brisk, mitigated, beneficial, popular, vigorous, (im)moderate, joyful, energetic, refreshing, astounding, delightful, laudable, stimulating, purposeful, meaningful, creative, productive, conciliatory, innovative, fantastic, orderly, praiseworthy, feverish, bee-like, hectic, frenzied, frenetic, frantic, turbulent, frequent, ceaseless, incessant, tireless, restless, harmless, febrile, staggering, taxing, gruelling, demanding, hyperkinetic, excessive, extensive, heavy, strenuous, copycat, arid, hard-core, suspicious, dubious, delinquent, furious, zany, odd, noticeable, dreadful, deadly, fiendish, despicable, foolish, harmful, contemptible, dangerous, annoying, purposeless, futile, aimless, wasteful, tedious, boring, dull, monotonous, routine, repetitive, lethal, sterile, meaningless, improper, covert, illicit, illegal, unethical, unacceptable, reprehensible, treasonable, enticing, sinister, questionable, misguided, hostile, tangential, violent, mundane, many-sided, multifarious, minimal, (non-)essential, basic, desperate, polyphasic, complex, high-level, low-level, high-impact, low-impact, light, solitary, extensive, self-motivated, inveterate, suppressed, subdued, restrained, restricted, forbidden, sustained, unprecedented, sporadic, groggy, down-to-earth, nocturnal, clandestine, behind-the-scenes, subversive, dissident, terrorist, underworld, underground, above-ground, day-to-day, political, social, educational, cultural, physical, recreational, sporting, natural, metabolic, cerebral, optional, compulsory, joint, collective, communal, ceremonial, indoor, outdoor

actor, actors, actress, actresses
engaging, touching, thrilling, convincing,
interesting, imposing, wide-ranging,
versatile, (un)adaptable, (in)flexible,
resourceful, adorable, affable, fine,
polished, accomplished, adept, perfect,
exquisite, splendid, superb, magnificent,
remarkable, confident, intense, handsome,
charismatic, lively, spirited, colourful,
flamboyant, skilful, top, leading,
world-class, legendary, glamorous,
celebrated, famed, renowned, well-known,
big-name, veteran, (well-)established,
outstanding, illustrious, sterling,
distinguished, persuasive, (in)effective,
(in)audible, (in)appropriate, bona fide,
genial, (in)significant, (un)intelligent, able,
great, good, gifted, talented, quick-witted,
stylish, well-respected, ambitious,
promising, rising, aspiring, fledgling,
would-be, unheard-of, little-known,
obscure, miscast, temperamental, bad,
artificial, weak, wooden, mannered,
synthetic, ranting, mercurial, ham(my),
conceited, unsung, self-effacing, poor,
regular, intuitive, instinctive, mobile, static,
serious, satirical, slapstick, athletic,
amateur, professional, apprentice,
understudy, versatile, physical, verbal,
comic, tragic, character, Method,
swashbuckling, stock, variety,
miscellaneous, avant-garde, contemporary,
modern, (un)realistic, post-realistic,
classical, lead, strolling, itinerant

adamancy See *stubbornness*

adaptability remarkable, uncommon,
superhuman, uncanny, eerie, mysterious,
queer, weird

adaptation, adaptations intelligent,
skilful, graceful, superb, perfect, smooth,
free, stark, clumsy, patchy, ham-fisted,
ham-handed, heavy-handed, shameless,
diverse, genetic

addict, addicts full-blown, hard-core,
senseless, mindless, abusive, chronic,
acknowledged, self-destructive, incurable,
potential

addiction true, (un)treatable,
(un)manageable, hopeless, unfortunate,
devastating, ruinous

addition, additions substantial, siz(e)able,
significant, notable, important, valuable,
worthy, welcome, unexpected

address, addresses (1: particulars of
where one lives) prestigious, august,
upmarket, (un)fashionable, confusing,
misleading, strange, (un)usual, fictitious,
permanent, temporary, foreign, local,
postal, correspondence, return,
accommodation

address, addresses (2: speech) See
also *speech* succinct, pertinent,
well-orchestrated, sonorous, high-flown,
mellifluous (mellifluent), grandiloquent,
extravagant, bombastic, powerful, fiery,
sharp-tongued, chilling, prophetic, major,
impromptu, inaugural, opening, closing,
keynote, welcoming, nation-wide,
commencement, plenary

adherence unswerving, loyal, devoted,
scrupulous, conscientious, firm, superb,
real, undoubted, persistent, obsessive,
strict, extreme, rigid, obstinate, adamant,
pertinacious, stubborn, inflexible,
impregnable, unshak(e)able, long-term,
uncertain, shaky, inconsistent

adherent, adherents See *adherence*

adjective, adjectives (un)common,
popular, traditional, sesquipedalian, apt,
right, (in)appropriate, (in)adequate,
(un)suitable, (un)savoury, (un)necessary,
excessive, hackneyed, trite, tired, flowery,
(un)flattering, wrong, obscure,
supernumerary, positive, comparative,
superlative, literal, figurative, collateral,
distributive, attributive, predicative,
proper, descriptive, quantitative, numeral,
demonstrative, interrogative, possessive,
pronominal, absolute, compound,
technical

adjustment, adjustments (un)easy,
smooth, simple, minor, noticeable,
(un)necessary, gradual, remarkable,
dramatic, peaceable, precise, profound,
difficult, hard, harsh, formidable,
complex, feverish, heavy, tough, jarring,
periodic, behavioural, procedural

administration, administrations See also
Appendixes A and B (in)efficient,
(in)competent, (in)capable, (ir)responsible,
venerable, clean, (im)practical,
(un)responsive, intelligent, (dis)organized,
freewheeling, harsh, bad, corrupt,
prodigal, inept, wasteful, bloated,
unwieldy, limp, lame-duck, central,
regional, local

administrator, administrators See *administration*

admiration rapt, enraptured, enthusiastic, excessive, unlimited, tremendous, boundless, unbounded, unreserved, abounding, overwhelming, deep, intense, long-lasting, awe-struck, silent, soft, genuine, honest, affectionate, chivalrous, sincere, honourable, utmost, keen, extraordinary, extravagant, glowing, gleaming, ardent, fervid, fervent, spirit-enhancing, outspoken, immediate, (un)grudging, sneaking, reluctant, conscious, mutual, natural

admirer, admirers doting, steadfast, steady, persistent, committed, avowed, avid, (over)ardent, warm, fervent, enthusiastic, exuberant, passionate, devout, devoted, keen, active, effusive, emphatic, obsessive, secret, (in)sincere

admission (1: statement confessing something) chilling, alarming, disappointing, stunning, surprising, startling, striking, tacit, implicit, silent, virtual, curious, candid, frank, sober, sensational, cautious, unexpected

admission (2: permitted entrance) easy, free, costly, cheap, reasonable, discretionary

adolescent, adolescents See *teenager*

adoption, adoptions (il)legal, (in)valid, (un)official, unanimous, (un)binding, long-term, traditional, independent, private, interracial, spiritual

adoration See *worship*

adult, adults full-grown, full-fledged, rational, (im)mature, consenting

advance, advancement (1: progress) See *progress*

advance (2: forward movement) irresistible, unhesitating, inexorable, inflexible, resolute, steady

advances (3: overture; personal approach) importunate, persistent, insistent, pressing, improper, unwelcome, troublesome, amorous

advantage, advantages overwhelming, overriding, surprising, lucrative, competitive, inestimable, formidable, untold, copious, substantial, prime, unique, decided, decisive, unquestionable, unequivocal, unmistakable, distinct, definite, apparent, real, obvious, seeming, relative, indirect, particular, main, principal, (un)attainable, (un)fair, petty, small, transitory, underhand, offset, numerical, mechanical

adventure, adventures hair-raising, frightening, breathtaking, exciting, thrilling, exhilarating, amazing, astounding, amusing, interesting, dashing, dazzling, titanic, risky, bold, lively, joyous, splendid, memorable, unforgettable, enormous, high, grand, real, true, unusual, wonderful, marvellous, fabulous, epic, remarkable, audacious, unique, extraordinary, unprecedented, once-in-a-lifetime, densely-coloured, prodigious, (un)affordable, hazardous, perilous, wild, reckless, weird, whimsical, frivolous, bizarre, desperate, fugitive, novelistic, fantastic(al), fanciful, romantic, amatory, amorous, gustatory, Rabelaisian

adventurer, adventurers quintessential, intrepid, fearless, dauntless, bold, daring, hardened, hard-core, rugged, inveterate, hilarious, nomadic, armchair

adverb, adverbs flat, simple, interrogative, conjunctive

adversary, adversaries See *opponent*

adversity, adversities See *misfortune*

advertisement, advertisements See also *commercial* enticing, eye-catching, gripping, unusual, elegant, witty, persuasive, catchy, sensational, splashy, bold, flaming, insincere, naïve, oily, phon(e)y, unctuous, oleaginous, vulgar, objectionable, personal

advertising aggressive, heavy, blatant, skilful, subliminal, false, misleading, institutional, national

advice sound, sage, informed, prudent, shrewd, wise, sensible, common-sense, sagacious, (in)judicious, clever, intelligent, astute, sober, quiet, well-meant, well-intentioned, kind(ly), invaluable, objective, impartial, disinterested, salutary, stoical, wholesome, expert, beneficial, useful, profitable, good, right, (un)reasonable, (un)reliable, (in)competent, (in)correct, cogent, insidious, (ir)responsible, (in)appropriate, constructive, (in)discreet, practical, pragmatic, (un)realizable, basic, forthright, direct, down-to-earth, seasonable, cautious, unforgettable, gratuitous, astringent, bland, blunt, foolhardy, ruinous, subversive, misleading, conflicting, abundant, professional, friendly, paternal, fatherly, (big-)brotherly, fraternal

adviser, advisers sound, disinterested, sage, trusted, impartial, sapient, wise, discerning, close, confidential, long-time, top, key, chief, principal, personal, economic, legal, military, professional, national-security

advocacy, advocacies See *advocate*

advocate, advocates unwavering, avowed, staunch, firm, avid, devoted, devout, eager, enthusiastic, fervent, fervid, fiery, strong, vigorous, forceful, emphatic, aggressive, passionate, zealous, vehement, ardent, energetic, formidable, fearless, relentless, unrelenting, influential, confrontational, loyal, trustworthy, effective, outspoken, eloquent, unambiguous, vocal, pioneer, leading, long-time, long-term

aeroplane, aeroplanes swishing, rattling, roaring, snarling, buzzing, rambling, screaming, incoming, outgoing, climbing, ascending, descending, circling, spinning, fast-sinking, receding, vanishing, high-flying, low-flying, slow-flying, flashing, oscillating, shaking, shuddering, bouncing, leap-frogging, fast-moving, scrambling, spluttering, sturdy, reliable, airworthy, flyable, manoeuvrable, agile, remarkable, giant, posh, luxury, luxurious, high-tech, advanced, sophisticated, (fully-)computerized, (un)stable, flyaway, (over)due, fog-bound, ill-fated, doomed, fugitive, malfunctioning, worn, frail, fragile, spindly, unflyable, disabled, rugged, cramped, rickety, antiquated, obsolete, icy, civil(ian), private, jet, ground-support, amphibious, single-engine, twin-engine, four-engine, fixed-wing, low-wing, turboprop, motorless, propeller(-driven), tail-heavy, nose-heavy, military, chase, pursuit, fighter, combat, battle, warfare, attack, reconnaissance, spy, spotter, passenger, commuter, patrol, rescue, supersonic, subsonic, two-seater, anti-submarine, recreational, commercial, transport, cargo, executive, (ultra-)light, radio-controlled, drug-running, bush, pilotless

affair, affairs comradely, friendly, intimate, long-running, high-key, low-key, serious, solemn, half-hearted, wild, stormy, tempestuous, troubling, sorry, disastrous, lamentable, messy, (en)tangled, mundane, (in)formal, practical, extramarital, domestic, legal, personal, civil, local, internal, external, foreign, public, national, international, pecuniary, temporal, spiritual, human

affectation absurd, foolish, childish, unnecessary, ridiculous, idle, unalloyed, pure, uninterrupted, abominable, detestable, distasteful, loathsome, hateful

affection, affections touching, unending, undying, long-standing, boundless, unbounded, undiminished, gentle, tender, genuine, true, sheer, deep, profound, inordinate, excessive, unconditional, special, unsullied, bonded, dutiful, laborious, constrained, dead, synthetic, sham, counterfeit, pretended, feigned, colourable, spurious, desultory, crazy, impulsive, amorous, latent, mutual, (un)reciprocal, one-sided, demonstrative, motherly, brotherly, avuncular, elementary

affinity, affinities See *relationship*

affirmation, affirmations stubborn, inflexible, obstinate, rigid, unyielding, strident, shrill, harsh, grating, joyous

affliction, afflictions See *distress*

affluence See *wealth*

affront, affronts See *insult*

aftermath mad, messy, chaotic, jarring, shocking, unsettling, agonizing, immediate

afternoon, afternoons See also *day* charming, enchanting, relaxing, exhilarating, pleasant, fine, soft, agreeable, pleasurable, enjoyable, delightful, relaxed, laid-back, lovely, gentle, delicate, tender, golden, idyllic, fresh, breezy, windless, windy, still, quiet, serene, cloudless, indolent, soft-aired, lazy, dozy, drowsy, sleepy, balmy, radiant, bright, sunny, warm, hot, sultry, scorching, sweltering, torrid, humid, steamy, muggy, grey, foggy, misty, drizzly, rainy, showery, wet, early, late

age, ages (1: stage of life) flourishing, prosperous, destitute, ripe, mature, old, advanced, tender, vulnerable, awkward, indeterminate, formative, chronological, middle, in-between, median, basal,

canonical, medical, voting, legal, mental,
educable, marriageable, reproductive,
breeding, child-bearing

age, ages (2: period) enlightened, heroic,
fabulous, (un)sophisticated, boorish,
permissive, prosaic, throw-away, bygone,
atomic, nuclear, space, computer,
motorized, pressured, high-tech, electronic,
digital, astrological, dynastic, industrial,
urban, Golden, prehistoric, megalithic,
Stone, Iron, ice

agenda, agendas sensible, time-efficient,
explosive, unpopular, crowded, heavy,
tight, (in)flexible, ambitious, radical,
wide-ranging, (in)formal, specific,
high-key, low-key, full, final, hidden

agent, agents voluntary, vicarious, secret,
undercover, fiscal, fiduciary,
plenipotentiary, foreign, reducing

aggression, aggressions crying, flagrant,
blatant, naked, outraged, ferocious, brutal,
vicious, treacherous, perfidious, intense,
excessive, boundless, recurrent, unabashed,
insatiable, dangerous, wolf-like, senseless,
inexcusable, gratuitous, outlaw, illegal,
unjustifiable, unjustified, unprovoked,
potential, military, territorial

agility amazing, surprising, astonishing,
astounding, remarkable, visible, evident,
incredible, unbelievable, extraordinary,
graceful, monkey-like, physical, mental

agitation, agitations feverish, frenetic,
apoplectic, boisterous, violent,
rampageous, undue, high, restless

agitator, agitators hard-core, hard-line,
militant, diehard, adamant, bellicose,
tough, reckless

agony, agonies piercing, searing,
stabbing, excruciating, indescribable,
intolerable, unendurable, insufferable,
unbearable, painful, wild, intense,
supreme, keen, poignant, protracted, deep,
vast, futile, mortal, physical

agreement, agreements beneficial,
amicable, cordial, informed, vital,
impressive, lasting, durable,
(un)favourable, balanced,
mutually-acceptable, verifiable, tacit, silent,
last-minute, surprise, (un)justifiable,
enforceable, unprecedented, disposable,
landmark, history-making, historic,
ironclad, rigid, balanced, prior, reluctant,
grudging, garrulous, hard-won, working,

collusive, implied, implicit, explicit,
confidential, (non-)binding, automatic,
slavish, (long-)overdue, massive,
substantial, voluminous, broad,
widespread, (non-)exclusive, far-reaching,
long-standing, fateful, stale, venal, servile,
hypocritical, instantaneous, patchwork,
vague, questionable, shaky, fragile,
delicate, flawed, grudging, faltering,
crumbly, infamous, unenforceable,
tattered, broken, dead, (un)conditional,
(un)guarded, preferential, consensual,
contractual, firm, (near-)total, unanimous,
mutual, formal, verbal, oral, rough,
outline, eight-point, high-level,
international, five-nation, bipartite,
tripartite, bipartisan, tripartisan, bilateral,
trilateral, multilateral, preliminary,
tentative, provisional, interim, collective,
(un)constitutional, (in)effectual, (il)legal,
peace, ceasefire, non-aggression,
cooperative, monetary, prenuptial,
premarital, parental, umbrella, bona fide

agriculture See also *farm* self-supporting,
(un)productive, bountiful, extensive,
(labour-)intensive, one-crop, diversified,
innovative, high-yield, high-cost, dry,
low-input, sustainable, high-technology,
organic, biodynamic, slash-and-burn,
regenerative

aid, aids unstinting, unconditional,
substantial, massive, lavish, adventitious,
long-term, safe, effective, adequate,
supernatural, seasonable, (im)partial,
valuable, immediate, forthcoming,
additional, temporary, inadequate,
sporadic, intermittent, scant(y), withheld,
covert, mutual, reciprocal, electronic,
(audio-)visual, hearing, digestive, financial,
pecuniary, humanitarian, technical,
military, logistical, foreign, emergency,
artificial; first

ailment, ailments See *illness*

aim, aims See also *goal* high, lofty, noble,
sublime, laudable, trustworthy,
(im)practicable, (un)achievable, easy,
unfailing, reliable, sure, apparent, certain,
unerring, difficult, dishonest, ignoble,
chaotic, paltry, clumsy, short-sighted,
immediate, final, ultimate, eventual, basic

air (1: mixture of gases) exhilarating,
refreshing, stimulating, bracing, stirring,
howling, seething, keen, brisk, windless,

breezy, (un)healthy, salubrious, pleasant, delicious, soft, light, crisp, perfumed, fragrant, odorous, sweet, (un)breathable, serene, crystalline, translucent, pearly, silvery, mild, fresh, clean, pure, pristine, unsullied, clear, pellucid, rare, thin, warm, icy, frosty, snowy, raw, cold, frigid, sunless, stale, still, silent, drowsy, dry, brittle, tumultuous, heavy, dense, thick, turbulent, thundery, turgid, ambient, bumpy, steamy, humid, moist, dank, hazy, dead, breathless, motionless, stagnant, dangerous, dirty, filthy, gritty, foul, tenuous, oleaginous, stinking, fetid, rancid, redolent, parched, hot, oppressive, sultry, corrupt, musty, stuffy, deathly, oxygen-thin, oxygen-poor, pestilential, murky, dusty, smoky, smoggy, cloudy, polluted, compressed, open, outdoor, indoor, liquid, cool, high, (sub)tropical

air, airs (2: appearance; manner) kingly, princely, sovereign, regal, majestic, august, lordly, aloof, dignified, grand, gracious, distinguished, consequential, prosperous, exalted, lofty, magnificent, superior, easy, cheerful, disengaged, cool, icy, contemptuous, indifferent, nonchalant, detached, languid, acrid, ironical, secretive, shadowy, complacent, abstract, uncompromising, haughty, arrogant, conceited, all-knowing, supercilious, affected, strutting, pensive, watchful, distracted

air, airs (3: tune; song) See *tune* and *song*

aircraft See *aeroplane*

airline, airlines See also *company* (1) glorious, established, full-fledged, fast-growing, (un)safe, (in)competent, (un)stable, (un)profitable, struggling, oversold, undersold, cash-strapped, troubled, failed, (non-)scheduled, state-owned, privatized, national, regional, passenger, commercial, civilian, military

airplane, airplanes See *aeroplane*

airport, airports See also *building* first-class, spacious, new, spanking, Art Deco, quiet, outlying, good-sized, small-craft, uncrowded, outmoded, shabby, congested, noisy, busy, chaotic, porterless, windswept, defunct, military, urban, municipal, commercial, domestic, international

air-raid, air-raids severe, fierce, violent, intense, sham, mock, false

alarm, alarms unnerving, shrill(ing), excessive, unnecessary, increasing, (non-)critical, frantic, abrupt, false, automatic

album, albums See *record*

alcohol, alcohols absolute, natural, pure, rubbing, industrial, grain, wood

alcoholic, alcoholics severe, persistent, obsessive, full-blown, hard-core, chronic, self-destructive, senseless, mindless, helpless, pathetic, abusive, incurable, potential, homeless, (un)reformed

alcoholism pervasive, endemic, chronic, epidemic, rampant, rife, prevalent, recurrent, transient, acute, violent, degrading, debasing, disgraceful, familial

alert, alerts credible, low-profile, high(-profile), instant, red, full, worldwide

alertness keen, clever, constant, frequent, persistent, consistent, assiduous, unfailing, rigorous, rigid, extreme, exacting, stringent, mental

alibi, alibis watertight, airtight, terrific, (im)plausible, feeble, questionable

alien, aliens (il)legal, clandestine, deportable, undesirable

allegation, allegations specific, serious, explosive, outrageous, preposterous, shocking, sensational, wild, despicable, (un)true, (in)conclusive, incredible, unbelievable, funny, ridiculous, absurd, irresponsible, heated, nasty, vindictive, malicious, unfair, spurious, false, shadowy, vicious, recurrent, criminal, libellous, slanderous

allegiance, allegiances See *loyalty*

allergy, allergies acute, extreme, severe, oppressive, troublesome, inconvenient, wearisome, environmental

alley, alleys stony, narrow, twisting, maze-like, lurid, repulsive, filthy, dusty, dust-choked, dark, dank, blind, back; Tin Pan

alleyway, alleyways See *alley*

alliance, alliances See *union*

alliteration consonantal, vocalic

allocation, allocations ordinal, piecemeal, random

allowance, allowances ample, lush, (il)liberal, (un)generous, (un)certain, little, measly, niggardly, small, short, scanty,

meagre, weekly, monthly, tax-free,
non-accountable, special, operating
allure, allures See *attraction*
allusion, allusions (un)self-conscious,
broad, stray, obscure, arcane, recondite,
esoteric, remote, ambiguous, disguised,
vague, injurious, hurtful, mischievous,
slanderous, venomous, autobiographical,
contemporary, topical, literary, classical,
historical, Biblical
ally, allies protecting, close, trustworthy,
dependable, steadfast, loyal, staunch,
long-standing, (in)valuable, vital, credible,
powerful, quiet, (un)reliable, wavering,
scheming, unwitting, principal, sometime,
erstwhile, temporary, former, previous,
putative, strategic, military
alphabet, alphabets impenetrable,
incomprehensible, perfect, international,
deaf-and-dumb, retrograde, indigenous,
modern, syllabic, phonetic, Cyrillic
altar, altars sacred, holy, divine,
magnificent, dignified, imposing, splendid,
majestic, splendorous, high, sacrificial
alteration, alterations See *change* (1)
alternative, alternatives refreshing,
appealing, (un)attractive, (un)sound,
(non-)viable, (un)workable, (in)appropriate,
(il)logical, (in)sensible, (im)practicable,
(un)real(istic), (un)reliable, (un)palatable,
(un)desirable, (un)justifiable,
(un)acceptable, (un)common, (un)certain,
(un)safe, (un)happy, (im)perfect, ideal,
obvious, possible, fanciful, poor,
unthinkable, stark, agonizing, painful,
melancholy, unanimous
amazement eager, intense, absolute, total,
utter, half, simple, blank, mute, silent,
unbelievable, incredible, extraordinary,
shocking, open-eyed, wide-eyed, squinting,
unconcealed, dazed
ambassador, ambassadors See *diplomat*
ambiguity, ambiguities subtle, tactful,
ingenious, sophisticated, calculated, artful,
crafty, devious, elusive, imperceptible, sly,
troubled, deliberate, (un)intentional,
syntactic
ambition, ambitions purposeful, worthy,
noble, laudable, grand, lofty, (sky-)high,
vaulting, towering, burning, compelling,
unwavering, overweening, deep,
monumental, excessive, passionate,
obsessive, neurotic, unimaginable,

inordinate, boundless, unbounded,
limitless, measureless, great, vast, heady,
wild, fierce, ravenous, deep-seated,
insatiable, determined, thriftless, raw,
life-long, constant, sheer, specific, dearest,
circumspect, modest, nervous, pitiful,
narrow, senseless, ruthless, merciless,
vicious, unscrupulous, armchair, satisfied,
(un)disguised, hidden, naked, legitimate,
popular, youthful, personal, materialistic,
worldly, imperial, territorial,
megalomaniacal
ambush, ambushes merciless, ruthless,
barbaric, barbarous, cruel, inhuman,
savage
amendment, amendments See *change* (1)
ammunition unexploded, heavy, military,
hunting, (semi-)fixed; verbal
amnesty, amnesties (un)conditional,
blanket, imminent, recent
amount, amounts large, huge, substantial,
handsome, considerable, (in)significant,
goodly, siz(e)able, tremendous, liberal,
vast, enormous, respectable, swelling,
copious, unheard-of, extraordinary,
increasing, inordinate, excessive, lavish,
prodigious, colossal, unimaginable,
unconscionable, obscene, outrageous,
monstrous, prodigious, incredible,
unbelievable, stupendous, formidable,
fearsome, amazing, surprising, astonishing,
daunting, terrific, overflowing, record,
(un)reasonable, (in)adequate,
(im)moderate, prudent, (dis)proportionate,
entire, exact, correct, precise, approximate,
(un)determined, (un)specified, undisclosed,
unstated, requisite, detectable, fixed,
unlike, (in)tolerable, unusual, scant, small,
meagre, ungodly, paltry, trivial, slight,
minuscule, infinitesimal, negligible,
(un)restricted, (un)limited, minute,
inadequate, lethal, total, aggregate
amusement, amusements (un)pleasant,
innocent, harmless, favourite, delicious,
sardonic, sceptical, (in)expensive, cheap,
idle, harmful, rueful, spiteful, malicious
anachronism, anachronisms crusty,
mossy, musty, fusty, antiquated, outdated,
deep-rooted, silly, embarrassing
analogy, analogies striking, astounding,
interesting, remarkable, memorable, apt,
(in)appropriate, conspicuous, strange,
pungent, false

analysis, analyses thoughtful, astute, perceptive, incisive, exhaustive, thorough, in-depth, profound, precise, (in)accurate, close, intimate, detailed, comprehensive, rich, (un)balanced, revealing, penetrating, prevailing, ruthless, relentless, merciless, sobering, sophisticated, empirical, full, (in)formal, (un)successful, constructive, prescient, prophetic, (in)valid, (in)adequate, (un)verifiable, (ir)rational, glib, cold-blooded, simple-minded, simplistic, sketchy, faulty, ponderous, superficial, murky, preliminary, ultimate, qualitative, quantitative, independent, scholarly, critical, chemical, metallurgical, judicial, statistical, numerical, clinical, genetic, theoretical, empirical, combinatorial, petrographic, microscopic, spectrographic, spectroscopic, spectrochemical, anthropometric

analyst, analysts astute, sober, profound, thorough, cool-headed, independent, financial, marketing, regulatory, military, strategic, political, legal

anarchist, anarchists mindless, senseless, heedless, reckless, impulsive, inconsiderate, indifferent, unmindful, unruly, wild

anarchy total, open, rampant, prevailing, baffling, mindless, senseless, unmindful, heedless, defiant, flagrant, insubordinate, mutinous, uncontrolled, unrestrained, unexampled, unprecedented, ethical, moral, criminal

ancestor, ancestors noble, distinguished, famous, maternal, paternal, direct, remote, distant, ephemeral, ultimate, indigenous, mythical

ancestry, ancestries See *ancestor*

anchor, anchors heavy, huge, rusty, foul, sheet, mushroom, stockless

anchorman, anchormen See *presenter*

anecdote, anecdotes amusing, entertaining, revealing, humorous, droll, hilarious, whimsical, zany, uplifting, pleasant, dewy, rounded, much-loved, much-told, well-attested, credible, curious, catchpenny, disparaging, behind-the-scenes, tawdry, worthless, senseless, pointless, aimless, trivial, petty, rambling, interlocutory

angel, angels holy, glorious, guardian, protecting, avenging, fallen, recording

anger overwhelming, consuming, devastating, excruciating, unthinking, unremitting, seething, rising, momentary, righteous, (un)justifiable, (in)explicable, (un)controllable, shrill, intemperate, extravagant, inordinate, immoderate, excessive, huge, tremendous, awful, frightful, awesome, furious, blind, bitter, ill-considered, unappeasable, implacable, conclusive, fierce, ferocious, formidable, vehement, passionate, gruff, violent, oblique, intense, fiery, pent-up, palpable, rebellious, delirious, solemn, cold, voiceless, sharp, impatient, subdued, tenuous, random, visceral

angle, angles precise, lopsided, gentle, true, shallow, slight, rakish, complementary, salient, adjacent, alternate, exterior, interior, facial, flat, interfacial, acute, right, obtuse, straight, solid, supplementary, dihedral, trihedral, polar, negative, oblique, plane, polyhedral, polarizing, positive, reflex, central

anguish See *suffering*

animal, animals clean(ly), edible, well-conditioned, sound, sacred, stately, majestic, spectacular, agile, active, nimble, gentle, sleek, graceful, amiable, docile, (a)social, pacific, placid, harmless, resourceful, thoroughbred, strong, sturdy, unclean, irrational, fretful, whimsical, unpredictable, excitable, nervous, feral, savage, fierce, unruly, (in)tractable, unapproachable, snarling, deadly, monstrous, ferocious, frightening, angry, awesome, fearsome, terrifying, alarming, terrible, tenacious, poisonous, dangerous, mean, vicious, bad-tempered, ill-tempered, surly, maniacal, cold-blooded, timid, (un)aggressive, antisocial, clumsy, scraggy, distasteful, inactive, effete, ruttish, live, rampant, rare, helpless, primitive, degenerate, stout, enormous, huge, great, colossal, monumental, bulky, massive, burly, large, lumpy, immense, digitigrade, dormant, gregarious, hardy, tough, heavy, prolific, solitary, reclusive, evasive, elusive, secretive, inarticulate, voracious, rapacious, ravenous, lop-eared, floppy-eared, bug-eyed, swift-footed, loose-limbed, bipedal, quadruped, four-footed, (long-)hoofed, joint-legged, leggy, short-tailed, long-tailed, curvicaudate,

shaggy, fluffy(-tailed), bobtailed,
crop-eared, hairy-eared, ring-streaked,
even-toed, backboned, hump-shouldered,
(spiral-)horned, many-celled, aliped,
bald(-faced), brindled, lean, wiry, weedy,
bony, tattered, emaciated, unusual, exotic,
bizarre, tam(e)able, domesticable,
adaptable, resilient, risible, receptive,
oestrous, ravenous, trunked, undersized,
littoral, lesser-known, terrestrial,
domestic(ated), (non-)migratory, coordinal,
(almost-)extinct, rare, arboreal, diurnal,
nocturnal, fossorial, prehistoric,
taxidermic, stuffed, flagellate, furry,
native, sacrificial, flesh-eating,
carnivorous, herbivorous, omnivorous,
rapacious, predatory, predacious, raptorial,
draught, ruminant, (near-)mythical,
(in)vertebrate, (one-)celled, multicellular,
bovine, farm, microscopic, amphibious,
marine, water, (semi)aquatic, planktonic,
ectothermic, endothermic, lab(oratory),
laboratory-reared, zoo-bred, captive, wild,
experimental, totemic, placental,
edentulous, dorsigrade, diplocardiac

animosity, animosities considerable,
deep, strong, intense, virulent, bitter,
vindictive, inordinate, inextinguishable,
unrelenting, heartless, relentless, ruthless,
merciless, long-standing, age-old, ancient,
lingering, open, covert, visceral, built-in,
ethnic, racial

ankle, ankles dainty, trim, slender, puffy,
weak, sore, swollen, lame

anniversary, anniversaries memorable,
remarkable, fitting, joyous,
(extra)ordinary, grim, bitter,
once-in-a-lifetime, once-in-a-millennium,
diamond, golden, silver, wedding

announcement, announcements
exuberant, breezy, weighty, major, special,
historic, landmark, dramatic, remarkable,
triumphant, triumphal, ringing, stunning,
startling, surprise, terse, solemn, tearful,
brief, curt, impulsive, spot, (il)legal,
(il)legitimate, formal, (un)official,
semi-official, high-volume, stentorian,
rapid-fire, splashy, coincidental, abrupt,
ominous, shattering, shocking, stunning,
bland, blunt, solemn, indignant, explicit,
open, positive, (un)predictable, absolute,
sweeping, broad, awful, meaningful,
meaningless, (un)popular, controversial,

defiant, rebellious, fraudulent, joint,
general, unilateral

announcer, announcers high-profile,
resourceful, flamboyant, star

annoyance, annoyances visible,
apparent, obvious, unbearable, intolerable,
unendurable, increasing, sudden,
(un)disguised, petty, excited, fretful,
aggressive, defensive

anonymity total, complete, strict, relative,
virtual, self-imposed, prudent

answer, answers soothing, reassuring,
(un)satisfying, convincing, revealing,
clear(-cut), adroit, competent, simple,
prompt, acute, imaginative, original,
sensitive, cogent, diplomatic, persuasive,
dutiful, appropriate, pat, right, correct,
straight, candid, frank, solid, immediate,
final, cut-and-dried, adequate, terse, deft,
clever, careful, incontrovertible, definite,
definitive, authoritative, resolute, decisive,
unequivocal, (in)conclusive, downright,
positive, categorical, unassailable, plain,
direct, straightforward, undisguised, smart,
sensible, intelligent, true, (un)satisfactory,
exact, accurate, forthright, perfect, gentle,
calm, kind, truthful, honest, consistent,
reluctant, evasive, meek, blunt, curt,
abrupt, flippant, stock, automatic,
dogmatic, standard, ultimate, mild,
non-committal, soft, monosyllabic,
prompted, silent, incredible, startling,
grave, impatient, guarded, cautious, slow,
studied, miraculous, quick, spot, ready,
uniform, wary, (un)predictable, surprising,
puzzling, querulous, complaining,
well-intentioned, knock-out, twofold,
suspicious, incorrect, caustic, inadequate,
slippery, indirect, wrong, censorious,
acrimonious, bitter, stinging, virulent,
ambiguous, casual, careless, daft,
nebulous, equivocal, fuzzy, murky, crude,
confusing, indefinite, circumspect,
haphazard, dry, indifferent, fatuous,
insufficient, less-than-polite, pert, saucy,
bold, impudent, tart, arrogant, loathsome,
sharp-tongued, surly, bad-tempered, rude,
offensive, gruff, thunderous, unfriendly,
inaccurate, faulty, erroneous, obdurate,
inexact, oblique, peevish, vague, partial,
confused, jargon-ridden, conflicting,
contradictory, affirmative, negative,
yes-or-no

ant, ants See also *insect* swift, silent, shiny, winged, wingless, dealate, predatory, black, (European) wood, red (Amazon), worker, soldier, warrior, army (legionary), guard, honey, bulldog, harvester, weaver, carpenter, fire
antagonism, antagonisms See *enmity*
antagonist, antagonists See *opponent*
anthem, anthems powerful, sepulchral, revolutionary, bellicose, militant, official, national, Olympic
anthology, anthologies See also *book* definitive, ambitious, comprehensive, enthusiastic, sensitive, generous, huge, engaging, (un)representative, random, varied
anticipation, anticipations panting, tickling, euphoric, pleasurable, enjoyable, pleasant, zestful, eager, rapt, excited, fond, rosy, electric, nervous, intense, tremendous, unbearable, frightening, fearful, thwarted, hasty, greedy
antics amusing, zany, lively, fevered, fantastic, farcical, absurd, grotesque, droll, odd, queer, crazy, boisterous, noisy, shambling, dizzying, frightening, disruptive, despicable, Punch-and-Judy
antipathy, antipathies violent, considerable, intense, strong, deep, inordinate, inextinguishable, covert, open, unworthy, bitter
antique, antiques authentic, fine, exquisite, superb, magnificent, splendid, fantastic, unique, peerless, exceptional, irreplaceable, (in)valuable, priceless, expensive, wonderful, singular, handsome, decorative, collectable (collectible), classic, turn-of-the-century, humble, sham, fake, reproduction
antiquities See *monument*
antiquity great, late, classical
anxiety, anxieties unremitting, overriding, overwhelming, consuming, ecstatic, feverish, impassioned, impatient, restless, acute, (in)tense, nervous, severe, grave, fitful, fretful, hysterical, tremendous, excessive, extreme, high, deep, persistent, chronic, habitual, transient, passing, momentary, brief, causeless, unmerited, illusory, imaginary, shadowy, unsubstantial, needless, unnecessary, complex, sombre, unbearable, painful, subtle, understandable, (un)accountable, inexpressible, blind, silly, diffident, unspoken, reticent, palpable, cerebral
apartheid humiliating, hurtful, ignoble, despicable, petty, small-minded, needless, total, explicit, implicit
apartment, apartments See *flat*
apathy See *indifference*
apology, apologies winning, soothing, tender, sincere, humble, elaborate, profuse, absolute, full, unqualified, earnest, respectful, shuffling, belated, shamefaced, embarrassed, stern, suppressive, wordless, unreserved, perplexed, confused, awkward, insincere, clumsy, weak, paltry, (un)conditional, (be)grudging, abject, routine, formal, written, public
apparition, apparitions puzzling, perplexing, baffling, bewildering, confounding, mystifying, dreadful, ghostly, enigmatic, mysterious, incomprehensible, inexplicable, unintelligible, vengeful
appeal (1: call for help) heart-rending, hard-hitting, agonizing, moving, rousing, stirring, conciliatory, heartfelt, fervent, emotional, impassioned, passionate, urgent, pressing, constant, last-ditch, final, pathetic, wild, frantic, dramatic, relentless, (un)successful, phon(e)y, lost, special, public, personal, direct-mail, relief, emergency
appeal (2: attraction) irresistible, undeniable, seductive, magnetic, ecstatic, tremendous, enormous, immense, strong, powerful, compelling, enduring, blooming, undiminished, timeless, phenomenal, (un)limited, relative, distinctive, specialized, exotic, broad(ened), widespread, demagogic, mass, popular, populist, global, universal, personal, romantic, sensuous, graphic, cathartic, charismatic, visceral, culinary
appearance, appearances lavish, nice, immaculate, splendid, respectable, welcome, timely, smart, crisp, neat, clean, orderly, wholesome, (un)healthy, dressy, larger-than-life, bright, gay, cheerful, lively, merry, remarkable, exceptional, captivating, striking, distinctive, glamorous, (pre)possessing, arresting, stunning, astounding, formidable, (un)impressive, serious, youthful, mature, kingly, wealthy, luscious, odd, abnormal, unusual, varied, unassuming, vulnerable,

sickly, emaciated, woebegone, wretched, ungainly, shabby, drab, foxy, grotesque, ludicrous, clownish, absurd, deceptive, disreputable, rakish, slovenly, untidy, uncouth, unkempt, careless, disordered, haggard, indecent, (un)seductive, freakish, hideous, outrageous, unpromising, ruffianly, gaunt, outward, physical; incessant, periodic, personal, public, professional, debut, surprise

appetite, appetites mighty, enormous, gargantuan, endless, limitless, unlimited, unfailing, uncontrollable, lusty, voracious, ravenous, (in)satiable, sharp, ferocious, rapacious, devouring, brutish, wolfish, healthy, hearty, greedy, keen, robust, inordinate, substantial, unbridled, avaricious, poor, grotesque, morbid, morose, raucous, finicky, discriminating, (im)moderate, shrunk, new-found, catholic, postprandial

appetizer, appetizers See also *food* intriguing, exquisite, irresistible, tasty, cheesy, spicy, tangy

applause warm, hearty, rapturous, frantic, ecstatic, enthusiastic, tumultuous, thunderous, stormy, wild, vigorous, high(est), loud, fervent, easy, justifiable, rhythmic, appreciative, complacent, spontaneous, instantaneous, polite, mild, feeble, spurious, spiritless, lukewarm, perfunctory, cathartic, public

appliance, appliances latest, convenient, labour-saving, energy-efficient, graceful, (un)affordable, (ir)reparable, (un)dependable, (un)reliable, cumbersome, faulty, defective, high-tech, digital, electric, electronic, cordless, knobless, free-standing, major, small, household, built-in, prosthetic

applicant, applicants See *candidate*

application, applications (1: personal or written request) impressive, serious, earnest, (in)complete, frivolous, multiple

application, applications (2: act of putting to use) scrupulous, fastidious, rigorous, careful, shrewd, (un)even, practical, immediate, broad, wide, infinite, rigid, tricky, wrongful

appointment, appointments (1: arrangement to meet) urgent, pressing, firm, scheduled, personal

appointment, appointments (2: act of appointing) significant, remarkable, impeccable, first-rate, outstanding, controversial, (un)renewable, permanent, sessional, contractual, term, back-up

appraisal, appraisals (dis)honest, (un)scrupulous, independent, fresh, fond, cool, low-key, precise, (in)accurate, (ir)regular, (un)balanced, (un)realistic, incisive, circumspect, cautious, prudent, discreet, detailed

appreciation, appreciations loving, thought-provoking, hearty, subtle, keen, profound, deep, thorough, sincere, generous, delicate, dispassionate, long-time, glowing, aesthetic, sensory

apprehension, apprehensions See *fear*

approach, approaches effective, workable, constructive, prudent, (in)sensible, (ir)rational, (im)proper, civilized, mature, watchful, wary, cautious, careful, thoughtful, gentle, measured, structured, exceptional, innovative, unique, fresh, new, novel, different, straightforward, direct, honest, subtle, diplomatic, conciliatory, sophisticated, foresighted, (in)flexible, open(-minded), even-handed, impartial, congruous, frank, moderate, simple, reasoned, no-nonsense, sound, ambitious, relaxed, joyful, spirited, breezy, unified, (ir)responsible, (in)tolerant, (un)friendly, benevolent, sympathetic, disastrous, secretive, false, overwrought, strict, rigid, heavy-handed, hard-line, ruthless, merciless, relentless, unrelenting, harsh, hard-nosed, tough, insidious, sneaky, stealthy, slovenly, narrow, single-minded, self-centred, short-sighted, more-erudite-than-thou, smarter-than-thou, affirmative, cold-hearted, fast, (im)modest, conservative, traditional, well-tried, (un)common, (un)conventional, (un)orthodox, radical, overzealous, sweeping, simplistic, (im)personal, (un)biased, technocratic, sledgehammer, circumspect(ive), diffident, carefree, lighthearted, cool, concealed, gradualist, soft-spoken, sycophantic, all-or-nothing, two-pronged, time-honoured, get-tough, juggernaut, alternative, sidelong, (in)formal, populist, integrative, confidential, entrepreneurial, real-world, hands-off, practical, pragmatic, methodical, systematic, analytical, speculative, critical, creative, collective, revisionist

approval, approvals hearty, strong, enthusiastic, vehement, full, popular, wholehearted, heartfelt, unreserved, overall, massive, overwhelming, far-reaching, well-advised, ill-advised, grim, (sort-of-)cautious, reluctant, grudging, tepid, lukewarm, rubber-stamp, dubious, sardonic, tacit, explicit, (un)expected, (un)conditional, (un)qualified, guarded, forcible, forced, pending, final, preliminary, formal, regulatory, mutual, unanimous, verbal

aptitude, aptitudes incredible, unbelievable, amazing, astounding, magnificent, splendid, remarkable, extraordinary, uncommon, (un)developed, natural, mechanical, special, scholastic

arbitration, arbitrations bitter, binding, enforced, voluntary, compulsory, commercial, industrial (labour), international

arcade, arcades glass-roofed, dim, colonnaded, concrete, classical

arch, arches imposing, (once-)grand, high, vast, monumental, giant, peerless, graceful, elegant, ornate, lacy, lace-metal, marble, sculptured, shady, rustic, blank, curving, ogival, vaulted, foiled, pointed, scalloped, corbelled, (many-)lobed, inverted, cubical, (un)sound, blind, triumphal, semi-circular, relieving, skew, round(ed), segmental, pectoral, elliptical, equilateral, rampant, Tudor, lancet (acute), ogee, basket-handle, trefoil, stilted, horseshoe, proscenium, Gothic, modernistic, Saracen, Roman(esque)

architect, architects bright, skilful, innovative, creative, inventive, imaginative, original, trendy, world-class, talented, gifted, first-rate, major, superb, well-known, notable, eminent, luminous, iconoclastic, avant-garde, traditional, conservative

architecture tasteful, distinctive, imaginative, functional, grand, lavish, rich, glorious, noble, fine, impeccable, impressive, monumental, soaring, striking, exquisite, brilliant, incomparable, expressive, solid, quality, substantial, magnificent, splendid, elegant, bold,

aristocratic, ornate, ornamental, decorative, florid, convivial, flamboyant, dazzling, traditional, (un)original, eccentric, plain, austere, mediocre, nondescript, lumpen, synthetic, flashy, ugly, defective, drab, primitive, indigenous, domestic, public, corporate, urban, civic, religious, pastel, mosaic, landscape, prehistoric, preclassical, (neo)classic(al), monastic, colonial, modern(ist), art nouveau, avant-garde, baroque, Gothic, Doric, Ionic, Corinthian, Rococo, Byzantine, Georgian, Islamic, Norman, Perpendicular, Renaissance, Romanesque, Roman, Tudor

archway, archways See *arch*

area, areas fascinating, intriguing, posh, élite, exclusive, choice, lush, elegant, affluent, rich, unique, crucial, key, prime, vital, sensitive, volatile, enjoyable, quiet, (un)safe, (in)secure, (un)settled, (un)productive, open, vast, extensive, (un)generous, (in)significant, subdividable, slummy, blighted, deprived, distressed, contested, depressed, congested, (over)crowded, populous, rambling, sprawling, dreary, seedy, sleazy, lawless, unprotected, dangerous, high-risk, inner-city, hazardous, eerie, derelict, shanty, honky-tonk, desolate, poverty-stricken, sleepy, little-known, unattractive, ghost, hostile, insurgent, outlying, remote, secluded, (in)accessible, hard-to-reach, unexplored, unmapped, uncharted, (drought-)stricken, adjacent, (un)recognizable, diverse, surrounding, (in)sensitive, vulnerable, gritty, barren, mountainous, marshy, swampy, grassy, pastoral, pasture, (once-)pristine, hilly, coastal, recreation(al), rural, urban, metropolitan, residential, suburban, administrative, geographic(al), ecological, time, search, rental, key, border, fringe, assembly; grey

argument, arguments convincing, telling, compelling, striking, exciting, cogent, original, reasonable, meretricious, tight, impregnable, demonstrative, conclusive, indubitable, valid, legitimate, sound, weighty, solid, strong, powerful, serious, straightforward, reasonable, shrewd, sophisticated, subtle, impressive, influential, important, practical, pragmatic, hard-nosed, forcible, forceful, potent, mighty, prevalent, choice, perceptive, high-minded, invulnerable, credible, plausible, precise, watertight, simple, provocative, admissible, logical, irresistible, irrefutable, persuasive, decisive, conclusive, influential, friendly, supple, spirited, novel, warm, mild, well-knit, (in)coherent, point-counterpoint, puerile, naïve, contentious, feeble, weak, acrimonious, false, dubious, specious, sceptical, loose, unfocused, nebulous, unseemly, shallow, unreasonable, spurious, tortuous, unsound, inconsequent(ial), illogical, fallacious, flimsy, shaky, tenuous, insignificant, intangible, tricky, invalid, irrelevant, implausible, threadbare, seamless, oft-repeated, stock, hackneyed, trite, inconsistent, brainless, insidious, disputable, debatable, unconvincing, unsupported, inconclusive, indefensible, ineffective, pedantic, tedious, senseless, unending, endless, protracted, insoluble, stringent, furious, insolent, rowdy, vicious, wrangling, red-hot, heated, tempestuous, ferocious, passionate, emotional, loud, wild, dissuasive, two-edged, double-edged, bread-and-butter, cumulative, academic, speculative, impromptu, moral, philosophical, domestic; teleological, ontological, cosmological

aristocracy See *aristocrat*

aristocrat, aristocrats commanding, masterful, powerful, well-acred, wealthy, thoroughbred, authentic, genial, born, beleaguered, false, arrogant, idle, debauched, degenerate, effete, decadent

arm, arms (1: limb) strong, muscled, muscular, thick, stout, sinewy, sallow, brawny, stuffy, stumpy, chubby, skinny, slender, reedy, stick-like, spindly, frail, naked, bare, scarless, hairless, hairy, upraised, open, flung, tipsy, consolatory, (over)protective, languid, numb, rigid, stiff, sluggish, turgid, swollen, spastic, flipper-like, lame, artificial, myoelectric

arm, arms (2: weapon) See *weapon*

army, armies gallant, invincible, determined, mighty, triumphant, victorious, great, poised, tank-heavy, ready, formidable, respectable, modern, vast, huge, mass, strong, tough, unified, undisciplined, (in)adequate, aggressive, menacing, hostile, lethal, small, little, tiny, resurgent, weak, weary, ragged, soft, unmanly, ragtag, scruffy, stricken, rebel(lious), revolutionary, mutinous, insurgent, seditious, underground, tank-led, motorized, mechanized, offensive, defensive, professional, all-volunteer, provisional, imperial, multinational, territorial, militia (reserve)

aroma, aromas rich, subtle, savoury, (un)pleasant, fine, sweet, flowery, subtle, sensational, seductive, tempting, enticing, tingling, tantalizing, irrepressible, irresistible, unmistakable, discernible, distinctive, remarkable, pervasive, penetrative, intense, deep, strong, heavy, gaudy, saucy, unusual, pungent, unbearable, greasy, yeasty, briny, smoky, juicy, spicy, herby

arrangement, arrangements careful, deft, elaborate, meticulous, methodical, perfect, close, definitive, rigid, inflexible, iron-clad, tenacious, compact, unique, orderly, systematic, workable, cosy, unusual, galling, vexing, face-saving, intricate, compound, (in)convenient, (un)suitable, (un)alterable, (un)necessary, hasty, hurried, crazy, furtive, traditional, independent, separate, private, reciprocal, preparatory, preliminary, climactic, alternative, contractual, collaborative, collective, trial, alphabetical, thematic

arrest, arrests close, wrongful, (un)lawful, false, arbitrary, violent, regrettable, mass, symbolic, political, house

arrival, arrivals prompt, (in)opportune, (un)timely, well-timed, (un)welcome, clamorous, new, incoming, anticipated, impending, (un)expected, sudden, early, late, unceasing, ill-timed, unnoticed

arrogance vaulting, majestic, unbridled, unrestrained, easy, wanton, surly, insolent, conceited

arrow, arrows straight, swift, dismal, fatal, bamboo, sharp, barbed, spent

art, arts enduring, everlasting, durable, imperishable, irreplaceable, priceless, pricey, sought-after, desirable, inestimable, useful, flourishing, superb, original, novel, unique, intriguing, fabulous, emollient, fledgling, eloquent, elegant, stylish, bad, pointless, pretentious, barbaric, raw, primitive, prehistoric, modern,

contemporary, age-old, ephemeral,
esoteric, exoteric, popular, traditional,
(un)common, unusual, extraordinary,
(un)insured, collectible, collaborative,
improvisational, local, oriental, élitist,
operative, creative, progressive,
commercial, industrial, saltatory, fine,
folk, tribal, pop(ular), plastic, decorative,
visual, optical, emblematic, household,
(non-)representational, magic(al),
descriptive, abstract, conceptual,
performance, performing, video,
(non-)verbal, linguistic, graphic, applied,
liberal, vernacular, mixed, imagist(ic),
ethnic, Fauvist, cubist, minimal, symbolist,
surrealist, impressionist(ic), expressionist,
propaganda, subversive, feminist;
black

art object, art objects See *artefact*
artefact, artefacts enchanting, fascinating,
charming, stunning, outstanding,
breathtaking, impressive, authentic,
original, unique, matchless, meaningful,
significant, important, fine, exceptional,
exquisite, magnificent, remarkable,
splendid, meticulous, rare, priceless,
deathless, (in)valuable, valued, inestimable,
incredible, unbelievable, intimate, delicate,
sal(e)able, collectable (collectible), crude,
unobtrusive, jewelled, enduring,
traditional, antique, archaeological,
pal(a)eontological, historical, primitive,
native, aboriginal, religious, cultural
artery, arteries narrowed, swollen, cut,
tender, vital, synthetic, coronary,
pulmonary, carotid, femoral, subclavian,
brachial, iliac, heart
article, articles (1: literary composition)
perceptive, insightful, well-argued, meaty,
informative, factual, erudite, in-depth,
comprehensive, authoritative, wise,
prescient, poignant, thoughtful,
provocative, insightful, intelligent,
outstanding, excellent, splendid, superb,
magnificent, masterly, elegant, charming,
fascinating, soul-stirring, timely, neutral,
balanced, (un)favourable, succinct, concise,
well-written, startling, cloying, formulaic,
lively, helpful, splashy, opaque, crusty,
controversial, sophomoric, offensive,
hard-hitting, one-sided, vindictive, vicious,
bombastic, boring, dull, dronish, obscure,
waggish, ironic, laudatory, lengthy,

full-page, two-page, detailed, ephemeral,
anonymous, valedictory, lead(ing)
article, articles (2: item) stock,
unaccustomed, miscellaneous
artifact, artifacts See *artefact*
artist, artists See also *painter* genuine,
true, sincere, prolific, productive, protean,
scrupulous, meticulous, consummate,
accomplished, skilful, first-rate, choice,
unique, innovative, perceptive, imaginative,
subtle, great, versatile, influential, master,
major, mature, remarkable, exceptional,
superlative, superb, outstanding,
important, world-class, world-renowned,
premier, famous, celebrated, well-known,
distinguished, (pre-)eminent, notable,
illustrious, established, humble,
impressionable, charismatic, flamboyant,
reclusive, solitary, aloof, volatile,
mercurial, temperamental, eccentric,
self-reliant, enterprising, detached,
impersonal, objective, long-forgotten,
impecunious, misunderstood,
unexceptionable, second-rate, mediocre,
unknown, little-known, unbeknown,
soi-disant, obscure, failed, unsuccessful,
effete, esoteric, commonplace,
contemporary, local, amateur,
professional, architectural, commercial,
folk, experimental, avant-garde, visual,
graphic, plastic, photographic, creative,
conceptual, cartoon, scenic, interpretative,
itinerant, Fauvist, abstract, symbolist,
cubist, impressionist(ic), expressionist,
minimal
ascent, ascents quiet, gentle, gradual,
slow, encouraging, abrupt, swift, sudden,
perilous, dangerous, steep, precipitous,
dizzying, continuous, initial
ash, ashes suffocating, mineral-laden,
ubiquitous, fine, foamy, powdery, prickly,
gritty, dry, hot, black, grey, fiery,
treacherous, abrasive, volcanic
aspect, aspects intriguing, fascinating,
pleasing, striking, distinct, vital, crucial,
impressive, glamorous, furtive, evasive,
shifty, sly, poignant, grim, dark,
unpleasant, troubling, ugly, repulsive,
surprising, puzzling, controversial,
redeeming, pertinent, ingrained, manifold,
outward
aspiration, aspirations See *ambition*
assailant, assailants See *attacker*

assassin, assassins See *murderer*
assault, assaults See *attack*
assembly, assemblies peaceable, rapt, riotous, secret, formal, unauthorized, unlawful, established, required, general, grand, representative, constituent, legislative, administrative, deliberative, judicial, national, tribal
assent, assents See *agreement*
assertion, assertions soothing, vehement, definite, positive, (un)safe, (in)correct, round, outspoken, bold, pompous, simplistic, questionable, doubtful, vague, erroneous, misleading, outlandish, dry, starchy, woolly
assessment, assessments frank, candid, clear(-eyed), (un)fair, (in)accurate, (un)realistic, (in)adequate, (in)conclusive, careful, fine, cautious, radical, glum, stringent, sombre, grim, gloomy, bleak, dire, chilling, dispiriting, disheartening, damning, erroneous, careless, muted, objective, subjective, comprehensive, initial, secondary, personal, professional
asset, assets squeaky-clean, precious, (in)valuable, valued, downstream, (un)profitable, huge, vast, substantial, tremendous, meagre, depressed, hidden, untraceable, ill-gotten, frozen, unsold, current (floating), quick, (in)tangible, (in)visible, disposable, physical, capital (fixed), net, personal, marital, matrimonial, financial
assignment, assignments See *task*
assistance, assistances See *support*
assistant, assistants (un)trustworthy, (un)reliable, (un)dependable, (in)competent, administrative, executive, technical, research, office, personal
association, association (1: an organization) See also *organization* profitable, non-profit, fraternal, educational, charitable
association, associations (2: companionship; connection) flattering, lasting, beneficial, fruitful, advantageous, convenient, (un)desirable, useful, positive, definite, unequivocal, intimate, (in)significant, strong, powerful, loose, flimsy, romantic, criminal, ignominious, simple, transitive, free
assortment, assortments See *collection*

assumption, assumptions (il)logical, (in)correct, sturdy, quaint, (un)fair, (un)realistic, basic, common, automatic, popular, widespread, sweeping, worn, naïve, dangerous, unfounded, faulty, shaky, wrong, erroneous, false, misguided, precarious, debatable, untestable, casual, arrogant, gratuitous, self-defeating, damaging, grim, implicit, underlying, unspoken, long-held, archaic
assurance, assurances cool, calm, lovely, bland, breezy, benevolent, ample, immense, absolute, categorical, powerful, innumerable, infectious, ironclad, tense, public, general, blanket
astonishment spluttering, stunning, speechless, dreamy, bleary, inexpressible, blank, wide(-eyed), open-eyed, unexpected, excited, enthusiastic, rapturous, serendipitous, infinite, absolute, utter, complete, total, enormous, sharp, intense, genuine, innocent, childlike, tart, indecisive, obtuse, mock
atheist, atheists hardy, staunch, steadfast, dogmatic
athlete, athletes tough, determined, heroic, well-conditioned, well-rounded, seasoned, perfect(ionist), superb, excellent, magnificent, outstanding, exceptional, indomitable, world-class, all-round, skilful, expert, agile, élite, great, sublime, high-profile, illustrious, top, leading, legendary, topnotch, well-known, superhuman, first-rate, celebrated, unbeatable, natural, keen, active, eager, passionate, avid, ardent, zealous, enthusiastic, earnest, fervent, serious, resolute, drug-free, steroid-free, skilled, talented, powerful, brilliant, handsome, competitive, muscular, compact, flexible, lithe, promising, (un)successful, (in)experienced, inept, stale, weary, worn-out, shy, robotic, demon, scratch, novice, amateur, professional, former, star, champion, recreational
athletics See *sport*
atmosphere, atmospheres uplifting, soothing, charming, engaging, pleasing, easygoing, relaxing, idyllic, blissful, genial, laid-back, propitious, favourable, supportive, intimate, cosy, placid, tranquil, calm, serene, genteel, reverential, uncrowded, quiet, congenial, (un)friendly,

warm, carefree, trouble-free, tension-free, unpressured, stable, peaceful, non-judgmental, liberal, sophisticated, cultured, homely, convivial, jovial, jubilant, festive, carnival, sinister, electrifying, evocative, unwholesome, f(o)etid, fickle, clouded, discouraging, stifling, claustrophobic, breathless, motionless, close, unstable, hectic, competitive, tense, confused, panicky, electric, menacing, sultry, high, thin, damp, gloomy, sullen, murky, sordid, dismal, drab, hateful, languorous, corrupting, repressive, volatile, distinctive, (non-)confrontational, rare, (ultra)dense, all-out, combustible, corrosive, primordial, special, sociable, mix-and-meet, dreamy, uncanny, mysterious, eerie, weird, supernatural; terrestrial, planetary, upper

atom, atoms immutable, fissionable

atrocity, atrocities disgusting, shocking, appalling, frightening, revolting, widespread, ugly, nameless, unspeakable, unmentionable, horrible, outrageous, terrible, awful, deplorable, disgraceful, frightful, odious, repellant, scandalous, calculated

attachment punctilious, unalterable, devoted, devout, staunch, unbounded, deep, strong, enduring, tender, satisfying, unshak(e)able, earnest, zealous, fervent, ardent, loving, loyal, sincere, serious, fierce, blind, religious, natural, emotional, sentimental, romantic

attack, attacks stupefying, slashing, devastating, swinging, annoying, scathing, chilling, blistering, ringing, unrelenting, grinding, biting, sweeping, daring, brazen, bold, defensive, inadvertent, commendable, low-key, virulent, gratuitous, unprovoked, unwarranted, unjustified, (un)justifiable, unfair, illegal, unlawful, violent, reckless, desperate, ferocious, scurrilous, frenzied, outrageous, formidable, frantic, intemperate, dastardly, sneak(y), secret, clandestine, insurgent, grisly, ghastly, hideous, deplorable, rude, sharp, strong, potent, stout, forceful, determined, wanton, harsh, fierce, hawkish, savage, bitter, acid, cruel, brutal, barbarous, relentless, ruthless, merciless, heartless, remorseless, pitiless, severe, scurrilous, vehement, spirited, venomous, furious,

pointed, ungenerous, serious, deadly, murderous, bloody, vicious, heavy(-handed), vitriolic, perfidious, predatory, clumsy, costly, unbearable, intolerable, impetuous, envious, rancorous, insidious, malicious, viperish (viperous), vindictive, splenetic, spiteful, slanderous, repugnant, fateful, abortive, veiled, deliberate, massive, all-out, full-scale, large-scale, small-scale, possible, likely, random, indiscriminate, mindless, senseless, pointless, futile, coming, unprecedented, tireless, sustained, persistent, systematic, periodic, recurrent, common(place), surprise, sudden, lightning, extraordinary, (in)direct, transient, incremental, withering, bare-knuckled, no-holds-barred, two-pronged, three-pronged, simulated, mock, sham, feigned, pretended, physical, verbal, sexual, felonious, military, frontal, flanking, aircraft, aerial, multiple, simple, amphibious, gun, (thermo)nuclear, chemical, microbial, poison-gas, missile, bomb, firebomb, terrorist, suicide, (un)premeditated, retaliatory, pre-emptive, reprisal, revenge, racial, indecorous, indecent, drunken, personal, xenophobic, verbal, hit-and-run, anonymous, precision, probing, eye-for-an-eye, hit-you-twice-as-hard; bilious, epileptic

attacker, attackers crazed, cowardly, treacherous, (un)known, still-unknown

attainment, attainments See *achievement*

attempt, attempts chivalrous, brave, bold, valiant, daring, heroic, audacious, innovative, constructive, serious, systematic, careful, (un)successful, ambitious, extravagant, breezy, unprecedented, (praise)worthy, valid, honest, creditable, strenuous, exhaustive, determined, resolute, (im)practical, elemental, conscious, clumsy, awkward, heavy(-handed), ham-handed, ham-fisted, sleazy, languid, extravagant, outrageous, frantic, pointless, dilatory, forceful, pathetic, ridiculous, pitiful, pitiable, desultory, hasty, disheartening, sad, failed, abortive, ill-judged, misguided, unsuccessful, ineffectual, imperfect, perfunctory, arrogant, inept, confused, blatant, ineffective, vain, futile, hopeless, fruitless, luckless, ill-fated, unfortunate, agonizing, grisly, boisterous, miserable, feeble, frail, faint, superficial, silly, insane, half-hearted, risky, senseless, ill-considered, shameful, violent, controversial, gruelling, disastrous, last-gasp, desperate, fierce, wilful, deliberate, involuntary, persistent, stubborn, incessant, unremitting, frequent, previous, past, subsequent, numerous, unfinished, continued, protracted, (un)organized, premature, tentative, last-ditch, solo

attendance diligent, faithful, assiduous, untiring, (near-)perfect, prompt, strong, good, average, sporadic, uneven, slim, thin, low, scant(y), insufficient, paltry, poor, meagre, measly, (ir)regular, optional, compulsory, mandatory, obligatory, required

attention, attentions caring, loving, intense, intensive, close, serious, earnest, rapt, diligent, meticulous, fastidious, assiduous, persistent, ardent, painstaking, inexhaustible, indefatigable, sustained, uninterrupted, undivided, infinite, constant, unwavering, unflagging, ongoing, increasing, sedulous, strict, studious, slavish, exacting, incisive, obsessive, responsible, scrupulous, dutiful, unobtrusive, whole, complete, excessive, lavish, considerable, thorough, absolute, adequate, skilled, prompt, urgent, immediate, careful, proper, (in)sufficient, enough, courtly, benevolent, tender, caressing, special, prideful, favourable, decisive, extraordinary, exuberant, unselfish, plodding, kindly, avuncular, decent, (un)welcome, fragmentary, scant, little, cursory, perfunctory, indifferent, inadequate, erratic, unwanted, inexplicable, flattering, grudging, full-time, curious, silent, unwarranted, wide(spread), world-wide, particular, (un)due, exclusive, inquisitive, public, personal, individual, professional, medical, religious

attentiveness abject, slavish, servile, subservient, submissive

attic, attics See *room*

attire See *clothes*

attitude, attitudes deferential, respectful, sound, sober, laudable, (un)favourable, hopeful, commendable, chivalrous, kindly, compassionate, positive, responsible, proud, optimistic, liberal, open-minded, magnanimous, patrician, aristocratic, élitist, tolerant, lenient, modest, humble, meek, wise, thoughtful, caring, helpful, appreciative, welcoming, patient, realistic, pragmatic, relaxed, placid, conciliatory, uplifting, benedictory, robust, no-nonsense, driving, perfectionist, selective, quiet, non-discriminatory, cordial, neutral, detached, objective, listless, clinical, tempering, platonic, easy, lax, tense, (un)clear, laissez-faire, firm, sanguine, incompatible, erratic, conflicting, bellicose, hostile, belligerent, aggressive, intransigent, combative, adversarial, destructive, defiant, threatening, suppliant, flippant, hesitant, stuffy, dilatory, obstructionist, supine, cynical, rude, ungenerous, insensitive, uncaring, selfish, indifferent, short-sighted, parochial, casual, negative, cavalier, scornful, haughty, (over)confident, cocksure, arrogant, condescending, patronising, snobbish, disdainful, (un)refined, possessive, truculent, pessimistic, judgmental, spiteful, pernicious, inflexible, unyielding, stubborn, unbending, unrelenting, belittling, ambiguous, self-centred, subjective, timid, undemocratic, implacable, callous, outrageous, peevish, petulant, censorious, lackadaisical, intolerant, unpleasant, indurate, obdurate, acidulous, contumelious, inhospitable, unhopeful, defeatist, obsolete, antediluvian, flighty, stern, unexpected, strange, ambivalent, depressed, holier-than-thou, empathetic, apologetic, free, happy-go-lucky, devil-may-care, careless, reckless, permissive, get-tough, hardline, hard-nosed, ingrained, fixed, predominant, pervasive, prevailing, fading, traditional, permanent, wait-and-see, sink-or-swim, hands-off, chip-on-the-shoulder, anachronistic, iconoclastic, (self-)defensive, philistine, philosophic, scientific, mental, xenophobic, sexist, racist, ageist

attraction, attractions enduring, outstanding, enchanting, compelling, dizzying, predominant, unique, singular, immense, big, ample, monumental, lush, irresistible, inescapable, subtle, marvellous, magical, imaginative, nebulous, curious, powerful, fiery, inexhaustible, impenetrable, hazardous, dangerous, fatal, favourite, meagre, mutual, molecular, stellar, cultural; central, main, prime, premier, star

auction, auctions glitzy, lengthy, hectic, wild, noisy, crazy, live, oral, impromptu, public, Dutch

audience, audiences hushed, rapt, captive, (in)attentive, (un)receptive, (un)responsive, (un)appreciative, delighted, discreet, (un)willing, ready, devoted, (un)sympathetic, (un)enthusiastic, (un)sophisticated, (un)intelligent, discriminating, great, rewarding, élite, distinct, select, limited, special, fashionable, chic, luxurious, bourgeois, silk-stocking, black-tie, dull, cold, indifferent, partisan, hostile, riotous, restive, unruly, tough, loutish, vulgar, rowdy, frivolous, uncultivated, unenlightened, crazy, gloomy, demonstrative, curious, vociferous, (un)happy, hard-bitten, contemptuous, incredulous, large, huge, vast, siz(e)able, mass, capacity, full-house, sold-out, sell-out, core, thin, small, scanty, microscopic, hard-to-reach, overflow, spontaneous, broad, wide(-ranging), mainstream, diversified, eclectic, global, world-wide, international

auditorium See *hall*

aunt, aunts See also *relation* maiden, unmarried, paternal, maternal, (un)favourite, meddlesome, prying, unofficial, adoptive, courtesy

austerity bruising, crippling, crushing, squeezing, disabling, damaging, severe, painful, unpopular, down-to-earth, collectivist

author, authors prolific, fertile, voluminous, extensive, tireless, indefatigable, painstaking, penetrating, versatile, successful, accomplished, remarkable, inimitable, adept, brilliant, spirited, superlative, major, ingenious, gifted, talented, felicitous, sagacious, first-rate, veteran, breakthrough, reclusive, dead, serious, committed, indulgent, preachy, standard, modern, ancient, old-fashioned, eminent, famous, celebrated, noted, well-known, distinguished, notable, reputed, luminous,

renowned, prominent, high-profile, readable, intricate, crabbed, perplexing, promising, hopeful, embryo, budding, rising, would-be, aspiring, struggling, hard-driven, anonymous, nominal, nameless, little-known, unknown, unbeknown, minor, second-rate, obscure, failed, distressed, necessitous, needy, unsuccessful, disreputable, abusive, humorous, miscellaneous, professional, hack, contemporary

authority, authorities (1: power to control) indisputable, undisputed, undoubted, unquestioned, unquestionable, rightful, accredited, appropriate, unimpeachable, unassailable, infallible, benevolent, (in)competent, (un)just, arbitrary, tenuous, slight, (self-)given, residual, transient, final, ultimate, supreme, high, temporary, vicarious, plenary, full, complete, absolute, unrestricted, immense, massive, pervasive, inherent, easy, unprecedented, unlimited, vicarious, local, central, legal, lawful, regal, tutelary, statutory, legislative, administrative, judicial, investigative, regulatory, parental, worldly, temporal, secular, moral, religious, spiritual, divine, tutorial

authority, authorities (2: expert) (best-)informed, excellent, ferocious, unerring, indisputable, indubitable, infallible, dependable, reliable, outstanding, international, top, reputable, ranking, established, reputed, (world-)renowned, illustrious, foremost, leading, (well-)known, noted, distinguished, eminent, good, self-styled

authorization, authorizations specific, valid, legal, legitimate, official

authorship true, authentic, definitive, genuine, reliable, successful, important, (in)famous, reputable, influential, prolific, substantive, esteemed, (un)distinguished, (un)disguised, renowned, original, permanent, major, minor, sole, unknown, doubtful, secretive, dubious, putative, established, proven, anonymous, pseudonymous, subsidiary, autonymous, multiple

autobiography, autobiographies See also *biography* and *book* fascinating, compelling, self-revealing, evocative, elaborate, juicy, breezy, affectionate, warm, clear-eyed, vigorous, eloquent, light-headed, (in)discreet, straightforward, concise, thumbnail, fragmentary, banal, mythomaniac, anecdotal, overt, plain-spoken, unsparing, ghost-written, ghosted

availability easy, wide, (un)restricted, (un)limited, (un)conditional, (in)definite, temporary

avalanche, avalanches thundering, rumbling, hurtling, swishing, glowing, devastating, fiery, unpredictable, murderous, volcanic

avarice sordid, vulgar, mercantile, ferocious, insatiable, insatiate, implacable, ruthless, unbridled, congenital

awakening, awakenings blunt, rude, rough, harsh, violent, bitter, slow, sudden, abrupt, groggy, premature, tardy, formal

award, awards substantive, substantial, fabulous, big, large(r-than-expected), major, grand, generous, top, prestigious, premier, valuable, honorary, just, even-handed, equitable, well-deserved, annual, literary

awareness keen, intense, profound, full, immediate, new, rueful, dim, painful, agitated, multifarious, intuitive, sensate, preternatural, f(o)etal, public

awe reverential, deferential, pious, religious, worshipful, sacred, mystical

awkwardness frigid, rigid, stiff, stony, wooden, ferocious, raw, rugged, demented, nervous, clumsy, painful, pitiful

axle, axles creaky, squeaky, broken

babbling, babblings incoherent, senile, feeble, shaky, infirm, doddering, senescent

babe, babes See *baby*

baby, babies bonny, sweet, beautiful, adorable, cheerful, stout, strong, vigorous, healthy, full-term, pink-cheeked, chubby(-cheeked), bouncing, fat, innocent, puny, scrawny, weak, helpless, defenceless, tiny, fragile, frail, emaciated, sickly, defective, flawed, undernourished, undersized, underdeveloped, premature, colicky, cranky, fussy, demanding, fretful, irritable, unpredictable, (un)responsive, bottle-fed, breast-fed, misbegotten, (un)born, new(born), suckling, abandoned, anencephalic, hydrocephalic, test-tube, adoptable, foster, blue

bachelor, bachelors confirmed, lik(e)able, sought-after, eligible, elusive, roguish, lonely, gay, young, middle-aged, elderly, pernickety, devil-may-care, roving-eyed, footloose, fancy-free

back, backs straight, bent, hump, hunch, sore, painful

backer, backers See *supporter*

background, backgrounds solid, intriguing, complex, diverse, depressing, sombre, modest, humble, poor, disadvantaged, sheltered

backing, backings See *support*

bacon See also *meat* back, streaky, lean, fat(ty), crisp(y), smok(e)y, (un)smoked, green

bag, bags fringed, capacious, bulging, portable, handleless, airtight, sealable, disposable, reusable, recyclable, moisture-absorbing, biodegradable, split, tattered, cumbersome, unwieldy, purse-like, leather, goatskin, cellophane, polyethylene, fabric, canvas, burlap, plastic, nylon, paper, mesh, string, soft, lightweight, opaque, woven, roll, envelope, accordion, box, beach, carrier, duffel (duffle), swagger, saddle, travel, ditty, grab, punch, medical, sleeping, carry-on, overnight, flight, shoulder, clutch, tote, hand, musette, evening, airsickness, flotation (buoyancy), intravenous (IV); diplomatic; rag

baggage See *luggage*

balance (equilibrium; steadiness) delicate, gingerly, harmonious, vital, healthy, perfect, exquisite, uncanny, reasonable, careful, thoughtful, workable, shaky, uncertain, disturbed, fragile, precarious, tremulous, dietary, dynamic, strategic, ecological

balcony, balconies shady, sunny, spotless, cool, dainty, quaint, dandy, ornate, beflowered, flower-lined, charming, spacious, scaly, shabby, wrap(a)round, semi-circular, horse-shoe, grillwork, ironwork, (wrought-)iron, cast-iron, iron-railed, wooden, stone-flagged, balustraded

baldness genetic, hereditary, partial, senile, premature, incipient

ball, balls (1: round body) hard, soft, bouncy, lively, gaudy, rubber(y), leather-covered, high

ball, balls (2: social gathering for dancing) See also *party* (2) wild, masked, dress, costume, grand, annual

ballad, ballads rousing, poignant, gorgeous, sweet, saccharine, melancholy, early, famous, well-known, woeful, traditional, romantic, popular, literary, bothy, broadside, topical, satirical

balloon, balloons colourful, bright, light, tossing, squeaky, runaway, (un)manned, compressible, hot-air, hydrogen, helium, captive (observation)

ballot, ballots See also *election* blank, secret, spontaneous, preferential, democratic

ban, bans long-standing, permanent, lifetime, comprehensive, worldwide, global, sweeping, (near-)total, blanket, outright, immediate, impending, porous, short-sighted, precautionary, discriminatory, (un)constitutional

band, bands decent, hearty, premier, up-to-the-minute, tireless, raucous, ragtag, concert, military, brass, (live-)rock, two-bit, polka, swing, calypso, jazz, dance, big

bandage, bandages (un)sterile, (un)medicated, clean, germless, hygienic, sanitary, plastic, fabric

bandit, bandits murderous, shameless, brutal, dangerous, cut-throat, savage, sanguinary, malevolent, masked, unlikely

bank, banks (1: establishment for keeping money) prestigious, major, leading, fast-growing, aggressive, strong, powerful, (un)sound, innovative, (un)profitable, insolvent, ailing, moribund, bankrupt, vulnerable, cash-starved, troubled, sleazy, central, commercial, merchant, mercantile, private, national, foreign, overseas, international, world, cantonal, chartered, central, state, high-street, issuing, joint-stock

bank, banks (2: land along a river) placid, slick, (un)walkable, forested, mangrove-tangled, craggy, rocky, sandy, muddy, grassy, mossy, sedgy, snowy, icy, frost-smooth, firm, green, lush, fertile, alluvial, flat, high, steep, precipitous, slippery

banknote, banknotes genuine, bogus, fake, counterfeit, difficult-to-counterfeit, tattered, greasy, immutable, extinct, worthless, high-denomination, big

bankruptcy, bankruptcies absolute, spectacular, imminent, fraudulent, (in)voluntary, formal, personal, corporate

banquet, banquets sumptuous, lavish, costly, magnificent, elegant, elaborate, long-winded, grand, splendid, exotic, testimonial, valedictory, imperial, regal, formal, official, annual

baptism, baptisms holy, solemn, sacramental, blessed, joyous, liturgical, traditional, Christian, submerging, vicarious, patriarchal, infant, youth, adult, private, public, group, assembly, family, interracial, ritualistic, ceremonial, simple, (in)valid, illicit, royal, oil-scented, candle-light, clinical

bar, bars See also *hotel* clubby, sociable, exclusive, cliquish, secluded, lively, bouncy, (un)comfortable, cheerful, flashy, cosy, (in)decent, rowdy, sleazy, funky, boisterous, rough, seedy, scruffy, raunchy, seamy, smok(e)y, patio, rooftop, stand-up, local, neighbourhood

barbarity, barbarities unbelievable, incredible, inconceivable (unconceivable), unthinkable, unspeakable

bargain, bargains blind, hard, rough, solid, tight, sharp, shrewd, incredible, unbelievable, fabulous, super, potential

bargainer, bargainers astute, subtle,

(in)adept, (un)skilled, (un)able, (un)trained, expert, dext(e)rous

bargaining, bargainings shrewd, aggressive, (un)realistic, stop-and-go, hard(-nosed), intense, tough, circumspect, surreptitious, secret, fierce, formidable, marathon, backroom, collective

bark, barking guttural, husky, throaty, high-pitched, rapid, endless, continuous, irksome

barracks fortified, walled, bleak, military

barricade, barricades See *barrier*

barrier, barriers formidable, (in)superable, (im)penetrable, (in)surmountable, (in)tractable, (im)passable, (un)bridgeable, (im)permeable, (in)effective, absolute, fateful, stiff, solid, massive, enormous, rigid, dense, incongruous, gaunt, pale, feeble, flimsy, makeshift, rubber-tyre, concrete, barbed-wire, partial, artificial, traditional, protective, defensive, regulatory, discriminatory, social, ethnic, racial, class, caste, geographic(al), regional, internal, (tran)sonic, thermal, commercial, ideological, natural, physical, mental, psychological, diplomatic, political, legal, bureaucratic, interprovincial, naval, language

base, bases (ultra)modern, secure, adequate, immense, sprawling, strategic, refuelling, launching

basement, basements bright, daylight, damp, dank, chilly, dark, windowless, musty, leaky, (un)finished, (un)developed, full, partial; bargain

basic, basics bare, austere, mere, minimum, simple, absolute

basis, bases firm, solid, credible, even-handed, impartial, mandatory, compulsory, optional, voluntary, broad, substantive, (ir)regular, semi-regular, ongoing, occasional, interim, temporary, permanent, (in)consistent, controversial, reciprocal, experimental, scientific, factual

basket, baskets exquisite, siz(e)able, bulky, cloth-lined, woven, hand-crafted, inverted, vase-shaped, elliptical, oval, flat, leaf-frond, wire, rattan, wicker, straw, sennit, birch-bark, bushel, Moses, sewing, laundry, shopping, bread, fruit, steamer, chip

bat, bats (small animal) undisturbed, mean, ugly, fierce, giant, blind, diurnal,

aliped, vampire, insectivorous,
carpophagous
bath, baths soothing, luxurious, elegant,
perfumed, tepid, (luke)warm, hot, thermal,
cold, Turkish, public, steam, medical,
curative, ceremonial, ritual
bather, bathers bikini-clad, nude, topless,
bare-breasted
bathing See *bath*
bathing suit See *swimsuit*
bathroom, bathrooms capacious, roomy,
marbled, marble-lined, steamy,
(in)adequate, luxurious, lavish, tasteful,
five-piece, en suite, full, half
bathtub, bathtubs shining, sparkling,
lucent, luminous, shiny, brilliant, giant,
corner, claw-foot, sunken, Roman-style
battery, batteries long-lasting,
rechargeable, dead, dry, solar, storage,
alkaline, general-purpose, mercury-free,
flat-plate, miniature
battle, battles noble, heroic, valiant,
Homeric, epic, memorable, momentous,
significant, notable, famous, historic,
dramatic, fierce, tough, uphill, wild, bitter,
vicious, violent, outrageous, deadly,
mortal, lethal, sanguinary, turbulent,
rip-roaring, stormy, intense, bang-up,
ungainly, bloody, ferocious, savage,
furious, hot, grim, awesome, gruesome,
ghastly, dogged, pertinacious, cruel,
siz(e)able, all-out, full-blown, ceaseless,
incessant, endless, unending, continuous,
constant, lengthy, sporadic, destructive,
bruising, gloves-off, long-range,
hard(-fought), (in)decisive, (in)conclusive,
crucial, critical, desperate, patchwork,
dubious, divisive, competitive, four-year,
fruitless, senseless, needless,
(un)conventional, (un)predictable,
(un)winnable, ill-fated, drawn(-out), set,
tactical, naval, frontier, hit-and-run, static,
mobile, sham, mock, make-believe, false;
propaganda, legal, diplomatic, ecumenical,
ritual, rhetorical
bay, bays blue, rocky, sandy, craggy,
landlocked, hill-bounded, palm-fringed,
island-studded, inner, shallow, sheltered
beach, beaches breathtaking, inviting,
enticing, alluring, charming, fascinating,
enchanting, dazzling, sparkling, gleaming,
glittering, sandy, white-sand, shingly,
shingle, pebbly, pebble, stony, rocky,

white-coral, (pearly-)white, golden,
powdery, powder-sugar, powder-soft,
smooth, silky, satiny, palmy, palm-shaded,
reef-protected, pretty, lovely, wonderful,
magnificent, splendid, superb, marvellous,
gorgeous, glorious, incomparable,
sensational, spectacular, flawless, fine,
beautiful, quaint, gentle, still, peaceful,
tranquil, pristine, clean, unsullied,
unblemished, undiscovered, unspoiled,
uncluttered, uncrowded, secluded, empty,
bare, lonely, inaccessible, postcard-perfect,
popular, sought-after, fashionable,
affluent, favourite, warm(-climate),
sun-struck, aquamarine, sweltering,
moonlit, tiny, slender, wide, broad, flat,
sloping, sweeping, long, curved, curving,
crescent(-shaped), steep, (un)swimmable,
seaweed-cluttered, chilly, misty, barren,
arid, wind-blown, wave-swept, polluted,
congested, (over)crowded, hotel-studded,
body-strewn, busy, noisy, uninhabitable,
public, private
beak, beaks See *bill* (3)
beam, beams (1: piece of wood or metal)
supporting, exposed, transverse, structural,
ornamental
beam, beams (2: a ray or column of light)
See *light*
bear, bears cuddly, playful, dext(e)rous,
elusive, agile, strong, surly, mighty, fierce,
ferocious, dangerous, awesome, lethal,
indomitable, unpredictable, ill-tempered,
cross, enraged, angry, aggressive, gruff,
hungry, omnivorous, adaptable, rangy,
short-faced, black, grizzly, Kodiak,
Alaskan, brown, polar, sloth (honey), sun,
Atlas, spectacled, performing, Russian;
panda; teddy
beard, beards neat, hoar(y), stubby, tufty,
curly, flowing, long, short, pointed, big,
rough, sandy, scraggy, scraggly, straggly,
shaggy, heavy, bushy, thick, full, scant,
thin, wispy, incipient, black,
pepper-and-salt, grey-haired, grizzled,
gingerbread, vast, tangled, patchy,
unkempt, ratty, scruffy, unruly, wild,
(full-)flowing, close-cut, uncut, goatee,
imperial, piratical, Vandyke
beast, beasts See *animal*
beat, beats rhythmic(al), syntactic,
syncopated, measured, tumultuous, rough,
loud, harsh, raucous, ragged, stormy,

deafening, compelling, (ir)regular, heavy, monotonous, insistent, menacing, threatening

beating, beatings sound, severe, indiscriminate, appalling, repugnant, vicious, unmerciful, merciless, ruthless, relentless, unrelenting, savage, brutal, fatal

beauty outstanding, haunting, enchanting, bewitching, fascinating, captivating, charming, unsparing, striking, dazzling, ravishing, astounding, astonishing, amazing, surpassing, raving, stunning, staggering, overwhelming, overpowering, breathtaking, abounding, flowering, glowing, radiant, luxuriant, exquisite, magnificent, supreme, singular, unexcelled, unsurpassed, unmatchable, unmatched, unequalled, incomparable, peerless, rare, exceptional, unusual, extraordinary, limitless, unlimited, unbelievable, incredible, remarkable, faultless, considerable, elegant, special, regal, ineffable, awesome, spectacular, phenomenal, legendary, timeless, perennial, lasting, enduring, unforgettable, unadorned, stark, goodly, superlative, superb, consummate, postcard, indescribable, inexpressible, aloof, rapturous, incisive, fading, fleeting, skin-deep, fragile, frail, tender, outward, inherent, artless, simple, unspoiled, untouched, sensuous, sultry, voluptuous, phantasmal, ethereal, hypnotic, magic, wild, natural, pastoral, scenic, aesthetic, transcendental, supernal, heavenly, divine, unearthly, native, personal, womanly, feminine, vocal; bathing

bed, beds warm, nice, soft, (un)comfortable, hard, low, high, massive, big, oversized, substantial, bumpy, spring, bouncy, (goose-)feather, crumpled, tumbledown, ramshackle, dilapidated, soiled, littered, dishevelled, disordered, (un)made, stripped, duvet-topped, sheetless, ornate, (semi-)reclining, adjustable, fold-down, foldaway, rollaway, collapsible, continental, rustic, truckle, trundle, twin, single, double, king-size, queen-size, wooden, metal, brass, canopied, mosquito-netted, water, air, funeral, four-poster, orthopaedic, posture-sprung, panel, respite, bridal, nuptial, chaste, virginal, amenity

bedtime customary, (ir)regular, (un)usual, fixed, early

bee, bees murmuring, humming, buzzing, droning, swarming, stinging, crawling, blinking, roving, hurrying, darting, shining, bothersome, murmurous, golden, vaporous, busy, stingless, persistent, aggressive, agitated, angry, fierce, feverish, instinctive, brainless, solitary, wild, parasitic, inquiline

beef See also *meat* high-quality, succulent, lean, home-grown, grain-fed, (fat-)marbled, corned

beer, beers refreshing, premium, popular, distinctive, smooth, deep, heady, strong, weak, small, insipid, heavy, dark, light, golden, vapid, thin, unusual, regular, tasteless, stale, flat, bland, flavourless, savourless, awful, (ice-)cold, icy, home-made, local, domestic, international, draught, soft, low-alcohol, (non-)alcoholic, regular, organic, eager, American-brewed, Dutch-brewed, Continental

beggar, beggars helpless, destitute, aggressive, importunate, persistent, pushy, unrelenting, unruly, belligerent, habitual, obsequious, sycophantic, subservient, dishonest, greedy, high-grossing, sign-holding, professional, itinerant

beginner, beginners hopeful, unpractised, unskilled, inexperienced, inexpert, awkward, clumsy, inept, callow, absolute

beginning, beginnings reassuring, (un)promising, (in)auspicious, (un)favourable, impressive, bright, good, fresh, propitious, hopeful, worrisome, discouraging, disheartening, fast, flying, false, hesitant, sinister, simple, humble, obscure, distinct, sluggish, ghastly, bumpy, shaky, rocky, faltering

behaviour, behaviours dutiful, impeccable, exemplary, (in)consistent, uniform, (ab)normal, amiable, demonstrative, graceful, (ir)responsible, (ir)rational, (un)reasonable, decent, desirable, model, sterling, accepted, mature, (in)correct, (im)proper, orderly, genteel, orthodox, cultured, calm, polite, sensible, pleasing, cordial, scrupulous, conscionable, (dis)courteous, gracious, (un)just, admirable, excellent, decorous, discreet, (un)accountable, (un)explainable, (in)explicable, (un)intelligible, well-bred, sincere, attractive, co-operative, respectable, seemly, (un)gentlemanly, (un)forgivable, (un)sophisticated, (in)appropriate, (un)ethical, (ir)responsible, (un)desirable, (dis)honourable, (un)acceptable, (un)friendly, (un)civilized, unprofessional, tasteless, aberrant, errant, unseemly, offensive, beastly, violent, brattish, stark, deplorable, reprehensible, despicable, abominable, petulant, abrupt, abusive, vindictive, brusque, deviant, delinquent, cowardly, boisterous, unruly, rowdy, unrestrained, disorderly, disturbed, capricious, uncontrolled, equivocal, disgraceful, reptilian, obstructive, (self-)destructive, forward, daredevil, reckless, daring, bold, thuggish, pushing, erratic, graceless, frivolous, furtive, freakish, illogical, infantile, infamous, immodest, pompous, mean, duplicitous, offhand, outlandish, outrageous, presumptuous, riotous, rebellious, rough, appalling, shocking, disgusting, sordid, sullen, mawkish, uncouth, clumsy, awkward, crude, coarse, vulgar, boorish, atrocious, cruel, suspicious, dubious, saucy, audacious, impudent, impertinent, impolite, rude, senseless, irregular, disruptive, psychotic, hysterical, paranoid, odious, hateful, displeasing, negligent, abusive, gruff, servile, obsequious, cringing, submissive, petty, peculiar, unconscionable, villainous, wild, wayward, manipulative, tyrannous, tyrannical, arbitrary, unbecoming, unsociable, antisocial, bearish, surly, shameful, regrettable, giddy, juvenile, adolescent, baby-like, childish, babyish, clingy, dependent, puzzling, perplexing, baffling, strange, bizarre, eerie, insincere, affected, unattractive, harassing, criminal, bellicose, combative, barbarous, vicious, predatory, dilatory, menacing, embarrassing, aggressive, egregious, unsporting, insulting, self-defeating, maladaptive, withdrawn, loose, degenerate, licentious, indecent, corrupt, unchaste, perverse, promiscuous, dissolute, depraved, unheard-of, (un)conventional, (ir)regular, (un)characteristic, (un)predictable, modifiable, mystifying, reticent, staid, changing, innate, impulsive, compulsive, instinctive, collective, learned,

voluntary, consummatory, social, sexual, autistic

being, beings inner, rational, reasonable, moral, intelligent, vocal, sentient, supernatural, (super)human, spiritual, aerial, spectral, (un)earthly, living, extra-terrestrial, imaginary, divine, Supreme

belief, beliefs fond, right, principled, (il)logical, (in)correct, (un)informed, genuine, sound, fundamental, basic, core, deep(-rooted), deep-seated, long-held, steadfast, wholehearted, conventional, traditional, firm, old-fashioned, infinite, permanent, undying, enduring, abiding, unwavering, unshak(e)able, unshaken, determined, rigid, strong, enthusiastic, fervent, intimate, passionate, heartfelt, sincere, (un)popular, cherished, explicit, wide-eyed, unavoidable, inevitable, necessary, spreading, current, prior, widespread, common, universal, general, prevalent, fanatical, sacrosanct, inviolable, uncompromising, adamant, arrogant, fierce, inordinate, desperate, adversarial, dubious, erroneous, mistaken, wrong, false, misguided, misleading, errant, absurd, superficial, fragile, deluded, vain, incomprehensible, unholy, harmful, fundamental(ist), fanatic(al), ineradicable, outworn, strange, esoteric, bizarre, spooky, incredible, unbelievable, fanciful, innocent, naïve, mischievous, heretical, superstitious, populist, central, inner, personal, religious, theological, spiritual, deistic, mystical, secular, ideological

believer, believers See also *belief* true, firm, passionate, ardent, devout

bell, bells tinkling, ringing, clanging, ticking, insistent, hard-struck, faulty, muffled, clay, metal, electric, prophetic, fateful

belly, bellies protruding, bulging, stout, swollen, bloated, beer, distended, enlarged, cramp-tortured, demanding

belongings See *possession*

belt, belts (super)wide, narrow, thick, elaborate, fancy, elastic, suede, leather, snakeskin, velvet, (brass-)studded, woven

bench, benches See also *seat* high-backed, elevated, hand-carved, cross-leg, undulating, mosaic, rustic, portable

bend, bends abrupt, sharp, hairpin, smooth, slight, gradual, sweeping

benefactor, benefactors benevolent, reliable, well-intentioned, well-meaning, marvellous, kind, generous, famous, renowned, great, first, mysterious, secret, anonymous, unknown, nameless, unexpected

benefit, benefits overriding, handsome, unqualified, substantial, staggering, amazing, astounding, inestimable, all-round, meaningful, practical, sound, major, important, (im)measurable, (in)significant, (un)limited, infinite, maximum, full, long-range, long-term, short-term, immediate, potential, additional, lasting, supreme, chief, special, peculiar, numerous, fringe, spin-off, (in)visible, (in)tangible, (un)clear, alleged, illusory, improper, minor, minuscule, accidental, unforeseen, short-lived, reciprocal, mutual, standard, cumulative, tax(able), pecuniary, monetary, economic, supplementary, personal, therapeutic, medicinal

benevolence See *charity* (1)

bequest, bequests See *legacy*

bet, bets, betting (un)safe, (un)cautious, (un)sure, riskless, risky, injudicious, ante-post

betrayal, betrayals blatant, ignoble, shameful, deep, uncaring, terrible, bitter

beverage, beverages See *drink*

bias, biases strong, heavy, impenetrable, pervasive, rife, overt, clear, apparent, (un)conscious, (un)intentional, (un)known, automatic, deep-rooted, built-in, disgraceful, vindictive, non-egalitarian, perceptual, personal, parental, racial, androcentric

bibliography, bibliographies definitive, authoritative, comprehensive, extensive, exhaustive, ultimate, impeccable, select(ive), respectable, valuable, useful, (un)dependable, (un)reliable, standard

bickering, bickerings unseemly, unbecoming, improper, inappropriate, indecorous, indecent, unreasonable, constant, endless

bicycle, bicycles shaky, rickety, stationary, wheeled, folding, collapsible, three-speed, ten-speed, mountain

bigotry militant, adamant, tough, quarrelsome, combative, open, unconcealed, cool, calculated, complete, irresponsible, absurd, sectarian, religious

bikini, bikinis See *swimsuit*

bill, bills (1: account of money owed) (in)correct, (over)due, outstanding, long-standing, massive, atrocious, outrageous, stiff, high, hefty, large, substantial, considerable, horrendous, appalling, incredible, unbelievable, exorbitant, walloping, whopping, soaring, inflated, (un)settled, (un)paid, receivable, uncollectible, monthly, day-to-day

bill, bills (2: draft of a proposed law) omnibus, controversial, legislative, (un)constitutional

bill, bills (3: beak of a bird) toothed, jagged, pointed, hooked, notched, pouched, depressed, decurved, (upward-)curving, downward-curving, straight, horny, strong, powerful, stout, long, short, slender, broad, wide, sharp, fierce, cruel, voracious

bill, bills (4: a piece of paper money) See *banknote*

biographer, biographers See *author* and *writer*

biography, biographies See also *book* definitive, creditable, substantial, insightful, landmark, ambitious, brilliant, masterly, valuable, graceful, trim, intimate, sympathetic, affectionate, worshipful, reverential, generous, balanced, judicious, eloquent, clear-eyed, objective, up-to-date, extensive, copious, mammoth, monumental, massive, careful, thorough, meticulous, well-documented, painstaking, accurate, serious, absorbing, fascinating, charming, compelling, satisfying, unflattering, equitable, searing, kitsch, readable, lively, vivid, popular, honest, full-scale, triple-decker, two-volume, detailed, concise, thumbnail, new, sensational, contentious, controversial, fictitious, fictionalized, one-dimensional, slanted, vengeful, mean-spirited, unbalanced, merciless, relentless, ruthless, lifeless, best-selling, hasty, chatty, conversational, anecdotical (anecdotal), revisionist, (un)authorized, official, prefatory, collective, historical, literary, critical

bird, birds twittering, chirping, squeaking,

hissing, shrieking, piping, croaking, singing, warbling, humming, babbling, blabbing, squawking, squalling, flapping, billing, descending, swaying, swerving, hopping, poking, tottering, wading, whirling, darting, soaring, standing, stalking, wandering, ruffling, snapping, charming, swift, dichromatic, majestic, regal, kingly, masterful, magnificent, elegant, graceful, exquisite, fearless, wild, domesticated, (care)free, captive, docile, delicate, healthy, vigorous, colourful, rufous, gaudy, sage, fabulous, chipper, cheerful, lively, restless, melodious, raucous, gregarious, lonesome, rare, pesky, tiny, toylike, chunky, ubiquitous, (un)common, unusual, offbeat, exotic, resilient, dozed, banded, (un)caged, mounted, threatened, aggressive, redolent, succulent, fruit-eating, seed-eating, insect-eating, insectivorous, hooded, bald(-faced), crested, long-necked, bald-headed, long-legged, short-legged, cerated, stubby-tailed, red-tailed, wide-billed, ruby-throated, gorged, plumaged, long-winged, flightless, squab, cage, game, aquatic, water, sea, oceanic, frigate, marsh, native, carpophagous, carnivorous, sedentary, migratory, terrestrial, territorial, nocturnal, altricial, precocial, diurnal, rasorial, cursorial, natatorial, zygodactyl, gallinaceous, apivorous, predacious, predatory, raptorial, rapacious, ratite, diplocardiac, decorative, adjutant, ant, national, passerine

birth, births noble, gentle, privileged, mean, humble, low, spectacular, celebrated, premature, unexpected, natural, (ab)normal, (un)safe, risky, (un)easy, difficult, traumatic, slow, painful, painless, virgin, vaginal, surgical, Caesarean; (il)legitimate, out-of-wedlock

birth control (un)available, (in)accessible, (in)effective, (un)safe, oral

birthmark, birthmarks (in)visible, obvious, congenital, vascular

birthrate, birthrates alarming, (record-)high, increasing, rising, falling, steady, slow, (un)reasonable, low, national

biscuit, biscuits dry, (semi)sweet, rich, delicious, scrumptious, cheesy, fancy, crumbly, round, thin, thick, hard, soft,

delicate, lace, crusty, crisp, brittle, home-made, plump, ginger, soda, ship's, tea, baking-powder, digestive, Bourbon

bite, bites swelling, tormenting, stinging, piercing, bone-deep, powerful, painful, hurtful, vicious, savage, rabid, poisonous, killing, deadly, fatal, desperate

bitterness inexorable, malignant, vengeful, gloomy, solipsistic, monstrous, unusual, terrible, oblique, dusty, frigid, sharp, deep, intense, enormous, infinite, lingering, impotent

black intense, pitch, slate, inky, ebony, midnight, blue, jet

blackness thick, intense, impenetrable, unpenetrable, impervious, unfathomable, inscrutable, unrelieved, velvety, predawn

blade, blades (razor-)sharp, sharp-edged, keen, pointed, broad, glittering, tapering, curved, boomerang-shaped, crescent-shaped, double-edged

blame See *charge* (1)

blasphemy sheer, subversive, repellent, repulsive, distasteful

blaze See *fire*

bleeding intense, profuse, copious, massive, unstoppable, unusual, irregular, suppressed, internal, external, intra-abdominal, haemorrhagic, spasmodic, haemophilic

blend, blends See *mix(ture)*

blessing, blessings (un)mixed, rich, unalloyed, grudging, reluctant, conditional, sacred, apostolic

blind, blinds See also *curtain* sleek, sophisticated, attractive, dramatic, slatted, (closely-)woven, fabric, roller, roll-up, wood-slat, horizontal, vertical, Venetian, Persian

blindness irrevocable, total, complete, partial, congenital, night, colour

bliss See *happiness*

blizzard, blizzards See *storm*

blockade, blockades heavy-handed, (in)effective, (in)efficient, (in)operative, aggressive, tight, temporary, indiscriminate, naval, armed, military, economic

blond (colour) platinum, light, medium, pale, ash, dirty

blood healthy, warm, whole, full, viscous, sticky, watery, thin, corrupt, life-saving, sacrificial, arterial, venous,

peripheral, occult (non-visible),
oxygen-full, oxygen-deficient, menstrual;
(im)pure, venomous, bad, young, blue,
aristocratic, noble

blood pressure exemplary, (ab)normal,
(un)stable, run-away, elevated, high, low,
symptomless, systolic, diastolic

bloodshed appalling, hateful, terrible,
frightful, fearful, awful, dreadful, grisly,
gruesome, senseless, unnecessary

blossom, blossoms See also *flower*
shuddering, fragile, delicate, tender,
fragrant, aromatic, odoriferous, variegated,
colourful, fresh, healthful, heavy, full,
snowy, parasitic, pallid, showy

blouse, blouses floral, middy, classic,
low, décolleté, floaty, flouncy, loose,
striped, open-necked, high-neck(ed),
cowl-neck, low-cut, ruffled, frilly, woven,
brocaded, slip-on, sleeveless, puffed-sleeve,
puffy-sleeved, short-sleeved, long-sleeved,
cap-sleeved, double-layered, wraparound,
wrap-and-tie, sheer, silk, twill, daring,
flimsy, gauzy, scanty, skimpy, immodest,
inappropriate, provocative, revealing,
sensual

blow, blows striking, devastating,
(bone-)crushing, smashing, telling,
appalling, finishing, agonizing, resounding,
ear-splitting, ear-piercing, glancing,
shocking, stupefying, punishing, blinding,
valiant, knock-down, vigorous, strong,
bitter, final, doughty, real, major, terrible,
dreadful, accidental, fell, fierce, smart,
sharp, severe, harsh, deep, solid, hard,
rough, serious, forceful, violent, heavy,
decisive, vital, disastrous, fateful, deadly,
mortal, fatal, cruel, vicious, wicked, nasty,
knockout, significant, fresh, long-term,
minor, spiteful, unexpected, double,
psychological

blue navy, royal, lofty, soft, tender, icy,
ice, frost, solid, electric, metallic, silvery,
steel, true, cobalt, greenish, greeny,
greyish, turquoise, teal, deep, cerulean,
azure, lilac, strong, intense, rich, pure,
luminous, vivid, bright, brilliant, vibrant,
dazzling, fiery, campanula, watery, pastel,
pale, pearl, indigo, methylene, peacock,
purple, purplish, whitish, powder,
light(ish), medium, mild, dark, iridescent,
china, porcelain, sapphire, smok(e)y, salty,
milky, basic, sky, sea, slate, slaty, bold,

serene, clear, translucent, transparent,
crystalline, crystal(-clear), limpid, alpine,
midnight, livid, vitriolic, ghostly, dusky,
(ultra)marine, gentian, delphinium,
speckled, bice, duck-egg, Wedgwood,
Prussian (Berlin, Chinese, Paris),
Cambridge, Oxford, Copenhagen

blunder, blunders See *mistake*

blush blabbing, revealing, telltale, virginal,
rosy, deep, tepid, sudden, spontaneous,
(un)conscious, unguarded; first

boast, boasts, boasting empty, silly,
impudent, immodest, earnest, forward,
brazen, brash, proud, incautious,
psychological

boat, boats rumbling, flying, wallowing,
chugging, floating, fast, open-topped,
open(-air), covered, pointed, sleek,
high-speed, seaworthy, easily-navigable,
sporty, custom-built, sturdy, stable,
staunch, watertight, stubby, beamy,
buoyant, upside-down, unwieldy, ungainly,
clumsy, frail, awkward, flimsy, fragile,
shabby, overcrowded, dilapidated, rickety,
leaky, shallow, midshore, offshore,
inter-island, weather-beaten, (un)navigable,
rakish, waterlogged, waterborne, inshore,
undersea, inflatable, collapsible,
aluminium, rubber, (walrus-)skin,
fibre-glass, glass-bottom, round-bottomed,
flat-bottomed, flat-keeled, mono-hulled,
multi-hulled, square-hulled, skin-hulled,
jolly, motor, power, steam, diesel-powered,
tug, packet, mosquito, torpedo,
commercial, recreational, sightseeing,
paddle(-wheel), gutta-percha

bobcat, bobcats See *cat*

body, bodies (1: physical structure of a
person or animal) healthy, sound, stout,
sturdy, stocky, hardy, neat, perfect,
well-shaped, (a)symmetric(al), well-built,
athletic, powerful, sinuous, sinewy,
muscular, muscled, thickset, strong,
remarkable, smart, willowy, pleasant,
gracious, delightful, graceful, slender, fit,
trim, sleek, delicate, gaunt, thin, light,
lithe, small-boned, compact, active, fatless,
tallish, weighty, bulky, chunky, corpulent,
squat, lumpish, dumpy, angular, cuboidal,
prone, supine, relaxed, prostrate,
inarticulate, firm, taut, floppy, stooped,
cushiony, inert, frail, weary, weak, sallow,
drowsy, diminutive, overgrown, limp,

misshapen, maimed, disabled, spastic, emaciated, exposed, tired, exhausted, jaundiced, ruined, shrunken, battered, wasted, swollen, organic, human

body, bodies (2: dead person or animal) fallen, dead, naked, frozen, bloated, (un)recognizable, (un)identifiable, unmarked, missing, lifeless, skeletal

body, bodies (3: group of persons or things) powerful, powerless, elected, elective, appointed, appointive, unicameral, deliberative, legislative, advisory, executive, corporate, multiracial, regulatory, watch-dog, umbrella, collective, inarticulate

boldness See *courage*

bomb, bombs undetectable, dirty, controversial, depth, long-range, deliverable, high-explosive, devastating, armed, home-made, makeshift, crude, ravaging, massive, huge, powerful, sophisticated, constant, fusion, remote-control, cluster, nuclear, (super-)atomic, hydrogen, neutron, time, incendiary, robot, buzz, tear, smoke, gas, fire, dynamite, demolition, car, fragmentation, aerosol, cobalt, rocket, gasoline, petrol, explosive, booby-trap, general-purpose, napalm, chemical, phosphorous, letter, parcel, pipe, mortar, fuel-air, aerial, percussion, barometric-pressure, stink, dummy

bombardment, bombardments devastating, intense, intensive, powerful, excessive, heavy, massive, pinpoint, (in)accurate, precision, precise, overt, indiscriminate, vicious, savage, ferocious, unmerciful, merciless, ruthless, pitiless, heartless, remorseless, relentless, unrelenting, round-the-clock, continuous, endless, unending, ceaseless, incessant, persistent, strategic, tactical, aerial

bombing, bombings See *bombardment*

bond, bonds (1: tie; band) enduring, close, tight, positive, warm, powerful, chummy, indissoluble, indefinable, (un)familiar, primal, temporary, incidental, momentary, fragile, loose, common, mysterious, atavistic, emotional, marital, parental, maternal, paternal, symbolic; chemical

bond, bonds (2: interest-bearing certificate) redeemable, mature, long-term, negotiable, convertible, fixed-rate, over-the-counter, gilt-edged, junk, high-yield, high-risk, savings, collateral, mortgage, income, trust, corporate

bondage See *slavery* and *servitude*

bone, bones hard, dense, delicate, soft, thin, brittle, fragile, bare, meatless, hollow, pitted, scarred, porous, compound, funny, occipital, frontal, parietal, pubic, pelvic, shin, heel, temporal, unciform, carpal, tarsal, distal, proximal, stirrup, knuckle, hominid, cancellate, zygomatic, osteoporotic, digital, hip

boo, booing humiliating, degrading, shameful, disgraceful, pathetic, lusty, loud, constant, continual, continued

book, books fascinating, entertaining, (un)interesting, challenging, compelling, engrossing, captivating, exhilarating, entrancing, engaging, sobering, (un)amusing, soothing, recondite, learned, instructive, informative, funny, upbeat, sal(e)able, comprehensible, easy, immense, masterful, important, sacred, breakthrough, successful, favourite, commendable, phenomenal, award-winning, crisp, provocative, sprightly, inspirational, worthy, enjoyable, timely, appropriate, solid, thorough, poignant, everlasting, fine, ambitious, extraordinary, moral, outstanding, singular, notable, exceptional, remarkable, unique, memorable, revolutionary, comprehensive, helpful, worthwhile, sober, wholesome, beneficial, realistic, unequalled, well-written, circumstantial, explosive, insightful, powerful, influential, indispensable, fundamental, noteworthy, reverential, mammoth, landmark, seminal, stunning, thoughtful, meaningful, profound, quality, impressive, up-to-date, suspenseful, straightforward, complex, out-of-the-way, difficult, demanding, light-hearted, inconsistent, fragmentary, unworthy, pedestrian, prosaic, amateurish, disappointing, terrible, slight, modest, trashy, stodgy, pedantic, tedious, contentious, loony, pornographic, evil, obscene, immoral, blasphemous, salacious, risqué, exploitative, disturbing, resentful, blinkered, libellous, seditious, subversive, treasonous, offensive, distasteful, stuffy, boring, dull, tiresome, wearisome, tedious, pretentious, scabrous, rotten, dry, stupid, unreadable, sultry, sensationalist(ic), simplistic, vicious, witless, tendentious, partisan, meandering, unpublishable, inaugural, first, forthcoming, scarce, rare, antiquarian, precious, new, second-hand, first-edition, full-length, curious, unusual, odd, controversial, (un)profitable, (in)accessible, posthumous, long-forgotten, ghost-written, (un)available, costly, contemporary, leather-bound, clothbound, gilt-edged, handsome, elegant, tall, unbound, musty, wobbly, old, well-worn, mouldy, pocket-size, slim, massive, heavy, cumbersome, hard-cover, soft-cover, glossy, coffee-table, bedside, pocket, adult, grown-up, juvenile, pop-out, library, reference, basic, source, travel, mass-market, comic, scholarly, scientific, trade, black, prayer, open, anecdotal, non-fiction, educational, recipe, scrap, log, style, symbolic(al), emblem, self-help, teach-yourself, sporting

bookcase, bookcases sectional, knockdown, adjustable, stationary, built-in

booklet, booklets See *brochure*

boom, booms welcome, surprising, unexpected, unprecedented, economic

boon, boons overwhelming, unalloyed, enormous, big, great, incalculable, obvious, unexpected

boost, boosts See *help*

boot, boots solid, sturdy, enormous, thick, heavy, lightweight, (thigh-)high, high-heeled, hip(-length), ankle(-high), low, army-style, waterproof, watertight, hobnailed, winged, square-toed, pointed, steel-toed, elastic-sided, dress, fancy, protective, rubber, leather, buckskin, calfskin, suede, lizard, vinyl, neoprene, lead, clumsy, outsize, squeaky, muddy, soil-dusty, slippery, slithery, unlaced, surgical, thermal, desert

border, borders peaceful, (un)safe, (in)secure, (un)stable, (un)settled, intact, tight, firm, precise, final, (il)logical, deep, extreme, utmost, furthest, outermost, far, rugged, wild, challenging, porous, straight-line, arbitrary, artificial, loose, modern, recent, post-war, volatile, dark, sleepy, permeable, (im)penetrable, (in)defensible, vulnerable, dense, crucial, traditional, exact, (in)determinate,

(un)clear, invisible, imperceptible, troubled, restless, tense, terrorist-prone, shrunken, pre-invasion, pre-war, mountainous, riverine, geographical, (un)official, (in)formal, political, administrative, electoral, international, territorial, national, regional, ethnic

bore, bores insufferable, unbearable, intolerable, unspeakable, unbelievable, incredible, terrific, hideous, monumental

boredom stifling, depressing, disheartening, dispiriting, irksome, awful, barren, dreary, dismal, miserable, comfortable, detached, acute, extreme, immense, monumental, dead(ly), evident, apparent, timeless, eternal, perpetual, unbroken, unending, unceasing, everlasting, endless, ceaseless, incessant

borrower, borrowers delinquent, (ir)responsible, reckless, profligate, wasteful, desperate, needy, blue-chip

borrowing, borrowings deep, (un)acknowledged, (ir)responsible, profligate, excessive, extravagant, runaway, reckless, wasteful

boss, bosses See also Appendixes A and B compassionate, (in)competent, influential, sympathetic, overbearing, amorous, truant

bottle, bottles refundable, returnable, recyclable, reusable, lightweight, plastic, stoneware, ceramic, glass, sparkling, sleek, long-neck, stirrup-spout, pear-shaped, potbellied, bulbous, stubby, knobby, gargantuan, decorated

boundary, boundaries See *border*

bounty, bounties See also *generosity, gift* and *reward* enduring, perpetual, endless, infinite, incalculable, ample, plenteous, fruitful, rich

boutique, boutiques See *shop*

bow, bows (1: weapon for shooting arrows) powerful, supple, pliant, over-strung, unstrung, (in)flexible, (double-)curved, composite, deadly

bow, bows (2: bending of the head or body) profound, deep, mighty, pompous, heavy, stiff, vigorous, brusque, jerky, slight, faint, little, low, courteous, apologetic, modest, perceptible, impassive, dignified, deferential, blatant, reverent, grateful

bowl, bowls exquisite, elegant, glazed, beaded, mould-blown, large(-footed), medium(-size), porous, heatproof, microwavable, microwave-safe, votive, pedestal

box, boxes capacious, strong, flimsy, weak, lightweight, cardboard, oblong, elongate, cubical, cylindric(al), oversized, stackable

boxer, boxers clean, dext(e)rous, adroit, tough, wiry, professional, amateur, featherweight, lightweight, middleweight, welterweight, heavyweight, flyweight

boy, boys See also Appendixes A and B serious-minded, studious, ingenious, gifted, precocious, resourceful, inventive, (in)discreet, (im)prudent, fine, (dis)obedient, fair-headed, gregarious, meek, effeminate, manly, muscular, (ir)responsible, (non-)aggressive, blatant, little, well-mannered, (im)polite, sharp, wide-awake, restless, white-headed, favourite, small-size, tender-faced, fair-haired, curly-headed, handsome, gawky, lanky, gangly, gangling, awkward, misguided, scrawny, boisterous, clamorous, impertinent, rumbustious, refractory, wayward, unruly, wild, undisciplined, noisy, red-blooded, unmannerly, (pre-)pubescent, adolescent, teenage, golden

boycott, boycotts massive, worldwide, (un)official, (in)effective, (in)efficient, (in)operative, economic

boyhood, boyhoods vivid, colourful, lively, spirited

bracelet, bracelets See also *jewel* spiky, spangly, gold, silver, copper, charm

bracket, brackets (punctuation) square, conditional, optional, angular, curly

braggart, braggarts confirmed, ingrained, chronic, habitual, thorough, inveterate, unending, egotistical

brain, brains quick, receptive, facile, carefree, lively, fervent (fervid), imaginative, crafty, scheming, unscholastic, sluggish, indolent, tired, exhausted, weary, sleepy, disordered, herniated, convoluted, vertebrate, oxygen-sensitive

brain-drain (un)desirable, (un)favourable, (un)fortunate, (dis)advantageous, (dis)agreeable, (un)fair, (un)just, unadvantageous, detrimental, reverse

brake, brakes squealing, noisy, stiff, faulty, defective, automatic, hydraulic, electric, mechanical, antilock

branch, branches swishing, rustling, swaying, thrashing, spreading, intertwining, twisting, (low-)hanging, snapping, patulous, prolific, leafy, thick(-leafed), dense, leafless, sapless, fruitless, (half-)bare, droopy, creaky, pendant, pendulous, errant, thorny, whippy, springy, delicate, slender, thin, gnarled, wide, bud-filled, tangled, bent, fallen, pliant, pliable, supple, divaricate

brandy, brandies See also *liquor* fine, smooth, neat, elegant, potent, aromatic, straight, silky, apple(jack), plum, cherry, apricot, liqueur

bravery See *courage*

brawl, brawls See *quarrel*

bread, breads crusty, pulpy, crumbly, flaky, crisp, chewy, soggy, sodden, (cotton-)soft, resilient, stodgy, heavy, rigid, rough, tough, warm, white, brown, black, (wafer-)thin, thick(-cut), plump, fresh(out-of-the-oven), piping-hot, savoury, tasty, aromatic, stale, mouldy, musty, rustic, flat, ring-shaped, wheaten, traditional, country-style, home-made, homely, commercial, standard, grainy, wholegrain, wholemeal, exotic, French, sacramental, American, Irish

breadwinner, breadwinners able, efficient, perfect, (ir)responsible, (un)successful, concerted, perpetual, haphazard, reluctant, hopeless, sole, main, absolute, partial, full-time, part-time

break, breaks soothing, refreshing, exhilarating, satisfying, pleasant, delightful, enjoyable, welcome, short-lived, complete, clean

breakdown, breakdowns annoying, infuriating, severe, serious, unavoidable, inevitable, sudden, unprecedented, unexpected, general, nervous, mental, mechanical

breakfast, breakfasts See also *meal* big, hearty, substantial, massive, prodigious, good, solid, square, leisurely, delightful, offbeat, nutritious, quick, light, (im)proper, skimpy, minimal, late-morning, fast-food, traditional, working

breakthrough, breakthroughs See also *success* amazing, tremendous, big, major, phenomenal, dramatic, first, real, medical, technological

break-up, break-ups acrimonious, nasty, messy, unpleasant, unfortunate, unexpected, sudden, dramatic

breast, breasts bouncing, spanking, startling, sensuous, provocative, assertive, naked, nude, bare, uncovered, exposed, clear, white, milky, creamy(-brown), lovely, tender, smooth, fine, pleasant, splendid, beautiful, graceful, sculptured, shell-like, meagre, small, underdeveloped, ample, bountiful, big, large, full, mature, firm, hard, taut, tight, flaccid, upright, high, up-pointed, upstanding, sharp, protrusive, round(ed), pouchy, shapeless, milk-swollen, dry, painful, lumpy, cancerous, cystic, prosthetic

breath, breaths rhythmic, tender, long, deep, profound, gargantuan, huge, sharp, shallow, eager, satisfied, ponderous, hasty, spluttering, quickening, shuddering, steaming, steamy, fiery, (un)easy, hard, painful, (catarrh-)choked, laboured, raspy, bubbly, gurgly, fresh, sweet, sour, intense, win(e)y, rancid, old, corrupt, rotten, bad, offensive, nauseous, fetid, stinking, rank, (un)pleasant, strong, abdominal

breathing serene, (un)steady, (im)proper, rhythmic, gentle, perceptible, (in)audible, stertorous, (un)easy, (ab)normal, (ir)regular, (un)quiet, unregulated, uncontrolled, slow, fast, rapid, difficult, deep, strong, heavy, (semi-)exhausted, laboured, tortured, shallow, short, harsh, hard, frantic, erratic, jerky, convulsive, jagged, ragged, grunting, open-mouthed

breed, breeds flourishing, vanishing, threatened, embattled, extinct, evanescent, superior, inferior, indigenous, distinct(ive), (un)identifiable

breeding impeccable, selective

breeze, breezes rising, passing, smacking, rustling, bracing, refreshing, soothing, pleasing, spanking, caressing, quartering, healthful, fresh, balmy, pure, crisp, brisk, lively, mild, tender, faint, slight, tepid, soft, slender, light, gentle, moderate, benign, friendly, vernal, welcome, grateful, sweet, fragrant, nippy, hoarse, strong, boisterous, stiff, sharp, steady, devious, unsettled, catchy, irregular, errant, wanton, wayward, random, desultory, lazy,

noxious, omnipresent, occasional, vesperal, landward, starboard, dry, warm, cool, chill(y), bone-chilling, southerly, southeasterly, westerly, northern, trade-wind-like, bucolic

brevity unusual, (un)acceptable, (ab)normal, exaggerated, bizarre, overdone, acid, testy, proverbial, legendary

bribe, bribes alluring, enticing, tempting, judicious, (in)discreet

brick, bricks (un)perishable, hard, rough, narrow, rectangular, red, mud, sand-lime, raw, clinker, decorative, Fletton, London

bride, brides bashful, shy, nervous, beautiful, (un)acknowledged, (un)avowed, prospective, secret

bridge, bridges low, high, overhead, spacious, reinforced, rehabilitated, new, substantial, four-lane, single-lane, tiered, two-tier, double-decked, many-arched, hump-backed, curving, graceful, handsome, mighty, spectacular, splendid, vital, (un)safe, (in)secure, fragile, weak, old, ancient, gaunt, shaky, rickety, creaky, rusty, rotten, swept-away, crude, narrow, temporary, girder(ed), statuary, vehicular, pedestrian, natural, rustic, (sand)stone, concrete, wooden, log, flyover, suspension, pontoon, arch(ed), floating

briefcase, briefcases elegant, leather, pigskin, eelskin, bulging, overflowing, dilapidated, lockable, zip-fastening

broadcast, broadcasts, broadcasting live, private, special, clandestine, nationwide, stereophonic, binaural, outside, overseas, local, regional, political, commercial

brochure, brochures easy-to-follow, (un)intelligible, informative, explanatory, slim, four-page, glossy, sensual, elegant, seductive, free, full-colour, preliminary, instruction, sales

brooding, broodings lonely, monkish, hermitical, secluded, depressed, forlorn

brook, brooks See *stream*

brother, brothers (un)affectionate, (un)loving, little, younger, elder, big, twin, half, whole, full, blood, foster, adopted, uterine; lay; soul

brow, brows handsome, broad, heavy, beetling, wrinkled, domed, precipitous, swarthy, dusky, dark, sparse, high, low

brown reddish, yellowish, greenish, greyish,

grey-orange, pinkish, purplish, blackish, golden, seal, deep, dull, pale, dingy, dormant, drab, dirty, muddy, strong, gentle, delicate, light, medium, dark(ish), chocolate, coffee, ginger, dingy, sandy, smok(e)y, mothy, coppery, blotchy, Vandyke

bruise, bruises touchy, painful, sore, unbearable, angry, livid

brutality, brutalities appalling, shocking, atrocious, hideous, ferocious, savage, repulsive, cruel, unrelenting, relentless, merciless, ruthless, remorseless, pitiless, heartless, senseless, incomprehensible, unimaginable, excessive, deliberate, sheer, ingrained, physical, emotional

bubble, bubbles gleaming, effervescent, gentle, pearly, iridescent, tiny, pinpoint, transient

bud, buds (half-)open, elongated, tight, axillary, cernuous, terminal; gustatory

budget, budgets legitimate, discretionary, tax-laden, bloated, gargantuan, huge, enormous, mammoth, massive, gigantic, extravagant, unlimited, limitless, (in)flexible, elastic, shoestring, anaemic, harsh, draconian, tough, strict, austere, no-frills, slim, paper-thin, penurious, frugal, pinchpenny, tight, (in)adequate, (in)sensible, debt-ridden, precarious, (un)balanced, well-balanced, (non-)accountable, supplemental, annual

buffalo, buffaloes wallowing, lolling, roaming, piebald, shaggy, water, Cape

buffet, buffets opulent, lavish, extravagant, sumptuous, bountiful, costly, wasteful, magnificent, imperial

bug, bugs See *insect*

building, buildings imposing, commanding, forbidding, fascinating, exciting, soaring, eye-catching, striking, stunning, enchanting, sumptuous, luxurious, lavish, elegant, sleek, graceful, ritzy, singular, distinctive, eclectic, handsome, dazzling, glittering, glimmering, gleaming, magnificent, stylish, fashionable, (centuries-)old, great, unique, idiosyncratic, revolutionary, ultramodern, exquisite, gritty, muscular, sturdy, solid, sound, indestructible, mighty, fancy, spectacular, stately, noble, lofty, majestic, expansive, capacious, commodious, (brand-)new, meretricious, attractive, ornate, splendid, impressive, enormous, massive, huge,

immense, monumental, stocky, grandiose, original, legendary, landmark, recognizable, noteworthy, venerable, operational, functional, utilitarian, tasteful, sleek, bland, chilly, flashy, gaudy, spiffed-up, cranky, wretched, hideous, crude, unsteady, unstable, flimsy, shaky, fragile, austere, dismal, drab, old, run-down, ramshackle, weather-worn, shabby, dowdy, gaunt, desolate, dead, defunct, congested, huddled, funky, gloomy, dreary, rambling, unsound, grimy, sooty, grey, decrepit, graceless, unattractive, ugly, irreparable, grotesque, ghostly, precarious, flimsy, outmoded, unfashionable, tasteless, sprawling, dilapidated, dingy, sleazy, low-slung, monolithic, stocky, surviving, low-lying, low-rise, high-rise, multistorey, two-block-long, squat, boxy, tall, skinny, prefabricated, sacred, empty, vacant, temporary, speculative, colonnaded, circular, rectangular, pyramid-roofed, main, fireproof, aseismic, unused, modernistic, futuristic, antique, historic, pioneer, heritage, neoclassical, turn-of-the-century, Romanesque, Gothic, baroque, art-deco, dark-timbered, false-fronted, densely-packed, cavernous, adjacent, commercial, industrial, municipal, office, corporate, residential, domestic, vernacular, squat

bull, bulls ill-tempered, irritable, ferocious, fearful, fearsome, cranky, frantic, stolid, enormous, colossal, massive, monstrous, clumsy, horned, frisky, range, winged, tame, sacrificial, Brahma

bullet, bullets stray, spent, tracer, standard, high-velocity, metal, rubber, plastic, mercury-tipped, silver

bully, bullies thrasonical, truculent, belligerent, cowardly, ferocious

burden, burdens light, easy, weightless, terrible, tremendous, enormous, considerable, colossal, heavy, crushing, devastating, unbearable, merciless, ruthless, pitiless, relentless, unrelenting, onerous, unconscionable, uneasy, impossible, awesome, constant, life-long, unwarranted, undue, unprecedented, economic, financial

bureaucracy, bureaucracies stifling, suffocating, exasperating, maddening, agonizing, baffling, uncaring, elaborate, cumbersome, complex, messy, awesome, terrible, formidable, oppressive, repressive, treacherous, massive, huge, large, enormous, endless, impenetrable, unresponsive, somnolent, lethargic, sluggish, top-heavy, privileged, dull, petty, faceless, swollen, bloated, crusty, tradition-bound, paternalistic, local, central, national, government

bureaucrat, bureaucrats grasping, high-ranking, senior, highly-paid, powerful, high-powered, seasoned, inflexible, obstructionist, bumptious, pompous, ambitious, tedious, negligent, inefficient, ineffective, corrupt, callous

burglar, burglars See *robber*

burial, burials solicitous, (im)proper, (in)decent, (un)ceremonious, elaborate, extravagant, honourable, peaceful, undisturbed, simple, quick, deep, primitive, pristine, anonymous, double, multiple, mass, private

burn, burns painful, superficial, deep, serious, substantial, hideous, horrible, first-degree, second-degree, third-degree

burst, bursts brittle, fitful, sporadic, spasmodic, convulsive, sudden, violent, explosive

bus, buses (over)due, late, early, sleek, oversized, chunky, shaky, decrepit, ramshackle, raucous, (un)reliable, local, private, public, communal, rural, city, cross-town, long-distance, night, double-decker, pay-as-you-enter; water

bush, bushes soaring, straggling, shrubby, thick, dense, scraggly, ragged, wiry, thorny, spiny, impenetrable, inhospitable, scrubby, dusty, tight, succulent, full-fruited, fruit, evergreen, deciduous

business (1: trade; commerce; buying and selling) booming, flourishing, thriving, surging, prosperous, brisk, lucrative, profitable, big, substantial, unchallenged, important, competitive, (un)stable, shady, stagnant, risky, dicey, tricky, multimillion-dollar, rough-and-tumble, waning, seasonal, slack, sluggish, strange, ephemeral, dead, spin-off, illicit, illegitimate, underground, high-risk, cut-throat, big

business, businesses (2: shop; commercial enterprise) flourishing, thriving, (in)active, new, small, medium-sized, big, prosperous, important, (un)successful, well-run, extensive, shaky, solid, sound, bread-and-butter, break-even, fledgling, defunct, independent, sideline, entrepreneurial, mail-order

business (3: task; duty; concern) all-important, dirty, secretive, pressing, urgent, rocky, dull, tough, complicated, risky, tricky, grim, hush-hush, frustrating, (un)official, private

businessman, businessmen See also Appendixes A and B high-flying, astute, honest, successful, affluent, shrewd, clear-sighted, discerning, energetic, perspicacious, ambitious, dynamic, aggressive, assertive, vigorous, hardworking, reputable, prosperous, no-frills, spunky, frisky, cautious, well-off, wealthy, blue-chip, realistic, practical-minded, self-made, no-nonsense, hard, prominent, influential, powerful, canny, world-class, (un)conscientious, (un)scrupulous, (un)ethical, greedy, crooked, dishonest, sleazy, seedy, unimaginative, unethical, hard-headed, hard-hearted, villainous, snide, high-powered, granite-faced, disreputable, hard-edged, mobile, entrepreneurial, small, super-rich, staid, harried, self-employed

businesswoman, businesswomen See *businessman*

butler, butlers traditional, family, aristocratic, (un)orthodox, wily, (in)experienced, obliging, devoted, reliable, generous, lordly, dignified, proud, stolid, impassive, expressionless, supercilious, conceited, pompous, fussy, hardworking, (in)valuable, amicable, admirable, retentive, ubiquitous, solitary, (un)self-conscious, pre-eminent, self-sufficient, fashionable, loyal, perfect, (in)offensive, heroic, inventive, resourceful, omniscient, discreet, unobtrusive

butter, butters hard, run, loose, creamy, salty, low-salt, sweet, fresh, strong, rancid, stale, molten, soft, frozen, lemon-flavoured, drawn

butterfly, butterflies quivering, panting, whirling, darting, floating, flashing, glittering, gay, dainty, beautiful, pretty, gilded, yellow, opal-winged, blue-winged, clear-winged, colourful, variegated, multicoloured, iridescent, evanescent, bright, brilliant, gaudy, theatrical, timid, nervous, drowsy, delicate, fragile, frail, powdery, light, swift, evasive, ungraspable, weary, common, migratory, nymphalid; social, literary

button, buttons pearl, gold, silver, brass, metal, fabric, shiny, filigreed, loose, fixed, adjustable, swirl

buttonhole, buttonholes dazzling, flamboyant, extravagant, resplendent, garish, gaudy, ostentatious, huge; bound, (in)visible

buyer, buyers heavy, eager, skittish, discerning, discriminating, (un)discriminate, (un)wise, aggressive, shrewd, canny, (un)willing, patient, avid, enthusiastic, gullible, frenzied, feverish, nervous, lack-lustre, prospective, potential, would-be, mystery, anonymous, speculative, solvent, first-time, dummy

buying See *buyer*

bystander, bystanders eager, alert, inquisitive, curious, confused, indifferent, passive, aloof, apathetic, cold, imperturbable, heedless, inconsiderate, innocent

cabin, cabins remote, lone(ly), roomy, spacious, one-room, snug, cosy, bright, dim, sturdy, rude, decrepit, weather-beaten, clapboard, starboard, log(-and-mud), cypress, thatched, roofed, rustic; port, deck

cabinet, cabinets (1: the executive body of a country) large, representative, unwieldy, (dis)loyal, (un)successful, split, coalition

cabinet, cabinets (2: a piece of furniture) See also *furniture* capacious, spacious, roomy, wide, low, tall, elegant, fusty, mouldy, musty, stuffy, freestanding, built-in, ash

cable, cables slender, thin, thick, heavy, twisted, Y-shaped, fibre-optic, submarine, coaxial, underground, electric

café, cafés pleasant, welcoming, lively, comfortable, intimate, cosy, colourful, charming, pricey, fancy, delightful, attractive, tranquil, (un)hygienic, smart, nice, favourite, cheery, orderly, elegant, glittering, trendy, venerable, classy, grand, posh, rich, sophisticated, urbane, fine, prestigious, handsome, plush, habitual, busy, spacious, tiny, little, modest, humble, appalling, dreary, shabby, smok(e)y, outdoor, open-air, terrace, rooftop, local, neighbourhood, mid-town, suburban, quayside, riverside, waterside, literary

cage, cages ornate, colourful, featureless, circular, funnel-shaped, wire, gaudy, garish, gloomy, smelly, filthy, confining

cake, cakes fluffy, flaky, light, dainty, delicious, rich, soft, moist, gooey, unleavened, flat, thin, thick, round, oblong, square, delicate, melt-in-the-mouth, assorted, sweet, luscious, heavenly, glorious, appetizing, lip-smacking, mouthwatering, ravishing, tempting, seductive, irresistible, crisp, sticky, sweet, creamy, nutty, plain, humble, brittle, bite-size, tasteless, mediocre, gigantic, special, patty, made-from-scratch, home-made, ready-mix, festal, fried, exotic

calamity, calamities See *disaster*

calculation, calculations elaborate, complex, intricate, detailed, meticulous, (in)correct, (in)accurate, tedious, rapid, casual, erroneous, stony, unfeeling, cold, mental, manual, mechanical, computer

calculator, calculators hand-held, pocket(-size), credit-card-size, full-function, electronic

calendar, calendars (in)accurate, intricate, complex, incongruous, illustrated, tear-off, perpetual, seasonal, electronic, heroic, ecclesiastical (Church), Gregorian, Hebrew (Jewish), Julian, Roman, Chinese, Hindu, Muslim (Islamic), Mayan, Republican (Revolutionary); Advent, Pirelli

calf, calves See also *cow* bleating, milk-fed, veal; unweaned, bone-thin

call, calls (1: short visit) lengthy, formal, occasional, unexpected, spontaneous, inopportune, mysterious, strange, perfunctory, inescapable, cold, exploratory, consultative, social

call, calls (2: cry; shout) raving, agitated, frantic, desperate, enraged, frenzied, forlorn, long, sharp, mating

call, calls (3: message; summons; invitation) intriguing, lengthy, occasional, inopportune, mysterious, extraordinary, seductive, frantic, agitated, threatening, disturbing, urgent, inescapable, anonymous, plaintive, high-pressure, abusive, nuisance, (un)expected, unauthenticated, hoax, incoming, internal, external, long-distance, domestic, overseas, person-to-person, reversed-charge

caller, callers See *visitor*

calm, calmness soothing, prevailing, imperturbable, unflappable, dignified, stoic, quiet, unhurried, clear-headed, serene, sullen, deep, dead, infinite, utter, absolute, impervious, cloistered, secluded, unruffled, dubious, deceptive, delusive, uneasy, ominous, tense, nervous, curious, astonishing, incomprehensible, unexpected, studied, drowsy, shattered, momentary, relative, outward, pastoral, Olympian

calumny, calumnies groundless, virulent, absurd, ridiculous, envious, bitter, venomous, acrimonious, blatant

camel, camels snuffling, snorting, snarling, groaning, grumbling, snapping, ambling, shuffling, gangling (gangly), lanky, frisky, surly, temperamental, dour, placid, domesticated, hamstrung, hump-backed, pack, Arabian (one-humped; dromedary), Bactrian (two-humped)

camera, cameras reflex, little, tiny, palm-sized, miniature, lightweight, sophisticated, foolproof, simple, compact, powerful, state-of-the-art, leading-edge, high-tech, hand-held, candid, sharp-eyed, manual, hidden, tripod-mounted, (un)steady, durable, ubiquitous, filmless, submersible, underwater, sonar, waterproof, telescopic, heat-sensitive, automatic, auto-focus, instant, still, electronic, panoramic, infrared, optical

camouflage masterful, skilful, clever, competent, ingenious, masterly

camp, camps fresh-air, cosy, well-kept, neat, simple, austere, spartan, lakeside, coastal, solitary, far-flung, remote, outlying, fetid, filthy, ramshackle, desolate, squalid, wretched, overflowing, sprawling, interracial, disused, jerry-built, makeshift, temporary, seasonal, summer, corrective, punishment, military; opposing, opposite, de facto

campaign, campaigns concerted, persistent, dogged, tough, all-out, strenuous, vigorous, shrill, energetic, aggressive, active, intensive, contentious, high-powered, broad, comprehensive, massive, widespread, large-scale, broad-based, city-wide, nationwide, countrywide, worldwide, daunting, strident, unbiased, (in)decisive, rousing, desultory, flamboyant, exuberant, (un)successful, valiant, victorious, elaborate, (in)effective, premeditated, low-budget, long-term, long-shot, non-stop, traditional, (un)popular, populist, one-man, moderate, lacklustre, low-key, vocal, raucous, tumultuous, frenetic, boisterous, frantic, hectic, feverish, zealous, diligent, ardent, loyal, complex, (public-)spirited, slick, splashy, vicious, rabid, aimless, abortive, futile, vociferous, dogged, tenacious, insurgent, unprecedented, chaotic, misguided, narrow-minded, dismal, dirty, mean, moribund, tricky, misleading, deceptive, treacherous, insidious, tendentious, bitter, nasty, relentless, merciless, ruthless, virulent, hostile, vacuous, vindictive, punitive, inexorable, volatile, rough-and-tumble, anti-intellectual, political, public-opinion, promotional, presidential, military, anti-crime, anti-alcohol(ism), anti-narcotics, anti-drug, anti-fur, whispering, public-relations, electoral, pre-election, door-to-door

campaigner, campaigners See *campaign*

camper, campers expert, skilful, (un)skilled, (un)trained, (in)competent, (dis)organized, avid, enthusiastic, amateur

campus, campuses See *university*

canal, canals open, closed, neutral, (un)safe, (un)navigable, (in)secure, (in)accessible, slow, tranquil, busy, winding, meandering, wide, deep, man-dug, man-made; alimentary, lateral, spinal, anal

cancer, cancers emerging, recurrent, widespread, invasive, serious, aggressive, dangerous, debilitating, deadly, fatal, fearsome, progressive, massive, advanced(-stage), developed, rare, palpable, (in)curable, (un)treatable, (in)operable, stealthy, stubborn, painful, painless, benign, malignant, colorectal, colonic, cervical, uterine, testicular, gastric, pancreatic, intestinal, vaginal, ovarian, lymphatic, endometrial, spinal, neural, rodentoid, breast

candidate, candidates viable, (un)welcome, (un)successful, (un)declared, (il)legitimate, (un)worthy, (un)deserving, (in)competent, (un)qualified, well-qualified, over-qualified, (un)acceptable, (un)promising, possible, (un)likely, (im)plausible, outstanding, hot, top(-flight), leading, major, strong, high-profile, favourite, long-shot, possible, potential, substantive, credible, specious, independent, rival, grey, weak, ill-starred, polarizing, desperate, (im)patient, optimistic, pessimistic, presidential, gubernatorial, mayoral, decanal, dark-horse, in-house

candle, candles flaming, flaring, bright, dim, alight, waxen, waxy, greasy, votive, tall, tallow; Roman

candour See *frankness*

candy, candies See *sweets*

cap, caps jaunty, flat(tish), puffy, frilly, squashy, soft, braided, peaked, brimless, cloth, felt

capability, capabilities See *ability*

capacity, capacities full, top, immense, infinite, limitless, (un)limited, unknown, unflagging, awesome, formidable, impressive, remarkable, uncanny; private, (un)official, advisory, fiduciary; thermal

cape, capes flowing, loose, fur, tweed, gold-brocaded, feathered, heavy, short, lengthy, hooded, detachable, reversible, separate, fixed, ermine

capital, capitals (1: money used in business) floating, dead, frozen, much-needed, (un)employed, idle, (un)invested, callable, (un)productive, paid-up, start-up

capital, capitals (2: a city serving as a seat of government) See also *city* (un)official, putative, provincial, regional, state, federal, territorial, constitutional, legislative, administrative, spiritual, colonial

capitalism democratic, unbridled, unrestrained, unfettered, free-market, bureaucratic

capitalist, capitalists devoted, greedy, insatiable, sleazy, corrupt, ruthless, old-fashioned

captor, captors brutal, ruthless, merciless, vigilant, cautious, wakeful, watchful

capture See also *captor* momentary, brief, sudden

car, cars shiny, deluxe, luxurious, luxury, plush, lush, spacious, glittery, prestigious, stately, expensive, costly, high-priced, spotless, roadworthy, trouble-free, (un)reliable, efficient, smart, streamlined, gleaming, chauffeur-driven, liveried, sleek, handsome, (un)stable, (un)steady, quiet, (un)comfortable, powerful, high-powered, good-quality, durable, rugged, top-of-the-line, exotic, flashy, tail-finned, competitive, swift, gas-hungry, vintage, phenomenal, bullet-proof, legendary, stylish, glamorous, classy, venerable, late-model, recent-model, antique, classic, peppy, high-performance, spanking, attractive, zippy, ostentatious, drivable, safe, well-travelled, one-owner, cute, economical, economy, inexpensive, no-frills, utilitarian, practical, fuel-efficient, environment-friendly, test-driven, unstable, unsafe, second-hand, mediocre, ungainly, decrepit, noisy, squealing, groaning, disabled, irreparable, knockabout, kidney-jarring, undrivable, cheap, troublesome, faulty, unglamorous, crumpled, dilapidated, beat-up, battered, crushed, bullet-ridden, abandoned, sedate, stuffy, dull, boxy, small, big, large, domestic, foreign, (sub)compact, front-wheel-drive, four-wheel-steering, two-wheel-steering, two-door, hatchback, four-cylinder, six-cylinder, eight-cylinder, automatic, open-topped, open-wheeled, one-seat, sporty, empty, vacant, driverless, fast, slow, stationary, south-bound, booby-trapped, armoured, convertible, open, electric, bumper, hydrogen, alternative-fuel, solar

card, cards (in)appropriate, hand-decorated, animated, (plastic-)laminated, distinctive, glossy, flash, vital, hot, strong, magnetic, bona fide, genuine, (in)valid, forfeit, fake, worthless, counterfeit, hand-made, ready-made, wild, post(al), all-purpose, birthday, Christmas, visiting, calling, business

cardigan, cardigans See *sweater*

care (1: attention) loving, understanding, satisfying, unremitting, unceasing, ceaseless, endless, supreme, utmost, extensive, infinite, excessive, constant, tender, meticulous, good, proper, fastidious, fine, conscientious, scrupulous, prompt, studious, affectionate, (un)satisfactory, attentive, (in)adequate, first-rate, first-class, high-quality, exemplary, elaborate, fabulous, provident(ial), zealous, assiduous, painstaking, exhaustive, unusual, extraordinary, solicitous, sophisticated, genuine, watchful, cautious, dutiful, reverential, religious, partial, cursory, minimal, torpid, superfluous, round-the-clock, acute, intensive, (in)accessible, long-term, brotherly, sisterly, motherly, fatherly, paternal, maternal, parental, medical, post-operative, prenatal, neonatal, pastoral, institutional, nursing, domiciliary, residential, palliative, respite, preventive, follow-up

care, cares (2: anxiety; worry) grave, weighty, momentous, burdensome, carking, onerous, earthly, household, domestic, worldly

career, careers flourishing, promising, blooming, fascinating, dazzling, rewarding, (un)satisfying, (un)congenial, brilliant, lustrous, bright, shining, luminous, glorious, singular, prolific, prosperous, lucrative, high-powered, distinguished, hard-won, triumphant, comfortable, blameless, independent, (well-)established, set, prodigious, spectacular, phenomenal, celebrated, fabled, illustrious, exceptional, remarkable, magnificent, wonderful, splendid, creditable, (in)glorious, (un)happy, clear-cut, (un)orthodox, chequered, varied, diversified, wide-ranging, versatile, multi-faceted, many-faceted, many-sided, bifurcate(d), colourful, flashy, sensational, lengthy, x-year, brief, truncated, meteoric, planetary, struggling, demanding, wandering, erratic, mysterious, enigmatic, bizarre, idle, vagrant, (un)stable, wayward, up-and-down, stormy, troubled, ignoble, shadowy, unpromising, once-promising, (un)eventful, (un)successful, dead-end, appalling, sagging, public, theatrical, dramatic, naval, academic, professional, corporate, auxiliary

carelessness subtle, sheer, apparent, seeming, unfeeling, shocking, disgraceful, shameful, wasteful, idle

caress, caresses soothing, conciliatory, tender, gentle, soft, pleasant, sweet, loving, rough, clumsy

cargo, cargoes See *goods*

caricature, caricatures (in)adequate, colourful, ridiculous, funny, camp, harsh, severe, overblown, bizarre, wicked, satirical

carnage, carnages frightening, appalling, shocking, terrible, ghastly, abhorrent, unprecedented, unimaginable, unbridled, savage, barbarous, merciless, gruesome, dreadful, horrible, grisly, frightful, baffling, abominable, hateful, senseless, wanton, wholesale

carpenter, carpenters (in)experienced, (un)skilled, inept, clumsy, awkward, cowboy

carpet, carpets See also *rug* luxury, plush, sumptuous, fine, sturdy, durable, shaggy, two-ply, worsted, flat-woven, shoddy, well-worn, scruffy, mossy, shabby, mangy, dusty, velvet, antique, magic, Persian

(Oriental), Brussels, Venetian, Turkish, Wilton, Art Deco, Axminster

carport, carports single, double, three-bay

carriage, carriages ornate, light, horse-drawn, one-horse, two-horse, horseless, pony, four-wheeled, two-seated, covered, open, recreational, ceremonial, hackney; railway

cart, carts heavy, two-wheeled, hand(-drawn), animal-drawn, toy, wooden, light

cartoon, cartoons amusing, animated, political, editorial, commercial

carving, carvings ornate, decorative, ornamental, floral, exquisite, splendid, magnificent, wonderful, remarkable, unusual, meticulous, flawless, perfect, elaborate, rich, baronial, intricate, quaint, deep, massive, obscure, painstaking

cascade, cascades See *waterfall*

case, cases (1: instance; condition) hopeless, fatal, unanswerable, (e)special, extreme, rare, gruesome, outrageous, egregious, notorious, mild, serious, critical, hypothetical, exceptional, sporadic, (un)reasonable, (ab)normal, (un)usual, (un)known, unexplained, complex, contagious, borderline, watershed

case, cases (2: lawsuit) circumstantial, interesting, notorious, high-profile, intriguing, controversial, (un)appealable, sensational, groundbreaking, unusual, landmark, skimpy, clear-cut, airtight, tough, complicated, perplexing, puzzling, spectacular, enormous, dangerous, difficult, tricky, bizarre, open, counterfeit, capital, criminal, civil, corporate, private

case, cases (3: argument) affecting, intense, plausible, persuasive, cogent

cash See also *money* petty, ready, cold, hard, residual, spot, instant, quick, meagre, spare, loose

castle, castles towering, rambling, forbidding, enchanting, fabulous, baronial, grand, glorious, lofty, luxurious, lovely, marvellous, wondrous, splendid, (once-)magnificent, sturdy, impregnable, lonely, storied, romantic, picturesque, spectacular, massive, enormous, old, spooky, venerable, capricious, gloomy, dank, (un)inhabitable, well-preserved, ruined, abandoned, haunted, fairy(-tale), marble-and-stone, ancestral, royal, feudal, Gothic, Baroque, Renaissance

casualty, casualties horrendous, horrible, terrible, frightful, heavy, high, unnecessary, uncalled-for; gastronomic, economic

cat, cats hissing, sprawling, darting, scratching, spinning, prowling, spluttering, purring, yowling, calling, sleeping, sleepy, predatory, feral, sabre-toothed, tame, ginger, tabby, bridled, tailless, digitigrade, sly, inquisitive, curious, purblind, restless, nervous, sleek, cute, short-haired, long-haired, contumacious, sphinx-like, lithe, pompous, fat, well-fed, pusillanimous, gaunt, mangy, (un)trained, uncollared, alley, road, stray, pet, domestic, Foreign, Shorthair, Blue, Abyssinian, Rex, Longhair, Himalayan, Siamese, Burmese, Maltese, Havana Brown, Angora, Manx, Russian, Persian

catastrophe, catastrophes See *disaster*

catch respectable, good, decent, lucrative, worthy, prestigious, enviable, unprecedented, record, (in)significant, picayune, meagre, labour-intensive, allowable, (non-)quota

cathedral, cathedrals See *church* (1)

cattle wandering, passing, obstreperous, noisy, unruly, blatant, prolific, scattered, rangy, sturdy, hardy, tough, healthy, attested, able-bodied, long-limbed, horned, pedigree, pure-bred, blooded, voracious, scrub(by), stunted, craggy, mangy, lank, slender, thin, scrawny, lean, skinny, emaciated, placid, pure, wild, captive, self-sustaining, dual-purpose, feral, upland, migratory

cauldron, cauldrons seething, boiling, foaming, steaming, bubbly, frothy, foamy, steamy

cause, causes (1: reason) clear-cut, precise, obvious, apparent, original, immediate, natural, deep-seated, root, fundamental, basic, primary, principal, major, central, leading, chief, main, assignable, (un)known, (un)certain, (un)determined, unidentified, hidden, complex, mysterious, enigmatic, (in)direct, (im)possible, bottom, reversible, correctable, curable, (im)probable, compelling, contributory, ultimate, final,

extraneous, elusive, highest, alleged, proximate; natural

cause, causes (2: aim) worthwhile, (un)worthy, (un)just, common, noble, passionate, moving, right(ful), righteous, moral, strong, (un)deserving, (un)popular, hopeless, questionable, phon(e)y, lost, peripheral, pet, ethnic, national, linguistic, cultural, political, altruistic

caution understandable, (un)wise, (un)necessary, discreet, discretionary, (un)enterprising, frugal, stealthy, unmitigated, unexpected, preparatory, initial, perpetual, permanent, lasting, deliberate, excessive, extreme, extra, sober(ing), (un)reasonable, snail-like

cave, caves intriguing, vast, spectacular, dank, chilly, murky, dark, shadowy, slippery, damp, warm, rocky, limestone, stuffy, dreary, gloomy, solitary, man-made, natural, hillside, secret, prehistoric, underground, subterranean, underwater, (under)sea

cavern, caverns See *cave*

ceasefire, ceasefires ambitious, durable, (in)effective, historic, immediate, urgent, wary, tenuous, shaky, fragile, elusive, failed, shattered, new, month-long, bilateral, unilateral, one-sided, official, (in)formal, total, (un)limited, (un)easy, temporary, permanent

ceiling, ceilings low, high, tall, towering, soaring, sloping, plaster, glass, grimy, gilt, ornate, decorated, sculptured, gold-flecked, filigreed, frescoed, coffered, cavernous, coved, (Gothic-)arched, vaulted, barrel-vaulted, fan-vaulted, ribbed, tent-like

celebration, celebrations glittering, rollicking, triumphant, glorious, upbeat, festive, rapturous, exuberant, joyous, euphoric, colourful, mammoth, marathon, full-scale, extravagant, spectacular, lavish, expensive, unabashed, ecstatic, spontaneous, raucous, boisterous, giddy, unrestrained, frenzied, delirious, wild, noteworthy, remarkable, extraordinary, uncommon, unique, living, (un)conventional, popular, subdued, funky, bittersweet, countrywide, preparatory, dual, annual, centenary, centennial, bicentenary, bicentennial, tercentenary, quatercentenary, hymeneal, nuptial, ecumenical, multifaith, ritual

celebrity, celebrities leading, top, chief, principal, popular, sought-after, best-dressed, worst-dressed, budding, incognito, small-scale, large-scale, instant, local, national, international, political, showbiz, Olympian

celibacy unbroken, continuous, uninterrupted, life-long, chosen, (in)voluntary, temporary, vowed, unaccountable, eccentric, fierce, sterile, painful, clerical, religious, doctrinaire

cell, cells (1: a small, close room) hard, bare, small, tiny, cement, windowless, fetid, stinking, humid, dark, dungeon-like, cramped, maximum-security

cell, cells (2: a tiny mass of living matter) healthy, immune, living, longevous, fatty, sponge-like, spore-like, flagellated, elongated, adhesive, residual, fragile, old, new, fresh, stiff, soft, embryonic, (im)mature, (ab)normal, (ir)regular, runaway, uncontrolled, hybrid, renegade, epithelial, malignant, cancer(ous), somatic, clastic, endodermal, epidermal, bacterial, reproductive, blood, sensory, basal, squamous, nasopharyngeal, ovarian, cervical, tubal, initial, meristematic

cell, cells (3: a device for generating electricity) wet, dry, dead, electrical, photoelectric, solar, fuel, primary (galvanic, voltaic), secondary, convective, open-circuit, nickel-cadmium, Daniel, Edison–Lalande

cellar, cellars damp, humid, dank, dark, close, clammy

cemetery, cemeteries immaculate, grandiose, marble-studded, impressive, calm, peaceful, sombre, bleak, scruffy, neglected, overgrown, outlying, national

censor, censors See *censorship*

censorship, censorships strict, austere, inflexible, oppressive, rigid, unrelenting, relentless, uncompromising, unyielding, heavy, constant, odious, abhorrent, detestable, loathsome, unjustifiable

censure, censures explicit, harsh, severe, caustic, hurtful, mild, token, unjustified, (un)deserved, public

centre, centres massive, state-of-the-art, (un)popular, metropolitan, regional, urban,

civic, bucolic, social, monastic, interpretive, cultural, commercial, financial, geographic(al), ecumenical

ceramic, ceramics stoneware, greenware, clay, porcelain, earthenware, slipware, creamware, redware, blackware, biscuit

ceremony, ceremonies overlong, impressive, beautiful, perfect, great, wonderful, splendid, magnificent, remarkable, spectacular, commanding, imposing, striking, amazing, elaborate, lavish, grandiose, ostentatious, expensive, tasteful, dignified, serious, grave, solemn, emotional, festive, joyous, smooth, rare, groundbreaking, exotic, sinister, grotesque, unnatural, forbidding, mysterious, sepulchral, wild, boring, cheap, flashy, low-key, (in)formal, indoor, outdoor, grand, special, nostalgic, traditional, antique, annual, religious, civil, sacred, nuptial, tribal, orgiastic

certainty, certainties inflexible, absolute, total, utter, complete, distant, virtual, practical, moral

certificate, certificates (un)authentic, (in)valid, fraudulent, fake, academic, medical, baptismal

chain, chains binding, continuous, endless, straight, intact, twisted, spidery, Y-shaped, iron, brass, bronze, steel

chair, chairs soft, easy, (un)comfortable, comfy, lazy, roomy, hefty, (un)reliable, (un)steady, deep, gilt, sumptuous, plump, luxurious, opulent, plush, overstuffed, stackable, adjustable, antique, decrepit, rickety, wonky, shaky, hard, stiff, wooden, metal, wicker, rattan, cane(-back), deal, wire-mesh, cast-iron, plastic-and-steel, moreen, canvas, chintz-covered, leather, backless, sling-back, grid-back, straight-back(ed), spindle-backed, oval-back, cross-leg, open-arm, squat, high, contour, vacant, ergonomic, occasional, wheeled, swivel, wing, hydraulic, electric, Sheraton, Chippendale, Wassily, Windsor, Hepplewhite, Morris; sedan; wheel; invalid; Bath

chairman, chairmen temporary, acting, honorary

chalet, chalets See *cottage*

challenge, challenges fascinating, exciting, interesting, rewarding, tempting, glaring, exhilarating, breathtaking, pressing, tantalizing, provocative, aggressive, successful, welcome, flat, real(istic), clamorous, blatant, stark, brazen, bold, stubborn, inescapable, unavoidable, inevitable, irresistible, indomitable, serious, fearless, awesome, heavy, stiff, tough, severe, cruel, formidable, awesome, worrisome, renegade, daring, jarring, risky, big, strong, tremendous, significant, enormous, immense, massive, Herculean, uphill, perpetual, unending, endless, never-ending, undiminished, supreme, ultimate, fundamental, (in)direct, implicit, explicit, new, last-ditch, upstart, unprecedented, impudent, unwinnable, elusive, abortive, insidious, warlike, sporadic, empty, proverbial, head-on, legal

champagne, champagnes See also *liquor* and *wine* dry, brut, sweet, (demi)sec, medium, pink, prickling, bubbly, tingly, tickling, cold, well-iced, authentic, celebratory

champion, champions grand, heroic, proud, invincible, undisputed, avowed, tireless, shining, enduring, early, budding, emerging, three-time, all-round, beaten, failed, single-minded, athletic, open, world, global, international, national, local, Olympic, pentathlon, decathlon

championship, championships prestigious, unprecedented, junior, senior, all-round, open, local, national, international, world

chance, chances exciting, promising, lucky, pleasant, lucrative, wondrous, splendid, excellent, real, considerable, substantial, strong, historic, reasonable, better-than-ever, certain, fifty-fifty, poor, slight, one-in-ten, remote, uncertain, marginal, minimal, slim, slender, five-per cent, precarious, negligible, zero, odd, diminishing, awful, ill-considered, off, second, final, last, only, sheer, outside, sporting

chandelier, chandeliers tinkling, swinging, dangling, dazzling, impressive, exquisite, splendid, lavish, elaborate, gorgeous, massive, enormous, big, heavy, flower-shaped, many-lustred, crystal, cut-glass

change, changes (1: changing) refreshing, constructive, welcome, salutary,

(un)pleasant, advantageous, beneficial, orderly, shifting, radical, drastic, dynamic, numerous, myriad, startling, extraordinary, unprecedented, subtle, genuine, concrete, exciting, dramatic, thorough, decisive, positive, peaceful, broad, extensive, comprehensive, far-reaching, sweeping, profound, (in)significant, major, mighty, appreciable, elaborate, enormous, tremendous, monumental, massive, huge, considerable, substantial, substantive, (im)measurable, staggering, breathtaking, stirring, gratuitous, durable, lasting, long-term, terminal, key, fundamental, basic, requisite, essential, indispensable, bold, (un)predictable, notable, remarkable, amazing, bewildering, astounding, astonishing, striking, startling, progressive, gradual, rapid, quick, speedy, spontaneous, abrupt, immediate, sudden, sharp, last-minute, impending, imminent, epochal, periodic, seasonal, continuous, obvious, noticeable, observable, perceptible, blatant, real, dizzying, tough, painful, cataclysmic, sullen, irrevocable, (un)stoppable, (ir)reversible, (ir)remediable, (un)avoidable, (in)evitable, turbulent, tumultuous, portentous, fateful, deliberate, sensible, specific, nominal, short-lived, minor, small, tiny, superficial, frivolous, trifling, inconsequent(ial), slight, pointless, contentious, objectionable, questionable, further, unsettling, over(due), measured, pronounced, marked, decided, restrictive, outward, external, cosmetic, surface, qualitative, physical, chemical, demographic, structural, revolutionary, evolutionary, cyclical, constitutional

change (2: money) correct, right, exact, loose, spare

channel, channels (1: a bed of running water) meandering, winding, twisting, tortuous, treacherous, current-torn, side, unobstructed

channel, channels (2: means of communication) (un)suitable, established, (il)legitimate, secret, (un)official

chaos distressing, frightening, limping, faltering, uncontrolled, unexampled, unprecedented, indescribable, incredible, unbelievable, perpetual, everlasting, complete, utter, total, absolute, constant, endless, incessant, unbounded, boundless, widespread, prevalent, dreadful, hellish, apparent, creative

chapter, chapters brief, scanty, punchy, lively, stirring, illuminating, (un)interesting, disconnected, heavy, dull, boring, detailed, introductory, final

character, characters (1: personal qualities; personage) See also Appendixes A and B appealing, lovely, pleasant, amiable, unimpeachable, heroic, unblemished, irreproachable, guileless, modest, forthright, imposing, colourful, humane, stable, impeccable, reformed, solid, decisive, resolute, determined, decided, distinct, resilient, puzzling, baffling, anomalous, crazy, weird, ambiguous, scary, singular, odious, negative, weak, despicable, warped, questionable, prosaic, vindictive, unstable, evil, bad, shady, caustic, wicked, unsavoury, tenacious, arrogant, petulant, autocratic, unusual, enigmatic, schizophrenic

character, characters (2: a person in a story, play) engaging, engrossing, refreshing, (un)original, vivid, vibrant, effective, rounded, life-like, human, (un)believable, (in)credible, (un)recognizable, (un)identifiable, three-dimensional, (in)consistent, intense, intricate, complex, larger-than-life, colourful, zany, (un)lik(e)able, (un)sympathetic, (un)popular, memorable, notable, timeless, good-natured, folksy, (un)lovable, grotesque, whimsical, bizarre, pivotal, central, predominant, major, minor, supporting, feminine, masculine, rich, (over)drawn, wooden, automatonlike, cardboard, blank, colourless, dimensionless, flat, one-dimensional, stereotyped, stereotypical, stock, obsolete, empty, sketchy, shallow, recurrent, representative, eponymous, authentic, mythic, fictitious, imaginary, composite, title, titular, cartoon

characteristic, characteristics overwhelming, abiding, appealing, endearing, striking, outstanding, distinguishing, distinctive, fixed, prominent, (pre)dominant, salient, positive, basal, chief, basic, fundamental, underlying, obvious, noticeable, notable, discernible, distinguishable, identifiable,

traceable, perceptible, peculiar, particular, special, unique, remarkable, marked, preponderant, (un)common, curious, whimsical, extraordinary, (un)pleasant, (un)desirable, (un)attractive, (un)enviable, contradictory, stubborn, intricate, stereotypical, inheritable, hereditary, ancestral, genetic, physical, racial, cultural, mental, genealogical, atavistic

characterization, characterizations painstaking, precise, (un)faithful, masterly, powerful, shrewd, complex, perfunctory, shallow

charge, charges (1: accusation) heavy, persistent, serious, capital, formal, positive, damning, old, long-standing, outstanding, specific, stunning, dire, provocative, sensational, (un)just, stark, obscure, grotesque, irresponsible, outlandish, groundless, baseless, far-fetched, forced, contrived, trumped-up, unfounded, phon(e)y, wrongful, false, dubious, base, contemptible, foolish, ridiculous, ludicrous, (un)proven, exaggerated, partial, (un)constitutional, legal, criminal, disciplinary

charge, charges (2: price asked) overdue, fixed, excessive, hefty, additional, minimum, supplementary, differential, standing, cover, service, terminal

charisma charming, dazzling, amazing, astonishing, astounding, stunning, radiant, powerful, talented, rare

charity (1: giving, kindness) ever-shining, supreme, heavenly, worthwhile, impulsive, boundless, unguarded, reckless, quixotic, cold-hearted, bloodless

charity, charities (2: benevolent organization) non-profit, voluntary, (non-)religious, (un)organized, registered, private, corporate, bona fide

charm, charms See also *attraction* enticing, captivating, bewitching, alluring, winning, flashing, fascinating, engaging, striking, endearing, compelling, surpassing, graceful, mesmeric, breezy, persuasive, masterful, unbeatable, irresistible, seductive, meretricious, unassuming, happy-go-lucky, relaxed, offhand, postcard, conspicuous, nameless, indefinable, vaunted, bluff, mighty, considerable, infinite, unending, enduring, remarkable, distinctive, special, curious, sinister, sardonic, rough-hewn, ebullient, superficial, deceptive, galling, low-key, cockeyed, quirky, deadly, inherent, inborn, native, manly, virile, physical, natural

chase, chases life-threatening, hair-raising, wild(-goose), high-speed, feverish, unsafe, dangerous, hazardous, fatal

chat, chats revealing, pleasant, humorous, witty, jocular, idle, light, casual, friendly, leisurely, desultory, mechanical, trifling, trivial, frivolous, futile, empty, mindless, parrot-like, unmeaning, meaningless, senseless, purposeless, endless, eternal, everlasting, incessant, perpetual, continuous, unceasing, lengthy, raucous, noisy, boisterous

chatter, chatters See *chat*

chauvinism See *patriotism*

cheat, cheats subtle, smart, ingenious, neat, treacherous, dastardly, foxy, snide, devilish, cunning, scurvy, despicable, rotten, sly, dishonourable, mischievous, crafty, base, low, rascally, abject, unscrupulous, dirty, nasty, mean, dext(e)rous

check, checks thorough, rigid, exhaustive, rigorous, strenuous, (im)proper, (in)appropriate, (ir)regular, (un)reasonable, intimidating, quick, random, cursory, superficial, perfunctory, routine, annual, occasional, periodic

cheek, cheeks damask, vermeil, (cherry-)red, crimson, ruddy, vivid, pink, rosy, rose-coloured, flushed, glowing, wholesome, milky, apple, hectic, sallow, wan, smooth, soft, cherubic, limp, round, oval, hollow, plump, fleshy, chubby, flabby, flaccid, fat, swollen, frostbitten, baggy, lean, thin, whiskered, fissured, puffed, fallen, shrunken, sunk(en), rugose, wrinkled, taut, haggard, chipmunk

cheekbone, cheekbones high, prominent, protrusive, chiselled

cheer, cheers rousing, deafening, (in)appropriate, good, tremendous, loud, enthusiastic, merry, fervent, heartfelt, vigorous, lusty, vociferous, wild, unruly, spontaneous, ragged, faint, half-hearted, reluctant, fickle

cheerfulness glowing, gushing, overflowing, bouncing, inexhaustible, indefatigable, effusive, brisk, buoyant, exuberant, ebullient, ecstatic, effervescent, giddy, hearty, calm, irreverent, impulsive, spontaneous, outward

cheering See *cheer*

cheese, cheeses creamy, rich, tasty, savoury, delectable, delicious, smooth, (semi-)soft, firm, hard, dry, (un)spreadable, runny, (un)ripe, mild(-tasting), medium, old, tart, piquant, nippy, sharp, tangy, funky, porty, pungent, strong-tasting, strong-smelling, aged, mature, snappy, mellow, maggoty, decayed, spiced, herbed, (mild-)flavoured, smoked, fine-grained, bland, low-fat, blue; synthetic, substitute, non-dairy

chef, chefs See *cook*

chemical, chemicals (un)stable, volatile, (in)efficient, powerful, potent, harmless, harmful, fearsome, hazardous, (non-)toxic, noxious, nasty, destructive, lethal, active, (in)soluble, waterproof, airborne, ozone-friendly, ozone-unfriendly, (non-)explosive, (non-)flammable, combustible, corrosive, agricultural, industrial, (in)organic, natural, synthetic, man-made, carcinogenic, base, precursor

cheque, cheques hefty, siz(e)able, substantial, fat, large, small, blank, detachable, bad, bogus, fraudulent, (in)valid, phon(e)y, fake, (un)cashable, bouncing, dud, personal, foreign, traveller's

chest, chests (1: part of the body) heaving, broad, flat, hollow, rounded, (over-)hairy, hairless, heavy, clear, tight, puffed-up, congested

chest, chests (2: large box) wide, broad, plump, commodious, flat, solid, heavy, portable, thin, soft, padded, fluffy, wooden, oak, cedar, pine, tin, metal, tea

chicken, chickens puling, squawking, cheeping, chirpy, fluffy, broody, recalcitrant, intensive-reared, free-range, live, plump, skinless, boneless, succulent, tender, soft, tasty, juicy, crisp, tough, stringy

chief, chiefs See *leader*

child, children screaming, crying, whimpering, beseeching, squalling, fretting, wailing, squealing, sobbing, howling, whining, well-fed, cherubic, sweet, innocent, charming, alert, docile, sensitive, considerate, harmonious, warm, affectionate, adorable, lovable, doll-like, playful, spirited, sprightly, exuberant, vivacious, gregarious, sociable, obedient, inquisitive, observant, curious, precious, non-aggressive, quiet, solicitous, sturdy, well-behaved, independent, self-reliant, (in)secure, pretty, buoyant, cheerful, light-hearted, healthy, dutiful, good, well-mannered, neat, rosy, remarkable, ingenuous, smart, talented, exceptional, gifted, precocious, robust, (un)pleasant, homely, truthful, demure, shining, guileless, sophisticated, tractable, delightful, privileged, resilient, jittery, difficult, irritable, fretful, whiny, uncommunicative, destructive, inconsiderate, noisy, naughty, restless, obstinate, pert, nasty, cheeky, bad, rough, troublesome, errant, shy, bashful, wayward, wilful, backward, boisterous, violent, bold, changeable, unpredictable, wretched, rash, impulsive, reckless, thoughtless, harum-scarum, ill-gotten, ill-bred, ill-favoured, incorrigible, pettish, perverse, stubborn, rebellious, hard-to-handle, unmanageable, uncontrollable, ineducable, spoilt, refractory, recalcitrant, saucy, mischievous, forward, disobedient, bad, naughty, contrary, fractious, impetuous, irresponsible, inactive, over-active, hyperactive, cranky, trouble-prone, ebullient, unruly, wild, rambunctious, rumbustious, fidgety, disruptive, obdurate, untoward, thankless, virulent, peevish, assertive, simple, sleepy, groggy, frail, fragile, sad-faced, sheepish-looking, sickly, sullen, sulky, unhealthy, delicate, hungry, shabby, ragged, weak(ly), anaemic, starving, malnourished, undernourished, fickle, wild-haired, barefoot, bedraggled, forlorn, frightened, unhappy, favourite, roly-poly, dumpy, squat, innocent, naïve, simple, trusting, talkative, wriggly, cross, little, diminutive, dependent, timorous, defenceless, adventurous, submissive, lost, missing, late-born, mixed-race, normal, problem, learning-disabled, handicapped, underprivileged, (mentally-)retarded, abused, forsaken, disadvantaged, troubled, disturbed, unfathered, posthumous, out-of-wedlock, bastard, illegitimate, adulterine, misbegotten, firstborn, changeling, fatherless, motherless, putative, natural, genetic, biological, single, only,

minority, minor, marasmic, dyslexic, autistic, spastic, psychotic, institutionalized

childbirth, childbirths See *birth*

childhood placid, (un)stable, contented, idyllic, true, privileged, sheltered, carefree, (un)happy, blighted, deprived, wretched, troubled, cheerless, appalling, miserable, grim, hellish, traumatic, chaotic, sickly, lonely, (ab)normal, fatherless, motherless, latchkey, seared, second, late, early, distant

chill, chills See *cold*

chimney, chimneys soaring, decorative, practical, functional, foul, filthy, steeple-like, pointed, conical, squat, stovepipe

chin, chins elegant, long, firm, dimpled, double, receding, square, cleft, clean-shaven, jutting, stubby, upswept, pronounced, determined

china, chinaware See also *porcelain*
delicate, fancy, brittle, fragile, unique, exquisite, vitreous, rare, antique, bone, fine, extraordinary, irreplaceable, decorative, ornamental, functional, commemorative, Ming

chocolate, chocolates See also *sweets*
tempting, mouthwatering, sinful, decadent, tasty, rich, luxury, hand-made, (un)sweetened, milk, dark, white, (semi)sweet, hot, liquid, solid, soft, hard, diabetic

choice, choices encouraging, enticing, appealing, exciting, (un)popular, masterly, careful, fit, inspired, expert, sensible, apt, deft, prudential, viable, astute, solid, genuine, (un)safe, (un)wise, (un)reasonable, (in)appropriate, (il)logical, (un)intelligent, well-informed, (un)informed, (un)clear, (un)satisfactory, (un)acceptable, odd, obvious, absolute, (un)qualified, right, wrong, handy, quick, fitting, (im)possible, overwhelming, (un)lucky, (a)typical, (un)limited, limitless, endless, myriad, comprehensive, plenteous, wide, little, narrow, careless, easy, stark, reluctant, inept, ill-informed, senseless, (in)constant, fickle, changeable, wavering, free, (in)convenient, desperate, natural, dynamic, (ir)revocable, (ir)reversible, compromising, arbitrary, controversial, incongruous, hard, difficult, tough, agonizing, bitter, painful, fatal, fateful, cursed, devilish, stunning, bewildering, discouraging, disappointing, thorny, quirky, delicate, permanent, voluntary, top, primary, number-one, first, foremost, specific, personal, unanimous, final, ultimate

chore, chores backbreaking, onerous, burdensome, weighty, tremendous, troublesome, tedious, dull, humdrum, boring, risky, complicated, repeated, put-off, simple, mundane, domestic, household, day-to-day

chorus, choruses merry, red-cassocked, discordant, dissonant, clamorous, raucous, male, female, mixed

Christian, Christians good, pious, fervent, staunch, devout, faithful, primitive, (non-)practising, (non-)observant, strict, committed, lapsed, born-again, fundamentalist, evangelical

Christmas, Christmases See also *feast* green, white, brown, colourful, good, lovely, delightful, cheerful, merry, memorable, stress-free, debt-free, glittering, hectic, cheerless, stressful, grim, antipodean, sunny

chronicle, chronicles See *history* and *record* (1)

church, churches (1: a building for public Christian worship) See also *building* soaring, terrifying, imposing, dazzling, fascinating, solid, flinty, (sand)stone, rock, adobe, beautiful, pleasant, lovely, tiny, small, miniature, peaceful, famous, renowned, celebrated, notable, glorious, magnificent, splendid, gracious, impressive, elaborate, gorgeous, monumental, massive, enormous, vast, spectacular, majestic, stately, grand, sumptuous, noble, sublime, venerable, distinctive, remote, thousand-seat, rock-hewn, squat, spiral, spired, pinnacled, peaked, square-towered, squat-towered, twin-towered, (gold-)domed, onion-domed, bulbous, red-roofed, tawny-roofed, frescoed, steepled, plain-windowed, floodlit, unspoilt, historic, ancient, (centuries-)old, rustic, grey, weather-worn, derelict, battered, monastic, medieval, national, Gothic, Baroque, Romanesque

church, churches (2: a particular body or division of Christians) charismatic, influential, (all-)powerful, non-denominational, mother,

long-established, well-established, early, present-day, Established, conservative, hierarchical, universal, national, official, mainline, dedicated, patriarchal, Christian, primitive, guild, collegiate, sedate, state, state-controlled, dictatorial, fundamentalist, (in)flexible, progressive, reactionary, episcopal, apostolic, Bible-thumping

cigarette, cigarettes smouldering, half-lit, cork-tipped, tailor-made, loose, contraband, potent, aromatic, stinking, king-size; herbal

cinema, cinemas See also *building* wide-screen, state-of-the-art, leading-edge, silent

circle, circles narrow, wide, inner, vicious, ever-decreasing, concentric, eccentric, polar, vertical

circulation, circulations endless, high, mass; poor, pulmonary, systemic

circumstance, circumstances flourishing, (un)promising, prosperous, fortuitous, easy, well-to-do, happy, (dis)honourable, right, (in)auspicious, (un)fortunate, (un)favourable, (un)propitious, (dis)advantageous, diverse, damnatory, unique, forced, sad, dividing, poignant, gruesome, miserable, embarrassed, suggestive, hard, adverse, futile, contracted, narrow, poor, inextricable, extreme, difficult, complicated, desperate, pressing, depressed, dire, depressing, harrowing, creepy, unusual, unlikely, peculiar, unforeseen, unexplained, unaccountable, powerless, fishy, (un)clear, cloudy, suspicious, questionable, bizarre, strange, mysterious, disadvantaged, (un)straitened, (un)controllable, untoward, turbulent, chaotic, strained, stressful, despicable, scurvy, troubling, trying, perilous, (un)expected, extenuating, attendant, similar, parallel, converging, dramatic, extraordinary, specific, special, precise, exact, external

circus, circuses thrilling, exciting, breathtaking, interesting, enchanting, delightful, raucous, boisterous, barbaric, three-ring, family, flea; Roman

citizen, citizens law-abiding, heritage-conscious, conservation-minded, concerned, thoughtful, viable, (dis)loyal, orderly, (ir)responsible, productive, respectable, peaceable, solid, good, valuable, exemplary, model, savoury, public-spirited, restive, affluent, well-pedigreed, distinguished, illustrious, prominent, leading, influential, eminent, great, honoured, average, ordinary, defenceless, innocent, simple, humble, second-class, inferior, middle-class, low-income, (il)literate, (un)wary, aged, senior, permanent, public, private, honorary, fellow, instant, world

city, cities brawling, teeming, thriving, booming, (once-)flourishing, imposing, glittering, sparkling, stunning, charming, appealing, fascinating, intriguing, captivating, enchanting, bewitching, exciting, attractive, seductive, busy, boisterous, tumultuous, immense, far-flung, monumental, great, colossal, huge, big, populous, vivacious, vibrant, exuberant, festive, dynamic, weighty, sanitary, safe, exotic, unique, giant, sophisticated, resplendent, glittery, sleek, neat, handsome, stylish, trendy, chic, graceful, elegant, gracious, civilized, refined, modern, cosmopolitan, omnivorous, dressy, kaleidoscopic, splendid, magnificent, free, prosperous, special, world-class, wide-avenued, sumptuous, hospitable, picturesque, stimulating, main, principal, major, proud, stately, majestic, regal, royal, lofty, fabled, fabulous, legendary, glorious, venerable, luxuriant, glamorous, wealthy, expensive, many-faceted, intimate, well-run, anodyne, uncrowded, quiescent, spacious, flashy, sprightly, family-orient(at)ed, residential, comfortable, (un)livable, (un)inhabitable, happy-go-lucky, dreamlike, romantic, casual, earthy, self-indulgent, delightful, lovable, lovely, beloved, squeaky-clean, corny, sedative, sombre, dour, sullen, insanitary, filthy, dull, somnolent, seedy, crime-ridden, dilapidated, smok(e)y, smoggy, smog-shrouded, polluted, suffocating, stuffy, (over)crowded, congested, cacophonous, rambling, swelling, sprawling, fast-growing, stressful, dingy, dowdy, shabby, frumpy, untidy, decrepit, drab, unassuming, desolate, depopulated, lonely, dangerous, tumbledown, decayed, grimy, confused,

worn-out, restive, restless, noisy, strident, plangent, turbulent, impetuous, frenetic, windswept, stodgy, boorish, old, clustered, stagnant, cardboard, recalcitrant, hostile, (wide-)open, impregnable, free, (mountain-)walled, fire-stricken, war-weary, dominant, rebel-held, threatened, riot-torn, gritty, medium-sized, striking, uncaring, static, ancient, antique, (pre)historic, medi(a)eval, foreign, history-rich, remote, outlying, distant, strange, inland, fair, tent(ed), nocturnal, one-industry, multiracial, holy, biblical, inner, maritime, mountain-nestled, mountain-fringed, industrialized, sea-girt, coastal, provincial, capital, satellite

civilization, civilizations old, ancient, classical, well-developed, (long-)established, unique, sophisticated, spectacular, glorious, superb, splendid, brilliant, thriving, flourishing, flowering, forward, affluent, mighty, dingy, dense, complex, complicated, moribund, past, bygone, effete, little-known, effeminate, material, backward, ill-understood, homogeneous, heterogeneous, dynastic, capitalist, oriental, Western; galactic

claim, claims solid, well-founded, (in)valid, (il)legitimate, (un)authentic, (un)just, (un)reasonable, (un)realistic, genuine, rightful, (un)lawful, (un)convincing, intriguing, tantalizing, significant, (in)credible, (un)sustainable, (im)plausible, (un)acceptable, (in)accurate, (un)supportable, (in)disputable, specious, explicit, amorphous, audacious, tenuous, unabashed, shameless, fictitious, feigned, false, bogus, fake, fraudulent, sham, phon(e)y, doubtful, dubious, suspect, questionable, erroneous, baseless, groundless, unfounded, hollow, treacherous, dishonest, crooked, misleading, conflicting, contradictory, deceitful, deceptive, absurd, bad, weak, lame, unwarranted, crazy, frivolous, arrogant, bizarre, inconsiderate, prior, frequent, multiple, persistent, special, widespread, expansive, populist, prophetic, vociferous, strident, wild, amazing, long-standing, melting, (un)important, enormous, hefty, exorbitant, excessive, extravagant, unrestrained, inflated, grandiose, outrageous, outlandish, skewed, modest, first, outstanding, compensable, proprietary, territorial, civil

claimant, claimants See *claim*

clamour untiring, unwearying, pressing, unremitting, unflagging, persistent, indefatigable, (un)justifiable

clan, clans See *tribe*

clapping See *applause*

clarity discerning, penetrating, amazing, striking, appealing, unusual, concise, insistent, graphic, simple, crystal, limpid, open, distinct, recognizable, unblemished, manifest, (un)ambiguous, doubtful

clash, clashes deadly, fatal, bloody, terrible, violent, armed, furious, ferocious, titanic, intense, explosive, (in)evitable, (un)avoidable, sporadic, accidental, consequent, brief, ethnic, racial, tribal, cultural, military

class, classes (1: a group sharing the same status) privileged, landed, moneyed, propertied, proprietary, titled, ruling, dominant, white-collar, select, élite, vibrant, prosperous, opulent, affluent, comfortable, leisured, leisurely, high(er), upper, middle, superior, inferior, low(er), underprivileged, untitled, mercantile, blue-collar, subordinate, servile, tight-knit, narrow, fast-growing, reactionary, feudal, rising, social, urban

class, classes (2: a body of students) full, (over)crowded, round-the-clock, sparse, small, (un)popular, attentive, reverential, lively, noisy, well-attended, regular, evening, night, tutorial, remedial, professional, graduating

classic, classics major, minor, established, popular, instant

classification, classifications elaborate, meticulous, convenient, careful, rigid, crude, symptomatic, systematic, methodical

clause, clauses (a division of sentence) main, subordinate, coordinate, consecutive, (non)restrictive, substantive, temporal, adjectival, adverbial

claw, claws extensile, retractile, toothed, hooflike, curved, sheathed, sharp, strong, stout, tremendous, massive, powerful, rigid, wicked, vicious, prehensile

clay, clays soft, moist, workable, malleable, stiff, impervious, silty, residual, sedimentary, stratified, molten, red, potters', China

cleanliness spotless, immaculate, meticulous, speckless, high, obsessive, haunting, abysmal, parochial, personal, public

clearness See *clarity*

clergy, clergyman See *priest*

clerk, clerks (un)trusted, (in)competent, (un)able, trustworthy, confidential, office, lay, parish

cleverness fiendish, diabolical, devilish, demoniacal, excessive, extreme, fierce, foxy, wicked

client, clients See *customer*

clientèle See *customer*

cliff, cliffs towering, sweeping, soaring, jutting, forbidding, impending, dizzying, frightful, awesome, gigantic, massive, huge, giant, majestic, stupendous, lofty, tall, scenic, spectacular, sheer, protective, steep, precipitous, abrupt, dominant, bold, sombre, rugged, sterile, waterless, unscalable, treacherous, inaccessible, scraggly, craggy, curving, circular, perpendicular, irregular, jagged, hewn, sculptured, waterfall-tasselled, sea-swept, wave-eaten, coastal, rocky, sandy, (lime)stone, chalk, clay, granite, sandstone

climate, climates bracing, relaxing, healthful, (un)healthy, (un)wholesome, beneficial, beneficent, bountiful, (in)hospitable, balmy, congenial, kindly, pleasant, amiable, genial, seductive, attractive, appealing, idyllic, (in)salubrious, sunny, perfect, ideal, gentle, benign, mild, favourable, moderate, equable, dry, clement, bland, warm, (dis)agreeable, wonderful, buoyant, exceptional, equable, diverse, (un)varying, uniform, (un)familiar, rainy, harsh, frigid, sickly, rigorous, severe, cool, wet, unforgiving, forbidding, wearing, inimical, alien, unfriendly, ineffable, soporific, frosty, oppressive, fierce, humid, damp, moist, baneful, unpredictable, capricious, variable, difficult, arid, (un)steady, seasonal, outdoor, (sub)tropical, alpine, highland, (sub)arctic, continental, polar, (sub)temperate, ecological; political

climax, climaxes emotional, sensational, harrowing, effective, spectacular, (un)expected, elusive

climb, climbing nimble, (un)successful, (un)safe, (un)steady, steep, stiff, sharp, giddy, tough, arduous, painful, difficult, laborious, painstaking, tiresome, formidable, titanic, horrendous, frightful, heroic, dramatic, hellish, flawless, perilous, dangerous, awesome, challenging, gruelling, dizzying, uphill, practice, artificial

climber, climbers agile, lithe, (in)flexible, avid, keen, victorious, tough, rugged, strong, heroic, expert, lead, veteran, (well-)trained, ill-trained, (in)experienced, (un)successful, intrepid, fearless, adamant, unyielding, fallen, panting, exhausted, worn-out, professional, amateur, champion

clinic, clinics reputable, modern, high-tech, state-of-the-art, rudimentary, spartan, sprawling, local, private, medical, antenatal, walk-in

clique, cliques tight, tenacious, influential, splinter, interdependent, identifiable, privileged, fascist, advantaged

cloak, cloaks regal, voluminous, oversized, big, hooded, invisible, snug, billowing, sweeping, flowing, swirly, comprehensive, sleeveless, dowdy, threadbare, shabby, torn, ragged

clock, clocks precise, (in)accurate, ornate, exquisite, magnificent, splendid, stately, slow, fast, unrepaired, (ir)repairable, rusty, rust-free, run-down, (un)set, unwound, self-winding, marble, soapstone, brass, ormolu, weight-driven, atomic, electric, musical, ornamental, miniature, digital, electronic, wind-up, astronomical, 400-day, quartz

clockwork regular, correct, harmonious, precise, proper, thorough, uniform, synchronous

closet, closets See *wardrobe* (1)

cloth, cloths coarse, rough, flimsy, durable, indestructible, serviceable, sleazy, tough, strong, damask, woollen, cotton, satin-weave, twill-weave, shaggy, jacquard, covert, balloon, threadbare, sensuous, glossy, waterproof, thorn-proof, light, heavy, plain, check, reversible, scratchy, damp, lint-free, pre-shrunk, burial, altar; bark, American

clothes, clothing modish, trendy, posh, elegant, prim, stylish, chic, fashionable, smart, way-ahead, extravagant, quality, bandbox-fresh, contemporary, trim, avant-garde, glamorous, high-profile, neat(-looking), natty, regal, fine, unique, distinctive, custom(-made), made-to-measure, adorable, decent, rich, sumptuous, opulent, expensive, unobtrusive, respectable, dazzling, quiet, presentable, exquisite, conservative, crushable, stretchy, serviceable, wearable, wrinkle-free, spick-and-span, sturdy, (im)proper, (in)appropriate, (un)suitable, (in)adequate, no-nonsense, snug, sensible, practical, utilitarian, versatile, simple, plain, subdued, unusual, rough-cut, cumbersome, bulky, tight, loose, enveloping, baggy, snazzy, boxy, square-shouldered, old-fashioned, unfashionable, outmoded, antiquated, dated, antediluvian, humble, seedy, shabby, dreary, dingy, run-down, stark, dowdy, threadbare, worn, tattered, torn, ragged, oversized, way-out, cast-off, second-hand, sodden, gritty, scruffy, soiled, chintzy, slovenly, unbecoming, unfit, wrong, crummy, fussy, over-florid, foppish, flamboyant, iridescent, flashy, tatty, garish, loud, showy, gaudy, kinky, hideous, hand-me-down, grubby, wrinkly, wrinkled, regular, mannish, unusual, heavy, light, sexy, immodest, sensual, provocative, inappropriate, daring, (un)revealing, close-fitting, loose-fitting, step-in, old, ready-made, square-shouldered, quilted, boxy, sombre, thin, scanty, full, simple, plain, ready-to-wear, conventional, off-the-rack, gender-neutral, sporty, sports, camouflage, military, civilian, (in)formal, casual, dressy, workaday, seasonal, synthetic, arctic, thermal, protective, fireproof, fire-resistant, fire-retarding, funerary, ceremonial, decorative, clerical, religious

cloud, clouds billowing, towering, passing, impending, reeking, black(-bellied), leaden, dull, dark, murky, variable, noctilucent, nacreous, luminous, diaphanous, (cotton-)white, (blue-)black, inky, sombre, sullen, grey, pastel, rosy, roseate, purple, golden(-coloured), glossy, chill, scattered, ragged, high-altitude, unattainable, podgy, opulent, thick, heavy, immense, vast, enormous, copious, ponderous, big, giant, mountainous, gargantuan, rough, turbulent, nebulous, long, viscous, lateral, vertical, lenticular, pot-bellied, globular, bulbous, narrow, immovable, fleecy, fluffy, puffy, cottony, billowy, patchy, wispy, lacy, fibrous, riven, thin, empty, little, light, magnificent, splendid, ugly, high, middle, low, curious, scuffy, dreary, dirty, acrid, sulphurous, radioactive, cosmic, convective, dust, dank, rain(y), rainbowed, rain-laden, steamy, vapoury, foggy, pensive, angry, ominous, depressing, easterly, layer, variable, cirrus, stratus, cumulus, nimbus, alto-cumulus, alto-stratus, cirro-stratus, cirro-cumulus, cumulo-nimbus, strato-cumulus

club, clubs exclusive, exclusionary, mandarin, prestigious, classy, posh, select, élite, stylish, trendy, tight, elegant, reputable, venerable, celebrated, world-famous, extravagant, pretentious, swank(y), remarkable, cosy, quiet, austere, relaxed, convivial, lively, powerful, vital, (un)successful, flashy, snazzy, sleazy, disreputable, dubious, hard-pressed, defunct, dank, musty, liquorless, (in)formal, executive, private, country, social, fraternal, political, professional, faculty

clue, clues tantalizing, puzzling, vexing, exciting, interesting, fascinating, (in)valuable, useful, strong, important, major, essential, critical, vital, valid, telltale, extraordinary, memorable, possible, simple, small, false, hidden, missing, casual, collateral, magnetic

clumsiness See *awkwardness*

coach, coaches (1: a closed four-wheeled carriage) elegant, elaborate, ornate, plush-seated, horse-drawn, imperial, royal, regal; motor, tourist; railway

coach, coaches (2: a tutor) exacting, demanding, imaginative, disciplinarian, communicative, inflexible, pedantic, dogmatic, arbitrary, fanatical, imperious, harsh, stern, able, capable, competent, efficient, devoted, dedicated, enthusiastic, natural, noted, well-known, veteran, retired, former, personal

coaching See also *coach* (2) rewarding, conscientious, innovative, (in)effective, intuitive, brilliant

coal glowing, incandescent, white-hot, clean-burning, live, smouldering, (jet-)black, brownish-black, hard, soft, dull, polluting, cob, sulphurous, bituminous, sub-bituminous, brown, anthracitic, steam, house

coalition, coalitions See *union*

coast, coasts scenic, picturesque, idyllic, spectacular, breathtaking, delightful, charming, sparkling, majestic, dramatic, dynamic, benign, undulating, rolling, steep, (non-)marshy, rocky, rock-ribbed, rock-bound, island-fringed, arid, barren, hard, harsh, jagged, craggy, rugged, fretted, forbidding, uninviting, impenetrable, receding, sweltering, unknown, undeveloped, uninhabited, exposed, pristine, wild, primitive, wind-swept, wind-worn, windward, stormy, battered, icebound, dreary, featureless, solitary, lonely, desolate, continuous, vast, outer

coastline, coastlines See *coast*

coat, coats mink, fur(-lined), astrakhan-collared, oilskin, woolly, camel-hair, sable, duffle, leather, buff, felt, worsted, melton, lamb, damask, buckskin, buffalo-skin, cashmere, canvas, frieze, splashy, snug, warm, rich, heavy, made-to-order, made-to-measure, stylish, neat, handsome, bespoke, lustrous, splendiferous, lightweight, classic, brand-new, ready-made, oversize, roomy, big, downy, shiny, flaring, flowing, huge, pepper-and-salt, one-button, two-button, single-breasted, double-breasted, covert, long, floor-length, calf-length, three-quarter(-length), knee-length, short-cut, trapeze-cut, stranded, high-collar, notch-collar, convertible, casual, oversized, conservative, cutaway, scant, flimsy, reversible, (swallow-)tailed, bald, dilapidated, dowdy, worn, disreputable, old, torn, ragged, threadbare, tattered, shabby, battered, old-fashioned, frumpish, frumpy, clumsy

cock, cocks shrilling, strutting, surly, fiery, crowing; heath, chaparral

code, codes cryptic, inviolable, tough; strict, stern, rigorous, ethical, moral, civil, penal; digital, postal

coffee, coffees refreshing, steaming, scalding, smooth, snappy, musty, nutty, rich, palatable, robust, full-bodied, strong, powerful, mellow, muddy, dilute, weak, brisk, frothy, thick, washy, watery, fresh(-ground), freshly-made, stale, undrinkable, loose, (finely-)ground, coarsely-ground, roast, ersatz, regular, fine, instant, black, white, milky, espresso, cappuccino, Turkish, Irish, Spanish, Viennese

coiffure, coiffures See *hair-do*

coin, coins current, rare, antique, historic, extinct, old, obsolete, genuine, authentic, collectible, eleven-sided, new-mint, brilliant, flashy, shiny, glistening, gleaming, shining, glittering, (un)tarnished, gold, silver, bronze, copper, counterfeit, spurious, false, bad, defective, worthless, worn, discoloured, bulky, clumsy, heavy, base, curious, decimal, subsidiary, special-edition, proof, commemorative

coincidence, coincidences intriguing, astonishing, startling, astounding, amazing, surprising, striking, intoxicating, sheer, remarkable, happy, delightful, (in)convenient, (un)fortunate, fishy, strange, odd, curious, eerie, outrageous, rare, exceptional, extraordinary, uncommon, unusual, phenomenal, miraculous, remarkable, singular, (un)likely, (im)possible, (im)probable, (im)plausible, (un)convincing, (in)credible, (un)believable, far-fetched, crass, mysterious, uncanny, fateful, serendipitous

cold (1: low temperature) exhilarating, stinging, biting, pinching, grinding, penetrating, deathly, fearful, atrocious, hellish, pitiless, heartless, ruthless, merciless, relentless, unrelenting, inclement, unbelievable, incredible, (knife-)sharp, intense, severe, fierce, harsh, brutal, bleak, extreme, deep, excessive, bitter, near-zero, icy, brittle, clammy, (un)common

cold, colds (2: illness) nasty, bad, miserable, frequent, recurrent, continual, chronic, persistent, prevalent, devastating, abominable, villainous, resistant, incurable, infectious, slight, shivery, feverish, seasonal, common, sinus, chest, head

coldness detached, withdrawn, apparent, aloof, indifferent, rude

collaboration, collaborations remarkable, responsible, fruitful, unstinting, total, full, close, growing, increasing, occasional, artistic, literary

collaborator, collaborators clever,

fruitful, (un)successful, impartial, fine, well-known, regular, unusual, close, (un)willing, (un)witting, suspected, uneasy, ill-assorted, corrupt, cunning, evil, traitorous, political, literary, artistic

collapse, collapses devastating, withering, wasting, disastrous, general, virtual, final, terminal, permanent, (long-)overdue, unexpected, general, nervous, emotional, physical, financial, economic

collar, collars standing, rolling, pointy, long, tall, high, deep, wide, enormous, double, wing, starched, rolled, notched, removable, capelike, (a)symmetrical, stand-up, stiff, turn-down, lace, guipure, immaculate, grubby, polo, wraparound, straight, draw-string, rounded, pinned, button-down, cervical, clerical, Italian, English, Vandyke, Peter Pan; white, blue, pink

colleague, colleagues former, erstwhile, esteemed, powerful, higher-status, influential, (un)reliable, (un)congenial

collectible, collectibles See *collection*

collection, collections striking, outstanding, intriguing, astounding, amazing, surprising, astonishing, dazzling, staggering, stunning, enchanting, fascinating, bewildering, (fast-)growing, baffling, perplexing, leading, foremost, prominent, premier, impressive, sumptuous, fantastic, fabulous, formidable, huge, vast, multitudinous, monumental, generous, massive, mammoth, numerous, large, enormous, extensive, rich, incredible, unbelievable, beloved, sought-after, prized, coveted, world-renowned, (in)valuable, priceless, irreplaceable, important, worthy, noble, sensitive, unique, exceptional, extraordinary, unusual, offbeat, one-of-a-kind, matchless, peerless, unparalleled, unexcelled, fine, exclusive, magnificent, exquisite, superb, stupendous, splendid, wonderful, remarkable, encyclop(a)edic, useful, luminous, miscellaneous, motley, multifarious, diverse, varied, homogeneous, heterogeneous, heteroclite, disparate, idiosyncratic, comprehensive, vivid, sprightly, timeless, antique, glitzy, (un)representative, volatile, static, rambling, meagre, scant, skeletal, pedestrian, iffy, useless, worthless, ramshackle, confusing, mad, crazy, odd, strange, bizarre, random, dusty, dull, art, family, corporate, private, public, popular, posthumous, permanent, archival

collector, collectors incurable, avid, keen, zealous, fervent, voracious, prolific, active, industrious, assiduous, skilful, (un)conscientious, unscrupulous, private, major, wealthy, (un)reflective, eccentric, impulsive, hurried

college, colleges See also *university* and *school* (non-)residential, Forces, denominational, private, well-regarded, reanimated, all-men, all-women, coeducational, sixth-form, community, commercial, agricultural, theological, business, further-education, technical

collision, collisions See also *accident* slight, massive, spectacular, fatal, violent, explosive, side, rear-end, head-on, mid-air

colony, colonies subservient, backwater, former, crown, penal, proprietary; lunar

colour, colours magnificent, exquisite, splendid, luscious, majestic, glorious, rich, full-bodied, strong, subtle, delicate, (in)congruous, consonant, consistent, warm, cheerful, gay, vital, vivid, vibrant, flamboyant, auspicious, elegant, (in)harmonious, matching, tasteful, (un)lovely, restful, earth(y), roan, mous(e)y, golden, dusky, dark(ish), sizzling, screaming, flaming, splashy, daring, bold, innovative, curious, incompatible, moderate, spectacular, inconspicuous, striking, muted, neutral, sober, plain, washy, pale, livid, drab, dim, dingy, dull, faint, dormant, dusty, complementary, deep, light, quiet, delicate, tender, languorous, grave, sombre, even, false, flame, mellow, spectral, spotty, odd, streaky, variegated, changeable, accidental, (a)chromatic, thin, flat, clear, ruddy, soft, off-key, insistent, compelling, (pre)dominant, radiant, brilliant, rippling, glowing, bright, loud, strident, intense, sharp, jerky, dazzling, stunning, garish, gaudy, showy, spurious, riotous, sensuous, abusive, translucent, limpid, sickly, dismal, bilious, distasteful, nauseating, absurd, (un)natural, extraordinary, curious, haunting, deceptive, everlasting, iridescent, opalescent, turbulent, luminous, gauzy,

sepia, reflective, autumnal, heat-absorbent, fast, solid, primary, fundamental, basic, local, prismatic, chromatic

colouring See *colour*

colours See *flag*

column, columns imposing, soaring, tall, high, lofty, heavy, massive, giant, gigantic, mighty, vertical, gold, ornamental, graceful, splendid, magnificent, narrow, slender, supporting, tumbling, ruined, battered, marble, lace-like, fluted, architectural, Egyptian, Roman, Doric, Ionic, Corinthian; vertebral, spinal

combat, combats See also *battle* and *war* (un)equal, fierce, ferocious, bloody, deadly, mortal, meaningless, senseless, close, hand-to-hand, single, (un)armed, impending, organized, mock, head-to-head, air, aerial; judicial

combatant, combatants See *warrior* and *soldier*

combination, combinations winning, striking, unique, wonderful, remarkable, fantastic, unusual, rare, curious, blockbuster, mix-and-match, odd, bizarre, knock-out

come-back, come-backs stunning, surprising, astounding, astonishing, amazing, remarkable, strong, incredible, unbelievable, unexpected, sensational

comedian, comedians entertaining, funny, zany, beloved, lovable, favourite, big-time, resourceful, (un)popular, (un)employable, flamboyant, irrepressible, well-paid, best-paid, poorly-paid, major, consummate, world-class, resourceless, durable, stand-up, alternative

comedienne, comediennes See *comedian*

comedy, comedies genuine, sophisticated, irresistible, first-class, delightful, brilliant, warm(-hearted), human(istic), cheerful, lively, vivacious, buoyant, extravagant, hilarious, uproarious, convulsive, frenetic, funny, sunny, exhilarating, amusing, diverting, facetious, light(-hearted), witty, whimsical, clever, amiable, gentle, refined, fantastic, sustained, deadpan, half-hearted, (in)elegant, noisy, tedious, ribald, bawdy, indecent, risqué, racy, crude, raunchy, silly, goofy, bizarre, dumb, raucous, fatuous, bleak, acidulous, self-deprecating, stark, dark, black, straight, serious, intellectual, high-camp, high, low, musical, physical, farcical, slapstick, bucolic, pastoral, rustic, folk, improvisational, satirical, sentimental, genteel, classic(al), romantic, fanciful, stand-up, episodic, surreal, social, Restoration

comfort, comforts cosy, sunny, elaborate, opulent, luxurious, baronial, spacious, solid, real, ineffable, everlasting, splendid, exquisite, genuine, civilized, superficial, cold, chilling, depressing, small, scant, modest, forsaken, comparative, relative, ultimate, creature, sensual, worldly, material, spiritual, religious, emotional, personal

command, commands total, consummate, absolute, unqualified, peremptory, (un)merciful, (ir)responsible, base, high, imperative, silent, divine, royal, unified, joint, central, single, direct

commander, commanders charismatic, capable, daring, powerful, formidable, tyrannical, dictatorial

commemoration, commemorations See *celebration*

comment, comments revealing, informed, reasonable, terse, concise, lucid, measured, just, suggestive, insightful, cogent, perceptive, informative, erudite, recondite, profound, luminous, (un)clear, (im)proper, (in)appropriate, apt, (in)sensitive, (un)fair, sympathetic, pointed, powerful, upbeat, snappy, succinct, pertinent, relevant, quotable, aphoristic, esoteric, analytical, cryptic, enigmatic, veiled, humorous, lively, throwaway, copious, extensive, indiscriminate, divergent, digressive, adverse, dour, outspoken, blunt, brusque, rude, coarse, heavy-handed, imperious, outrageous, off-screen, unreasonable, wry, snide, malicious, catty, spiteful, jaundiced, resentful, scathing, blistering, lacerating, caustic, tangential, partisan, partial, sarcastic, incisive, mocking, ironic, unctuous, flattering, acid, snappish, troubling, uncalled-for, breathless, impromptu, casual, off-the-cuff, running, direct

commentary, commentaries See *comment*

commerce See *trade* (1)

commercial, commercials See also *advertisement* witty, graphic, oily, unctuous, oleaginous, persuasive, insincere, deceptive, misleading, (in)effective

commercialism crass, cynical, insensitive, unfeeling, vulgar, unrefined, excessive, rampant, dominant, prevalent, unrestrained, reduced

commission, commissions x-member, preliminary, special, fact-finding, investigative, royal, rogatory, papal

commitment, commitments unflinching, binding, sticking, sweeping, unfailing, unending, long-standing, increasing, growing, long-term, lifetime, lifelong, permanent, unabated, undiminished, unrestrained, intense, firm, decisive, resolute, close, serious, categorical, definite, unequivocal, genuine, whole-hearted, unqualified, open-handed, open-ended, concrete, profound, deep, hard-nosed, solid, full, staunch, dogged, ferocious, unshak(e)able, irreversible, irrevocable, implacable, enthusiastic, passionate, idealistic, constructive, laudable, major, large, outstanding, unavoidable, inevitable, fundamental, special, monastic, stand-by, quiet, solemn, clear, simple, lukewarm, half-hearted, small, token, fading, wavering, momentary, marital, unilateral, military, financial, visceral, intellectual

committee, committees independent, select, mammoth, siz(e)able, x-member, special, unwieldy, crucial, sensitive, powerful, influential, watchdog, key, blue-ribbon, (in)effective, fractious, parochial, moribund, all-party, consultative, advisory, executive, administrative, disciplinary, congressional, legislative, preparatory, revisory, policy(-setting), joint, ad hoc, central

commodity, commodities See *goods*

common sense compelling, convincing, moving, pressing, telling, potent, powerful, sound

communication, communications peaceful, (un)healthy, (in)adequate, (in)efficient, (in)effective, meaningful, thoughtful, real, (ab)normal, private, privileged, two-way, constant, non-existent, sporadic, chequered, faulty, poor, rudimentary, clandestine, intimate, confidential, incriminating, frustrating, instant, global, telepathic, (non-)verbal, symbolic, social, military, electronic, telegraphic, postal, telephonic, radio, televisual, computer

communicator, communicators able, powerful, skilful, convincing, compelling, dynamic, energetic, forceful, natural, born

communiqué, communiqués authoritative, upbeat, cheerful, bland, final, draft, military

Communism progressive, military-style, totalitarian, unadulterated, rigid, hard-core, hard-line, old-line, dogmatic, doctrinaire, monolithic, suffocating, fading, failing, fragile, reformist, atheistic, godless, orthodox

Communist, Communists See also *Communism* overt, die-hard, dedicated, loyal, passionate, fanatical, hard-line

community, communities flourishing, prosperous, affluent, sleek, chic, unique, progressive, liberal, cosmopolitan, attractive, exciting, modern, (un)stable, traditional, family-orient(at)ed, self-sufficient, self-governing, self-contained, self-supporting, interdependent, Utopian, humane, just, comfortable, viable, vital, graceful, healthy, solid, sober, small, tiny, minuscule, diminutive, large, siz(e)able, (ever-)growing, fast-growing, roisterous, wild, vibrant, diverse, complex, stiff, instant, dreary, sedate, distinct, (in)coherent, outlying, remote, far-flung, satellite, neighbouring, clannish, cliquish, close(-knit), insular, parochial, contentious, riven, split, troubled, high-profile, low-profile, (in)significant, multicultural, biracial, mixed-race, polyglot, native, aboriginal, ethnic, refugee, immigrant, urban, rural, rustic, world-wide, primitive, (semi)nomadic, transient, resident, political, diplomatic, cultural, black, biblical, religious, spiritual, ecclesiastical, monastic

commuter, commuters See *traveller*

companion, companions boon, bonny, engaging, valued, perfect, merry, cheerful, jovial, jolly, gay, dear, genial, loyal, constant, inseparable, longtime, delightful, amiable, (un)pleasant, (dis)agreeable, (un)desirable, (un)congenial, (un)interesting, (un)wholesome, boring, tiresome, low, coarse, bad, vulgar, (un)sociable, ancient, (in)frequent, live-in, sexual

company, companies (1: business) See also *firm* giant, big, large, wildcat, major, small, mid(dle)-size, medium-size, expansionist, promising, flourishing, fast-growing, billion-dollar, unwieldy, high-quality, monolithic, spun-off, (well-)established, powerful, (in)efficient, customer-orient(at)ed, debt-free, creditworthy, viable, dynamic, innovative, (un)profitable, pervasive, aggressive, diversified, united, venerable, independent, market-driven, faltering, struggling, (once-)failing, money-losing, distressed, troubled, debt-laden, shaky, obscure, fledgling, (un)successful, insolvent, private-sector, public-sector, family-controlled, family-financed, state-owned, parent, subsidiary, holding, export-orient(at)ed, industrial, commercial, pharmaceutical, fiduciary, global, multinational, international

company, companies (2: an organization of musical or dramatic performers) accomplished, (well-)established, prestigious, venerable, active, first-class, (in)capable, (in)efficient, resident, touring, strolling, theatrical, amateur, professional

company (3: a group of persons) stimulating, entertaining, attractive, affectionate, good, lively, convivial, jocund, glad, playful, congenial, genial, friendly, choice, august, notable, illustrious, glamorous, mixed, (un)desirable, (un)welcome, (un)pleasant, (un)healthful, (dis)agreeable, extravagant, dull, low, vulgar, coarse, mean, wretched

comparison, comparisons discriminating, (in)valid, (im)plausible, (un)favourable, (un)fair, (im)partial, (im)precise, (in)exact, (in)accurate, (un)reliable, apt, close, far-fetched, overblown, shoddy, flawed, gratuitous, illusory, invidious, inept, dubious, odious, tongue-in-cheek, unavoidable, inevitable, direct

compassion See *pity*

compensation, compensations cushy, (un)fair, (un)just, better, belated, immediate, meagre, low, high, hefty, rich, generous, excessive, (un)reduced, set, full, partial, individual, financial, monetary, workman's

competence sheer, prodigious, superb, enviable, unequalled, incomparable, extraordinary, marvellous, remarkable, astonishing, outstanding, flawless, demonstrable, notable, noteworthy, unobtrusive

competition, competitions healthy, friendly, (un)fair, (un)just, brisk, tremendous, high, robust, close, extreme, strong, vigorous, aggressive, harsh, stiff, tough, rigorous, desperate, keen, sharp, intense, fierce, feverish, hot, steamy, all-out, full-fledged, weighty, pure, tenacious, ferocious, gruesome, rabid, unrelenting, relentless, merciless, ruthless, pitiless, heartless, vicious, cut-throat, unscrupulous, unbelievable, head-to-head, constant, long-standing, cruel, increasing, rising, growing, bruising, gruelling, blistering, unfettered, vain, incalculable, formidable, heated, formal, open, (now-)defunct, regional, national, international, world-class, foreign, global, athletic

competitiveness See *competition*

competitor, competitors worrisome, fierce, tough, suppressive, cut-rate, formidable, ferocious, dominant, far-reaching, hot, consistent, tireless, determined, resolute, tenacious, stubborn, aggressive, vicious, deadly, new, eligible, rival

compilation, compilations See also *collection* engaging, intriguing, staggering, stunning, astonishing, dazzling, meticulous, scrupulous, laborious, authoritative, vast, massive, monumental, extensive, incredible, fantastic, coveted, unparalleled, unexcelled, encyclop(a)edic, tedious

complainer, complainers loud, constant, confirmed, chronic, habitual, professional

complaint, complaints rising, sweeping, predominant, number-one, common, familiar, frequent, serious, angry, loud, resigned, bitter, relentless, tiresome, consistent, persistent, ultimate, everlasting, endless, (un)authentic, (il)legitimate, unfounded, groundless, false, spurious, sham, vague, (in)significant, minor, petty, frivolous, vexatious, irrational, individual, universal, primary, official, formal

complexion, complexions glowing, radiant, fresh, dewy, (un)healthy, (un)wholesome, youthful, smooth, coarse, dark, swarthy, florid, ruddy, sanguine,

unblemished, pasty, sickly, sallow, ashen, pallid, pale, deathly, spotty, luminous, clear, fair, high-coloured, milky, off-colour, olive, ivory, creamy

complexity, complexities baffling, staggering, incredible, unbelievable, prodigious, nightmarish, awesome, labyrinthine, Gordian

compliance, compliances total, strict, (in)sincere, (un)enthusiastic, (un)willing, early, half-hearted, weak, tepid, feigned, grudging

complication, complications alarming, life-threatening, devastating, labyrinthine, intricate, hideous, serious, long-term, everlasting, chronic, benign, potential

compliment, compliments charming, touching, warm, genial, pretty, ultimate, superb, graceful, gracious, elaborate, stupendous, flaming, flowery, florid, exuberant, lavish, excessive, extravagant, profuse, generous, (in)sincere, (un)restrained, well-timed, best-timed, borderline, fanciful, left-handed, dubious, doubtful, fulsome, flattering, empty, double-edged, two-edged, backhanded, ironical, ambiguous, sweeping, broad, routine, sly

component, components essential, fundamental, crucial, vital, active, primary, indispensable, pivotal, requisite, sensitive, organic, chemical, base

composer, composers See *musician*

composition, compositions exceptional, original, unequalled, unique, taut, complex, whimsical, extemporaneous, musical, chemical, physical, written

composure unfaltering, imperturbable, unflappable, calm, serene, cool, admirable, remarkable, professional, formal

compromise, compromises shrewd, clear-sighted, ingenious, subtle, artful, brilliant, achievable, amiable, (un)tenable, (im)possible, (un)workable, (in)effective, (un)happy, (un)acceptable, (un)satisfactory, (un)palatable, (un)easy, (un)reasonable, unique, essential, unavoidable, inevitable, tentative, fragile, delicate, elusive, objectionable, painful, tortured, far-reaching, face-saving, last-ditch, reluctant

computer, computers ambitious, elaborate, advanced, complex, complicated, sophisticated, inscrutable, self-conscious, high-speed, powerful, (un)reliable, foolproof, innovative, programmable, high-performance, recalcitrant, obsolete, outdated, mainframe, desktop, laptop, mini, analog(ue), digital, hybrid, hand-held, portable, pocket, rugged, built-in, ballistic, primary, personal, optical, electronic, high-end, mid-range, IBM-compatible, micro

comrade, comrades See *companion*

concealment, concealments sly, artful, astute, canny, crafty, sneaky, cunning, foxy, stealthy, furtive, secret(ive), duplicitous, surreptitious, cautious, clandestine

conceit, conceits See *vanity*

concentration, concentrations consuming, full, immense, enormous, tremendous, heavy, intense, intensive, tight-lipped

concept, concepts See also *idea* unique, innovative, novel, new, radical, abstruse, (un)ambiguous, specious, murky, muddy, vague, fuzzy, strange, alarming, repugnant, static, fluid, narrow, conventional, eons-old, reactionary, outdated, outmoded, universal, central, fundamental, scientific, theoretical

conception, conceptions popular, superficial, misguided, dualistic, visual, symbolic, impressionistic

concern, concerns burning, debilitating, pressing, rising, growing, increasing, overwhelming, overriding, on-going, touching, lingering, underlying, enduring, lifelong, neurotic, grave, assiduous, legitimate, valid, real, genuine, understandable, (un)justifiable, earnest, indulgent, imminent, urgent, immediate, prime, capital, chief, principal, prime, primary, utmost, major, paramount, dominant, supreme, apparent, obvious, tremendous, strong, vital, deep, profound, widespread, massive, serious, sharp, guarded, definite, specific, sole, unexpected, tender, minor, minimal, frivolous, scant, picayune, petty, mean, undue, irrational, silly, common, mutual, earthly, temporal, mundane

concert, concerts full-bodied, tremendous, prestigious, first-class, public, formal, annual, philharmonic, rock, pop, outdoor, open-air, impromptu, symphony, festival, benefit, Advent Christmas, carillon, memorial, gala, inaugural

concession, concessions key, substantial, fundamental, dramatic, far-reaching, big, major, enormous, tough, remarkable, (un)important, (in)significant, (un)limited, additional, exclusive, partial, minor, face-saving, territorial

conclusion, conclusions breathtaking, sobering, moving, surprising, (un)happy, victorious, firm, obvious, foregone, climactic, prudent, reasoned, unarguable, inevitable, unavoidable, inescapable, irrefutable, (il)legitimate, mordant, strong, (in)correct, (il)logical, natural, dramatic, premature, (un)believable, (in)credible, (im)plausible, (un)reasonable, (un)likely, far-reaching, easy, secure, arbitrary, poignant, reluctant, (un)provable, wan, absurd, false, fallacious, faulty, hasty, abrupt, pitiful, slippery, bleak, bitter, stark, bizarre, gloomy, apocalyptic, erroneous, alarming, shocking, unsettling, damning, distressing, (un)expected, guarded, interpretive, speculative, deliberative, overall, initial, tentative, final

condemnation, condemnations open, sharp, angry, unmeasured, wholesale, bitter, obstinate, tough, harsh, powerful, scathing, stinging, sweeping, deafening, fiery, shrill, priggish, joint, blanket, moral, religious

condition, conditions (1: the present state of things; circumstances) tip-top, immaculate, ideal, perfect, exceptional, superb, normal, elaborate, optimum, optimal, passable, hopeful, comfortable, fine, (un)settled (un)stable, variable, (un)enviable, (un)favourable, (in)auspicious, (dis)agreeable, (un)safe, (in)sanitary, (un)hygenic, (un)pleasant, (un)fortunate, (un)correctable, flaccid, arduous, harsh, intolerable, unbearable, cruel, tough, trying, discouraging, difficult, stressful, regretful, pitiable, distressing, alarming, abysmal, foul, dismal, fatal, unspeakable, terrible, ignominious, deplorable, wretched, lethargic, despondent, morbid, poor(-to-very-poor), acute, delicate, grim, disturbed, unsettling, bizarre, abnormal, squalid, humbling, dire, barren, crammed, crowded, odious,

disgusting, Augean, horrible, serious,
critical, dangerous, strained, uncertain,
disordered, chaotic, mysterious, horrific,
desperate, bothersome, degrading,
emaciated, appalling, punishing, precarious,
brutal, abominable, inhuman, subhuman,
death-like, bleak, incurable, hopeless,
forlorn, adverse, hostile, rugged, spartan,
destitute, desolate, inadequate, beggarly,
ruined, broken-down, atrocious, scary,
hazardous, onerous, prevailing, chronic,
permanent, transient, current, (pre-)existent,
fluctuating, exotic, rare, primitive,
pervasive, underlying, static, comatose,
pristine, primordial, living, atmospheric,
climatic, physical, geographic(al)

condition, conditions (2: stipulation)
underlying, long-standing, preferential,
(un)favourable, (un)acceptable, absolute,
stern, ruthless, strict, stiff, far-fetched,
key, minimum, Draconian

conduct decent, chaste, impeccable,
irreproachable, faultless, good, generous,
right, (im)moral, (dis)honourable,
meritorious, distinguished, rational,
becoming, conscientious, exemplary,
dignified, noble, stately, diplomatic, loyal,
sage, straight, (un)principled,
commendable, steady, (in)considerate,
(im)proper, (un)acceptable, (un)ethical,
(im)prudent, (un)professional, permissible,
blam(e)able, culpable, awkward,
disgusting, anomalous, disorderly, bad,
disreputable, hideous, lurid, mean, callous,
disgraceful, mysterious, flagitious,
ungenerous, shabby, devious, deviant,
shameful, frivolous, ignorant,
discreditable, deplorable, inexcusable,
immoral, wicked, evil, unbecoming, cheap,
disappointing, riotous, outrageous,
indecent, unseemly, infamous, shameless,
gruff, venal, loose, contemptible,
unpardonable, exceptionable,
objectionable, indecorous, irreligious,
harsh, ruthless, vindictive, reprehensible,
malicious, odious, repulsive, hateful,
offensive, opprobrious, wild, turbulent,
questionable, negligent, unprofessional,
reckless, light, democratic, sexual

confederation, confederations See *union*

conference, conferences (un)productive,
(in)conclusive, (un)successful, high-status,
dramatic, wartime, moving, glittering,

extravagant, mammoth, pretentious, tense,
heated, secret, (un)scheduled, surprise,
impromptu, periodic, full-fledged,
full-dress, open-ended, (in)formal,
national, international, multicountry,
celebrated, (un)ceremonious, upcoming,
annual, biennial, centenary, rare, summit,
scholarly, academic

confession, confessions full, sincere,
heartfelt, devout, earnest, veracious,
candid, bald, explosive, startling, stunning,
terrible, virtual, tacit, voluntary,
unprecedented, sudden, auricular, rueful,
tearful, futile, dangerous, false, bogus,
tortured, embarrassed, private, gunpoint,
free, ceremonial, ritual

confidant, confidants long-time, trusty,
trustworthy, esteemed, faithful, reliable,
dependable

confidence, confidences utter, total,
full, deep, boundless, intimate, unreserved,
undaunted, clear, easy, exuberant,
buoyant, unsuspecting, childlike, absolute,
implicit, utmost, supreme, immortal,
brimming, incredible, unbelievable,
overwhelming, hard-edged, abounding,
growing, increasing, emerging, bold,
unflappable, unshak(e)able, unshaken,
steadfast, strong, strict, fierce, solemn,
supernal, cocksure, overweening, reckless,
conceited, premature, bubbly, shaky, slim,
reeling, short-lived, unquestioned,
unreasoned, mutual, spousal, public

confinement, confinements cramped,
improper, indefinite, solitary

confirmation, confirmations unequivocal,
unquestionable, incontrovertible,
indisputable, unmistakable, clear, solid,
definite, independent, official, triumphant

conflict, conflicts threatening, flaring,
never-ending, unending, protracted,
unabated, constant, endless, continuous,
drawn-out, perpetual, full-scale, desultory,
divisive, sleepless, pitiless, ruthless,
merciless, heartless, relentless, unrelenting,
fanatical, acrimonious, unavoidable,
inevitable, insoluble, intractable,
inconclusive, unresolved, open,
fundamental, basic, wide, stern, intense,
riotous, fierce, brutal, bloody, grisly,
deadly, murderous, ruinous, disastrous,
internecine, perilous, ugly, nasty,
appalling, agonizing, excruciating,

deep-seated, inner, explosive, complicated, potential, conspicuous, apparent, myriad, lopsided, armed, military, global, national(ist), nationalistic, secessionist, internal, regional, civil, racial, factional, (inter)tribal, ethnic, personal, marital, religious, political, ideological, procedural

conformity, conformities strict, severe, dogmatic, arbitrary, coercive, bland, torpid, casual, cultural

confrontation, confrontations clear, outspoken, open, direct, breathless, dramatic, serious, intense, major, lengthy, occasional, possible, (in)evitable, (un)avoidable, (un)healthy, hopeless, sterile, unnecessary, single-minded, ugly, catty, spiteful, grinding, searing, burning, costly, aggressive, provocative, hostile, explosive, violent, bloody, bitter, perilous, deadly, tragic, painful, divisive, armed, military

confusion, confusions engrossing, utter, complete, total, thorough, general, pervasive, widespread, considerable, illimitable, limitless, boundless, inexplicable, pointless, ruinous, inextricable, fevered, hopeless, dark, vague, bitter, wild, chaotic, pernicious, terrible, dire, monstrous, riotous, ludicrous, unnecessary, unparalleled, idiotic, joyful, temporary, self-conscious, mental, social

congestion overwhelming, unremitting, harassing, growing, nasal, bronchial, traffic, postal

congratulation, congratulations warm, hearty, heartfelt, sincere, cordial, unstinted, exuberant

connection, connections apt, potent, deep, intimate, long-standing, apparent, (in)distinct, vague, suspicious, startling, unexpected, wrong, right, powerful, privileged, synaptic, shadowy, disputable, (in)direct, causal, tenuous, circumstantial

conquest, conquests See *victory*

conscience, consciences impeccable, wholesome, (over)scrupulous, (super)sensitive, strong, free, clear, clean, (un)easy, vivid, restless, guilty, terrible, elastic, pliant, tender, impressionable, queasy, squeamish, personal, individual, collective, social, moral

consensus, consensuses See also

agreement clear, fundamental, broad, overwhelming, rare, remarkable, impressive, astonishing, surprising, amazing, growing, fragile, national

consent See *agreement*

consequence, consequences (un)pleasant, subtle, natural, real, measured, profound, far-reaching, mighty, incalculable, momentous, dramatic, inevitable, unavoidable, inescapable, (un)foreseeable, (un)predictable, uncertain, unintended, indirect, long-range, long-term, innocuous, aberrant, ominous, awesome, horrific, terrific, frightful, frightening, terrible, pernicious, destructive, dreadful, dismal, ugly, adverse, negative, harmful, painful, bleak, grim, severe, serious, grave, dire, harsh, fatal, perilous, dangerous, perverse, disastrous, catastrophic, calamitous, devastating, brutal, staggering, explosive, undesirable, unthinkable, foolish, perplexing, ambiguous, global, (un)expected, ultimate

conservationist, conservationists See *environmentalist*

conservatism staid, complacent, demure, sedate, inherent, innate, passionate, rigid, plodding, political

conservative, conservatives unyielding, rock-ribbed, inflexible, adamant, arch, staunch, firm, starchy, irreconcilable, old-guard, Disraelian

consideration, considerations compelling, overriding, basic, profound, careful, close, active, sober, complete, paramount, fair, equitable, weighty, big, major, main, immediate, influential, ulterior, maximum, utmost, first, last, important, active, reasonable, determinative, tactical, monetary, moral, ethical, perceptual, aesthetic

consistency, consistencies unbending, unyielding, uncompromising, inflexible, (un)alterable, (un)modifiable, impressive, admirable, rigid, austere, adamant, persistent, puritanical, relentless, strict

consolation See *sympathy*

consonant, consonants alveolar, (un)voiced, voiceless, lateral, cacuminal, guttural, palatal, dental, labial, sibilant, liquid, velar, nasal, plosive, fricative

conspiracy, conspiracies See *plot* (1)

constitution, constitutions (1: physique)

(cast-)iron, strong, powerful, robust, muscular, bony, (un)healthy, underdeveloped, delicate, fastidious, frail, weak

constitution, constitutions (2: system of government) just, democratic, sovereign, mixed, (un)written, theocratic, draft

construction, constructions sturdy, (un)safe, quality, sound-proof, heavy-duty, loose, faulty, shoddy, substandard, fragile; hammering

consultant, consultants See *expert*

consultation, consultations close, closed-door, secret, furtive, whispered, urgent, complicated, brief, leisurely, comprehensive, fruitful, fruitless; in-home, domiciliary, hospital, private

consumer, consumers See also *customer* careful, cautious, frugal, (im)prudent, (un)wary, ardent, sophisticated, queasy, unsuspecting, docile, extravagant, spendthrift, debt-laden, heavy, big, voracious, health-minded, health-conscious, price-conscious, recession-wary, panicky, jittery, nervous, skittish

consumption growing, soaring, galloping, staggering, preposterous, excessive, incessant, inordinate, (in)frequent, conspicuous, (un)reasonable, (im)moderate, optimum, frivolous, (un)limited, scant, domestic, overseas, global, overall

contact, contacts (un)fruitful, (un)friendly, (un)pleasant, (un)ethical, (in)discreet, careful, immediate, close, intimate, intense, (in)direct, (in)valuable, positive, top-level, high-level, daily, excessive, extensive, unceasing, (ir)regular, (in)frequent, formal(istic), casual, accidental, inadvertent, intermittent, lengthy, tenuous, initial, tentative, vague, distasteful, careless, risky, shady, clandestine, furtive, secret, treasonous, (un)limited, (un)restricted, (un)protected, eye-to-eye, economic, cultural, social, personal, physical, amorous, sexual, homosexual, bisexual, extraterrestrial

contamination, contaminations invisible, mysterious, radioactive, bacterial, chemical, industrial, septic

contemplation, contemplations pleasurable, calm, quiet, silent, serene, hushed, inexpressible, vague, motionless,

noiseless, pacific, restful, secluded, undisturbed, transcendental, mystic

contempt burning, blistering, seething, withering, corrosive, unfriendly, mistrustful, distasteful, surly, disdainful, vaunted, abhorrent, indifferent, cynical, flippant, gleeful, icy, haughty, arrogant, lofty, regal, lordly, sprawling, total, utter, avowed, naked, open, flagrant, brusque, blunt, marked, evident, obvious, noticeable, undisguised, silent, unperturbed, ingrained, passionate, vivid, angry, dark, bitter, unrelenting, relentless, merciless, ruthless, pitiless, heartless, unlenient, unhappy, stony-eyed, singular

contender, contenders leading, principal, top, serious, strong, formidable, obstinate, stubborn, determined, resolute, formidable

content, contentment blissful, silent, serene, quiet, calm, delicious, sweet, complete, utter, sublime, deep, measureless, immeasurable, unusual

contention, contentions See *dispute* and *strife*

contest, contests (un)equal, (un)fair, (un)even, nasty, intemperate, close, keen, vigorous, tough, gruelling, tiring, raucous, one-sided, acrimonious, bitter, three-cornered, mortal, close-fought, knock-out, frantic, sharp, fierce, competitive, local, national, international

contraceptive, contraceptives long-lasting, (in)effective, (un)safe, (un)available, (in)accessible, oral

contract, contracts juicy, lucrative, profitable, remunerative, plum, rich, hefty, massive, multimillion-dollar, major, comprehensive, exclusive, terminable, severable, voidable, (in)dissoluble, (un)enforceable, (in)valid, novel, fraudulent, unconscionable, quasi, aleatory, bipartite, bilateral, constructive, sound, executory, long-term, consensual, onerous, exclusive, verbal, open-ended, prenuptial, rental, master, gratuitous, rolling

contradiction, contradictions clear, obvious, apparent, (in)direct, flat, flagrant, blatant, poignant, emphatic, troubling, excruciating, seeming, glaring, jarring, baffling, curious, endless; rude, cheeky

contrast, contrasts intriguing, flaring, striking, startling, unnerving, swelling, jarring, stunning, unique, stark, telling, sharp, marked, violent, fantastic, extreme, total, dramatic, instructive, welcome

contribution, contributions striking, telling, meaningful, positive, genuine, valuable, worthy, helpful, insightful, important, (in)significant, hefty, monumental, massive, immeasurable, substantial, siz(e)able, vast, wide-ranging, vital, profound, conspicuous, impressive, main, outstanding, remarkable, generous, munificent, magnificent, splendid, incontestable, unique, distinctive, unprecedented, unparalleled, unusual, selfless, unselfish, valid, steady, regular, lasting, (im)perishable, (un)limited, voluntary, unnoticed, unrecognized, decisive, small, negligible, feeble, meagre, paltry, intermittent, doubtful, anonymous, political, monetary, charitable

contributor, contributors generous, munificent, distinguished, unselfish, authoritative, expert, siz(e)able, large, small, voluntary, (ir)regular, (in)frequent; sole, (un)paid, academic, freelance

control, controls purposeful, careful, unified, (ir)responsible, firm, tight, uncontested, thorough, overwhelming, full, total, complete, exclusive, absolute, pervasive, stringent, rigid, strict, stiff, tough, rigorous, severe, autocratic, precise, substantial, considerable, effective, (un)limited, (in)sufficient, permanent, sole, weak, soft, slack, behind-the-scenes, dubious, spurious, diminishing, relaxing, nebulous, ineffective, cursory, virtual, ultimate, final, optimal, central, covert, partial, voluntary, mandatory, regulatory, administrative, statutory, tactical, manual, remote, parental, muscular, budgetary

controversy, controversies heated, intense, vigorous, (un)necessary, (un)welcome, unabated, enduring, long-time, centuries-old, protracted, continual, pressing, growing, raging, (long-)smouldering, flaring, considerable, enormous, major, key, overblown, widespread, acrid, nasty, bitter, furious, scandalous, national, political, artistic, critical

convention, conventions (1: practice or custom) See also *custom* outworn, rigid, (in)flexible, social

convention, conventions (2: conference) See also *conference* annual, biennial, founding, inaugural, business, nominating

convention, conventions (3: agreement) See *agreement*

conversation, conversations (un)edifying, uplifting, exhilarating, stimulating, penetrating, flowing, running, interesting, sparkling, swirling, relaxing, solid, sententious, calm, quiet, crisp, playful, vivacious, sprightly, joyous, jocose, animated, excited, swirly, fervent, brisk, lively, bright, brilliant, witty, deep, close, intimate, serious, grave, intense, erudite, high-minded, learned, meaningful, profitable, incisive, elegant, spicy, rich, forcible, keen, refined, genial, easy, free, heartfelt, steady, varied, casual, light, breezy, laconic, tiresome, drowsy, discursive, disjointed, dull, stuffy, disputatious, flat, insipid, random, stupid, frivolous, pointless, spiritless, hurried, snatchy, lengthy, fitful, desultory, abrupt, vapid, distasteful, inanimate, boring, stilted, insufferable, halting, lagging, tangled, bawdy, unprofitable, fruitless, futile, idle, circular, three-way, verbatim, social, general, private, (in)formal; criminal

conversationalist, conversationalists See also *conversation* entertaining, amusing, stimulating, avid, brilliant, tremendous, great, big, glib, smooth, fluent, eloquent, shrewd, indefatigable, inexhaustible, tireless, relentless, lengthy, diffuse, compulsive

converser, conversers See *conversationalist*

conversion, conversions See *change* (1)

convict, convicts See *criminal* and *prisoner*

conviction, convictions (1: being convinced) unwavering, unflinching, immutable, unshak(e)able, firm, fixed, (deeply-)rooted, well-established, long-standing, lifelong, age-old, (dead-)serious, intense, deep, perfect, complacent, mature, conscientious, courageous, evident, overweening, unreasoned, unbearable, ghastly, passionate, corrosive, powerful, strong, sturdy, stubborn, enormous, waning, innate, personal, ideological, religious

conviction, convictions (2: the act of convicting of a crime) wrongful, false, unjust, dramatic, sensational, criminal

cook, cooks able, fantastic, competent, expert, great, famed, renowned, trendy, health-conscious, creative, serious, first-class, terrible, poor, licensed, born, natural, professional, amateur

cookie, cookies See *biscuit*

cooking See also *cuisine* discriminating, first-class, expert, vibrant, innovative, imaginative, heavenly, (in)adequate, quick, thrifty, simple, plain, delectable, tasty, no-nonsense, rich, heady, even, distinctive, hot, fiery, complex, outdoor, home, mother's, traditional

cooperation, cooperations encouraging, praiseworthy, friendly, sociable, (un)fruitful, unstinted, full, vital, close, ready, whole-hearted, helpful, crucial, overt, unprecedented, spectacular, remarkable, increasing, growing, sweeping, minimal, (un)achievable, elusive, prickly, bilateral, supranational, military

copy, copies clean, perfect, fair, exact, faithful, identical, certified, true, freak, illicit, bootleg, (in)accurate, (in)correct, (il)legible, good, rough, duplicate, triplicate, quadruplicate, quintuplicate, sextuplicate, back-up, draft, working; complimentary, advance; rare

cord, cords stiff, tight, loose, sturdy, elastic, fibrous, intertwining, twisted, knotted, tasselled, (pompon-)studded, electric, vocal, spinal, umbilical

corner, corners comfortable, cosy, snug, pleasant, warm, shady, secure, quiet, restful, secluded, secretive, obscure, remote, (in)accessible, tight, blind, square

corporation, corporations See also *company* (1) giant, major, conglomerate, élite, immense, big, siz(e)able, high-powered, mighty, dominant, (un)successful, (un)profitable, flourishing, regenerate, ruthless, greedy, uncaring, quasi-public, closed, multinational, international, private

corps diplomatic, medical, cadet, élite

corpse, corpses icy, putrefying, nameless

correction, corrections substantial, major, (in)significant, extensive, textual, fundamental, tremendous, considerable, appreciable, welcome, last-minute, minor, slight, further, obvious

correspondence, correspondences (letters) wide-ranging, thoughtful, delightful, candid, exciting, entertaining, prolific, voluminous, endless, (ir)regular, desultory, constant, (dis)continued, (un)interrupted, platitudinous, esoteric, underground

correspondent, correspondents swashbuckling, punctual, exact, well-disposed, reluctant, negligent, irate, distant, peripatetic, itinerant, roving, local, overseas

corridor, corridors long, narrow, dark, dank, treacherous, tiled

corruption, corruptions staggering, suffocating, stunning, flourishing, rampant, massive, pervasive, widespread, large-scale, total, serious, spectacular, high-level, endemic, blatant, brazen, shameless, unspeakable, rapacious, petty, discreet, low-level, alleged, organized, undetected, political, official; textual

cosmetics old-fashioned, oil-based, water-based, oil-free, fragrance-free, (un)scented, over-the-counter, smelly, liquid, hypoallergenic, non-comedogenic, non-allergenic, theatrical, ceremonial

cost, costs (ever-)increasing, rising, soaring, staggering, galloping, overwhelming, (hyper-)inflationary, explosive, excessive, enormous, considerable, substantial, astronomical, immense, high, lofty, horrendous, colossal, incalculable, runaway, major, steep, vast, prohibitive, exorbitant, fearful, awesome, hideous, appalling, ruinous, incredible, unbelievable, unjustified, (un)reasonable, (un)acceptable, (im)moderate, minimal, little, low, minor, nominal, low-budget, direct, actual, estimable, inescapable, aggregate, total, exact, explicit, intangible, extraneous, extra, hidden, superfluous, initial, operational, administrative, capital, prime

costume, costumes See also *dress* opulent, sumptuous, spectacular, elaborate, lavish, courtly, gorgeous, magnificent, splendid, vivid, picturesque, romantic, bohemian, colourful, bright, quaint, fanciful, glittering, flamboyant, fantastic, conspicuous, impressive, striking, charming, attractive, distinctive, spangled, (sequin-)studded, (in)appropriate, outlandish, rakish, jaunty, out-and-out, dashing, garish, vulgar, ridiculous, voluminous, flowing, sporty, theatrical, ceremonial, symbolic, authentic, traditional, national, native, ethnic, tribal, period

cottage, cottages tiny, little, elegant, charming, quaint, pretty, picturesque, (un)sheltered, snug, cosy, hom(e)y, shady, idyllic, romantic, tranquil, quiet, neat, tidy, well-appointed, (once-)cheerful, homely, remote, out-of-the-way, solitary, secluded, abandoned, (un)inhabitable, yonder, crude, humble, lowly, ramshackle, rickety, heartless, terraced, rustic, country, rural, ski, Alpine, Swiss

couch, couches See *sofa*

cough, coughs rasping, grating, racking, sputtering, rattling, hacking, lingering, long, slow, low, deep, tight, hoarse, husky, harsh, hard, dry, itchy, nasty, obstinate, stubborn, persistent, intractable, pertinacious, spasmodic, frequent, perpetual, (ir)regular, bad, fitful, throaty, convulsive, wheezy, explosive, violent, fearful, productive, phlegmatic, bronchial, whooping, psychogenic

coughing See *cough*

council, councils (im)potent, interim, governing, grand, advisory, privy, progressive, executive, ecumenical, national, regional, tribal, revolutionary, professional, consultative, judicial, parish, town, borough, county, district, city

counsel, counsels See *advice*

counselling See also *counsellor* one-on-one, premarital, medical, academic, educational, psychological, marriage, bereavement

counsellor, counsellors See also *counselling* sage, wise, sound, sapient, discerning, effective, firm, disinterested, impartial

countenance, countenances radiant, affable, gracious, pleasant, mild, benign, noble, steady, debonair, suave, refined, peaceful, carefree, cheerful, dignified, raffish, impassive, dreary, glum, gloomy, grim, grave, melancholy, sad, doleful, woeful, pitiful, funereal, stern, mute,

grisly, formidable, ill-favoured, firm, coarse, vulgar, rugged

country, countries mountain(ous), wooded, landlocked, Alpine, littoral, agricultural, grassy, arid, fenny, low, prostrate, rugged, vast, swampy, rolling, undulating, even, (un)stable, hapless, lawless, unruly, fractious, troubled, riot-torn, strife-torn, repressive, progressive, turbulent, volatile, crisis-ridden, unified, united, free, independent, neutral, (once-)mighty, security-conscious, aggressive, freebooting, expansionist, (non-)belligerent, war-weary, war-torn, enemy-held, fragile, industrial, agricultural, (fast-)growing, peripheral, underdeveloped, undeveloped, benighted, backward, destitute, poor, poverty-stricken, famine-stricken, ailing, fading, prosperous, advanced, (resource-)rich, oil-rich, diverse, varied, go-ahead, open, immense, neighbouring, conterminous, contiguous, minuscule, cautious, barbaric, uncivilized, lawless, ungovernable, unmanageable, self-sufficient, tradition-bound, placid, peaceful, serene, nascent, new, old, class-ridden, remote, exotic, bicultural, multi-ethnic, unknown, tolerant, capitalist, socialist, communist, secular, religious, insular, tributary, colonial, imperial

countryside See also *country* charming, ravishing, breathtaking, lovely, pleasant, (un)exciting, beautiful, pretty, magnificent, splendid, placid, quiet, tranquil, serene, peaceful, secluded, drowsy, cheerful, lush, verdant, bountiful, treeless, bare, village-dotted, surrounding, rolling, undulating, open, arid, rugged, forlorn, wretched, cheerless, desolate, grim, cold, mountainous, Alpine

coup, coups See *move* and *action*

coup d'état, coups d'état decided, (un)successful, abortive, failed, short-lived, overdue, minor, major, surprise, brutal, misguided, disastrous, bloody, bloodless, old-style, reactionary, right-wing, left-wing, illegitimate, illegal, unconstitutional

couple, couples charming, interesting, healthy, happy, responsible, honeymoon, inseparable, (un)matched, mismatched, (now-)estranged, incompatible, unhappy, distressed, feuding, young, middle-aged, elderly, gregarious, newly-married, (un)married, interracial, mixed, interfaith, childless, (in)fertile, expectant, heterosexual, homosexual, gay, lesbian, working, dancing, courting

couplet, couplets pointed, balanced, flowing, tautly-knit, assertive, rhymed, five-stress, decasyllabic, heroic, closed, open, short, long, anapaestic, Alexandrine, Augustan

coupon, coupons valuable, money-saving, (in)valid, (ir)redeemable

courage astounding, astonishing, amazing, surprising, unwavering, unrelenting, unfaltering, unflinching, (un)flagging, infinite, indomitable, invincible, unshak(e)able, undaunted, boundless, unbounded, signal, singular, blasé, incandescent, incorruptible, incredible, unbelievable, fiery, intrepid, enormous, great, infinite, supreme, sublime, superb, magnificent, splendid, real, remarkable, exceptional, matchless, extraordinary, rare, preternatural, exemplary, unexampled, uncommon, transcendent, reckless, vainglorious, swashbuckling, bullying, lonely, moral, physical, instinctive; Dutch

course, courses (1: forward movement; direction) straight, steady, irreversible, obvious, circuitous, even, upward, downward, wavy, independent, right, wrong, eastward, westward, erratic, reverse, serpentine, zigzag, narrow, downhill, disastrous, foolish, (un)predictable, treacherous, devious, obstacle-laden

course, courses (2: series of lectures) innovative, (un)interesting, dull, high-pressure, high-level, (in)complete, exhaustive, gruelling, rigorous, tough, difficult, intensive, special, trendy, indispensable, time-consuming, structured, formal, independent, optional, compulsory, mandatory, stock, run-of-the-mill, rare, elementary, introductory, elective, prerequisite, (non-)credit, (non-)transfer(able), live-in, refresher, academic, technical, commercial, vocational

court, courts (1: place where legal cases are heard) deferential, tough, lenient, (in)competent, independent, secular, ecclesiastical, clerical, military, civil, supreme, criminal, county, juvenile, local, moot, special, superior, district, provincial, federal, municipal, highest, ecclesiastical, rabbinic(al), World, European

court, courts (2: residence of a sovereign; formal assembly held by a sovereign) illustrious, sumptuous, prerogative, legendary

courtesan, courtesans amiable, attractive, ambitious, aspiring, enterprising, infamous, vile, lecherous, lewd, sexy, alluring, enticing, tempting, expensive, high-class, high-priced, upmarket

courtesy, courtesies elaborate, charming, affectionate, warm, inborn, natural, instinctive, innate, inbred, habitual, common, simple, regal, (un)studied, shy, perfunctory, indifferent, superficial, distracted, due, old-world, professional

courtier, courtiers glittering, obsequious, obedient, servile, fawning, flattering, subservient, sycophantic

courtship, courtships storybook, whirlwind, impetuous, precipitate, long-drawn-out, difficult, aggressive, provocative, unrestrained, pushy, unconventional

courtyard, courtyards lush, vine-trellised, flowered, delightful, immaculate, neat, elaborate, spectacular, expansive, shady, enchanting, tranquil, elegant, giant, overgrown, wild, inner, open, arcaded, tiled

cousin, cousins close, full, first, second, third, distant, kissing

coverage impeccable, (in)adequate, extensive, comprehensive, pervasive, worldwide, scant(y), (un)balanced, unbiased, (un)favourable, live, blanket

cow, cows wandering, ambling, stray, brindle(d), dapple(d), shaggy, black-and-white, coppery-red, spotted, striped, pedigree(d), plump, lean, skinny, weedy, gaunt, wiry, dry, (un)productive, milch, dairy, milk, Friesian, Guernsey, Jersey, Aberdeen, Angus; sacred

coward, cowards sanguine, base, despicable, contemptible, paltry, mean, worthless, swaggering, braggart, abject, grovelling, degraded, craven, arrant, utter, notorious, spiritless, mean-spirited, out-and-out, wretched, moral

cowardice swinish, base, dastardly, contemptible, disgraceful, shameful, dishonourable

cowboy, cowboys tough, hardy, bowlegged, cocky, proud, shifty, opportunistic, lone(some), western

crab, crabs scrambling, crawling, walking, prowling, pugnacious, pot-bellied, stick-legged, ten-legged, soft-shelled, giant, tiny, crimson, blue, purplish-red, reddish-brown, marine, bristly (horse), edible, spider, Japanese, Dungeness

craft, crafts flourishing, vanishing, skilled, intricate, useful, mass-produced, authentic, precarious, traditional, domestic, rural, ethnic

craftsman, craftsmen gifted, expert, skilful, fine, superb, delicate, intricate, accomplished, consummate, ingenious, competent, master, experienced, qualified, trained

craftsmanship breathtaking, fine, superb, excellent, remarkable, exquisite, splendid, magnificent, rare, vintage, exacting, meticulous, intricate, intrinsic, delicate, traditional, age-old, old-fashioned, cunning, rude

crash, crashes ear-piercing, ear-splitting, resounding, grinding, dizzying, mortifying, frightening, terrible, terrific, thunderous, violent, tremendous, spectacular, low-impact, (non-)frontal, fiery, fatal, tragic; marital

craze, crazes interesting, growing, spreading, passing, vanishing, age-old, latest, short-lived, brief, national, dietary

cream, creams (dairy-)fresh, luscious, sweet, seductive, delicious, tempting, irresistible, lavish, rich, heavy, thick, stiff, concentrate, light, frothy, sour, salty, perishable, stale, (non-)greasy, medicated, artificial, natural, cold, emollient, vanishing, cosmetic, therapeutic, depilatory

creation, creations inspired, ingenious, imaginative, innovative, original, unusual, fantastic, latest, simple, remarkable, striking, gargantuan, deceptive, gawky, clumsy, awkward

creature, creatures hulking, husky, massive, elegant, graceful, sturdy, baffling, enchanting, strange, fantastic, enigmatic, mysterious, unsung, exotic, bizarre, amorphous, peaceful, harmless, gentle, lik(e)able, lovable, (un)friendly, beloved, (non-)aggressive, meddlesome, benighted, rapacious, feral, wild, brutal, venomous, deadly, remarkable, nameless, wormy, contemptible, pitiable, awkward, odd-looking, clumsy, (un)intelligent, miserable, wretched, vocal, solitary, elusive, reclusive, prolific, four-footed, multilegged, spindly-legged, many-celled, one-celled, finned, winged, nocturnal, existential, magical, mythical, mythological, primitive, primitivistic, prehistoric, ancient, primordial, living, (a)social, aerial, aquatic, planktonic, amphibious, seraphic, larval; fellow

credential, credentials heady, credible, well-established, outstanding, impressive, impeccable, indisputable, irreproachable, unimpeachable, solid, upper-crust, (in)appropriate, modest, flimsy, suspicious, questionable, official, professional, educational, military, financial

credibility poor, fragile, new-found

credit (financial trustworthiness) impeccable, good, flexible, cheap, (un)easy, scarce, endless, close, measly, commercial, revolving

creditor, creditors generous, persistent, insistent, aggressive, nervous, reproachful, unrelenting, unfeeling, villainous, importunate, stubborn, large, major, innumerable, bona fide

creed, creeds prevailing, superficial, old, hoary, mossy, sanctimonious, political, personal

creek, creeks See *stream*

creeping stealthy, cautious, clandestine, secretive, serpentine, snaky, sly, sneaky, noiseless

crew, crews select, (hand-)picked, heroic, dedicated, spirited, fine, superb, accomplished, (in)experienced, (in)competent, (un)skilled, inept, subdued, insubordinate, (dis)obedient, mutinous, wild, gaunt, missing, professional

cricket, crickets chirping, shrilling, crying, cheerful

crime, crimes shocking, startling, revolting, disgusting, glaring, preposterous, dreadful, heinous, foul, diabolic(al), atrocious, outright, malicious, serious, severe, grave, sordid, hideous, terrible, horrible, unpardonable, violent, vicious, monstrous, unspeakable, senseless, mindless, complex, tangled, horrible, grisly, abominable, abhorrent, repugnant, frightful, gruesome, ghastly, flagrant, cold, scandalous, inexpiable, lurid, nameless, infamous, black, spectacular, notorious, sensational, passional, brutal, satanic, fiendish, hellish, evil, detestable, execrable, antisocial, outrageous, hateful, mercenary, (un)sophisticated, two-bit, inhuman, unnatural, horrendous, lucrative, high, common, widespread, rampant, innumerable, flourishing, rising, calculated, premeditated, victimless, undetected, unreported, gang-related, hard-core, high-risk, low-risk, petty, capital, teenage, juvenile

criminal, criminals arch, brazen, atrocious, heinous, desperate, elusive, petty, tough, unconscientious, unrelenting, relentless, heartless, merciless, pitiless, ruthless, psychopathic, violent, violence-prone, habitual, unfeeling, callous, obdurate, hardened, unrepentant, impenitent, clever, cunning, inflexible, dangerous, depraved, (un)natural, notorious, known, reputed, big-name, high-profile, active, hard-core, arrant, out-and-out, panicky, recalcitrant, vicious, predatory, embittered, suspected, common, extraditable, homicidal

crisis, crises menacing, harrowing, distressing, devastating, staggering, growing, impending, unfolding, deep, acute, grave, crucial, indefinable, complicated, unresolved, broad, vast, squalid, ugly, raucous, full-blown, momentary, temporary, minor, (in)evitable, (un)avoidable, unprecedented, unexpected, sudden, long-range, global, hemispheric, national, domestic, regional, personal, constitutional, military, political, financial, fiscal, economic, emotional

criterion, criteria (un)reliable, (un)acceptable, (in)appropriate, (in)flexible, strict, restrictive, vague, (un)certain, specific, established, objective, diagnostic

critic, critics masterly, competent, learned, scholarly, knowledgeable, sapient, seasoned, frank, (un)discerning, (un)discriminating, (in)discriminate, mild, tolerant, capable, (im)partial, (un)prejudiced, dispassionate, careful,

consistent, (un)conscientious, authoritative, influential, powerful, astute, shrewd, reflective, engaging, wise, constructive, leading, distinguished, prominent, rearguard, perennial, persistent, articulate, vocal, vigorous, vociferous, outspoken, dauntless, sharp(-tongued), hostile, grumpy, peevish, sulky, harsh, severe, adverse, dismissive, jealous, rancorous, pedantic, hidebound, dogmatic, judgmental, censorious, acerbic, mischievous, sneering, cynical, captious, carping, misguided, unimaginative, destructive, unrelenting, relentless, pitiless, ruthless, heartless, remorseless, merciless, intolerant, fierce, anonymous, (post-)modernist, impressionistic

criticism, criticisms engaging, genial, insightful, pointed, solid, reasonable, elaborate, profound, constructive, sustained, positive, tolerant, (un)informed, enthusiastic, rhapsodical, impassioned, ecstatic, pithy, lenient, substantial, weighty, sound, (in)valid, (un)subtle, mild, gentle, artful, prudent, responsible, favourable, charitable, muted, reserved, cautious, guarded, restrained, sharp, incisive, keen, trenchant, spicy, corrective, direct, acute, blunt, outspoken, outgoing, (un)fair, (in)competent, able, careful, (un)justifiable, (un)deserved, unwarranted, uncalled-for, (un)friendly, (un)reasonable, (in)tolerable, (in)temperate, impersonal, objective, dispassionate, disappointing, pungent, vehement, hostile, inimical, capricious, adverse, harsh, vociferous, loud, destructive, personal, trivial, feeble, contemptible, tepid, heavy, savage, fierce, cruel, intolerant, vile, spiteful, malevolent, venomous, acrimonious, virulent, vitriolic, caustic, acid-tongued, bitter, severe, disingenuous, penetrating, piercing, unrelenting, biting, stinging, cutting, blistering, scathing, devastating, carping, unyielding, unvarnished, mordant, sarcastic, piquant, tongue-in-cheek, irresponsible, uncharitable, derisive, abusive, oblique, indignant, frenzied, unfavourable, sorry, growing, widespread, considerable, (over)drawn, specific, public, tabloid, (con)textual, interpretative, impressionistic, generic, literary, new, (post)modern, sociological, dialectic, canonical

crocodile, crocodiles grunting, scrambling, lurking, sluggish(-looking), aggressive, enormous, American, Siamese, Australian

crop, crops bounteous, bountiful, plentiful, bumper, exceptional, siz(e)able, vintage, surplus, rich, abundant, luxuriant, healthy, good, record, heavy, excellent, spectacular, promising, high-quality, choice, decent, satisfying, lucrative, profitable, exportable, life-sustaining, stable, varied, stunted, poor, scanty, fair, low, failed, meagre, subsistence, withered, fallow, scraggly, water-thirsty, chemical-intensive, dead, sodden, insect-prone, average, staple, major, chief, principal, catch, (bi)annual, salt-tolerant, labour-intensive, water-intensive, commercial, domestic, traditional, experimental, alternate, alternative, alternating, occasional, seasonal, organic, cash

cross, crosses trefoil, Latin, Calvary, patriarchal (archiepiscopal), papal, Greek, Celtic, Maltese, fleury, moline, quadrate, potent, pectoral, wayside, roadside, ansate, hooked, crooked, Nazi, Egyptian, St Andrew's, St George's, Lorraine

cross-examination, cross-examinations tense, unrelaxed, heated, rigorous, thorough, meticulous, minute, inclement, unrelenting, relentless, ruthless, heartless, merciless, slashing

crow, crows calling, squalling, squawking, noisy, croaky, hoarse, black, clever, fearless, predatory, hooded, carrion

crowd, crowds vast, enormous, dense, large, siz(e)able, innumerable, gigantic, big, great, small, meagre, thin, modest, orderly, peaceful, peaceable, (un)friendly, well-behaved, warm, supportive, silent, (im)patient, mixed, motley, heterogeneous, euphoric, delighted, enthusiastic, jolly, exultant, jubilant, festive, exuberant, crazy, frenzied, (dis)enchanted, insensitive, boisterous, rowdy, unruly, disorderly, wild, uproarious, noisy, rough, abrasive, hysterical, delirious, angry, irate, ardent, bloodthirsty, panic-stricken, awe-stricken, suspicious, riotous, tumultuous, grief-stricken, murderous, gawkish, turbulent, hostile, partisan, restless, agitated, excited, overflow, sellout

crown, crowns gleaming, glittering, spiky, thorny, conic(al), golden, solid-gold, magnificent, historic, royal, imperial, triple, Papal

crudity, crudities mortifying, humiliating, unhinged, untoward, shameful, unbearable, insufferable, intolerable, unspeakable

cruelty, cruelties shocking, appalling, unfeeling, distressing, evil, feline, infernal, sinful, heinous, malignant, sadistic, unchecked, persistent, horrible, calculated, blatant, downright, naked, treacherous, devilish, abominable, wanton, random, wolfish, heartless, merciless, ruthless, pitiless, relentless, unrelenting, inhumane, insensate, severe, grievous, deliberate, unjustifiable, causeless, malicious, unnatural, brutish, unmoved, monstrous, atrocious, hideous, unimaginable, inconceivable, unbelievable, incredible, indescribable, wicked, savage, fierce, ferocious, unremitting, morbid, physical, mental

cruise, cruise See *trip*

crusade, crusades See *crusader*

crusader, crusaders active, ardent, eager, (over)zealous, devout, dedicated, emotional, fanatic(al), feverish, zestful, indomitable, vain, (a)moral, religious, political, social

cry, cries grating, piercing, shuddering, heartbreaking, heart-rending, blood-curdling, boisterous, joyous, strident, vociferous, feeble, weak, faint, loud, high-pitched, barbaric, queer, eerie, strange, inarticulate, rhythmic, awful, dreadful, frantic, throaty, sharp, anguished, shrill, bitter, grievous, sorrowful, doleful, dolorous, sad, mournful, wretched, sepulchral, harsh, raucous, hoarse, uncontrollable, irrepressible, fitful, spasmodic, convulsive, hysterical, agitated, frenzied, desperate, plaintive, idiotic, long, drawn-out, intermittent, ceaseless, endless, unending, unheard, inner, muffled, far, futile, unmistakable, primal, guttural

crying See *cry*

cue, cues subtle, tactful, tactless, tantalizing, plain, positive, (non)verbal, visual

cuisine, cuisines See also *cooking*
intriguing, challenging, exciting, unique,

heady, audacious, creative, inventive,
imaginative, iconoclastic, exotic, great,
exquisite, sumptuous, superb, splendid,
magnificent, fine, decent, delicate,
ingenious, trendy, distinctive, solid, robust,
hearty, rich, fragrant, glorious, vaunted,
pretentious, spicy, hot, fiery, varied,
eclectic, complex, complicated, bland, dull,
egregious, low-fat, lean, typical, authentic,
haute, classic, nouvelle, regional, ethnic,
kosher, national, local
culprit, culprits suspected, presumed,
principal, primary
cult, cults fashionable, lucrative, maniacal,
disturbing, short-lived, litigious, terroristic,
satanic, religious, spirit, cargo
culture, cultures flourishing, living,
enduring, persistent, strong, dominant,
rich, vibrant, sophisticated, (un)civilized,
advanced, unique, (in)accessible,
mysterious, baffling, dazzling, colourful,
glorious, (once-)proud, stubborn,
idiosyncratic, distinct(ive), homogeneous,
disparate, simple, intact, emerging,
surviving, dying, vanishing, obsolete,
outdated, forgotten, dull, trite, inbred,
mainstream, conventional, traditional,
contemporary, preliterate, prehistoric,
megalithic, primitive, native, indigenous,
aboriginal, (semi)feudal, nomadic, local,
folk, communal, common, urban, alien,
physical, pastoralist, computer, pop,
popular, biblical, literal, oral
cunning foxlike, foxy, canny, artful,
astute, shrewd, sly, crafty, devious,
dext(e)rous, evasive, guarded, judicious,
resourceful, prudent, diplomatic, deadly,
elephantine, Machiavellian
cup, cups brimming, brimful, insidious,
dainty, thick, gold-rimmed, two-handled,
double-handled, handleless, inverted,
opaque, porcelain, china, clay, earthen,
polystyrene, Styrofoam, disposable,
ceremonial
cupboard, cupboards capacious,
commodious, large, roomy, walk-in, fitted,
spacious, fusty, mouldy, musty, stuffy,
bare, empty, full
cure, cures See also *treatment* (1)
promising, unfailing, infallible, simple,
sudden, magic, miraculous, full, (un)sure,
(in)effectual, (im)possible, (in)complete,
permanent, (in)expensive, (un)known,

universal, ancient, traditional,
experimental, effete, painful, illusive,
quack, natural, holistic, herbal, preventive,
psychic, spiritual, miracle
curfew, curfews strict, stringent, tight,
24-hour, round-the-clock, daytime,
all-night, dusk-to-dawn, indefinite, virtual,
blanket, wide, military
curiosity keen, intense, extreme, restless,
burning, innate, unbridled, microscopic,
legendary, incredible, unbelievable, wary,
anxious, eager, unabashed, overwhelming,
unflagging, unrelenting, relentless,
enormous, honest, understandable,
childlike, idle, grotesque, detached,
undiscriminating, gauche, clumsy, tactless,
morbid, prurient, widespread, mute,
insatiable, unquenchable, (un)restrained,
unsatiated, ungratified, undeveloped,
unrivalled, pointed, shocked, universal,
natural, scientific
curl, curls stiff, tight, loose, abundant,
short, crisp, silvery, golden, flaxen,
bouncing, tumbling, unruly, wanton,
rebellious, refractory, stubborn, permanent
currency, currencies soaring, rising,
commanding, buoyant, muscular, strong,
sturdy, powerful, sound, high-yield,
safe-haven, major, (un)stable, sagging,
fallen, anaemic, weak, fragile, shaky,
worthless, valueless, useless, dysfunctional,
vulnerable, wildcat, obsolete, extinct,
scarce, single, common, (un)popular,
counterfeit, (non-)convertible,
(un)exchangeable, spendable, foreign,
local, key, soft, hard, fractional, decimal,
fiduciary, full-bodied, representative
current, currents flowing, circling,
conflicting, twisting, strong, powerful,
mighty, tremendous, prodigious, swift,
feeble, weak, gentle, slack, slow, sluggish,
(un)predictable, (un)reliable, terrific,
(un)expected, tricky, fierce, vicious,
wicked, deceptive, treacherous, perilous,
demonic, coastward, southwest,
underlying, bottom, tidal, aerial, fluvial,
marine, inshore, thermionic, direct,
induced, pulsating, alternating, electric,
dynamic
curriculum, curricula solid, (un)balanced,
well-balanced, (ir)relevant, (in)flexible,
comprehensive, broad, multi-dimensional,
imaginative, textbook-driven, rigid, tough,

vaunted, antiquated, outmoded, out-of-date, complex, tedious, core, ordinary, traditional, developmental, inclusionary, academic

curse, curses vociferous, tempestuous, clamorous, horrid, strident, boisterous, obstreperous, blatant, constant, lifelong, voluble

curtain, curtains exquisite, attractive, pretty, sleek, sophisticated, dramatic, (well-)matching, fine, opulent, heavy, massive, steep, impenetrable, (un)lined, brocaded, frilly, silk-fringed, loose, attached, floor-length, ceiling-mounted, shorty, wall-wide, floral, plain, fabric, brocade, one-way, double, reverse-stripe, ready-made, handmade, translucent, transparent, sheer, lace, lacy, filmy, eyelet, stationary, gauze, textured, scalloped, gingham, billowing, dreary, (hour-)glass, crisscross, drop, shirred, ruffled, layered, pouffed, tabbed, casual

curtsy (curtsey), curtsys (curtseys) elegant, graceful, stylish, appropriate, charming, nimble, courtly, quick

curve, curves long, sharp, graceful, gentle, faint, sweeping, deceptive, wicked, sinuous, snaky, characteristic, concave, caustic, normal (Gaussian)

cushion, cushions See also *pillow* plush, loose, attached, floral, vibrating, air, inflatable, decorative, ornamental

custody (un)determined, joint, temporary, open, protective, military

custom, customs prevailing, prevalent, time-honoured, long-held, long-standing, traditional, venerable, discerning, sensitive, dated, outmoded, obsolete, mutable, extinct, dead, old, ancient, centuries-old, old-fashioned, superstitious, colourful, characteristic, weird, arcane, peculiar, grim, odd, different, exotic, strange,

quaint, primitive, savage, barbarous, barbaric, eastern, western, local, tribal, native, aboriginal, pagan, religious, formal, national, provincial, alien, funerary

customer, customers (ir)regular, (in)frequent, steady, habitual, constant, established, long-standing, large, creditworthy, blue-chip, favoured, valuable, prestigious, high-profile, loyal, repeat, long-term, faithful, eager, appreciative, demanding, fastidious, assiduous, (dis)satisfied, unsatisfied, disgruntled, disappointed, (un)discerning, (un)pleasant, awkward, wayward, greedy, skimpy, mean, stingy, (un)happy, occasional, small, tough, stubborn, recession-wary, budget-conscious, price-conscious, delinquent, early-bird, potential, would-be, prospective, corporate; queer

cut, cuts deep, nasty, serious, bad, painful, skin-deep; Draconian

cutback, cutbacks devastating, debilitating, extensive, substantial, massive, enormous, huge, fundamental, severe, drastic, savage, deep, major, minor, financial, economic

cutlery bone-handled, ivory-handled, (food-)stained, silver-plated, gold-plated

cycle, cycles recurring, never-ending, endless, unbroken, persistent, multitudinous, downward, self-destructive, (ir)regular, alternating, varying, inexorable, frantic, vicious, hydrologic(al), cosmic, celestial, lunar, biological, reproductive, menstrual, oestrous, climatic, ceremonial, trade

cynicism exuberant, extravagant, reverent, unreserved, unrestrained, conceited, puppyish

dagger, daggers See also *sword* heavy, broad, razor-sharp, curved, double-edged, silver-sheathed, studded, ornate, business-like, traditional, ceremonial

dam, dams overflowing, gigantic, colossal, massive, hydroelectric, timber, metal, hollow, earth, man-made, semihydraulic

damage major, substantial, big, extensive, enormous, colossal, immense, massive, pervasive, widespread, incalculable, untold, (long-)lasting, enduring, long-range, long-term, permanent, serious, severe, heavy, brutal, mindless, senseless, staggering, appalling, devastating, dreadful, fearful, catastrophic, calamitous, (ir)reparable, (ir)reversible, (ir)retrievable, (un)controllable, (un)avoidable, (in)evitable, cumulative, growing, latent, potential, unforeseen, wanton, deliberate, intentional, wilful, malicious, resultant, residual, minuscule, minimal, minor, superficial, modest, (un)limited, evident, material, ecological, environmental, cerebral, neurologic(al), emotional, psychological, physical, structural

damages swingeing, (in)significant, big, stiff, estimable, (un)specified, aggravated, general, exemplary, punitive, compensatory, monetary

dance, dances rapturous, joyful, joyous, cheerful, merry, gay, lively, brisk, giddy, rapid, (lightning-)fast, ecstatic, unique, fine, seemly, proper, suitable, meticulous, graceful, rhythmic, staccato, enthusiastic, rollicking, thumping, whirling, whirlwind, (high-)spirited, frenzied, frenetic, impromptu, spontaneous, compulsive, marchlike, stately, dignified, old-fashioned, old-time, authentic, splendid, exuberant, florid, effervescent, round, vigorous, pelvic, passionate, modern, romantic, slow, light, listless, popular, sacred, hysterical, grotesque, hilarious, boisterous, uproarious, noisy, graceless, stiffish, interminable, delirious, wild, abandoned, unrestrained, uninhibited, provocative, sensuous, orgiastic, crude, vulgar, exotic, naked, nude, burlesque, erratic, lewd, casual, social, traditional, (in)formal, martial, freestyle, solo, balletic, ceremonial, festive, ritual, dervish, break, folkloric, symbolic, expressionist, classical, traditional, aerobic, Gothic, oriental

dancer, dancers swaying, wavering, swinging, whirling, strutting, bounding, spinning, flying, inspired, accomplished, graceful, elegant, superb, magnificent, fine, surefooted, agile, springy, lithe, supple, frenzied, diminutive, world-class, award-winning, legendary, stellar, unique, promising, thrilling, showy, flash, common, clumsy, graceless, ponderous, weary, costumed, leading, première, professional, solo, native, fancy, exotic, table, erotic, nude, go-go, topless, lyrical, classical

dancing See *dance*

dandy, dandies mincing, simpering, fantastic, egregious, snobbish, arrogant, snooty, supercilious, haughty

danger, dangers grave, positive, serious, extreme, appalling, pre-eminent, great, dreadful, frightful, deadly, mortal, innumerable, long-term, constant, ever-present, potential, impending, imminent, immediate, actual, real, apparent, inherent, (un)common, threatening, lurking, growing, discerning, minor, temporary, imaginary, yellow

dark, darkness growing, descending, pitch, hideous, dismal, grim, thick, profound, deep, impenetrable, unutterable, abysmal, intense, abject, utter, complete, absolute, total, perpetual, infinite, partial, inky, dimensionless, hushed, silent, eerie, windy, chill(y), humid, squally, rainy, foggy, moonless, predawn, Egyptian

data See *information*

date, dates approximate, memorable, noteworthy, (in)significant, (un)important, unforgettable, auspicious, portentous, tentative, conjectural, due, firm, fixed, definite, specific, (in)exact, (un)questionable, (il)legible, first, magnetic, target

daughter, daughters perfect, sweet, innocent, (un)dutiful, (in)considerate, (un)grateful, (dis)obedient, defiant, teenage, adolescent, marriageable, foster, natural, adoptive, putative

dawn, dawns breaking, unfolding, fragrant, fiery, pink, crimson, reddish, rosy, cool, cold, freezing, clear, grey, hazy, misty, drizzly, pearly, lonely, murky, bleak, thunderous, ephemeral

day, days ideal, idyllic, fresh, breezy, windless, balmy, sunny, unclouded, cloudless, shiny, calm, still, quiet, placid, fine, delicate, tender, gentle, soft, mild, bright, brilliant, clear, serene, limpid, crisp, perfect, unblemished, flawless, fair, agreeable, cheerful, untroubled, undistressful, easy, indolent, magnificent, golden, proud, exciting, big, glorious, admirable, marvellous, splendid, delightful, peaceful, exhilarating, profitable, useful, tremulous, lively, joyful, (un)pleasant, pleasing, productive, lucky, enchanting, gratifying, memorable, spacious, propitious, (in)auspicious, favourable, cushy, prosperous, flourishing, affluent, red-letter, halcyon, eligible, busy, field, dramatic, ineffable, blue, dreamy, sleepy, soporific, languid, dozy, drowsy, sunless, grey, hazy, overcast, dull(ish), cloudy, misty, foggy, sultry, scorching, blistering, searing, sweltering, stifling, suffocating, breathless, breezeless, hot, stuffy, airless, steamy, torrid, (baking-)hot, muggy, humid, warm, stormy, thundery, blustery, gusty, windy, windswept, tempestuous, tumultuous, blizzardly, squally, sombre, wintry, black, dark, dismal, gloomy, raw, hellish, dreary, wet, rainy, showery, drippy, drizzly, damp, chilly, frosty, parky, frigid, chilling, nippy, snowy, snow-gripped, crummy, grim, groggy, soggy, cheerless, oppressive, threatening, gruelling, intolerable, interminable, precarious, unvarying, careless, rough, anxious, frenetic, hectic, agonizing, empty, tedious, boring, fateful, trying, hard, fatal, disconsolate, heady, repressive, lawless, chaotic, strenuous, ill-fated, melancholy, devastating, traumatic, ghastly, unlucky, dismal, lean, blue, depressing, disappointing, ill-omened, upside-down, effete, decadent, wretched, undramatic, woozy, long, broad, consecutive, entire, whole, livelong, full, new, (un)eventful, youthful, young(er), childish, heady, giddy,

sappy, adventuresome, mad, lazy, aimless, unprofitable, lost, blank, busy, decisive, natural, make-or-break, pioneer, far-away, far-off, long-ago, bygone, appointed, working, parting, calendar (civil), church, flag, lay, quarter, natal, wedding, nuptial, sidereal, rainy, high-tech, low-tech, juridical, meatless, holy, memorial, Yule, Ember

daylight See also *light* blinding, broad, full, open, clear, sunless, rose-grey

deadline, deadlines tight, tough, firm, strict, ultimate, putative, arbitrary, publishing

deadlock, deadlocks tense, difficult, critical, awkward, knotty, complex, impenetrable, nasty, perplexing, puzzling, serious, stubborn, political

deafness creeping, annoying, partial, complete, temporary, permanent, chronic

deal, deals (un)profitable, lucrative, (dis)advantageous, (dis)honest, square, good, perfect, (il)legal, (un)lawful, premier, firm, shrewd, astute, audacious, mammoth, unbeatable, explicit, (un)fair, (in)valid, raw, cosy, cynical, sour, (in)adequate, preposterous, tricky, shaky, illicit, controversial, underhand, clandestine, secret, under-the-table, behind-the-curtains, tacit, queer, murky, dubious, questionable, shady, crooked, fraudulent, lousy, dormant, complicated, complex, (im)possible, imminent, dead, all-round, unanimous, bilateral, reciprocal, tentative, last-minute, square, sector(i)al, ad hoc

dealer, dealers reputable, helpful, knowledgeable, square, (dis)honest, (un)friendly, (un)scrupulous, dodgy, artful, sleek, shady, shadowy, low-level, freewheeling, (un)snotty, sales-hungry, private, authorized

dealing, dealings straight, virtuous, (dis)honest, (un)just, (im)proper, (in)sincere, disingenuous, crooked, secret, dark, shady, shadowy, wicked, villainous, nefarious, evil, light, heavy, turbulent, political

death, deaths heroic, (un)dignified, honourable, illustrious, peaceful, quiet, humane, restless, clawing, virulent, unfeeling, civil, violent, crushing, swift,

languishing, lingering, premature,
untimely, sudden, (too-)early, slow,
imminent, impending, instant(aneous),
agonizing, devastating, horrible, terrible,
awful, grim, needless, senseless, wretched,
tragic, (un)avoidable, (un)preventable,
(in)evitable, (in)escapable, sure, certain,
reversible, wrongful, unjustified, gruesome,
bizarre, grisly, ghastly, suspicious,
mysterious, stalking, (un)expected,
unexplained, unreported, unconfirmed,
inadvertent, merciful, (un)natural,
accidental, incidental, clinical, ritual,
perinatal, neonatal, asthmatic; thermal;
living, white

debate, debates searching, edifying,
fruitful, valid, (dis)orderly, keen, lively,
spirited, vigorous, animated, brisk, warm,
passionate, impassioned, moving, careful,
thorough, intelligent, substantive,
conclusive, fundamental, (in)effective,
sententious, reasoned, full(-dress),
full-fledged, wide, tame, intense, intensive,
interminable, vigorous, fiery, hot, heated,
scorching, rugged, frenzied, loud, stormy,
anguished, indignant, angry, furious,
raucous, acrimonious, rancorous, hoary,
bitter, divisive, corrosive, hysterical,
contentious, volatile, esoteric, inconclusive,
indecisive, unresolvable, long-standing,
sputtering, swelling, raging, drawn-out,
long(-winded), endless, marathon,
continuous, disjointed, incoherent,
rambling, bruising, debilitating, gruelling,
agonizing, two-hour, wild, ferocious,
fierce, rowdy, raucous, languid, stifled,
dull, tedious, emotional, intellectual,
internal, philosophical, political, fiscal,
public, open, formal, partisan,
parliamentary

debater, debaters expert, skilful,
quick-witted, clever, effective, alert, keen,
ardent, fierce

debris burning, smouldering, flying,
whirling, floating, water-borne,
flood-borne, impenetrable, scattered, loose,
unsightly, volcanic, radioactive

debt, debts crushing, dizzying, staggering,
tormenting, alarming, walloping,
enormous, astronomical, monumental,
mountainous, inestimable, incalculable,
hefty, massive, extensive, formidable,
immoderate, heavy, ponderous,

outrageous, worrisome, growing,
long-standing, out-of-control, disgraceful,
just, (un)due, (un)payable, (un)repayable,
(un)collectable, (ir)recoverable,
(un)reasonable, (in)supportable,
(un)lawful, long-term, short-term,
(un)serviceable, (un)manageable, new, old,
floating, (long-)outstanding, musty, bad,
mature, higher-grade, bonded, common,
public, national, domestic, foreign,
external

debut, debuts exhilarating, triumphant,
auspicious, impressive, strong, sensational,
unforgettable, spectacular, seamless,
bruising, glitzy, pugnacious, star-studded,
opening, electoral

decade, decades See also *period* waning,
last, previous, future, next, current, present

decay ghastly, incipient, inchoate,
rampant, pervasive, potential, putrid,
bacterial, senile, moral; beta, radioactive

deceit, deceits unabated, harmless,
elaborate, pious, cunning, calculating,
crafty, devious, deliberate, intentional,
serious, Machiavellian

decency, decencies charming, becoming,
elegant, gracious, graceful, dignified,
proper, simple, common, fundamental

deception, deceptions See *deceit*

decision, decisions significant, pivotal,
crucial, landmark, earth-shaking, stunning,
unprecedented, fundamental, big,
monumental, dramatic, surprising,
enormous, historic, important, flawless,
right, sound, calculated, shrewd,
hard-headed, (in)appropriate,
(in)competent, (un)wise, (im)prudent,
(in)discreet, (ir)responsible, disinterested,
(un)stable, capable, (un)reasonable,
(in)efficient, (un)reliable, sensible,
informed, inspired, meaningful, candid,
irrevocable, firm, hard-and-fast,
unyielding, cast-iron, definite, clear,
distinct, momentous, (un)timely, snap,
bold, drastic, lenient, costly, simple,
honourable, irretrievable, (ir)reversible,
(un)negotiable, cautious, solitary, stunning,
(un)fortunate, (un)just, (un)fair,
(in)equitable, neutral, fair, (im)partial,
(un)prejudiced, unbiased, binding, major,
inevitable, unavoidable, ineluctable,
(un)necessary, wavering, top-level,
eventful, impetuous, (un)easy, hard, tough,

procrastinating, lingering, tardy, difficult, previous, visceral, spot, impulsive, sudden, instant, speedy, fast, rapid, swift, quick, hurried, hasty, rush, rash, high-risk, risky, dicey, immediate, instantaneous, split-second, snap, (in)significant, notable, (un)popular, everyday, day-to-day, mundane, preliminary, final, ultimate, last-minute, weak-minded, impossible, positive, deliberate, controversial, questionable, wrong, arbitrary, indifferent, stupid, boneheaded, foolish, poor, precipitate, capricious, erratic, foul, unbearable, headstrong, impolitic, mindless, heedless, reckless, desperate, bizarre, feckless, apocalyptic, catastrophic, fateful, conflicting, excruciating, agonizing, painful, radical, tactical, judicial, moral, personal, individual, unilateral, collective, unanimous, ad hoc

deck, decks lower, orlop, promenade, upper, top, weather, bridge, poop

declaration, declarations See *announcement*

decline drastic, sharp, dramatic, precipitous, steep, permanent, irreversible, irretrievable, (in)evitable, (un)avoidable, abrupt, rapid, swift, progressive, gradual, unprecedented, massive, widespread, short-term, long-term, steady, staggering, alarming, cataclysmic, tragic, ruinous, catastrophic, calamitous, lamentable, depressive, ragtag, (in)significant, slight, economic, social, moral, cyclic

décor, décors bold, exotic, iconoclastic, lavish, sleek, tasteful, glitzy, rich, magnificent, splendid, (un)congenial, right, wrong, excessive, incongruous, bland, surreal, modern, ante-bellum

decoration, decorations charming, exquisite, quiet, festive, seductive, fanciful, picturesque, quaint, artful, skilful, clever, deft, (un)attractive, stylish, tasteful, ornate, elaborate, lavish, luxurious, busy, garish, odd, floral, pendant, hanging, suspended, zoomorphic, interior, exterior

decorator, decorators See *artist*

decorum singular, rare, curious, meticulous, rigid, austere, rigorous, inflexible, strenuous, strict, unbending, unrelenting, unyielding

decrease tremendous, enormous,

dramatic, whopping, alarming, (in)significant, rapid

decree, decrees decisive, final, absolute, occasional, irreversible, irrevocable, nisi, peremptory, statutory, judicial, declaratory

dedication (1: devotion) See *devotion*

dedication, dedications (2: inscription prefixed to a book) See *compliment*

deed, deeds (1: an act) good, noble, heroic, glorious, illustrious, knightly, chivalrous, brave, valiant, great, extraordinary, epic, honourable, legendary, newsworthy, dramatic, (un)eventful, unsung, rash, ill, dark, evil, wicked, bad, harmful, murderous, ruthless, atrocious, black, horrible, outrageous, warlike, foul, scoundrelly, dastardly, disloyal, cowardly, repulsive, ugly, villainous, fraudulent

deed, deeds (2: legal document) (un)authentic, official, original

deer bleating, wandering, bounding, fleeing, skulking, bulging, rutting, shining, fawning, herd-abandoned, calm, timid, peaceable, sociable, sleek, slender, fleet, wild, tufted, spotted, white-lipped, white-tailed, black-tailed, red, fallow

defeat thumping, resounding, crushing, devastating, stunning, mortifying, overwhelming, humiliating, staggering, telling, haunting, decisive, disastrous, ignominious, shameful, disgraceful, unmitigated, inglorious, ignoble, dishonourable, worst, calamitous, bitter, painful, irrevocable, serious, assured, undoubted, straight, certain, virtual, impending, final, total, utter, massive, practical, electoral, personal, political, national

defect, defects glaring, conspicuous, radical, gross, serious, grave, major, considerable, devastating, latent, patent, insidious, (ir)reparable, undetected, uncorrected, untreated, minor, superficial, congenital, genetic, physical, metabolic, neurological, mental, visual, structural

defence, defences unflinching, unyielding, ardent, fervent, passionate, impassioned, animated, spirited, tenacious, dogged, strong, stout, vigorous, strenuous, sturdy, gallant, impregnable, invincible, firm, ferocious, bitter, frantic, staunch, tireless, weak, little, (in)adequate, (un)satisfactory, (un)successful, threatened, tepid, clubby, concerted, instantaneous, last-ditch, civil, coastal, national

defender, defenders brave, staunch, stalwart, sturdy, firm, stout, indomitable, ferocious, dogged, ardent, fiery, militant

defiance peaceful, quiet, spirited, fierce, persistent, reckless, unthinkable, unflinching, clear, open, vocal, bold, blatant, garrulous, grave, taut

deficiency, deficiencies glaring, conspicuous, latent, (ir)reparable, serious, severe, sad, genetic, mental, cognitive, physical, congenital, neurological, nutritional

deficit, deficits increasing, growing, soaring, swelling, devastating, menacing, staggering, towering, glaring, large, siz(e)able, vast, huge, dramatic, gargantuan, tremendous, incalculable, hefty, heavy, stiff, appreciable, massive, enormous, terrific, chronic, persistent, perpetual, undiminished, unusual, uncontrolled, uncontrollable, runaway, hopeless, irretrievable, irresponsible, critical, stubborn, (un)foreseeable, temporary, structural, fiscal

definition, definitions imaginative, pithy, quirky, clear-cut, precise, (in)adequate, (un)satisfactory, (in)accurate, (in)expressible, deft, simple, complex, tendentious, broad, elastic, outdated, rigid, restrictive, prescriptive, specific

deformity, deformities gross, extreme, congenital, hereditary, inborn, innate, (un)acquired, physical

degree, degrees (1: step or stage; extent); extraordinary, certain, remarkable, rare, great, high, substantial, infinitesimal, low, varying, intolerable, culpable

degree, degrees (2: academic title) advanced, higher, high-powered, belated, fake, bogus, fraudulent, first, honorary, conjoint

deity, deities See *god*

delay, delays annoying, maddening, exasperating, aggravating, baffling, untoward, troublesome, unfavourable, unfair, costly, serious, vexatious, disastrous, odd, extraordinary, critical, unconscionable, strange, excessive, undetermined, substantial, (un)accountable, major, customary, (un)common, (un)usual, habitual, chronic, bureaucratic,

(in)excusable, endless, interminable, long, lengthy, hours-long, three-day, two-hour, minor, brief, short, (un)intentional, (in)frequent, (un)avoidable, (in)evitable, (in)tolerable, (un)bearable, (un)reasonable, irresponsible, unexplained, (un)expected

delegate, delegates (un)acceptable, accredited, foreign, high-ranking, high-level, six-person, plenipotentiary, signatory, papal, apostolic, diplomatic

delegation, delegations See *delegate*

deliberation, deliberations See *discussion* and *debate*

delicacy, delicacies choice, costly, exotic, unique, rich, much-sought, prized, ambrosial

delight, delights unspeakable, unutterable, exalted, dizzy, rare, vain, rapturous, unqualified, unabashed, puckish, voluble, unalloyed, unmitigated, breathless, keen, special, incomparable, unprecedented, uncommon, unimpaired, sheer, irresistible, intense, undisguised, incredulous, expansive, perennial, constant, infinite, unfading, unending, unbounded, never-failing, ultimate, anticipatory, fearful, impish, childish, simple, mindless, sardonic, vicious, surreptitious, perverse, orgiastic, sadistic, sensuous, sensory, sensual, scenic, aesthetic, culinary, epicurean

delinquency, delinquencies juvenile, academic, geriatric, moral

delinquent, delinquents See also *delinquency* raging, apathetic, indifferent, impassive, (in)corrigible, (un)reformable, (un)changeable, (un)manageable, (un)responsive, (un)cooperative, (un)repentant, first-time, repeat, juvenile

delivery, deliveries (1: a distribution; a handing over) (un)reliable, safe, speedy, rapid, fast, prompt, immediate, forward, staggered, special, express

delivery, deliveries (2: a birth) See also *birth* easy, trouble-free, problem-free, difficult, life-threatening, breech, vaginal, surgical, Caesarean

deluge, deluges See *flood*

delusion, delusions long-standing, haunting, astonishing, pure, beautiful, daft, silly, foolish, reckless, gross, monstrous, dangerous, unfortunate, strange, common, popular, momentary, fundamental

demagogue, demagogues See *agitator*

demand, demands (ever-)increasing, soaring, rising, growing, surging, ravenous, voracious, heavy, extensive, exorbitant, mighty, enormous, large, great, high, strong, fantastic, higher-than-expected, inordinate, outlandish, excessive, insatiable, ambitious, countless, limitless, (un)limited, intense, strident, unconscionable, stringent, tough, good, long-standing, unceasing, incessant, ceaseless, endless, unending, central, irrepressible, (un)acceptable, (im)moderate, (un)reasonable, (un)realistic, cocky, brazen, multifarious, straightforward, clear, key, core, basic, onerous, adamant, vociferous, gruelling, heartless, merciless, pitiless, ruthless, relentless, unrelenting, unyielding, unwavering, unquenchable, non-negotiable, importunate, gruelling, inexorable, hot, overwhelming, sweeping, meteoric, stagnant, modest, low, minimum, weak, sluggish, slack, tumbling, factitious, unnatural, vague, fictitious, artificial, troublesome, extortionate, (un)lawful, well-timed, pent-up, gratuitous, urgent, pressing, insistent, abrupt, loud, shrill, clamorous, widespread, global, worldwide, emphatic, conflicting, contradictory, irreconcilable, uncompromisable, paradoxical, absolutist, voracious, future, underlying, vehement, unprecedented, domestic, societal, social, ethical

demeanour, demeanours See *behaviour* and *conduct*

democracy, democracies free, maximum, liberal, libertarian, full-fledged, wide, genuine, true, authentic, real, (un)stable, (non-)functional, durable, peaceful, working, traditional, mature, budding, fledgling, emerging, young, embryonic, neophyte, rocky, fragile, elusive, weak, social, participatory, parliamentary, constitutional, representative (indirect), multiparty, multiracial, pluralistic, paternalistic, tribal, Thespian

demolition, demolitions imminent, inevitable, (un)avoidable, certain, inescapable, regrettable, mindless, doomed, fated, (un)scheduled

demon, demons canny, cunning, arch,

mischievous, crafty, sly, ruthless, officious, evil, ghostly, satanic, personal

demonstration, demonstrations (1: parade; a show of military force) calm, silent, unarmed, peaceful, non-violent, joyous, spontaneous, (in)effective, frantic, noisy, fiery, raucous, exuberant, interminable, unprecedented, dramatic, memorable, sporadic, small, large(-scale), mass(ive), city-wide, huge, siz(e)able, violent, ugly, nasty, bloody, sombre, solemn, hateful, uncontrollable, unruly, disorderly, militant, defiant, spectacular, fearless, hostile, angry, furious, explosive, persistent, desultory, sporadic, faltering, flag-waving, sign-waving, (il)legal, multiracial, public

demonstration, demonstrations (2: an outward expression or display) vivid, impressive, radiant, animated, colourful, spirited, vibrant, signal, significant, conclusive, unequivocal, ample, rare, garish, showy

demonstrator, demonstrators See *demonstration* (1)

den, dens secluded, cloistered, hermitic, hidden, sheltered, solitary, squalid, wretched

denial, denials strong, wholesale, complete, flat, vehement, strenuous, stiff, severe, bitter, vociferous, staunch, passionate, hot, unqualified, truthful, cautious, (un)convincing, not-very-convincing, direct, outright, consistent, persistent, sharp, brusque, straightforward, utter, unconditional, positive, explicit, truculent, blanket, categorical, steadfast, tongue-tied

denomination, denominations mainline, tiny, perdurable, dissident, contentious, indigenous, native, religious

dénouement, dénouements See *plot* (2)

dentistry cosmetic, restorative, prevent(at)ive

denunciation, denunciations scorching, scathing, stinging, seething, vigorous, vitriolic, harsh, total, absolute, explicit, blunt, public, angry, furious, swift, well-worn, standard

departure, departures (1: going away) sad, emotional, painful, (dis)orderly, grand, (un)ceremonious, quiet, smooth, reluctant, sudden, abrupt, hurried, hasty, rash, precipitate, (un)timely, imminent, (un)expected, unexplained, surprise, tardy

departure, departures (2: changing) daring, challenging, triumphant, courageous, venturesome, audacious, brave, fearless, foolhardy, drastic, radical, dramatic, notable, (in)significant

dependence, dependency complete, utter, total, heavy, extensive, feather-brained, silly, childish, forced, humiliating, compulsive, mutual

deportation, deportations (il)legal, (un)orthodox, imminent, immediate

deposit, deposits (1: money deposited) substantial, big, (non-)refundable, secure, recoverable, insurable

deposit, deposits (2: layer of solid matter) rich, inexhaustible, loose, (un)stratified, fluvial, silty, mineral, alluvial, allochthonous, autochthonous, argillaceous, subterranean, commercial

depression (1: economic) profound, deep, chronic, (decade-)long, stubborn, severe, marked, serious, full-blown, major, painful, devastating, grim, global

depression (2: emotional) crushing, debilitating, chronic, recurrent, occasional, mild, severe, extreme, grave, serious, acute, profound, deep, difficult, inescapable, lingering, black, manic, suicidal, endogenous

deprivation, deprivations appalling, troubling, shocking, conspicuous, woeful, pitiful, rude, considerable, severe, perilous, utter, emotional, sensory, material, financial, sexual, social

depth, depths baffling, dizzying, vertiginous, inexhaustible, unfathomable, fathomless, bottomless, abysmal, immeasurable, tremendous, hidden, murky, dark, obscure, labyrinthine, gloomy, innermost, dank, nether; Gothic

derelict, derelicts pathetic, pitiful (pitiable), ragged, contemptible, despicable, lamentable, virtual

descendant, descendants (in)direct, veritable, (il)legitimate, lineal, linear

descent, descents sheer, steep, rapid, dizzying, vertiginous, perilous, dangerous, risky, traumatic, slow; hereditary

description, descriptions flowery, lively, living, vivid, curious, roseate, elaborate, eloquent, comprehensive, straightforward, lucid, clear, succinct, exact, precise, laconic, thumbnail, brief, concise, meticulous, unimpeachable, imaginative, impressive, masterly, deft, unparalleled, delicate, thorough, true, faithful, candid, frank, penetrating, (un)coloured, compelling, charming, enchanting, fruity, glowing, ecstatic, animated, eager, (in)accurate, lifelike, lush, lyrical, effusive, extravagant, hilarious, fastidious, rapturous, sensitive, sententious, lovable, strange, minute, complete, full, detailed, blow-by-blow, hard-edged, evocative, beautiful, (in)appropriate, long-winded, poignant, gory, harrowing, perplexing, sketchy, superficial, vague, colourless, pictorial, graphic, factual, poetic, anthropomorphic

desert, deserts scorching, seething, sweltering, searing, burning, scorched, parched, unending, endless, immense, enormous, vast, boundless, golden, bare, empty, bleak, (hyper)arid, semiarid, unsparing, forbidding, unforgiving, trackless, featureless, barren, sere, desolate, derelict, stark, flat, grim, bone-dry, inaccessible, impassable, far-flung, austere, harsh, rigorous, inhospitable, lifeless, uninhabited, awesome, unmerciful, merciless, ruthless, pitiless, heartless, relentless, unrelenting, primitive, hushed, still, sandy, rocky, mountainous, spiny, shale, pitted, torrid, hot, tropical, cactus-strewn, salt; cultural

design, designs striking, vivid, impressive, (in)efficient, sleek, graceful, elegant, trendy, delicate, superb, magnificent, splendid, superlative, deluxe, elaborate, opulent, lavish, marvellous, impeccable, well-proven, award-winning, exquisite, vintage, simple, basic, flamboyant, meticulous, precise, ornate, colourful, inlaid, thoughtful, fanciful, imaginative, dazzling, authentic, inventive, innovative, novel, original, unusual, one-of-a-kind, revolutionary, radical, avant-garde, state-of-the-art, leading-edge, provocative, bold, neat, rare, brilliant, ingenious, fancy, distinctive, unfettered, familiar, ordinary, traditional, classic, (un)conventional, conservative, contemporary, modern, (un)restrained, austere, spare, ascetic, indigenous, foreign, insidious, run-of-the-mill, mundane, functional, practical, utilitarian, (in)artistic, (in)complete, (in)adequate, overwrought, bombastic, busy, indecipherable, intricate, sloppy, faulty, defective, odd, sinuous, (curvi)linear, uncompromising, decadent, naïve, primitive, frothy, fluid, modular, running, incised, graphic, high-tech, computer-aided, industrial, structural, interior, scenic, floral, abstract, symmetrical, geometric, diagonal, hexagonal, symbolic, futuristic, Art Deco, paisley, Gothic, Victorian, Georgian

designer, designers shrewd, brilliant, (un)successful, famous, celebrated, eminent, notable, noted, top, best-known, well-known, honoured, major, big, distinguished, legendary, prestigious, sought-after, superb, talented, influential, innovative, revolutionary, bold, outrageous, generative, intrepid, dazzling, eccentric, erratic, obscure, would-be, interior, architectural, industrial, graphic

desire, desires overweening, overwhelming, overpowering, consuming, burning, intoxicating, yearning, flaming, compelling, unwavering, (un)quenchable, (in)satiable, (in)controllable, (un)controllable, (un)conquerable, immoderate, inordinate, boundless, exorbitant, utter, keen, enthusiastic, secret, deep(-seated), single-minded, restless, sincere, genuine, honest, frenzied, (un)healthy, wild, fervent (fervid), empty, amorphous, inmost, wistful, (ir)resistible, passionate, ardent, intense, understandable, inexpressible, unworthy, low, sharp, keen, eager, vehement, voluptuous, lusty, coarse, violent, unholy, earthy, mutable, fickle, base, impish, mischievous, rapacious, culpable, foolish, insane, stubborn, vain, obsessive, mundane, worldly, strong, dual, (un)natural, missionary, innermost, unremitting, long-standing, long-term, long-range, re-emerging, fleeting, pressing, waning, impatient, sudden, impetuous, unattainable, pent-up, disappointed, hidden, vague, peculiar, compulsive, convulsive, basic, primary, primeval, innate, atavistic, instinctual, instinctive, carnal, sexual, personal, ancestral

desk, desks (dis)orderly, (un)tidy, executive-size, enormous, mammoth, ornate, battered, rickety, creaky, antique, pedestal

desolation, desolations depressing, grim, gloomy, dismal, dreary, awful, immense, infinite, extreme, utter, total, complete, magnificent, stark, irrevocable, irretrievable, tortured, lunar

despair grinding, crushing, blinding, black, bleak, dark, bewildered, bitter, unrelenting, relentless, inarticulate, unproductive, reckless, silent, crazy, wild, grave, no-way-out, oppressive, hellish, utter, (near-)total, profound, deep, pervasive, widespread, excessive, growing, creeping, momentary, initial

despot, despots domineering, unbending, overbearing, messianic, charismatic, privileged, imperious, powerful, power-mad, (power-)crazed, power-hungry, absolute, all-out, unchallenged, dictatorial, brutal, tyrannous, unscrupulous, cruel, pitiless, heartless, remorseless, merciless, ruthless, relentless, unrelenting, iron-fisted, murderous, monstrous, bloodthirsty, bloody, thuggish, oppressive, dangerous, implacable, wily, devious, defiant, arrogant, vain, paranoiac, paranoid, incompetent, erratic, capricious, whimsical, aggressive, ambitious, petty, greedy, rapacious, grasping, corrupt, benevolent, detestable, hideous, abhorrent, insulting, feudal, colonial, Bolshevik

despotism See *despot*

dessert, desserts tempting, ravishing, captivating, lip-smacking, mouthwatering, refreshing, eye-appealing, eye-catching, impressive, spectacular, luxurious, sumptuous, monumental, irresistible, delicious, dainty, sinful, seductive, decadent, scrumptious, delightful, delectable, flavourful, zesty, excellent, perfect, impeccable, luscious, sweet, nonpareil, unequalled, unsurpassed, unforgettable, ethereal, glorious, legendary, chic, favourite, cold, humble, simple, bland, gooey, creamy, fruit(y), jelly-like, (raisin-)rich, (un)healthy, high-calorie, high-fat, low-calorie, low-fat

destination, destinations alluring, bewitching, exciting, glamorous, viable, easy, distant, far-flung, final, (high-)end, ultimate, specific, precise, well-defined, new, (un)popular, (un)known, little-known, unstated, vague, leading, foremost, (un)usual, exotic, favoured, intended, ill-defined, tourist(ic)

destiny, destinies See *fate*

destitution See *poverty*

destruction, destructions overwhelming, utter, complete, total, absolute, mass, extensive, massive, monumental, wholesale, widespread, devastating, unabated, unimaginable, untold, apocalyptic, irrevocable, irretrievable, indiscriminate, wanton, deliberate, wilful, insidious, treacherous, nightmarish, alarming, appalling, unnerving, unsettling, pitiful, awful, ferocious, useless, unthinking, demented, mad, insane, maniacal, senseless, mindless, needless, ruthless, pitiless, remorseless, heartless, merciless, relentless, unrelenting, periodic, systematic, long-term, eventual, physical, environmental

detachment judicious, cool, icy, calm, disinterested, dispassionate, benign

detail, details telling, revealing, compelling, intriguing, gritty, informative, florid, exquisite, perfect, close, exact, specific, intimate, precise, pertinacious, rigorous, meticulous, thorough, distinct, discernible, perceptible, vivid, memorable, rich, fresh, sensational, abundant, lengthy, voluminous, myriad, innumerable, great, elaborate, ample, full, complete, mountainous, circumstantial, authentic, (in)adequate, (ir)relevant, (im)pertinent, (un)important, (in)significant, unsparing, nerve-wracking, grisly, gruesome, horrible, horrific, appalling, shocking, excruciating, stupefying, unsavoury, sordid, morbid, intricate, cumbersome (cumbrous), complex, murky, curious, scant, scarce, minute, little, tiny, small, minor, bare, sketchy, vague, immaterial, trifling, trivial, petty, fleeting, assiduous, lurid, gory, eerie, colourful, thrilling, offbeat, inconsequential, fictitious, technical, photographic, graphic, de rigueur

detective, detectives enterprising, tenacious, smart, resourceful, (un)successful, intrepid, dauntless, fearless, daring, brave, bold, plucky, mysterious, armchair, undercover, fictional, fictitious, private, investigative

detention, detentions humane, secure, lengthy, preventive, forcible, preferential, (un)lawful, (il)legal, military, administrative

deterioration tremendous, substantial, considerable, alarming, acute, inexorable, rapid, eventual, (un)avoidable, (un)preventable, (in)evitable, irreversible, overall, structural

determination unflinching, unflagging, unyielding, unwavering, unbending, unswerving, unabashed, undiminished, stern, gritty, steely, rocky, stony, sturdy, hard, invincible, unshak(e)able, inflexible, definite, resolute, stiff, dogged, iron, unquenchable, inexorable, indomitable, steadfast, fixed, unalterable, obstinate, stubborn, persistent, firm, bull-headed, single-minded, fierce, burning, incredible, unbelievable, strong, tough, rugged, full, merciless, grim, sheer, solemn, quiet, moderate, high-minded, honest, admirable, patient, principled, manic, demonic, final, waning, wavering, smouldering

deterrence See *deterrent*

deterrent, deterrents vexing, frightening, trying, testing, extreme, ultimate, crucial, effective; nuclear

detestation See *hate*

devastation, devastations See *destruction*

development, developments exciting, interesting, surprising, stunning, startling, promising, encouraging, hopeful, constructive, innovative, seminal, positive, remarkable, momentous, sensational, dramatic, full-scale, massive, (in)significant, (un)welcome, (im)proper, impressive, (in)complete, normal, (un)steady, sustainable, (ir)reversible, new, recent, subsequent, (un)foreseeable, pertinent, irrelevant, peripheral, divergent, extraneous, rampant, unchecked, rapid, extraordinary, sinister, worrisome, worrying, troubling, turbulent, adverse, ominous, grave, disastrous, cataclysmic, indigenous, architectonic, prenatal, economic, social, cognitive, evolutionary, geothermal, adolescent, physical, mental; urban

device, devices clever, ingenious, ultimate, state-of-the-art, leading-edge, diabolical, time-saving, beneficial, labour-saving, simple, complicated, (in)effective, (im)practicable, (in)accurate, old, hoary, modern, simulative, (un)sophisticated, hands-off, built-in, automatic, artificial, electrical, (electro)mechanical, medical, mnemonic, electronic, analytic, measuring, testing, eavesdropping, explosive, artistic, poetic, oratorical

devil, devils horned, crafty, wicked, vicious, murderous, evil, hideous, infernal, incarnate, satanic, Luciferian, Mephistophelian(-ean)

devotee, devotees assiduous, obsequious, solicitous, diligent, impassioned, great, fanatical

devotion, devotions unyielding, unflinching, unswerving, unwavering, unflagging, unshak(e)able, unceasing, untiring, overwhelming, undying, lasting, enduring, long-standing, lifelong, eternal, constant, deep, immense, enormous, extreme, fanatic(al), patriarchal, stubborn, exacting, selfless, intense, relentless, limitless, unsparing, total, inordinate, whole-hearted, misplaced, ferocious, wild, rabid, fervent, enthusiastic, passionate, obsessional, exceptional, single(-minded), frank, honest, genuine, legendary, high-minded, assiduous, supreme, unabashed, diligent, obsequious, silent, solicitous, suicidal, mutual, filial, holy, religious

dew, dews refreshing, gentle, hoary, pristine, bright, fresh, cool, heavy, thick

diagnosis, diagnoses encouraging, (un)favourable, astute, heartbreaking, shocking, troubling, critical, fateful, definitive, (im)proper, (in)correct, (in)accurate, complex, elusive, uncertain, fuzzy, controversial, early, tentative, final, biological, clinical, computational, mathematical, differential, physical, preoperative

dialect, dialects pure, lively, twangy, emphatic, distinct, distinctive, boisterous, low, thick, rough, uncouth, fast, unintelligible, antique, archaic, local, regional, sectional, black, Hibernian

dialogue, dialogues sparkling, humbling, vivacious, lively, vintage, polished, vital, rich, smooth, terse, witty, (un)natural, life-like, well-written, fruity, deadpan, unanchored, protracted, insipid, pretentious, dry, wooden, lifeless, stilted, strained, jaded, gross, jocular, realistic, naturalistic, conversational, off-stage, vernacular, face-to-face, Socratic

diamond, diamonds glittering, shining, refulgent, radiant, genuine, priceless, costly, expensive, rare, real, true, perfect, flawless, one-carat, big, egg-sized, false, rough(-cut), (un)cut, hard, fancy-coloured, marquise, blue, yellow, natural, synthetic, industrial; black

diarist, diarists See *writer*

diary, diaries detailed, long, voluminous, candid, secretive, intermittent, revealing, intimate, self-absorbed, ponderous, (in)complete, meagre, pencilled, daily, appointment

dictator, dictators See also *despot* old-style, durable, powerful, imperious, domineering, absolute, virtual, legendary, charismatic, brutal, corrupt, privileged, tyrannous, unscrupulous, ruthless, merciless, pitiless, heartless, remorseless, relentless, unrelenting, irresponsible, oppressive, repressive, unconscionable, squeamish, vain, petty, unpredictable, loathsome, odious, overbearing, rapacious, thuggish, iron-fisted, steel-fisted, coup-resistant, invincible, unchallenged, much-feared, deranged, self-appointed

dictatorship, dictatorships benevolent, incompetent, unstable, erratic, capricious, whimsical, ruthless, pitiless, heartless, remorseless, merciless, relentless, unrelenting, oppressive, repressive, uncontrollable, brutal, tough, harsh, paranoid, bloody, hideous, pernicious, abhorrent, overbearing, greedy, hidebound, infamous, monstrous, virtual, expansionist, imperious, military, one-party, totalitarian, socialist, Marxist

diction chaste, correct, elegant, felicitous, fresh, delicate, precise, perfect, formal, stiff, affected, stilted, laboured, bloated, epigrammatic, poetic

dictionary, dictionaries authoritative, comprehensive, exhaustive, substantive, definitive, unique, helpful, decent, up-to-date, out-of-date, (un)reliable, mighty, ponderous, monumental, compact, single-volume, one-volume, two-volume, detailed, unabridged, general, bilingual, biographical, technical, legal, medical, scientific, etymological, standard, pocket

diet, diets (un)appetizing, strict, restrictive, aggressive, unrelenting, relentless, ruthless, pitiless, merciless, radical, excessive, ascetic, abstemious, jejune, rigorous, pernicious, steady, ideal, sure-fire, (in)flexible, (im)moderate, wholesome, nutritious, (un)healthy, (un)healthful, (in)adequate, (un)sensible, (in)discriminate, (im)proper, (un)suitable, (in)valid, (in)temperate, (im)prudent, (un)safe, (un)balanced, well-balanced, varied, lenient, (un)natural, all-natural, low, lean, bare, spare, scanty, meagre, minimal, fastidious, bizarre, nasty, absurd, impulsive, unpalatable, tasteless, traditional, standard, (un)conventional, (ab)normal, unaccustomed, vital, primary, special, disheartening, monotonous, bland, low-carbohydrate, low-fat, low-cholesterol, low-sodium, (sodium-)restricted, salt-restricted, low-salt, (salt-)reduced, sugar-reduced, protein-rich, meatless, heart-healthy, low-calorie, calorie-reduced, high-fibre, gluten-free, high-fat, fatty, sugar-laden, therapeutic, medicinal, vegetarian, Vegan, kosher, soft

dieter, dieters serious, determined, enthusiastic, (un)wise, (in)sensible, undeterred, rigid, frequent, habitual

dieting See *diet*

difference, differences (1: the state of being unlike) bracing, striking, glaring, swelling, unnerving, shocking, stark, radical, critical, crucial, dramatic, profound, deep, tremendous, palpable, wide, definite, spectacular, basic, fundamental, essential, principal, main, chief, primary, enormous, vast, interesting, genuine, substantive, effective, clear, obvious, noticeable, vivid, vital, (in)distinguishable, (in)discernible, (im)perceptible, (in)visible, (in)appreciable, undefined, subtle, irreversible, durable, humiliating, minute, small, benign, academic, surface, (in)significant, decided, marked, qualitative, ideological, cultural, social, economic, semantic, generic, phonemic

difference, differences (2: disagreement) intractable, serious, deep(-seated), deep-rooted, broad, wide, sharp,

(in)surmountable, (ir)reconcilable, crucial, fundamental, substantial, enormous, (in)significant, inevitable, unavoidable, volatile, academic, small, (in)visible, (im)perceptible, ugly, long-standing, momentary, protracted, sectarian, ideological, polemical

difficulty, difficulties insuperable, formidable, considerable, noticeable, discouraging, (in)surmountable, stubborn, (in)extricable, (in)soluble, invincible, extreme, grave, serious, heavy, formidable, perplexing, terrible, dreadful, pressing, increasing, (un)expected, slight, run-of-the-mill, basic; financial, pecuniary

diffidence anxious, embarrassed, confused, desperate, awkward, uneasy

dignity, dignities austere, solemn, grave, full, immense, proper, inalienable (unalienable), unassailable, doffing, weighty, regal, royal, queenly, elegant, quiet, calm, unruffled, intact, cold, askew, mellow, quixotic, homespun

dilemma, dilemmas compelling, abiding, vexing, racking, agonizing, excruciating, frightening, striking, serious, urgent, classic, unusual, curious, intractable, inextricable, insoluble, dire, forlorn, hopeless, awful, awesome, complex, knotty, guilt-fraught, painful, nightmarish, ridiculous, dubious, deplorable, dismal, dreadful, terrible, ugly, wicked, vicious, woeful, perilous, unsolved, personal, ethical, moral, legal, Parnassian

dimension, dimensions enormous, large, majestic, Olympian, (in)finite, diminutive, (un)realistic, engaging, fresh, frightening, awesome, record, unbelievable, incredible, specified, rooted, fractional; fourth

dining room, dining rooms See *restaurant*

dinner, dinners See also *meal* festive, complete, vinous, bibulous, elaborate, elegant, snug, fancy, gourmet, candlelight, candlelit, romantic, sumptuous, lavish, decadent, full-dress, black-tie, long-winded, grand, special, superb, delightful, excellent, unsurpassed, wonderful, splendid, fantastic, magnificent, hearty, relaxed, leisurely, quiet, intimate, nice, pleasant, satisfying, delectable, delicious, scrumptious, tasty, succulent, savoury, late, frugal, boring, passable, atrocious, frozen, fattening, typical, orthodox, traditional, customary, usual, impromptu, stand-up, informal, casual, (semi-)formal, sit-down, alfresco, testimonial, social, business, state

dinosaur, dinosaurs old-world, extinct, antediluvian, lizard-hipped, bird-hipped; industrial

diplomacy, diplomacies shrewd, genteel, gentle, quiet, smooth, imaginative, true, genuine, innovative, creative, artful, peaceful, exquisite, secret, dogged, tenacious, obstinate, tough, heavy-handed, intense, hot, hectic, frantic, (in)conclusive, misguided, high-level, (non-)military, personal, multilateral, international

diplomat, diplomats top(-ranking), prominent, eminent, well-known, important, well-placed, legendary, exceptional, astute, shrewd, tactful, seasoned, consummate, brilliant, finished, patrician, eloquent, smooth-spoken, smooth-tongued, avuncular, plodding, phlegmatic, dour, emotionless, immune, veteran, roving, resident, career, foreign

direction, directions (1: course taken) same, opposite, (un)specified, specific, particular, random, (un)predictable, misguided, reversed, clockwise, anti-clockwise, counter-clockwise, northward, southward, eastward, westward, northerly, southerly, easterly, westerly

directions (2: information; instruction) careful, simple, clear, explicit, distinct, definite, precise, exact, (in)comprehensible, complicated, puzzling, intricate, firm, wanting, missing, lacking

director, directors canny, shrewd, astute, knowing, extraordinary, vigorous, (in)effectual, energetic, high-minded, brilliant, pragmatic, (in)experienced, (un)promising, innovative, sagacious, (in)accessible, visionless, wily, cunning, dummy, associate, (non-)executive

directory, directories See *guide* (1)

disability, disabilities widespread, overriding, severe, partial, (un)known, premature, temporary, chronic, permanent, physical, mental, sensory, psychiatric, musculoskeletal; legal

disadvantage, disadvantages obvious, great, immense, incalculable, infinite, persistent, hopeless, concomitant, strategic, economic, biological, technological

disagreement, disagreements jarring, lingering, frank, outspoken, vehement, heated, strong, emphatic, substantial, fundamental, profound, deep, perennial, vicious, bitter, serious, complete, slight, initial, internal, marital, domestic, ethnic, national, communal

disappearance, disappearances baffling, puzzling, perplexing, mysterious, enigmatic, incomprehensible, inexplicable, unaccountable, suspicious, irretrievable, sudden, graceful, virtual

disappointment, disappointments distressing, galling, vexing, crushing, blistering, staggering, bitter, harsh, uneasy, tragic, furious, sad, grievous, cruel, brutal, painful, rude, terrible, severe, acute, keen, gross, desperate, deep, profound, slight

disapproval unequivocal, outspoken, frank, mild, stern, strong, emphatic, vehement

disarmament genuine, one-sided, unilateral, bilateral, mutual, multilateral, nuclear

disaster, disasters heart-rending, sickening, appalling, staggering, grave, significant, irreparable, grim, dreadful, sure, terrible, horrific, unparalleled, (un)controllable, (un)preventable, inevitable, unavoidable, inexplicable, incredible, unbelievable, singular, enormous, incalculable, unimaginable, large(-scale), colossal, spectacular, major, unlooked-for, recurring, unforeseen, unexpected, unprecedented, lurking, impending, imminent, sudden, unnameable, potential, unfolding, unpardonable, unqualified, unmitigated, full-fledged, total, complete, fatal, deadly, mysterious, national, international, natural, seismic, financial, economic, atmospheric, maritime, nuclear, ecological, environmental

disbelief silent, helpless, sullen, stunned, dazed, wide-eyed, shocked, pained, powerful, wild, crushing, apparent, initial

disciple, disciples avid, fervent, zealous, ardent, impassioned

disciplinarian, disciplinarians natural-born, fierce, domineering, overbearing, oppressive, merciless, pitiless, ruthless, heartless, relentless, unrelenting, iron-fisted

discipline, disciplines (un)profitable, firm, tight, strict, rigid, unflagging, iron, rigorous, stern, harsh, tough, severe, exacting, brutal, (in)effective, temperate, abstemious, lax, daily, tremendous, ascetic, monastic, doctrinal, personal

disclosure, disclosures stunning, stupefying, intriguing, full, indiscreet, candid, inflammatory, (un)expected, unauthorized, public

discomfort, discomforts See *pain*

discontent growing, rumbling, flaring, smouldering, genuine, deep, strong, sour, awful, popular

discord, discords See *disagreement*

discount, discounts huge, substantial, fantastic, breathtaking, astounding, cash, staff

discovery, discoveries heart-stirring, astonishing, astounding, amazing, surprising, stunning, startling, dazzling, tantalizing, intriguing, exciting, interesting, glamorous, successful, significant, enormous, valuable, useful, fruitful, important, real, dramatic, noteworthy, consequential, revolutionary, historic, unbelievable, incredible, wonderful, remarkable, phenomenal, momentous, fabulous, legendary, fortunate, lucky, delightful, appropriate, fond, (un)pleasant, belated, timely, fresh, serendipitous, chance, coincidental, accidental, unexpected, new, increasing, sensational, apropos, curious, sinister, singular, extraordinary, macabre, gruesome, grisly, horrible, arcane, chilling, rapid-fire, confused, hysterical, shocking, useless, unpleasant, painful, archaeological, historical, medical, scientific

discrepancy, discrepancies See *difference* (1)

discretion, discretions nice, charming, affable, appropriate, considerate, delightful, elegant, pleasant, refined, thoughtful

discrimination, discriminations subtle, outright, blatant, apparent, overt, (un)common, (un)conscious, invidious, hurtful, unjustified, unjustifiable, unacceptable, pervasive, systematic, deep-rooted, alleged, (un)intended, reverse, racial, religious, de facto

discussion, discussions animated, spirited, lively, enthusiastic, intense, intensive, deep, profound, vigorous, sensitive, alert, frank, sophisticated, edifying, meaningful, meaty, rational, positive, learned, elaborate, useful, heart-to-heart, warm, fruitful, unhurried, quiet, (un)pleasant, civilized, serious, understanding, systematic, solemn, no-holds-barred, substantive, exhaustive, weary, loose, flawed, interminable, acrimonious, stormy, noisy, vociferous, sterile, fruitless, ponderous, rudimentary, casual, perfunctory, irrelevant, irrational, complex, impersonal, brief, endless, lengthy, excessive, deadly, (in)formal, secret, arcane, two-hour, peripatetic, man-to-man, face-to-face, bilateral

disdain See *contempt*

disease, diseases devouring, wasting, withering, catching, death-dealing, limiting, debilitating, devastating, frightening, puzzling, baffling, depressing, agonizing, spreading, lurking, full-blown, inveterate, ascertainable, cruel, pestilent, gruesome, obnoxious, deadly, (non-)fatal, mortal, lethal, insidious, rare, acute, high-risk, major, irreversible, progressive, slow, obstinate, complex, severe, widespread, prevalent, rampant, (ir)recoverable, (in)curable, (ir)remediable, (un)preventable, (un)treatable, (un)controllable, (in)eradicable, (un)stoppable, (un)beatable, dangerous, deep-seated, painful, (un)common, virulent, poisonous, eruptive, nasty, harsh, awesome, scary, dreadful, fearful, horrible, loathsome, hideous, reportable, inextirpable, unidentified, unspecified, undetected, (un)suspected, (still-)unresolved, (un)confirmed, self-inflicted, self-induced, exclusionary, (un)insurable, specifiable, latent, incipient, (auto)immune, refractory, recurrent, premature, (a)symptomatic, inflammatory, expensive, mysterious, mystery, cryptogenic, esoteric, strange, passing, organic, malign(ant), benign, minor, trivial, seasonal, inheritable, hereditary, genetic, congenital, acute, chronic, local, infectious, contagious, communicable, transmissible, quarantinable, terminal, endemic, epidemic, pandemic, social, medical, clinical, mental, physical, corporeal, psychosomatic, protozoan, nutritional, vitamin-deficiency, functional, occupational, mosquito-borne, parasitic, ulcerative, degenerative, iatrogenic, intestinal, glandular, bacterial, viral, oesophageal, verminous, cardiac, cardiovascular, pulmonary, circulatory, respiratory, rheumatic, coeliac, coronary, articular, infantile, mental, manic, febrile, venereal, gastrointestinal, tropical, industrial, skin, arterial, myocardial, thromboembolic, neuromuscular, feral, ischaemic, periodontal

disfigurement severe, grotesque, bizarre, eerie, cruel, painful, ruthless, merciless

disgrace humiliating, overwhelming, total, utter, deep, unqualified, positive, irretrievable, indelible, (un)deserved

disguise, disguises puzzling, intriguing, convincing, clever, impenetrable, exquisite, thin, transparent, apparent, useful

disgust sickening, angry, bitter, ineffable, unspeakable, unmitigated, unconquerable, utter, supreme, utmost, extreme, greatest

dish, dishes (1: any particular food) mouthwatering, appetising, enticing, tempting, exciting, intriguing, savoury, tasty, flavourful, fresh, delectable, delicious, pleasant, delightful, zesty, piquant, extravagant, hom(e)y, pretty, delicate, admirable, elegant, impressive, lusty, legendary, exquisite, fabulous, splendid, magnificent, impeccable, perfect, decent, decorous, princely, robust, select, exotic, colourful, innovative, quintessential, traditional, classic, favourite, staple, representative, standard, basic, fragrant, garlicky, spicy, (un)usual, (less-)renowned, (un)familiar, time-consuming, unsavoury, fattening, tony, pungent, gam(e)y, odd, healthful, nutritious, natural, vegetarian, fat-free, cholesterol-free, meatless, main, side, quick, easy, light, seasonal, national, regional, ethnic, festive, ceremonial

dish, dishes (2: a plate) See *plate*

dishonesty appalling, dreadful, terrible, awful, disgraceful, shameful, flagrant

disillusion, disillusionment See *disappointment*

dislike, dislikes inherent, violent, fierce, invincible, intense, hearty, cordial, temperamental, strong, singular, vehement, zealous, morbid, secret, unconcealed,

evident, palpable, open, deep(-rooted), fundamental, unconditional, mute, mutual, racial

dismay utter, complete, helpless, blank, mock

dismissal, dismissals abrupt, prompt, unceremonious, arrogant, summary, wrongful, arbitrary, forceful, (un)planned, (un)just, (un)fair, (un)lawful, (il)legal, (un)constitutional, constructive

disobedience defiant, stubborn, disloyal, disregardful, wilful, mutinous, rebellious, treacherous, unruly, massive, civil

disorder, disorders widespread, prevalent, endemic, chronic, flagrant, dreadful, extreme, severe, total, complete, utter, bohemian, rare, (un)treatable, (ir)reversible, debilitating, immune, intractable, complex, grievous, negligent, violent, fatal, progressive, degenerative, depressive, sadistic, trophic, nutritional, circulatory, respiratory, organic, genetic, congenital, metabolic, (gastro)intestinal, sensory, medical, physical, mental, emotional, functional, neuromuscular, behavioural, personality, psychological, neurological, psychiatric, nervous, somatic; ethnic, social, civil

disparity, disparities See *difference* (1)

display, displays breathtaking, dazzling, glittering, thrilling, startling, fascinating, stunning, dizzying, blinding, compelling, (un)edifying, overwhelming, mammoth, spectacular, phenomenal, resplendent, graceful, elaborate, grand(iose), monstrous, innovative, unprecedented, unusual, extraordinary, rare, magnificent, remarkable, splendid, lavish, luxurious, skilful, great, impressive, (in)effective, proud, awesome, ceremonious, tasteful, attractive, vibrant, colourful, well-chosen, animated, masterful, (in)formal, theatrical, aggressive, daring, vulgar, blatant, stark, pretentious, vaunted, garish, gaudy, showy, ostentatious, puerile, childish, tasteless, chaotic, loud, unseemly, sickening, grisly, exotic, spartan, permanent, international, (un)characteristic, humbling, cultural, archaeological, agricultural, aerial, pyrotechnic, ritual, metronomic

disposition, dispositions sanguine, serene, calm, quiet, cheerful, animated, buoyant, easy(-going), tolerant, undemanding, kindly, friendly, sociable, gentle, even, fine, happy(-go-lucky), merry, genial, docile, pacific, peaceful, peaceable, placid, optimistic, sweet, sunny, smooth, generous, (un)pleasant, personable, good-natured, strong, inveterate, steady, open, candid, simple, unguarded, timid, moody, restless, errant, wandering, roving, loafing, unsettled, pugnacious, critical, sour, dense, stubborn, selfish, intractable, surly, passive, rapacious, greedy, predatory, arrogant, extortionate, venomous, spiteful, malignant, jealous, envious, quick-tempered, irritable, quarrelsome, impulsive, rebellious, volatile, saturnine, thoughtless, unpleasant, unruly, savage, vicious, indolent, sluggish, truant, amorous, communicative, solitary

dispute, disputes animated, warm, spicy, heated, vehement, vigorous, serious, endless, drawn-out, protracted, (decades-)old, long(-standing), venomous, acrimonious, rancorous, intricate, nasty, bizarre, bitter, surly, vicious, ugly, complex, thorny, considerable, major, mighty, noisy, angry, intractable, (un)negotiable, controversial, minor, casual, superficial, (un)resolved, tactical, factious, territorial, ethnic, tribal, domestic, internal, verbal, civil, legal

disregard See also *disrespect* haughty, lofty, sublime, high, patrician, blithe, wanton, open, blatant, flagrant, callous, unfeeling, cool, obtuse, insolent, reckless, heedless, contumelious, obscene, contemptuous, cavalier, complete, total, utter, absolute, grotesque, singular, conscious, wilful

disrepair ruinous, deplorable, desperate, dismal, dreadful, painful, shocking, woeful, cheerless

disrespect See also *disregard* reckless, saucy, uncivil, clumsy, rude, contemptuous, discourteous, impertinent, insolent, irreverent, contumelious, brutal, wilful

disruption, disruptions crushing, blistering, distressing, galling, vexing, unpleasant, rude, cruel, furious, careless, catastrophic, major, massive, obvious, constant, momentary

dissatisfaction deep, sharp, bitter, open, public, grave, fundamental, widespread

dissent See *difference* (2)

dissertation, dissertations See *research* and *study*

dissident, dissidents See *rebel*

distance, distances stupefying, huge, great, long, substantial, considerable, interminable, formidable, extraordinary, good, vast, fabulous, inestimable, chasmic, (un)reasonable, (un)safe, discreet, striking, measurable, faint, little, short, deceptive, minimum, maximum, angular, perpendicular, focal, horizontal, mean, middle, polar, aesthetic, artistic

distinction, distinctions (1: difference) sharp, clear-cut, (over)subtle, casuistic, sophistic(al), fine(-drawn), invidious, (im)palpable, nice, delicate, minute, trifling, refined, arbitrary, precise, pivotal, crucial, rigid, further, apparent, (im)perceptible, class, qualitative, quantitative, fundamental

distinction (2: honour) apparent, unique, prestigious, invidious, dubious, social

distortion, distortions grave, serious, massive, blatant, unfair, deliberate, malicious, intentional, awful, frightful, wicked, vicious, mean, weird, perceptual

distraction, distractions See *disruption*

distress alarming, crushing, hideous, deep, profound, acute, sore, pallid, impotent, widespread, uttermost, genuine, squalid, visible, apparent, conspicuous, manifest, obvious, minor, incidental, accidental, chronic, degenerative, emotional, spiritual, nervous, psychological, physical, abdominal, pecuniary, financial

distribution, distributions (un)even, (in)equitable, (un)equal, (un)limited, (non-)partisan, wide, rat(e)able, random, chaotic, (ab)normal, (dis)orderly, (dis)organized, regional, geographic(al), bimodal, binomial, chi-square

district, districts plush, fashionable, exclusive, posh, glamorous, trendy, elegant, aristocratic, middle-class, classy, handsome, tony, peaceful, prosperous, agreeable, glitzy, animated, legendary, disadvantaged, seedy, squalid, blighted, infamous, disreputable, raunchy, grim, dirty, poverty-stricken, slum(my), rough, unfashionable, dilapidated, crumbly, tatty, dreary, deprived, run-down, unsavoury, rough-and-tumble, scruffy, busy, frontier, outlying, remote, cramped, populous, large, autonomous, residential, municipal, urban, rural, judicial, commercial, financial, electoral, red-light

distrust See *suspicion*

disturbance, disturbances hilarious, serious, grave, considerable, violent, enraged, persistent, major, small, petty, trifling, trivial, slight, minor, strange, potential, internal, domestic, public, civil, ethnic, emotional, physical, environmental, geologic(al)

disturber, disturbers wanton, deliberate, imprudent, inconsiderate, indifferent, rash, heedless, thoughtless, reckless, unruly, wild

dive, dives hair-raising, rugged, deep, steep, high, forward, backward, reverse, inward, twist, perfect, (half-)parabolic

diver, divers avid, serious, unprotected, hapless, amateur, professional, first-time, champion, certified, free, competitive, deep-sea, scuba

diversion, diversions exciting, thrilling, interesting, genial, healthy, wholesome, cheerful, edifying, favourite, quaint, upper-crust, exclusive, popular, feverish, (dis)agreeable, (un)pleasant, insipid, boring, sleazy, seedy, squalid, cheap, nocturnal

diversity, diversities dazzling, amazing, astonishing, startling, astounding, staggering, bewildering, fascinating, stunning, marvellous, remarkable, rich, incomparable, unparalleled, colourful, casual, ethnic, cultural, genetic, economic

dividend, dividends cumulative, fixed, floating, unwarranted

diving See *dive*

division, divisions (1: share; split) hard-and-fast, rigid, (in)equitable, (un)equal; cell

division, divisions (2: difference) bitter, dire, sharp, growing, deep, profound, racial, ethnic

divorce, divorces amicable, civilized, no-pain, simple, (un)easy, messy, bitter, acrimonious, venomous, painful, hurtful, nasty, devastating, final, interlocutory, (il)legal, no-fault, civil, religious

docility See *submission* and *obedience*

doctor, doctors (in)competent, capable, kind, good, skilful, reliable, qualified, resourceful, serviceable, astute, (un)successful, (un)able, (in)experienced, (in)efficient, (un)skilled, dedicated, conscientious, caring, compassionate, (well-)trained, licensed, clever, detached, negligent, outstanding, eminent, top-notch, (un)practising, full-fledged, (un)orthodox, local, rural, outpatient, resident, substitute, clinical, osteopathic, personal

doctrine, doctrines (in)effective, basic, (un)conventional, traditional, fundamental(ist), long-standing, rigid, extreme, noxious, pernicious, (in)sincere, false, odd, subversive, abusive, (un)sound, obscurantist, heretical, immoral, Christian

document, documents authentic, proper, valid, original, genuine, important(-looking), significant, valuable, seminal, crucial, vital, essential, basic, unique, landmark, articulate, sensitive, (top-)secret, confidential, privileged, concluding, pertinent, (ir)relevant, spurious, sham, fallacious, phon(e)y, fake, fictitious, bogus, false, counterfeit, deceptive, misleading, missing, surviving, extant, attainable, disposable, moving, controversial, effectual, polemic, probatory, notarial, (il)legal, (un)classified, internal, human, manuscript, scholarly, preparatory

documentary, documentaries See *film*

documentation meticulous, scrupulous, authoritative, careful, fastidious, painstaking, (in)adequate, turgid, faulty, dazzling, historical

dog, dogs whimpering, barking, howling, snarling, yelping, fawning, snapping, straying, galloping, waddling, prancing, prowling, (drug-)sniffing, snuff(l)ing, panting, spinning, prostrate, friendly, playful, energetic, perky, exuberant, eager, bouncy, frisky, lively, alert, nimble, agile, lithe, statuesque, sleek, graceful, digitigrade, intelligent, husky, vigorous, muscular, powerful, cute, intelligent, loyal, lovable, adorable, gregarious, affectionate, faithful, smart, obedient, attentive, protective, pedigree, rare, pure(bred), precious, expensive, gentle, docile, endearing, beloved, popular, cuddly, cuddlesome, well-behaved, well-mannered, well-bred, (un)trained, placid, calm, barkless, (un)collared, deliberate, prize, spoilt, hoity-toity, crazed, nippy, growly,

whiny, rabid, stray, vicious, ferocious,
mad, mean, tough, mixed-breed, mongrel,
wormy, stocky, fat, overweight, cowardly,
lazy, scruffy, smelly, wild, silly, feisty,
stubborn, sleepy, violent, underbred,
savage, fierce(-looking), ill-natured,
mad, nasty, restless, fearsome,
ferocious(-looking), hostile, dangerous,
tough, rumbustious, disobedient,
uncontrollable, snappish, (love-)starved,
abandoned, ring-tailed, whip-tailed,
silky-coated, hairy, furry, shaggy, scrawny,
scraggly, skinny, slender, lean, bony,
(rib-)thin, emaciated, mangy, long-haired,
wire-haired, smooth-haired, spotted,
large-headed, lop-eared, floppy-eared,
long-bodied, short-legged, web-footed,
hungry, starving, wheezy, crotchety, guide,
military

dogma, dogmas See *doctrine*

doll, dolls favourite, translucent, life-like,
animated, mechanical, (fast-)talking,
jabbering, computer-driven, stuffed, fabric,
straw, corn-husk, china, porcelain, paper,
bright-haired, home-made, mass-produced,
periwigged, stocking, rag, two-in-one,
cork, antique, rococo

dollar, dollars high-flying, climbing,
soaring, surging, strengthening, flourishing,
buoyant, strong, powerful, muscular,
erratic, volatile, resilient, red-hot, shaky,
downsize, weak, anaemic, beaten-down,
fallen, bouncing, plunging, (nose)diving,
soft, overvalued, devalued, almighty,
hard-earned, stained, tattered, creasy,
crisp, commemorative, paper

dolphin, dolphins chirping, squeaking,
groaning, swimming, springing, twisting,
prancing, frolicsome, friendly, wild, dusky,
canny, sleek, graceful, captive, common,
spotted, bottle-nosed, rough-toothed,
hump-backed

domain, domains See *area*

dome, domes soaring, towering, gleaming,
lofty, majestic, splendid, magnificent,
impressive, colossal, gargantuan, giant,
gigantic, massive, transparent, (un)stable,
plastered, golden, copper, stone,
distinctive, blocky, planetarium-like,
cowled, rounded, circular, elongated,
hemispherical, onion(-shaped),
igloo-shaped, ribbed, polygonal, geodesic

dominance overwhelming, overbearing,
prevailing, paramount, perfect, complete,
lengthy, endless, forceful, suffocating,
autocratic, despotic, imperious, cerebral,
cultural, regional

domination See *dominance*

dominion See *authority* and *rule*

donation, donations liberal, generous,
unselfish, huge, substantial, (in)significant,
minuscule, tax-free, cash, financial,
private, individual, corporate, charitable,
anonymous

donkey, donkeys swaying, gentle, placid,
patient, sure-footed, nimble, frisky,
peevish, recalcitrant, obstinate, stubborn,
ill-tempered, cantankerous, stupid,
scrawny, wild, domestic

donor, donors liberal, generous, hearty,
extravagant, lavish, bountiful, cheerful,
ungrudging, unrestrained, charitable, kind,
open-handed, philanthropic(al),
well-meaning, major, magnanimous,
(un)willing, (un)reluctant, repeat, potential,
anonymous; universal

doom, dooms See also *fate* impending,
inextricable, impassable, hopeless,
inevitable, perpetual, awful, painful,
grievous, shameful

door, doors elaborate, studded, ornate,
graceful, curved, arched, windowless,
open, closed, shut, (air)tight,
corrugated-metal, iron-studded,
(well-)guarded, rusty, worn, shabby,
creaky, light, heavy, vaultlike, wide, vast,
massive, monumental, interior, exterior,
inner, outer, rear, back, side, single,
double, pocket, storm, front, foldaway,
folding, swinging, sliding, dummy,
overhead, revolving, bow, louvred,
automatic, French, Dutch, screen

dosage, dosages (ab)normal, (un)safe,
(in)effective, stiff, potent, generous,
liberal, large, high, hefty, excessive,
massive, lethal, fatal, deadly, slow,
measured, fixed, steady, precise, minute,
small, low(-level), sub-threshold, multiple,
cumulative, heady, painful, painless,
requisite, required, urgent, acute, oral

dose, doses See *dosage*

doubt, doubts haunting, hanging,
besetting, rising, lingering, waning,
agonizing, maddening, chilling, fearful,
grave, genuine, serious, deep, enormous,
profound, persistent, corrosive, little,

slight, (un)reasonable, cruel, widespread, fresh, internal, external, instinctive

dough rising, firm, thick, strong, manageable, workable, pliable, light, soft, smooth, glossy, cohesive, sticky, twirly

dove, doves See also *bird* and *pigeon* cooing, billing, harmless, innocent

downfall, downfalls mountainous, precipitous, disastrous, final, ultimate, sudden, political

dozen, dozens round, full, (in)complete; baker's

draft, drafts (sketch; outline) See *outline*

drainage (in)consequent, (in)appropriate, (im)proper, (in)adequate

drama, dramas See also *play* serious, heavy, esoteric, serial, comic, farcical, tragic, satiric(al), poetic, realistic, romantic, naturalistic, expressionistic, religious, mystic, absurd(ist), sentimental, avant-garde, problem, dogmatic, doctrinaire, closet, legitimate, intense, slice-of-life, eschatological, contemporary, classic(al), musical, folk, suspense, psychological, mood, costume

dramatist, dramatists premier, major, exquisite, brilliant, prolific, gifted, talented, veteran, first-rate, marvellous, superlative, first-class, established, distinguished, honoured, esteemed, famous, celebrated, (pre-)eminent, noted, well-known, notable, prominent, renowned, promising, aspiring, budding, embryo, would-be, obscure, struggling, minor, unknown, failed

drape, drapes See *curtain*

drawback, drawbacks inherent, intrinsic, essential, fundamental, real, obvious, hidden, undeniable, unquestionable, indisputable

drawer, drawers tidy, neat, top, bottom, secret, concealed, hidden

drawing, drawings freehand, sketchy, edgy, rough, full-scale, large-scale, delicate, evocative, elegant, remarkable, magnificent, splendid, primitive, humorous, satirical, whimsical, schematic, mechanical, panoramic, linear

dread, dreads See *fear*

dream, dreams idyllic, pleasant, delicious, sweet, fond, vivid, fantastic, ultimate, prophetic, (un)realizable, (un)attainable, (un)obtainable, (un)achievable, bold, passionate, untarnished, good, lifelong, deathless, perpetual, enduring, sustaining, haunting, lingering, burning, feverish, frenzied, ardent, recurrent, persistent, portentous, fragile, ephemeral, transient, evanescent, airy, rummy, wispy, quixotic, unreal, imaginary, hazy, incomprehensible, inexplicable, unnarratable, inchoate, limitless, boundless, grandiose, overblown, oversize, big, wild, distant, wavering, wistful, fearful, scary, appalling, disordered, bizarre, weird, strange, fantastic, crazy, lunatic, ridiculous, absurd, far-off, bad, unrestful, impalpable, insidious, demented, demonic, delirious, unsubstantial, insubstantial, dead, delusive, elusive, impossible, improbable, empty, idle, senseless, meaningless, hopeless, wrong, fading, pointless, endangered, immemorial, (long-)cherished, unbroken, ruminative, meditative, private, personal, youthful, American, Arthurian

dress, dresses ravishing, bewitching, striking, becoming, gorgeous, magnificent, splendid, terrific, spectacular, fabulous, immaculate, (hand-)decorated, modish, fashionable, high-fashion, snappy, stylish, elegant, handsome, graceful, swanky, snug, slinky, smart, attractive, dainty, snazzy, neat, delicate, correct, costly, rich, fitted, chic, appropriate, sophisticated, luxurious, lustrous, full, fancy, lovely, medium-price, practical, serious, wash(able), coquettish, outsize, flyaway, cool, flamboyant, simple, ordinary, plain, new, novel, unusual, (parti-)coloured, flowered, polka-dot, sleek, stretch, cut-out, scoop-neck, tight-necked, low-necked, high-necked, cowl-necked, halter-neck, strapless, floor-length, full-length, full-skirted, knee-length, plaid, frilly, floppy, loose, flowing, voluminous, straight, unwaisted, waistless, fluttery, apron-like, high-waisted, low-waisted, décolleté, belted, ruffled, trimmed, piped, sleeveless, big-sleeved, long-sleeved, (skin-)tight, drop-back, drop-waist, bias-cut, low-cut, two-piece, trapeze(-style), slimming, wide-swinging, swingy, print, summery, whitish, fussy, plain-blue, silken, chiffon, taffeta, serge, lace, satin, gingham, sequined, quilted, appliquéd, beady, seersucker, vulgar, shapeless, unfitted, baggy, frumpy, flashy,

showy, outlandish, tawdry, wacky,
tattered, torn, shabby, odd, crazy, dowdy,
unflattering, old-fashioned, outmoded,
bedraggled, soiled, slinky, flimsy, skimpy,
immodest, inappropriate, daring,
provocative, (leg-)revealing, sexy, sensual,
wild, scanty; academic, clerical,
ceremonial, (semi-)formal, informal,
mournful, national

dressing, dressings appetizing, creamy,
low-calorie, lemony, piquant, house,
Italian, French, Greek, Indian

drink, drinks refreshing, soothing,
pleasing, cool, steaming, bubbly,
effervescent, fizzy, delightful, exquisite,
(un)pleasant, tasteful, flavourful,
(non-)nutritive, pure, premium, potent,
strong, stiff, full-bodied, heady, authentic,
thick, lusty, frothy, zesty, pungent,
piquant, light, weak, shilpit, insipid,
tasteless, flavourless, watery, vapid, stale,
flat, humble, bitter, chalky, slimy, spicy,
innocuous, ubiquitous, national, social,
occasional, seasonal, tropical, short, long,
tall, intoxicating, alcoholic, narcotic, diet,
soft, diuretic, soporific, medicinal,
complimentary

drinker, drinkers discerning,
(im)moderate, (in)temperate,
(ir)responsible, slight, occasional,
sophisticated, traditional, social, habitual,
chronic, hard, obdurate, hearty,
compulsive, heavy, unpleasant,
unrepentant, suicidal, inveterate, solitary

drinking See also *drinker* (ir)responsible,
(in)temperate, excessive, copious, deep,
hearty, hard, disruptive, social, ritual

drive, drives (1: motivation; energy)
unremitting, unceasing, compelling,
sweeping, concerted, unified, appropriate,
insatiable, boundless, endless, ceaseless,
relentless, clear, (un)conscious, greedy,
ruthless, aggressive, high-pressure,
monomaniacal, covert, unbridled, complex,
subconscious, inner, internal,
single-handed, single-minded, mindless,
insane, irrational, fervid, feverish, frenetic,
frenzied, ill-considered, misguided,
indiscriminate, low, innate, natural,
competitive, implicit, explicit, compulsive,
acquisitive, possessive, entrepreneurial,
emotional, sexual, biological, personal,
diplomatic, military

drive, drives (2: a trip in a car or carriage)
See *ride*

driver, drivers careful, cautious, expert,
confident, guiltless, sober, dependable,
(un)safe, (in)competent, (in)experienced,
(un)qualified, (un)licensed, (ir)responsible,
nervous, heavy-footed, lane-hopping,
careless, unpredictable, madcap,
short-tempered, aggressive, reckless,
negligent, drunk, dazed, bad, hit-and-run,
daredevil, guilty, average

driving careful, cautious, expert, smooth,
defensive, (in)experienced, flawless,
unpredictable, treacherous, (un)safe,
intrepid, careless, reckless, erratic,
dangerous, atrocious, drunk(en),
(ir)responsible, aggressive,
long-distance

drizzle, drizzles See *rain*

drone, drones (dull, monotonous tone)
somnolent, soporific, dull, somniferous,
stuporous, murmurous, sonorous

drop, drops (decline) See *decline*

drought, droughts devastating, menacing,
crushing, withering, punishing, pernicious,
disastrous, terrible, severe, acute, extreme,
(years-)long, persistent, extensive,
widespread, ferocious, pitiless, cursed, big,
endemic, recurrent, frequent, occasional,
annual, grassless

drug, drugs See also *medicine* and
narcotic (un)safe, powerful, (im)potent,
(in)effective, essential, life-saving, wonder,
miracle, miraculous, (in)appropriate,
harmless, mild, (in)accessible, (il)licit,
(il)legal, (un)proven, unidentified,
standard, under-the-table, over-the-counter,
pervasive, habit-forming, (non-)addictive,
tricyclic, serious, harmful, dangerous,
pernicious, toxic, raw, synthetic, soluble,
pleasurable, intravenous, recreational,
experimental, proprietary, restorative,
analeptic, therapeutic, repository, opiate,
palliative, psychotropic, antipsychotic,
psychoactive, neuroleptic, anti-depressant,
immunosuppressive, toxic, purgative,
carminative, analgesic, decongestant,
anaesthetic, chemotherapeutic,
anti-rejection, anti-inflammatory,
antihistamine, antiarrhythmic,
anticonvulsant, antifebrile, antitussive,
antiviral, antiretroviral, antifungal,
(non-)prescription, pharmaceutical,

narcotic, anaphrodisiac, barbiturate, diuretic, diaphoretic, emetic

drug trafficker, drug traffickers See *criminal*

drum, drums rattling, rolling, throbbing, thundering, muffled, bucket-shaped, tight, ceremonial

drunk, drunks habitual, confirmed, inveterate, obvious, notorious, boisterous, belligerent, violent, obnoxious, brutal, uncommunicative

drunkard, drunkards See *drunk*

drunkenness habitual, notorious, pervasive, rife, rampant, prevalent, epidemic, endemic, blatant, violent, beastly, bestial, public

dryness bone-crushing, parched, scorched, vapid

duck, ducks sitting, quacking, waddling, splashing, gossipy, croaky, ululant, playful, plump, ruddy, tuftless, red-breasted, pintailed, ring-necked, tufted, wild, domestic, diving, mountain, blue, black; lame, dead

duel, duels epic, second-round, ill-matched, abortive, deadly

dullness desperate, deadly, forlorn, grim, appalling, languid, vapid, intolerable, unbearable

dune, dunes rolling, shifting, growing, spreading, flaming, spectacular, active, wavy, short-lived, grassy, coastal, sand

dupe, dupes easy, innocent, unwitting, unsuspecting, helpless, unarmed, gullible, hapless

dust, dusts suffocating, blinding, stinging, blasting, inexorable, fluffy, loose, powdery, flour-like, fine, microscopic, gritty, sandy, coarse, crystalline, smoky, oily, ashy, ashen, acrid, dense, incoherent, (non)inflammable, abrasive, deadly, airborne, atmospheric, cosmic, interstellar, radioactive, volcanic

duty, duties (obligation) (un)endurable, unshirkable, inescapable, stressful, detestable, tedious, manifest, stern, perfunctory, painful, burdensome, heavy, onerous, rightful, weary, oppressive, harassing, grim, differential, imperative, unpleasant, myriad, manifold, wide-ranging, multifarious, troublesome, doleful, distressing, dreary, steadfast, distasteful, derogatory, active, bounden, mandatory, obligatory, fundamental, ordinary, everyday, commonplace, menial, sacred, professional, editorial, administrative, clerkly, official, moral, patriotic, parental, filial, wifely, husbandly, domestic, civil, civic, fiduciary, ceremonial

dwelling, dwellings See *house*

dye, dyes permanent, fixed, (sun-)fast, brilliant, natural, plant-based, mineral, synthetic, direct, substantive, radio-opaque

dynasty, dynasties illustrious, legendary, fabled, rich, flourishing, reactionary, ruling, royal, regal, imperial

eagerness See *enthusiasm*

eagle, eagles hissing, flying, soaring, circling, swooping, nestling, perching, agile, proud, majestic, imperial, predatory, wedge-tailed, bald (bald-headed, white-headed), golden, harpy, ring-tailed

ear, ears (1: the organ of hearing) upright, erect, flat, rounded, bushy, slit, flapping, pendulous, pierced, fringed, pointed, tattered, cocked, wriggly, droopy, floppy, crinkly, tiny, big, outsize, stiff, sore, deaf, outer (external), middle, inner (internal); electronic, bionic

ear (2: the sense of hearing; sensitivity to musical tone) quick, keen, outstanding, brilliant, exquisite, sensitive, sharp, favourable, fine, discriminating, unerring, delicate, remarkable, loving, sympathetic, willing, receptive, (un)responsive, acute, pitch-perfect, deaf

earnings See *income*

earring, earrings See also *jewel* and *ornament* hanging, dangling, matching, fetching, charming, attractive, elegant, fashionable, discreet, heavy, pendant, clip(-on), diamanté

earth, earths (1: soil) See *soil*

earth (2: planet) See also *planet* revolving, blue, green

earthquake, earthquakes rumbling, rocking, jarring, rattling, devastating, striking, large(-scale), huge, gigantic, major, siz(e)able, giant, big, great, mammoth, massive, colossal, monster, powerful, strong, savage, violent, deadly, destructive, disastrous, catastrophic, cataclysmic, calamitous, serious, terrible, awesome, killer, unprecedented, (in)frequent, impending, moderate, small, underwater

ease total, consummate, extreme, effortless, relative, gracious, pleasant, carefree, crisp, arrogant, obvious, apparent, natural

eater, eaters light, slow, frugal, skimpy, fastidious, particular, discriminating, fussy, picky, finicky, dainty, (in)sensible, (im)moderate, fast, tremendous, hearty, adventurous, compulsive, gluttonous, voracious, sloppy, messy

eating good, happy, leisurely, pleasurable, hearty, (un)healthy, excessive, tremendous, gluttonous, endless, ceaseless, noisy, ravenous, compulsive, light, fastidious, (in)sane, (in)sensible, (im)moderate,

eccentric, eccentrics See *eccentricity*

eccentricity, eccentricities engaging, harmless, wild, peculiar, explosive, bizarre, aberrant, abnormal, characteristic, distinctive, grotesque, queer, enigmatic, whimsical, legendary, deliberate, unconscious, self-conscious

echo, echoes swishing, rustling, sweeping, resounding, haunting, fading, hollow, light, faint, puny, strong, huge, continuous, endless, (double-)repeated, multiple, desultory, ghastly; seismic

eclipse, eclipses partial, total, solar, lunar, annular

economist, economists esteemed, noted, notable, distinguished, well-known, renowned, famous, superlative, eminent, celebrated, first-rate, pragmatic, (un)orthodox, liberal, conservative, academic, political; home

economy, economies booming, flourishing, (fast-)growing, fast-moving, improving, thriving, good, rosy, stable, prosperous, exuberant, vibrant, robust, recession-proof, sound, vigorous, healthy, viable, diverse, productive, sturdy, powerful, buoyant, brisk, dynamic, huge, laissez-faire, free-market, market-driven, self-contained, resurgent, progressive, sophisticated, advanced, affluent, resilient, open, state-run, command, resource-dependent, spiky, soft, sour, flat, uncertain, desperate, wheezy, arthritic, jittery, chaotic, unruly, disorderly, bearish, underdeveloped, backward, febrile, wobbly, shaky, fragile, prostrate, anaemic, sick(ly), weak, slow, dismal, abysmal, complex, once-flourishing, languishing, sp(l)uttering, sagging, tottering, faltering, sinking, withering, slumbering, struggling, limping, rigid, obsolete, stale, (long-)dormant, stagnant, sluggish, laggard, moribund, (hyper)inflated, inflation-prone, uncompetitive, creaky, inefficient, comatose, recalcitrant, decrepit,

downtrodden, (war-)battered,
(war-)exhausted, recession-racked,
cramped, depressed, retarded, tattered,
strained, stricken, troubled, ruined,
shattered, stalled, hamstrung, unhinged,
bloated, runaway, (near-)bankrupt,
consumer-driven, barter-driven, mixed,
rural, capitalist, socialist, statist,
political, global, national, domestic,
agricultural

ecstasy, ecstasies exhilarating, wild,
unrestrained, irrepressible, uncontrollable,
untrammelled, unbridled, inexpressible,
dizzy, infinite, spontaneous, momentary,
stupefied, dreamy, sleepy, blissful, blithe,
delightful, delicious, exuberant, exalted,
enjoyable, heedless, joyful, rapturous,
utter, celestial, transcendental, spiritual,
perverse, evil

Eden See also *heaven* latter-day, other

edge, edges clean, (un)even, smooth,
thin, fine, (razor-)sharp, keen, hard,
precarious, brittle, crumbly, extreme,
inner, outer, projecting, convex, transverse,
serrate(d), ragged, jagged, flanged,
cushioned, steel, obsidian; cutting, leading,
trailing

edifice, edifices See *building*

editing See also *editor* assiduous,
perceptive, informative, intrusive, careful,
meticulous, conscientious, persevering,
punctilious, diffident, cautious,
(in)sensitive, (in)adequate, severe,
nit-picking, ham-fisted, careless, cursory,
indifferent, superficial, rough, textual

edition, editions magnificent, splendid,
authoritative, definitive, exhaustive,
comprehensive, final, new, recent, timely,
original, long-lost, three-volume, deluxe,
leather-bound, impressive, special, popular,
cheap, bilingual, trilingual, polyglot,
samizdat, paperback, hard-cover, limited,
school, pocket, diplomatic, quarto,
collected, omnibus

editor, editors See also *writer* and
journalist exact(ing), careful, thorough,
impeccable, creative, perceptive,
punctilious, conscientious, meticulous,
authoritative, persevering, pedantic,
(un)imaginative, incomparable, crusty,
indulgent, helpful, kindly, blue-pencilling,
roving, senior, assistant, executive,
managing, metropolitan, deputy, chief,
freelance, copy, house, desk,
commissioning

editorial, editorials See *article* and *essay* (1)

education quality, superior, good, solid,
all-round, broad, rounded, thrilling,
above-average, rigorous, Oxbridge,
Ivy-League, élitist, accomplished,
congenial, modern, utilitarian, satisfying,
meaningful, (im)perfect, (in)adequate,
(un)suitable, desultory, poor, sub-average,
little, inferior, shallow, superficial, limited,
minimal, glancing, mediocre, (in)accessible,
(un)orthodox, (in)formal, private, mass,
cross-cultural, religious, pious, secular,
rural, compulsory, bread-and-butter,
moral, outdoor, single-sex, basic, liberal,
adult, vocational, remedial, special,
private, public, parochial, professional,
physical, technical, sectarian,
(pre-)elementary, preschool, secondary,
higher, advanced, further

educator, educators See *teacher*

effect, effects stunning, startling, striking,
overpowering, enchanting, stimulating,
exhilarating, soothing, uplifting, tempering,
healing, restorative, beneficial, healthy,
protective, salutary, genuine, masterful,
impressive, glorious, dramatic, recherché,
happy, positive, decisive, undisputed,
miraculous, hypnotic, magnetic, magic(al),
uncanny, deceptive, treacherous, insidious,
deleterious, pernicious, deadly, adverse,
harmful, alarming, chilling, wearing,
catastrophic, severe, unhealthy, depressive,
negative, unhappy, detrimental, ill, dire,
incongruous, (in)appropriate, unbecoming,
deterrent, disincentive, disruptive, perilous,
serious, malign, horrible, horrendous,
disastrous, worrisome, divisive, debasing,
demoralizing, devastating, debilitating,
perverse, awesome, galling, ruinous,
depressing, staggering, lethal, caustic, fast,
immediate, unmistakable, appreciable,
marked, noticeable, discernible, evident,
obvious, apparent, (in)visible, far-reaching,
(ever)lasting, long-lasting, long-term,
marginal, modest, meagre, short-lived,
minimum, maximum, unwitting,
(in)significant, drastic, telling, potent,
immediate, profound, inevitable,
unavoidable, stupefying, unpredictable,
practical, potential, considerable,
measurable, tremendous, massive, residual,

lingering, primary, major, minor,
immediate, pervasive, cumulative, additive,
integrative, overall, opposite, retroactive,
side, toxic, corrosive, catalytic, mesmeric,
magnetic, metrical, noxious, therapeutic,
thermic, aphrodisiac, visual, geopolitical,
net, keystone

effects (possessions; belongings) See
possession

efficiency astounding, amazing,
astonishing, outstanding, marvellous,
remarkable, flawless, perfect, superb,
enviable, unequalled, incomparable,
extraordinary, streamlined, ruthless,
maximum, peak, prompt, quiet, smooth

effort, efforts promising, rewarding,
astonishing, persevering, painstaking,
outstanding, unremitting, ceaseless,
unceasing, endless, unflagging, unstinting,
(un)fruitful, (un)profitable, conciliatory,
stupendous, long-drawn-out, tangible,
all-out, utmost, genuine, honest,
well-intentioned, thorough, skilful, heroic,
valorous, valiant, gallant, exemplary,
noble, worthy, laudable, praiseworthy,
humanitarian, philanthropic, benevolent,
terrific, powerful, pivotal, vast, massive,
tremendous, immense, great, mammoth,
enormous, superhuman, Herculean,
whole-hearted, mitigative, hearty, decisive,
definite, energetic, earnest, zestful, spirited,
(over-)zealous, daring, ingenious, dogged,
ambitious, innovative, (in)effectual,
(in)effective, unequivocal, strong,
pertinacious, systematic, (un)productive,
constructive, united, unified, elaborate,
studious, constant, ongoing, successive,
demanding, tireless, untiring, arduous,
strenuous, vigorous, (in)adequate,
conclusive, studied, unbelievable,
incredible, (un)successful, conscientious,
patient, unabashed, aggressive,
enterprising, intense, intensive, steady,
die-hard, staggering, ferocious, persistent,
determined, deliberate, conscious, flat,
limited, modest, humble, sterile, abortive,
desultory, sporadic, spasmodic, haphazard,
unavailing, elusive, vain, useless, reckless,
fruitless, barren, wasted, futile, crude,
clumsy, confused, inconclusive, lame,
tremulous, timid, tedious, stilted, pestilent,
puny, feeble, half-hearted, shoddy,
faltering, superficial, duplicitous,

clandestine, secret, covert, illegal,
heavy-handed, tense, frantic, rare,
desperate, last-ditch, lonely, personal,
face-saving, apparent, exhaustive,
last-minute, muscular, no-holds-barred,
intermittent, maiden, incipient, straining,
agonizing, lifelong, stubborn, relentless,
ruthless, merciless, outrageous, grotesque,
belated, short-lived, unrecognized,
concerted, (il)legitimate, collective, joint,
cooperative, collaborative, mutual,
physical, diplomatic

effrontery, effronteries See *insolence*

egg, eggs raw, fresh, free-range, stale,
viable, (un)fruitful, (in)fertile, sterile,
double-yoke, fatty, brown, white, speckled,
new-laid, broken, cracked, (well-)beaten,
lightly-beaten, soft-boiled, hard-boiled,
rotten, decayed, spoiled, bad, addled,
ersatz; artificial, wooden, china

ego, egos big, fat, ample, great,
tremendous, monumental, (over)large,
enlarged, inflated, frustrated, Olympian,
political; alter

egomania besetting, harassing, haunting,
obsessive, dominant, intrusive,
troublesome, chronic

elder, elders See *old person*

election, elections See also *ballot* free,
meaningful, (un)democratic, flawless,
open, straight, peaceful, (dis)honest,
(un)fair, (in)conclusive, (un)satisfactory,
(il)legal, (in)valid, (in)decisive, hung, snap,
fraudulent, crooked, sham, mock, dubious,
controversial, abortive, meaningless,
restrictive, demoralizing, close, dumb,
dirty, bitter, fractious, hard-fought, fiery,
chaotic, quadrennial, head-to-head, crucial,
historic, emotional, turbulent, landslide,
competitive, sobering, gratuitous,
forthcoming, next, last, imminent,
previous, flawed, (un)tainted, primary,
run-off, local, general, municipal,
domestic, cantonal, regional, provincial,
federal, national, legislative, parliamentary,
presidential, pluralistic, multi-party,
multi-candidate, non-party, direct, secret

electrician, electricians See *worker*

elegance breathtaking, surpassing,
exquisite, simple, modest, facile, unique,
exceptional, extraordinary, rare, flawless,
discreet, understated, sartorial, fastidious,
artful, artless, careful, careless, casual,

(un)studied, vapid, (in)formal, instinctive, moneyed, sensuous

elegy, elegies See *poem*

element, elements distinctive, constituent, vital, significant, essential, crucial, important, key, fundamental, strong, invariable, stable, (un)desirable, (dis)agreeable, objectionable, disruptive, rare, inert, complex, conspicuous, identifiable, intrinsic, homogeneous, heterogeneous, underlying, colourless; physical, spiritual, mathematical, meteorological; heavy, chemical, metallic, gaseous, metal, radioactive, negative, transuranic

elephant, elephants trumpeting, snorting, screaming, shuffling, ambling, rumbling, wading, wallowing, performing, rutting, frolicsome, peaceable, calm, gentle, harmless, tame, docile, slow, solitary, captive, growing, enraged, furious, recalcitrant, lumbersome, (un)trained, (un)domesticated, aggressive, wild, giant, enormous, gigantic, massive, magnificent, majestic, harmful, rogue, bull, African, Asian (Indian); white

elevator, elevators See *lift*

elimination, eliminations partial, total, complete, possible, virtual, imminent, eventual

élite, élites tightly-knit, status-conscious, glittering, moneyed, privileged, tiny, small, narrow, exclusive, powerful, aristocratic, political, intellectual, literary, creative, diplomatic

eloquence suave, persuasive, irresistible, seductive, powerful, flinty, brilliant, Ciceronian, artless, artificial, pompous, natural, pyrotechnic, emotive, forensic

embargo, embargoes See *sanction*

embarrassment, embarrassments bloodcurdling, degrading, awkward, red-faced, shameful, bewildered, acute, real, total, heavy, intense, severe, painful, pained, curious, whimsical, faint, temporary, long-term, continual, enormous, deprecatory; pecuniary, monetary

embrace, embraces profound, deep, full, big, long, exuberant, firm, tight, affectionate, fond, loving, warm, emotional, passionate, infatuated, tender, ready, silent, doting, surreptitious,

impulsive, earnest, stiff, congratulatory, protective, motherly, welcoming

embroidery, embroideries fine, delicate, dainty, elegant, elaborate, minute, skilful, exquisite, magnificent, splendid, open, cutwork, wool, canvas, bead, metal

emergency, emergencies dire, extreme, real, normal, desperate, disastrous, formidable, life-threatening, medical, national, domestic

emigrant, emigrants See *immigrant*

eminence, eminences shining, commendable, conspicuous, distinguished, evident, illustrious, noted, impressive, lofty, supreme, political, social, academic, athletic, scientific

emotion, emotions lofty, high, genuine, (in)sincere, deep, long-lasting, abiding, enduring, permanent, easy, mixed, morbid, strange, poignant, musing, effusive, windy, sthenic, violent, fervent, intense, strong, (too-)powerful, overpowering, overwhelming, explosive, visceral, raw, pent-up, inexpressible, unexplainable, unbearable, tragi-comic, weak, positive, negative, hostile, false, cheap, shallow, lewd, conflicting, ambivalent, complex, connotative

emotionalism infantile, puerile, childish, silly, immature

emphasis, emphases rightful, heavy, determined, constant, ceaseless, ruthless, merciless, relentless, unrelenting, shifted, disproportionate, maudlin, fundamental

empire, empires flourishing, glorious, proud, great, vigorous, powerful, mighty, vast, colossal, ambitious, sagging, faltering, dissolving, vanishing, shaky, troubled, powerless, defunct, colonial, corporate, multinational, commercial

employee, employees See also *worker* (hand-)picked, model, innovative, hardworking, punctual, sleep-deprived, (un)productive, outstanding, valued, tireless, (un)skilled, traditional, lifetime, average, blatant, reckless, low-wage, mid-level, entry-level, striking, prospective, private-sector, public-sector, contingent, full-time, part-time, temporary, probationary, permanent, salaried, trial

employer, employers fair, kind, lenient, easy, hard, exacting, strict, harsh, severe, unfeeling, life-long, large, paternalistic

employment, employments steady, (more-)stable, active, gainful, remunerative, high, stagnant, (half-a-)lifetime, temporary, casual, occasional, seasonal, permanent, full-time, part-time, (ir)regular, scarce, starveling, servile, degrading

emptiness vast, infinite, eerie, weird, scary, ghastly, terrible, awful, bleak, harsh, stark, barren, suffocating, pointless

encounter, encounters See also *meeting* casual, chance, (im)probable, amicable, lively, meaningful, providential, memorable, historic, epic, crucial, (un)safe, close, mean-spirited, banal, painful, bizarre, awkward, meaningless, fierce, impending, face-to-face, dangerous, illicit, strange, romantic, sexual

encouragement, encouragements loving, unflagging, valuable, perpetual, constant, endless, ceaseless, zestful, (in)sincere, half-hearted

end, ends salutary, triumphant, desirable, (un)avoidable, (in)evitable, pitiful, crazy, absurd, gruesome, hapless, unfortunate, wretched, extreme, bitter, brutal, apparent, poignant, distinct, early, imminent, (long-)overdue, abrupt, premature, untimely, quick, sorry, horrible, divisive, (ir)rational, (in)comprehensible, (un)necessary, (in)conclusive, (in)appropriate, climactic, predeterminate; loose, dead; receiving

endeavour, endeavours See *effort*

ending, endings victorious, tame, spectacular, perfect, quiet, upbeat, (un)happy, sad, tearful, tragic, deplorable, pitiable, miserable, inevitable, disappointing, harrowing, unforgettable, ambiguous, elusive, superficial, dull, (il)logical, (in)appropriate, (in)conclusive, contrived, surprise; masculine; chorus

endorsement See *approval*

endurance sturdy, remarkable, considerable, enormous, austere, brave, silent, quiet, manful, heroic, stolid, stoic, meek, Spartan, physical

enemy, enemies keen, inveterate, insidious, bitter, caustic, vindictive, perfidious, treacherous, dour, implacable, diabolical, vociferous, rancorous, unscrupulous, vengeful, pursuing, plodding, redoubtable, formidable,

dauntless, fearless, intrepid, dangerous, lethal, murderous, deadly, mortal, devastating, heartless, remorseless, pitiless, merciless, ruthless, relentless, unrelenting, grim, anonymous, elusive, secret, open, powerful, mighty, unbeatable, arrogant, key, primary, arch, immortal, lasting, perpetual, timeless, eternal, constant, lifelong, longtime, old, erstwhile, inexorable, irreconcilable, prostrate, helpless, defenceless, submissive, wakeful, watchful, vigilant, sworn, fancied, real, immediate, inexorable, potential, natural, hereditary, mutual, common, public

energy, energies abounding, unbounded, boundless, unbridled, unremitting, unflagging, (un)renewable, inexhaustible, unquenchable, irrepressible, undiminished, ample, enormous, continuous, (super)abundant, prodigious, bottomless, restless, tireless, untiring, formidable, demonic, titanic, gigantic, huge, tremendous, intense, fervid, brisk, robust, ubiquitous, indomitable, indefatigable, unfaltering, implacable, gritty, exuberant, youthful, diligent, untamed, pent-up, buoyant, effervescent, infectious, astonishing, amazing, astounding, turbulent, inordinate, palpable, dormant, manic, abrasive, economical, rotational, high-octane, loving, jaded, moribund, waste, diminishing, waning, vital, alternative, latent, creative, sunlit, solar, hydroelectric, atomic (nuclear), (geo)thermal, wind, radiant, potential, luminous, binding, mechanical, sexual, erotic, kinetic, translational, chemical, electrical, acoustic, dynamic, static

enforcement uncompromising, unyielding, unrelenting, relentless, ruthless, pitiless, heartless, merciless, heavy-handed, tough, stiff, rigorous, effective, strict, rigid, stringent, half-hearted, lax, military

engagement, engagements (1: employment) binding, impending, favoured, multifarious, public

engagement, engagements (2: pledge of marriage) See *marriage*

engine, engines rasping, screaming, roaring, rumbling, humming, grinding, chugging, snarling, spluttering, thumping, throbbing, surging, running, smoking, steam-snorting, high-powered, powerful, stout, ferocious, low-cost, (fuel-)efficient, compact, radical, auxiliary, compound, indomitable, heavy, lightweight, portable, (un)conventional, red-hot, runaway, stalled, stationary, idle, quiet, husky, wheezy, screeching, droning, puffing, (ir)reparable, sluggish, dead, defunct, rusty, faulty, inefficient, solar, steam, jet, diesel, internal-combustion, reciprocating, pilot, radial, traction, pneumatic, synchronous, rotary, hot-air, valve-in-head, long-shafted, four-cylinder, four-cycle, four-stroke, two-cycle, two-stroke, (gas-)turbine, air-cooled, aero, hydraulic, free-piston, five-horsepower, auxiliary, beam, inboard, outboard

engineer, engineers sound, acoustical, aerodynamic, aeronautical, agricultural, architectural, ceramic, chemical, civil, electrical, environmental, genetic, geotechnical, hydraulic, solar, industrial, locomotive, mechanical, metallurgical, marine, nuclear, sanitary, structural, mining

engineering See also *engineer* advanced, innovative, high, state-of-the-art, leading-edge, futuristic, superior, sophisticated, creative, expressive, computer-aided; social

English (language) flawless, impeccable, meticulous, accentless, unaccented, (im)proper, (im)perfect, excellent, good, elegant, sophisticated, crisp, clear, plain, perspicuous, lucid, quaint, delightful, unadulterated, rhythmic, poetic, rudimentary, better, passable, readable, (in)correct, (in)adequate, understandable, (un)intelligible, misspelt, corrupt, distorted, bad, rusty, halting, unsteady, broken, shattered, laboured, rugged, stiff, poor, soft-spoken, sing-song, archaic, liturgical, ordinary, formal, stereotypical, Basic, (non-)standard, sub-standard, pidgin, Old, Middle, Modern, remedial, vocational, business, black

enigma See *mystery*

enjoyment, enjoyments blissful, inexhaustible, glorious, obvious, evident, peaceful, simple, innocent, rough, unctuous, short-lived, momentary, passing, fleeting, swift, tarnished, sinful, sensual, mental, nostalgic

enmity, enmities understandable, inordinate, inextinguishable, unrelenting, relentless, merciless, pitiless, heartless, ruthless, deep, age-old, ancient, considerable, intense, strong, bitter, vindictive, virulent, deadly, unworthy, covert, open, vague, amorphous, regional

enormity, enormities monstrous, colossal, monumental, tremendous, terrible

enquiry, enquiries See *inquiry*

enrolment, enrolments increasing, rising, soaring, flourishing, stagnant, (un)stable, fluctuating, excessive, peak, maximum, minimum

enterprise, enterprises See also *undertaking* and *project* thriving, gainful, lucrative, (un)profitable, money-making, cost-effective, (in)efficient, leading-edge, state-of-the-art, methodical, persistent, vital, viable, substantial, large, ambitious, venturous, venturesome, self-sustaining, hazardous, perilous, arduous, daring, staggering, expensive, nightmarish, fledgling, delicate, sleazy, shady, shadowy, dubious, depraved, unproven, tattered, state-run, mixed, free, individual, private, charitable, scholarly, commercial

entertainer, entertainers See also *performer* beloved, favourite, (un)popular, resourceful, major, legendary, durable, world-class, consummate, flamboyant, well-paid, best-paid, poorly-paid, (un)employable, (un)scheduled, resourceless, impromptu

entertaining See *entertainment*

entertainment, entertainments heartwarming, sparkling, wholesome, safe, clean, favourite, terrific, gracious, glamorous, lavish, luxurious, spectacular, prodigious, amiable, (dis)agreeable, (il)legitimate, (in)offensive, sleazy, seedy, squalid, cheap, (in)formal, diverse, live, impromptu, musical, theatrical, popular, family, late-night, electronic, pop

enthusiasm unflagging, untiring, uncompromising, seething, sweeping, overflowing, overwhelming, swaggering, unabated, heady, intense, solid, inexhaustible, enormous, unbounded, boundless, rapturous, ecstatic, exuberant, jubilant, dedicated, wholehearted, frantic, (red-)hot, wild, irrepressible, unquenchable, ungovernable, restless, unqualified, passionate, boisterous, buoyant, infectious,

contagious, splendid, furious, factitious,
spontaneous, remarkable, brash, guileless,
naïve, genuine, (in)sincere, (un)pretentious,
waning, pent-up, sparing, incredible,
unbelievable, nervous, sporadic, mild,
quiet, wide-eyed, boyish, youthful,
personal

enthusiast, enthusiasts burning, fervent,
feverish, ecstatic, zealous, passionate,
staunch, hard-core, visionary, dreamy,
fanciful, insane, unrealistic, unpractical,
Utopian, idealistic, romantic, unashamed

entity, entities harmonious, viable, stable,
unified, single, discrete, distinct, separate,
independent, (im)personal, artistic,
political, organizational

entrance (1: place or means of entry)
welcoming, bright, main, principal, high,
grand, impressive, spectacular, towering,
narrow, bottleneck, cramped, pillared,
arched, (twin-)towered, covered, draped,
tiled, ceremonial, separate, private, outside

entrance (2: the act of entering) striking,
impressive, effective, dramatic, theatrical,
spectacular, grand, triumphal, supreme,
whirlwind, flamboyant, breezy, auspicious,
abrupt, sudden, unexpected, exclusive,
(un)lawful

entreaty, entreaties See *plea*

entrepreneur, entrepreneurs high-flying,
ambitious, hardworking, industrious,
energetic, decisive, diligent, reputable,
daring, leading, large-scale, self-made,
self-taught, self-reliant, canny, astute,
shrewd, inspired, mercurial, restless,
natural, born, prosperous, (super-)rich,
affluent, well-heeled, wealthy, flamboyant,
colourful, quintessential, prototypical,
potential, aspiring, budding, (un)successful,
resurgent, acquisitive, single-minded,
crooked, dishonest, disreputable

entry, entries See *entrance* (2)

environment, environments stimulating,
inviting, (in)hospitable, (in)tolerant,
(un)kind, elegant, splendid, exotic, ideal,
supportive, peaceful, (un)safe, (in)secure,
(un)healthy, (im)proper, (ab)normal,
(un)stable, undisciplined, self-contained,
self-sustaining, unspoiled, pollution-free,
smoke-free, congenial, caring, warm,
fruitful, pristine, benign, luxurious,
resilient, sparse, dreamlike, unique,
distinctive, yeasty, harsh, rough, wild,
fierce, tough, rotten, demanding,
unrelenting, relentless, ruthless, merciless,
pitiless, cruel, capricious, delicate, fragile,
vulnerable, difficult, trying, stressful,
intense, hostile, implacable, uncertain,
(un)predictable, right, wrong, restrictive,
hermetic, sombre, (non-)threatening,
(un)hurried, internal, external, physical,
chemical, native, natural, pastoral,
geographic(al), social, urban, (a)esthetic,
working, political, technological

environmentalist, environmentalists
dedicated, staunch, ardent, avid, eager,
anxious, militant, zealous, alert, watchful,
tireless

envoy, envoys extraordinary, accredited

envy consuming, corrosive, unrestrained,
inordinate, childish, absurd, hidden

epic, epics lush, picaresque, folk,
literary

epidemic, epidemics See also
disease raging, devastating, puzzling,
insidious, silent, (un)stoppable,
(un)controllable, unabated, hideous, severe,
painful, terrible, costly, deadly, global,
unprecedented, viral

epigram, epigrams glittering, sparkling,
stunning, flippant, smart, pointed,
polished, urbane, pert

episode, episodes See *story*

epitaph, epitaphs tender, witty, biting,
mock, extempore, pompous

epoch, epochs See *era*

equal, equals perfect, rough, intellectual

equilibrium See *balance*

equipment, equipments modern,
advanced, up-to-date, sophisticated,
high-quality, high-tech, solid-state,
state-of-the-art, leading-edge,
labour-saving, life-saving, costly,
expensive, expendable, delicate, sensitive,
scarce, heavy, new, special, unusual,
strange, lavish, right, wrong, (ir)reparable,
(ir)replaceable, (in)adequate,
(un)dependable, (un)reliable,
(un)serviceable, (im)proper, complex,
bulky, crude, dangerous, obsolete,
outdated, out-of-date, archaic, antiquated,
decrepit, rusting, malfunctioning, defective,
faulty, basic, standard, (non-)essential,
home-made, mechanical, rental, electronic,
electric, industrial, commercial, military,
recreational, protective, sensory

era, eras (un)eventful, beautiful, glamorous, sophisticated, fashionable, fascinating, gracious, leisurely, vibrant, bitter, rigorous, tumultuous, turbulent, suffocating, shadowy, flagitious, vicious, (fitness-)crazed, unfolding, passing, vanishing, receding, new, modern, old, ancient, foregone, bygone, long-gone, predynastic, pre-revolution(ary), post-revolution(ary), pre-war, post-war, Grecian, Jewish, Chou, Olympic, Roman, Seleucid, Maccabean, Vikrama, Christian, Diocletian, Islamic, geological, glacial, Pleistocene, Pal(a)eozoic, Cenozoic

erosion, erosions imminent, potential, eventual, rapid, accelerated, relentless, excessive, spectacular, patchy, natural (geological)

errand, errands (un)pleasant, (un)avowable, (un)known, routine, daily, festive, mournful, frantic

error, errors cardinal, capital, serious, major, fundamental, gross, grave, grievous, costly, abominable, awful, unpleasant, fatal, obtrusive, outrageous, vulgar, disastrous, monstrous, absurd, ridiculous, inexcusable, unpardonable, ignorant, queer, dreadful, tragic, distasteful, noxious, common, prevalent, systematic, unnecessary, abundant, conspicuous, patent, blatant, glaring, obvious, manifest, evident, flagrant, plain, distinct, clear, undetected, trifling, trivial, minor, slight, small, venial, elementary, basic, simple, unimportant, probable, fresh, vital, venerable, palpable, sensible, collective, typographical, factual, grammatical, textual, contextual, tactical, procedural, human, clerical, volitional; genetic

erudition solemn, pompous, pedantic, scholarly, encyclopaedic

eruption, eruptions stunning, spectacular, huge, big, colossal, full-scale, massive, violent, explosive, awesome, terrible, horrible, catastrophic, disastrous, cataclysmic, spontaneous, successive, major, minor, volcanic; skin, dermatological

escalation, escalations dramatic, heady, giddy, dizzy(ing), heedless, capricious, wild, unfortunate, bitter

escape narrow, hairbreadth, providential, miraculous, effective, opportune, futile, lucky, desperate, sensational, spectacular, daring, breathtaking, natural, near, close, precarious, rapid, quick, timely, ready, sudden, last-minute, subtle, smooth

essay, essays (1: literary composition) revealing, compelling, useful, masterly, skilful, lively, thoughtful, high-minded, insightful, provocative, studied, thorough, accurate, readable, cross-grained, offbeat, zany, opaque, obscure, chatty, patchy, crusty, didactic, occasional, personal, photographic, informative, critical, familiar, descriptive, reflective, interpretive, persuasive, anonymous, dedicatory

essay (2: effort; attempt) See *effort* and *attempt*

establishment, establishments See *institution* (1)

estate, estates broad, vast, trim, grand, gracious, palatial, secluded, meagre, exclusive, ten-acre, (un)settled, insolvent, ducal, ancestral, hereditary, landed, country, fiduciary, feudal, leasehold, freehold, defeasible, monastic; real; third, fourth

esteem unbounded, great, high, low, small, mutual, public, universal, posthumous

estimate, estimates informed, knowledgeable, credible, right, (un)reliable, (in)accurate, independent, sober, conservative, uncritical, rosy, optimistic, pessimistic, grim, disheartening, low, high, preposterous, (un)equivocal, unbiased, (un)safe, first, uncertain, rough, current, (un)official, wrong, sketchy, problematic, woozy, detailed, supplementary, comprehensive, overall, preliminary

estrangement See *difference* (2)

ethic, ethics relentless, fierce, rigid, (in)flexible, rigorous, strict, unyielding, stringent, binding, arguable, professional, biomedical, environmental, human

evacuation, evacuations massive, (un)necessary, forced, compulsory, (in)voluntary, emergency; colonic

evaluation, evaluations careful, (un)fair, (im)partial, objective, unbiased, dispassionate, discerning, tough, (un)necessary, constructive, fruitful, fruitless, simplistic, total, complete, imminent, optional, compulsory, routine, analytical

evasion, evasions skilful, cunning, deceptive, plausible, specious, tactical

evening, evenings See also *day*
relaxing, charming, enchanting, calm, still, quiet, serene, clear, undisturbed, peaceful, cosy, pleasant, nice, enjoyable, delightful, wonderful, marvellous, enchanted, agreeable, lovely, beautiful, exquisite, ideal, perfect, soft, mellow, fresh, balmy, convivial, cheerful, happy, rollicking, mild, lazy, starlit, starless, moonless, silvery, romantic, elegant, suave, hom(e)y, boring, dull, uneventful, dreary, drab, damp, chill(y), cool, crisp, overcast, misty, drizzly, raw, steamy, muggy, humid, dismal, miserable, sweltering, social, sociable, festive, big-time

event, events exciting, intriguing, dazzling, glittering, interesting, challenging, bewildering, stunning, breathtaking, stupendous, (in)significant, (un)important, monumental, crucial, decisive, momentous, pivotal, singular, major, main, newsworthy, glamorous, spectacular, pre-eminent, blue-ribbon, landmark, watershed, world-renowned, great, grand, notable, dramatic, epochal, mighty, big, providential, heroic, triumphant, blessed, joyful, happy, pleasurable, lovely, star-studded, stylish, popular, glorious, sacred, cosmopolitan, profound, tremendous, special, memorable, unforgettable, notorious, vivid, tumultuous, unusual, unprecedented, extraordinary, exceptional, remarkable, unpredictable, unforeseen, tangible, real, imaginary, auspicious, propitious, favourable, portentous, serendipitous, coincidental, (un)related, classic, contemporary, probable, actual, homespun, (il)logical, (in)formal, routine, regular, recurrent, antecedent, preliminary, subsequent, sprawling, unfolding, seasonal, (un)likely, rare, unique, peculiar, once-in-a-lifetime, lonely, biannual, semi-annual, biennial, bicentennial, distant, imminent, future, recent, current, contemporary, synchronous, quirky, (un)familiar, spontaneous, eternal, ephemeral, prosaic, commonplace, (un)remarkable, unpopular, complex, irrevocable, jarring, crazy,

outlandish, regrettable, controversial, worrisome, burdensome, (anxiety-)provoking, unsettling, alarming, stirring, gruelling, daring, overwhelming, strident, stressful, horrific, horrible, fateful, tragic, dotty, traumatic, terrible, cataclysmic, painful, upsetting, emotional, patriotic, international, literary, historic(al), critical, sporting, cultural, terrestrial, celestial, astronomical, meteoritic, geological, supernatural, astrological, fund-raising, social, official, tourist-orient(at)ed

evidence, evidences (un)convincing, compelling, unquestionable, indisputable, irrefutable, unmistakable, incontrovertible, sound, solid, hard, definite, pivotal, critical, crucial, dramatic, eloquent, (un)reliable, empirical, expert, trustworthy, clear(-cut), corroborative, strong, discreditable, untainted, abundant, enormous, substantial, ample, cogent, confirmatory, (un)persuasive, (un)reasonable, (in)adequate, (un)acceptable, (un)satisfactory, immediate, good, valid, verifiable, supporting, (in)conclusive, weighty, credible, persuasive, objective, first-hand, damning, uncorroborated, staggering, growing, increasing, surrounding, overwhelming, wide, predominant, heartening, firm, positive, definite, specific, factual, concrete, palpable, tangible, visible, graphic, obvious, manifest, evident, intimate, usable, striking, startling, surprising, admissible, extant, actual, mixed, indirect, collateral, internal, probable, principal, (in)accessible, procurable, attainable, producible, available, fragmentary, fresh, gory, grim, ugly, alarming, moral, presumptive, full, explosive, flamboyant, indecisive, complex, hearsay, fallacious, faulty, erroneous, dubious, suspect, questionable, misleading, murky, perjured, tenuous, scant(y), weak, marginal, insufficient, slight, little, slender, flimsy, spotty, irrelevant, vague, ambiguous, controversial, conflicting, problematic, additional, unearthed, unproven, undocumented, unsupported, anecdotal, ocular, potential, cumulative, experimental, documentary, contextual, preliminary, supplementary, circumstantial, direct, primary, statistical, historical, archaeological, archival, prima-facie, forensic, material, physical, scientific, observational, clinical, electronic, photographic, stratigraphic, spectroscopic

evil, evils crying, coming, lurking, necessary, attendant, chronic, concomitant, consequent, visionary, imaginary, unreal, unthinkable, unimaginable, indescribable, dismal, monstrous, insidious, multifarious, disastrous, wilful, social

evolution, evolutions steady, perpetual, slow, convergent, (in)complete, unmarkable, social, ideological, natural, historical, organic

exaggeration, exaggerations extravagant, bizarre, eccentric, wild, serious, (un)pardonable, slight, jocular, humorous, grotesque, overdrawn, surrealistic

examination, examinations (1: test of knowledge) gruelling, anxiety-provoking, high-pressure, stiff, rigorous, rigid, competitive, nefarious, exhaustive, comprehensive, mid-year, final, supplemental, mid-term, terminal, oral, viva voce, multiple-choice

examination, examinations (2: inspection) (in)conclusive, intent, close, proper, searching, thorough, vigorous, rigorous, meticulous, detailed, exhaustive, comprehensive, strict, rigid, exact, narrow, thoughtful, objective, startling, hasty, cursory, repeated, routine, preliminary, essential, basic, fundamental, microscopic, physical, neurological, forensic, post-mortem, critical, medical

example, examples compelling, shining, sterling, glaring, striking, speaking, telling, stunning, outstanding, explicit, clear, conspicuous, notable, noticeable, flagrant, stand-out, eminent, vivid, star, peerless, unmatched, lustrous, illustrative, concrete, splendid, remarkable, magnificent, juicy, opportune, memorable, bright, famous, ideal, sublime, dramatic, monumental, supreme, premier, prime, up-to-date, classic, solitary, single, singular, sole, numerous, quick, additional, far-fetched, fuzzy, misleading, (un)impressive, (in)appropriate, (un)satisfactory, (un)important, (in)convenient, (un)suitable, (in)significant, (un)cited, specific

exasperation See *anger*

excellence, excellences sterling, unsurpassed, unexampled, unprecedented, extraordinary, outstanding, shining, enduring, enviable, remarkable, academic

exception, exceptions overriding, glaring, glittering, striking, conspicuous, obvious, remarkable, notable, resolute, rare, solitary, unique, possible, one-time

excess, excesses overflowing, exorbitant, abundant, immoderate, inordinate, intemperate, lavish, profligate, unrestrained, wretched, indulgent, ridiculous, mischievous, sensual, hedonistic, gastronomic

exchange, exchanges free, vital, beneficial, useful, (un)restricted, (un)limited, difficult, domestic, cultural, fair

excitement, excitements whirling, throbbing, trembling, all-consuming, glorious, heavy, feverish, ecstatic, boisterous, confused, clumsy, witless, hysterical, violent, rampageous, lugubrious, doleful, enormous, tremendous, considerable, incredible, unbelievable, strange, palpable, infectious, undue, tense, sheer, lasting, perpetual, non-stop, short-lived, sudden, brittle, (un)restrained, latent, mass, vicarious, physical

excursion, excursions See *trip*

excuse, excuses (in)valid, (il)legitimate, genuine, good, perfect, sound, (in)credible, colourable, (im)plausible, (un)acceptable, (un)convincing, (un)reasonable, (un)worthy, (un)common, (un)likely, handy, classic, old, time-worn, obvious, transparent, laboured, rotten, ready(-made), convenient, poor, preposterous, flimsy, lame, fictitious, pallid, thin, slim, suspicious, glib, shaky, slick, slight, piffling, frail, specious, false, phon(e)y, clumsy, artful, cunning, crafty, disingenuous, idiotic, silly, muttering, petulant, unobtrusive

execution, executions (capital punishment) grisly, brutal, pitiless, ruthless, heartless, remorseless, merciless, relentless, unrelenting, inhuman, arbitrary, deliberate, unlawful, illegal, systematic, mass, summary, ritual, political, (extra)judicial

executive, executives shrewd, motivated,

ingenious, brilliant, top-flight, savvy,
daring, dynamic, affable, high-paid,
well-paid, top, senior, high-powered,
high-ranking, high-flying, junior-level,
flamboyant, uptight, busy, diligent,
industrious, hardworking, cautious,
(un)successful, (un)pleasant, (in)efficient,
(in)competent, inept, failed, mediocre,
forceful, airborne, chief, business,
financial

exercise, exercises wholesome, healthy,
healthful, challenging, purposeful,
sustained, vigorous, all-out, intensive,
intense, high-impact, rigorous, strenuous,
excessive, severe, heavy, taxing,
excruciating, demanding, high-level,
(im)moderate, (im)modest, low-level,
mild, special, habitual, daily, nightly,
weekly, early-morning, boring,
repetitive, (ir)regular, (in)sufficient,
(un)pleasant, rhythmic, cerebral, mental,
relaxation, warm-up, physical, gymnastic,
remedial, therapeutic, salutary,
post-natal, antenatal, aerobic, anaerobic,
ambulatory

exercising See *exercise*

exertion, exertions See *effort*

exhaustion See *fatigue*

exhibit, exhibits See *exhibition*

exhibition, exhibitions sparkling,
dazzling, stunning, enchanting,
landmark, masterly, first-rate, elaborate,
delectable, resplendent, prestigious,
ambitious, imaginative, evocative,
provocative, unusual, rare, monumental,
panoramic, interactive, condescending,
vulgar, indecent, distasteful, ostentatious,
pretentious, recent, centennial,
permanent, indoor, outdoor, open-air,
travelling

exhortation, exhortations ringing,
inspirational, right-minded,
bloody-minded, mean, vicious, wicked,
evil, diabolic(al), devilish, infernal,
Luciferian, religious, patriotic

exile, exiles (1: banishment)
(un)comfortable, (un)restricted, painful,
disgraceful, bitter, provisional, temporary,
permanent, indefinite, internal, external,
self-imposed, voluntary, (en)forced,
political, rural

exile, exiles (2: banished person) wandering,
poverty-stricken, homesick, internal

existence, existences See also *life*
blessed, peaceful, carefree, happy-go-lucky,
full, humdrum, dull, monotonous,
exasperating, insipid, cheerless, drab,
colourless, squalid, miserable, wretched,
bleak, austere, harsh, painful, modest,
hand-to-mouth, frugal, meagre,
impecunious, threadbare, Spartan, brief,
finite, continued, tame, self-serving,
haphazard, perilous, solitary, age-old,
physical, corporeal, earthly, mortal,
vegetable

exit, exits (un)dignified, (un)graceful,
(un)ceremonious, dramatic, theatrical,
spectacular, flamboyant, forcible, sudden,
hasty, quick, ignominious

exodus, exoduses swelling, steady,
sudden, chaotic, marked, mass

expanse, expanses forbidding, sweeping,
wide, vast, ample, great, empty,
(un)limited, barren

expansion, expansions small, modest,
steady, gradual, robust, further,
widespread, feverish, explosive, relentless,
runaway, wanton, unbridled, heady,
tremendous, rapid, self-destructive,
ongoing, territorial

expectation, expectations tickling,
rising, high, great, heroic, happy,
(un)realistic, momentary, impatient,
breathless, widespread, new, constant, low,
heavyweight, sanguine, fond, traditional,
(il)legitimate, (un)real, conflicting,
extravagant, fantastic, inflationary,
unrealistic, impossible, wild, vain,
unfounded, naïve, empty, false,
precarious, grim, tormenting,
medium-term

expedition, expeditions (un)fortunate,
(un)lucky, (un)forgettable, (un)successful,
fruitful, fruitless, adventurous, perilous,
ill-fated, disastrous, ambitious, grandiose,
remarkable, three-week, modest, nefarious,
wicked, punitive, false, lost, exploratory,
botanical, oceanographic, archaeological,
scientific, military, colonizing

expenditure, expenditures
(un)profitable, extravagant, ruinous,
prodigal, profitless, wasteful, reckless,
heedless, negligent, unbudgeted, eligible,
total, capital, out-of-pocket

expense, expenses light, trifling,
alarming, staggering, enormous,

considerable, unwarrantable, needless, unseemly, (un)justifiable, (il)legitimate, (un)avoidable, questionable, extraordinary, extravagant, heedless, onerous, exorbitant, horrendous, prohibitive, ravenous, profligate, fixed, (in)significant, uncontrolled, unforeseen, (un)expected, one-time, public, personal, miscellaneous, incidental, out-of-pocket, contingent, current, household, travelling, business, overhead, operating, capital

experience, experiences thrilling, breathtaking, overwhelming, satisfying, exhilarating, exciting, fascinating, rewarding, uplifting, salutary, beneficial, meaningful, rich, instructive, educative, valuable, extensive, tremendous, broad, wide, enormous, considerable, large, deep, remarkable, dramatic, incandescent, seminal, formative, ripe, exotic, exquisite, (un)pleasant, joyous, pleasurable, motley, varied, intense, vivid, first-hand, hands-on, real-world, wonderful, marvellous, privileged, exceptional, hoary, unforgettable, memorable, restricted, (in)communicable, pitiable, sordid, nasty, bitter, harsh, hard-won, devastating, scary, killing, moving, unusual, (un)common, strange, profound, intense, engaging, (all-)consuming, climactic, unbelievable, incredible, sobering, (un)limited, long, irritating, vertiginous, novel, unique, universal, traumatic, claustrophobic, hellish, unsettling, gruelling, heartburning, heart-rending, nerve-racking, harrowing, frightening, depressing, bleak, ghastly, boring, painful, unbearable, humiliating, humbling, mortifying, jarring, unnerving, frustrating, meaningless, scathing, bitter-sweet, stressful, scary, gory, flawed, unsatisfactory, scant, bewildering, poignant, disagreeable, distasteful, heady, difficult, shocking, humble, vagabond, bruising, previous, prior, frequent, fleeting, day-to-day, vicarious, inner, private, cultural, educational, chalkface, secular, worldly, religious, spiritual, mystic, moral, amoral, sensory, sensuous, sensual, emotional, visual, aesthetic

experiment, experiments promising, worthwhile, clever, ingenious, imaginative, crucial, (in)conclusive, radical, innovative, landmark, unprecedented, novel, historic, ambitious, spectacular, daring, tantalizing, astonishing, fascinating, curious, critical, (in)significant, routine, empirical, controversial, arduous, complicated, long, large-scale, small-scale, bizarre, barren, futile, inconsequential, fragile, sloppy, venturesome, (in)humane, (un)successful, reckless, hazardous, risky, dangerous, short-term, long-term, preliminary, dead-end, double-blind, control, chemical, scientific, linguistic, psychological, binomial

expert, experts sought-after, busy, (best-)informed, unerring, infallible, international, leading, ranking, reputable, noted, outstanding, reputed, genuine, foremost, top, renowned, illustrious, (well-)known, distinguished, self-styled

explanation, explanations penetrating, compelling, incisive, sharp, direct, clear, plain, lucid, coherent, luminous, straightforward, viable, genial, cogent, tangible, good, feasible, elaborate, detailed, scrutable, succinct, poignant, patient, pellucid, transparent, persuasive, understandable, provocative, novel, (un)reasonable, (in)adequate, (im)proper, (un)convincing, (un)believable, (im)plausible, (im)precise, (un)satisfactory, (im)probable, (un)likely, (ir)rational, (in)comprehensible, (un)conventional, laconic, terse, wordy, long-winded, laboured, cautious, veiled, rote, dominant, contradictory, foolish, ridiculous, absurd, vague, discrepant, dubious, apocryphal, ill-considered, fuzzy, clumsy, awkward, far-fetched, prosaic, tortuous, initial, immediate, alternative, full, partial, periphrastic, fatalistic, causal, official

exploitation, exploitations inappropriate, improper, inapt, infelicitous, incongruous, tasteless, unbecoming, unrelenting, relentless, ruthless, merciless, pitiless, remorseless, heartless

exploration, explorations ambitious, formal, long, (ever-)increasing, leisurely, vigorous, arduous, systematic, panoramic, treacherous, risky, solitary, polar, undersea, on-site, (un)manned, scientific

explorer, explorers early, first, great, legendary, heroic, brave, bold, adventurous, intrepid, daring, determined, thorough, quintessential

explosion, explosions devastating, rocking, tearing, deafening, thunderous, loud, terrible, terrific, horrific, horrendous, awful, tremendous, huge, spectacular, titanic, stupendous, astonishing, violent, deadly, fatal, cataclysmic, muffled, multiple, premature, instantaneous, spontaneous, simultaneous, unremitting, harmless, urban, chemical, stellar; phreatic

explosive, explosives sensitive, powerful, efficient, (un)detectable, difficult-to-detect, high(-performance), low, primary, plastic, liquid

export, exports soaring, rising, vigorous, competitive, lucrative, massive, large-scale, siz(e)able, skimpy, stagnant, sagging, frustrated, illicit, illegal, invisible, national

exposure, exposures vast, widespread, prominent, momentary, constant, long-term, short-term, accidental, unforeseen, unprotected, unsafe; indecent; multiple; chemical

expression, expressions (1: a look on the face) angelic, beatific, winsome, innocent, candid, genial, decent, tender, amused, (un)happy, good-humoured, (un)refined, (in)discreet, radiant, rapt, misread, regretful, prissy, lacklustre, sombre, sober, solemn, serious, pensive, questioning, quizzical, bewildered, confused, vacant, vacuous, blank, impassive, glazed, stony, dreamy, dumb, stupid, inane, wistful, harsh, accusatory, stern, grim, forbidding, grave, melancholy, down(cast), dejected, dispirited, morose, gloomy, sullen, ill-humoured, rueful, queasy, sorrowful, mournful, doleful, woeful, lugubrious, no-nonsense, quiet, sad, coarse, dour, doubtful, undecided, fleeting, anxious, weary, grievous, threatening, hangdog, cowering, ashamed, facial, ocular

expression, expressions (2: a saying) facile, candid, good-humoured, (un)refined, (in)discreet, felicitous, concise, (im)precise, rapturous, smooth, effusive, vivid, apt, forcible, catchy, hackneyed, commonplace, trite, memorable, stupid, inane, inept, vacant, wistful, harsh, accusatory, stern, grim, grave, sober, morose, gloomy, ill-humoured, sorrowful, doleful, lugubrious, spontaneous, base, coarse, obscene, profane, dour, pejorative, antic, doubtful, fulsome, anxious, jittery,

uneasy, tense, threatening, prosaic, favourite, (in)frequent, (non-)standard, figurative, slang

expulsion degrading, humiliating, ignominious, dishonourable, disgraceful, scandalous, shameful, forceful, inevitable, unavoidable, imminent, eventual

extermination, exterminations wanton, unimaginable, indiscriminate, deliberate, wilful, maniacal, nightmarish, ruthless, merciless, remorseless, pitiless, heartless, relentless, unrelenting, needless, systematic, methodical, total, mass, impending, imminent, inevitable, threatening

extradition, extraditions (un)appealable, (un)warranted, (un)justifiable, (un)expected, imminent, eventual, inevitable, impending, threatening

extravagance, extravagances vigorous, wild, febrile, crass, preposterous, reckless, scandalous, sinful, unconscionable, insensate, wanton, prodigal, unbounded, vainglorious, heedless, thoughtless, blindfold, needless, glorious, astounding

extravaganza, extravaganzas See *show*

extreme, extremes frenetic, frenzied, frantic, absurd, self-defeating, other, opposite, antithetical

extremist, extremists intransigent, intractable, radical, irreconcilable, recalcitrant, uncompromising, wild, headstrong, obstinate, wilful, bolstered, religious

eye, eyes flashing, glowing, glittering, sparkling, gleaming, shining, winking, slumbering, languishing, swimming, (love-)darting, discerning, (in)discriminating, longing, weeping, gaping, spying, questing, burning, laughing, smiling, (wide-)staring, goggling, popping, bulging, speaking, yearning, searing, pleading, beseeching, questioning, (un)blinking, stinging, roving, darting, scanning, prying, melting, unflinching, piercing, penetrating, captivating, hypnotic, amiable, iridescent, pellucid, colourless, pallid, jaundiced, bloodshot, (blood-)red, red-rimmed, pink-lidded, rose-dark, bluish, (china-)blue, sea-blue, brunet, almond, (liquid-)brown, ginger-brown, smoky(-brown), ash-coloured, grey, tawny, dark, sloe, green(ish), hazel, sapphire, sullen, mottled, slit, bleary, dazed, tremulous, haggard, wrinkled, watery, weird, stony, flinty, lustreless, sterile, rodent, predatory, luscious, porcine, lambent, naked, liquid, bright, ardent, lustrous, pellucid, intense, radiant, glossy, moist, lashless, visionless, sightless, blind, starry, striking, remarkable, clear, dull, beady, glassy, fixed, intent, near-sighted, hollow, limpid, magic, prominent, protuberant, sunken, slant, bulbous, hawk-like, rabbity, ferret, squinty, cavernous, deep(-set), wide-set, elongated, dilated, enlarged, wide, baggy, huge, exquisite, heavy, goggle, lacklustre, misty, tarantula-like, froggy, ulcerated, short-sighted, heavy-lidded, thick-lashed, shadowless, swollen, wide-awake, unblinking, jaunty, vivacious, blissful, soulless, expressionless, still, languid, languorous, sensitive, withdrawn, impassive, emotionless, washed-out, dejected, sombre, anguished, sorrowful, tearful, downcast, dim, novice, observant, appreciative, imperious, droopy, lugubrious, puffy, mortal, reverted, besotted, averted, thoughtful, keen, incisive, precise, candid, frank, drowsy, sleepy, sleep-deprived, mute, peevish, mercurial, enigmatic(al), unfathomable, practised, accustomed, untrained, sharp, penetrative, quick, perceptive, prim, telescopic, baleful, evil, unfocused, meditative, dreamy, distracted, speculative, indeterminate, crinkly, wary, inscrutable, (ever-)watchful, astonished, ubiquitous, vacuous, alert, protective, earnest, ardent, slow, excited, dense, morose, sardonic, covetous, envious, contemptuous, derisive, scornful, furtive, stealthy, frightened, hostile, belligerent, oblique, evasive, beery, hungry, playful, restless, shifty, warm, radiant, soulful, expressive, fiery, weak, weary, scratchy, inflamed, sore, rheumy, exhausted, liquor-clogged, wistful, wild, authoritative, assertive, possessive, forceful, stoical, worshipful, distrustful, incredulous, inquisitorial, imbecilic, myopic; mental

eyebrow, eyebrows shaggy, thick, bushy, rough, big, beetle, jutting, projecting, stiff, singular, caterpillar, Mephistophelian(-ean)

eyeglasses See *glasses*

eyelash, eyelashes ingrowing, ingrown, long, false, fake, curly, thick, scanty, dark, silken

eyelid, eyelids winking, heavy, slumb(e)rous, droopy, hairless, wrinkled

eyesight, eyesights See *vision* (1)

fable, fables See *story*

fabric, fabrics plain, subtle, delicate, rich,
fine, translucent, filmy, gauzy, diaphanous,
smooth, (velvety-)soft, ciré, glossy, wiry,
heavy, strong, robust, durable,
long-lasting, hard-wearing, coarse, stiff,
rough, scratchy, (semi-)opaque, sheer,
see-through, crisp, cool, unique, radiant,
lustrous, colourful, fancy, decorative,
elastic, light(weight), weather-proof,
rain-proof, water-repellant, water-resistant,
shrink-proof, shrink-resistant, absorbent,
washable, easy-care, wrinkle-free,
colour-fast, reversible, porous, canvas-like,
gauze-like, bulky, woolly, silky, graphite,
quality, sumptuous, superb, luxurious,
elegant, sprightly, crinkly, wrinkly,
static-resistant, crease-resistant,
flame-retardant, chintz, floral, moiré,
multi-print, unfinished, stencilled, sprigged,
(candy-)striped, figured, corded,
(hand-)woven, hand-knit, machine-made,
loose-woven, (flame-)stitched, ribbed,
twilled, twill-weave, plain-weave,
complex-weave, linen, acetate, cotton,
textile, silk, rayon, vane, woollen,
synthetic

fabrication, fabrications malicious,
evil-minded, wicked, spiteful, vicious,
admitted, palpable, transparent

façade, façades glittering, imposing,
astounding, exciting, outstanding, striking,
stunning, impressive, majestic, graceful,
glitzy, sedate, deceptive

face, faces rosy, ruddy, pinkish,
dark(-complexioned), rust-hued, coppery,
(sun-)brown, swarthy, (snow-)white,
sallow, pale, pallid, flushed, discoloured,
colourless, chalky, waxen, ashen, pallid,
tan(ned), wan, green, glowing, sun-worn,
grey, beaming, smiling, fresh, unlined,
(sweat-)bright(ened), radiant, brilliant,
mirthful, blissful, pleased, florid, seraphic,
gentle, calm, placid, serene, lively,
vivacious, (un)friendly, affable, animated,
beautiful, sweet, pretty, handsome,
(un)attractive, enchanting, dignified,
kindly, open, honest, expressive,
intellectual, intelligent, interesting, candid,
frank, simple, trustful, glad, humorous,
humour-saturated, sunshiny, benevolent,
confident, supercilious, bilious, dour,
furtive, morose, haggard, lewd, tearful,
tearless, grim, sinister, solemn, serious,
stern, craggy, sad, sullen, sour, rueful,
frowning, gloomy, intense, uneasy, drowsy,
torpid, expressionless, cold, phlegmatic,
stiff, rigid, fixed, immobile, impassive,
unmoved, tight-lipped, glassy, indifferent,
rugged, harsh, sober, false, passionless,
dispassionate, emotionless, straight,
earnest, thoughtful, exhausted, tired,
strained, (tight-)drawn, weary, wearied,
(work-)worn, sweat-streaked, forbidding,
unfriendly, angry, inscrutable, baffling,
shocking, startled, commanding,
(grief-)stricken, pained, sulky, grubby,
clean-shaven, wrinkle-free, homely,
(un)prepossessing, saturnine, old, wry,
deadpan, visionary, rubicund, wholesome,
cherub(ic), lean, anaemic, wasted,
emaciated, lacerated, grave, voluptuous,
impish, expansive, round, chunky, bloated,
meagre, flabby, floppy, broad, beaky,
bony, thick-jowled, long, taut, gaunt,
baby, chubby, podgy, swollen, lumpy,
rough, full, fat, plump, stolid, dull, hard,
flat, thin(-fleshed), hanging, contorted,
coarse-featured, chiselled, raw-boned,
high-cheeked, strong-jawed, distorted,
(still-)boyish, rough-hewn, cavernous,
concave, wrinkled, twisted, puffy, angular,
leathery, downy, frizzly, frowsy,
weather-worn, weather-beaten, weathered,
unlined, bespectacled, blank, pathetic,
pimply, (red-)pimpled, (pock-)marked,
pockpitted, freckled, ghastly, deathly, pale,
dished, lifeless, apathetic, passive,
inanimate, immovable, imperturbable,
unreserved, overcast, plain, disagreeable,
sour, wincing, peevish, pugnacious,
bad-tempered, malevolent, predatory,
withdrawn, diffident, strange, well-known,
(un)familiar, ugly, droll, ethereal,
downcast, ill-favoured, mobile, unreadable,
piquant, porcine, twitching, flushed,
twisted, tear-stained, battered, bleeding,
nondescript, scorched, petulant, imbecile,
ascetic

facility, facilities exceptional, exemplary,

state-of-the-art, unique, (un)limited, (in)adequate, (un)suitable, decent, extensive, complete, attractive, sophisticated, terrific, élite, unbelievable, incredible, existing, lacking, bare, rudimentary, outdated, awkward, compatible, communal, recreational, educational, cultural, toilet

fact, facts tantalizing, fascinating, refreshing, encouraging, certain, positive, obvious, first-hand, incontestable, undeniable, indisputable, irrefutable, confirmable, (un)confirmed, undisputed, intransigent, provable, ominous, accomplished, salient, pertinent, invaluable, (in)significant, (ir)relevant, supporting, demonstrable, notable, singular, concrete, circumstantial, fundamental, essential, intriguing, empirical, inescapable, ineluctable, absolute, (un)known, unpleasant, unfortunate, stark, bare, blunt, crude, cold, humdrum, bitter, painful, hard, harsh, terrible, monstrous, brutal, ghastly, hideous, trivial, curious, decisive, living, plain, dry, inexorable, unalterable, sober(ing), dour, dismal, grim, crushing, staggering, devastating, little-known, overriding, verifiable, perceivable, startling, alarming, puzzling, surprising, perplexing, shadowy, doleful, shaky, simple, ultimate, discouraging, (un)doubted, suppressed, (un)related, unreported, material, elementary, actual, public, basic, essential, primary, scientific

faction, factions moderate, articulate, radical, rival, powerful, bitter, rogue, isolable, dissident, breakaway, rebel, splinter, disparate, schismatic, emerging, warring, violence-prone, hard-line, fundamentalist, political, guerrilla

factor, factors ominous, (un)known, (un)common, decisive, decided, positive, influential, significant, major, critical, crucial, central, overriding, dominant, vital, salient, prominent, conspicuous, striking, unquestionable, unmistakable, big, powerful, volatile, unpredictable, considered, (un)measured, detrimental, unifying, threatening, complicated, interwoven, innumerable, discrete, countervailing, immediate, outside, external, (in)tangible, contributory, limiting, intractable, oppressive, discouraging, aggravating, cyclical, formative, causative, hereditary, environmental, genetic, psychological

factory, factories (in)efficient, modern, advanced, high-tech, up-to-date, state-of-the-art, leading-edge, sophisticated, fabulous, functional, prestigious, viable, cost-efficient, cubbyhole, booming, (un)successful, (un)safe, (in)operable, smokeless, mammoth, many-storeyed, rambling, old, run-down, obsolete, obsolescent, outmoded, defunct, dead, decrepit, bleak, dilapidated, out-of-date, idle, (long-)abandoned, strike-bound, prefabricated

faculty, faculties (1: ability; power) dormant, imaginative, judicative, rational, intuitive, mental, critical

faculty, faculties (2: teaching staff) See *teacher* and *professor*

fad, fads interesting, growing, spreading, passing, dying, vanishing, short-lived, adulatory, ideological, behavioural, dietary

failure, failures resounding, utter, total, complete, absolute, partial, enormous, spectacular, colossal, big, abysmal, sterile, dire, abject, cataclysmic, consistent, costly, expensive, flat, bitter, dead, conspicuous, signal, ultimate, shameful, ignominious, wretched, miserable, calamitous, disastrous, catastrophic, tragic, regrettable, pathetic, lamentable, pitiable, deplorable, disheartening, distressing, frightening, unqualified, hopeless, forlorn, dismal, ghastly, ugly, notable, apparent, consequential, (un)accountable, honourable, inevitable, unavoidable, eventual, practical, virtual, critical, marital; mechanical, autonomic, respiratory, cardiopulmonary, circulatory, renal

fair, fairs thronging, buzzing, rollicking, dazzling, teeming, colourful, myriad, lively, huge, crowded, busy, frenzied, boisterous, raucous, chaotic, annual, agricultural, industrial

fairness scrupulous, conscientious, fastidious, meticulous, eminent, conspicuous, impartial, equitable, judicious, exact, due, fundamental, questionable

fairy, fairies dainty, kind, good, noble, evil, wicked, household

faith enduring, abiding, unblinking, (un)wavering, (un)faltering, undying, unbending, unquestioning, unshak(e)able, steadfast, rigorous, strong, firm, stubborn, inflexible, ardent, extravagant, intact, pure, full, saving, blind, living, total, profound, deep, valiant, cheerful, unabated, undiminished, perfect, good, bad, dogmatic, dominant, age-old, ancient, perennial, traditional, voluntary, implicit, precarious, wobbly, sinking, (un)shaken, newfound, anti-intellectual, pacifist, religious, institutional

fall, falls dizzying, precipitous, steep, sharp, sudden, abrupt, inopportune, headlong, dangerous, shameful, ignominious, disgraceful, cyclic

falls See *waterfall*

falsehood, falsehoods malicious, perfidious, contemptible, atrocious, flagrant, deliberate, rousing, flat, extraordinary, patent, absurd

fame (thoroughly-)deserved, well-earned, splendid, magnificent, illustrious, bright, gigantic, glittering, lasting, enduring, deathless, immortal, imperishable, undiminished, high, wide(spread), steady, unexpected, sudden, overnight, mortal, declining, posthumous

familiarity, familiarities easy, close, intimate, calm, cosy, customary, habitual, usual, excessive, unreserved, unrestrained, unlimited, limitless, unwelcome, impertinent, contemptuous

family, families caring, loving, upstanding, good, supportive, wonderful, decent, well-bred, nice, refined, intact, close(-knit), tightly-knit, (re)united, fine, stable, respectable, worthy, hospitable, old, happy, royal, noble, ruling, aristocratic, titled, powerful, important, dynastic, bourgeois, illustrious, renowned, distinguished, prominent, great, remarkable, leading, high-status, high-born, affluent, wealthy, landed, moneyed, prosperous, well-to-do, well-heeled, well-off, rich, conservative, sociable, forceful, far-flung, struggling, needy, impecunious, private, whole, large, big, troubled, dysfunctional, strife-torn, scandalous, infamous, feckless, bizarre, alcoholic, intact, immediate, foster, surrogate, adoptive, natural, avuncular, ersatz, nuclear, traditional, (over)extended, single-child, two-child, single-parent, two-parent, hybrid, mother-led, mother-driven, one-earner, two-earner, one-income, two-income, double-income, suburban; Mafia-type

famine, famines agonizing, devastating, blighting, catastrophic, grim, apocalyptic, mighty, great, giant, mass, terrible, vicious, widespread, needless, agricultural

fan, fans (1: an object for making a current of air) swishing, humming, whirling, oscillating, (in)efficient, beautiful, fine, (hand-)painted, powerful, palm-leaf, cardboard, folding, hand(-held), electric, decorative, oriental

fan, fans (2: a fanatical supporter) gushing, screaming, applauding, doting, steadfast, steady, persistent, committed, avowed, avid, (over)ardent, fervent, enthusiastic, exuberant, passionate, devout, devoted, supportive, loyal, long-time, serious, die-hard, hysterical, rabid, raucous, boisterous, violent, obsessive, appreciative, disappointed, livid, myriad, fickle

fanatic, fanatics ascetic, humourless, strident, determined, formidable, obstinate, zealous, rabid, manic, mad, frenetic, frenzied, unreasonable, narrow-minded

fanaticism See also *fanatic* sordid, vile, contemptible, mean, ignoble

fancy, fancies copious, strong, decided, lively, fine, original, capricious, wild, wayward, unsubstantiated, idle, loose, footless, odd, whimsical, passing, sudden, exquisite, aerial, visionary

fantasy, fantasies whimsical, playful, wild, campy, extravagant, excitable, dreamlike, wistful, vivid, idle, ultimate, blurring, comforting, golden, exotic, delightful, pleasant, self-important, self-indulgent, inexplicable, outlandish, violent, dangerous, desolate, gruesome, twisted, recurring, daft, daffy, infantile, silly, idiotic, sheer, apocalyptic, nightmarish, harrowing, morbid, aberrant, (in)voluntary, creative, romantic, sensuous, perverse, erotic, sexual, adulterous, private; Gothic

farce, farces See also *play* (1) lively,

entertaining, screaming, side-splitting, knockabout, flat-out, fast-tempo, macabre, black, coarse, raucous, deplorable, worthless, broad, wild, popular, bucolic

fare, fares (1: the sum paid for a journey) steep, half, reduced, cut-rate, full, unrestricted, double, excursion, charter, round-trip, return, special, promotional, competitive

fare (2: food; diet) See *food*

farewell, farewells moving, touching, sorrowing, rousing, teary, tearful, sad, emotional, passionate, impetuous, robust, frenzied, fond, warm, gentle, tender, breezy, sentimental, nostalgic, painful, long, reluctant, pathetic, cordial, affectionate, friendly, bittersweet, final

farm, farms See also *farmland* and *agriculture* thriving, prosperous, well-to-do, debt-ridden, mortgage-free, (in)fertile, (un)productive, (un)successful, viable, many-acred, old-fashioned, diversified, mixed, quaint, neat, well-ordered, thrifty, beloved, peaceful, drought-stricken, under-productive, failing, lonely, solitary, remote, outlying, rambling, one-man, pastoral, (non-)organic, experimental, collective, state-run; county, poor

farmer, farmers work-hardened, sturdy, diligent, industrious, (un)productive, (un)scientific, (in)efficient, (un)skilled, (un)successful, small-scale, large-scale, busy, small(-time), little, traditional, conventional, old-time, progressive, innovative, independent, (over-)extended, drought-stricken, troubled, (heavily-)indebted, hard-pressed, dispossessed, penniless, illiterate, semi-literate, sedentary, peasant, gentleman, private, organic, ecological

farming See also *farm* and *agriculture* advanced, sophisticated, innovative, lucrative, (un)productive, (in)efficient, traditional, conventional, mainstream, old-fashioned, risky, part-time, high-yield, cost-effective, high-cost, (un)successful, backbreaking, (labour-)intensive, extensive, large-scale, dry(land), irrigated, arable, small-plot, rudimentary, primitive, futile, chemical, organic, biodynamic, slash-and-burn, one-crop, diversified, mixed, hydroponic, industrial

farmland, farmlands See also *farm* fertile, open, rolling, peaceful, comfortable, featureless, vanishing

fascination, fascinations compelling, alluring, charming, bewitching, enticing, rapt, irresistible, powerful, hypnotic, mesmeric, silent, incredible, unbelievable, marvellous, particular, endless, everlasting, enduring, eternal, curious, peculiar, queer, morbid

fashion, fashions (1: of clothes) current, latest, trendy, new, up-to-date, avant-garde, prevailing, fantastic, colourful, multifaceted, high, top-name, fine, (pseudo-)cerebral, (un)exciting, strange, peculiar, queer, extreme, cliquish, radical, frivolous, outrageous, fickle, faddish, flashy, fleeting, passing, funky, fluctuating, popular, neutral, classic, collegiate, feminine, teenage

fashion, fashions (2: manner) See also *manner* haphazard, random, perfunctory, clandestine, secret, traditional, orderly, efficient, unique, time-honoured

fast, fasting extended, forced, self-imposed, traditional, sunset-to-sunset, dawn-to-sunset, annual

fat, fats waxy, mushy, soft, hard, fake, dietary, (un)saturated, polyunsaturated, monounsaturated, subcutaneous

fatality, fatalities See also *death* sole, only, single, on-the-job, industrial, accidental

fate, fates lofty, glorious, merciful, pitiful, (un)happy, (un)fortunate, (un)kind, benign, reassuring, progressive, explicit, adverse, wayward, jarring, untoward, sad, dreadful, dreary, gloomy, dark, malignant, oppressive, evil, lamentable, unenviable, cruel, tragic, destructive, implacable, unrelenting, relentless, pitiless, ruthless, heartless, merciless, remorseless, brutal, hostile, mysterious, inscrutable, enigmatic, problematic, unpredictable, unclear, uncertain, extraordinary, strange, unavoidable, inevitable, uncontrollable, impending, imminent, intervening, hanging, ultimate, common, universal

father, fathers loving, caring, affectionate, kind(ly), devoted, dedicated, (un)fit, demonstrative, fond, weighty, indulgent, dour, harsh, (over-)exacting, strict, demanding, stern, trying, severe, disciplinarian, authoritative, overbearing, domineering, autocratic, pompous, unkind, cruel, tyrannical, despotic, incestuous, unfit, ineffectual, abusive, failed, negligent, improvident, putative, biological, natural, adoptive, foster, surrogate; founding, city

fatigue overwhelming, haunting, persistent, extreme, excessive, profound, total, severe, terrible, desperate, unrelenting, relentless, ruthless, merciless, pitiless, incurable, chronic, mental, emotional, physical

fatigues (work clothes) See *uniform*

fault, faults See *mistake*

favour, favours preposterous, undue, special, extra, reciprocal, big, huge, enormous, royal, personal, political, sexual

favouritism See *bias*

fear, fears haunting, overpowering, rising, growing, chilling, crushing, debilitating, blinding, heart-rending, intense, acute, violent, hearty, abject, terrible, awful, dreadful, vacant, dark, scrupulous, premonitory, indescribable, inexpressible, impalpable, nameless, clammy, tremendous, gloomy, morbid, panic, mortal, hourly, endemic, grisly, stark, abject, dire, explosive, confused, bare, helpless, capricious, desperate, speculative, substantive, legitimate, pervasive, widespread, rampant, omnipresent, chill, cold, stony, aerial, (un)substantial, extreme, guilty, abiding, persistent, continual, constant, perpetual, momentary, lingering, lurking, ingrained, deep-seated, deep-rooted, instinctive, inborn, natural, habitual, understandable, legitimate, abnormal, paranoiac, paranoid, slavish, crazy, childish, puerile, irrational, foolish, ludicrous, absurd, petty, clumsy, unconscious, genuine, well-placed, well-founded, unfounded, ungrounded, groundless, unjustified, baseless, fantastic, idle, imaginary, unrealistic, inordinate, righteous, overblown, shadowy, obsessive, superstitious, short-lived, long-held, unresolved, unspoken, inarticulate, raw, mortal, holy, womanish, reverential, pathological, visceral

feast, feasts See also *festival* whopping, dazzling, lavish, hearty, costly, sumptuous, abundant, bountiful, splendid, regal, elaborate, huge, gargantuan, fragrant, luscious, memorable, interminable, enjoyable, delightful, modest, boisterous, rambunctious, unruly, (in)formal, communal, fixed, (im)movable, cultural, ceremonial

feat, feats amazing, astounding, astonishing, staggering, dazzling, demanding, big, landmark, rare, extraordinary, remarkable, explosive, innovative, valorous, prodigious, wonderful, stupendous, splendid, magnificent, marvellous, glorious, impressive, spectacular, fantastic, incredible, unbelievable, uninhibited, crazy, zany, mean, technical

feather, feathers glossy, iridescent, small, hard, innumerable, soft, delicate, fluffy, weightless, light, bristle-like, speckled, spiky, capricious, auricular

feature, feature (1: appearance of the face) appealing, alluring, endearing, pretty, chiselled, characteristic, distinctive, distinguishing, striking, noticeable, prominent, conspicuous, obvious, remarkable, specific, special, rugged, salient, sharp, pronounced, irregular, gaunt, delicate, small, soft, modest, sunken, haggard, sodden, coarse, heavy, strong, massive, lumpen, malleable, immobile, motionless, passive, bronze-like, angular, hard-edged, telltale, flat, plain, blunt, ascetic, repulsive, simian, craggy, pockmarked, contorted, distorted, malformed, waxen, feminine, facial

feature, features (2: characteristic) intriguing, exciting, striking, amazing, interesting, distinguishing, outstanding, advantageous, attractive, (un)amiable, innovative, nice, salient, conspicuous, obvious, distinctive, universal, prominent, dominant, noticeable, recognizable, permanent, unchanging, standard, (ir)regular, specific, special, discriminative, peculiar, differential, unique, redeeming, repulsive, physical, anatomical, natural, geographical, geological, morphological, architectural, social, religious, organizational

federation, federations See *union*

fee, fees (un)affordable, (un)reasonable, whopping, rising, extortionate, hefty, huge, siz(e)able, steep, stiff, exorbitant,

outrageous, gargantuan, handsome,
(in)significant, skimpy, round, numerous,
up-front, prospective, (un)accountable,
(un)palatable, disguised, optional,
mandatory, deductible, annual, flat,
regular, supplementary, supplemental,
premium, legal, medical, membership,
application, advisory

feeding daily, regular, forcible,
intravenous, tubal, regurgitative

feeling, feelings exhilarating, thrilling,
(un)sympathetic, (un)friendly, lofty,
delicious, restful, wonderful, gentle,
tender, exquisite, hopeful, genuine, warm,
luxuriant, marvellous, kindly, freaky,
(bone-)deep, ungovernable, pervasive,
overriding, staggering, indescribable,
inexplicable, top-of-the-world, poignant,
hostile, chilly, adverse, eerie, ambivalent,
bitter, hard, ill, panicky, scary, frightened,
nervous, shaky, bad, strong, dull, heavy,
pressing, raw, vulnerable, ruffled, fretful,
washy, uneasy, uncomfortable,
antipathetic, unkindly, mixed, tense,
violent, hopeless, despairing, inmost,
intense, acute, drowsy, sinking,
light-hearted, heady, light-headed, funny,
curious, strange, queer, eerie, uncanny,
giddy, faint, listless, sick, long-held,
conflicting, sanctimonious, chilling,
unsettling, upsetting, harrowing, prickling,
tantalizing, stinging, menacing, ghastly,
terrible, awesome, awful, lasting,
momentary, visceral, traumatic, paranoid,
voluptuous, erotic, unearthly, incredible,
unbelievable, deep-seated, pent-up, mutual,
inner, instinctive, intuitive, negative,
positive, (un)controllable, superstitious,
fatalistic, suicidal, universal, mystical,
religious, poetic, parental

fellow, fellows See Appendixes A and B

felon, felons See *criminal*

feminism See also *feminist* assertive,
clear-eyed, considerate, ill-informed,
rudimentary, radical, rabid, intellectual

feminist, feminists mild, active, avowed,
committed, aggressive, fervent, ardent,
militant, radical, fanatical, fighting,
instinctive (instinctual), intellectual

fence, fences towering, tall,
(eight-foot-)high, surrounding, straggling,
temporary, permanent, neat,
weather-beaten, heavy, flimsy, crude,

shabby, wobbly, broken-down,
(im)movable, collapsible, grilled,
ornamental, protective, (woven-)wire,
wire-mesh, barbed-wire, razor-wire,
heavy-mesh, chain-link, bamboo, electric,
high-voltage, (wrought-)iron, steel(-pole),
stone, wood, palisade, zigzag, woven,
invisible, electronic; psychological

ferocity staggering, intoxicating,
maddening, crushing, raging, devastating,
unrelenting, barbaric, fiendish, merciless,
cruel, unrestrained, bestial, brutish,
diabolic(al), inhuman, pitiless, ruthless,
vicious, relentless

fertilizer, fertilizers complete, organic,
mineral, biological, synthetic, artificial,
commercial, chemical, nitrogen

festival, festivals See also *feast* elaborate,
elegant, extravagant, lavish, spectacular,
fantastical, non-stop, long-standing,
current, international,
internationally-known, famous,
world-class, prestigious, significant, small,
solemn, annual, quadrennial, seasonal,
musical, choral, film, sacred, religious,
secular, cultural, ecclesiastical, outdoor,
harvest

feud, feuds unending, long-standing,
lasting, ongoing, lingering, drawn-out,
sterile, complex, internecine, bitter,
unrelenting, relentless, heartless,
remorseless, ruthless, merciless, pitiless,
senseless, violent, intense, dreary, raucous,
brutal, bloody, political, ideological,
family, internal, ethnic, tribal, corporate

feudalism tenacious, theocratic, medieval

feuding See *feud*

fever, fevers soaring, high, persistent,
tenacious, resistant, obstinate, chronic,
sthenic, irritative, hectic, searing,
debilitating, wasting, (non-)fatal, violent,
nervous, low-grade, slight, tertian,
rampant, continued, continuous, reduced,
intermittent, remittent, fitful, relapsing,
recurrent, (ir)responsive, viral, nocturnal,
diurnal, obscure, artificial, enteric,
surgical, cerebral, cerebrospinal, childbed,
puerperal, abortive, symptomatic, low,
scarlet, yellow, rheumatic, glandular,
undulant (Malta, Mediterranean),
rickettsial, haemorrhagic

fibre, fibres elastic, lustrous, sensual,
tough, fine, soluble, woven, natural,

mineral, vegetable, animal, cellulose, synthetic, twisted, polyester, cotton, nylon, flax, nerve, carbon, dietary

fiction, fictions See also *novel* and *story* vivid, precise, (un)healthy, trashy, escapist, phantasmagoric, fabulous, speculative, science, spy, pulp, space, autobiographical, romantic, classical, detective

fidelity See *loyalty*

field, fields (1: land) lush, loamy, (in)fertile, (un)productive, (jade-)green,verdant, generous, tidy, open, far-flung, extensive, big, large, fresh, waving, sloping, rolling, shimmery, clean, bare, barren, arid, cropless, fallow, tawny, (winter-)brown, scrubby, erodible, windy, wet, cold, comfortless, stubble, weedy, grassy, stubby, hilly, adjacent, contiguous, scrubby, humble, untended, sodden, waterlogged, flooded, (stone-)terraced, sun-baked, parched, (cow-)dotted, hydrothermal; Elysian

field, fields (2: scope) fast-changing, virgin, new, fresh; integrated

fiend, fiends See *devil*

fight, fights gruelling, tiring, unrelenting, flaring, spluttering (sputtering), intense, intensive, full-scale, all-out, strong, heavy, savage, vicious, fierce, ferocious, bitter, internecine, furious, hot, harsh, violent, bloody, terrible, brutal, stubborn, useless, endless, ceaseless, non-stop, huge, no-holds-barred, single-minded, free, chaotic, roaring, noisy, desultory, protracted, sporadic, rugged, uphill, three-cornered, valiant, brisk, victimless, (un)fair, (un)equal, (un)balanced, one-sided, united, mock, head-on, hand-to-hand, last-ditch, (under)sea, ethnic, factional, street-to-street, professional

fighter, fighters splendid, stalwart, tough, powerful, fierce, savage, pertinacious, merciless, pitiless, ruthless, heartless, remorseless, relentless, unrelenting, violent, vicious, tenacious, restless, fidgety, dedicated, (un)dependable, solitary

fighting See *fight*

figure, figures (1: number) See also *number* heartening, encouraging, staggering, astonishing, astounding, surprising, startling, swelling, phenomenal, astronomical, horrendous, preposterous, ridiculous, prodigious, handsome, magic, bleak, worrisome, alarming, disappointing, gloomy, grim, actual, firm, (un)alterable, approximate, (in)correct, discouraging, (un)true, (in)significant, (un)reliable, (in)valid, deceptive, rising, high, low, overall, normal, preliminary, final, round

figure, figures (2: shape) svelte, astral, trim, slender, petite, tiny, wiry, (ultra-)slim, skeletal, thin, spare, clean, sleek, well-proportioned, splendid, hourglass, graceful, flamboyant, solid, lovely, light, plastic, firm, rigid, upright, perfect, slight, squat, busty, compact, buxom, ample, full, plump(ish), obese, abundant, fattish, roly-poly, spry, stocky, thick, muscular, sinewy, robust, broad-backed, low-sized, bulging, manly, feminine, girlish, recumbent, sombre, ungainly, gaunt, frail, fragile, lanky, terra-cotta, shadowy, ghostly, shady, (well-)rounded, dim, faint, indefinable, wasted, willowy, lithe, odd, grotesque, solitary, soldierly, lurking, hulking, stooping, reclining, crumpled, gnarled, life-size, irregular, clumsy, awkward, many-sided, geometric(al), opulent, multilateral, plane, two-sided, three-sided, four-sided, angular, curvilinear, three-dimensional, solid, hollow, lay

figure, figures (3: person) See also Appendixes A and B fascinating, charming, compelling, appealing, unique, incomparable, unparalleled, innovative, prominent, well-known, great, major, leading, towering, pivotal, singular, influential, mighty, distinguished, remarkable, splendid, powerful, strong, exalted, heroic, glamorous, larger-than-life, immortal, enduring, world-famous, lik(e)able, popular, beloved, colourful, credible, commanding, haunting, (un)prepossessing, independent, remote, shadowy, lonely, solitary, enigmatic, macabre, shambling, messianic, stocky, eccentric, puzzling, taunting, fuzzy, outrageous, controversial, ungainly, huge, (in)distinct, reserved, sorry, uncouth, disagreeable, spectral, central, key, literary, public, athletic, (non)religious, cultural, historic(al), political, business, comic, tragic, social, folk, legendary, allegorical, mythological, mythical, composite, underworld, cult

figurehead, figureheads respectable, venerable, honourable, estimable, creditable, presentable, reputable, well-beloved

file, files (un)tidy, bulging, growing, voluminous, bulky, thick, comprehensive, detailed, permanent, lifelong, bogus, extant, surviving, missing, open, closed, confidential, (top-)secret, personal, official, electronic

film, films fascinating, charming, entrancing, ravishing, stunning, fine, robust, powerful, strong, exciting, artful, informative, comprehensive, well-made, well-wrought, expensive, big-budget, fabulous, marvellous, remarkable, splendid, magnificent, irresistible, provocative, moving, sensational, (un)successful, memorable, serious, accomplished, sumptuous, lavish, eloquent, subtle, wholesome, Oscar-winning, award-winning, award-deserving, major, smash, great, landmark, vintage, seminal, classic, epic, legendary, swell, blockbuster, hit, cranky, odd, terrific, nifty, sword-and-sorcery, slapstick, bittersweet, splashy, ostentatious, pretentious, pedantic, controversial, abysmal, worthless, lifeless, insipid, leaden, failed, harrowing, (un)forgettable, lame, prissy, disjointed, well-meaning, incendiary, gruesome, bloodthirsty, lugubrious, plotless, sprawling, taut, crass, empty-headed, pointless, lousy, suspense-filled, suspenseful, daring, foreign-language, small-budget, low-budget, scary, stodgy, suggestive, erotic, indecent, blue, pornographic, dirty, obscene, X-rated, first-run, grainy, black-and-white, full-length, feature, silent, sound, wide-screen, big-screen, giant-screen, photographic, documentary, educational, instructional, promotional, ideological, historical, swashbuckling, realistic, surrealist

fin, fins flaring, billowing, stinging, floppy, flappy, spiny, movable, triangular, curved, translucent, stilt-like, wing-like, fragile, sturdy, pectoral, dorsal, pelvic, caudal, tail, anal

finance, finances See also *money* solid,

(un)stable, balanced, exhausted, shaky, compensatory

financing (in)appropriate, short-term, long-term, interest-free, assumable

find, finds exciting, astonishing, astounding, startling, puzzling, perplexing, fabled, rich, spectacular, exceptional, rare, great, significant, landmark, replicable, historic, archaeological

finding, findings telling, revealing, encouraging, groundbreaking, startling, striking, astounding, surprising, astonishing, puzzling, staggering, enticing, sensational, significant, impressive, positive, monumental, curious, (in)consistent, controversial, specific, objective, confirmatory, disappointing, devastating, troubling, shocking, primary, preliminary, provisional

fine, fines paltry, low, lenient, heavy, hefty, severe, stiff, strict, punitive, crushing, (un)just, (in)equitable, (un)fair, set

finesse inborn, innate, natural, instinctive, admirable, remarkable, elegant, exquisite, refined, subtle, wonderful

finger, fingers dainty, delicate, ringless, (magenta-)nailed, stubby, pudgy (podgy), muscular, stocky, thick, plump, slender, spatulate, short, long, slim, spidery, scrawny, wiry, crusty, bony, gaunt, gnarled, cocked, stretched, webbed, clubbed, itchy, numb, stiff, oily, sticky, jammy, spread, (non)functional, sore, painful, quick, light, nimble, agile, deft, smart, skilled, sensitive, inept, awkward, clumsy, tickling, throbbing, tingling, twitching, warning, accusatory, condemnatory, reproachful, first, index, second, third, little, ring

fingernail, fingernails neat, elegant, long, short, stubby, ingrown, ingrowing, depressed, flat, chewed, broken, shell-like, spoon-like, purple, dry, brittle

fingerprint, fingerprints distinctive, composite, latent; genetic

fire, fires roaring, hissing, spluttering, snapping, sizzling, raging, raking, glaring, twinkling, sparkling, flaring, glowing, burning, spreading, tumbling, withering, dying, expiring, smouldering, smoking, lambent, candescent, healthy, bright, vivid, brisk, charming, warm, cheerful, cosy, gentle, corrosive, explosive, contagious, hot, impetuous, destructive, ruinous, disastrous, tragic, devastating, deadly, vicious, diabolical, horrendous, terrible, angry, furious, fierce, ferocious, wild, great, huge, spectacular, mammoth, monster, monstrous, massive, prodigious, hellish, intense, orange, red, neon-red, crimson, purplish, tawny, snappy, treacherous, mysterious, suspicious, incendiary, accidental, casual, man-made, smoky, ashy, smudgy, smokeless, flameless, naked, dim, slow, small, low, dead, (un)quenchable, (in)extinguishable, (un)manageable, (un)containable, (un)controllable, stubborn, unpredictable, liquid, viscous, quick, accidental, poetic, rapid, open-hearth, open(-air), volcanic; ethereal; Greek

firearm, firearms See *gun*

fireplace, fireplaces roaring, bright, (in)efficient, impressive, (un)attractive, ornate, handsome, arched, soaring, floor-to-ceiling, enormous, massive, bulky, antique, working, tiled, marble, slate, granite, brick, rock, (cut-)stone, wood, gas, electric, feature, fresh-air, corner-mounted, see-through

firework, fireworks sizzling, hissing, soaring, sparkling, dazzling, loud, soundless, colourful, spectacular, impressive, showy

firing (in)effective, intense, dying, deliberate, accidental, sporadic, occasional, indiscriminate, practice, live

firm, firms venerable, successful, reputable, solid, substantial, giant, big, major, profitable, flourishing, thriving, sound, secure, safe, prestigious, pre-eminent, capital-rich, efficient, expanding, heavyweight, (well-)established, high-technology, bloated, independent, going, fledgling, upstart, ailing, obscure, money-losing, struggling, faltering, solvent, inefficient, small, medium-sized, state-run, family-run, family-held, multinational, international, foreign, local, private, subsidiary, industrial, mercantile, commercial, banking, counselling, consulting

fish, fishes (fish) tempting, teasing, tantalizing, biting, darting, squirting, diving, swimming, splashing, meandering, wallowing, writhing, flashing, glistering, frantic, rare, scarce, salient, elongated, graceful, broad-bellied, sharp-finned, fancy-finned, pug-faced, sharp-toothed, speckled, mottled, (dark-)striped, red-fleshed, golden, silvery, opalescent, translucent, iridescent, shimmery, fancy, colourful, sinister, outlandish, grotesque, droll, preposterous, raw, watery, succulent, dry, bony, boneless, spiny, rubbery, wriggly, swirly, skirmy, slithery, slimy, live, fresh, abundant, numberless, spawning, good-sized, marketable, edible, delectable, plump, juicy, hardy, resilient, smooth-skinned, firm-fleshed, freshly-caught, quick-frozen, skinless, solid, tough, inedible, putrid, stale, pale, measly, (non-)poisonous, venomous, rotten, (lead-)tainted, stinking, swollen, smelly, diseased, spent, migratory, freshwater, salt-water, deep-water, deep-sea, ocean, marine, labyrinth, soft-finned, spiny-finned, sparoid, anadromous, catadromous, cartilaginous, oviparous, cannibalistic, predatory, tropical, wild, transparent, electric, larval, anemone, scorpaenoid, percoid, serranid, carangid, cyprinodont, cyprinoid, teleost

fisherman, fishermen brave, sturdy, coarse, hard-bitten, deep-sea, inshore, fresh-water, commercial, nomadic, seasonal

fishery, fisheries large-scale, rich, lucrative, profitable, inshore, offshore, longshore, (il)legal, freshwater, salt-water, deep-water, virgin, commercial

fishing lucrative, profitable, bountiful, coarse, freshwater, salt-water, inshore, offshore, longshore, coastal, topwater, (il)legal, still, seasonal, commercial, recreational

fist, fists pummelling, hammering, formidable, big, mighty, gnarled, tight, angry; iron

fjord, fjords slim, tiny, deep(-cut), calm, brackish, spectacular, dramatic, magnificent, wild, sheltered, isolated, steep-walled, winding, land-locked

flag, flags flying, flaunting, snapping, flapping, triangular, square, oblong, swallow-tailed, decorative, vibrant, ragged, bedraggled, soiled, tattered, crumbling, school, national(ist), military, regimental; white, chequered

flame, flames See also *fire* roaring,
wavering, spluttering (sputtering),
spreading, piercing, darting, surging,
rising, shooting, blinding, raging, burning,
devouring, consuming, smok(e)y, swirling,
(in)extinguishable, (un)quenchable,
immitigable, eternal, evanescent, errant,
fierce, fussy, lambent, (non)luminous,
vivid, monstrous, scanty, naked, uplifted,
languid, slow, sickly, slight, yellow, pale,
livid, orange, mauve, crimson, blue

flash, flashes bewildering, blinding,
bright, candescent, explosive, sudden,
instantaneous, momentary, intermittent,
occasional, recurrent, sinuous, stark

flat, flats ultra-modern, smart, coquettish,
new, superb, fashionable, luxurious,
opulent, prestigious, palatial, spectacular,
sumptuous, imaginative, lofty, swank,
commodious, spacious, roomy, decent,
respectable, prim, well-kept, tidy, snug,
tailor-made, balconied, waterfront,
beachfront, well-appointed, redone,
less-than-palatial, half-decent,
(un)affordable, modest, low-rent,
incommodious, barren, spartan,
unpretentious, unimaginative, tiny,
cavernous, claustrophobic, poky, old,
stuffy, dark, dingy, dilapidated, crummy,
cramped, shabby, miserable, squalid,
dismal, filthy, run-down, drab, seedy,
mean, frowzily-curtained, burnt-down,
quirky, council, walk-up, walk-in, attic,
basement, sixth-floor, penthouse,
bachelor(-pad)

flatterer, flatterers See *flattery*

flattery, flatteries sickening, disgusting,
cringing, fawning, grovelling, obsequious,
graceful, judicious, senseless, sedulous,
saccharine, extravagant, grotesque, servile,
fulsome, abject, mean, dishonest, insincere,
amusing

flavour, flavours authentic, (un)palatable,
(un)pleasant, (dis)agreeable, superb,
splendid, magnificent, delicate, mild,
smooth, sweet, saccharine, delicious, rich,
subtle, racy, tart, (sub)acid, sharp, unique,
unusual, strange, odd, unaccustomed,
distinctive, distinct, (in)distinguishable,
(in)definable, spicy, briny, full, yeasty,
fruity, brisk, crisp, nutty, musty, snappy,
smok(e)y, salty, gamy, robust, tantalizing,
tempting, smooth, mellow, herbaceous,

tangy, exotic, drowsy, sweet–sour, acidic,
bitter, coarse, brassy, metallic, strange,
wine-like, discouraging, (long-)lasting,
natural, artificial

flaw, flaws See also *defect* minute, tiny,
subtle, substantive, gigantic, huge,
conspicuous, obvious, glaring, basic,
unsettling, serious, dangerous, fatal,
suspected, genetic

fleet, fleets large, hostile, élite,
(treasure-)laden, naval, fishing

flesh gleaming, warm, tender, smooth,
silky, proud, firm, solid, flabby, flaccid,
quaggy, scrawny, skinny, pale, porous,
numb, ripe, juiceless, bloodless, wizened,
putrid, gangrenous, slimy, scabby; mortal

flight, flights (1: journey made by air)
smooth, nice, scenic, (un)spectacular,
memorable, shake-down, turbulent, rough,
clumsy, bumpy, gruelling, harrowing, long,
dull, tedious, doomed, ill-fated, direct,
non-stop, long-haul, low-altitude,
high-altitude, swift, (in)frequent, no-frills,
regular, charter(ed), unmanned, morning,
night, daily, (un)eventful, hazardous, epic,
incoming, outgoing, smoke-free, solo,
(un)available, round-trip, return,
round-the-world, intercontinental,
transcontinental, transoceanic,
transatlantic, trans-Pacific, cross-country,
southward, northbound, international,
domestic, commercial, recreational,
inaugural, lunar, (super)sonic, (sub-)orbital

flight, flights (2: movement through the
air) graceful, unerring, unimpeded,
accurate, soaring, curving, upward,
downward, horizontal, level,
(javelin-)straight, low-altitude,
high-altitude, low-level, spectacular,
buoyant, (sub-)orbital, high-speed

flight, flights (3: hasty departure)
headlong, hurried, panicky, precipitate,
inglorious, shameful, disgraceful,
moonlight

flirtation, flirtations aggressive,
provocative, pushy, persistent,
unrestrained, whirlwind, impetuous,
precipitate, storybook, mild, harmless

flood, floods roaring, raging, gushing,
surging, foaming, swelling, devastating,
terrible, fierce, ferocious, tragic,
disastrous, destructive, calamitous,
cataclysmic, catastrophic, lethal, miserable,

sudden, short-lived, record, stormy, torrential, mighty, enormous, monstrous, knee-deep, swollen, steamy, silt-laden, unabated, unchecked, unprecedented, widespread, spotty, seasonal, periodic

flooding See *flood*

floor, floors (1: ground surface) gleaming, shining, spotless, immaculate, level, buttery, (un)even, sagging, sloping, bare, worn, steel-plate, inlaid, decorative, rich-hued, scooped-out, earth(en), mud, wood(en), hardwood, granite, cement, concrete, marble, mosaic, stone, slate, rubber, cold, damp, fuggy, cracked, well-worn, flimsy, squeaky, mossy; ocean

floor, floors (2: storey) ground, first, second, third, upper, attic, mezzanine

flour, flours strong, soft, plain, high-protein, stone-ground, wholewheat, instant, all-purpose, corn, rice

flow, flows steady, smooth, graceful, orderly, continuous, ceaseless, free, profuse, copious, heavy, massive, voluminous, prodigious, (ab)normal, (in)adequate, frenetic, turbulent, precipitous, wild, diminishing, (un)interrupted, umbilical, menstrual; cash, trade, production

flower, flowers blooming, charming, dazzling, striking, bright, lovely, dewy, healthful, healthy, gay, vernal, fresh, fabulous, odoriferous, nectar-rich, fragrant, sweet-scented, colourful, dainty, attractive, pretty, beautiful, handsome, delicate, soft, fragile, exquisite, magnificent, splendid, rare, exotic, luxurious, high-priced, sublime, majestic, regal, incomparable, forceable, long-lasting, short-lived, variegated, self-coloured, sky-blue, pink-red, pale-violet, yellowish-green, multicoloured, proliferate, semi-double, spiked, thorny, tiny, symmetrical, compound, composite, spurred, nodding, swirly, sessile, agglomerate, open, long-stemmed, stemless, ninefold, four-petalled, many-petalled, interwoven, overblown, disepalous, dispermous, monoclinous, diclinous, hybrid, fertile, festive, frilly, alien, nocturnal, diurnal, alpine, showy, swaying, slumbering, droopy, sleepy, crumpled, rough, waxy, scruffy, limp, (half-)dead, unkempt, scentless, artificial, wayside, wild, insectivorous, tropical, woodland, roadside, indoor, water, cardinal, acropetal, herbaceous, basipetal, bipetalous, anandrous, anisomerous, isomerous, asepalous, cernuous, averse, adverse, bipinnate, cruciate, dimerous, monadelphous, bulbous, tetramerous, capitate, capitular, tubular, cyclic

fluctuation, fluctuations temporary, passing, unruly, uncontrollable, turbulent, violent, wild

fluency graceful, elegant, dext(e)rous, easy, neat, natural

fluid, fluids gushing, (crystal-)clear, thin, tenuous, viscous, dense, rare, watery, bubbly, milky, oily, gluey, musky, vital, subtile, frictionless, colourless, odourless, perfect, homogeneous, incompressible, volatile, potable, synovial, gastric, spermatic, extracellular, serous, cerebrospinal, noxious, acidic, seminal, amniotic, vaginal, bodily, spinal, hydraulic

flying graceful, graceless, clumsy, awkward, blind, acrobatic

foam bubbly, creamy, scummy, white, effervescent, (non)biodegradable

focus, focuses (foci) primary, distinct, clear, coherent, harmonious, intense, sharp, central

foe, foes See *enemy*

fog, fogs haunting, rolling, loitering, descending, tumbling, billowing, blinding, smothering, thickening, shrouding, shifting, spectral, dreadful, dismal, dense, thick, heavy, clingy, swirly, impenetrable, limitless, severe, pea-soup, murky, black, grey, pallid, hazy, cool, ice, snow-laced, freezing, wet, clammy, lifeless, thin, light, patchy, pearly, luminous, (un)seasonable, frequent, sudden, putrid, coastal, frontal

foliage See *leaf*

folk, folks See also *people* simple, country; Beaker

follower, followers faithful, loyal, devout, dedicated, ecstatic, enthusiastic, unquestioning, obedient, slavish

folly, follies See *stupidity*

fondness growing, (ever)lasting, enduring, unfailing, ceaseless, endless, imperishable, perennial, unshak(e)able, persistent, extreme, inordinate, stubborn, genuine, unaggressive, perverse, pixilated, impetuous, newfound, unaccountable

food, foods (in)adequate, (im)proper, hearty, wholesome, nourishing, nutritious, nutritive, healthful, health(y), whole, unprocessed, healing, valuable, sustaining, low-calorie, preservative-free, chemical-free, pesticide-free, fat-free, cholesterol-free, low-salt, low-sodium, low-fat, unadulterated, (calcium-)rich, light, mild, natural, organic, elegant, colourful, finicky, fresh, sappy, juicy, succulent, fabulous, simple, favourite, delicate, (in)digestible, (un)inviting, captivating, alluring, tempting, satisfying, appetizing, appealing, attractive, imaginative, hearty, subtle, dainty, edible, pure, luxurious, costly, choice, prized, masterly, aromatic, special, sophisticated, delightful, splendid, magnificent, sublime, superb, divine, heavenly, scrumptious, delicious, tasty, high-taste, zesty, flavourful, delectable, palatable, savoury, toothsome, mouthwatering, lip-smacking, fine, superior, good, adequate, solid, crunchy, crisp(y), textured, thick, chunky, fitting, hot, spicy, soft, tender, chewy, starchy, sugary, tangy, salty, oily, garlicky, acidic, rich, creamy, fatty, fattening, fat-laden, high-fat, plain, tasteless, mediocre, abominable, inedible, insipid, bland, refined, unwholesome, unhealthful, unhygienic, complicated, sugar-rich, lacklustre, worthless, queasy, repellent, unattractive, uninteresting, stale, terrible, wretched, coarse, poor, inferior, dreadful, heavy, stodgy, greasy, soggy, mushy, limp, cold, miserable, improper, distasteful, flavourless, slimy, questionable, putrid, bad, rotten, unfit, rotting, revolting, perishable, (un)popular, homely, unusual, potted, (un)traditional, abundant, (in)sufficient, superfluous, taboo, basic, staple, primary, principal, robust, rustic, home-grown, (in)tolerable, oven-ready, everyday, (non-)kosher, vegetarian, ethnic, macrobiotic, fast

fool, fools raving, blinking, fond, credulous, helpless, hopeless, witless, arrant, big, gross, perfect, consummate, complete, stark, positive, downright, thorough, plain, born, egregious, motley, natural, insensate, cockeyed, idiotic, incoherent, vain, obstinate, ridiculous, ineffable, disastrous, congenital

foolishness See *stupidity*

foot, feet (1: bodily part) slouching, stamping, clumping, dainty, nimble, indefatigable, strong, large, huge, elephantine, immense, monstrous, rough, knobby, webbed, cracked, bulbous, swollen, swelling, aching, sore, motionless, numb, itchy, weary, uncertain, wobbly, stockinged, shoeless, smelly, cold, wet, hind, front, truncated, reptilian, (too-)flat, artificial, prosthetic

foot, feet (2: unit of length) cubic, square, linear

foothill, foothills See *hill*

footnote, footnotes detailed, copious, exhaustive, terse, concise, memorable, (un)intelligible, explanatory

footprint, footprints fresh, clear, visible, startling, suspicious, fishy, incriminatory, accusatory, hominoid

footstep, footsteps crisp, soft, quiet, silent, noiseless, soundless, slow, short, long, loud, quick, noisy, laborious, heavy, wavering, faltering, quickening, hurrying, shuffling, muffled, alien, stealthy, following, sinister

forbearance See *patience*

force, forces uniting, guiding, restraining, unifying, cohesive, effective, overwhelming, compelling, imposing, impulsive, influential, superior, enormous, tremendous, siz(e)able, substantial, monumental, epic, titanic, amazing, astounding, astonishing, unabated, durable, irresistible, inconceivable, mighty, awesome, potent, powerful, massive, pervasive, full, deterrent, shocking, formidable, ferocious, (un)just, (un)justifiable, (un)reasonable, excessive, unnecessary, unwarranted, lethal, deadly, destructive, hostile, antagonistic, opposing, possessive, main, sheer, immanent, opposable, unstoppable, irrepressible, invincible, energetic, emphatic, mysterious, heavy, muted, significant, crushing, brute, bullish, barbaric, evil, pernicious, vociferous, explosive, vital, fundamental, repulsive, divisive, propulsive, special, auxiliary, élite, fighting, multinational, multilateral, expeditionary, insurgent, rebellious, strategic, (para)military; political, elemental, physical, spiritual, psychic, material, outside, external, projectile, ejective, electromotive, motive, gravitational, magnetomotive, centrifugal, centripetal, geologic(al), cataclysmic, tectonic, (non-)nuclear, (aero)dynamic, static, parallel

forecast, forecasts glowing, sunny, rosy, roseate, (in)accurate, meticulous, infallible, unequivocal, (un)reliable, sage, time-honoured, long-term, short-term, (in)credible, dire, bleak, grim, devastating, bearish, bullish, gloomy, failed, futuristic, meteorological, economic

forecasting See *forecast*

forehead, foreheads striking, open, honest, wrinkled, sweaty, hot, massive, receding, bronzed, towering, high, cliff-like, wide, broad, expansive, protuberant, jutting, bulging, projecting, knotty, bulbous, low, thoughtful

foresight penetrating, admirable, cautious, careful, reliable, shrewd, well-advised

forest, forests sheltering, protecting, protected, lofty, bountiful, productive, luxuriant, evergreen, verdant, lush, thick, dense, heavy, tangled, gnarled, shaggy, wild, inexhaustible, renewable, shadowy, tranquil, peaceful, undisturbed, silent, still, lifeless, (long-)dead, enchanted, fairy-tale, unsullied, unpolluted, valuable, splendid, magnificent, mighty, regal, moon-broken, pure, virgin, intact, undiscovered, impenetrable, pathless, trackless, dangerous, treacherous, vanishing, stunted, old-growth, brittle, dark, suffocating, forbidding, sopping, humid, damp, moist, steamy, scrubby, oozy, slimy, gloomy, ghostly, lonely, deep, vast, broad, endless, extensive, open, vespertine, deciduous, (sub)arctic, fossil, black, dry, atavistic, primitive, prim(a)eval, primordial, pristine, coniferous, pine(-scented), estuarine, hilly, mountain(ous), tropical, coastal, marshy, cathedral, native, national, boreal, maritime, riverine, rain

forgery, forgeries obvious, (un)detectable, audacious, meticulous, palpable, skilful, clever, worthless, pale, cheap, clumsy, inartistic

forgiveness saintly, compassionate, clement, merciful, charitable, tolerant, generous, indefatigable, unvindictive, gracious, mutual, Christian

form, forms (1: shape) See *shape*

form, forms (2: printed document) simple, straightforward, involved, complex, complicated, arcane, mysterious, baffling, puzzling, enigmatic, incomprehensible, (un)necessary, (over-)wordy, repetitive, intrusive, impertinent, official

formality, formalities stifling, suffocating, maddening, uncaring, rigid, inflexible, ponderous, profound, excessive, elaborate, intricate, complex, complicated, cumbersome, snarled, massive, lengthy, endless, unnecessary, mere, empty, brief, minimal, nominal, legal

formula, formulas (formulae) unrelenting, unyielding, inexorable, rigid, dogmatic, complicated, intricate, fundamental, old, new, (un)known, rare, equitable, profitable, revolutionary, radical, set, stereotyped; mathematical, algebraic, asymptotic(al), chemical

fort, forts (im)pregnable, (in)accessible, (in)expungeable, (un)conquerable, (im)penetrable, (in)defensible, high-walled, shell-proof, stern, formidable, mighty, extraordinary, elegant, majestic, gallant, stately, imposing, commanding, lofty, gigantic, massive, solid, strong, old, big, fairy-tale, tranquil, ghostly, stone, mountain, hilltop, coastal, strategic, weak, frail, crumbly, medieval

fortress, fortresses See *fort*

fortitude See also *courage* outstanding, great, increasing, diminishing, manlike, manly, Roman; intestinal

fortune (1: wealth) staggering, breathtaking, fabulous, substantial, vast, colossal, enormous, huge, immense, siz(e)able, inexhaustible, ample, handsome, considerable, plentiful, tidy, snug, (once-)fabled, ill-gotten, unclaimed, fast, bankrupt, moderate, uncertain, overnight

fortune (2: luck) smiling, good, wonderful, marvellous, extraordinary, soaring, miraculous, bright, (un)favourable, (un)propitious, bad, adverse, detrimental, elusive, fickle, faithless, waning, shifting, sagging, wayward

fortune-teller, fortune-tellers (un)skilful, (un)skilled, clever, able, smart, (im)plausible, (un)convincing, persuasive

forum, forums vigorous, dynamic, refreshing, powerful, spirited, zealous, unbiased, open, public, national, international

foundation, foundations (1: basis) durable, dependable, firm, strong, solid, supple, (in)secure, (un)trustworthy, (un)safe, (un)stable, weak, flimsy, crumbly, old, ancient

foundation, foundations (2: endowment) philanthropic, benevolent, charitable, educational, humanitarian, humane, non-profitable

fountain, fountains tinkling, whispering, gushing, floating, (ever-)flowing, sprouting, splashing, elaborate, lavish, affluent, carved, tiled, salient, fantastic, lovely, unusual, famous, glorious, natural, man-made, baroque, pyramidal, domed; drinking

fowl, fowls See *bird*

fox, foxes wary, cagey, wily, cunning, crafty, sly, elusive, omnivorous, light-footed, rare, red, grey, desert (kit), town, arctic (white), blue

fraction, fractions ordinary, partial, tiny, minute, infinitesimal, irreducible; continued, decimal, simple (common, vulgar), (im)proper, equal, compound (complex)

fracture, fractures hairline, simple (closed), compound (open), multiple, greenstick, vertebral

fragrance enchanting, appealing, exciting, satisfying, delicious, seductive, irresistible, beautiful, marvellous, clean, fresh, sweet, delicate, fine, elegant, subtle, obvious, blunt, heady, heavy, deep, thick, strong, overpowering, haunting, torturing, oppressive, pungent, unsavoury, stale, sickly, unbearable, languorous, ephemeral, weak, faint, elusive, mysterious, exotic, (un)familiar, intangible, floral, woody, piny, musky, oily, musty, distinctive, unforgettable, lasting, (long-)lingering, modern, (semi-)oriental

frame, frames (1: a surrounding part or border) sharp-cornered, triple, massive, elegant, gilt, ornate, elaborate, fancy, garish, gaudy, handmade

frame, frames (2: bodily construction) heavy, robust, muscular, stout, broad, bulky, massive, big, gigantic, stocky, overweight, obese, pudgy, slight, tiny, skinny, lanky, loose, trim, shrunk, elfin, cold, ungainly, spidery

frankness refreshing, bracing, disarming, breathtaking, surprising, astonishing, astounding, amazing, unusual, blunt, utter, sincere, warm, taut, evident, remarkable, obsessive, acid, brutal, naïve

fraud, frauds deliberate, callous, blatant, barefaced, outright, gross, absolute, extreme, all-out, gigantic, unqualified, unmitigated, widespread, rampant, actual, apparent, constructive, electoral, criminal

freedom, freedoms flowering, unencumbered, real, perilous, (ir)responsible, giddy, gypsy, rascally, untrammelled, new-found, (hard-)won, elusive, short-lived, lost, basic, fundamental, relative, comparative, limitless, (un)limited, partial, total, absolute, moral, religious, political, academic, intellectual

frequency, frequencies startling, astounding, astonishing, amazing, growing, rising, increasing, alarming, frightening, maddening, significant, common, habitual, persistent, nightmarish; low, reduced, medium, high, radio, angular, base, audio

freshness delicious, dewy, crisp, vivid, youthful, vernal, open-air

friend, friends intimate, beloved, bosom, close, well-matched, congenial, firm, delightful, affectionate, constant, loyal, staunch, (stead)fast, attached, lifelong, stalwart, steady, inseparable, sincere, loving, trusty, devoted, dear, constant, warm, faithful, unfailing, tender, (e)special, exceptional, sympathetic, near, (much-)valued, valuable, favoured, select, particular, unsycophantic, like-minded, reassuring, familiar, candid, judicious, level-headed, (un)reliable, (in)considerate, honest, hospitable, influential, powerful, high-powered, high-profile, high-placed, well-placed, posh, illustrious, useful, former, (long-)lost, quondam, erstwhile, long-ago, long-time, old-time, one-time, sometime, unworthy, false, so-called, dubious, fair-weather, deceitful, treacherous, faithless, perfidious, disloyal, unfaithful, officious, personal, childhood, school, college, mutual, political

friendship, friendships See also
friend disarming, warm, sincere, strong,
cordial, mutual, close, intimate, mature,
true, perfect, firm, (un)steady, (un)stable,
steadfast, precious, selfless, durable,
unwavering, long(-standing), lasting,
abiding, intact, unparalleled, profound,
deep, harmonious, (all-)embracing,
short-lived, broken, false, casual, unlikely,
seeming, indiscreet, acrid, immediate,
spurious, nettlesome, formal, strict,
notorious, extravagant, Platonic

fright, frights See *fear*

frivolity, frivolousness light-minded,
light-headed, light-hearted, giddy,
irrelevant, petty, childish, puerile,
youthful, silly, feather-brained,
scatter-brained

frog, frogs chirping, screaming,
hammering, singing, skipping, croaking,
screeching, tiny, torpid, green (spring)

front, fronts broad, solid, united, strong,
fragile, bloody, fluid, cruel; sea, ocean,
water; popular, global, common, political;
warm, cold, polar

frontier, frontiers See *border*

frost, frosts tenacious, stubborn, sharp,
hard, rimy, chilling, killing, early,
untimely, inopportune, unseasonable,
dissolving, glistering, glazed, granular,
hoar, white, black, air, aerial

frown, frowns set, immovable, rigid, stern,
grim, forceful, faint, pinched, permanent

fruit, fruits firm, fleshy, shiny, colourful,
tempting, juicy, luscious, fresh, sound,
mature, (over)ripe, succulent, plump, fine,
lush, refreshing, racy, delicious, sweet,
delectable, mellow, flavourful, savoury,
tasty, sugary, tangy, sticky, crisp, crunchy,
(in)edible, harvestable, strange, exotic,
unusual, scarce, rare, (in)dehiscent,
spurious, conical, (two-)winged, podlike,
squarish, pointed, moniliform, perishable,
smooth, silken, green, immature,
undeveloped, unripe(ned), underripe, sour,
subacid, aggregate, multiple, low-calorie,
abundant, woody, seedy, seedless,
clingstone, freestone, downy, hard,
thin-skinned, smooth-skinned, soft, fallen,
(weather-)cracked, insipid, tasteless,
flavourless, rotten, withered, wizened,
pesticide-laden, maggot-eaten, maggoty,
wormy, malignant, seasonal, contraband,

tropical, indigenous, local, wild, citrus,
dry, eating, forbidden; simple; first

frustration, frustrations profound, deep,
vast, immense, unbounded, continual,
extreme, intense, angry, bitter, relentless,
pent-up, swelling, clumsy, sheer, obvious,
inevitable, unavoidable, understandable,
small, sexual

fuel, fuels combustible, (in)flammable,
(un)tainted, (un)polluted, volatile,
synthetic, fossil, high-grade, low-grade,
high-octane, low-octane, solid, liquid,
chemical (exotic), sulphurous, radioactive,
nuclear, fissionable, (un)leaded

fulfilment gratifying, engaging, pleasing,
satisfying, cheerful, pleasant, agreeable,
storybook, personal

fume, fumes nauseating,
(lung-)threatening, (lung-)searing,
suffocating, stifling, overpowering,
dizzying, stinking, foul-smelling, acrid,
telltale, undesirable, hazardous, dangerous,
deadly, lethal, toxic, poisonous, choking,
invisible, odourless, hot, chemical,
gaseous

fun great, unadulterated, sheer,
good-natured, harmless, wholesome,
robust, boisterous, smashing, rollicking,
free-wheeling, uproarious, hilarious,
spectacular, brisk, endearing, (un)civilized,
timeless, buffoonish, silly, merciless,
irreverent, childish, light-hearted

function, functions overriding, prime,
central, crucial, vital, precise, definite,
(im)proper, (un)reliable, (ab)normal,
(un)stable, (il)legitimate, apparent,
specified, testable, measurable, exclusive,
occasional, adaptive, revisory, social,
legislative, bodily, sexual, reproductive,
ceremonial, ritual, physiological,
characteristic; asymptotic(al), cosine

functioning See *function*

fund, funds public, common, idle,
disposable, high-yield, joint, scanty,
meagre, untold, (un)limited, (in)sufficient,
additional, loose, (un)specified,
(in)adequate, illicit, (un)necessary,
revolving, consolidated, mutual, charitable,
humanitarian, memorial

fundamental, fundamentals See *basis*

funding See also *fund* full, substantial,
available, static, (un)stable, (in)sufficient,
(un)favourable, (un)limited, (in)adequate,

(un)predictable, (in)equitable, meagre, fickle, initial, partial, external

funeral, funerals haunting, impressive, splendid, magnificent, (un)remarkable, huge, dignified, stately, dramatic, peaceful, sombre, traumatic, painful, emotional, frenzied, affecting, (un)pompous, festive, costly, (in)expensive, tiresome, scrambling, passing, simple, military, state, official, public, private, mass, mock

fur, furs valuable, luxurious, rich, splendid, magnificent, fluid, soft, smooth, sleek, sensual, shapely, springy, curly, bristly, wiry, shaggy, thick, dense, coarse, patchy, fragile, glittering, lustrous, glossy, silky, dark-brown, grey(ish), charcoal, reddish-orange, blackish, silver-tipped, white-tipped, blotched, spotted, marsupial; fake, artificial, nylon, fun

furnace, furnaces glowing, seething, fiery, sooty, vertical, cylindrical, (forced) warm-air, air-blown, industrial, atomic, solar, coal-fired, coke-fired, oxygen-fired, oil-fired, open-hearth

furniture, furnishing, furnishings plush, luxurious, lavish, sumptuous, glamorous, first-rate, high-quality, astonishing, tasteful, attractive, elegant, imaginative, interesting, nice, clean-cut, delicate, (un)comfortable, stylish, snappy, ornate, unique, extraordinary, fabulous, soft, solid, dependable, durable, sturdy, (long-)lasting, top-of-the-line, (hand-)painted, hand-crafted, well-crafted, eclectic, heteroclite, easy, diagrammatic, adaptable, simple, plain, ascetic, (un)attractive, clinical, occasional, household, ample, cushiony, (velvet-)cushioned, metal-legged, bossy, plastic-veneer, custom-made, mass-produced, steam-bent, wrought, used, second-hand, dingy, rickety, derelict, shabby, clumsy, bulky, cumbrous, ugly, hideous, unglamorous, sparse, bombé, rustic, antique, classic, (neo-)traditional, (ultra)modern, modernist, contemporary, colonial, Empire-style, Sheraton, Georgian, Art Deco, Romanesque, sectional, bentwood, metal, wicker, rattan

fury See *rage*

future, futures shining, promising, rose-coloured, radiant, rosy, bright, cheerful, hopeful, desirable, glorious, auspicious, prosperous, positive, assured, secure, (un)stable, magnificent, rich, abundant, tremendous, long, foreseeable, calculable, precarious, troubled, clouded, cloudy, unsettling, uncertain, unknown, unwritten, indefinite, iffy, doubtful, scary, fearful, unpredictable, unrealizable, surprising, solvent, immediate, (not-too-)distant, long-term, bleak, dim, grim, murky, black, dismal, gloomy, forbidding, aimless; financial

gaiety, gaieties exhilarating, blissful, blithe, delightful, placid, exuberant, exalted, enjoyable, rapturous, cheerful, joyful, heedless, flippant, wild, unrestrained, unconstrained, impetuous, strenuous, excited, boisterous, irrepressible, untrammelled, unbridled, uncontrollable, rompish, spontaneous, unwonted, strained, forced, affected, idle, drunken, youthful, natural

gain, gains solid, steady, real, decisive, tangible, impressive, stupendous, considerable, siz(e)able, tremendous, enormous, hefty, (in)significant, huge, phenomenal, substantial, spectacular, remarkable, rich, massive, major, durable, new, further, additional, potential, supposed, sudden, long-term, short-term, (il)licit, sordid, fraudulent, ill-gotten, spotty, little, small, trifling, minor, modest, (un)limited, hard-won, capital, territorial, geopolitical, professional, personal, private, financial, monetary, material, artistic, numerical

galaxy, galaxies lumpy, spiral, elongated, turbulent, distant, unexplored

gale, gales See *wind*

gallery, galleries renowned, (long-)established, superb, elegant, spectacular, ambitious, outstanding, prestigious, artist-run, small-budget, private, privately-run, state-run, avant-garde, experimental, national, municipal, metropolitan, local; long

gamble, gambles tempting, daring, calculated, adventurous, fearless, bold, desperate, risky, dangerous, foolhardy, rash, reckless, heedless, foolish, deadly, big, intense

gambler, gamblers See also *gamble* casual, compulsive, incurable, driven, regular, keen, congenital, notorious, sharp, shrewd, wily, sly, crafty, unscrupulous, small-time, (un)lucky, hysterical, desperate

gambling addictive, compulsive, excessive, (im)moderate, (il)legal, (un)popular, (in)accessible, (un)controllable, (un)organized, state-run

game, games amusing, entertaining, diverting, exciting, absorbing, thrilling, challenging, (un)winnable, perfect, leisurely, boisterous, light-hearted, (un)popular, rudimentary, square, hard, cheerful, (dis)honest, one-sided, lopsided, intricate, elaborate, secular, ferocious, fair, crazy, pointless, stupid, tough, strenuous, knockabout, noisy, rip-roaring, rough, wild, violent, unequal, rattling, faddish, (il)legal, dramatic, goalless, imaginary, flipping, wicked, tight, perennial, endless, crucial, vital, decisive, touch-and-go, rough-and-tumble, gentlemanly, catty, ubiquitous, addictive, dangerous, sedate, deadly, innocuous, (un)safe, dusty, hot, sweaty, frantic, high-stakes, flawless, errorless, successive, impromptu, back-to-back, pick-up, play-off, championship, two-handed, four-handed, intercollegiate, interscholastic, indoor, outdoor, intramural, extramural, recreational, amateur, professional, national, universal, first-round, dicey, tactical, political, motivational, cat-and-mouse, electronic, athletic, Olympic, Pythian

gang, gangs howling, roving, powerful, rampageous, (ultra-)violent, rowdy, boisterous, raffish, vulgar, active, mindless, insidious, vengeful, rival, visible, Mafia(-style), teenage, youth, urban; old

gaol, gaols See *prison*

gap, gaps huge, immense, measurable, big, large, great, vast, wide, profound, deep, demonstrable, perceptible, visible, conspicuous, evident, apparent, glaring, yawning, forbidding, turbulent, fundamental, open, extreme, narrow, (un)bridgeable, impassable, mysterious, puzzling, awkward, serious, irrational, cold, cultural

garage, garages (in)secure, separate, single, double, triple, integral, attached, detached, enclosed, (un)heated, drive-in, underground, domestic, private, commercial

garb, garbs See *clothes*

garbage See *rubbish*

garden, gardens grand, spectacular, lavish, smiling, prolific, lush, verdant, overflowing, delightful, pretty, prim, neat, trim, weedless, graceful, elegant, handsome, attractive, beautiful, fascinating, glowing, wondrous, lovely, blissful, peaceful, serene, silent, hushed, secluded, solemn, bounteous, fragrant, magnificent, superb, splendid, pleasant, glorious, distinctive, idyllic, never-never, pest-free, low-maintenance, extensive, showy, spacious, rambling, sprawling, rolling, modest, year-round, shady, tree-shaded, weedy, shabby, sordid, unkempt, desolate, decrepit, sparse, barren, murky, muddy, overgrown, wild, private, public, formal, experimental, market, sculptured, sunken, back, front, rear, vegetable, fruit, rose, kitchen, roof(top), hanging, botanical, zoological, herb, organic, alpine, miniature, (cut-)flower, interior, indoor, hydroponic, undersea, pristine, Elysian, Edenic

gardener, gardeners avid, keen, obsessive, inexhaustible, indefatigable, tireless, champion, weekend, amateur, professional, market, organic, ornamental, topiary

gardening See *gardener*

garment, garments See *clothes*

garret, garrets See *room*

gas, gases billowing, noxious, noisome, poisonous, toxic, explosive, deadly, dangerous, lethal, harmful, suffocating, (eye-)stinging, scalding, searing, thin, rare, dense, (in)visible, sour, hot, soluble, elastic, buoyant, tasteless, colourless, odourless, liquefiable, (in)flammable, (in)combustible, natural, synthetic, inert, industrial, laughing, olefiant, radioactive, greenhouse, cosmic, interstellar, intestinal

gasoline See *petrol*

gate, gates yawning, imposing, massive, magnificent, light, heavy, narrow, wide, weathered, creaky, wooden, steel, (wrought-)iron, cast-iron, stone, lion-crowned, five-barred, back, inner, outer, front, head, main, central; Pearly

gathering, gatherings peaceful, (dis)orderly, intimate, distinguished, glittering, convivial, cheerful, wintry, cheerless, noisy, monstrous, huge, enormous, large, small, thin, spontaneous, scraggly, promiscuous, (in)formal, (non-)partisan, chummy, exclusive, sit-down, stand-up, indoor, outdoor,

(il)legal, traditional, ceremonial, family, tribal, clan

gaze, gazes piercing, penetrating, searching, exploring, teasing, unwinking, unwavering, steadfast, steady, fixed, stony, steely, dreamy, pensive, serene, innocent, direct, wide, intense, solemn, earnest, benign, guileless, shiny-eyed, sterile, dull, soulful, level, frozen, unhurried, inquisitive, curious, crystal, fawning, owlish, hawkish, feline

gazelle, gazelles slender(-horned), graceful, soulful, swift, agile, gentle, beautiful, light-brown

gem, gems See also *jewel* precious, valuable, priceless, imperishable, enduring, scratch-proof, imperial, spectacular, magnificent, remarkable, splendid, unusual, staggering, exceptional, rare, beautiful, high-grade, investment-quality, dazzling, sparkling, lustrous, translucent, clear, clean, opaque, (pear-)shaped, multi-faceted, many-faceted, (well-)polished, (un)set, uncut, rough, semi-precious, sal(e)able, low-grade, phon(e)y, snide, contraband, indigenous, exotic, industrial, synthetic

gene, genes working, (un)healthy, (ab)normal, malevolent, faulty, defective, regressive, missing, bacterial, viral, cancer-causing, human; selfish

general, generals tyrannical, dictatorial, arbitrary, (in)experienced, cagey, extraordinary, irate, former, cardboard, ci-devant, retired

generalization, generalizations sweeping, wholesale, amusing, entertaining, indiscriminate, meaningless, fatuous, faulty, rash

generation, generations rising, growing, succeeding, subsequent, new, unborn, future, sullen, (un)lucky, embittered, reckless, rootless, (non)committal, computer-(il)literate, lost, elder, younger

generosity overwhelming, magnificent, dramatic, proverbial, eager, unselfish, big-hearted, amazing, remarkable, wonderful, astounding, unusual, unworldly, lavish, unbounded, boundless, excessive, rich, inordinate, prodigal, unquenchable, uncontrollable, unregulated, unguarded, courteous, imprudent, thoughtless, irrational, unreasoning, rash, ridiculous, instant, impulsive

genius, geniuses (1: a person with exceptional ability) budding, erratic, maverick, veritable, true, universal, underpaid, poverty-stricken

genius (2: extraordinary intellectual power) penetrating, trenchant, perceptive, incomprehensible, precocious, overwhelming, sublime, vivid, versatile, many-sided, multiple, awesome, unparalleled, astounding, swaggering, fanciful, imaginative, creative, poetic, lyric, medical, mechanical

genre, genres unique, matchless, rare, exceptional, eccentric, bizarre, odd, uncommon, literary

gentleman, gentlemen perfect, finished, well-bred, affable, courteous, gallant, chivalrous, polite, true, fine, courtly, attentive, elegant, reverend, self-styled; gentleman's

gentleness charming, affectionate, warm, calm, timorous, humble, modest, indulgent, false, incongruous, manly, inviolable, inborn, natural, innate, inbred, habitual, instinctive

gentlewoman, gentlewomen See *lady*

germ, germs spreading, alarming, invasive, pernicious, infectious, nasty, deadly, lethal, latent, dormant

gesture, gestures charming, moving, impressive, chivalrous, courteous, heroic, generous, thoughtful, tactful, goodwill, consolatory, conciliatory, doting, friendly, responsive, efficient, (im)proper, (in)appropriate, (in)significant, magnificent, noble, gracious, magnanimous, grand, handsome, elaborate, extravagant, exuberant, expansive, unconfined, imaginative, (in)hospitable, (un)graceful, nimble, nippy, hearty, brisk, lively, fluent, (in)expressive, sullen, wordless, quiet, masterful, exquisite, last-minute, well-timed, timely, unprecedented, (un)expected, (long-)overdue, memorable, bold, apparent, stunning, darting, lightning, impulsive, jerky, hostile, violent, imperious, angry, bizarre, playful, puzzling, careless, insouciant, stiff, clumsy, awkward, ungainly, uncouth, effeminate, listless, imitative, characteristic, typical, unsteady, wild, frantic, frenzied, excited,

emphatic, determined, exaggerated, helpless, hopeless, useless, pointless, meaningless, ill-advised, unavailing, forceful, powerful, imperative, commanding, peremptory, authoritative, domineering, haughty, proud, dismissive, supplicating, inimical, obscene, deprecatory, aggressive, provocative, repetitive, nervous, goofy, harsh, curious, scornful, rude, derisive, disdainful, sardonic, wooden, cold, irregular, threatening, broad, sweeping, small, tiny, reflexive, token, opening, acrobatic, symbolic, dramatic, theatrical, histrionic, pantomimic, mimetic, mimic, fluid; populist, humanitarian, political

ghost, ghosts haunting, stirring, warning, sneering, solemn, sultry, hideous, horrible, unpleasant, restless, uneasy, crazy, pale, visible, famous, well-known, friendly, exorcizable

giant, giants alarming, towering, portly, tall, enormous, colossal, huge, ghostly, fearsome, awesome, absolute, destructive; reptilian

gift, gifts (1: talent) See *talent*

gift, gifts (2: present) useful, lovely, unique, enviable, princely, munificent, generous, open-handed, splendid, magnificent, fabulous, (un)reasonable, charming, captivating, practical, unusual, handsome, goodly, gracious, large, lavish, prestigious, enormous, special, (un)welcome, hearty, (un)acceptable, (in)appropriate, thoughtful(ly-chosen), fitting, enduring, living, random, tremendous, inestimable, priceless, pricey, ultimate, uncanny, fatal, niggardly, trifling, trivial, small, free, useless, anonymous, surprise, unexpected, unsolicited, prophetic, monetary, honorary, ceremonial, ritualistic, reciprocal, anniversary, betrothal

gipsy, gipsies See *gypsy*

giraffe, giraffes ambling, galloping, swift, wandering, meditative, huge, lanky, lordly, stately, gentle, mild-mannered, graceful, long-necked, knobby-horned, voiceless

girl, girls See also *woman* and Appendixes A and B charming, fascinating, enchanting, bewitching, luscious, attractive, beautiful, pretty, dainty, fresh-faced, blooming, well-formed, graceful, willowy, leggy, comely, amiable, presentable, winning, adorable, sweet, nice, gossamer, admirabie, respectable, chaste, virginal, virtuous, upright, energetic, bubbly, effervescent, vivacious, lively, vibrant, sprightly, high-spirited, winsome, well-mannered, desirable, proper, angelic, modest, demure, shy, coy, naïve, green, hom(e)y, country-bred, meticulous, obliging, unattractive, homely, plain, flirtatious, demented, brazen, flashy, impudent, abandoned, brash, go-go, forward, lusty, (un)sophisticated, boisterous, flighty, giggly, callow, inexperienced, untrained, giddy, obstinate, inflexible, impetuous, madcap, pert, forward, wayward, alluring, enticing, fair, limber, lanky, shilpit, little, puny, slim-waisted, sickly, slight, slender, plump, buxom, roly-poly, strapping, big, shapeless, sentimental, dreamy, visionary, romantic, tomboy(ish), bachelor, nubile, (un)marriageable, cover, minor, pubescent, adolescent, teenage(d); au pair

giver, givers, giving See *donor*

glacier, glaciers hanging, melting, smooth, stable, mighty, massive, immense, small, icy, stubborn, continental, tributary

glamour bewitching, captivating, charming, enchanting, fascinating, glittering, gleaming, dazzling, shining, luminous, lustrous, attractive, meretricious, spurious, superficial, social

glance, glances piercing, searching, passing, fleeting, running, withering, knowing, loving, sweeping, parting, longing, amorous, flirtatious, lustrous, bashful, tender, eager, wary, sharp, astute, shrewd, brief, hasty, rapid, quick, sudden, casual, cursory, perfunctory, serpentine, nervous, startled, fearful, scared, responsive, malignant, baleful, wistful, sultry, saucy, voluptuous, oblique, suspicious, mere, occasional, chilly, soulful, upward, forward, backward, outward, sideward, sidelong, sideways, superficial, angry, significant, straight, (un)steady, uneasy, surreptitious, furtive, secret, stealthy, stolen, covert, startled, moody, quizzical, interrogative, wordless, surly, murderous, coquettish, wishful, frantic, malicious, covetous, mischievous,

contemptuous, exploratory, deliberate, inevitable, unavoidable

gland, glands tiny, swollen, tubelike, soft, fleshy, (in)active, overactive, underactive, exocrine, endocrine, parathyroid, mammary, pineal, pituitary, salivary, parotid, prostate, uropygial, suprarenal (adrenal, renal), thyroid, ductless, sebaceous, metatarsal, genital, hypothalamic, temporal, eccrine, apocrine

glare (1: bright light) brilliant, lurid, gaudy, garish, flashy, steely, meretricious, tawdry, implacable, obstructive, blinding, pitiless, intolerable, unbearable, crystalline, intense

glare, glares (2: stare) See *stare*

glass (1: substance) brittle, fragile, ground, splintery, durable, heatproof, heat-resistant, tempered, multilayer, thick, green, flexible, clear, transparent, translucent, reflective, flawed, cut, spun, Venetian, volcanic, burning, lead (flint), safety (shatter-proof), flat, bulletproof, structural, optical, invisible, photosensitive, photochemical, one-way

glass, glasses (2: an article made of (1) radiant, stubby, rounded, stemmed, stemless, flute, tall, fragile, (cut-)crystal, lead-crystal, early, present-day

glasses (spectacles) strong, powerful, oversize(d), steel-rimmed, metal-rimmed, horn-rimmed, gold-rimmed, silver-rimmed, wire-rimmed, heavy-rimmed, black-rimmed, rimless, tortoiseshell, thick, fancy, designer, round, owlish, heavy, bitty, loose-lensed, clear, misty, grubby, dark, safety, bi-focal (divided), polarized, corrective, telescopic

glassware See *glass* (2)

glaze shiny, glossy, glasslike, metallic

gleam, gleams radiant, glamorous, liquid, bright, quicksilver, dim, faint, tiny, fixed, mischievous, wicked

glimmer, glimmers See *gleam*

glimpse, glimpses tantalizing, intriguing, interesting, fascinating, rare, insightful, intimate, unique, subtle, poignant, detailed, fleeting, momentary, fractional, fragmentary, faint, distant, first-time, final, occasional, superficial, evanescent

globe, globes golden, crystal, translucent, spherical, terrestrial, celestial

gloom stifling, chilling, disheartening,

surrounding, unremitting, impenetrable, unadulterated, deep, vast, weighty, murky, morbid, dyspeptic, depressive, ponderous, solemn, circumambient, claustrophobic, shuttered, unwonted, uncertain, Stygian

glory, glories everlasting, perpetual, priceless, winsome, inimitable, excessive, unimaginable, real, former, past

glove, gloves leather, plastic, suede, piqué, fur(-lined), kid, rubber, latex, pristine, liner, stiff, skin-tight, full-length, fingerless, well-worn, clumsy, discoloured, disposable, surgical, protective, back-up, velvet

glow, glows bewitching, dazzling, shining, lingering, persistent, immeasurable, luminous, candescent, lucid, bright, radiant, gentle, tender, faint, soft, rosy, ruddy, healthy, sunny, happy, golden, crimson, fitful, eerie, fresh, warm, deep, autumnal, nacreous

goal, goals worthwhile, (un)worthy, commendable, laudable, (in)appropriate, (ig)noble, admirable, straightforward, great, high, ambitious, valid, real, predominant, chief, main, primary, principal, fundamental, central, uppermost, important, positive, clear(-cut), precise, specific, obvious, tangible, definite, tremendous, immediate, final, ultimate, eventual, overriding, modest, common, critical, easy, difficult, alluring, (un)justifiable, short-term, long-term, short-range, long-range, lifelong, long-standing, quixotic, identifiable, measurable, achievable, (un)realistic, (un)reachable, (un)attainable, (un)approachable, (im)possible, (im)plausible, (un)reasonable, (un)acceptable, broad, shifting, hidden, invisible, elusive, fuzzy, clumsy, short-sighted, pointless, modest, humble, limited, single(-minded), drab, utilitarian, perverse, malicious, unspoken, (pre)determined, (un)met, avowed, implicit, explicit, professional, personal, strategic

goat, goats bleating, skipping, bouncing, prancing, wandering, voracious, omnivorous, milking, sharp-horned, sure-footed, glossy, jumpy, destructive, silly, unpredictable, wayward, elusive, capricious, wild, feral, domestic, gaunt,

mountain, long-eared, Cashmere, Angora

God all-powerful, almighty, omniscient, omnipotent, omnipresent, exalted, high, great, mighty, wise, absolute, sublime, alive, eternal, everlasting, immortal, ineffable, one, beneficent, merciful, compassionate, forgiving, clement, relenting, tremendous, benign, gracious, aware, subtle

god, gods living, protective, benevolent, discerning, awesome, mysterious, sylvan, false, capricious, wrathful, angry, avenging, menacing, cruel, (im)personal, tutelary, worldly, celestial, supernal, pagan, animist, Aztec

goddess, goddesses See *god*

gold gleaming, shining, sparkling, pure, filled, solid, true, real, genuine, fine, free, simple, graphic, impure, alluvial, molten, wrought, unalloyed, unadulterated, ductile, pale, Dutch, white, antique; fool's

golfer, golfers See *athlete*

good-bye See *farewell*

goodness absolute, complete, perfect, natural, innate, moral

goods select, (better-)quality, high-quality, attractive, outstanding, (un)satisfactory, essential, exotic, esoteric, sweated, (non-)perishable, (non-)edible, (non-)durable, (un)profitable, (un)sal(e)able, (un)available, marketable, merchantable, exportable, returnable, low-cost, scarce, precious, made-to-order, utilitarian, domestic, shoddy, faulty, bogus, phon(e)y, high-priced, expensive, pricey, low-quality, poor-to-medium-quality, run-of-the-mill, precarious, dangerous, hazardous, clandestine, bootleg, (il)legal, contraband, hot, (un)declared, unclaimed, hard-to-get, low-priced, worldly, taxable, dutiable, customable, bonded, duty-free, capital, soft, brown, white, dry, luxury, basic, dress, electronic, (non-)military

goose, geese gaggling, hissing, honking, yelping, waddling, strutting, noisy, silly, white-fronted, bar-headed, wild, domestic, migratory, blue, Canada

gossip, gossips fascinating, astounding, informed, harmless, juicy, merry, naughty, malicious, pernicious, catty, spiteful, raucous, insidious, vicious, evil, dirty, rotten, mean, petty, unseemly, prurient, incestuous, idle, trivial, lowly, muted, wild, salacious, constant, eternal, common, local, latest, underhand

governess, governesses esteemed, admirable, (un)trained, (in)competent, (in)judicious, conscientious, careful, careless, old-fashioned

government, governments honest, clean, (un)just, (in)efficient, (il)legitimate, strong, powerful, popular, open, fair, compassionate, conciliatory, good, (un)stable, unshak(e)able, viable, long-term, (un)representative, broad-based, (in)effective, moderate, (un)democratic, (ir)responsible, previous, present, incoming, outgoing, current, central, multiracial, non-partisan, pliant, ineffectual, slothful, inattentive, corrupt, fragile, weak, shaky, turbulent, powerless, moribund, arbitrary, absolute, monolithic, repressive, narrow, paternalistic, harsh, hard-line, authoritarian, totalitarian, despotic, dictatorial, iron-fisted, tyrannical, militaristic, fractious, tottering, crumbly, revolutionary, all-powerful, lawless, sleazy, white-minority, local, leftist, rightist, capitalist, socialist, communist, liberal, parliamentary, monarchial (monarchical), royal, coalition, three-party, three-man, shadow, civilian, military, de facto, incumbent, interim, provisional, caretaker, provincial, federal(ist), central, regional, territorial, majority, minority, secessionist, (un)constitutional

gown, gowns See also *dress* exquisite, sumptuous, lavish, stately, splendid, full-length, strapless, sleeveless, high-waisted, sterile, frilly, floor-length, floating, fluttery, traditional, formal, bridal, academic, surgical, hospital, legal, baptismal, christening, ceremonial

grace, graces charming, bewitching, elegant, serene, easy, refined, artless, pleasant, unstudied, mannered, natural, wonted, usual, habitual, customary, opulent, outward, extrinsic, inherent, intrinsic, inner, kingly, social

graciousness See *grace*

gradation, gradations imperceptible, slight, gradual, subtle

grain, grains ripe, smutty, thick-clustered, grass-like, high-yield, high-protein, low-fibre, rotten, whole, cereal

grammar, grammars perfect, (in)correct,

sloppy, wobbly, synchronic, diachronic, generative, descriptive, prescriptive (normative), case, transformational, systemic, phrase-structure, categorial

grandeur, grandeurs incomparable, matchless, eminent, august, dignified, distinguished, majestic, epic, down-at-heel, shabby, scenic

grandfather, grandmother See *grandparent*

grandparent, grandparents elderly, old, crusty, frail, (over-)doting, lonely, geriatric, maternal, paternal, adoptive

grant, grants generous, large, small, paltry, global, government, initiatory, one-time

grape, grapes See *fruit*

grasp easy, precise, firm, iron, tenacious; (in)adequate

grasping See *grasp*

grass, grasses fast-growing, straggling, luscious, lush, verdant, emerald, (lime-)green, abundant, thick, luxuriant, rank, hard(y), strong, drought-tolerant, firm-stemmed, crisp(y), yielding, shaggy, tantalizing, succulent, aromatic, fresh, fibrous, soft, delicate, tender, young, lank, scanty, sparse, threadbare, meagre, tall, long, short, harsh, rough, bamboo-like, reedy, wiry, spiky, flossy, lifeless, colourless, salty-coloured, brown, winter-worn, frosty, (un)cut, thirsty, siliceous, perennial, aquatic, plastic, synthetic, culmiferous

grassland, grasslands See *grass*

gratification, gratifications pleasurable, enjoyable, pleasant, rapturous, zestful, vicarious, instant, personal, sensual

gratitude deep, profound, profuse, effusive, tremendous, enormous, immense, infinite, imperishable, undying, enduring, eternal, sincere, heartfelt, warm, true, inexpressible, tangible, fulsome

grave, graves immaculate, well-kept, grandiose, impressive, decorated, silent, still, calm, undisturbed, nameless, (un)marked, unidentified, (un)identifiable, unlocated, unknown, hidden, clandestine, secret, shallow, fresh, simple, crude, unkempt, watery, lonely, double, multiple, collective, mass, communal, common

graveyard, graveyards See *grave*

gravy, gravies savoury, pleasant, lumpless,

fat, rich, greasy, lumpy, thick, thin, runny, dark, light

greed sobering, venomous, ferocious, larval, insatiable, insatiate, implacable, ruthless, outright, naked, measured, unbridled, vulgar, individual, mercantile, capitalist

green solid, bold, vibrant, vivid, lush, brilliant, bright, intense, deep, blackish, reddish, purplish, yellowish, bluish, greyish, clear, icy, teal, iridescent, bottle, dull, pale, sombre, vernal, emerald, pea, almond, olive, lime, lemon, lettuce, (spear)mint, apple, aqueous, sea, jade, tender, delicate, pastel, light, medium, dark, misty, luminous, luminescent, mottled, dappled, kelly, poison, hunter, jungle, forest, grass, silver(y), acidic, metallic, wrinkled, celadon, frond-like, lichen-like, dusty, pearl, bice, chrome, fawn, Paris, Sherwood

greeting, greetings pleasant, charming, affectionate, friendly, warm, cordial, intimate, sultry, sensual, enthusiastic, tumultuous, tactile, sugary, fawning, innocuous, stereotyped, traditional, (in)formal, (un)usual, customary, undemonstrative, subdued, lukewarm, frigid, cool, cold, chilly, frosty, icy, dry, wintry, belated, personal, Yuletide

grenade, grenades See *bomb*

grey rusty, smok(e)y, sooty, dark, charcoal, dusky, pasty, ash(en), silver(y), bluish, pinkish, dusty, murky, misty, light, dove, pearl, medium, dull, pale, slate, metallic, leaden, steel(y), iron, pewter, soft, graphite, purplish, brownish, pastel, shadow, eerie, mouse, pied, diaphanous, Oxford

grief, griefs distressing, agonizing, heart-rending, swelling, overwhelming, overpowering, sore, appalling, infinite, stony, frantic, poignant, violent, convulsive, deep, intense, brief, lasting, protracted, inconsolable, dumb, corrosive, passionate, severe, unbearable, bitter, excess(ive), immoderate, uncontrollable, boundless, massive, mighty, immense, frenzied, inarticulate, unmitigated, inexpressible, intimate, (in)sincere, counterfeit, fresh

grievance, grievances long-lasting, long-standing, lingering, genuine,

(il)legitimate, gratuitous, petty, trivial, nettlesome, political, ethnic, nationalist, personal

grin, grins See also *smile* ingratiating, engaging, dazzling, sparkling, sunny, cheery, gleeful, bright(-eyed), amiable, affable, pleasurable, friendly, complacent, contented, shy, toothy, toothless, sardonic, sarcastic, sneering, lopsided, leering, easy, broad, big, large, wide, tremendous, languid, languorous, feeble, faint, weary, wry, sheepish, tipsy, fatuous, stupid, idiotic, boyish, perky, ghoulish, cocky, elfin, wicked, mischievous, rakish, impish, naughty, sly, conspiratorial, infectious, whitish

grip, grips strong, firm, iron, inexorable, irreversible, tenacious, ferocious, relentless, steady, skilful, diligent, fastidious, exclusive, manly, massive, tremendous, wiry, clammy, slack, temporary, tentative, tender, tenuous, listless, limp, shaky, hooked, deadly

groan, groans inarticulate, hollow, harsh, distressful, heartbreaking, heart-rending, grievous, sorrowful, dolorous, mournful, agitated, frenzied, choked, stifled, muffled, anguished

ground, grounds sliding, sloping, (un)level, (un)even, rough, rugged, cracked, broken, naked, soft, (un)stable, (un)steady, solid, firm, (iron-)hard, moist, virgin, raw, bare, brown, maiden, silty, fertile, cultivable, marshy, swampy, sodden, soggy, spongy, watery, hummocky, rocky, stony, slow, sloppy, lumpy, hostile, miry, shaky, sacred, holy, (un)tried, broken, recreation, testing; familiar, common, middle, sure

grounds (1: the area around and belonging to a house or building) immaculate, tidy, manicured, well-kept, verdant, lovely, unkempt, extensive, surrounding, bucolic(al)

grounds (2: basis for belief, action, or argument) (in)sufficient, (un)reasonable, (un)justifiable, flimsy, logistical, humanitarian, moral

groundwork See *foundation*

group, groups harmonious, peaceable, amicable, moderate, (in)significant, exclusive, prestigious, outstanding, select, élite, (under)privileged, disadvantaged, deprived, influential, orderly, lively, active, legendary, independent, representative, diverse, miscellaneous, disparate, mixed, motley, eclectic, fervent, tenacious, rival, like-minded, interdependent, centrist, activist, diehard, militant, paramilitary, radical, armed, fascist, suppressive, belligerent, extremist, clandestine, subversive, underground, insurgent, rebellious, dissident, pugnacious, virulent, vocal, loud, siz(e)able, fast-growing, fledgling, distinct, distinctive, (un)identifiable, unknown, shadowy, sparse, tiny, narrow, sedentary, scraggly, fractious, unruly, unsavoury, loose, fundamentalist, individualistic, tight(-knit), close(ly)-knit, (un)sociable, (non-)partisan, mainline, (inter)national, sectional, political, conservative, minority, majority, (multi)cultural, (multi)racial, ethnic, native, indigenous, ethnolinguistic, polyglot, fringe, ad hoc, experimental, humanitarian, advisory, tribal, ecclesiastical, ecumenical, high-risk, self-help, peer, feminist, gender, performing, paramilitary, rebel, splinter, environmental, religious, church, umbrella, anti-nuclear, (ultra-)nationalist, ginger, satanic, investigative

grove, groves See *wood* (2)

growth, growths amazing, astonishing, astounding, dizzying, frenetic, meteoric, rapid, wanton, wild, unbridled, explosive, vigorous, robust, dynamic, phenomenal, mighty, exceptional, runaway, massive, substantial, solid, tremendous, prodigal, unceasing, ceaseless, non-stop, long-term, continual, sustained, sustainable, steady, enduring, consistent, indefinite, sedate, imperceptible, morbid, disproportionate, chaotic, unprecedented, negative, flagging, slow, anaemic, (in)complete, stagnant, (un)healthy, (im)moderate, potential, economic, industrial, spiritual, cancerous

grudge, grudges malicious, petty, cruel, bitter, ill-natured, lurking, sheer, covert, aforethought

grumbling chesty, inarticulate, indistinct, unnecessary, needless, fruitless, endless

guarantee, guarantees credible, reliable, solid, effective, positive, rigorous, airtight, ironclad, binding, (un)conditional, illusory, three-year, lifetime, constitutional, money-back, written, legal

guard, guards snarling, rifle-toting, hulking, hulky, burly, beefy, plumed, attentive, cautious, observant, open-eyed, wakeful, sleepless, wide-awake, vigilant, alert, merciful, strict, edgy, nervous, abusive, brutal, vicious, detestable, sadistic, remorseless, ruthless, merciless, heartless, pitiless, relentless, unrelenting, listless, paramilitary, (un)armed, personal; advance, rear; national

guardian, guardians protecting, watchful, attentive, faithful, conscientious, scrupulous, sagacious, venerable, effective, zealous, temporary, permanent, fiduciary, legal, in loco parentis

guer(r)illa, guer(r)illas fierce, bloody, nihilistic, dangerous, murderous, merciless, ruthless, heartless, pitiless, remorseless, relentless, unrelenting, desperate, reckless, bold, audacious, crazed, lethal, nationalist

guess, guesses shrewd, wild, right, wrong, (in)correct, mistaken, bad, good, (un)safe, cautious, round, random, blind, inspired, (un)reasonable, likely, tempting

guest, guests eminent, high-profile, favourite, sought-after, delightful, enjoyable, perfect, (un)welcome, gracious, unexpected, unwanted, intrusive, unbidden, long-winded, exacting, ill-mannered, boring, (ir)regular, (in)frequent, occasional, casual, transient, paying, overnight, surprise

guidance proper, sapient, wise, sage, shrewd, discerning, perspicacious, expert, intelligent, safe, fallacious, considerable, educational, vocational, professional, spiritual, moral, celestial

guide, guides (1: book) authoritative, informative, indispensable, essential, (well-)organized, impeccable, respectable, (un)reliable, (un)dependable, (in)accurate, (un)safe, handy, in-depth, detailed, comprehensive, compact, (well-)illustrated, standard, tear-out

guide, guides (2: person) (un)reliable, (un)trustworthy, (un)qualified, (in)experienced, (im)pudent, strident, self-styled, uniformed, official

guideline, guidelines basic, (un)realistic, (un)feasible, (im)practical, stringent, tough, ultra-safe, (un)safe, (un)clear, vague, complex, lax, well-defined, ill-defined, antiquated, established

guilt, guilts overwhelming, reprehensible, inappropriate, conscious, intense, residual, individual, communal, national

guitar, guitars See also *musical instrument* thrashing, acoustic, electric, bass, classical, flamenco

gun, guns stuttering, roaring, smoking, heavy, powerful, formidable, destructive, sophisticated, vintage, ready, ancient, obsolete, old-fashioned, cockeyed, light, minute, portable, self-propelled, single-barrelled, short-barrelled, long-barrelled, double-barrelled, twin-barrelled, four-barrelled, multibarrelled, clip-fed, belt-fed, high-velocity, swivel, (semi-)automatic, plastic, anti-aircraft, (sub-)machine, toy, tail, tranquillizer

gunfire, gunfires devastating, killing, unerring, unfailing, steady, destructive, murderous, deadly, bloody, brutal

gunman, gunmen desperate, bold, audacious, fierce, dangerous, bloody, lethal, murderous, reckless, crazed, ruthless, pitiless, heartless, remorseless, merciless, relentless, unrelenting

gymnast, gymnasts See *athlete*

gypsy, gypsies strolling, wandering, unsettled, scattered, transient

habit, habits inveterate, deep(-rooted), deep-seated, lifelong, permanent, (in)frequent, (ir)regular, (un)usual, (near-)normal, tenacious, obstinate, stubborn, rigid, unconquerable, incorrigible, irreclaimable, incurable, enticing, scrupulous, systematic, methodical, (un)steady, subconscious, powerful, studious, good, favourite, enjoyable, congenial, sensible, frugal, restrained, convivial, (in)temperate, ultra-temperate, beneficial, salutary, healthful, (un)healthy, (un)productive, (dis)organized, lavish, extravagant, luxurious, profligate, hopeless, permissive, moody, erratic, idle, empty, thoughtless, repulsive, maddening, abominable, uncouth, dangerous, lethal, deadly, injurious, self-destructive, filthy, addictive, unpalatable, unseemly, loathsome, expensive, shameful, vile, wasteful, bad, sloppy, frowzy, disgusting, hateful, detrimental, harmful, hurtful, pernicious, nasty, erotic, voluptuary, dissipated, splenetic, evil, vicious, dubious, destructive, repellent, ferocious, faulty, costly, annoying, undesirable, vagrant, dated, inexplicable, curious, extraordinary, singular, eccentric, eerie, odd, bizarre, ridiculous, insular, previous, dying, vanishing, primitive, pure, desultory, uncertain, unsettled, mimic, imitative, gregarious, sedentary, scholarly, dietary, work(ing), personal, cultural, social, sexual, mental

habitat, habitats (un)productive, (in)hospitable, (in)adequate, elegant, unique, rich, fine, vital, crucial, critical, prime, choice, (un)disturbed, unspoiled, diminishing, vanishing, poor, swampy, curious, natural, (sub)arctic, riverine, upland

hair blond (blonde), blondish, dark-blond, ash-blond, swarthy, (ruddy-)brown, reddish-brown, yellow-brown, golden-brown, light-brown, tawny, coppery, (jet-)black, salt-and-pepper, chestnut(-coloured), amber, ginger, raven, mous(e)y, auburn, brunette, rust-coloured, jet-black, deep-black, reddish(-golden), snowy, hoary, fair, russet, raven-black, titian, greyish, honey-gold, honey-coloured, flame-coloured, (snow-)white, silvery, silver-streaked, carroty, flaxen, sleek, platinum, gleaming, shining, lustrous, luminous, shiny, glossy, billowy, wavy, curly, crimpy, tufted, crisp, kinky, spiky, lank, frizzy (frizzly), fuzzy, slick, downy, shaggy, fluffy, slinky, stringy, unruly, fly-away, (un)manageable, hard-to-manage, recalcitrant, resilient, kittenish, rippling, streaming, flowing, flying, billowing, straggling, straggly, lovely, beautiful, attractive, healthy, feelable, thick, heavy, abundant, luxuriant, sumptuous, vigorous, thin, sparse, scrawny, wispy, soft, smooth, floppy, straight, loose, tumbling, receding, vertical, oily, cottony, woolly, silky, silken, crepe, waist-length, shoulder-length, sparse, coarse, sandy, reedy, rough, stiff, twisted, tangled, stubby, dry, brittle, wiry, bristly, crinkly, clustering, blowzy, messy, untidy, nondescript, tatty, scrubby, unkempt, bedraggled, unsightly, gypsyish, sprouting, ingrowing, superfluous, incised, facial, pubic, artificial

haircut, haircuts smart, fashionable, simple, short, plain, severe, close, strange, bizarre, wild, punk-style, square-edged, layered

hair-do, hair-dos bouffant, resplendent, massive, new, modish, trendy, high-style, elaborate, unique, favoured

hairstyle, hairstyles See *hair-do*

hall, halls glorious, palatial, sumptuous, grandiose, great, exquisite, huge, spacious, vast, wide, cavernous, wondrous, glittery, glittering, lofty, baroque, vaulted, tapestried, marble-floored, glass-walled, skylit, ornate, decorated, airy, solemn, hushed, gloomy, windowless, ill-lit, dusky, dark, clapboard, narrow, mazelike, dingy, central, main, monolithic, baronial, municipal, community, communal, parochial, ceremonial, festival, recreation, rehearsal

hallucination, hallucinations vivid, daft, silly, reckless, foolish, strange

hallway, hallways See *hall*

halo, haloes surrounding, glowing,

glittering, shining, gleaming, glorious, golden, angelic

halt, halts See *stop*

hand, hands (1: bodily organ) caring, loving, helping, caressing, healing, kindly, tender, open, gracious, facile, eager, immaculate, graceful, adroit, deft, dext(e)rous, nimble, airy, expansive, upstretched, widespread, soft, fine-skinned, dainty, delicate, ring-laden, hairy, horny, (rock-)hard, strong, powerful, muscular, commanding, large, enormous, huge, small, tiny, lank, slender, skinny, thin, limp, frail, firm, gnarled, chapped, chubby, broad, meaty, puffy, podgy, squabby, stumpy, (mauve-)veined, knotty, knobby, bony, long-boned, aged, leathery, stiff-fingered, long-fingered, white-knuckled, sun-dark, freckled, plump, quick, supple, limber, grimy, oily, sticky, clammy, dirty, smeary, filthy, clean, wet, dry, sweaty, greasy, blood-stained, white, violent, harsh, rude, pure, busy, bare, free, cold, heavy, clumsy, shaking, numb, frozen, idle, (un)steady, still, quiet, languid, languorous, restraining, tireless, untiring, sore, bloated, swollen, contorted, arthritic, rough, coarse, raw; iron

hand, hands (2: writing; style) See also *handwriting* free, shaky, rapturous, indolent, lazy, careless, (un)trained

hand, hands (3: worker) (un)trained, (in)experienced, mutinous, deck, green, old

handbag, handbags See *bag*

handicap, handicaps limiting, confining, unsettling, glaring, severe, immense, substantive, serious, considerable, gross, permanent, mild, slight, physical, mental, emotional, psychological, neurological, genetic, congenital

handicraft, handicrafts See *artefact*

handkerchief, handkerchiefs dainty, scented, floppy, cotton, linen, silk, lawn, lace, cambric

handle, handles ornate, smooth, rough, rusty, broken, loose, tapered

handling able, masterful, masterly, skilful, deft, careful, delicate, tactful, (in)sensitive, expeditious, cautious, special, (un)professional, (in)competent, inept, sloppy, tactless, shaky, clumsy, awkward, erratic

handshake, handshakes cordial, warm, genial, earnest, big, firm, steady, sturdy, strong, boneless, spineless, limp, dead, cool, brusque, peremptory, old-fashioned, (un)conventional, secret, masonic

handwriting, handwritings impeccable, graceful, beautiful, attractive, florid, plain, sharp, minute, cursive, fluid, bold, (in)conspicuous, crabbed, cramp(ed), fair, (un)even, (il)legible, (un)readable, (in)distinct, (in)decipherable, execrable, vexatious, spidery, awful, bad, shaky, shocking, appalling, rounded, angular, connected, interrupted, sloping, running, slanting, sprawling, scrawling, cursive, backhand(ed), italic, calligraphic, copperplate

happening, happenings See *event*

happiness unalloyed, exultant, buoyant, radiant, luminous, shining, perfect, consummate, supreme, unflagging, unclouded, ideal, deep, intense, eternal, everlasting, unending, endless, real, unutterable, unspeakable, ineffable, essential, tender, fragile, elusive, fleeting, short-lived, transient, unexpected, unlooked-for, delirious, domestic, conjugal, connubial, primordial, celestial, heavenly, divine

harassment maddening, annoying, exasperating, unremitting, increasing, unbearable, ruthless, relentless, mischievous, malicious, vicious, cruel, sexual

harbour, harbours charming, idyllic, picturesque, scenic, spectacular, quaint, (bluff-)sheltered, (well-)protected, colourful, lively, all-important, vital, limpid, still, calm, (un)safe, (in)hospitable, commodious, spacious, convenient, fine, crucial, narrow(-necked), deep-water, landlocked, ice-bound, secluded, tidal, natural, inner

hardship, hardships appalling, severe, serious, desperate, cruel, intractable, unbearable, incredible, unbelievable, unimaginable, inconceivable, unspeakable, undue, (un)endurable, beneficial, emotional, mental, physical, financial, economic

harm, harms overwhelming, (long-)lasting, immense, great, infinite, serious, irreparable, irremediable, irrevocable, inestimable, incalculable, unimaginable, wrongful, malicious, small, potential, bodily, physical, emotional

harmony, harmonies relaxing, enduring, (ever)lasting, permanent, uninterrupted, eternal, perfect, faultless, maximum, excellent, heavenly, blissful, unprecedented, relative, inner, inward, shaky, delusive, (inter)racial, ethnic, domestic

harshness unrelenting, unfeeling, jarring, forbidding, exacting, biting, annoying, cutting, unmitigated, savage, brutal, blunt, inappropriate, (un)necessary, crude, coarse, grim, merciless, relentless, ruthless, unkind

harvest, harvests plenteous, plentiful, good, abundant, copious, bountiful, bounteous, bumper, record, exceptional, rich, excessive, unlimited, generous, (un)ripe, (un)predictable, poor, small, scanty, bleak, bitter, disastrous

haste breathless, frantic, deadly, excessive, mad, vast, feverish, remarkable, undue, improper, blind, indecent, unseemly, indiscriminate, rash, tearing, devilish, terrible

hat, hats jaunty, smart, trim, dainty, pretty, attractive, distinctive, stunning, handsome, stylish, dashing, elegant, plutocratic, (in)appropriate, (im)proper, (un)suitable, spectacular, light, supple, slippery, veiled, rimless, brimless, stiff-brimmed, broad-brimmed, big-brimmed, wide-brimmed, wide, round, squarish, peaked, close-fitting, bell-shaped, turn-down, conical, cylindrical, crested, three-cornered, deep, big, ponderous, enormous, oversized, inconspicuous, narrow, pointed, handmade, brocaded, tasselled, floppy, fur-lined, ostrich-plumed, high-crowned, low-crowned, gold-laced, silver-laced, lacy, festive, transparent, summery, traditional, shady, straw, silk, felt, velvet, (rabbit-)fur, beaver, (patent-)leather, birch-bark, terry-cloth, sagging, crumpled, tawdry, garish, gaudy, shabby, pert, saucy, shapeless, funny, eccentric, weird, ridiculous, bizarre, (un)becoming, outmoded, atrocious, mouldy, sweaty, (sweat-)stained, creased, crushable, hard, (half-)cocked, tin, military, emblematic, ceremonial, tricorn(e), Florentine

hate, hates profound, deep(-seated), deep-rooted, unutterable, inveterate, black,

rabid, venal, fierce, rancorous, impatient, obsessive, visceral, bitter, poisonous, implacable, persistent, intense, powerful, pent-up, fiery, virulent, fervent, vehement, bizarre, fanatical, unalterable, unrestrained, unbridled, unqualified, inexpiable, unrelenting, relentless, merciless, ruthless, heartless, pitiless, unreasoning, inexplicable, stupid, blind, incredible, unbelievable, hidden, explicit, naked, pure, boiling, smouldering, abiding, enduring, undying, old, traditional, endemic, spasmodic, universal, personal, mutual, tribal, sectarian, ethnic, racial, religious, mortal

hatred, hatreds See *hate*

haunt, haunts See *resort*

haven, havens See *retreat* (2)

havoc See *destruction* and *confusion*

hawk, hawks flying, soaring, circling, swooping, flapping, majestic, bright-eyed, watchful, broad-winged, banded, ferruginous, sharp-shinned, red-tailed, red-shouldered, red-backed, rough-legged, predatory, tame

hay high-quality, musty, wet, dry, fresh-cut, new-mown, tawny-golden

hazard, hazards (un)common, real, heady, grave, serious, positive, nasty, perilous, deadly, possible, imaginary, temporary, constant, potential, threatening, diminishing, minor, occupational, environmental, toxic, chemical, physical, moral

haze, hazes See *mist*

head, heads level, balanced, cool, turgid, stuffy, sweating, aching, splitting, throbbing, roundish, long, high, erect, disproportionate, shaven, tonsured, balding, hairless, massive, bulbous, leonine, domed

headache, headaches (head-)splitting, distressing, piercing, blinding, throbbing, excruciating, stunning, thumping, severe, serious, troublesome, intense, violent, high-intensity, hurtful, painful, giant, awful, terrible, nasty, vicious, tremendous, big, considerable, extraordinary, mysterious, miserable, persistent, stubborn, intractable, chronic, recurrent, (in)frequent, sudden, periodic, occasional, slight, mild, benign, feigned, bilious, melancholic, post-traumatic, organic, vascular, allergic, frontal, hypertensive

heading, headings See *headline*

headline, headlines screaming, startling, sensational, catchy, bold, strident, large-type, dominant, splashy, pithy, breathless, wrong, misleading, disturbing, ominous, sardonic, sarcastic, front-page

headquarters sprawling, temporary, permanent, underground, regimental, administrative

headteacher, headteachers See also *teacher* legendary, charismatic, pugnacious, truculent, combative, belligerent, beleaguered

healing, healings See *cure*

health glowing, perfect, optimal, good, marvellous, remarkable, robust, vigorous, sturdy, unimpaired, rude, rugged, excessive, exuberant, radiant, tolerable, precarious, intemperate, weak, delicate, ill, low, feeble, fragile, frail, uncertain, fluctuating, failing, convalescent, physical, mental, psychological, spiritual, occupational, holistic, oral, personal

heap, heaps See *pile*

hearing (1: the power of perceiving sound) excellent, (in)substantial, (im)perfect, normal, functional, good, partial, poor, defective, rudimentary, restricted, restorable

hearing, hearings (2: opportunity to be heard) (un)fair, (un)sympathetic, exhaustive, painful, (un)scheduled, preliminary, public, disciplinary

heart, hearts loving, warm, benevolent, affectionate, generous, large, stout, brave, clean, pure, innocent, (un)merciful, joyful, sanguine, open, tolerable, compassionate, understanding, (in)sensitive, (un)feeling, (un)sympathetic, (un)casuistic, noble, free, unhateful, cheerful, gay, tender, gentle, grateful, overflowing, trusting, excitable, susceptible, light, contrite, flinty, callous, hard, obdurate, sore, simple, soft, well-disposed, impervious, immovable, still, emotionless, hostile, stony, cold, frozen, frigid, leaden, cruel, timid, timorous, rocky, slippery, profound, mute, sleeping; throbbing, thumping, sinking, burning, failing, faltering, ailing, sound, muscular, (un)healthy, (un)fit, (un)stressed, troubled, diseased, bloated, swollen, congestive,

shapeless, weak, poorish, tired, flaccid, (in)efficient, implantable, artificial, skippy, runaway; faint, black, heavy; social

heart attack, heart attacks minor, moderate, warning, ephemeral, major, big, severe, acute, desperate, new, old, impending, recurrent, first, second, debilitating, life-threatening, massive, full-blown, full-scale, catastrophic, (non-)fatal, anterior

heartbeat, heartbeats galloping, fast, slow, (ir)regular, fluttery, erratic, faint, thready

heartburn, heartburns annoying, painful, bothersome, uncomfortable, intense, chronic

heat scalding, scorching, blistering, blasting, sizzling, overpowering, excruciating, debilitating, blinding, cloying, flaming, burning, withering, suffocating, stifling, sweltering, staggering, soaring, searing, gruelling, stupefying, stunning, unremitting, prickly, torrid, sultry, killer, murderous, savage, brutal, ferocious, indolent, sullen, (un)reasonable, (in)tolerable, (in)sufferable, (un)bearable, unrelenting, relentless, ruthless, merciless, heartless, pitiless, oppressive, convulsive, fierce, vicious, diabolical, devilish, infernal, windy, steamy, soggy, horrid, terrible, terrific, awesome, awful, hard, dry, thick, tremendous, excessive, intense, taut, muggy, unusual, exceptional, record, extreme, fiery, violent, severe, incandescent, languid, (in)direct, (un)seasonal, mellow, moderate, gentle, sensible, low, medium, high, radiant, strawy, red, specific, steam, solar, equatorial, white, black, tropical; atomic, latent; prickly

heating (in)adequate, (im)proper, (in)sufficient, bad, central, electric, hot-air, warm-air, energy-saving, steam, radiant (panel), solar

heaven, heavens blissful, indulgent, unbounded, boundless, eternal, glorious, (un)merciful, blue, high, seventh

hedge, hedges quick, lush, dense, thick-set, low, high, three-foot, well-trimmed, (un)tidy, withered, quickset, ornamental

heel, heels quick, rough, clacking, spiky, stiletto, high, low, flat, wedge, Cuban

height dizzying, staggering, commanding, soaring, lofty, glorious, formidable, awesome, frightful, fearful, heady, dizzy, giddy, ethereal, enormous, unimaginable, excessive, perilous, (un)usual, (ab)normal, average, adjustable, physical; academic

heir, heirs (un)lawful, (il)legitimate, (un)worthy, true, rightful, apparent, presumptive, lineal, single, sole, missing

heirloom, heirlooms See *possessions* and *property*

helicopter, helicopters buzzing, screaming, circling, climbing, soaring, swaying, wavering, huge, nimble, jet, single-rotor, twin-rotor, military

hell raging, burning, scorching, flaming, fiery, unadulterated, veritable, eternal, living

helmet, helmets close(-fitting), heavy, hard, stone-proof, plastic, heavy-metal, steel, leather, horned, plumed, conic(al), protective, pith, cork, medi(a)eval, industrial, Greek, German, Roman, Viking

help steadfast, enormous, constant, generous, gratuitous, (in)valuable, priceless, tremendous, real, cheerful, enthusiastic, hearty, ungrudging, indispensable, vital, constructive, instrumental, special, timely, additional, immediate, positive, on-going, further, forthcoming, reluctant, seasonable, reciprocal, outside, professional, financial, voluntary, spiritual, divine, rehabilitative

helper, helpers (un)likely, (un)willing, ready, eager, reluctant, voluntary, (un)paid, domestic

helping, helpings See *serving*

helplessness See *inability*

hen, hens rustling, squawking, darting, scratching, broody, haughty, free-range, battery, bantam, game, Cornish, Leghorn

herb, herbs beneficent, mild, wild, tropical, perennial, dry, fresh, aromatic, exotic, pungent, delicious, savoury, tasty, (in)edible, brambly, baneful, poisonous, unnamed, assorted, medicinal, culinary, anodyne, antiphlogistic, antispasmodic, aperient, aphrodisiac, carminative, cathartic, demulcent, diaphoretic, diuretic, emetic, expectorant, h(a)emostatic, hypnotic, irritant, nervine, oxytoxic, stomachic, sudorific, tonic, vermifugal, vulnerary

herd, herds See *cattle*

herdsman, herdsmen wandering, roving, nomadic, (un)wary

heritage, heritages proud, worthy, sacred, rightful, abundant, rich, precious, priceless, magnificent, splendid, palpable, warlike, unique, distinctive, ambiguous, ambivalent, common, social, cultural, artistic, musical, architectural, national, racial, ethnic, aboriginal, native, militaristic, colonial, natural, genetic, biological, culinary

hermit, hermits dour, unsociable, determined, reclusive, solitary, complete

hero, heroes plucky, dauntless, undauntable, brave, chivalrous, glamorous, glowing, nifty, venerable, quintessential, genuine, real, authentic, unqualified, undisputed, popular, populist, sympathetic, charismatic, blooming, conquering, famous, larger-than-life, mighty, irrepressible, flawless, nameless, flesh-and-blood, rough-and-tumble, dubious, ineffectual, proven, putative, eponymous, fabled, fabulous, mythic(al), mythological, folk, legendary, military, (inter)national, tribal, fictional

heroine, heroines See *hero*

heroism See also *hero* sublime, selfless, remarkable, extraordinary, legendary, personal

hesitancy, hesitation vacillating, faltering, wavering, persistent, timid, diffident, frightened, half-hearted, spiritless, disagreeable, (ever-so-)slight, uncharacteristic, painful

hiding See *concealment*

hierarchy, hierarchies rigid, inflexible, age-old, traditional, social

highlight, highlights See *event*

highway, highways See also *road* modern, super, magnificent, major, principal, primary, spectacular, scenic, busy, well-travelled, strategic, two-tier, double-decker, all-weather, two-lane, four-lane, multi-lane, concrete, gravel, dirt-and-gravel, limited-access, impassable, dangerous, lonely, arterial, coastal

hike, hikes See *walk*

hiker, hikers See *walker*

hiking See *walk*

hill, hills sloping, rolling, plunging, clear-cut, silent, scenic, gentle, graceful, stupendous, voluptuous, viny, lush, green, verdant, fleury, flowering, flowered, flower-decked, vine-covered, heath-covered, (pine-)forested, fir-fringed, woody, wooded, timbered, grassy, volcanic, glacier-formed, sandy, rocky, chalky, spongy, coastal, bucolic, rustic, humpbacked, flat-topped, steep(-sided), deep-sided, low, spinal, curvaceous, convex, rounded, open, muddy, dusty, dust-shrouded, dirt, craggy, solemn, desolate, gaunt, bleak, grim, misty, dark, harsh, arid, bare, naked, barren, treeless, jagged, rugged, bumpy, arduous, precipitous, treacherous, slippery, sharp, thin, hidden, blind, windy, wind-worn, windswept, winter-clad, snowy, snow-free, ancient, perpetual, everlasting, eternal, dun-colour(ed), long, slight, nameless, (in)visible, yonder, sere, prim(a)eval

hint, hints tantalizing, tactful, subtle, astute, shrewd, latent, obvious, broad, plain, clear, helpful, (un)generous, insulting, foul, slanderous, cruel, sly, foxy, slight, slender, vague, veiled, proleptic

historian, historians erudite, learned, resourceful, copious, prolific, voluminous, robust, scholarly, judicious, sympathetic, talented, gifted, careful, accurate, pedantic, living, dead, eminent, celebrated, famous, noted, well-known, distinguished, foremost, leading, stand-up, peripatetic, hireling, professional, popular, academic, narrative

history, histories haunting, fascinating, intriguing, sprawling, regal, impressive, (in)glorious, unique, vivid, lively, idyllic, (un)authentic, complex, intricate, chequered, shrouded, turbulent, tumultuous, troubled, rocky, unstable, unsettled, traumatic, shameful, scandalous, painful, bloody, catastrophic, profane, lying, bogus, strange, obscure, incisive, intense, detailed, lengthy, voluminous, limited, scant, spare, unfolding, faceted, dry, obtuse, pictorial, photographic, written, spoken, oral, conventional, revisionist, meditative, biographical, anecdotal, narrative, natural, geological, geographic(al), academic, scholarly, saintly, religious, national, visual, early, ancient, ancestral, frontier, local

hitch, hitches (1: knot) half, rolling

hitch, hitches (2: difficulty) last-minute, technical, unexpected

hobby, hobbies satisfying, interesting, diverting, pleasing, (time-)absorbing, (time-)consuming, obsessive, favourite, enjoyable, profitable, pointless, peculiar, (un)common, (un)usual, particular, expensive, selected, hom(e)y, pet

hold, holds tenacious, stubborn, tough, tight, firm, strong, pernicious, tenuous, slight, fragile, uncertain, precarious

hole, holes gaping, huge, siz(e)able, deep, shallow, tiny, narrow, jagged, crumbly, circular, conical, messy, bottomless, precipitous, blind, black, hand-dug

holiday, holidays enjoyable, delightful, lovely, gay, (un)pleasant, (un)happy, (un)satisfactory, perfect, glamorous, sensational, safe, trouble-free, hassle-free, worry-free, (well-)deserved, welcome, pricey, low-cost, long, short, brief, spontaneous, tiring, enervating, disappointing, special, regular, movable, annual, once-in-a-lifetime, legal, national, statutory, religious, ceremonial; Roman

homage respectful, honourable, deferent(ial), proper, appropriate, due, meek, abject, obsequious

home, homes See also *house* comfortable, cosy, snug, well-ordered, well-kept, immaculate, spotless, neat, gracious, spacious, commodious, luxurious, posh, stately, impressive, dignified, palatial, respectable, tasteful, decent, opulent, lovely, inviting, magnificent, lavish, prestigious, affluent, prosperous, spectacular, aristocratic, handsome, ornate, romantic, energy-efficient, modern, fine, (un)affordable, stable, attentive, joyful, secure, loving, suburban, secluded, two-storey, baroque, permanent, temporary, brick, cinder-block, chalet-style, modest, frugal, poverty-stricken, (un)inhabitable, rundown, dismal, lonely, sedate, outlying, weekend, summer, group, mobile, ancestral, starter, second, matrimonial, single-family, historic, ante-bellum; convalescent; abusive, dysfunctional

homecoming, homecomings See *return*

homeland, homelands ancestral, hereditary, tribal, traditional, immemorial, independent, adoptive, adopted

homesickness tormenting, acute, hopeless, intense, oppressive

homicide, homicides See *killing*

homosexual, homosexuals secret, clandestine, closet(ed), open, self-declared, practising

honesty unquestioned, unimpeachable, unfailing, unparalleled, unchangeable, uncompromising, unflinching, unswerving, scrupulous, impregnable, trenchant, exceptional, singular, transparent, rigid, strict, harsh, ruthless, sheer, simple, blunt, complete, disarming, certifiable, patent

honey pure, clear, transparent, light-coloured, amber, dark, smooth, creamy, thick, crystalline, spicy, wild

honeymoon, honeymoons idyllic, peaceful, blissful, delightful, enjoyable, happy, Elysian, Edenic

honour, honours everlasting, spotless, stainless, immaculate, impeccable, bright, foremost, chief, top, high(est), signal, incredible, unbelievable, singular, exceptional, rare, special, overwhelming, welcome, dubious, tarnished, (un)deserved, national, personal, academic, scholastic, funerary, posthumous

hoof, hoofs (hooves) cloven, elongate(d), tapered

hooligan, hooligans See *gang*

hope, hopes never-failing, swelling, rising, towering, dangling, living, unfailing, pleasing, shining, shiny, cheerful, sanguine, optimistic, bright, (un)reasonable, genuine, serious, fond, heart-warm, earnest, fervent, fervid, feverish, widespread, expansive, high, boundless, limitless, golden, eternal, resurgent, constant, mature, wistful, tremulous, wild, quixotic, unreal, indifferent, fresh, unrepentant, unfounded, unrealistic, lingering, sinking, forlorn, vain, futile, thin, slim, slender, scant, faint, dim, vague, tenuous, desperate, blind, precarious, wan, fallacious, false, idle, slight, frail, small, sterile, misleading, deceptive, delusive, illusory, empty, abortive, uncharitable, short-lived, long-held, newborn, immediate, ultimate, last

hopefulness See *hope*

horizon, horizons enchanting, charming, captivating, fascinating, pleasing, far, visible, immense, wide, broad, (razor-)thin, empty, blank, high, unobstructed, monotonous, faraway, distant, crimson, colourless, shimmery, misty, hazy, dim; soil, calcic, salic; sensible, personal, celestial

horn, horns (1: a device that makes a loud sound) shrieking, blasting, bleating, sounding, screaming, deafening, skull-splitting, strident, contrapuntal, basset, French, English

horn, horns (2: a hard, pointed growth on the head of an animal) goring, flat, smooth, long, straight, spiral, lyre-shaped, twisted, curved, curving, mounted, stout, massive, stubby, extravagant, lethal

horror, horrors See also *fear* indescribable, unutterable, inconceivable, unimaginable, unspeakable, unbelievable, insupportable, unbearable, oppressive, unabridged, ghastly, relentless, helpless, absolute, supreme, persistent, pale, fastidious

horse, horses snuffling, dashing, prancing, galloping, running, vaulting, jaunting, stalking, flying, bounding, ambling, thrashing, pedigree, thoroughbred, blooded, easy-going, placid, amiable, docile, calm, tractable, (un)manageable, recalcitrant, fine, magnificent, mettlesome, (high-)spirited, lively, skittish, lithe, sleek, goodly, frisky, spunky, digitigrade, plump, muscular, strong, sturdy, powerful, exceptional, full-formed, fleet, big, well-fed, alert, trusty, (professionally-)trained, swift, tame, standard-bred, sulky, crotchety, eccentric, nervous, balky, spooky, cantankerous, hidebound, mangy, sorry, frail, contemptible, pitiful, headstrong, hard-mouthed, stubborn, obstinate, broken-down, stale, underbred, vicious, mean, bad-tempered, nasty, windbroken, decrepit, scrawny, scraggy, scruffy, worn-out, leggy, lean, flea-bitten, heady, wiry, restive, sway-backed, long-legged, rangy, razor-backed, shaggy, rugged, (un)broken, (un)bridled, (un)tied, (un)castrated, untrained, unruly, intractable, unapproachable, wild, riderless, roan, piebald, pinto, spotted, mottled, bay, pied, sorrel, dappled, chestnut, shiny, wheezy, gaited, runaway, fast, winning, losing, unraced, world-class, tournament-class, low-goal, dark, wheel, riding, working, walking, ceremonial, Shire, Arabian; Trojan (wooden)

hospital, hospitals modern, fine, prestigious, élite, (brand-)new, overwhelming, (over)crowded, rudimentary, sprawling, tertiary, 200-bed, non-profit, for-profit, state-run, private, local, general, regional, community, mobile, field, military, long-term, short-term, proprietary, government, mental, surgical, psychiatric, geriatric, pediatric, veterinary, teaching, training, convalescent, auxiliary, specialist, maternity, forensic

hospitality cordial, unostentatious, lavish, generous, effusive, extravagant, grand, legendary, memorable, unequalled, peerless, charming, warm(-hearted), selfless, characteristic, proverbial, traditional, natural, indiscriminate, reckless, promiscuous, easy, eager, cool, Homeric

host, hosts See also *hostess* engaging, consummate, genial, thoughtful, warm, friendly, pleasant, congenial, gracious, courteous, tactful, honey-tongued, tactless, thoughtless, (in)hospitable

hostage, hostages spirited, helpless, innocent, political

hostess, hostesses See also *host* attractive, fascinating, charming, graceful, pleasing, perfect, impressive, delightful, consummate, experienced, well-connected, prominent, loquacious, gracious, unflappable, calm, composed, imperturbable

hostility, hostilities open, frank, outright, overt, covert, veiled, growing, lurking, smouldering, long-standing, abiding, age-old, eternal, latent, active, visceral, implacable, pent-up, relentless, unrelenting, unyielding, combative, savage, senseless, mindless, inexplicable, deliberate, distasteful, slight, pacific, traditional, racial, ethnic, mutual

hotel, hotels luxurious, luxury, deluxe, superluxe, sumptuous, first-class, posh, exclusive, plush, rich, smart, palatial, top, swank(y), gorgeous, attractive, luscious, glittering, gleaming, stylish, fashionable, classy, magnificent, exquisite, world-class, glamorous, elegant, ritzy, fastidious, impeccable, fascinating, forbidding,

venerable, five-star, pricey, stately, gracious, distinguished, flamboyant, flashy, splashy, vintage, well-established, legendary, fabled, fabulous, historic, huge, grand, charming, quaint, comfortable, well-appointed, well-run, choice, grandmotherly, old-fashioned, friendly, intimate, spanking-new, once-grand, tiny, massive, high-rise, central, midtown, sugary, sprawling, rambling, cold, (im)personal, (in)expensive, budget-priced, cheap, second-class, second-rate, informal, modest, nondescript, unassuming, unpretentious, dingy, drab, dubious, dicey, run-down, seedy, shabby(-looking), sleazy, tatty, uncared-for, dirty, filthy, untidy, seamy, dilapidated, old, beat-up, dour, stuffy, smelly, (half-)empty, Gothic, Renaissance, chalet-style, rustic, residential, commercial (transient), tourist

hour, hours See also *hours* seasonable, inopportune, soft, idle, harassing, fleeting, fateful, empty, vacant, disengaged, endless, consecutive, dying, inordinate, meridian, scant, full, small, solid, twilight, eleventh, fatal, ill-spent, wasted, unearthly, unholy, witching, fine, rush, zero; sidereal, solar

hours waking, extended, sedentary, crucial, last, gruelling, glorious, long, frequent, (ir)regular, (un)acceptable, (in)flexible, school, office, sleeping, working, canonical, peak, off-peak, daylight, business, wee, pre-dawn

house, houses nice, modern-built, pretty, charming, quaint, dream, fine, immaculate, elegant, elaborate, tasteful, smart, lovely, fantastic, wonderful, exquisite, splend(o)rous, opulent, fabulous, luxurious, sumptuous, stately, palatial, majestic, patrician, palace-like, grand(iose), imposing, deluxe, respectable, outstanding, gorgeous, attractive, fancy, fashionable, comfortable, cosy, snug, well-appointed, pleasant, substantial, solid, sturdy, strong, ample, commodious, roomy, spacious, enormous, exciting, delightful, attractive, cute, quaint, trim, well-built, quality(-built), gracious, smashing, big, huge, great, large, substantial, expansive, neat, well-kept, well-tended, sheltered, splendid, superb, magnificent, remarkable, unique, attractive, exquisite, custom-built, (in)sanitary, (un)healthful, (un)healthy, central, (in)habitable, lodgeable, restorable, (ir)reparable, (in)adequate, staid, plain, boxy, kitschy, gingerbread, (un)pretentious, unassuming, modest, small, simple, desolate, dingy, dilapidated, run-down, decrepit, poverty-stricken, shoddy, shabby, dreary, mean, rough, untidy, humble, meagre, rude, unadorned, mangy, dismal, wretched, shaky, rickety, ugly, ramshackle, squalid, bleak, desolate, burnt-out, forlorn, tumbling, sagging, uninhabitable, low-cost, seedy, flimsy, primitive, extemporaneous, derelict, (time-)weathered, grey-weathered, dank, dark, draughty, crowded, remote, lone, adjacent, neighbouring, bare, (un)sheltered, uninhabited, contiguous, rambling, sprawling, ranch-style, high-peaked, stilted, low-slung, open-plan, square-bayed, bow-fronted, branch-roofed, slate-roof, flat-topped, low-roofed, tile-roofed, stone-roofed, (stone-)tiled, wooden, (half-)timbered, gabled, prefabricated, adobe, stone, red-brick, all-brick, (mud-)brick, wood-clad, square-timbered, (timber-)frame, wood-frame, stucco, wood-trim, well-timbered, log, lacy, (concrete-)floored, (un)furnished, (un)affordable, vacant, empty, untenanted, rent-free, (long-)paid-for, newly-built, hurricane-proof, fire-proof, fan-cooled, solar-heated, energy-efficient, haunted, duplex, multistorey, unattached, (semi-)detached, Colonial(-style), Georgian, Edwardian, contemporary, period, historic, rustic, ranch, split-level, tri-level, row (town), terraced, verandahed, porticoed, pillared, spooky, two-storeyed, sod, ancestral, country, dream; charnel, halfway, disorderly, bawdy, tap, public, religious; open

housekeeper, housekeepers clean, admirable, esteemed, immaculate, fastidious, spick-and-span, saving, frugal, old-fashioned, slack, sluttish, messy, (in)efficient, careful, careless, (in)competent, (ir)responsible, (un)trustworthy, (un)tidy, dishy, live-in, (non)resident, (un)paid

housewife, housewives See *wife*

housework See *work*

housing well-appointed, decent, (un)affordable, (in)adequate, (ir)regular,

durable, public, low-cost, low-income, low-rent, high-density, tumbledown, dilapidated, crumbling, (sub)standard, permanent, temporary, transitional, family, rental, mobile

hue, hues See *colour*

hug, hugs See *embrace*

human, humans fallible, errant, erring

humidity cloying, staggering, punishing, drizzly, oppressive, thick, high, low, soft, maximum, actual, relative, absolute

humiliation, humiliating wounding, degrading, abject, supreme, deep, frequent, ignominious, infamous, disgraceful, inglorious, shameful, uneasy, vulgar, terrible, public

humming tuneful, melodious, (in)harmonious, pleasant, soft, smooth, sonorous, sweet, untuneful, tuneless, loud, noisy, eerie, murmurous, apian, bee-like

humour literate, discursive, intellectual, vigorous, genial, true, lambent, subtle, rich, (un)pleasant, (un)refined, (un)civilized, subliminal, delightful, quaint, lively, perceptive, effervescent, hearty, robust, warm, unobtrusive, quiet, gentle, delicate, mellow, bright, shining, good, quixotic, sanguine, homespun, natural, offhand, easy-going, madcap, impulsive, broad, infectious, pervasive, irrepressible, irresistible, feisty, sportive, indulgent, zany, keen, racy, folksy, playful, witty, oblique, wisecracking, jittery, cynical, (un)forced, deadpan, loud, ribald, riotous, rowdy, bawdy, slapstick, whimsical, arch, second-hand, mordant, dry, earthy, voluptuous, gross, crude, acerbic, barnyard, offensive, grim, wry, spinous, sardonic, lascivious, tart, bitter, sick, tired, sharp, piquant, salty, ironic, sinister, callous, acid, biting, ill-natured, squalid, sordid, sly, impish, devilish, puckish, odd, weird, heavy-handed, clumsy, awkward, waggish, tongue-in-cheek, mischievous, wicked, roguish, self-directed, self-deprecating, self-effacing, quirky, low, black, raunchy, farcical, comic, witty, mock-serious, interlocutory

hump, humps projecting, prominent, grotesque, disfiguring, unsightly

hunger unrelenting, excruciating, biting, vexing, turbulent, insatiable, poignant, keen, sharp, rabid, ravenous, staunch, fierce, extreme, real, urgent, widespread, mountainous

hunter, hunters avid, fervent, clever, deft, competent, venturesome, daring, crafty, stout, hardy, rotund, expert, (il)legal, wandering, solitary, nomadic, aboriginal, recreational

hunting magnificent, splendid, excellent, intensive, intense, heavy, unrelenting, relentless, indiscriminate, wasteful, (un)controlled, unregulated, (il)legal, unethical

hurricane, hurricanes See *storm*

hurry tearing, breathless, frantic, mad, vast, remarkable, undue, improper, indecent, indiscriminate, desperate, rash, feverish, devilish, terrible, dreadful, excessive, deadly

hurt, hurts See *harm*

husband, husbands gallant, devoted, fine, good, perfect, ideal, model, quintessential, kind-hearted, loving, supportive, protective, dutiful, thoughtful, diligent, fitting, doting, beloved, (un)faithful, (dis)loyal, (in)attentive, (un)manageable, anxious, unassailable, selfish, uxorious, indomitable, errant, volatile, feckless, worthless, thriftless, nagging, jealous, chauvinistic, abusive, recalcitrant, violent, violence-prone, unsuspecting, inconsolable, prospective, former, common-law, long-distance

hush, hushes See *silence*

hut, huts trim, little, stray, primitive, rude, crude, modest, spartan, simple, lowly, humble, foul, squalid, dirty, filthy, fetid, miserable, wretched, gloomy, cramped, precarious, flimsy, dirt-floored, tumbledown, rickety, shaky, ramshackle, dilapidated, sordid, uncouth, weather-beaten, smok(e)y, ablaze, dome-shaped, domed, open-fronted, terraced, circular, straw, thatch(ed), thatch-roofed, palm-thatched, palm-fringed, bark-walled, prefabricated, plywood, wooden, grass, adobe(-walled), mud(-walled), tin, corrugated-metal, stilt-legged, (stove-)heated, beach, rural, movable, makeshift, Nissen, Quonset

hygiene (im)proper, rudimentary, basic, oral, dental, personal, mental

hymn, hymns stirring, captivating, edifying, uplifting, noble, charismatic, imaginative, graceful, lovely, soft, vigorous, select, glorious, zealous, moral, didactic, solemn, pious, sacred, spiritual, religious, devotional, blessed, divine, immortal, enthusiastic, melodious, memorable, (non-)metrical, popular, familiar, authentic, (un)orthodox, centonate, sectarian, partisan, fanatical, controversial, sacrilegious, sanctimonious, profane, obscene, uncouth, flimsy, graceless, contemptible, sensual, sentimental, spontaneous, resilient, short, manageable, memorizable, long, vernacular, (un)poetic, congregational, processional, doctrinal, celebratory, liturgical, mystical, ritualistic, redemptive, apostolic, primitive, old, ancient, modern, personal, private, public, national, (un)scriptural, (un)original, evangelical, dissenting, sacramental, latitudinarian, miscellaneous, occasional, morning, evening, Eucharistic, Christian

hypocrisy, hypocrisies sickening, nauseating, revolting, crude, blatant, arrant, obvious, meek, sweet, oleaginous, unctuous, malicious, self-righteous

hypocrite, hypocrites oily, bland, unctuous, pious, specious, shameless, contemptible, smooth-faced, smooth-tongued, sanctimonious

hysteria convulsive, fitful, maniac(al), neurotic, spasmodic, unrestrained, wild

ice thin, thick, rough, slushy, brash, solid, rigid, smooth, loose, crumbly, (half-)formed, sparkling, dazzling, crystal, clear, luminescent, implacable, permanent, severe, bitter, (un)safe, (im)passable, fickle, treacherous, slippery, deadly, silent, water, winter, surface, coastal, artificial, natural, black, dry, glacial, Arctic, Pleistocene

idea, ideas time-saving, resounding, stimulating, intriguing, animating, promising, winning, soothing, enterprising, appealing, captivating, fascinating, attractive, irresistible, splendid, magnificent, sensible, nice, unique, marketable, workable, foolproof, seminal, incisive, good, clear, vivid, graphic, right, perfect, practicable, innovative, newfangled, new, fresh, novel, original, unprecedented, creative, imaginative, prudent, vigorous, yeasty, resourceful, honourable, basic, simple, clear-cut, definite, golden, advanced, progressive, grand, lofty, exultant, noble, excellent, impressive, great, feasible, big, monumental, clever, brilliant, bright, constructive, fine, shrewd, sophisticated, sound, tremendous, provocative, worthwhile, prodigious, laudable, commendable, praiseworthy, tough-minded, youthful, (in)adequate, (un)wise, (in)distinct, (in)tangible, (im)practical, (un)realistic, (un)healthy, (un)tenable, aggressive, consistent, cheesy, bewildered, harmful, ruinous, erroneous, troublesome, preposterous, awful, hazy, misty, mistaken, wrong, dim, abstruse, (un)ambiguous, specious, murky, muddy, fuzzy, misleading, deceptive, vague, (in)distinct, musty, far-fetched, lousy, dumb, crank, outlandish, preposterous, outrageous, goofy, crackpot, wild, crazy, cockeyed, bizarre, eccentric, odd, offbeat, remote, ridiculous, scrappy, second-rate, harebrained (hairbrained), foolish, senseless, trite, vulgar, difficult, loopy, lopsided, hallucinatory, cranky, ghastly, monstrous, oppressive, foggy, repugnant, desultory, random, stale, antiquated, reactionary, outmoded, outdated, commonplace, stereotypical, false, nebulous, inchoate, incipient, slight, wicked, inconceivable, revolutionary, radical, heretical, contrary, liberal, superstitious, lax, unwarranted, modern, faint, broad, limited, tolerant, conflicting, connected, incipient, dominant, prim, strait-laced, prudish, puritanical, old-fashioned, (un)conventional, century-old, eons-old, common, futuristic, prevalent, prevailing, overriding, haunting, all-consuming, unchanging, immutable, unearthly, fantastic, fixed, innate, rough, mysterious, fanciful, quixotic, foreign, alien, distant, obsessional, bold, elusive, extreme, ethereal, favourite, ready-made, underlying, central, fundamental, pet, generic, abstract, romantic, perceptual, philosophic(al), theoretical, scientific

ideal, ideals ethereal, celestial, sacrosanct, utopian, fine, exquisite, bright, shining, high, noble, dignified, lofty, exalted, sublime, worthy, precious, worthwhile, wistful, exacting, impossible, false, existential, romantic, religious, political, collective

idealism See *ideal*

identification, identifications positive, (im)proper, easy, unconscious, difficult, conjectural, fake, visual, ethnic

identity, identities healthy, positive, true, primary, original, unmistakable, unalienable, distinctive, unique, fragile, vulnerable, eroded, separate, lasting, permanent, fixed, fictitious, secret, monolithic, dual, cultural, linguistic, individual, tribal, ethnic, national, racial, regional

ideology, ideologies good, (un)orthodox, (in)flexible, rigid, tired, failed, defunct, bad, dangerous, pernicious, conflicting, oppressive, totalitarian, objective, subjective

idiom, idioms elegant, precise, prepositional, verbal

idiot, idiots See *fool*

idleness weary, tedious, careless, aimless, barren, empty, fruitless, hollow, lethargic, unproductive, void, worthless

idler, idlers incorrigible, unchangeable,

unreformable, refractory,
good-for-nothing, worthless
idol, idols popular, instant, long-lost,
false, clay-footed, teen; pagan
ignorance abysmal, gross, immeasurable,
dense, utter, absolute, extreme,
catastrophic, crass, profound, intense,
impenetrable, unfathomable, monumental,
great, vast, widespread, pathetic, pitiful,
sad, woeful, distressing, lamentable,
shameful, unfortunate, sorrowful,
deplorable, blatant, plain, sheer,
pure, sublime, supreme, prodigious,
blissful
illiteracy distressing, appalling, deplorable,
lamentable, pathetic, pitiful, sorrowful,
woeful, unfortunate, widespread,
functional, cultural, historical,
geographic(al), gastronomical
illiterate, illiterates See *illiteracy*
illness, illnesses light, simple, minor,
slight, mild, (in)sufferable,
(un)manageable, sham, imaginary, feigned,
self-inflicted, sulky, clear-cut,
(un)specified, (un)predictable,
(un)treatable, (in)curable, (un)complicated,
grave, painful, sharp, dangerous, severe,
major, intractable, serious, deep-seated,
persistent, growing, progressive, terrible,
hopeless, desperate, widespread, fearful,
dire, hard, acute, critical, run-of-the-mill,
(un)common, strange, mysterious,
undetermined, unspecified, violent, lethal,
catastrophic, significant, unrelenting,
relentless, ruthless, heartless, pitiless,
merciless, insidious, incipient, constant,
recurrent, protracted, long-term, long-stay,
(near-)fatal, debilitating, devastating,
agonizing, mundane, rare, sedentary,
chronic, somatic, genetic, hereditary,
degenerative, contagious, infectious,
terminal, environmental, food-borne, viral,
muscular, physical, bodily, organic,
metabolic, mental, psychiatric,
manic-depressive, psychotic,
psychosomatic, spiritual, occupational,
recreational, aerial, diarrhoeal, iatrogenic,
respiratory
illusion, illusions astonishing, haunting,
compelling, smooth, stupendous, beautiful,
rosy, pure, blessed, strange, queer,
grotesque, daft, silly, foolish, idiotic,
reckless, unfortunate, dangerous,

momentary, past, magical, romantic,
optical, hormonal
illustration, illustrations sophisticated,
lavish, exuberant, profuse, copious, ample,
vivid, crisp, racy, superb, splendid,
magnificent, remarkable, whimsical,
decorative, variorum, graphic
image, images soothing, (un)flattering,
captivating, compelling, haunting,
overriding, touching, glowing, striking,
startling, dazzling, glittering, vivid,
vibrant, upbeat, enviable, elaborate,
larger-than-life, ethereal, glamorous,
brilliant, squeaky-clean, good,
(un)substantial, powerful, indelible,
prevalent, persistent, obsessive,
long-standing, impressive, wholesome,
meaningful, positive, unforgettable,
persuasive, too-good-to-be-true,
well-defined, (crystal-)sharp, clear, distinct,
singular, remarkable, magnificent,
splendid, dovish, glitzy, gaudy, vanishing,
fleeting, fading, sagging, lingering,
wavering, cracking, hazy, vague, obscure,
graven, exact, precise, stark, vaunted,
popular, touching, unmistakable, integrate,
old-fashioned, traditional, protean, reverse,
whimsical, tarnished, negative, gruesome,
nightmarish, sinister, insidious, deceptive,
treacherous, harrowing, appalling,
shocking, depressing, bleak, seamy, false,
weak, fragile, ephemeral, tired, time-worn,
tattered, battered, bad, unseemly, spitting,
ghostly, macabre, eerie, bland, shadowy,
stodgy, wavy, brusque, rusty, incongruous,
molten, mordant, emblematic, living, real,
romantic, mythic, symbolic, mental,
virtual, public, domestic, personal,
historical, abstract, graphic, (audio-)visual,
three-dimensional, physical, photographic,
holographic, auditory, eidetic, split
imagery, imageries See *image*
imagination, imaginations wandering,
roving, teeming, mobile, opulent, ebullient,
prolific, profuse, enormous, unrestricted,
remarkable, startling, fertile, fecund,
over-active, hyper-active, exuberant, vital,
vivid, lively, quick, pregnant, fruitful,
powerful, fervent, fervid, prodigious,
combustible, bold, frenetic, febrile,
fevered, restless, loose, clairvoyant,
roseate, intimate, incipient, cynical,
hard-bitten, open-eyed, classic, morbid,

turbid, confused, disordered,
(non-)mimetic, childish, erotic,
reproductive, productive (creative), passive,
sensuous, retrospective

imbalance, imbalances glaring, flagrant,
conspicuous, obvious, utter, severe,
overwhelming

imitation, imitations meticulous,
audacious, skilful, clever, (in)adequate,
(in)accurate, inept, passable, ignorant,
servile, slavish, pale, cheap, clumsy,
shoddy, worthless, unfair, humorous,
sprightly, obvious, blatant, avowed,
extempore

immaturity silly, naïve, obtrusive,
impertinent, offensive, selfish, babyish,
childish, boyish, infantile, juvenile, young,
youthful

immensity, immensities stunning,
staggering, overwhelming, huge, colossal,
vast, tremendous

immigrant, immigrants early, recent,
jobless, hard-bitten, desperate, destitute,
poverty-stricken, deportable, (il)legal,
undocumented, fake, phon(e)y, bogus,
sham, dubious, prospective, would-be,
potential, stateless, wealthy, privileged,
(un)skilled, first-generation, independent,
rural, entrepreneur(ial), landed

immigration large-scale, siz(e)able,
mass(ive), explosive, meagre, clandestine,
(il)legal, free, open, closed, strict,
(un)desirable

immodesty impudent, presumptuous, rude,
saucy, brazen, bold, shameless, arrogant,
contemptuous, haughty, insulting,
offensive, overbearing

immorality, immoralities corrupt,
depraved, dissolute, indecent, lewd,
licentious, loose, lustful, vile, wanton,
squalid, rampant, obvious, wilful, sensual,
sexual

immortality enduring, eternal,
imperishable, infinite, lasting, undying,
unfading, imperishable, permanent, brief,
vicarious

immunity, immunities natural, active,
passive, de facto, diplomatic

impact, impacts powerful, widespread,
far-reaching, lasting, proven, positive,
serious, growing, immediate, initial,
beneficial, profound, primary, major,
tremendous, enormous, massive,

significant, considerable, substantial, large,
big, full, timely, dramatic, direct, overall,
cumulative, ultimate, possible, discernible,
noticeable, negligible, slight, minimal,
trivial, marginal, incidental, negative,
crushing, deplorable, devastating,
disappointing, horrible, phon(e)y

impairment, impairments limiting,
glaring, unsettling, substantive, serious,
severe, immense, considerable, huge,
enduring, gross, permanent, mild, slight,
physical, genetic, congenital, neurological,
mental, psychological, visual

impartiality studious, diligent, thoughtful,
uncompromising, disinterested,
dispassionate, unimpassioned

impasse, impasses See *deadlock*

impatience long-standing, increasing,
growing, open, intense, vigorous, phrenetic
(frenetic), frantic, frenzied, sharp,
desperate, gruff, susurrant, rustling,
pugilistic(al)

impediment, impediments See *obstacle*

imperialism dilapidated, crumbly,
moribund, disreputable, brazen, aggressive,
fascist(ic), retrogressive, cynical, economic

impertinence See *rudeness*

implement, implements See *tool*

implication, implications intriguing,
solid, subtle, numerous, enormous,
far-reaching, wide(spread), broad, full,
profound, deeply-rooted, important,
significant, obvious, incredible,
unbelievable, grave, chilling, devastating,
alarming, unsettling, worrying, staggering,
ominous, disastrous, regrettable, scary,
negative, sinister, personal, social

impoliteness See *rudeness*

import, imports rising, soaring, siz(e)able,
robust, top-price, bargain, exclusive,
foreign

importance prime, premier, primary,
paramount, enormous, vital, crucial,
critical, great, cardinal, supreme,
sovereign, incalculable, immeasurable,
utmost, vast, overwhelming, greatest, high,
extraordinary, (e)special, undeniable,
urgent, enduring, lasting, infinite,
earth-shattering, transcendent, intrinsic,
marked, secondary, slight, marginal

impossibility, impossibilities monstrous,
huge, enormous, virtual, physical

impression, impressions enduring,

lasting, (long-)abiding, overwhelming, haunting, lurking, lingering, recurrent, ineffaceable, indelible, ineradicable, imperishable, permanent, profound, deep, immediate, unforgettable, dominant, strong, unmistakable, distinct, clear, vivid, lively, sharp, memorable, positive, widespread, pervasive, broad, tremendous, considerable, large, first, instantaneous, pleasing, satisfactory, subjective, unintentional, distorted, erroneous, mistaken, misguided, misleading, deceptive, wrong-headed, grotesque, negative, false, illusory, elusive, fleeting, passing, momentary, short-lived, feeble, (in)concise, (in)accurate, (un)favourable, antagonistic, abstract, artistic, visual, sensuous, sensory; obverse, reverse

imprint, imprints See *impression*

imprisonment, imprisonments unlawful, illegal, unconstitutional, false, wrongful, inhuman

improbability, improbabilities apparent, (im)plausible, (un)convincing, (un)believable, (in)credible, (un)likely, remote, gross, wild, strange, striking

improvement, improvements astonishing, amazing, surprising, stunning, considerable, huge, vast, (in)significant, substantial, immense, tremendous, phenomenal, major, drastic, extensive, unprecedented, unheard-of, genuine, dramatic, marked, tangible, distinct, definite, recognizable, obvious, noticeable, discernible, observable, (in)visible, conspicuous, measurable, sustained, steady, consistent, progressive, undoubted, unquestionable, certain, decided, unmistakable, constant, overdue, gradual, imperceptible, slight, marginal, modest, structural, functional, cosmetic, incremental

imprudence See *indiscretion*

impudence See *insolence*

impulse, impulses overwhelming, fiery, aggressive, hasty, giddy, heedless, reckless, vehement, violent, wild, powerful, inexhaustible, irresistible, resistless, fantastic, capricious, careless, rash, awful, sudden, momentary, wayward, ballistic, suicidal, single, inborn, instinctive, natural, specific, emotional, nationalist, creative, sexual

inability total, helpless, awkward, indefensible, pathetic, regretful, glaring, fretful, utter, flagrant, dizzying, congenial, (un)natural

inaccuracy, inaccuracies glaring, inadvertent, careless, sloppy, slipshod, apocryphal, deceptive, misleading

inactivity dull, indolent, lethargic, listless, lifeless, passive, slothful, sluggish, protracted, extended

incense, incenses soothing, sweet-smelling, aromatic, fragrant, musky

incentive, incentives alluring, enticing, inviting, inciting, stimulating, attractive, strong, powerful, tremendous, high, rich, vital, generous, hefty, positive, new, special, ultimate, fading, financial, monetary

incidence, incidences See *frequency*

incident, incidents interesting, amusing, memorable, remarkable, laughable, ludicrous, ridiculous, (un)pleasant, (un)fortunate, absurd, whimsical, bizarre, eerie, painful, horrific, shocking, frightening, gruesome, traumatic, explosive, fatal, ghastly, untoward, chilling, ugly, suspicious, banal, minor, major, average, sporadic, sequential, unrecorded, poetic

inclination, inclinations See *tendency*

incoherence raving, clumsy, enigmatic(al), illogical, inchoate, incongruous, irrational, vague, wild

income, incomes siz(e)able, substantial, considerable, large, handsome, appreciable, comfortable, respectable, snug, solid, ample, tidy, spectacular, unlimited, limitless, vital, perpetual, luxuriant, steady, secure, stable, assured, (ir)regular, (in)adequate, (in)sufficient, fair, increasing, fluctuating, additional, uncertain, median, moderate, stagnant, modest, tiny, exiguous, small, meagre, paltry, skimpy, slender, low, sluggish, precarious, tumbling, residual, excludable, discernible, visible, ostensible, discretionary, current, prospective, projected, unearned, fraudulent, independent, annual, total, gross, net, effective, taxable, pre-tax, after-tax, tax-free, disposable, portable, (un)spendable, real, pecuniary (monetary), rental, household, joint, personal, supplemental, alternative

incompetence breathtaking, glaring, mortifying, vexatious, blatant, obvious, gross, flaky, unbelievable, incredible, intolerable, unendurable, unbearable, unpardonable, manageable; mental

inconvenience appalling, mortifying, subtle, inappropriate, unwieldy, slight, minor, manageable, (un)bearable, (un)endurable, (in)tolerable, vexatious

increase, increases whopping, staggering, striking, alarming, astounding, startling, spectacular, tremendous, substantial, appreciable, (im)moderate, (un)reasonable, excessive, explosive, hefty, massive, siz(e)able, unstoppable, unprecedented, dramatic, sharp, worrisome, distressing, steep, (in)significant, perceptible, visible, noticeable, marked, apparent, gradual, steady, marginal, slight, little, paltry, potential, twofold, fourfold, hundred-fold, million-fold, incremental, overall, exponential

increment, increments substantial, tremendous, appreciable, hefty, siz(e)able, (in)significant, paltry, small, double, unearned, annual, merit, across-the-board

indebtedness See *obligation*

indecency mild, veiled, gross, brutal, bawdy, coarse, offensive, unbecoming, vulgar, uproarious, unsuitable, unseemly, smutty

independence complete, full, utter, outright, absolute, ultimate, fierce, stern, stubborn, unpurchasable, gritty, healthy, sturdy, refreshing, flamboyant, bloodless, growing, eventual, partial, nominal, intermittent, short-lived, brief, shaky, precarious, uncommitted, unconstrained, unencumbered, unrestricted, hard-won, (hard-)earned, long-thwarted, unilateral, financial, regional, spiritual

index, indexes comprehensive, massive, analytical, asyndetic; **(indices)** opsonic, orbital, refractive

indication, indications clear, significant, strong, substantial, growing, positive, favourable, early, scant, sketchy, implicit, tacit, underlying, outward

indictment, indictments damning, devastating, scathing, stinging, blistering, solid, severe, heavy-handed, (in)valid, insidious, bold, unthinkable, blanket, criminal

indifference utter, complete, extreme, benign, sublime, apparent, real, open, unequivocal, intrinsic, inherent, cool, cold, cruel, impassive, insensitive, phlegmatic, unfeeling, contemptuous, callous, strange, headstrong, persistent, pervasive, steely, balmy, studied, affected, wry; ethical

indigestion galloping, embittering, acute, chronic, difficult, persistent, recurrent

indignation See *anger*

indiscretion, indiscretions foolish, careless, ill-advised, audacious, imprudent, injudicious, rash, silly, heedless, thoughtless, innocent, minor, trifling, youthful

individual, individuals See *person*

individuality, individualities See *characteristics*

indolence See *laziness*

indulgence, indulgences excessive, luxurious, cheap; plenary, partial

industrialization intense, intensive, comprehensive, breathtaking, astounding, post-war

industry, industries (1: manufacturing; business) gigantic, huge, enormous, vast, prolific, mature, high-tech(nology), technology-intensive, viable, sustainable, (in)efficient, (un)healthy, full-fledged, independent, rewarding, lucrative, (un)profitable, robust, competitive, long-lived, (long-)established, unregulated, engrossing, thriving, seething, booming, swaggering, budding, fledgling, struggling, lagging, ailing, (long-)depressed, hard-pressed, embattled, battered, troubled, antiquated, stagnant, moribund, obsolete, obsolescent, outdated, dead, inefficient, precarious, uncertain, vulnerable, (near-)bankrupt, broken, low-tech, traditional, new, mid-size, unsung, seasonal, (un)safe, hazardous, dangerous, labour-intensive, indigenous, local, domestic, state-run, small, infant, minor, major, self-financing, private, cyclical, primary (extractive), secondary (fabricating), tertiary (distributive), ancillary, heavy, light, key, pivotal, basic, nuclear, manufacturing

industry (2: hard work; diligence) painstaking, persevering, hardworking, diligent, constant, energetic, lively, vigorous, voracious, zealous, indefatigable, steadfast, unremitting

inefficiency See *incompetence*

inequality, inequalities long-standing, gaping, glaring, flagrant, gross, terrible, unfair, disproportionate, dire, alleged, social, racial, economic, sexual

inertia monumental, massive, substantial, colossal, spineless

infancy puling, whimpering; relative

infant, infants See *baby*

infatuation, infatuations fiery, feverish, frenzied, frantic, helpless, delirious, crazy, insane, irrational, foolish, lunatic, evident, lifelong

infection, infections deadly, (near-)fatal, lethal, brawny, virulent, serious, acute, silent, persistent, inflammatory, painful, overwhelming, lingering, painless, mild, (un)controllable, uncontrolled, (un)avoidable, recurrent, long-term, lifelong, chronic, latent, dormant, opportunistic, systematic, mysterious, undetermined, bizarre, everyday, primary, symptomatic, subclinical, epidemic, contagious, viral, fungal, bacterial, respiratory, pulmonary, chlamydial, intestinal, pelvic, urinary, genital, gastrointestinal, water-borne

inference, inferences conjectural, deductive, denotative, (un)reasonable, (ir)rational, (il)logical

inferno, infernos See *hell*

infidelity, infidelities perfidious, blatant, insulting, obvious, vainglorious, suspected, repeated, unforgivable, marital, conjugal, sexual

infinitive, infinitives perfect, complementary, passive, split

inflammation, inflammations acute, severe, dreadful, painful, sore, (non-)bacterial, subcutaneous, laryngeal, rectal

inflation, inflations rising, soaring, galloping, staggering, roaring, raging, sizzling, growing, explosive, fast, high, uncontrollable, runaway, wild, serious, outrageous, ruinous, double-digit, full-tilt, unreal, rapacious, rampant, persistent, chronic, recent, global, world-wide, (im)moderate, low, subdued, slackening, hidden, zero

influence, influences restraining, tempering, unifying, beneficial, seminal, formative, productive, positive, salutary, (un)desirable, real, marked, enormous, immense, considerable, outsize, inordinate, decisive, absolute, substantial, ubiquitous, pervasive, strong, potent, powerful, heavy, unmeasured, undiminished, sustained, commanding, profound, vital, effectual, growing, prevailing, far-reaching, unescapable, inescapable, unmistakable, quiet, ineradicable, permanent, abiding, (long-)lasting, major, minor, exterior, extraordinary, undue, weak, tenuous, flimsy, minimal, marginal, trivial, zero, impulsive, disparate, insidious, baneful, shaky, pernicious, unsavoury, discordant, oppressive, discouraging, disheartening, lingering, worrisome, sordid, adverse, disruptive, malign, baleful, injurious, pestiferous, evil, degenerative, awesome, divisive, hostile, unhealthy, negative, noxious, deleterious, detrimental, inimical, subliminal, extraneous, interactive, subconscious, genetic, astral, astrological, mythical, natal, cultural, environmental, partisan, political

influx, influxes See *flow*

informant, informants taciturn, reticent, uncommunicative, reliable, silent, (un)paid

information (un)reliable, (in)accurate, right, (in)correct, (il)legal, (il)legitimate, (in)complete, (un)necessary, (ir)relevant, (in)adequate, (in)credible, (un)believable, meaty, solid, valuable, crucial, vital, critical, welcome, timely, useful, helpful, essential, first-hand, up-to-date, pertinent, (un)clear, definite, precise, specific, explicit, concrete, fascinating, intriguing, detailed, in-depth, full, straight, remarkable, (un)pleasant, startling, astounding, surprising, exclusive, privileged, gratuitous, additional, substantive, further, sketchy, cursory, sparse, meagre, minimal, out-of-the-way, special, increasing, (in)accessible, (un)available, mysterious, ambiguous, complicated, distorted, unbiased, false, wrong, faulty, discreditable, deceptive, damning, alarming, troubling, upsetting, misleading, conflicting, contradictory, innocuous, useless, second-hand, new(-found), elementary, slanderous, anecdotal, inside(r), advance, preliminary, background, intelligence, basic, factual, linear, logical, practical, sensitive, confidential, private, personal, quantitative, qualitative

infringement, infringements glowing, glaring, raging, burning, gross, infamous, odious, scandalous, atrocious, vicious, wanton, wicked, blatant, flagrant, calculated

ingenuity See *skill*

ingratitude coarse, crude, gross, rank, base, incalculable, gruff, insolent, distasteful, black

ingredient, ingredients basic, fundamental, essential, prime, key, staple, crucial, principal, central, primary, requisite, (un)important, (un)necessary, (in)effective, vital, (in)active, dynamic, (un)common, (in)distinctive, best, secret, exclusive, favourite, mysterious, exotic, robust, good-quality, fine, proper, safe, healthy, wholesome, beneficial, natural, (garden-)fresh, seasonal, lusty, mouthwatering, missing, optional, supplementary, additional, substituted, artificial, obtainable, (un)available, deleterious

inhabitant, inhabitants original, native, first, aboriginal, indigenous, long-time, first-known, permanent, mixed-blood, oldest

inheritance, inheritances fabulous, fine, rich, worthy, worthless, small, rightful, legal, private, collective; biological

inheritor, inheritors See *heir*

initiative, initiatives worthy, imaginative, generous, bold, unimpeded, fresh, well-intentioned, first, quixotic, dramatic, diplomatic, private, individual

injection, injections (un)warranted, fatal, lethal, blast, solid (direct), intravenous, hypodermic

injury, injuries slight, minor, subtle, involuntary, wanton, (un)justifiable, serious, severe, major, extensive, massive, acute, terrible, horrendous, permanent, grievous, unnecessary, (un)avoidable, (in)evitable, devastating, excruciating, undetermined, untreated, detectable, local, multiple, traumatic, life-threatening, career-threatening, accidental, athletic, bodily, internal, personal, musculoskeletal, whiplash

injustice, injustices grave, crying, hideous, cruel, brutal, gross, glaring, blatant, flagrant, considerable, out-and-out, complete, outright, unqualified, utter, deliberate, continual, rank [used pejoratively], social, racial

ink, inks indelible, ineffaceable, permanent, washable, invisible (sympathetic), wet, dry, metallic, Indian

inn, inns See also *hotel* flavourful, exquisite, rowdy, favourite, old-style, wayside, rural

innocence amiable, simple, pristine, pure, unstained, uncorrupted, wide-eyed, child-like, boyish, naïve, fearless, honest, bland, good-humoured, unsuspecting, guileless, disarming, total, evident, stupid, idiotic

innovation, innovations startling, daring, challenging, striking, tempting, remarkable, unheard-of, unlimited, wild, significant, (ad)venturous, venturesome, audacious, bold, fearless, cautious, ingenious, imaginative, creative, high-tech, technical, technological

innuendo, innuendoes subtle, astute, shrewd, sly, foxy, crafty, snide

inquiry, inquiries careful, (in)discreet, (in)adequate, exhaustive, thorough, extensive, full(-scale), wide-ranging, broad-based, in-depth, tough, keen, impending, immediate, inevitable, messy, suspicious, curious, prying, unquenchable, controversial, unscientific, inconclusive, independent, internal, free, initial, preliminary, (in)formal, (un)constitutional, judicial, scholarly, scientific, public

insanity See *madness*

insect, insects buzzing, chirping, crawling, prowling, skulking, flying, swarming, biting, annoying, tormenting, stinging, beneficial, helpful, harmless, shiny, glossy, tiny, (sheath-)winged, two-winged, wingless, crepuscular, flat-bodied, stout-bodied, leaf-shaped, disjunct, skittish, lithe, nimble, restless, sluggish, airborne, predatory, ravenous, rapacious, voracious, carnivorous, pernicious, dangerous, poisonous, venomous, lethal, deadly, destructive, mean, vicious, bad, harmful, detrimental, infective, importunate, bothersome, unpleasant, indomitable, hostile, pesky, pestiferous, parasitic, pesticide-resistant, bloodsucking, infamous, angry, widespread, migratory, larval, dealate, aquatic, diurnal, nocturnal, hemipterous, heteropterous, homopterous, dipterous, brachypterous, neuropterous, hymenopterous, coleopterous

insight, insights sharp, shrewd, keen, profound, deep, astounding, remarkable, valuable, unusual, unique, rare, acute, (non)predictive, imaginative, preternatural, revealing, tantalizing, intriguing, refreshing, dispiriting, rueful, personal, psychological

insignificance trifling, trivial, puny, petty, relative, contemptible, flimsy, inconsequential, lightweight

insincerity, insincerities nauseating, disgusting, revolting, sickening, repugnant, venal, mercenary, deceptive, deceitful, false, specious, double-faced, two-faced

insinuation, insinuations See *hint*

insistence compelling, demanding, persevering, pressing, urging, unwavering, passionate, scrupulous, (in)sincere, subtle, bold, dogged, vehement, determined, rigid, steely, emphatic, persistent, stubborn, fanatical, gnat-like, piteous, angry, irksome, irritable, stolid, endless, perverse, disingenuous, arrogant, duplicitous

insolence unblushing, barefaced, presumptuous, uncivil, supercilious, intolerable, unbearable, insufferable, brazen(-faced), shameless, callous, audacious, severe, heartless, thoughtless, crude, outrageous, arrant, audacious, brash, bumptious, contemptuous, offensive, oblique, downright

insomnia gross, chronic, transient, occasional, imaginary, stark

inspection, inspections close, thorough, rigorous, tough, stringent, careful, (in)frequent, (ir)regular, routine, cursory, perfunctory, shoddy, secondary, double, quality, statutory, on-site

inspiration, inspirations quick, sudden, spiritual, prophetic, divine, superhuman, supernatural, ephemeral, artistic

instability, instabilities wavering, fluctuating, quavering, reeling, rocking, shivering, shuddering, swaying, swinging, tottering, disastrous, adverse, untoward, wobbly, quaking, shaky, loose, perilous,

risky, timorous, tremulous, inherent, long-term, global, atmospheric, political, nervous, emotional

instance, instances solitary, rare, unique, singular, exceptional, striking, fresh, normal, capital

instant, instants See *moment*

instinct, instincts unerring, unfailing, sound, perceptive, astute, profound, deep-seated, strong, basic, primal, primitive, blind, vagrant, elemental, natural, spiritual, fighting, sexual, maternal, parental, filial, gregarious, self-protecting, protective, migratory, entrepreneurial, political

institute, institutes See *college* and *school*

institution, institutions (1: established practice or social custom) valuable, valid, venerable, hallowed, prized, élite, enduring, prevailing, living, well-established, dynamic, unique, powerful, mysterious, human

institution, institutions (2: organized society) big, strong, powerful, large, well-established, self-supporting, troubled, weak, failing, shaky, social, charitable, benevolent, financial

instruction (teaching; education) See also *teaching* (1) and *education* congenial, intensive, (in)adequate, minimal, supplementary, interlocutory, cursory, religious

instructions (directions; orders) definite, positive, firm, (in)sufficient, (un)clear, (in)appropriate, simple, explicit, unequivocal, (im)precise, meticulous, detailed, lengthy, thorough, minute, particular, general, comprehensive, strong, forceful, last-minute, customized, step-by-step, top-level

instructor, instructors See *teacher*

instrument, instruments sophisticated, time-honoured, indispensable, fine, sterile, delicate, sensitive, (in)accurate, (in)adequate, (in)effective, (im)potent, all-purpose, disposable, sharp-edged, unusual, offbeat, exotic, pliable, complex, unwieldy, crude, blunt, faulty, musical, exact, scientific, technical, optical, obstetric, negotiable, surgical; historical

insulation rigid, blanket, reflective, electrical, thermal

insult, insults humiliating, exasperating,

galling, grievous, wanton, serious, cruel, insolent, malicious, merciless, heartless, pitiless, ruthless, relentless, unrelenting, inclement, rank, shameful, intolerable, brutal, coarse, gross, ultimate, signal, shocking, terrible, petty, off-colour, heedless, gratuitous, unjustifiable, unwarranted, uncalled-for, direct, studied, inadvertent, unwitting, unconscious, unreal, tremendous, exquisite, deliberate, (un)intentional, (un)intended, calculated, premeditated, supposed, imaginary, open, personal

insurance, insurances (in)adequate, (in)expensive, (un)obtainable, (un)available, (un)affordable, (in)valid, mandatory, optional, extra, blanket, comprehensive, fraternal, private, social, industrial, medical, mutual, marine, dental, legal

insurgent, insurgents See *rebel*

insurrection, insurrections See *rebellion*

integration, integrations unifying, uniting, close, one-way, political, economic, cultural, linguistic

integrity immaculate, impeccable, flawless, spotless, stainless, unsullied, unblemished, intact, scrupulous, incorruptible, unparalleled, indomitable, (un)questionable, high, human, personal, territorial, professional, artistic, scientific

intellect, intellects See *mind*

intellectual, intellectuals studious, gullible, highbrow, working-class

intelligence, intelligences sharp, keen, alert, sensitive, remarkable, amazing, high, superior, uncanny, full-level, precocious, flinty, normal, (above-)average, moderate, limited, subnormal, untutored, intuitive, innate, inborn; artificial

intemperance excessive, extravagant, extreme, inordinate, violent, wild, dissipated, sodden, unredeemed

intensity, intensities blistering, boiling, burning, bulging, breathtaking, consuming, fulminating, exciting, seething, swelling, ardent, extreme, immoderate, high, palpable, low, subdued

intent, intents grand, laudable, good, pacific, peaceable, peaceful, loving, (dis)honourable, (ig)noble, messianic, sincere, fervent, serious, earnest, firm, avowed, deliberate, obvious, (un)clear, outrageous, provocative, hostile, guilty, felonious, satanic, bad, deadly, perfidious, treacherous, deceitful, evil, malign, devious, suspicious, plunderous, hidden, underlying

intention, intentions See *intent*

interaction, interactions harmonious, conciliatory, cordial, affable, agreeable, friendly, intense, sociable, social, face-to-face

intercourse (1: communication) See *communication*

intercourse (2: sexual relations) See *sex* (2)

interest, interests (1: desire; well-being) fascinated, consuming, absorbing, overriding, overwhelming, all-pervasive, profound, deep, keen, intense, intensive, excessive, frantic, active, strong, colossal, tremendous, prodigious, close, substantive, great, considerable, ardent, (dis)passionate, true, real, genuine, legitimate, vital, tireless, honest, intrinsic, warm, sincere, enthusiastic, avid, fresh, rising, growing, extraordinary, long-term, perennial, permanent, eternal, abiding, enduring, unfailing, unflagging, unceasing, long-standing, ever-living, lifelong, spirited, insatiable, poignant, lively, alert, warm, sympathetic, wide(-ranging), broad, general, common, particular, special, mutual, convergent, wide-ranging, varied, multiple, diversified, diverse, multifarious, manifold, eclectic, catholic, incidental, tangential, singular, shrewd, spasmodic, pragmatic, worldly, latent, sectional, peculiar, potential, adventitious, primary, possessory, understandable, cautious, (un)selfish, mercenary, pungent, conflicting, incongruous, sensational, outside, passing, temporary, short-lived, ephemeral, peripheral, momentary, shifting, resurgent, faddish, passive, shallow, trivial, withering, waning, fading, relaxing, surface, mild, faint, languid, little, minimal, negligible, moderate, tepid, half-hearted, marginal, narrow, lukewarm, unexpected, unabated, beneficial, financial, intellectual; mutual, public

interest, interests (2: sum paid for the use of money) substantial, high, hefty, inflated, extortionate, punitive, simple, compound, usurious, tax-exempt

interference, interferences well-intentioned, officious, brazen, rash, injudicious, excessive, serious, unveiled, unprecedented, unexpected, aggressive, intolerable, unbearable, undesirable, unwarranted, unintentional, inadvertent, foreign, atmospheric

interpretation, interpretations penetrating, (in)accurate, innovative, original, (un)reasonable, double, multiple, broad, various, captious, long-standing, traditional, conventional, standard, (un)orthodox, modified, narrow, loose, rigid, (in)flexible, blunt, daring, (un)common, (un)usual, violent, distorted, arbitrary, capricious, uncertain, erroneous, contradictory, reassuring, oral, private, literal, alternative

interrogation, interrogations (in)tense, heated, incessant, constant, protracted, marathon, rigorous, mean-spirited, inclement, unrelenting, relentless, heartless, remorseless, merciless, ruthless, fruitless

interruption, interruptions continual, annoying, aggravating, vexing, exasperating, irksome, constant, incessant, brief, casual, abrupt, murmurous, unwelcome, distasteful, unacceptable, unwanted, insensitive

interval, intervals stated, specified, fixed, lucid, periodic, (ir)regular, random, unpredictable, rare; geologic(al)

intervention, interventions fruitful, benignant, timely, concerted, (in)appropriate, (un)acceptable, fruitless, incongruous, unfortunate, ill-timed, heavy(-handed), unprecedented, forceful, covert, naked, surprise, sudden, unexpected, outside, imperial, minimum, maximum

interview, interviews edifying, penetrating, revealing, entertaining, wide-ranging, tantalizing, fascinating, interesting, frank, (un)friendly, (in)effective, intensive, exhaustive, in-depth, detailed, substantive, extended, long, audacious, face-to-face, unprecedented, rare, memorable, (in)formal, (un)usual, banal, unpropitious, chilly, rambling, excursive, digressive, difficult, gruelling, hubris-laden, high-handed, clandestine, on(off)-the-record, live, radio, television, on-screen, sit-down, personal, door-to-door, two-part, back-to-back, background

interviewer, interviewers seasoned, (in)experienced, inquisitorial, intrusive, pugnacious, aggressive, reverential, deferential

intimacy, intimacies transcendent, amiable, congenial, friendly, amicable, cordial, genial, sharp, uneasy, increasing, enduring, lasting, forbidden, illicit, primal, emotional, verbal, physical, sexual, social

intolerance fanatic(al), unreasonable, visionary, ethnic

intoxicant, intoxicants See *liquor*

intrigue, intrigues See *plot* (1)

introduction, introductions glowing, flattering, graceful, vibrant, vivid, brilliant, enthusiastic, impassioned, lively, radiant, terse, precise, prolix, formal

intrusion, intrusions annoying, aggravating, vexing, exasperating, irksome, brash, impertinent, impudent, insolent, rude, unwelcome, unwarranted, distasteful, unacceptable, unwanted, unauthorized, cold, manipulative, assertive, insensitive, sacrilegious

invader, invaders (un)welcome, parasitic, barbaric, barbarian, brutal, uncivilized, accursed, treacherous, stealthy, potential, alien, foreign

invalid, invalids chairbound, bedfast, bedridden, confirmed, confined, incurable, chronic, permanent, total, lifelong, incorrigible, hopeless, helpless, depressed, miserable, optimistic, cheerful

invasion, invasions peaceful, violent, vicious, barbaric, barbarian, brutal, uncivilized, abhorrent, outrageous, insidious, treacherous, wicked, unacceptable, criminal, ruthless, relentless, unrelenting, devastating, traumatic, ill-fated, extensive, full-scale, mass(ive), all-out, blatant, open, virtual, veritable, sudden, lightning, periodic, sporadic, potential, imminent, impending, retaliatory, sea-borne, amphibious

invective, invectives See *abuse*

invention, inventions exciting, fascinating, interesting, intriguing, tantalizing, astounding, astonishing, marvellous, wonderful, remarkable, unbelievable, incredible, miraculous, revolutionary, ingenious, creative, successful, modern, new, timely, pure, improbable, unwitting, marketable, versatile, time-saving, practical, (un)necessary, sprawling, berserk, whimsical, antic, fanciful, odd, singular, freakish

inventiveness See *invention*

inventor, inventors original, ingenious, imaginative, eccentric, nameless, unknown

inventory, inventories imposing, striking, stunning, impressive, comprehensive, detailed, (in)complete

investigation, investigations fruitful, close, in-depth, thorough, intense, intensive, exhaustive, serious, skilled, vigorous, rigorous, meticulous, systematic, painstaking, detailed, elaborate, sweeping, wide-ranging, extensive, full(-scale), far-reaching, far-flung, nationwide, major, massive, ongoing, current, immediate, three-month, subsequent, initial, high-level, warrantless, minor, controversial, (in)adequate, (in)competent, independent, impartial, (un)fair, (in)complete, cursory, hasty, speedy, damning, shoddy, fruitless, internal, bona fide, open, on-site, on-the-spot, judicial, criminal, forensic, clinical, critical, scientific

investigator, investigators meticulous, thorough, (un)fair, (un)prejudiced, independent, special, intrepid, criminal, private, financial

investment, investments secure, (un)safe, worry-free, good, sagacious, meaningful, (un)sound, (un)wise, (in)judicious, (in)sensible, astute, solid, sure(-fire), savvy, smart, cautious, conservative, superb, (in)flexible, diversified, multifarious, lucrative, (un)profitable, (un)reliable, attractive, ambitious, high-return, unfettered, substantial, hefty, heavy, huge, massive, modest, active, tangible, short-term, long-term, (un)affordable, (un)fortunate, initial, ongoing, unparalleled, unequalled, high-risk, risky, tricky, nail-biting, hot, passive, bad, poor, ill-fated, costly, sluggish, iffy, (in)direct, capital, equity, agrarian, foreign

investor, investors veteran, daring, aggressive, confident, seasoned, brainy, smart, sharp, astute, shrewd, careful, cautious, avid, active, volatile, serious, enthusiastic, reclusive, offshore, conservative, novice, big, major, large, small, cash-laden, cash-rich, reluctant, frisky, spunky, leery, sceptical, half-hearted, self-satisfied, ecstatic, euphoric, confused, agitated, anxious, edgy, nervous, jittery, panicky, nail-biting, scared, frightened, glum, optimistic, pessimistic, greedy, money-hungry, careless, gullible, helpless, potential, long-term, private, individual, joint, institutional, foreign

invitation, invitations thoughtful, warm, hearty, gracious, courteous, coveted, irresistible, intriguing, obliging, flattering, tardy, half-hearted, (un)welcome, (hand)written, (in)formal, standing, oral, personal

involvement, involvements active, intimate, intense, heavy, deep, disastrous, (un)fortunate, (un)justifiable, (in)direct, total, partial, emotional, personal, military

iron red-hot, (rust-)pitted, reduced, molten, wrought, corrugated, fluted, galvanized, malleable, cast

irony, ironies bantering, delicate, tender, gentle, mild, subtle, deft, restrained, lofty, benevolent, (in)tolerable, calculated, double-edged, mordant, caustic, bitter(sweet), cruel, painful, powerful, explosive, rasping, sly, jaundiced, crashing, tragic, sad, devastating, glaring, resonant, big, queer, ultimate, laconic, self-deprecating, cosmic, romantic, dramatic, verbal (rhetorical), Socratic

irregularity, irregularities redolent, widespread, abounding, endemic, shameful, unacceptable, disgraceful, outrageous, conspicuous, procedural

irrelevance, irrelevances hopeless, tangential, digressive, inconsequential, inappropriate

irresponsibility, irresponsibilities incredible, gross, heedless, careless, foolish, imprudent, reckless, thoughtless

irritation, irritations vexing, stinging, maddening, exasperating, ghastly, dark, intense, major, minor, petty, small, ridiculous, constant, continued, soporific; (sub)cutaneous

island, islands charming, enchanting, tempting, seductive, sensuous, marvellous, beautiful, lovely, placid, peaceful, calm, tranquil, easy-going, romantic, storybook, paradisiacal, Edenic, Elysian, dream-like, balmy, idyllic, sublime, lonely, secluded, remote, distant, far-flung, outlying, gaunt, bleak, desolate, obscure, uncharted, unexplored, uninhabited, unsullied, unblemished, unspoiled, barren, naked, treeless, palmy, lush, verdant, fertile, forested, wooded, park-like, reedy, sand(y), rocky, mountainous, desert, volcanic, limestone, coastal, mangrove, conifer-clad, coral, marshy, freshwater, tiny, small, siz(e)able, (in)significant, main, rolling, steep-sided, cliff-sided, steep-cliffed, vast, sparse, unpretentious, (in)habitable, unprotected, strategic, indefensible, hostile, wild, primitive, rugged, leeward, wind-swept, wind-racked, shoreless, offshore, adjacent, neighbouring, furthest, nearest, strategic, myriad, unassailable, fabled, imaginary, make-believe, fictional, artificial, tropical, subpolar, subantarctic, equatorial

isolation devastating, debilitating, tough, terrible, desolate, dreary, rugged, depressed, forlorn, hopeless, hermetic, profound, complete, total, partial, relative, virtual, wilful, voluntary, self-imposed, enforced, forcible, amiable, idyllic, splendid, serene, centuries-old, lonely, protective, bucolic, mystic, social, racial, historic, geographic(al), physical, diplomatic

issue, issues (1: a disputed matter) weighty, vital, crucial, critical, decisive, central, key, top-priority, primary, chief, fundamental, dominant, prominent, paramount, great, big, major, live, immediate, hot, incendiary, burning, serious, powerful, potent, explosive, incendiary, combustible, (in)significant, substantial, substantive, tempestuous, nettlesome, sensitive, emotive, pressing, urgent, prickly, thorny, tricky, sticky, touch(y), messy, problematic, compelling, intriguing, real, distinct, familiar, current, topical, present, contemporary, futurist, long-standing, overriding, agonizing, perplexing, vexing, troubling, troublesome, difficult, tough, intractable, unmanageable, contentious, unresolved, convoluted, complex, controversial, provocative, divisive, acrimonious, rancorous, (once-)taboo, volatile, engaging, advantageous, prosperous, arbitrable, dead, broad, obscure, false, prosaic, insignificant, incidental, indirect, peripheral, fading, fleeting, flaring, extraneous, political, legal, ethical, emotional, conceptual, local, provincial, national, international, side, public, social, humanitarian

issue, issues (2: a publication) informative, unprecedented, recent, forthcoming, latest, current, back, free, trial, premier, première, first, inaugural, pilot, maiden, subsequent, final, special, anniversary

itch, itching, itchiness annoying, agonizing, harrowing, persistent, appalling, intolerable, unbearable

item, items specific, miscellaneous, irreplaceable, hard-to-get, rare, cryptic, (un)identifiable, unidentified, (un)classified, commemorative

itinerary, itineraries exact, fixed, firm, rigid, (in)flexible, vague, strenuous, gruelling, undiscoverable, detailed, globetrotting, selective, alternative

ivory gleaming, raw, live, dead, ill-gotten, elastic, brittle, frail

jacket, jackets See also *coat* jaunty,
warm, snug, custom-made, fitted,
easy-fitting, close-fitting, loose-fitting,
ill-fitting, small-shouldered, high-button,
single-button, one-button, two-button,
three-button, zip-up, (un)lined,
straight-cut, reverseless, collarless,
high-collar(ed), high-necked, flat-back,
raglan-sleeved, scanty, husky, outsize,
hip-length, waist-length, double-breasted,
single-breasted, belted, check, classic,
ample, baggy, boxy, shapeless, lightweight,
suede, sheepskin, buckskin, sharkskin,
(imitation-)leather, tweed, denim, jean,
velvet, corduroy, cotton-twill, down-filled,
raffia, plaid, knit, quilted, fur-trimmed,
bullet-proof, outer

jail, jails See *prison*

jailer, jailers brutal, brute, brutish,
merciless, ruthless, bestial, abominable,
barbarous, barbaric, inhuman, swinish,
unfeeling, patient, vigilant

jam, jams (1: thick preserve) pure,
delicious, tasty, sweet, sugary, fruity,
jellied, firm, thick, lumpy, runny, watery,
syrupy, mouldy, thin, regular, tart,
sugarless, home-made

jam, jams (2: things, people, etc., crowded,
together) See also *traffic* intractable,
stubborn, obstinate, chaotic, frenetic,
huge, unmanageable, uncontrollable,
terrible, horrendous, dreadful

janitor, janitors See *worker*

jar, jars wide-mouthed, open-mouthed,
narrow-necked, wavy-handled,
two-handled, lidded, tripod, cracked,
sealed, leaky, (air-)tight, lustrous,
earthen(ware), stoneware, alabaster,
lacquer-ware, (black-)glazed, ornamental,
Canopic

jaw, jaws tenacious, powerful, strong,
massive, lean, toothed, toothless, square,
wide, projectile, projecting, jutting,
hanging, nether, vice-like, undershot,
grinding, swinging, biting, agape, crooked,
vicious, fearsome, horrible, lower, upper,
bucket; pharyngeal

jealousy, jealousies intense, fierce,
savage, vulgar, insane, petty, mean,
narrow, wretched, destructive, corrosive,
extreme, covert, evident, naked, resentful,
(in)excusable, flaming, unquenchable,
troublesome, unreasoning, baseless,
endless, complex, lurking, pathological,
sibling, sexual, marital, professional, ethnic

jerk, jerks twitching, inadvertent,
unintentional, casual, involuntary,
unpredictable, occasional, odd, random,
sporadic, choppy, bouncy, palmodic,
spasmodic

jest, jests See also *joke* merry, sharp,
sarcastic, abusive, caustic, biting, harsh,
scurrilous, derisive, incisive, flippant,
inconsequential

Jew, Jews devout, full-fledged, dogmatic,
strict, fundamentalist, traditionalist,
(non-)observant, (non-)Orthodox,
ultra-Orthodox, ultra-religious,
(non-)religious, liberal, (non-)practising,
lapsed, born-again, secular(ized), Sabra
(native-born), Diaspora, Sephardic,
Ashkenazi, Hasidic, Israeli, Messianic;
Wandering

jewel, jewels, jewellery See also *gem*
glamorous, remarkable, superb, splendid,
magnificent, exquisite, rich, opulent,
attractive, fetching, striking, befitting,
charming, obtrusive, intricately-made,
elaborate, ornate, original, hand-crafted,
handmade, unusual, stunning, staggering,
modish, stylish, fashionable, delicate,
quaint, fine, (in)valuable, priceless,
(semi-)precious, expensive, costly,
one-of-a-kind, gemstone, antique, serious,
chunky, bold, intricate, filigreed,
many-faceted, enamel, bone, paste, shell,
simple, pretentious, ostentatious, brilliant,
bright, sparkling, gleaming, dazzling,
glittering, flashy, gaudy, meretricious,
tawdry, garish, showy, artificial, ersatz,
sham, imitation, fake, shoddy, vulgar,
cheap, preposterous, identifiable,
traditional, old-fashioned, second-hand

job, jobs (1: position) (in)secure, lifetime,
permanent, (un)steady, (un)stable, fixed,
regular, enduring, durable, full-time,
lucrative, high-paying, well-paying,
better-paying, profitable, plush, dream,
top, fat, challenging, fussy, satisfying,
stimulating, rewarding, congenial, good,

meaningful, cushy, easy, comfortable, nice, (un)desirable, glamorous, quality, responsible, prestigious, respectable, vital, (un)conventional, non-routine, white-collar, ceremonial, professional, skilful, (semi)skilled, demanding, stressful, high-stress, tense, powerful, tenuous, scarce, plentiful, workaday, ordinary, low-paying, low-wage, minimum-wage, poverty-wage, lowly, nondescript, precarious, chancy, risky, hazardous, perilous, unskilled, low-stress, menial, hack, sweaty, wearing, consuming, harsh, strenuous, frenetic, brutal, monotonous, humdrum, meaningless, dirty, temporary, seasonal, short-term, part-time, occasional, casual, summer, odd, redundant, assembly-line, blue-collar, behind-the-counter, front-counter, clerical, entry-level, dead-end, manufacturing, agricultural, service-sector, private-sector, public-sector, administrative, supervisory, technical, paying

job, jobs (2: task) masterful, first-rate, terrific, superb, splendid, magnificent, remarkable, perfect, fabulous, marvellous, good, thorough, precise, creditable, commendable, responsible, rewarding, (dis)agreeable, careful, neat, sensitive, formidable, significant, spectacular, monumental, vast, enormous, mammoth, stressful, demanding, painstaking, distasteful, rush, myriad, above-board, careless, spivvy, messy, shoddy, patch-up, slapdash, odious, dreary, deplorable, cowboy

joint, joints (1: the point where two bones are joined) sore, painful, swollen, inflamed, creaky, bleeding, (im)movable, arthritic, sacroiliac

joint, joints (2: a device by which things are joined together) universal, dovetail

joke, jokes witty, funny, delicious, enjoyable, light-hearted, mild, risible, crisp, amusing, facetious, hilarious, bluff, refined, clean, solemn, popular, time-honoured, hoary, everlasting, eternal, wry, stock, (long-)standing, stale, customary, (well-)known, well-worn, hackneyed, much-repeated, often-repeated, dull, drab, dry, insipid, morbid, poor, trite, forced, strained, rueful, tedious, clumsy, feeble, pointless, ineffectual,

heartless, pitiless, merciless, ruthless, relentless, unrelenting, cruel, sly, grim, ghastly, horrible, sick, lame, far-fetched, grisly, banal, brutal, costly, dark, dolorous, puerile, adolescent, tongue-in-cheek, trenchant, clear-cut, nippy, acerbic, cutting, biting, incisive, bitter, caustic, ironic, untimely, inopportune, unreasonable, blue, bawdy, broad, indecent, undignified, indelicate, coarse, dirty, risqué, inappropriate, tasteless, repellent, off-colour, obscene, raw, ripe, salacious, vulgar, rude, repulsive, offensive, suggestive, (in)comprehensible, sexist, ethnic, racial, racist, private, practical, off-hand, hit-or-miss, conceptual

joking See *joke*

journal, journals See also *magazine* prestigious, sober, responsible, authoritative, esteemed, (well-)established, reputable, fledgling, earthy, irreverent, sensational, (in)accessible, interdisciplinary, multidisciplinary, scholarly, academic, learned, literary, professional, medical, scientific, trade, special-interest

journalism high-class, solid, honest, credible, painstaking, skilled, no-nonsense, humane, (un)ethical, unbiased, (in)accurate, fine, compelling, interpretive, investigative, forceful, pack, sensational, shabby, superficial, scurrilous, crude, virulent, anonymous, public-service, hack, freelance, yellow, pictorial

journalist, journalists veteran, nimble, maverick, perceptive, investigative, innovative, distinguished, well-known, eminent, prominent, seasoned, experienced, aspiring, up-and-coming, enterprising, obscure, nosy, meddling, freeloading, wily, insensitive, swashbuckling, hard-bitten, grubby, local, regional, freelance, independent

journey, journeys soothing, smooth, safe, gay, enjoyable, delightful, charming, exciting, perfect, fascinating, stupendous, remarkable, memorable, unforgettable, unprecedented, epic, legendary, nostalgic, ambivalent, indescribable, intriguing, worthwhile, interminable, wearisome, weary, tiring, bone-banging, gruelling, harrowing, appalling, dreadful, hideous, tedious, arduous, exhaustive, laborious, tortured, torturesome, torturous, difficult, tortuous, rough, tumultuous, tempestuous, stormy, dreary, luckless, fateful, treacherous, perilous, risky, haphazard, scary, frightening, venturesome, adventurous, daring, courageous, hectic, restless, mysterious, eccentric, futile, unbelievable, incredible, exotic, lonesome, lonely, nocturnal, far, distant, six-day, slow, final, outward, circular, round, return, trade, business, interplanetary, overland, transatlantic, subterranean, lunar, homeward, maiden, spiritual, magical, mystical, mythical, epic

joy, joys satisfying, overwhelming, overflowing, exceeding, unbounded, boundless, endless, infinite, immense, abundant, unbridled, unrestrained, immeasurable, unabashed, carefree, unsullied, unadulterated, unalloyed, unmitigated, perfect, unutterable, indescribable, inexpressible, unspeakable, ineffable, incredible, unbelievable, exuberant, sheer, pure, childlike, exquisite, intense, extreme, heartfelt, voluptuous, ecstatic, noisy, wild, aggressive, reckless, springy, bouncing, swaggering, blundering, speechless, priceless, undreamed-of, new-found, instantaneous, sudden, transient, passing, brief, elusive, lasting, permanent, revelatory, melancholy, heavenly, earthly, fiendish, sensuous, sensual, seedy, lurid

jubilee, jubilees See *anniversary*

judge, judges wise, shrewd, perspicacious, upright, conscientious, honest, just, fair(-minded), incorruptible, impartial, objective, disinterested, clement, merciful, compassionate, gentle, kind, forgiving, lenient, merciless, strict, severe, hard, stern, grave, solemn, sober, irascible, corrupt, venal, dishonest, prejudiced, partial, district, associate, puisne, appellate, supernumerary

judg(e)ment, judg(e)ments accurate, sound, correct, sensible, balanced, level-headed, well-reasoned, (im)mature, flawless, mellow, sane, clear, definitive, good, informed, subtle, shrewd, perspicacious, discerning, unbiased, (un)just, (un)fair, careful, (in)appropriate, rational, succinct, cautious, dissenting, dismissive, cutting, reversible, landmark,

according, wavering, premature, crude, unpractised, inexperienced, raw, harsh, questionable, debatable, one-sided, (non-)partisan, (im)partial, sketchy, faulty, uneducated, cold, uncanny, snap, reckless, hasty, rash, premature, poor, superficial, (un)reliable, deliberate, jaundiced, distorted, clouded, bad, austere, sweeping, final, declaratory, declamatory, several, severable, unchallenged, unanimous, collective, practical, instinctive, intuitive, subjective, critical, professional, moral, triage

jug, jugs handsome, two-handled, earthenware, stoneware, pottery, ceramic, china, porcelain, Toby

juice, juices refreshing, fresh, cool, nutritious, delicious, pure, potent, strong, stiff, heady, zesty, piquant, pungent, lusty, authentic, soporific, light, weak, shilpit, insipid, vapid, watery, stale, gastric, milky, win(e)y, unsweetened, frozen, suckable

jump, jumps startling, stunning, surprising, sudden, quick, rapid, dext(e)rous, clean, clever, dramatic, vigorous, unlikely, (un)reluctant, errant, deadly, two-foot-high, standing, high, broad, vertical, long, triple, quadruple

jumping See *jump*

jungle, jungles See also *forest* dense, deep, sprawling, teeming, vigorous, luxuriant, lush, scrub, resilient, verdant, steamy, sultry, remote, virgin, roadless, treacherous, lethal, impassable, impenetrable, intact, uncharted, undisturbed, untouched, rugged, tangled, mountainous, hilly, equatorial, primeval, primordial, bamboo; urban, concrete, asphalt

jurist, jurists unbiased, (un)prejudiced, fair(-minded), (im)partial, dispassionate, disinterested, (in)corruptible, (ir)responsible, (un)conscientious, implacable, unfair, corrupt, venal, (dis)honest, unconvinced, petit (petty, trial), grand, hung, special (blue-ribbon)

jury, juries See *jurist*

justice ideal, even-handed, equal, fair, reasonable, justifiable, (im)partial, unbiased, strict, indifferent, capricious, scant, flawed, rough(-and-ready), belated, remunerative, fundamental, abstract, distributive, retributive, procedural, poetic, individual, social, economic, natural, criminal

justification, justifications compelling, (in)sufficient, (un)reasonable, (il)legitimate, (il)legal, rightful, (un)sound, (in)valid,

(un)warranted, (un)necessary, (in)sufficient, voiced, obvious, minimal, spurious, scientific

juxtaposition, juxtapositions peculiar, strange, curious, odd, ungainly, awkward, clumsy, (un)characteristic

kangaroo, kangaroos bouncing, thumping, boxing, graceful, spur-tailed, nail-tailed, red-necked

key, keys duplicate, spare, master, skeleton

kidnapping, kidnappings daring, brazen, bold, fearless, perilous, dangerous, venturesome, venturous, adventurous, adventuresome, risky, rash, treacherous

killer, killers See *murderer*

killing, killings unrepentant, brutal, bloody, treacherous, villainous, felonious, atrocious, horrific, grisly, unscrupulous, cold-blooded, sickening, despicable, brutal, brutish, insidious, impersonal, reckless, futile, senseless, random, wanton, indiscriminate, rash, systematic, wholesale, widespread, foul, infamous, inhuman, unprovoked, unnecessary, unlawful, illegal, accidental, (in)voluntary, (un)intentional, unrelenting, relentless, ruthless, pitiless, remorseless, heartless, merciless, blameless, shameless, shameful, unsolved, (un)planned, (un)premeditated, (drug-)related, uncontrolled, sectarian, reprisal, tit-for-tat, ritual, double, triple, serial, ambush, terrorist

kind, kinds special, particular, rare, various, different, (un)usual, (un)familiar

kindness affectionate, affable, amiable, compassionate, good-natured, sincere, true, genuine, open-hearted, profuse, excessive, innate, inbred, generous, loving, gracious, unexampled, unprecedented, unparalleled, unlooked-for, unexpected, proverbial, sympathetic, benevolent, charitable, (un)characteristic, (un)equivocal, suspicious, questionable

king, kings legitimate, lawful, rightful, true, bounteous, sage, statesmanlike, formal, gracious, regnant, magnificent, portly, dignified, (all-)powerful, sacred, legendary, autocratic, tyrannical, fierce, virtual, powerless, weak, degenerate, uncrowned, titular, constitutional, hereditary, ceremonial

kingdom, kingdoms thriving, flourishing, prosperous, peaceable, vast, majestic, glorious, independent, autonomous, sylvan, ancient, short-lived, hereditary, mythical, legendary; animal, vegetable, mineral

kiss, kisses smacking, transcendent, exquisite, light, soft, tender, gentle, delicate, loving, warm, amorous, passionate, impassioned, impetuous, impulsive, solemn, slow, deep, generous, big, drowsy, smothering, full-mouthed, long(-drawn), protracted, trenchant, restrained, cool, withdrawn, noisy, hungry, sloppy, abrasive, electrifying, ceremonious, consolatory, parting, first, dry, wet, French, cousinly, sisterly, brotherly, motherly, fatherly, avuncular

kitchen, kitchens trendy, modern, contemporary, cosy, bright, cheery, quality, lovely, neat, fabulous, impeccable, gleaming, (in)efficient, cavernous, spacious, large, huge, family-size, compact, diminutive, tiny, sordid, insanitary, country-style

kitten, kittens See also *cat* cute, warm, adorable, furry, fluffy, jumpy, frisky, playful, frolicsome, merry, gay, sportive, curious, feeble, weak, nervous

knave, knaves See *rogue*

knee, knees pretty, round, shapely, knobb(l)y, bare, sore, aching, stiff, trick, shaky, unyielding, rubbery, weak, thin, dodgy, bent, swollen, arthritic, problem, bended

knife, knives sharp, keen(-edged), lethal, stout, blunt, dull, rusty, rusted, thin-bladed, fixed-blade, long-bladed, broad-bladed, double-bladed, serrated, cleaver-like, single-edged, two-edged, double-edged, (semi)circular, curved, straight, whacking, steel, flint, bamboo, pearl-handled, bone-handled, buckhorn, hoof, electric, cordless, switchblade, pocket, folding, laser, surgical, all-purpose, utility, ceremonial

knight, knights dauntless, intrepid, stalwart, audacious, valiant, doughty, heroic, brave, daring, fearless, bold, courageous, gallant, noble, high-spirited, chivalrous, zealous, legendary, irreproachable, errant, recreant, false, cowardly, mounted, mailed

knitting plain, purl, unravelled, weft,

hand, machine, cable, Aran, Fair Isle;
French

knob, knobs heavy, crystal, brass

knock, knocks, knocking soft, slight,
hesitant, loud, violent, frantic, feverish,
persistent, muffled; shrewd, hard,
severe

knot, knots tight, firm, hard, intricate,
inextricable, stumpy, telltale, ornamental,
(un)safe, (in)secure, loose, running (slip),
four-in-hand, square (reef), triple,
Gordian; French

knowledge proper, precise, competent,
intimate, empirical, first-hand,
comprehensive, vast, extensive, widespread,
encyclopaedic, prodigious, exhaustive,
mature, thorough, expert, significant,
instructive, profound, advanced, detailed,
uncanny, minute, intimate, valuable,
priceless, (in)adequate, (in)sufficient,
reassuring, precocious, explicit, attainable,
rudimentary, elementary, shaky,
superficial, second-hand, glancing, sketchy,
desultory, incomplete, imperfect, mediocre,
passable, middling, slight, small, scant,
(un)limited, skimpy, second-rate,
superficial, useless, amateur, unconscious,
untapped, working, practical, factual,
theoretical, cumulative, innate, universal,
intuitive, public, general, common,
fundamental, basic, pure, self-taught,
material, certain, prior; carnal

label, labels informative, conventional, stereotypical, (il)legible, colourful, elusive, slippery, deceptive, false, warning, cautionary

labelling See *label*

laboratory, laboratories prestigious, sophisticated, state-of-the-art, leading-edge, forensic, portable

labour, labours See *work*

labourer, labourers See *worker*

labyrinth, labyrinths See *maze*

lack appalling, troubling, aggravating, shocking, glaring, egregious, conspicuous, noticeable, evident, utter, woeful, pitiful, critical, deficient, perilous, risky, chronic

ladder, ladders swaying, (un)steady, (un)stable, (in)flexible, rickety, shaky, tricky, narrow, wooden, metal, aluminium, welded, steadied, straight, hook, rope, multipurpose, foldaway, rolling, scaling, aerial, starboard, sectional; corporate, social, evolutionary

lady, ladies highborn, portly, courtly, titled, dignified, esteemed, venerable, imposing, stately, grand, courteous, benevolent, hospitable, gracious, elegant, fashionable, designer-dressed, sophisticated, perfect, affable, fine, beautiful, genteel, affected

lake, lakes sparkling, twinkling, gleaming, placid, calm, still, tranquil, serene, peaceful, quiet, dormant, languid, (un)ruffled, choppy, scenic, spectacular, dramatic, breathtaking, splendid, magnificent, gorgeous, moonlit, lovely, blue, turquoise, emerald, mirror-like, (diamond-)clear, crystal-clear, limpid, transparent, circular, crescent-shaped, windswept, icy, frozen, salty, glassy, gassy, remote, lonely, unusable, lifeless, pristine, ancient, private, tiny, small, narrow, vast, wide, enormous, huge, great, large, spacious, oxbow, (30-foot-)deep, shallow, saline, salt-rich, brackish, acid(ic), dead, navigable, fishless, glacier-fed, spring-fed, river-fed, rain-filled, receding, marine, tricorn, natural, artificial, man-made, scummy, land-locked, glacial, volcanic, sunken, underground, mountain, sylvan, (sub)alpine, recreational

lamb, lambs bleating, baaing, scampering, gambolling, chipper, gentle, meek, quiet, uncomplaining, shorn, woolly, fleecy, newborn, premature, cade, karakul, sacrificial, pet, Paschal, Passover, Canterbury; Persian

lamp, lamps flickering, dangling, globular, sombre, bronze, porcelain, ceramic, leaded-glass, bamboo-filament, high-performance, electric, incandescent, gas, oil, paraffin, halogen, pilot, safety, standing, tungsten, tail, astral, signal, adjustable, portable, clamp-on, mercury-vapour, fluorescent, low, pin-up, neon, quartz, kerosene, votary, votive, solar

land, lands prime, good, (in)fertile, (un)productive, loamy, bountiful, lush, (un)fruitful, rich, fat, abundant, verdant, idyllic, ageless, arable, (ir)reclaimable, harvestable, cultivable, tillable, usable, fallow, marginal, contorted, unspoiled, bare, barren, waste, desolate, bleak, gaunt, grim, sere, hard, rough, harsh, uncompromising, unyielding, ungenerous, tenacious, recalcitrant, stubborn, obstinate, exhausted, thirsty, parched, water-starved, sunburnt, (semi-)arid, bad, cracked, roadless, trackless, thorny, sterile, poor, intractable, untended, derelict, untilled, uncultivated, unimproved, stubble, scrubby, run-down, worthless, valueless, windswept, riparian, erodible, erosion-prone, alkaline, saline, alluvial, rugged, craggy, swampy, boggy, peaty, tussocky, moonscape, mountainous, raw, wild, pristine, virginal, primitive, undeveloped, untamed, unvisited, forbidding, hummocky, haggard, rock-strewn, (de)forested, wooded, bucolic, palm, treeless, rolling, sloping, undulating, flat, (un)even, bumpy, up-and-down, submarginal, far-off, remote, open, distant, unknown, mysterious, cherished, (un)popular, (un)developed, (un)inhabitable, (in)hospitable, uninviting, war-torn, strange, exotic, primeval, ancestral, foreign, native, commonable, communal, biblical, farm, rural, pasture, pastoral, recreational, industrial, Crown, foster, marginal, blown-out; Never-Never, Cloud-Cuckoo

landing, landings happy, fine, magnificent, splendid, remarkable, extraordinary, spectacular, smooth, graceful, soft, beautiful, perfect, (ab)normal, (un)scheduled, (un)planned, (un)safe, hard, blind, bumpy, jerky, tough, bad, low, miracle, precautionary, emergency, bone-jarring, low-visibility, disastrous, crash, partial, amphibious, nose-down, wheels-down

landlady, landladies attentive, (un)just, proud, inquisitive, prying, fussy, fastidious, greedy, hard(-hearted), heartless, obdurate, oppressive, rapacious, grasping, long-time, non-resident, absentee

landlord, landlords See *landlady*

landmark, landmarks outstanding, prominent, pre-eminent, unique, distinctive, recognizable, conspicuous, enduring, venerable, vintage, famous, memorable, best-known, notorious, obscure, national, historic

landscape, landscapes awe-inspiring, imposing, striking, fascinating, charming, enchanting, pleasing, baffling, startling, dreamy, ethereal, blissful, evocative, diaphanous, postcard, beautiful, picturesque, scenic, panoramic, dramatic, romantic, fantastic, splendid, magnificent, spectacular, glorious, grandiose, peerless, radiant, vast, broad, surrounding, great, fine, (un)pleasant, serene, tranquil, still, silent, cosy, lunar, moonlit, shimmery, varied, tree-studded, pine-studded, bush-clogged, fertile, fecund, fresh, verdant, green, umber, ochre, pastel, flat, steep, undulating, rolling, soaring, leonine, harsh, pitiless, heartless, merciless, ruthless, relentless, unrelenting, uninviting, inhospitable, hostile, boring, unpeopled, unspoiled, ghostly, arid, torrid, dry, scorched, treeless, tawny, blank, bald, stark, empty, barren, dead, dun, bleak, grim, desolate, melancholy, sombre, gloomy, dismal, sordid, squalid, wild, hellish, chaotic, scruffy, dingy, soggy, timeless, immutable, transitory, remote, lonely, lonesome, primal, primordial, primeval, ancient, domesticated, contorted, wrinkled, rugged, blasted, abandoned, wasted, claustrophobic, unstable, fragile,

desert, mountain, natural, wooded, limestone, stony, dusty, swampy, chalky, political, natural, pastoral, rural, urban, man-made, alpine; impressionist

landscaping imaginative, creative, inventive, ingenious, meticulous, professional

lane, lanes through, shady, shadowy, muddy, dirt, narrow, steep, rambling, twisty, crooked, secluded; traffic

language, languages vibrant, vivid, vigorous, living, picturesque, straightforward, refined, polished, elegant, graceful, polite, restrained, copious, pliant, flowing, lapidary, easy, pure, plain, clear, pellucid, explicit, limpid, memorable, simple, laconic, (in)comprehensible, (in)decipherable, articulate, measured, terse, precise, concise, succinct, incandescent, tactile, tasty, delicate, upbeat, colourful, elaborate, shapely, flamboyant, showy, pompous, grandiloquent, ornate, flowery, turgid, pretentious, rhythmical, (un)musical, high-flown, roundabout, flash, artificial, breathy, breakneck, aphoristic, passionate, impassioned, wooing, emotive, graphic, vehicular, heroic, ritual, cryptic, soft, torrential, strange, unique, stereotyped, influential, dominant, dying, dead, extinct, archaic, dormant, esoteric, (in)flexible, wooden, innovative, befitting, (in)decent, (im)proper, (in)appropriate, (un)suitable, (un)printable, (dis)respectful, mean, trite, appalling, crude, raw, foul, vile, insulting, offensive, abusive, pungent, acrimonious, low, taunting, opprobrious, scurrilous, ribald, disgusting, shameful, base, debased, evil, sultry, immoral, obscene, risqué, bawdy, violent, corrupt, bizarre, unctuous, prosaic, nasty, profane, blasphemous, vulgar, coarse, unrepeatable, inflammatory, incendiary, damning, contemptuous, impure, strong, tough, uncompromising, graphic, ambiguous, convoluted, obscure, ordinary, common(place), prevailing, everyday, workaday, unrecognized, stilted, natural, oral, written, liturgical, medical, legal, gestural, tonal, sonic, vernacular, slangy, musical, poetic, isolating, first, adoptive, hybrid, descriptive, expressive, rhythmical, symbolic, figurative, metaphorical, demonstrative, pidgin, technical, universal, foreign, alien, parent, native, aboriginal, ancestral, national, state, local, ethnic, formal, official, diplomatic, parliamentary, grammarless, non-verbal, (un)inflected, guttural, cognate, tonic, vocalic, private, inclusive, Romance

lantern, lanterns powerful, feeble, collapsible, portable, fixed, butane, kerosene, petrol, oil, magic, dark, Chinese, Japanese

lapel, lapels sagging, wide, narrow

lark, larks See also *bird* cheerful, gay, happy, jolly blithe, singing, hovering

laser, lasers powerful, flexible, portable, airborne, crystal, nose-turret, high-energy, free-electron, X-ray, video, surgical, argon, carbon dioxide, helium–neon

laugh, laughs enchanting, engaging, winning, roaring, side-splitting, horse, big, huge, giant, deep, ripe, fruity, luscious, attractive, hearty, merry, soft, decent, good, light(-hearted), jocund, forthright, genuine, whole-hearted, generous, rich, clear, merry, jovial, jolly, vigorous, melodious, sonorous, staccato, loud, shrill, high(-pitched), uproarious, raucous, uncontrollable, interminable, irrepressible, strident, dry, sharp, harsh, riotous, boisterous, contagious, infectious, idiotic, mawkish, pitiful, insolent, demoniac, wry, wacky, sarcastic, sardonic, scornful, sneering, mocking, sly, confiding, blushing, nervous, incredulous, provocative, empty, artificial, ready

laughter hearty, wholehearted, soft, (un)easy, conspiratorial, deep, merry, gay, cheerful, gleeful, light-hearted, delighted, glad, wholesome, ripe, rich, high-spirited, splendid, superb, sumptuous, explosive, immoderate, (half-)hysterical, irrepressible, uncontrollable, incessant, uninterrupted, involuntary, uneasy, coarse, wild, inextinguishable, raucous, boisterous, inordinate, broad, free, unruly, frenzied, uproarious, gusty, riotous, excessive, convulsive, appreciative, shrieking, roaring, tinkling, mocking, leering, derisive, irreverent, hideous, ironic, unseemly, inappropriate, vulgar, ribald, bawdy, indiscriminate, loud, shrilly, mischievous, malicious, sly, unkind, pointed, frequent, contagious, intense, nervous, grim, inward,

spontaneous, snide, tinselly, (un)restrained, uncontrolled, shallow, infectious, provocative, magical, girlish, impish, demoniac(al), bacchanalian, Homeric

law, laws honourable, venerable, solid, (in)adequate, (un)justifiable, (in)operative, (in)effective, (im)perfect, (in)convenient, uniform, (un)equal, protective, humane, compassionate, liberal, (in)flexible, protectionist, lenient, easy, slack, lax, (un)enforceable, strict, severe, chilling, oppressive, repressive, rigorous, harsh, stringent, tough, stiff, brutal, exacting, prohibitive, restrictive, tight, pitiless, merciless, heartless, ruthless, relentless, unrelenting, inexorable, inviolable, unbreakable, infrangible, irrefragable, rigid, puritanical, intrusive, defunct, obscure, musty, long-standing, immutable, old-fashioned, out-of-date, outmoded, outdated, flawed, defective, invalid, controversial, haphazard, weak, fading, foolish, crazy, eccentric, ridiculous, loony, (un)written, unspoken, universal, fundamental, national, rabbinical, religious, ecclesiastical, empirical, civil, martial, positive, public, property, substantive, sumptuary, moral, penal, agrarian, blue, criminal, military, (un)constitutional, common, dry, feudal, electoral, international, marine, maritime, natural, organic, Poor, primordial, moratory, physical, punitive, retroactive, retrospective, ex post facto, executory, mercantile, corporeal, parliamentary, provincial, federal, sanitary, Draconian, Salic, Mosaic, Roman; periodic, phonetic; lynch (swamp)

lawlessness See *anarchy*

lawn, lawns tidy, neat, luxuriant, lush, springy, deep, spacious, well-kept, (well-)trimmed, crew-cut, green, velvet, verdant, emerald, drought-resistant, sloping, rolling, angular, fenced, thin, overgrown, weedy, wild, brown, sunburned, parched, scraggly, untidy

lawsuit, lawsuits See *case* (2)

lawyer, lawyers competent, sharp, able, adroit, bright, articulate, sharp-witted, acute, masterful, loquacious, ubiquitous, dynamic, persuasive, brilliant, prominent, leading, high-priced, veteran, (un)successful, (in)experienced, full-fledged, practising, ambitious, incipient, budding, briefless, foxy, aggressive, wily, astute, shrewd, sharp-eyed, slick, crafty, cunning, sly, wayward, corrupt, dishonest, dishonourable, unethical, crooked, irreverent, unconscientious, unscrupulous, greedy, wilful, (un)trustworthy, court-appointed, tax, criminal, corporate, matrimonial, banking, constitutional, international

layer, layers (in)distinct, undermost, outer(most), (im)permeable, tiny, delicate, skimpy, thick, thin, impermeable, fluffy, sedimentary, protective, epidermic (epidermal)

lay-off, lay-offs abrupt, drastic, mass(ive), major, permanent, temporary

laziness shocking, appalling, easy-going, unenterprising, habitual, chronic, accustomed, disgraceful, scandalous, shameful, comatose, languid, slothful, soporific, vacuous

lead molten, crude; red, white; black

leader, leaders benevolent, vigorous, energetic, high-minded, sensible, seasoned, experienced, promising, rising, adept, wonderful, remarkable, pragmatic, accessible, extraordinary, peerless, exceptional, ideal, great, legendary, dynamic, moderate, (un)savoury, (in)effectual, able, competent, capable, effective, prestigious, invaluable, superb, reform-minded, reformist, successful, strong-willed, unflappable, patient, calm, trustworthy, decisive, uncompromising, determined, reactive, lik(e)able, lovable, amiable, beloved, (un)popular, personable, born, natural, charismatic, visionary, inspired, hit, top, high-ranking, key, maximum, paramount, authentic, undisputed, unchallenged, unrivalled, rightful, democratic, patriotic, supreme, prominent, innovative, unconventional, maverick, wily, undaunted, diehard, indomitable, autonomous, outspoken, forceful, virile, fearless, (all-)powerful, dominant, tough(-minded), unsentimental, glamorous, strong, fiery, articulate, bold, influential, unifying, rebel, revolutionary, secessionist, factious, megalomaniacal, underground, clandestine, terrorist, visionless, doddering, irresolute, craven, misguided, fractious, deceitful, hypocritical, two-faced, double-faced, incompetent, corrupt, controversial, dogmatic, opinionated, hard-headed, hysterical, shadowy, mercurial, formidable, imperious, authoritarian, autocratic, hard-line, unbending, ruthless, pitiless, heartless, merciless, relentless, unrelenting, power-mad, self-styled, self-serving, iron-fisted, arbitrary, despotic, dictatorial, arrogant, militant, unwanted, indecisive, weak, pliant, malleable, nominal, meddlesome, potential, interim, rival, titular, temporal, secular, religious, spiritual, moral, church, fundamentalist, intellectual, tribal, native, aboriginal, national, social, military, civilian, civic, political, corporate, de facto

leadership benevolent, inspirational, effective, constructive, creative, innovative, no-nonsense, heroic, dynamic, vigorous, charismatic, popular, smooth, genuine, successful, adequate, strong, decisive, determined, (un)stable, iron-willed, firm, clear, implacable, tough, hard-line, outstanding, responsible, reformist, reform-minded, liberal, moderate, vibrant, colourful, consensual, inclusive, stressful, adventurous, budding, slipping, turbulent, clandestine, underground, irresponsible, poor, visionary, crazy, recalcitrant, nominal, collective, moral, national, hereditary, patriarchal

leaf, leaves rustling, gleaming, shining, (low-)growing, broad-spreading, shaking, variegated, dark-green, yellow(ish), autumn-red, coppery, golden, steely, luminous, iridescent, fresh, attractive, floral, decorative, handsome, (in)edible, aromatic, fragrant, firm, erect, broad, balmy, succulent, exuberant, abundant, luxuriant, lush, dense, astringent, fleshy, pulpy, woolly, papery, hairy, downy, feathery, glossy, tender, slender, crisp, crinkly, adventitious, seed, basal, radical, primordial, rudimentary, finely-lobed, (five-)lobed, mottled, whorled, notched, sharp-pointed, (spiny-)toothed, spiked, veined, plaited, bifid, deflexed, dissected, sodden, ribbed, incised, cleft, segmented, curved, elephantine, prickly, needle-like, curly, acinaciform, (sword-)flat, lacy, intricate, simple, compound, existing, new, dead, assurgent, droopy, floppy, decayed, rotten, weeping, limp, wiry, blistery, coarse, averse, adverse, acerate, linear, lanceolate, elliptic, ensiform, oblong, cultrate, cuneate, oblanceolate, undulate, verticillate, denticulate, ovate, obovate, spatulate, pandurate, bilobate, binate, bipartite, deltoid, cordate, reniform, bijugate (bijugous), lyrate, peltate, hastate, sagittate, (odd-)pinnate, palmate (trifoliolate), deciduous, distichous, evergreen, acropetal, basipetal, dorsiventral; bay

leaflet, leaflets See *pamphlet*

league, leagues (group of teams) dynamic, competitive, regular, big, major, minor, little, national

leap, leaps breathtaking, graceful, (ir)regular, forward, upward, high, giant, gigantic, quantum, tremendous, boundless, dramatic, enthusiastic, playful, awesome, frantic, desperate, fatal, dare-devil, rash, reckless

learner, learners quick, fast, slow, backward, late

learning painstaking, solid, thorough, profound, advanced, wide, passionate, limited, independent, self-directed, humane, crucial, fruitless, sterile, rote, multisensory

lease, leases long-term, short-term, five-year, (un)renewable, repairing

leather, leathers fine, supple, pliant, flexible, (butter-)soft, shiny, plush, thick, tough, raw, patent, suede, imitation, Russian

leave, leaves one-month, short-term, long-term, open-ended, extended, (un)paid, sick, medical, sabbatical, terminal, compassionate, parental, convalescent, administrative; French

lecture, lectures See also *speech* impressive, provocative, informative, striking, commanding, interesting, enjoyable, popular, (un)imaginative, dull, tedious, wearisome, monotonous, repetitive, repetitious, lengthy, sterile, diffuse, wordy, rumble-voiced, moral, demonstrative, obligatory, plenary

lecturer, lecturers See *speaker*

leg, legs graceful, (un)shapely, nice, elegant, beautiful, pretty, lovely, refined, fine, stout, full, firm, solid, strong, athletic, muscular, beefy, sinewy, thickly(-muscled), limber, silky, smooth, lithe, nimble, bare, stockingless, (well-)exposed, tender, slim, slender, flabby, limp, scrawny, reedy, stick-like, spindly, elongate(d), skinny, bony, rubbery, bandy (bow), dangling, hairy, hairless, hair-free, numb, sore, sallow, shaky, trembly, wobbly, stiff, rigid, motionless, sluggish, gnarled, stumpy, dumpy, podgy, plump, stubby, lumpy, squabby, squat, languid, hollow, forked, raw, inflamed, swollen, mottled, flipper-like, spidery, crooked, lame, malformed, hind, front, stilt(-like), thoracic

legacy, legacies ample, plenteous, sumptuous, vast, abundant, bounteous, substantial, monumental, massive, uplifting, lavish, luxuriant, opulent, rich, precious, valuable, irreplaceable, priceless, worthy, worthwhile, precious, affluent, incredible, unbelievable, magnificent, splendid, remarkable, dazzling, fine, unspoiled, elusive, fragile, worthless, bitter, grim, sorry, piteous, terrible, murky, corrosive, specific, general, residual, permanent, enduring, haunting, lingering, fading, vanishing, (un)expected, literary, cultural, colonial

legend, legends enduring, lasting, living, secure, hoary, ancient, venerable, noble, glamorous, superstitious, apocryphal, shadowy, implausible, fabulous, fictional, fictitious, false, idle, meaningless, unmeaning, unsubstantiated, unwritten, local, popular, picturesque, traditional, epic(al), mythical, mythological, tribal, fairy, Arthurian

legislation vital, progressive, (un)just, (un)reasonable, well-intentioned, comprehensive, complex, oppressive, burdensome, tyrannical, coercive, repressive, tough, discriminatory, vindictive, stringent, controversial, antiquated, innocuous, harmless, restrictive, punitive, retrospective, ex post facto, protectionist, compulsory, bicameral

legislature, legislatures See also *parliament* rubber-stamp, unicameral, bicameral, local, regional, civil

leisure elegant, glorious, abundant, scanty,

slow, unhurried, unhasty, intensive, wearisome

lender, lenders See *creditor*

length, lengths excessive, inordinate, horrendous, focal, uniform, variable

lens, lenses clear, translucent, powerful, high-powered, heavy, soft, hard, plastic, gas-permeable, oxygen-permeable, wide-angle, toric, prescription, corrective, industrial-strength, cylindrical, myopic, magnetic, electrostatic, electromagnetic, anastigmatic, microscopic, telescopic, photographic, fish-eye, crystalline, rigid, crown, aplanatic, anamorphic, apochromatic, achromatic, bifocal, zoom, telephoto, contact, objective (object), concave (diverging, negative), convex (converging, positive), double-concave, double-convex, biconcave, biconvex, plano-concave, plano-convex, convexo-concave, concavo-convex

lesson, lessons salutary, compelling, valuable, exemplary, fine, unforgettable, never-to-be-forgotten, fundamental, powerful, forceful, costly, painful, bitter, brutal, tough, harsh, sharp, grim, dark, chilling, humbling, tedious, difficult, boring, hard-earned, well-deserved, graphic; moral

letter, letters supportive, welcome, charming, nice, tactful, sprightly, snappy, graceful, candid, frank, agreeable, thoughtful, moving, affectionate, touching, warm, heart-warming, impassioned, passionate, intimate, friendly, polite, refined, polished, concise, conciliatory, noble, valiant, respectful, authentic, elegant, civil, judicious, meaningful, cheerful, entertaining, lively, humorous, hilarious, exuberant, grateful, anguished, revealing, entreating, pleading, begging, supplicant, suppliant, resilient, spurious, threatening, upbraiding, sharp, harsh, vehement, gushing, sententious, scathing, iridescent, gossiping (gossipy), chatty, discursive, playful, rude, pathetic, equivocal, scurrilous, pornographic, scatological, obscene, abusive, irate, taunting, blistering, bitter, defamatory, acrimonious, virulent, obsequious, tedious, gross, blunt, scandalous, disgusting, revolting, rambling, sprawling, mischievous, dry, harmful, impersonal, senseless, incendiary, illiterate, indignant, cheerless, uncivil, inappropriate, indiscreet, ominous, business-like, fugitive, irretrievable, dead, surviving, sal(e)able, (il)legible, indecipherable, dog-eared, (in)frequent, previous, forthcoming, outstanding, urgent, pressing, detailed, four-page, reminiscent, long-expected, unanswered, unsigned, unclaimed, unacknowledged, hand-written, undated, unposted, fake, encyclical, verse, clandestine, strong, business, bread-and-butter, covering, consolatory, official, private, express, circular, follow-up, personal, confidential, side, day, night, monitory, open, valedictory, congratulatory, sentimental, anonymous, testimonial; dead

level, levels staggering, soaring, peak, record, maximum, lofty, high, elevated, deep, phenomenal, masterful, sustainable, allowable, permissible, (un)acceptable, true, (un)steady, (un)even, (un)desirable, (in)tolerable, (un)palatable, outlandish, fantastic, inflated, unheard-of, (un)usual, (un)realistic, (ab)normal, (un)healthy, (un)detectable, (un)distinguishable, fluctuating, plunging, low, (im)modest, precarious, shameful, dangerous, critical, insulting, frightening, worrisome, scary, rudimentary, stratospheric

liar, liars consistent, pernicious, unmitigated, blundering, unblushing, inveterate, common, congenital, consummate, compulsive, manifold, frequent, habitual, (long-)established, incorrigible, veritable, glib, abject, worthless, contemptible, despicable, arrant, downright, thoroughgoing, out-and-out, timid, conscious, unconscionable, unscrupulous, unprincipled, black-hearted, terrible, devious, mean, pathological

libel, libels criminal, civil

liberalism unretrenched, unabashed, moderate

liberty, liberties absolute, unwarrantable, unwarranted, untrammelled, hard-won, new-found, personal, individual, civil, moral, political, constitutional, national

library, libraries irreplaceable, priceless, valuable, unique, fine, superb, fascinating, large, vast, extensive, substantial, tremendous, massive, impressive, extraordinary, sacrosanct, inviolable, luxurious, renowned, quiet, helpful, useful, busy, noisy, dusty, modern, small, spare, (in)accessible, cosy, antiquated, electronic, open-stack, public, private, special, mobile, home, personal, portable, provincial, state, national, government, city, legislative, local, regional, municipal, community, business, university, college, school, departmental, medical, scientific, theatrical, memorial, genealogical, professional, children's, depository, prison, art, music, law, toy, pet, museum, technical

licence, licences (1: permission) (in)valid, lapsed, (non-)transferable, perpetual, long-term, short-term, royalty-free, non-exclusive, worldwide, special, restricted

licence (2: freedom) poetic, artistic, creative

lid, lids air-tight, twist-off, child-proof

lie, lies whopping, whacking, swingeing, bouncing, astonishing, rousing, big, monstrous, slick, wily, flagrant, outrageous, egregious, arrant, downright, outright, absolute, total, stolid, blatant, bald(-faced), barefaced, shameless, brazen, preposterous, out-and-out, flat, palpable, obvious, conscious, shabby, mean, vulgar, black, harmful, poisonous, wicked, malicious, pernicious, damnable, hateful, envenomed, atrocious, obnoxious, repugnant, stupid, terrible, lurid, heinous, deliberate, misleading, tawdry, undisguised, foul, impudent, intolerable, unbearable, unacceptable, indefensible, unjustifiable, brash, cowardly, damnedest, bold, frantic, vicious, unconscionable, scandalous, innocent, harmless, protective, white

life, lives satisfying, rewarding, flourishing, exciting, astonishing, teeming, glittering, glamorous, glorious, honourable, virtuous, holy, saintly, devotional, sinless, decent, moral, clean, pure, wonderful, comfortable, harmonious, exemplary, orderly, organized, balanced, idyllic, stable, magnificent, distinguished, productive, industrious, hard-working, resourceful, shifty, active, contented, healthy, tranquil, safe, secure, peaceful, relaxing, leisurely, carefree, sweet, regular, temperate, civilized, meaningful,

purposeful, significant, full, unblemished, straight, simple, frugal, austere, (un)settled, (un)profitable, (un)pleasant, unruffled, congenial, blameless, charmed, easy, luxurious, rich, sober, benign, rosy, vibrant, toilsome, fevered, chequered, varied, diverse, diversified, colourful, two-sided, many-sided, turbulent, hectic, fast-paced, heady, busy, restless, (un)complicated, erratic, tumultuous, raucous, strenuous, eclectic, straight, traditional, normal, ordinary, intense, livable, endurable, straggling, inactive, withdrawn, muted, solitary, lonely, lone, cloistered, retired, everlasting, contemporaneous, corrupt, depraved, sensual, frivolous, reprobate, rakish, loutish, sybaritic, dysfunctional, misspent, vagabond, voluptuous, dissolute, dissipated, wild, licentious, worthless, prosaic, vagrant, vacant, empty, vacuous, fruitless, unobtrusive, sinful, debauched, wicked, profligate, scandalous, inglorious, seamy, flat, eventless, uneventful, stiff, sessile, deadly, precarious, unbearable, intolerable, incomprehensible, mad, crazy, chaotic, desolate, stormy, contradictory, unexceptional, stale, vicious, evil, bleak, dismal, dreary, unsafe, insecure, uncertain, chancy, risky, dangerous, rough, undaunted, hard-fought, lamentable, deplorable, grievous, rugged, shattered, outrageous, careless, false, deceitful, hypocritical, double, repetitive, unchanging, miserable, humdrum, monotonous, dull, restrictive, unsteady, sedentary, rural, urban, bucolic, future, migratory, transitory, peripatetic, celibate, married, family, reproductive, private, public, social, daily, everyday, day-to-day, civil, military, mercantile, materialistic, common, communal, inner, indoor, outdoor, contemplative, eternal, mental, ectoplasmic, (semi-)nomadic; aquatic, planktonic, microscopic

life-style, life-styles patrician, grand, opulent, ostentatious, lavish, luxurious, regal, privileged, gracious, refined, (un)healthy, (in)sane, (un)safe, (un)balanced, (im)prudent, cosy, unique, flamboyant, enjoyable, comfortable, unhurried, secure, carefree, uninhibited, open-ended, modest, simple, exotic,

self-indulgent, fat, stagnant, lazy,
sedentary, (in)active, hyperactive, busy,
stressful, rugged, (un)complicated,
workaholic, (un)traditional,
(un)conventional, (in)flexible, (in)formal,
casual, transient, vanishing, mobile,
slapdash, vegetative, dull, unthinking,
passive, (un)acceptable, alternative,
materialistic, private, secretive, loose,
hedonistic, decadent, promiscuous,
outdoor, native, indigenous

lift, lifts bumpy, electric, shop, outdoor,
direct-traction, glass(-sided)

light, lights blinding, glittering, glaring,
sparkling, glowing, twinkling, dazzling,
flaming, flashing, blinking, wavering,
searing, powerful, strong, bright, brilliant,
luminescent, shimmery, glimmery, shrill,
vibrant, limpid, intense, dense, hard,
harsh, insufferable, unbearable,
full-spectrum, marvellous, visible, naked,
stark, steady, crimson, ochrous, darkish,
coppery, white, peachy, translucent,
candescent, clear, undiluted, lurid,
lambent, glare-free, sullen, dim, faint, soft,
subdued, mellow, pale, murky, sickly,
weak, feeble, pallid, pale, thin, misty,
molten, elusive, fading, waning, transient,
dappled, jagged, fibrous, eerie, weird,
bizarre, unearthly, uncanny, mysterious,
nightmarish, gaudy, poor, cold,
(in)adequate, oblique, (in)direct, indoor,
outdoor, natural, artificial, warning, tail,
side, brake, seasonal, kaleidoscopic,
achromatic, shadowless, laser, fluorescent,
polar, auxiliary, ultraviolet, neon, city,
night, strobe (stroboscope), zodiacal,
auroral, flashing, southern, northern,
green, red, offshore, photographic, festive,
Klieg (Kleig)

lighthouse, lighthouses round, square,
six-sided, eight-sided, (candy-)striped, rare,
modern, powerful, automatic,
atom-powered, abandoned

lighting See *light*

lightning, lightnings gleaming, flashing,
blinding, intermittent, rapid, quick, swift,
violent, lethal, steely, jagged, forked
(zigzag, chain)

likelihood remote, improbable, slight,
high, maximum, every

likeness, likenesses flattering, striking,
speaking, good, exact, perfect, truthful,

formidable, inveterate, remote, superficial,
slight, uncanny

liking, likings reciprocal, strong,
(un)healthy, (un)wholesome, morbid

limb, limbs See also *hand* (1) and *leg*
trembling, writhing, stiffening, powerful,
pouchy, turgid, swollen, scraggly, gangly,
tumid, rudimentary, undeveloped, naked,
artificial, bionic, electronic, spastic,
arthritic, distal, proximal

limit, limits (un)reasonable, (un)acceptable,
(in)tolerable, (un)bearable, discernible,
permissible, vulnerable, strict, tough,
severe, rigid, lax, mandatory, supposed,
temporary, clear, legal

limitation, limitations annoying, grinding,
aggravating, distressing, harassing,
(un)reasonable, (un)acceptable,
troublesome, vexatious, traditional,
physical, mental, intellectual

line, lines right, straight, direct, rigid,
unwavering, wavy, wiggly, undulating,
heavy, continuous, (ir)regular,
(in)definable, (in)visible, now-visible,
perpendicular, oblique, slanting, diagonal,
concurrent, forward, structural, transverse,
wiggly, squiggly, hazy, fine, sleek, frail,
(un)broken, jagged, hard, vertical,
horizontal, asymptotic, converging,
starting, dividing, unbalanced,
genealogical, dead, side, isogonal, agonic,
pure, equinoctial, geodesic; assembly;
main; bottom; firing; hot; receiving;
umbilical, intravenous; seismic

liner, liners See *ship*

lingerie See *underwear*

linguistics diachronic, synchronic,
comparative, structural, descriptive,
historical

link, links definite, strong, close, (in)direct,
key, (un)breakable, (in)dissoluble,
(in)extricable, subtle, vibrant, vital,
far-reaching, extensive, tangible,
discernible, evident, apparent, obvious,
ostensible, consistent, sole, odd, grotesque,
secret, obscure, mysterious, intermediate,
intricate, complex, tangled, common,
possible, weak, remote, tenuous, frail,
suggestive, dubious, questionable,
(long-)binding, missing, symbiotic, genetic,
historic, physical, mental, personal,
umbilical

lion, lions roaring, snarling, wandering,

biting, reclining, rampant, couchant, lean, fluffy, rangy, tawny, dusky, swarthy, muscular, majestic, brave, courageous, valiant, fearsome, fierce, savage, ferocious, lazy, nomadic, caged, domesticated

lip, lips ruby, rubious, coral, rosy, (rose-)red, blood-red, blue-red, cherry(-red), purple, blue, bluish, vivid, beautiful, rich, warm, sensual, sensuous, alluring, luscious, petulant, aloof, rose-leaf, (well-)chiselled, cleft, curled, in-bred, bevelled, broad, flat, tiny, pursy, fine, thin, smooth, velvety, soft, bony, hard, strong, coarse, blubber, full, plump, heavy, thick, fat, huge, big, large, simian, stiff, taut, languid, sleepy, pendulous, loose, sloppy, pouty, flaky, protruding, gaping, precise, dry, moist, juicy, chapped, cracked, wrinkled, parched, swollen, scarred, whiskered, nether, lower, upper, prehensile

liqueur, liqueurs See *liquor*

liquid, liquids flowing, pouring, steaming, bubbly, effervescent, oily, milky, watery, pasty, syrupy, sticky, frothy, (un)stable, (im)pure, volatile, washy, hardened, thick, thin, sour(ish), briny, viscous, cloudy, murky, clear, bright, translucent, fine, solvent, (in)soluble, water-soluble, (im)miscible, subtile, transparent, mobile, homogeneous, colourless, odourless, tasteless, fragrant, pleasant-smelling, aromatic, pungent, deadly, sterile, toxic, (in)flammable, combustible, poisonous, menacing, organic, synthetic, corrosive, antiseptic, hygroscopic, lachrymatory

liquor, liquors smooth, clear, pure, fine, exquisite, top-brand, hard, spirituous, rare, fruity, pungent, rich, full-bodied, strong, powerful, potent, searing, fiery, lethal, deadly, dangerous, harmful, injurious, ruinous, contraband, alcoholic, duty-free

list, lists full, (in)complete, exhaustive, extensive, lengthy, staggering, lavish, detailed, unending, endless, inclusive, up-to-date, ongoing, (in)flexible, growing, (in)accurate, meticulous, impressive, preliminary, partial, selective, selected, supplementary, suggestive, interesting, free, short, long, perfunctory, grim, mental, civil, honour, wine, voting, active, waiting, mailing; back; critical; civil

listener, listeners attentive, interested, supportive, sympathetic, avid, consistent, respectful, wonderful, tireless, surreptitious, curious, (un)inquisitive

listening intense, breathless, enthusiastic, intent, zealous, sombre; easy

literacy basic, functional, precocious

literature, literatures consummate, pure, rich, lasting, spirited, pious, profane, obscene, libertine, subversive, archetypal, classic, modern, contemporary, indigenous, oral, (non-)fictional, narrative, comparative, poetic, pastoral, folk, juvenile, didactic, informative, intellectual, committed, escapist, diversionary, imaginative

litter See *rubbish*

livelihood, livelihoods lucrative, bare, precarious, uncertain, mendicant, meagre, secondary

living, livings expansive, lush, luxury, (in)decent, (un)healthy, good, graceful, gracious, (un)safe, high, purposeful, careful, sacramental, joyous, easy-going, carefree, plain, casual, precarious, uncertain, haphazard, bare, slender, meagre, hand-to-mouth, frugal, fast, indecent, sordid, slipshod, subhuman, careless, furtive, riotous, wild, (un)restrained, sequestered, secluded, day-to-day, daily, routine, contemporary, inner, communal, urban, suburban, rural

living conditions See *condition* (1)

lizard, lizards rustling, darting, creeping, crawling, sleepy, swift, cold-blooded, fringe-toed, frilled, striped, collared, spiny, flaky, poisonous, bloodthirsty, terrestrial, diurnal

load, loads tottering, tiring, crushing, mountainous, peak, substantial, heavy, bulky, massive, hefty, ponderous, enormous, big, fearful, formidable, disproportionate, full, partial, light, (un)manageable, dead

loaf, loaves See also *bread* fresh, stale, undersize, oversize, flat, round, plump, dense, crusty, soft, speckled, standard, ornate, gourmet, exotic, gingerbread, farmhouse, fruit, batch, pan, coburg, Jewish, English, French; meat

loan, loans substantial, big, large, huge, goodly, considerable, extravagant, (im)moderate, multimillion-dollar, generous, petty, small, modest, sound, outstanding, mature, high-interest, low-interest, interest-free, low-cost, variable-rate, short-term, intermediate-term, long-term, (in)flexible, (un)forgivable, instant, outright, anonymous, sour, bad, uncollectible, delinquent, insolvent, shaky, troubled, hopeless, risky, fraudulent, fake, commercial, home-equity, day-to-day, sectoral, open-ended, soft

lobby, lobbying shrewd, formidable, unconquerable, (in)effective, dynamic, forceful, feverish, vigorous, frantic, well-connected, professional

lobster, lobsters See also *fish* crawling, creeping, clawless, hoary; spiny (rock)

location, locations unique, exotic, unrivalled, great, strategic, central, prime, prestigious, superior, remarkable, spectacular, fabulous, enviable, fantastic, (in)convenient, good, fine, advantageous, fortuitous, picturesque, felicitous, (in)auspicious, sought-after, (un)favourable, (un)desirable, (il)logical, (un)suitable, safe, remote, hard-to-reach, out-of-the-way, (in)accessible, vulnerable, temporary, hypothetical, scattered, bad, precarious, desolate, backwater, undesired, (top-)secret, (still-)undisclosed, (un)specified, (un)known, (yet-to-be-)chosen, exact, precise, geographic(al), geologic(al), bucolic, strategic

lock, locks (1: a fastening for a door) secure, foolproof, stiff, tricky, insecure, electric, warded, Yale

lock, locks (2: a portion of hair) golden, soft, curly, flowing, rebellious, wild, disorderly

locomotive, locomotives diesel, steam, gas-turbine, electric, ignition

lodging, lodgings See *house*

log, logs huge, mossy, yule

logic clear, irrefutable, incontrovertible, unfaltering, compelling, subtle, inexorable, unyielding, unrelenting, cold, faulty, tortuous, twisted, fuzzy, perverse, spurious, strange, futile, conventional, traditional, modern, intuitive, inductive, deductive, symbolic (mathematical), Aristotelian

loneliness harrowing, distressing, depressing, worrying, painful, awful, terrible, indescribable, incredible, unbelievable, uneasy, unbearable, intolerable, embittered, desolate, forlorn, barren, dry, hard, intense, immense, abject, immutable, monkish, secluded, unrelieved

longing, longings fond, profound, intense, wistful, nostalgic, unbearable, desperate, vague, strange, curious, sudden, irresistible, inexpressible, immortal, nameless, instinctive, universal

look, looks cheerful, joyful, jubilant, pretty, good, lively, flower-like, comely, attractive, appealing, bewitching, charming, enchanting, luscious, angelic, radiant, placid, serene, grateful, sympathetic, thoughtful, tender, forgiving, glamorous, amorous, amatory, fond, loving, searching, piercing, incisive, fixed, steadfast, steady, stony, sinister, expectant, unbending, blank, flat, unflinching, distant, absent, abstracted, grumbling, sober, careful, close, concerned, anxious, contented, gay, frank, knowing, incredulous, imperious, lingering, rangy, outdoor(sy), anguished, alert, true, wistful, pensive, resigned, eager, earnest, solemn, stern, offbeat, troubled, agitated, dreamy, sceptical, suspicious, mysterious, enigmatic, incomprehensible, inscrutable, waggish, determined, pale, thin, sharp, fierce, severe, hard, startled, furtive, fleeting, stealthy, secret(ive), quirky, revealing, meaning, knowing, reflective, bewildered, firm, intense, intent, misty, astute, shrewd, realistic, statuesque, hollow-eyed, whimsical, quizzical, monitory, admonitory, condemnatory, reproachful, interrogative, bold, immodest, aloof, impudent, cautionary, wistful, gloomy, bleak, sullen, dour, languishing, glum, sulky, sad, miserable, distressed, black, crazed, cowed, perfunctory, withering, disdainful, scornful, contemptuous, sneaking, cunning, jealous, mean, spiteful, affronted, pained, sheepish, embarrassed, dull, disturbed, withdrawn, desperate, pleading, sly, fishy, deceitful, deceptive, repulsive, rugged, vicious, mischievous, sour, nasty, pained, wicked, scorching, scowling, angry, enraged, resentful, hostile, unfriendly, inimical, guilty, ireful, ghastly, dissatisfied, grumbling, vindictive, vacuous, dry, wan, woebegone, threatening, venomous, curdling, cloudy, fearful, timorous, unwholesome, owlish, hawk-like, faraway, sideways, sidelong, close-up, backward, quick, graphic, comprehensive, come-hither

loophole, loopholes sacrosanct, inviolable, sacred, legal

lorry, lorries light, heavy, supplies-laden, bunting-clad, six-metre-long, four-wheel-drive, ten-ton, derelict, rattletrap, rumbling, whining, open, diesel, flatbed, low-loader, highway, tank(er), multi-stop, refrigerator, pick-up, tar-laying, grain-hauling, juggernaut, tip-up

loser, losers clear-cut, good, gallant, cheerful, bad, discontented, ultimate

loss, losses (ir)reparable, (ir)recoverable, (ir)retrievable, (ir)redeemable, (ir)remediable, oppressive, wasteful, grievous, worrisome, horrendous, steep, deep, siz(e)able, appreciable, enormous, tremendous, incalculable, immeasurable, inestimable, huge, massive, widespread, extensive, large(-scale), big, hefty, acute, significant, major, gigantic, record, unprecedented, thumping, traumatic, complete, absolute, heavy, severe, dramatic, stinging, bitter, painful, incredible, unbelievable, heartburning, heart-rending, inconsolable, unappeasable, terrible, disastrous, catastrophic, devastating, stunning, crushing, staggering, drastic, steady, permanent, chronic, fatal, deadly, humbling, humiliating, continuous, outright, functional, actual, intimate, previous, sudden, dead, temporary, momentary, (un)acceptable, negligible, trifling, minimal, one-time, comparative, cumulative, consequential, accidental, short-term, paper, material, monetary, capital, operating, partial, total, conceptual

lot, lots (an area of land) See at end of *site*

lotion, lotions soothing, antiseptic, mild, potent

lottery, lotteries (il)legal, controversial, global, international, worldwide, on-line, electronic

loudspeaker, loudspeakers blasting, raucous, concealed, built-in

lounge, lounges See *room*

love, loves abiding, enduring, unfailing, undying, (ever)lasting, burning, (un)demanding, overwhelming, binding, caring, unquestioning, pure, genuine, real, perceptive, tender, fond, reverent, torrid, unquenchable, unshaken, unshak(e)able, indissoluble, permanent, eternal, abundant, immeasurable, boundless, rapturous, earnest, ardent, passionate, affectionate, fervent, intense, frantic, fierce, profound, deep, (un)conditional, desperate, unquestionable, ideal, blind, obsessional, unearthly, integral, mutual, full-blown, extreme, inherent, inborn, defiant, hopeless, stormy, tempestuous, new-found, lost, (im)pure, furtive, secret, unabashed, shameless, shameful, wavering, changeable, sloppy, shallow, superficial, false, childish, poignant, bitter-sweet, destructive, fatal, unreturned, unanswered, unrequited, unsanctioned, open, imperative, possessive, obsessive, sentimental, romantic, Platonic, spiritual, holy, sacrificial, concupiscent, brotherly, fraternal, sisterly, fatherly, paternal, mother(ly), maternal, parental, conjugal, physical, incestuous, adulterous, free, lustful, steamy, erotic, carnal, gay, homosexual, lesbian

love-letter, love-letters See also *letter* burning, torrid, ardent, passionate, fiery, impassioned, warm

love-making gratifying, enjoyable, pleasurable, sybaritic, rapturous, unsurpassed, non-stop

lover, lovers caring, billing, longing, infatuated, hot, constant, ardent, devoted, fond, tender, passionate, fervent, attentive, idyllic, solicitous, romantic, sentimental, chaste, capricious, reckless, irresistible, moonstruck, star-crossed, ill-fated, unlucky, inarticulate, bashful, reluctant, backward, disconsolate, designing, false, inconstant, fickle, changeable, casual, old-time, quondam, would-be, alleged, secret, physical, Platonic, illicit, live-in

loyalty, loyalties unswerving, unflinching, undeviating, unquestioning, unwavering, never-failing, fanatic, granitic, blind, misplaced, abused, strong, intense, firm, deep-rooted, lifelong, scrupulous, genuine, exceptional, uncritical, unquestioned, obsessive, indisputable, fierce, ferocious, slavish, canine, high(er), waning, ebbing, little, tenuous, dubious, (un)shaken, labile, dual, partisan, marital, personal, tribal

luck remarkable, wonderful, unbelievable,

incredible, phenomenal, unexpected, good, unhoped-for, unprecedented, adverse, ill, bad, foul, (un)favourable, tough, worsening, blind

luggage tough, portable, light, heavy, overweight, cumbersome (cumbrous), bulky, excessive, superfluous, incoming, outgoing, unaccompanied, unlabelled, unclaimed, unchecked, bomb-laden, broken, torn, soiled, personal, on-line

lull, lulls See *calm*

lumber See also *wood* (1) softwood, hardwood, rough, raw, unprocessed

lunch, lunches See also *meal* ample, huge, hearty, profligate, sumptuous, lavish, abundant, full-course, long, elegant, fattening, light, fine, meagre, frugal, hot, cold, lacklustre, traditional, set-price, lakeside, fieldside, buffet, picnic, stand-up, business(man's), work-related, working, state

luncheon, luncheons See *lunch*

lung, lungs (in)efficient, (un)healthy, scarless, pinkish, slate-coloured, blotchy, scarred, mottled, wheezy, consumptive, cancerous

lure (1: charm) See *charm*

lure, lures (2: artificial bait) enticing, shimmery, glimmery, shiny, brightly-coloured, colourful

lust, lusts virile, insatiable, unsatisfiable, uncontrollable, obsessive, thick, predatory, unrestrained

lustre, lustres glistering, glistening; sheeny, unfaded, undulled, untarnished

luxuriance teeming, affluent, abundant, constant, extravagant, exuberant, lavish, sumptuous

luxury, luxuries blissful, sybaritic, profuse, unimaginable, ostentatious, superfluous, unmeaning, meaningless, senseless, ludicrous, unbelievable, incredible, unashamed, inappropriate, decadent, forbidden, sinful, superficial, dispensable, unequalled, expensive, (un)affordable, discreet, comparative

lying See also *lie* copious, conscious, incorrigible, outright

lyric, lyrics See also *poem* moving, powerful, salty, wry, suave, well-known, memorable, changeable, short, (un)rhymed, amatory, graphic, suggestive, obscene, dramatic, mystical, musical

machination, machinations See *plot* (1)

machine, machines ingenious, (in)efficient, wonderful, astonishing, remarkable, incredible, unbelievable, revolutionary, advanced, sophisticated, state-of-the-art, leading-edge, labour-saving, sleek, versatile, foolproof, (im)practical, self-contained, self-acting, intricate, complicated, implacable, hands-off, polyphase, automatic, heavy, sturdy, ravenous, monstrous, gargantuan, hot, simple, zany, small-scale, large-scale, special, bulky, idle, clangorous, defective, worn-out, antiquated, outdated, obsolete, archaic, dead, creaky, steam-powered, wind-powered, solar, thermal, coin-operated, hydraulic, electronic, inductive, synchronous, cryptographic, robotic; military

machinery See *machine*

madness raving, dizzying, utter, abject, fabulous, ruddy, hopeless, flat, ultimate, addled, wild, delirious, deranged, witless, sheer, stark, arrant, quintessential, irrevocable, suicidal, alcoholic, intrinsic, congenital, hereditary; midsummer

magazine, magazines prominent, respectable, venerable, illustrious, intelligent, serious, influential, distinctive, prestigious, glamorous, esteemed, world-class, meretricious, authoritative, profitable, slick, highbrow, esoteric, traditional, snappy, oversize, home-made, up-to-date-fashionable, glossy, gaudy, tawdry, garish, flashy, newsy, raunchy, brassy, brash, tony, faddy, hot, sensationalistic, broad, popular, general-interest, (in)accessible, (now-)defunct, solvent, ailing, failing, troubled, cash-strapped, fledgling, short-lived, radical, contraband, irreverent, obscure, frothy, saucy, dull, dronish, dissident, weekly, bi-weekly, tri-weekly, semi-weekly, monthly, bi-monthly, semi-monthly, yearly, bi-yearly, semi-yearly, quarterly, regional, national, international, pictorial, illustrated, gossipy, naughty, girlie (girly), adult, pornographic, sex(-orient(at)ed), dirty, filthy, smutty, sleazy, disreputable, life-style, (high-)fashion, feminist, little, small-circulation, paid-circulation, satiric(al), intellectual, professional, literary, periodical, in-flight, geographic(al), expatriate

magic charming, bewitching, instant, awesome, powerful, white, black, sympathetic, cabalistic

magician, magicians adept, skilful, dext(e)rous, deft, clever, experienced, great, whiz-bang, amateur, professional

magistrate, magistrates See *judge*

magnet, magnets powerful, weak, natural, horseshoe, bar, U-shaped

magnificence imposing, surpassing, extraordinary, exalted, grand, elegant, glorious, awesome, imperial, majestic, splendid, spectacular, stately, sublime, sumptuous, indescribable

magnitude, magnitudes infinite, enormous, tremendous, great, unparalleled, proportionate, apparent, absolute

maid, maids (female servant) See also *servant* (in)competent, (ir)responsible, (un)trustworthy, trim, affable, spunky, impudent, saucy, pert, clumsy, slovenly; general

mail See also *letter* (un)welcome, (un)reliable, (ir)regular, unpredictable, morning, afternoon, express, air, surface, first-class, second-class, third-class, dead, direct, electronic, inland, overseas, personal, confidential

maintenance (service) meticulous, scrupulous, conscientious, (im)proper, careful, (in)adequate, careless, poor, cheap, costly, short-term, long-term, (in)essential, routine, (ir)regular, preventive

majesty, majesties incomparable, peerless, sublime, glorious, dignified, grand(iose), stately, statuesque, divine, regal, imperial, royal, kingly, princely, queenly, ceremonial

majority, majorities overwhelming, great, large, siz(e)able, heavy, thumping, swingeing, whopping, predominant, resounding, comfortable, handsome, substantial, (rock-)solid, record, clear, unprecedented, lopsided, massive, huge, vast, strong, powerful, commanding, influential, formidable, triumphant,

outright, silent, compact, fragile, shaky, narrow, slim, paper-thin, simple, absolute, overall, working, built-in, electoral

make-up elegant, discreet, (un)obtrusive, prominent, curious, heavy, gaudy, garish, brassy, liquid, pancake, cosmetic, theatrical, stage, circus, character, clown

malady, maladies See *disease*

malaise virulent, incurable, chronic, acute, intermittent, general, pervasive, persistent, haunting, compelling, regular, physical, nervous, neurotic

malefactor, malefactors See *criminal*

malice See also *hate* unreasoning, covert, overt, aforethought, premeditated, petty, ill-natured, bitter, cruel, sheer, personal

man, men See also Appendixes A and B masculine, womanly, effeminate, aged, middle-aged, affluent, natural, new, private, moribund, outdoor, primitive, prissy, prim, right-hand, urban, rural, masterful, your-mother-would-love-you-to-date, bring-home-to-mother, self-educated, self-made, clean-shaven, balding, considerable, superior, rugged, hairy, well-built, able-bodied, muscular, tough, solitary, independent, unworldly, self-effacing, primeval, cadaverous, free, mortal, individual, common, collective; straw, front, end; con; Neolithic, Pal(a)eolithic, Neanderthal

management, managements (un)intelligent, (un)sound, (in)competent, careful, (un)skilled, (un)wise, tough-minded, loving, paternalistic, good, aggressive, new, sloppy, careless, slothful, inept, arrogant, distant, bureaucratic, poor, bad, upper, industrial, personnel, market, financial, strategic, general, business

manager, managers articulate, astute, brilliant, (in)competent, (in)efficient, energetic, hands-on, inept, top, senior, middle, district, area, corporate, general, business, industrial

mandate, mandates clear, broad, huge, open-ended, limited, narrow

manhunt, manhunts massive, intensive, large-scale, nationwide

mania, manias See *craze* and *madness*

maniac, maniacs unreasoning, crazy, crazed, demented, deranged, dangerous, violent, psychotic

manifestation, manifestations refreshing, open, apparent, evident, obvious, undisguised, overt, tactile, tangible, direct, verbal

manipulation, manipulations clever, dext(e)rous, skilful, deft, cunning, foxy, smooth, facile, neat, underhand, indirect, callous, ruthless

manipulator, manipulators See *manipulation*

manner (individual style; method) friendly, decisive, resolute, dignified, kind, moving, touching, orderly, attractive, elaborate, refined, elegant, polished, professional, calm, composed, subdued, alert, lively, humane, light-hearted, easy-going, high-spirited, jaunty, exemplary, masterly, responsible, folksy, winning, charming, persuasive, considerate, unpretentious, unimpeachable, neat, perspicuous, succinct, straightforward, unassuming, tender, regal, courtly, baronial, lofty, proud, technocratic, simple, painstaking, singular, distinctive, (un)obtrusive, self-deprecating, matronly, impassioned, sedate, usual, grave, detached, laughing, unceremonial, casual, commanding, authoritative, determined, insistent, cautious, adult, (self-)complacent, flamboyant, effervescent, vivacious, hammy, offhand, arrogant, imperious, pompous, harsh, forbidding, grim, discouraging, gruff, crude, rough, surly, rude, icy, cold, unfriendly, snobbish, helter-skelter, confused, hurried, irresolute, outward, artificial, insincere, officious, meddlesome, stiff, peremptory, dictatorial, prepossessing, possessive, blustery, inhumane, superficial, bureaucratic, cumbersome, threatening, provocative, aggressive, humourless, frantic, irresponsible, negligent, reckless, humiliating, affected, silly, stealthy, fractious, restless, whimsical, odd, bizarre, silken, sinuous, stag(e)y, uncivilized, useemly, vainglorious, hesitant, withdrawn, unresponsive, undisciplined, aloof, opportunistic, furtive, sloppy

manners (social behaviour) affable, courteous, good, nice, pleasant, natural, genial, elegant, grand, courtly, florid, suave, debonair, (im)proper, perfect, (un)acceptable, (un)polished, (un)refined, impeccable, correct, respectable, (un)cultured, taking, winning, endearing, unpretending, homely, conventional, provincial, rustic, countrified, stiffish, undemonstrative, awkward, gross, bad, vulgar, harsh, coarse, ill, appalling, outrageous, atrocious, shocking, crude, awkward, rude, uncouth, abominable, affected, rotten, social

manoeuvre, manoeuvres subtle, nimble, shrewd, clever, skilful, deft, dext(e)rous, sophisticated, precise, intense, frantic, full-scale, secret, hidden, wily, sly, cunning, crafty, devious, evasive, inept, self-serving, daring, brutal, subterranean, tactical, political

manoeuvring See *manoeuvre*

mansion, mansions forbidding, imposing, charming, sprawling, rambling, expansive, enormous, multistorey, palatial, castled, sumptuous, stately, great, handsome, elegant, luxurious, plush, lavish, splendid, magnificent, heavenly, old, ancient, secluded, mysterious, sepulchral, rustic, steep-roofed, turreted, gabled, colonial(-style), neoclassical, ante-bellum, medieval, Georgian, Palladian

manslaughter See *killing*

manufacture, manufacturing See also *industry* (1) (non-)durable, flexible, computer-aided, computer-assisted, industrial, heavy

manuscript, manuscripts precious, valuable, priceless, pricey, irreplaceable, marketable, publishable, authentic, genuine, real, bona fide, rare, one-of-a-kind, extant, aged, ancient, original, (il)legible, foul, corrupt, fake, paper, papyrus, historical, literary, musical

map, maps spectacular, superb, magnificent, (un)clear, (in)comprehensible, (un)readable, substantive, detailed, factual, state-of-the-art, leading-edge, modern, up-to-date, (un)reliable, (in)accurate, (in)appropriate, informative, decorative, crude, outdated, dog-eared, visionary, rectangular, two-panel, large-scale, small-scale, (shaded-)relief, contour, panoramic, three-dimensional, double-sided, two-sided, fold-out, thematic, high-tech, computer-drawn, electronic, official, administrative, (geo)political, physical, geologic(al),

topographic(al), celestial, aerial, historical, pocket, road, route, local, antique, intergalactic, satellite, world, (general-)reference, archaeological, military, aeronautical

marble, marbles imperishable, mottled, banded, variegated, (multi-)coloured, discoloured, white, black, grey, pale, pink, pink-and-white, reddish, greenish, lucent, luminescent, serpentine, powdery, fossiliferous, statuary

march, marches interminable, endless, wearisome, difficult, forced, onward, forward, backward, (il)legal, (un)authorized, phon(e)y, irreversible, steady, quick, 10,000-strong, regimental, military, ceremonial, demonstration, protest

marcher, marchers proud, agile, weary, exhausted, reluctant, undisciplined, unruly, banner-waving, protest

mark, marks (visible indication or sign) distinguishing, peculiar, (in)visible, (un)recognizable, indelible, lasting, ubiquitous, faint, minimum, black, livid; high-water, low-water; diacritical, editorial

market, markets (1: trade; the field of business) surging, flourishing, thriving, fast-growing, booming, tempting, leading, strong, large, buoyant, remarkable, orderly, active, brisk, vibrant, lively, easy, favourable, bullish, optimistic, (red-)hot, big, (un)healthy, (in)efficient, (un)competitive, powerful, dynamic, aggressive, lucrative, infinite, insatiable, soft, ready, borderless, (wide-)open, unfettered, free, irrepressible, ubiquitous, upscale, (un)stable, untapped, virgin, adaptable, eager, whiplash, skittish, turbulent, volatile, unsettled, uncertain, unpredictable, crucial, entry-level, competitive, unprecedented, pent-up, nervous, arcane, liquid, quiet, calm, jittery, wild, frenzied, rambunctious, unruly, panic-stricken, panicky, shaky, wobbly, lethargic, lackadaisical, flat, dispirited, depressed, thin, small, weak, restricted, limited, cheap, lifeless, dead, inactive, grey, languid, tight, lousy, dismal, unfavourable, stringent, fragile, stiff, thin, choppy, slow, slack, sluggish, stagnant, moribund, cut-throat, closed, potential, captive, world(wide), foreign, local, overseas, offshore, national, non-domestic, global, mass, broad, financial, speculative, wholesale, retail, grey, underground, black, common, commercial, spot, forward

market, markets (2: a place for selling and buying) thronging, buzzing, teeming, rollicking, sprawling, labyrinthine, crowded, busy, frenzied, chaotic, raucous, cacophonous, lively, earthy, down-to-earth, colourful, garish, dusty, booth-lined, covered, awninged, open(-air), street, outdoor, indoor, waterfront, morning, traditional, local, neighbourhood, wholesale, retail

marketing See *market* (1)

marketplace, marketplaces See *market* (2)

marriage, marriages satisfying, flourishing, lasting, enduring, rewarding, ongoing, wonderful, perfect, great, blessed, lucky, joyful, genuine, splendid, enjoyable, happy, blissful, honourable, healthy, harmonious, strong, close, (un)stable, viable, correct, lifetime, long-time, 25-year, intact, romantic, story-book, fairy-tale, advantageous, egalitarian, (un)workable, (un)fortunate, puzzling, childless, potential, turbulent, tempestuous, tumultuous, intolerable, (now-)broken, kaput, errant, traumatic, disastrous, short-lived, brief, dead(-end), unwise, irregular, shallow, immature, improvident, unsuitable, desultory, dull, boring, loveless, non-sexual, celibate, tense, unequal, stormy, hopeless, infirm, shaky, rickety, irreparable, umpteen, improper, unfortunate, ferocious, strained, ill-fated, doomed, failed, broken, dysfunctional, expedient, profitable, (non-)adulterous, disposable, impulsive, sacramental, inter-faith, interracial, mixed, conventional, traditional, companionate, diplomatic, strategic, consensual, dynastic, morganatic, instant, civil, shotgun, clandestine, proxy, secret, (il)legal, (il)legitimate, (un)lawful, (in)valid, sensuous, polygamous, common-law, open, heterosexual, same-sex, mass, adventurous, runaway, two-career, long-distance, sham, putative

marsh, marshes outlying, vast, open, silent, still, shallow, fertile, rich, fresh, brackish, loose, soupy, boggy, soggy, spongy, fenny, swampy, sedgy, ice-rimmed, windswept, pond-pocked, treeless, treacherous, uliginous, wet, coastal, inland, tidal, tidewater, salt, pristine

martyr, martyrs holy, blissful, saintly, pure, virgin, selfless, dedicated, latter-day, unsung, unknown, misunderstood, blessed, secular

marvel, marvels See *wonder* (2)

mask, masks inscrutable, fantastic, grotesque, odd, fiendish, humorous, long-nosed, fierce-looking, weird-looking, leering, two-sided, distorted, twisted, sterile, makeshift, metal, aluminium-foil, papier-mâché, scrap-paper, copper, brass, clay, rubber, chin-and-cheek, face, life, death, ceremonial, gauze, surgical, dramatic, theatrical, comic, tragic, funerary

masquerade, masquerades dazzling, flamboyant, garish, gaudy, elaborate, extravagant, resplendent; mere

mass, masses (1: a quantity of matter) homogeneous, conglomerate, leaden, inert, inactive, weighty, labyrinthine, crumpled, tangled, confused, unformed, impenetrable, (super)dense, solid, loose, molten, incoherent, irregular, formless, shapeless, meaningless, characterless, lumpy, frothy, pasty, pulpy, spongy, pliable

mass, masses (2: a large body of people in a compact group) suffering, toiling, seething, huddled, ignorant, unruly, unwashed, dangerous, broad, discontented

Mass, Masses (3: a celebration of Communion) solemn, three-hour, open-air, outdoor, special, pontifical, nuptial, memorial, Low, High, Solemn, Requiem, Votive

massacre, massacres ghastly, terrible, frightful, grisly, despicable, disgraceful, foul, abhorrent, unimaginable, unspeakable, brutal, brutish, barbaric, unprecedented, shameful, shameless, infamous, unprovoked, expedient, bloody, ritual

massage, massaging refreshing, soothing, stimulating, welcome, effective, lengthy, gentle, sensuous, sensual, pleasurable, illicit, rhythmic, traditional, therapeutic, indoor, outdoor, warm, cardiac

mast, masts tall, taut, rusted, raked, fold-down, main, fore, second, third, jury

master, masters easy, lenient, kind, sympathetic, good, nice, trusting, grand, regal, taciturn, unassailable, hard, unfeeling, stern, cruel, harsh, strict, severe, awful, exacting, (un)sympathetic, rightful, colonial; undisputed, legendary; Old

masterpiece, masterpieces invaluable, inestimable, priceless, singular, unique, undoubted, seminal, exquisite, magnificent, rare, colossal, timeless, ageless, lost, found, admitted, doubtful, popular, classical, artistic, literary

mastery See *skill*

mat, mats straw, rush, flax, grass, palm(-leaf), wicker, bamboo, reed, (hand)woven, door

match, matches (1: a pair suitably associated; a marriage union) excellent, precise, perfect, ideal, lucky, (un)suitable, mercenary

match, matches (2: a contest; a game) keen, spirited, impressive, big, glitzy, needle, crucial, play-off, charity

match, matches (3: a small stick tipped with material that is easily set on fire by friction) wooden, strike-anywhere, safety, sulphur

mate, mates ideal, steady, (un)faithful, (in)tolerable, (un)desirable, useful, sensuous, would-be

material, materials (1: substance of which a thing is made) thick, bulky, earthy, shoddy, serviceable, quality, sturdy, durable, indestructible, (im)perishable, advanced, exotic, waterproof, fireproof, (un)desirable, hazardous, dangerous, lethal, deadly, (non)flammable, (in)combustible, incendiary, explosive, fire-resistant, caustic, toxic, absorbent, (ultra-)light, elastic, resilient, flexible, pliable, yielding, soft, brittle, flimsy, filamentous, impervious, horny, calcareous, fibrous, nylon-like, fine-grained, porous, loose, compressible, (bio)degradable, powdery, raw, primary, secondary, man-made, synthetic, natural, organic, fibred, haemic, (non-)magnetic, (non-)plastic, sapraemic, residual, abrasive, fissionable, galactic, thermoplastic, radioactive, (non-)metallic, siliceous, chondritic, meteoritic, extraterrestrial; genetic

material (2: information to be used in a book, etc.) (in)accurate, (in)accessible, hard-to-access, (ir)relevant, (im)plausible, (in)credible, objective, subjective, objectionable, critical, factual, graphic, documentary, tabular, illustrative, topical, historical, scientific, research, background

material, materials (3: fabric) See *fabric*

materialism uncompromising, degrading, grasping, debasing, disgraceful, rapacious, greedy, coarse, vulgar, crude, crass, callow, degenerate, gross, ignoble, rude, uncivilized, uncultivated, unpolished, raw, frantic, obscene, dialectical

matter, matters (1: a subject under consideration) vital, priority, life-or-death, weighty, serious, grave, delicate, urgent, pressing, momentous, (un)important, (in)consequential, (in)significant, complex, complicated, intricate, confused, troubling, half-hearted, trivial, trifling, small, petty, light, simple, frivolous, commonplace, mundane, everyday, worldly, temporal, private, laughing, jesting, personal

matter (2: a substance) See *substance*

mattress, mattresses soft, hard, firm, inflatable, foam, spring, water, single, double, king-size

maturity responsible, rare, prime, (in)complete, full-blown, full-grown, precocious, late, sexual, menstrual, emotional

maze, mazes twisting, bewildering, puzzling, baffling, perplexing, enigmatic, intricate, inextricable, complex, involved, twisted, tangled, incomprehensible, impenetrable, endless, veritable, real, sleazy, Daedalian, labyrinthine; bureaucratic, political

meadow, meadows sloping, rolling, balding, flowering, flowery, grassy, marshy, spongy, swampy, lush, rich, velvety, glorious, emerald, bright, sunlit, sunny, breezy, pretty, tranquil, drowsy, parched, snowy, wild, high, level, flat, (un)even, broad, outlying, alpine, mountain, water

meal, meals satisfying, appealing, appetizing, captivating, tempting, inviting, nourishing, sumptuous, lavish, luxurious, exquisite, fabulous, magnificent, elaborate, decent, elegant, deluxe, splendid, impeccable, perfect, terrific, hearty, full,

substantial, tremendous, copious, huge,
square, big, hefty, abundant, siz(e)able,
large, enormous, massive, gargantuan,
prodigious, profligate, lingering, long,
slow, leisurely, multi(ple)-course,
five-course, full-course, delicate, seductive,
attractive, varied, imaginative, savoury,
tasty, delectable, delicious, mouthwatering,
lip-smacking, wonderful, delightful,
unsurpassed, excellent, good, colourful,
sensational, pleasurable, cheerful, luscious,
great, out-of-the-ordinary, memorable,
ethereal, fresh, nutritious, healthful,
healthy, sensible, light, (in)digestible,
fat-free, low-carbohydrate, high-protein,
carbohydrate-rich, (un)balanced, fattening,
greasy, fat-heavy, meatless, (im)proper,
solid, liquid, hot, frozen, ready-made,
uneaten, scratch, offbeat, versatile,
spur-of-the-moment, midday, late, early,
matutinal, noonday, set-price, favourite,
semi-formal, stiff, (ir)regular, normal,
scheduled, typical, uniform, brief, outdoor,
hurried, (in)formal, nominal, insufficient,
frugal, budget, inexpensive, thrifty,
economical, passable, slight, slender,
simple, small, paltry, scanty, meagre, poor,
modest, sketchy, niggardly, miserable,
execrable, abominable, dreadful, revolting,
monotonous, lack-lustre, unvarying, same,
(in)edible, dismal, tasteless, unsavoury,
disappointing, limp, gourmet, kosher,
nouvelle-cuisine, vegetarian, ceremonial,
celebratory, buffet-style, all-you-can-eat,
one-dish, communal

meaning, meanings plain, (un)clear,
unmistakable, innovative, timorous,
convolute(d), complex, perplexing, obscure,
cloudy, indeterminate, portentous,
multi-layered, vague, ambiguous,
inaccessible, mistaken, misunderstood,
held, general, particular, special, personal,
opposite, double, intrinsic, core, essential,
primary, secondary, surface, original,
latent, literal, learned, recondite,
casuistical, ulterior, symbolic, lexical,
connotative

meanness abject, sordid, vile, base,
contemptible, despicable, ignoble,
malicious, malignant, shameful, vicious,
wicked

means (1: method; process) foolproof,
(ir)rational, honest, novel, sophisticated,

(in)adequate, (in)effectual, (un)available,
casual, roundabout, devious, cunning,
deceitful, underhand, secret, clandestine,
dishonest, sinuous, violent, anachronistic

means (2: money; resource; wealth)
(in)secure, (in)adequate, independent,
private, slender, slight, humble, varied

measure, measures (1: a step taken;
proceeding) peaceful, pacific, correct,
(in)appropriate, (in)effective, (in)effectual,
telling, spectacular, resolute, (un)reliable,
(in)adequate, (in)sensible, (un)acceptable,
(sub)standard, vigorous, dramatic,
salutary, (in)sufficient, (un)enforceable,
(un)justifiable, innovative, (un)suitable,
(un)necessary, (un)welcome, significant,
common-sense, prudent, pragmatic,
practical, simple, heroic, prompt, urgent,
speedy, startling, sobering, unprecedented,
bold, desperate, indispensable, essential,
concrete, radical, decisive, stringent, stiff,
harsh, repressive, Draconian, extreme,
sweeping, violent, strict, optional,
compulsory, mandatory, obligatory, tough,
forcible, forceful, strong, drastic,
uncompromising, finger-in-the-dyke,
hazardous, wishy-washy, arbitrary, potent,
permissive, fraudulent, discriminatory,
blunt, crude, vindictive, half, partial,
transitional, preparatory, halfway,
stop-gap, temporary, interim, tentative,
special, additional, extraordinary,
alternative, retaliatory, disciplinary,
punitive, coercive, voluntary, defensive,
reformatory, reformative, reformist,
sanitary, hygienic, protective, preventive,
curative, remedial, corrective, conservation,
energy-saving, protectionist, security,
emergency, surveillance, panic, cost-saving,
cost-effective, cosmetic, administrative,
legal, relief

measure, measures (2: a unit, standard,
or system used) precise, careful, exact,
correct, refined, subtle, authentic,
(in)accurate, superficial, square, dry,
liquid, cubic, circular, linear (long),
dimensional

measurement, measurements See
measure (2)

meat, meats raw, rare, underdone,
medium-rare, well-done, chewy, burnt,
sun-cured, wind-dried, (vacuum-)packed,
hormone-treated, tender, fine, top-quality,

choice, prime, pink, pliant, succulent,
juicy, zesty, fresh, good, flavourful, tasty,
savoury, delicious, toothsome, scrumptious,
boneless, nutritious, lean, low-cholesterol,
sinewy, stringy, coarse(-grained), firm,
green, marbled, standard, utility, leathery,
hard, tough, dry, fatty, greasy, tasteless,
high, gam(e)y, day-old, flyblown, putrid,
rotten, putrescent, rancid, rank, disgusting,
diseased, tainted, measly, measled,
foul-smelling, putrescible, white, dark, red,
cold

mecca, meccas favourite, beloved,
offbeat, traditional

mechanic, mechanics ingenious,
proficient, courteous, adept, accomplished,
dext(e)rous, smart, masterful, resourceful,
(un)qualified, (un)skilled, (in)experienced,
(in)competent, (un)scrupulous, (dis)honest,
stupid, inept, automotive

mechanism, mechanisms See *system*

medal, medals prestigious, illustrious,
solitary, lowly, bogus, gold, silver, bronze,
competitive, commemorative, prize,
(long-)service, war, military; putty

meddling See *interference*

media free, uncensored, state-run,
uncontrolled, unbridled, popular,
sensationalist(ic), pervasive, adaptable,
versatile, babbling, trashy, sycophantic,
mainline, news, mass, electronic

mediation, mediations (non-)binding,
patient, confidential, incisive, trenchant,
clear-cut, crisp

mediator, mediators able, adept, expert,
outstanding, top, credible, trustworthy,
objective, detached, disinterested, aloof,
impartial, unbiased, forceful,
(self-)appointed

medication See *medicine* (1)

medicine, medicines (1: drug) See also
drug suave, active, powerful, strong,
potent, heavy, efficacious, crucial,
miraculous, wonder-working, life-saving,
God-sent, internal, external, oral, liquid,
generic, brand-name, proprietary(patent),
(im)proper, (dis)agreeable, bitter, curative,
(in)effective, (in)effectual, nasty,
unpalatable, distasteful, traditional,
(un)conventional, antiquated,
over-the-counter, (non-)prescription,
experimental, herbal, nauseous, restorative,
sedative, soporific, soothing, intravenous

medicine, medicines (2: the science of
treating disease) traditional,
(un)conventional, (non-)orthodox,
mainstream, high-tech, slap-happy, quack,
preventive, internal, psychosomatic,
forensic (legal), geriatric, pulmonary,
emergency, cardiac, behavioural, trauma,
occupational, industrial, general, folk,
veterinary, ayurvedic, holistic, alternative,
manipulative, reproductive,
complementary, molecular, nuclear, herbal,
physical, natural, allopathic, clinical,
hom(o)eopathic, high-altitude

mediocrity comfortable, (in)tolerable,
average, inferior, second-rate, second-class,
profound, universal

meditation, meditations rambling,
absorbing, engrossing, motionless, fixed,
profound, deep, solitary, pensive,
reflective, rapt, purposeful, transcendental,
church-like, prayerful, spiritual, cogitative

meditativeness See *meditation*

meeting, meetings well-conducted,
orderly, friendly, cordial, harmonious,
quiet, subdued, (un)pleasant, hopeful,
fruitful, constructive, convivial, brisk,
intensive, fortuitous, snap, mysterious,
startling, surprise, chance, casual,
perfunctory, accidental, protracted,
lengthy, long(-winded), marathon, short,
brief, gigantic, decisive, weighty, crucial,
climactic, historic, dramatic, memorable,
first-ever, high-level, high-powered,
unauthorized, teetotal, non-partisan,
down-to-earth, face-to-face, anti-climactic,
business-like, urgent, upcoming, untoward,
unruly, acrimonious, chaotic, stormy,
rocking, boisterous, turbulent, raucous,
tiresome, pathetic, tempestuous,
passionate, emotional, tense, frosty,
ill-fated, discordant, intolerable, futile,
fruitless, unplanned, unscheduled,
unexpected, uninterrupted, unattended,
backroom, confidential, secret, clandestine,
surreptitious, sporadic, weekly, monthly,
yearly, annual, once-a-decade, bi-weekly,
fortnightly, triennial, quarterly, plenary,
plenum, one-to-one, closed-door, private,
general, public, special, (ir)regular, broad,
open, joint, emergency, exploratory,
discretionary, obligatory, preliminary,
initial, opening, wind-up, ceremonial,
summit, multifront, extraordinary, official,

(in)formal, business, organizational, procedural, pre-summit, crisis, mediation, community, mass, celebratory

melancholy settled, thoughtful, inexplicable, strange, affected, feigned, bittersweet, morbid, pathological, Darwinian

melodrama, melodramas See also *tragedy* (2) and *play* (1) muted, overheated, murky, full-throated, scatological, stock, outrageous

melody, melodies stimulating, charming, haunting, yearning, flowing, rippling, soothing, harmonious, rhythmic, pretty, pleasant, graceful, lovely, hymn-like, impassioned, singable, memorable, merry, energetic, catchy, soft, unearthly, vapid, boring, tedious, dull, lifeless, syncopated, unheard, shopworn, basic

member, members See also Appendixes A and B dynamic, (in)active, (un)desirable, established, respectable, honourable, venerable, valuable, constructive, solid, illustrious, high-profile, prominent, upstanding, maverick, controversial, low-profile, dissenting, unelected, chartered, senior, junior, old, new, full(-status), (non-)voting, provisional, regular, rank-and-file, (non-)permanent, alternative, alternate, potential, paid-up, associate, corporate, honorary, life(time), bona fide, participating, common, external, corresponding, statutory, advisory

membership, memberships fledgling, (un)limited, (un)stable, lapsed, temporary, life, honorary; grass-roots

memoir, memoirs See *memory* (1) and *autobiography*

memo(randum), memos See *note* (2)

memorial, memorials massive, gigantic, awesome, granite, bronze, attractive, eloquent, lasting, enduring, durable, permanent, perpetual, marble, brass

memory, memories (1: recollection) stirring, moving, (self-)revealing, entertaining, tantalizing, charming, lovely, fond, pleasant, wonderful, warm, heartfelt, fragrant, rosy, golden, idyllic, ecstatic, exuberant, delightful, rich, touching, tender, hallowed, blissful, lasting, abiding, enduring, permanent, special, intimate, hom(e)y, precious, insouciant, satisfying, affectionate, rose-tinted, provocative,

(long-)dormant, deep, sharp, keen, vivid, clear, (in)distinct, indelible, evanescent, fresh, recent, early, distant, far-reaching, clustering, overwhelming, compelling, rollicking, fleeting, fading, receding, unfaded, faint, tenuous, nebulous, vaporous, misty, vague, hazy, dim, clouded, shadowy, surreal, dream-like, dreamy, pensive, mercurial, elusive, fragmentary, rambling, garrulous, dominant, sensitive, poignant, sharp(-edged), magical, potent, close, unusual, incredible, extraordinary, sacred, larky, confused, dreadful, grim, sombre, wistful, galling, harrowing, distressing, chilling, haunting, ugly, ghastly, nightmarish, unpleasant, uneasy, unbearable, bitter, horrific, terrible, bad, harsh, treacherous, painful, bittersweet, traumatic, suppressed, delirious, wilful, introspective, fictional, childhood, boyhood, living, graphic, nostalgic, historic, amorous, personal, common

memory, memories (2: ability to remember) strong, powerful, tenacious, retentive, stupendous, impeccable, (un)erring, (in)fallible, (un)reliable, remarkable, exceptional, phenomenal, singular, inexhaustible, long(-term), good, astonishing, amazing, prodigious, conscious, selective, faulty, fragile, failing, bad, shocking, short(-term), collective, verbal, photographic, visual, episodic, semantic, iconic, echoic

menace, menaces See *threat*

mention honourable, deferential, respectful, specific, passing, casual, cursory, oblique, obscure, whimsical

menu, menus tempting, elaborate, lavish, extravagant, rich, sumptuous, expensive, special, unusual, smart, balanced, splendid, eclectic, complete, expansive, comprehensive, extensive, inventive, sprightly, exotic, adventurous, mouthwatering, standard, fail-safe, unpretentious, simple, meagre, sparse, monotonous, alternative, continental, ethnic, vegetarian

merchandise See *goods*

merchant, merchants prosperous, shrewd, active, alert, foremost, quality, prominent, (un)scrupulous, (dis)honest, wily, snide, crooked, (un)successful

merit, merits enduring, lasting, unpretending, outstanding, congenial, special, unusual, limitless, intrinsic, relative, (un)questionable, (un)equivocal, unrecognized, unrewarded, dubious, artistic

merriment See *gaiety*

mess, messes slovenly, chaotic, total, mixed, incomprehensible, awful, disgraceful, scandalous, dreadful, hideous, horrible, pretty, ghastly, unholy, unplanned, financial

message, messages unifying, conciliatory, gracious, upbeat, cheerful, hopeful, optimistic, meaningful, influential, important, vital, authoritative, subliminal, expressive, terse, laconic, concise, pointed, subtle, (un)clear, frank, blunt, (im)perceptible, unmistakable, vague, (un)equivocal, (un)ambiguous, cryptic, streamlined, explosive, strong, powerful, tough, stern, stiff, specific, particular, eternal, ominous, mournful, platitudinous, positive, serious, uncompromising, sober(ing), alarming, chilling, disquieting, apocalyptic, cautionary, overriding, pervasive, stony, unfeeling, heartless, obdurate, defiant, suppliant, sombre, grim, tart, irresponsible, quibbling, meaningless, inexpressive, urgent, strident, swift, rapid, laggard, (top-)secret, lengthy, long-winded, squiggly, wordless, unspoken, written, incoming, oral, vocal, verbal, personal, collective, universal, divine, promotional; mixed

messenger, messengers swift, wing-footed, sure, (un)reliable, special, diplomatic

metal, metals rugged, tough, coarse, screechy, tenacious, stubborn, intractable, cohesive, strong, heavy, light(-weight), powdery, soft, hot, heat-resistant, gleaming, shiny, filmy, crystalline, pure, molten, (non-)corrugated, jagged, twisted, versatile, recyclable, valuable, (quasi-)precious, semi-precious, plentiful, active, common, base, noble, white (antifriction), yellow, scrap, rare-earth, road, (non-)magnetic, (non-)ferrous, ferromagnetic, fine, ductile, malleable, primary, monovalent, alkali, electropositive

metaphor, metaphors compelling, effective, illustrative, imaginative, felicitous, well-chosen, apt, overriding, evocative, powerful, vivid, poignant, (in)appropriate, unprecedented, unique, (un)familiar, rhetorical, bombastic, arcane, dead, sensuous, innocent, tactile, ill-chosen, loose, mixed, sustained, poetic, polysynthetic; personal

method, methods unique, ingenious, (in)efficient, foolproof, infallible, valid, efficacious, (dis)honest, straightforward, scrupulous, fair, sophisticated, innovative, clear, productive, suitable, appropriate, accurate, precise, meticulous, thorough, perfect, exact, systematic, newfangled, modern, up-to-date, revolutionary, fresh, handy, (in)direct, facile, practical, practicable, simple, least-cost, particular, alternative, leading, rigorous, spectacular, (in)formal, (un)reliable, (un)acceptable, (in)effective, tried, superior, inferior, sensational, blatant, ancient, traditional, (un)conventional, (un)orthodox, regular, old-fashioned, outmoded, antiquated, obsolete, squalid, slipshod, crude, futile, strong-arm, extremist, brutal, violent, tough, awkward, unhandy, questionable, wasteful, deceitful, crooked, unscrupulous, cunning, crafty, astute, sly, doubtful, uncomradely, devious, clandestine, backdoor, underhand, dishonest, furtive, roundabout, unsuited, flawed, expensive, established, (well-)tried, favoured, rule-of-thumb, experimental, comparative, scientific, deductive, evolutionary, clinical, scholarly, high-tech, pragmatic, prescriptive, catechetical, Machiavellian; historical, Socratic

metre, metres (measured rhythm in verse) crude, rocking-horse, iambic, trochaic, dactylic, spondaic, anapaestic, amphibrachic, alliterative

microphone, microphones (in)visible, hidden, small, faulty, cordless, personal, pencil (studio), lavallière (lapel), non-directional, bi-directional, uni-directional, dynamic, crystal, carbon

microscope, microscopes powerful, high-energy, electron, optical, simple, compound, binocular, holographic

migration, migrations leisurely, scattered, quick, long, extended, unending, arduous, extraordinary, immense, dramatic, amazing, (un)usual, (un)limited, mass(ive), reverse, altitudinal, annual, (twice-)yearly, seasonal, prehistoric, sea-borne, urban, internal, interprovincial, intercontinental, international, economic; chain

mile, miles vertical, standard, geographic (nautical, air), international, Roman, statute

militancy unbending, fighting, quarrelsome, adamant, bellicose, combatant, combative, tough, warlike

milk fresh, sweet, smooth, wholesome, rich, creamy, thick, thin, cool, cold, tepid, warm, hot, low-fat, fat-free, curdly, ropy, clammy, tainted, stale, iron-poor, rancid, powdered, fermented, condensed, tinned, evaporated, certified, malted, bottled, (un)sweetened, sour, UHT, pasteurized, full-cream, skimmed, top, whole, raw; glacier

millionaire, millionaires philanthropic, parvenu, upstart, snob, demented, reckless, heedless, profligate, wasteful, effete, decadent, self-made, instant, paper

minaret, minarets See *tower*

mind, minds commanding, towering, soaring, dazzling, piercing, penetrating, engaging, inquiring, questioning, discerning, discriminating, searching, far-reaching, omnivorous, incisive, perceptive, judicious, sanguine, sober, sound, pure, clean, alert, agile, subtle, powerful, strong, exhaustless, brilliant, energetic, well-informed, gifted, original, orderly, (ice-)clear, lucid, luminous, quick, tidy, precise, broad, open, comprehensive, plastic, pliable, practical, subtle, versatile, active, keen, acute, eager, flexible, superior, abnormal, exceptional, extraordinary, nimble, robust, sane, spacious, supple, fecund, fruitful, fertile, prolific, prodigious, ingenious, clever, deft, independent, lively, liberal, tranquil, serene, mobile, (un)balanced, (un)reasonable, (ir)rational, sedulous, impartial, right, straightforward, exalted, receptive, (un)conscious, yielding, daedal, easy, curious, impressionable, (un)quiet, perfervid, animated, reeling, febrile, fanciful, whimsical, busy, tired, unfathomed, unpredictable, unbent, warped, impure, perverse, unclean, dirty, sluggish, torpid, dull, literal, (drink-)sodden, unimaginative, woolly,

sub-average, vacuous, vacant, blank, empty, unreplenished, chasmic, idiotic, stupid, foolish, inane, nasty, parochial, narrow, small, stunted, uneducated, artless, sick, diseased, slow, giddy, stagnant, numb, illiberal, one-track, shallow, inactive, unsound, weak, feeble, barren, unfurnished, unfruitful, unresting, wandering, hazy, vagrant, insane, distracted, addled, deranged, disordered, troubled, disturbed, confused, demented, tormented, little, callous, mean, petty, murky, unformed, twisted, wayward, evasive, discursive, creative, inventive, imaginative, rational, analytical, enumerative, pictorial, carnal, metaphysical, philosophic(al), romantic, empirical, inductive, intuitive, inquisitive, photographic, judicial, critical, methodical; subliminal

mine, mines (1: a pit from which minerals are dug) operating, active, rich, (un)productive, (un)profitable, viable, decrepit, dust-laden, unlocated, undiscovered, exhausted, abandoned, dead, acoustic, open-pit, open-cast, hydraulic, bituminous

mine, mines (2: an encased explosive) deadly, finger-size, land, magnetic, contact, anti-personnel, submarine, pressure

mineral, minerals soluble, fusible, fibrous, glassy, colourless, homogeneous, (non-)metallic, submetallic, secondary, diagnostic

minimum, minima irreducible, bare, absolute, lowest, smallest, critical

minister, ministers See *priest*

minority, minorities small, tiny, fragile, (in)significant, fast(est)-growing, substantial, siz(e)able, privileged, affluent, thoughtless, intense, silent, vociferous, vocal, (in)visible, (un)identifiable, defenceless, uncomplaining, (un)representative, targeted, forgotten, downtrodden, dissatisfied, disgruntled, underprivileged, disadvantaged, deprived, racial, ethnic, ethnocultural, domestic, religious, cultural, linguistic, (in)voluntary

minute, minutes flying, loitering, suspenseful, contemplative, indeterminable, magical

miracle, miracles amazing, astounding, marvellous, superb, wondrous, wonderful, veritable, genuine, authentic, real, true, virtual, possible, presumptive, alleged, dubious, contemporary, blessed, God-given, supernatural, providential

mirror, mirrors waving, glittering, bright, shiny, limpid, sparkling, reflective, flawless, ornate, (hand-)bevelled, dinky, dull, flawed, cracked, scabrous, three-sided, three-sectioned, floor-to-ceiling, grand, oversized, oval, aplanatic, rear-view, one-way, two-way, concave, convex, Venetian, Art Deco, Art Nouveau, parabolic, pocket, cheval; magic

mirth intoxicating, cheery, festive, gleeful, hilarious, jolly, joyous, whimsical, broad, unrestricted, free, unconfined, riotous, uproarious, innocent, farcical

miscarriage, miscarriages (in pregnancy) heartbreaking, heart-rending, agonizing, life-threatening, disappointing, distressing, sad, pitiful, unfortunate, ill-fated, ill-timed, early, late

mischief, mischiefs harassing, annoying, ingenious, merry, wanton, malicious, potent, evil, elfish, impish, detrimental, foxy, harmful, hurtful, injurious, malevolent, prankish, roguish, spiteful, venomous, wicked, deliberate, irresponsible, childish, puerile, infantile, schoolboy

misconception, misconceptions See *delusion*

misconduct beastly, bestial, delinquent, offensive, wicked, wilful, deliberate, outrageous, disgraceful, shameful, felonious, professional, judicial, sexual

miser, misers griping, grasping, greedy, avaricious, rapacious, acquisitive, covetous, parsimonious, stingy, avid, tight, villainous

misery, miseries crushing, agonizing, grinding, overwhelming, widespread, deep, savage, sharp, stark, sordid, squalid, mean, forlorn, abject, ghastly, black, oppressive, gross, utter, complete, unalloyed, pure, irreparable, untold, inexpressible, everlasting, long-term, querulous, unmerited

misfortune, misfortunes appalling, devastating, overpowering, grinding, overwhelming, total, miserable, unspeakable, temporal, undeserved,

successive, manifold

mishap See *accident* (1)

misjudgement, misjudgements See *mistake*

mismanagement staggering, glaring, flagrant, gross, chaotic, widespread, epic, disgraceful, shameful, criminal

mismatch glaring, blatant, flagrant, obvious, utter, outrageous, apparent

missile, missiles hurtling, devastating, deadly, powerful, lethal, sophisticated, smart, (in)accurate, (un)reliable, risky-to-use, elusive, wayward, unwieldly, obsolete, shoulder-held, programmed, unmanned, spherical, combat, defensive, training, interceptor, (un)guided, wire-guide, nuclear, nuclear-tipped, nuclear-capable, strategic, mobile, (high-)explosive, subsonic, cluster, self-driven, underwater, low-flying, sea-to-sea, anti-tank, anti-ship, anti-aircraft, anti-missile, cruise, submarine, air-defence, air-to-air, surface-to-surface, air-to-surface, surface-to-air, air-to-subsurface, ground-to-air, short-range, medium-range, intermediate-range, long-range, orbital, intercontinental, (anti-)ballistic

mission, missions honourable, noble, worthwhile, sacred, peaceable, flawless, singular, triumphant, quixotic, serious, vital, fateful, urgent, specific, uncertain, vainglorious, arrogant, secret, hazardous, risky, dangerous, unnerving, demanding, costly, sensitive, impossible, sole, primary, final, several-fold, high-powered, check-out, investigative, fact-finding, diplomatic, humanitarian, mercy, rescue, recruiting, surveillance, reconnaissance, military, attack, sweep, defensive, life-saving, behind-the-scenes, spying, espionage, peace-keeping, last-hope, messianic

mist, mists rolling, hanging, floating, overlying, deep, heavy, thick, severe, dense, perpetual, (long-)lasting, early-morning, hazy, foggy, surreal, dreamlike, dreamy, sudden, directionless, invisible, opaline, opal(escent), white, dark, dead-coloured, dust-coloured, dust-bright, sunlit, glittering, shimmery, clear, translucent, transparent, diaphanous, luminous, brilliant, faint, fragrant, silvery,

smok(e)y, murky, dusty, sooty, cold,
chill(y), freezing, humid, cylindrical,
cottony, warm, torrid, hot, wet, steamy,
dewy, vaporous, swirly, tenuous,
gossamer, evanescent, (feather-)soft,
light, thin, briny, maritime, corrosive,
sepia

mistake, mistakes glaring, striking,
flagrant, obvious, big, monumental,
gargantuan, enormous, colossal, gross,
grave, major, great, drastic, appalling,
shocking, atrocious, wretched, horrific,
horrible, terrible, fundamental, crucial,
serious, genuine, egregious, outrageous,
lamentable, regrettable, deplorable,
(in)excusable, (un)pardonable, hideous,
sore, grievous, silly, absurd, stupid,
thoughtless, clumsy, unforeseeable,
unfortunate, careless, laughable, ridiculous,
whimsical, fantastic, grotesque, innocent,
childish, ghastly, curious, costly, evident,
conspicuous, impossible, ineradicable,
correctable, irredeemable, (in)curable,
(in)corrigible, (ir)remediable, dispensable,
tragic, fatal, calamitous, recurrent, rare,
unconscious, honest, accidental, reciprocal,
common, universal, human, natural,
historic, strategic, logistical

mistreatment See *abuse*

mistrust See *suspicion*

misunderstanding, misunderstandings
jarring, lingering, unfortunate, deplorable,
sore, total, widespread, perennial, gross,
vehement, strong, fundamental, huge,
substantial, slight, wilful

misuse See *abuse*

mix(ture), mixtures tantalizing, startling,
heady, select, (in)harmonious, (un)usual,
incongruous, inconsonant, singular,
extraordinary, mysterious, curious,
indiscriminate, confused, oddball,
incoherent, complex, motley, eclectic,
volatile, sloppy, combustible, explosive,
bubbly, frothy, syrupy, (in)dissoluble

moan, moans (be)wailing, groaning,
sighing, sobbing, eerie, low, suppressed,
continuous, deep, pathetic, diabolical

moaning See *moan*

mob, mobs howling, screaming,
(fast-)growing, good-natured,
undisciplined, disorderly, truculent,
raucous, unruly, tumultuous, noisy, surly,
angry, irate, enraged, violent, wild,

mutinous, frenetic, excited, enthusiastic,
patriotic

mobility adaptable, flexible, free, fluid,
unrestrained, unrestricted, uncontrolled,
musculo-skeletal

mobilization See *organization*

mockery, mockeries insulting, jeering,
sneering, insolent, strident, vociferous,
harsh, unutterable, scornful, buoyant,
salubrious, ashen, good-natured

mode, modes See *fashion* (1) and *style* (3)

model, models (1: one who poses for an
artist or photographer) attractive,
glamorous, graceful, incomparable, wispy,
emaciated, sexy, delicious-looking,
voluptuous, aspiring, successful, desirable,
professional, commercial, photographic

model, models (2: standard to be
imitated) perfect, absolute, universal,
inimitable

model, models (3: a small copy of
something) rare, scale, small-scale,
half-scale, lookalike, appropriate,
animated; computer

moderation clear-headed, thoughtful,
perceptive, sagacious, judicial, rational,
commendable, sensible

modesty becoming, forbearing, yielding,
self-effacing, unassuming, humiliating,
retiring, disarming, charming, graceful,
terse, polite, characteristic, airy, innocent,
virgin, chaste, virtuous, bashful, demure,
oblique, humble, meek, shy,
(un)ostentatious, (in)sincere, false, extreme,
infinite, overdone, inherent, inborn, innate

moisture steamy, clammy, dank, muggy,
soggy, atmospheric

moment, moments propitious,
(in)auspicious, (un)favourable,
(in)appropriate, right, (im)proper,
(in)opportune, fruitful, creative,
(in)judicious, exquisite, climactic, crucial,
vital, decisive, critical, transcendent,
sublime, supreme, (in)convenient, ecstatic,
rapturous, thrilling, stirring, vivid, radiant,
shining, happy, exuberant, jubilant,
golden, exultant, triumphant, unique,
unsurpassed, lucid, tender, calm, decent,
positive, rare, enchanted, proud, precise,
exact, same, fundamental, dramatic,
historic, memorable, intense, singular,
extraordinary, touching, odd, brief, magic,
pivotal, fitting, stunning, unforgettable,

incredible, unbelievable, intimate, unpredictable, evanescent, short-lived, passing, fleeting, amazing, idle, expectant, tense, harsh, awful, appalling, awkward, tricky, embarrassing, uneasy, nervous, fervid, depressive, apprehensive, disquieting, excruciating, painful, forlorn, lonely, ghastly, hideous, dark, low-ebb, sickening, ominous, awesome, fateful, lamentable, awkward, rocky, furious, wrathful, giddy, careless, reflective, convulsive, anguished, emotional, psychological, strategic; magnetic

monarch, monarchs See also *king* beloved, (un)popular, (un)approachable, ideal, benevolent, malevolent, cruel, terrible, heartless, absolute, puissant, mighty, (all-)powerful, autocratic, despotic, dictatorial, would-be, puppet, merry, reluctant, constitutional, hereditary

monarchy, monarchies benign, centuries-old, fairy-tale, anachronistic, irrelevant, authoritarian, absolute, constitutional (limited), representative, parliamentary, dual, feudal, puppet, surviving

monastery, monasteries ascetic, secluded, inaccessible, out-of-the-way, remote, unapproachable, solitary, reclusive, contemplative, mountainous, c(o)enobitic, conventual, monkish, oblate, Byzantine

money, moneys (monies) plentiful, (easily-)available, ready, easy, extra, spare, tight, scarce, close, foreign, bogus, counterfeit, false, enticing, tempting, (un)confiscable, repayable, recallable, hard-earned, ill-gotten, (un)tainted, narcotics-tainted, mystery, advance, reserve, hush, smart, seed, blood, earnest, paper, pocket, pin, maundy, prize, reward, blackmail, spending, call, commodity, conscience, ransom, start-up, protection, key, tax-free, credit, fiat, fiduciary, factional, full-bodied, big, hard, soft, representative, standard, discretionary, set-up, expense; electronic

monitoring careful, thorough, exhaustive, (im)proper, (in)appropriate, (ir)regular, (un)reasonable, perfunctory; foetal

monk, monks mendicant, ascetic, c(o)enobitic, simple, secluded, cloistered, solitary, silent, meditative, contemplative, serene, shaven-headed, cowled, guardian, low-ranking, novice, holy, Benedictine, Carthusian, Cistercian, Franciscan, Dominican, Augustinian, Cluniac, Buddhist

monkey, monkeys jabbering, babbling, chattering, snarling, scrambling, swaying, swinging, prancing, prowling, resplendent, garrulous, merry, agile, intelligent, inquisitorial, evil-tempered, mischievous, tricky, (un)manageable, intractable, woolly, shaggy, hairy, reclusive, unobtrusive, captive, tame, arboreal, snub-nosed, pig-tailed, ring-tailed, stump-tailed, buffy-headed, green, orange, spider, miniature

monotony stifling, depressing, disheartening, dispiriting, unrelenting, unvarying, boring, irksome, tedious, tiresome, wearisome, barren, deadly, unbearable, listless, languid

monster, monsters lurking, overwhelming, shocking, awful, dreadful, hateful, heinous, hideous, horrid, ugly, frightful, horrible, scary, grotesque, strange, unnatural, fantastic, unspeakable, queer, bizarre, grisly, gruesome, horrid, terrible, fearsome, other-worldly, surreal, inhuman, prey-laden, devouring, vicious, pugnacious, venomous, dreadful, deformed, giant, enormous, gigantic, monumental, titanic, mighty, fabled, mythical

month, months lunar, solar, bissextile, nodical, synodical, vernal, anomalistic, sidereal, calendar

monument, monuments spectacular, stupendous, magnificent, splendid, remarkable, unique, matchless, singular, exceptional, grand, noble, mighty, gigantic, massive, lavish, impressive, fascinating, irreplaceable, famous, ancient, monolithic, megalithic, classical, old, (pre)historic, historical, enduring, living, fitting, familiar, marble, stone, tabular, formal, challenging, gaudy, decrepit, rusting, sooty, scarred, cracked, sacred, secular, national, cultural, tourist, futuristic, funerary, equestrian

mood, moods jolly, jubilant, jovial, convivial, merry, genial, mirthful, cheerful, upbeat, joyous, amiable, friendly, agreeable, happy, bullish, festive, celebratory, buoyant, bright, optimistic, hopeful, exuberant, exhilarant, carefree, mellow, responsive, expansive, playful, skittish, welcoming, serene, subdued, blessed, bland, ambivalent, conciliatory, pensive, nostalgic, retrospective, slumb(e)rous, defensive, conversational, reminiscent, remorseful, repentant, contrite, restless, pervasive, dominant, prevailing, unpredictable, frenetic, patriotic, revolutionary, apprehensive, cautious, anxious, shifting, boastful, loquacious, contagious, uneasy, tense, brittle, touchy, disgruntled, feisty, fractious, stormy, surly, captious, carping, contentious, bitchy, militant, warring, bellicose, belligerent, quarrelsome, ebullient, pugnacious, hostile, violent, bleak, black, dark, grey, sombre, sullen, dreary, barren, wanton, irresponsible, lazy, huffy, sulky, overbearing, haunting, melancholy, sad, gloomy, morose, dejected, dispirited, depressed, pessimistic, despairing, perverse, fickle, distraught, dismal, raspy, crotchety, cranky, vengeful, bitter, sour, ugly, foul, incalculable, sentimental, sensuous, valedictory

moon, moons awe-inspiring, tremendous, fantastic, glorious, gigantic, bright, brilliant, (bone-)white, ochre(ous), golden, smoky, (blood-)red, pale, faint, dim, wan, frosted, horned, woolly, changeable, capricious, reborn, three-quarter, (in)crescent, gibbous, low, shy, new, half, full(-bellied), old, harvest, tropical

moonlight expansive, splendid, magnificent, brilliant, bluish, silvery, golden, greyish, lambent, soft, mellow, faint, weak, harsh

moor, moors barren, bleak, gloomy, greyish, ghostly, dank, damp, lonely, desolate, wild, extensive, heathery, panoramic

moorland, moorlands See *moor*

morale sagging, cracking, high, low, poor, damaged, broken, shattered, (un)sustainable

moralist, moralists rigid, inflexible, relentless, unrelenting, uncompromising, unyielding, charismatic

moralizing boring, sententious, excessive, repetitious, pompous, monotonous, tiresome, bromidic, tedious, wearisome

morality chaste, decent, noble, proper, upright, virtuous, stern, repressive, (in)flexible, (un)questionable, outdated, traditional, conventional, personal, ethical, sexual, Puritan, Victorian

morals impregnable, formidable, invulnerable, puritan, indifferent, loose, lax, corrupt, ingrained

morbidity disgusting, unhealthy, unwholesome, sickly, scrofulous, morose, cadaverous, ghastly, dark, deadly, diseased, gloomy, grisly, gruesome, abhorrent, repellent, repulsive, loathsome, repugnant

morning, mornings See also *day* sparkling, brilliant, bright, golden, perfect, exquisite, cheerful, balmy, serene, calm, lovely, sweet, brisk, fine, limpid, clear, sunny, opal, crisp, dreamy, misty, mist-shrouded, foggy, dewy, dew-wet, steamy, groggy, cold, cool, raw, freezing, frosty, icy, hot, hazy, overcast, rimy, drizzly, rainy, drippy, humid, damp, sombre, grey, sultry, hectic, heady, blustery, bleak, dreary, stormy, gusty, windy, windswept, early, late

mortality, mortalities (in)significant, inescapable, imminent, in-hospital, neonatal, infant

mortgage, mortgages heavy, hefty, stiff, (in)flexible, bad, open-end, adjustable-rate, assumable, tacit, underlying, first, second, chattel, residential, open, closed, endowment, vendor-take-back, reverse

Moslem, Moslems See *Muslim*

mosque, mosques See also *building* arcaded, (gold-)domed, golden-domed, mosaic-rich, elegant, graceful, striking, centuries-old, enormous

mosquito, mosquitoes See also *insect* vicious, skittish, pesticide-resistant, pernicious, blood-sucking, swarming, swollen, larval, nocturnal, diurnal, crepuscular, malarial

mother, mothers (over-)doting, fond, affectionate, devoted, (over-)protective, attentive, alert, (over-)anxious, defensive, patient, diligent, dedicated, observant, competent, rational, attached, practical, forbidding, extraordinary, strict, firm, obsessive, weary, careworn, distressed, distraught, agitated, mortified, grumpy, abusive, negligent, unfit, incompetent, tempestuous, manipulative, formidable, overbearing, possessive, domineering, nosy, working, stay-at-home, pregnant, expectant, new, single, unwed, biological, genetic, legal, natural, real, adoptive, foster, putative, surrogate, gestational, emblematic

motion (1: movement) winding, rocking, swaying, whirling, twisting, undulating, stirring, sweeping, oscillatory, vertiginous, swift, unhurried, fluid, dreamy, retrograde, queasy, quick, brisk, slow, uninterrupted, ceaseless, constant, perpetual, springy, jerky, violent, slight, liquid, fluent, overhand, (ir)regular, sidelong, enthusiastic, spontaneous, up-and-down, (un)steady, repetitive, to-and-fro, back-and-forth, spiral, side-to-side, active, passive, wasted, rhythmic, link, alternate, perpetual, spiral, rotary, circular, sinuous, uniplanar, linear, rectilinear, curvilinear

motion (2: a proposal for action) worthwhile, purposeful, non-confidential, privileged, subsidiary, incidental, main, procedural

motivation, motivations See *drive* (1)

motive, motives bona fide, genuine, (un)clear, plain, (ir)rational, sound, pure, subtle, laudable, lofty, honest, respectable, prudent, (un)questionable, pressing, strong, powerful, sufficient, deep, emulous, (in)appropriate, (in)adequate, important, necessary, (im)plausible, ostensible, prime, primary, ulterior, underlying, hidden, veiled, inexplicable, mixed, complex, mercenary, esoteric, flinty, sinister, impure, crude, vile, sordid, base, mean, contemptible, grovelling, malicious, poor, selfish, greedy, secret, obscure, recondite, stated, established, political, pecuniary, psychopathic, ideological, psychological, physiological

motor, motors See *engine*

mountain, mountains enduring, towering, soaring, cloud-piercing, imposing, awe-inspiring, forbidding, surrounding, rolling, sloping, dizzying, steep, precipitous, high, lofty, haughty, sublime, tall, uplifted, grand, huge, vast, prodigious, brawny, lovely, splendid, magnificent, majestic, regal, glorious, fantastic, castellated, picturesque, spectacular, hypnotic, leonine, scenic, incredible, unbelievable, ineffable, velvety,

serene, sleepy, flat-topped, irregular, squat, sinuous, anomalous, lunar, spiny, toothy, (blade-)sharp, forked, fissured, craggy, rugged, rock-strewn, jagged, stern, piny, (rain-)forested, pine-clad, redwood-studded, palm-fledged, oak-covered, beech-covered, lush, verdant, green, pastel, marble(-rich), glacier-carved, white-capped, snow-capped, snow-crowned, snow-tipped, snow-peaked, snow-blasted, snow-draped, snow-streaked, snow-bound, whiteheaded, storm-shrouded, windswept, shattered, eroded, cloud-tattered, mist-captive, mist-veiled, misty, protective, formidable, wild, brutal, remote, untouched, (un)inhabitable, (un)climbable, (im)passable, (un)explorable, unstable, avalanchy, treacherous, hostile, barren, sere, desolate, gaunt, bleak, arid, stark, naked, bald, fragile, coastal, tropical, lava, volcanic, granite, shale, sacred

mountaineer, mountaineers See *athlete*

mourner, mourners (in)sincere, impassioned, emotional, agitated, hypocritical, wild, unrestrained, hysterical, maniac(al)

mouse, mice cheeping, roving, skulking, timorous, wee, meek, mute, quiet, unperturbed, nimble, agile, fleet, fast, facile, aggressive, destructive, troublesome, tractable, docile, domesticated, house, field, nocturnal, white, deer (white-footed), meadow

moustache, moustaches dashing, twitching, flaring, cheerful, joyful, flippant, rakish, smart, neat, handsome, fashionable, distinct(ive), fierce, fearsome, heavy, large, big, luxuriant, thick, profuse, curled, curly, bushy, brushy, coarse, stubby, soft, stiff, brisk, bristly, droopy, twirly, wriggly, cavalry, old-fashioned, sly, scrawny, thin, small, salt-and-pepper, golden, ginger, smoke-stained, (tobacco-)yellow, blond, long, wispy, twisted, trimmed, tapered, unkempt, scruffy, scraggy, handlebar, false, walrus, toothbrush, pork-chop, incipient, adolescent, Teutonic

mouth, mouths firm, cherry, scarlet, (bone-)dry, parched, tight, slack, loose, flaccid, gaping, agape, voluptuous, lascivious, warm, eager, ready, thin, wide, enormous, protrusive, prominent, well-shaped, plum-like, elliptical, flinty, lipless, turned-down, toothless, long-toothed, (semi-)dewlapped, misshapen, grim, sulky, big, loud, stupid, foul, puckish, foamy, slobbery, slabbery

move, moves innovative, smart, right, safe, cautious, wise, astute, shrewd, judicious, prudent, foresighted, concrete, positive, significant, (mis)calculated, conciliatory, magnificent, splendid, stunning, aggressive, persuasive, unprecedented, unusual, (un)warranted, provocative, inevitable, unavoidable, overdue, excessive, momentous, controversial, reluctant, incomprehensible, bold, daring, foolhardy, precipitous, scary, risky, timid, expedient, quick, hasty, rash, undiscriminating, clumsy, abortive, futile, wrong, false, disastrous, cynical, secret, unnecessary, serious, costly, desperate, repressive, ominous, belated, surprise, tentative, interim, political, strategic, tactical, retaliatory, precautionary, concessionary, defensive, symbolic

movement, movements (1: motion; moving) gracious, leisurely, unhurried, slow, lethargic, lithe, supple, limber, smooth, delicate, flowing, graceful, (un)steady, fluid(ic), free, brisk, progressive, onward, migratory, strategic, tactical, stately, harmonious, rhythmical, spontaneous, swaying, slight, tiny, vague, harsh, laboured, calculated, meticulous, hypnotic, snaky, twisting, writhing, snapping, rotary, limping, spastic, abrupt, flashy, jerky, slinky, jumpy, restless, erratic, disjointed, flabby, sluggish, loose, hesitant, (un)predictable, uncertain, languid, languorous, drowsy, massive, monstrous, inartistic, clownish, strenuous, unsteady, clumsy, awkward, meditative, ponderous, graceless, casual, deliberate, seductive, stealthy, offensive, circular, sidewise, (anti-)clockwise, inward, backward, outward, back-and-forth, convulsive, compulsive, muscular, corrective

movement, movements (2: tendency) purposeful, creative, viable, cohesive, nascent, budding, fledgling, (re-)emerging, growing, influential, broad(-based), multifarious, well-funded, tight-knit, strong, great, least-known, extraordinary, mass, spontaneous, uncontrolled, resurgent, unco-ordinated, self-proclaimed, populist, revolutionary, fundamentalist, underground, radical, extreme, unsavoury, left-of-centre, left-wing, right-wing, resistance, dissident, barbarian, voluntary, grass-roots, indigenous, (now-)moribund, reform, nihilistic, chauvinist, feminist, pro-life, human-rights, civil-rights, anti-nuclear, suffragist, anti-fur, environmental, anti-war, peace, ethnic-pride, anti-slavery, independence, secessionist, racist, religious, charismatic, totalitarian, temperance, youth, rebel, political, artistic, guerrilla, liberation, cubist, fitness

movie, movies See *film*

mower, mowers See also *machine* and *engine* hand, power(-driven), gas, electric, self-propelled, rotary, ride-on, one-wheel, reel

mowing machine, mowing machines See *mower*

mud, muds grainy, oozy, slimy, murky, slippery, thick, turbid, deep, heavy, tenacious, sticky, viscous, hardened, putrid, curative

mule, mules obstinate, stubborn, ungovernable, unyielding

murder, murders bloodcurdling, shocking, lurid, cruel, spectre-like, cold-blooded, foul, sensational, savage, brutal, barbaric, bestial, unnatural, horrible, grisly, gruesome, ghastly, frightful, dreadful, terrible, abominable, hateful, mindless, senseless, motiveless, wanton, random, indiscriminate, bizarre, violent, outrageous, cowardly, treacherous, paranoid, unsolved, mysterious, baffling, unprovoked, unjustified, aggravated, wilful, deliberate, premeditated, double, triple, multiple, wholesale, (non-)capital, first-degree, second-degree, contract, machine-gun, retaliatory, ritual, copycat, serial, carbon-copy; blue

murderer, murderers remorseless, cold-blooded, vicious, hardened, terrible, vile, dangerous, unrepentant, inflexible, savage, bestial, brutal, frenzied, quiet, silent, random, notorious, would-be, alleged, potential, loose, fugitive, wanted, unconvicted, extraditable, natural-born, mass, multiple, first-degree, self-confessed, psychotic, psychopathic, professional, juvenile, serial

murmur, murmurs purling, humming, grumbling, groaning, mumbling, muttering, whimpering, undulating, trembling, tremulous, deep, melodious, inarticulate, unintelligible, vague, indistinct, low, soft, disjointed, uneasy, bleak, susurrant, susurrous, alcoholic; cardiac

muscle, muscles sagging, bulging, strong, well-developed, enormous, powerful, rocky, massive, bulky, high-tension, tight, hard, rigid, stiff, firm, taut, ropy, soft, smooth, flaccid, flabby, limp, skeletal, pliable, pliant, inelastic, weak, tense, delicate, smooth, torn, achy, sore, loose, inert, enlarged, (over-)developed, well-developed, wasted, cramped, tired, distal, proximal, intrinsic, extrinsic, rotational, voluntary (striated), involuntary (unstriated), facial, cardiac, skeletal, risible, pectoral, dorsal, intercostal, scalene, transverse, abdominal, lower-back, biceps, triceps, calf; military

museum, museums intriguing, interesting, fascinating, charming, fine, superb, famous, renowned, (long-)established, reputable, major, tremendous, (in)efficient, remarkable, spectacular, gigantic, elegant, ambitious, interactive, privately-funded, state-funded, state-run, mainstream, unusual, (un)traditional, small, hamstrung, soporific, (over)crowded, eccentric, local, metropolitan, state, national, municipal, cultural, science, war, ethnic, archaeological, prehistoric, architectural, industrial, general, history, art, natural, folk(lore), open-air, transport, postal, thematic, (neo)classical, oceanographic

music uplifting, ravishing, relaxing, soothing, moving, penetrating, searching, haunting, captivating, (be)witching, inviting, tinkling, rippling, enduring, gentle, refined, sweet, sublime, lush, beautiful, delightful, luscious, aerial, ethereal, astral, celestial, heavenly, divine, inspired, grand, marvellous, sacred, impressive, gorgeous, quality, highbrow, descant, serious, sophisticated, maverick, cerebral, delicious, lovely, lively, gay, cheerful, joyful, pure, unadulterated, serene, soft, dream-like, dreamy,

light(-hearted), slumb(e)rous, romantic, light, vital, top-quality, disciplined, potent, innovative, tuneful, florid, colourful, seductive, irrepressible, memory-laden, memorable, unusual, unearthly, eerie, muffled, sensuous, voluptuous, powerful, vigorous, fast, eclectic, derivative, tame, slow, melancholy, soulful, wailing, minor-key, sad, solemn, blues, sombre, ominous, plaintive, spooky, passionate, trance-like, funky, mood, funereal, mourning, unaccompanied, traditional, cantabile, contrapuntal, new, syncopated, modernistic, low-key, rollicking, rap, (toe-)tingling, tremulous, upbeat, downbeat, mighty, tonal, psychedelic, restless, angular, cacophonous, vibrant, heavy, barbarous, wild, fiery, raucous, harsh, sharp, bouncy, energetic, hoarse, ephemeral, strident, loud, high-pitched, shrill, thund(e)rous, ear-piercing, ear-splitting, harsh-sounding, thumping, deafening, blasting, heavy-metal, clangorous, frantic, brutal, ragged, disjointed, vulgar, corny, boring, repetitive, dull, humdrum, cheap, trashy, unimaginative, big-band, beat, rock(-and-roll), acid-rock, drum, disco, electronic, electroacoustic, concrete, bottled, metal, piped, canned, orchestral, instrumental, vocal, chamber, consort, choral, synthesizer, classical, modern, art, folk, pop(ular), indigenous, rustic, honky-tonk, country, contemporary, mensural, polyphonic, thematic, theme, incidental, light, sentimental, new-age, processional, recessional, written, sheet, operatic, serial, (a)tonal, passion, soul, liturgical, sacred, gospel, devotional, secular, martial, field, patriotic, absolute, stringed, jazz, swing, salsa, reggae, hip-hop, taiko, live, rococo, water, dance, baroque, background, street, national, funeral, preludial, postludial

musical instrument, musical instruments old, original, early, period, venerable, portable, complex, acoustic, long-necked, hexagonal, one-stringed, four-stringed, unstrung, (un)stringed, wind, woodwind, brass, percussion, reed, transposing, electric, electrophonic

musician, musicians captivating, dazzling, spirited, intense, ardent, virtuoso,

accomplished, polished, consummate,
competent, talented, fine, brilliant, gifted,
remarkable, exceptional, great, influential,
thorough, finished, dext(e)rous, skilful,
skilled, trained, sophisticated, sterling,
first-rate, major, courtly, phenomenal,
legendary, perfect, solid, sober, popular,
successful, noted, notable, celebrated,
distinguished, well-known, famous,
(pre-)eminent, active, temperamental,
esoteric, aspiring, rising, struggling,
controversial, stale, mendicant, failed,
(not-so-)long-haired, versatile, professional,
amateur, free-lance, classical, jazz, rock,
pop, itinerant, street

Muslim, Muslims pious, devout, faithful,
staunch, fervent, zealous, zealot, strict,
true, orthodox, (non-)observant,
(non-)practising, puritanical,
fundamentalist, militant, (in)tolerant,
hard-line, lapsed, Sunni, Shi'a (Shi'ite)

mustache, mustaches See *moustache*

mutiny, mutinies See *rebellion*

mutter, mutters See *murmur*

mystery, mysteries baffling, puzzling,
perplexing, intriguing, tantalizing,
fascinating, astounding, bewildering,
compelling, enduring, abiding,

surrounding, prevailing, haunting,
lingering, exasperating, annoying,
unfolding, deep, unfathomable,
bottomless, fathomless, inexplicable,
inscrutable, inextricable, intractable,
enigmatic, impenetrable, incomprehensible,
obscure, elusive, dark, abysmal, dusky,
intricate, unapproachable, suspenseful,
sensational, vast, big, real, utter, eternal,
deep, profound, insoluble, troublesome,
awesome, gruesome, ghastly, grim,
macabre, complete, ongoing, holy,
unravelled, unfathomed, unsolved,
unresolved, untangled, unexplained,
shrouded, veiled; pagan, Orphic

myth, myths ancient, hoary, venerable,
popular, time-honoured, pervasive,
persistent, prevalent, widespread, common,
ingrained, enduring, sustaining, cloying,
potent, outsized, colossal, nostalgic,
counter-productive, injurious, repulsive,
unfounded, fantastic, classic,
established, cultural, aetiological,
supernatural, theogonic, explanatory,
aesthetic

mythology, mythologies primitive,
popular, abundant, powerful, inexpressible,
incomprehensible, tribal

nail, nails (1: fastening device) rusty, crooked, bent, exposed, stubborn, headless, common, finishing, casting, flooring (screw), box, wire, counter-sunk, shingle, roofing, lath, horseshoe, upholstery, hob, brad, flathead, cut, duplex-head, finger, double-headed (scaffold), screw-drive

nail, nails (2: fingernail) See *fingernail*

name, names (re)sounding, high-sounding, strange-sounding, Latin-sounding, amusing, intriguing, amazing, eye-catching, endearing, fitting, apt, (in)appropriate, solid, sensible, illustrious, famous, stellar, undefiled, regal, noble, honoured, pedigreed, prestigious, beautiful, (in)elegant, melodious, sonorous, resonant, resplendent, vowel-laden, misspelled, elusive, real, fictitious, assumed, phon(e)y, feigned, false, borrowed, folksy, mysterious, (un)familiar, (un)common, unusual, exotic, archaic, whimsical, silly, odd, idiotic, colourful, old-fashioned, hard-to-pronounce, (un)pronounceable, (un)recognizable, characteristic, arcane, euphemistic, fair, bucolic, bland, pedestrian, unlovely, catchy, masculine, feminine, misleading, confusing, (un)complicated, chilling, disgraceful, opprobrious, earthy, unrefined, irreverent, infamous, ineffable, adopted, family, first (given, Christian), middle, maiden, personal, generation, milk, baptismal, pet, pen, stage, legal, official, (non)technical, figurative, place, cover, code; generic, trade, proprietary; big, household; proud, clean, good

nap, naps restorative, restful, usual, short, prolonged, protracted, much-needed, obligatory, daily, mid-day

narcotic, narcotics (il)legal, illicit, addictive, insidious, debilitating, soothing, subtle, raw, exotic, hypnotic, anaesthetic, anodynic, comatose, nepenthean, somniferous, soporiferous, stupefactive, stuporous, torporific

narrative, narratives authentic, graceful, colourful, vivid, lively, racy, brisk, flowing, rapid, (richly-)detailed, sweeping, orderly, supple, heart-rending, chilling, agonizing, teasing, succinct, clear, plain, distracting, meandering, unending, dreamlike, evocative, disconnected, (un)sympathetic, (in)contestable, false, repetitive, prolix, injurious, well-told, melodramatic, suspenseful, epic, (non-)linear, first-hand, first-person, third-person, factual, historical

narrator, narrators charming, accomplished, skilled, skilful, talented, omniscient, central, chatty

narrow-mindedness parochial, bigoted, prejudiced, dogmatic, pedantic, petty, shallow, strict, sectarian, provincial

nation, nations powerful, mighty, strong, confident, peaceful, pacific, neutral, unaligned, non-aligned, progressive, reform-minded, affluent, rich, thriving, vibrant, benign, advanced, developed, resource-rich, independent, sovereign, coherent, (un)stable, undivided, unified, united, populous, keystone, (inter)dependent, rigid, once-mighty, conservative, aggressive, belligerent, militant, adversary, reclusive, (long-)polarized, downtrodden, battered, cowed, stricken, strife-torn, fragmented, war-weary, helpless, weak, barbarous, young, budding, new, sprawling, fledgling, emerging, tiny, little, benighted, less-developed, hard-up, primitive, (dirt-)poor, have-not, begging, pariah, undernourished, recipient, industrial, seafaring, trading, bilingual, island, buffer, producer, consumer, monolithic, polymorphous, tribal

nationalism proud, vehement, fervent, passionate, strong, extreme, dyed-in-the-wool, touchy, virulent, irrational, narrow, strident, deep-seated, rampant, resurgent, defensive, jingoistic, parochial, militaristic, religious

nationalist, nationalists ardent, staunch, impassioned, inflamed, dedicated, obsessive, (im)moderate, hardline, extremist, uncompromising, rampant

naturalist, naturalists dedicated, devoted, zealous, amateur

nature, natures (1: individual character or disposition) truthful, veracious,

honourable, trusting, forgiving,
affectionate, sensitive, lovable, benevolent,
good, kindly, charitable, generous,
vivacious, cheery, magnanimous,
easy-going, light-hearted, breezy, casual,
carefree, lively, flexible, friendly,
gregarious, contagious, amiable,
angst-ridden, social, responsive, amorous,
passionate, emotional, romantic, facile,
pacific, peaceful, peace-loving, reserved,
retired, austere, confiding, trustful, shy,
wary, susceptible, (un)resisting, yielding,
submissive, compliant, zany, wayward,
truant, protean, many-sided, diffuse,
complex, unresolved, tempestuous,
impulsive, unappealing, possessive, cold,
indifferent, devious, insensitive, irascible,
vague, ambiguous, distorted, avaricious,
deceitful, condescending, overbearing,
frivolous, flighty, stubborn, wilful, quirky,
grotesque, resistant, unfriendly, capricious,
aggressive, combative, fighting,
unflappable, perverse, acquired, (in)artistic,
inner; second

nature (2: natural unspoiled scenery or
countryside) See *scene* and *countryside*

neatness dainty, adroit, elegant, exact,
fastidious, immaculate, precise, orderly,
proper, shapely, smart, spick-and-span,
spotless, trim, well-groomed, studied

necessity, necessities See *need*

neck, necks graceful, fine, scrawny,
scraggy, lean, thin, skinny, slim, slender,
sinuous, serpentine, long, thick, taut,
stumpy, crinkly, muscular, sculptured, wry,
arched, limp, sore, aching, stiff, drawn,
sunburned, swollen, snowy, dirty, scruffy,
swanlike

necklace, necklaces See also *jewel*
heavy, chain, bead(ed), feathered, shell,
cameo, ornate, floral, precious, valuable,
cheap, inexpensive, short, (over)long

necktie, neckties silk, tweed, polyester,
wool(len), string, striped, spotted, print,
wide, soft, quirky, conservative, subdued,
restrained, discreet, elegant,
(un)fashionable, bright, colourful,
flamboyant, dashing, flashy, garish, loud,
wild, whimsical, crude, sprightly, black,
white, bow, ascot, windsor, tartan, paisley,
pattern, rep

need, needs crying, overriding,
overpowering, burning, compelling,

consuming, persevering, pressing,
staggering, lasting, distressing, dire,
voracious, sore, stern, anxious, feverish,
bitter, inexorable, constant, immediate,
urgent, instant, hurried, imperative,
desperate, drastic, essential, big, basic,
fundamental, primal, base, vital, critical,
great, absolute, exigent, imperious, real,
positive, conceivable, apparent, obvious,
distinct, acute, grim, deep(est), ingrained,
neurotic, undeniable, indispensable,
inevitable, unavoidable, irresistible,
authentic, stringent, iron, specific,
temporary, day-to-day, insatiable,
inextinguishable, ongoing, diverse,
unconscious, unforeseen, actual, little,
prosaic, questionable, modest, unhealthy,
sordid, disorderly, bitter, ignoble, pitiable,
lamentable, tragic, ghastly, material,
economic, cultural, bodily, internal,
psychological, devotional, spiritual,
nutritional, biological, instinctive, special,
individual, personal, universal

needle, needles sharp, thin, hollow,
two-tined, disposable, ice, electric,
magnetic, hypodermic, etching

negation, negations unyielding,
inveterate, adamant, obstinate

neglect appalling, disgusting, distressing,
shocking, unfeeling, unconscionable,
shameful, culpable, dishonourable,
scandalous, disgraceful, ineradicable, cold,
gross, dire, dreadful, malign, wilful,
deliberate, (un)conscious, benign, cheerful,
sheer, utter, seeming, apparent, criminal,
contributory

negligence, negligences See also *neglect*
criminal, contributory

negotiation, negotiations, negotiating
(in)effective, (un)fruitful, (un)productive,
(im)proper, substantive, peaceful,
conciliatory, cordial, good-faith, lucid,
(non-)polemical, open-handed, serious,
steady, delicate, intense, heated, fevered,
feverish, hectic, frantic, laborious,
painstaking, arduous, wearisome, tedious,
baffling, tough, suspenseful, stressful,
nerve-racking, sp(l)uttering, tumultuous,
dramatic, hurried, hasty, complicated,
complex, intricate, difficult, tense, glacial,
tortuous, controversial, unpredictable,
acrimonious, contentious, fragile, troubled,
stormy, fruitless, last-ditch, comprehensive,

broad, wide-ranging, marathon, (in)valid, fundamental, preliminary, exploratory, formal, secret, behind-the-scenes, hushed, face-to-face, (in)direct, slow-moving, slow-paced, drawn-out, sluggish, protracted, continued, stop-and-go, ongoing, open-ended, follow-up, round-table, bilateral, trilateral, high-level, top-level, summit, exploratory, trade; pillow

negotiator, negotiators seasoned, able, credible, tough, unyielding, hard-bitten, no-nonsense, noncommittal, key, top, ace, weary, pallid, frustrated, bitter

neighbour, neighbours obliging, courteous, cooperative, quiet, popular, thoughtful, peaceful, peaceable, harmonious, private, (un)friendly, (un)welcome, curious, nosy, prying, inquisitive, gossipy, hostile, troublesome, fractious, pugnacious, feuding, predatory, rapacious, nettlesome, next-door, nearby, nearest, immediate

neighbourhood, neighbourhoods posh, chic, classy, trendy, fashionable, elegant, graceful, premier, wealthy, upscale, opulent, pricey, well-off, prosperous, estimable, proud, (un)liv(e)able, fine, respectable, fascinating, fancy, gracious, (un)desirable, (un)attractive, (un)prepossessing, established, stable, built-up, close-knit, genteel, funky, bohemian, varied, lively, individualistic, grotty, marginal, quiet, (dis)orderly, (un)safe, (un)friendly, (un)familiar, run-down, bleak, moribund, tough, rough, nasty, troubled, lethal, crime-ridden, brawling, waning, congested, seedy, poor, squalid, immediate, transient, residential, urban, inner-city, suburban, working-class, blue-collar, middle-class, white-collar, black, whites-only, ethnic, interracial, racist, single-family

nerve, nerves (un)steady, iron, steely, tense, taut, twitchy, short, hypersensitive, shaky, calmed, unstrung, high-strung, over-strung, pinched, raw; depressor, main, tiny, whitish, sensory (afferent), auditory, olfactory, sciatic, visual, sub-orbital, facial, cardiac, cranial, trigeminal, optic(al), phrenic, pneumogastric, ophthalmic, peripheral, abducens, accessory, acoustic, parasympathetic

nervousness See *anxiety*

nest, nests pendulous, conic(al), papery, bulky, tangled, empty, cosy, (un)stable, established, crude, slight, flimsy, insubstantial, artificial, man-made, plastic, mud, subterranean

net, nets scrambling, nylon-mesh, weblike, handmade, machine-made, fine-meshed, long-handled, flimsy, deadly, fatal

network, networks See *system*

neutrality strict, scrupulous, impartial, fair, disinterested, objective, non-partisan, unallied, unbiased, unprejudiced, vaunted, traditional, regional

news refreshing, exhilarating, encouraging, exciting, thrilling, rattling, startling, surprising, amazing, astounding, moving, stunning, stupefying, fast-breaking, blessed, (un)beneficial, (un)welcome, hopeful, cheerful, cheery, good, excellent, glad, (un)pleasant, joyful, upbeat, (un)favourable, great, electric, firm, dependable, trustworthy, reliable, authentic, sensational, incredible, unbelievable, wonderful, remarkable, fantastic, vital, unexpected, memorable, serious, chief, quiet, urgent, current, topical, recent, late(st), fresh, dramatic, momentous, (red-)hot, second-hand, stale, copious, mixed, hard, soft, cold, bad, sad, grim, gloomy, melancholy, dismal, ominous, dreadful, awful, grave, tough, macabre, disgraceful, dire, unsettling, unnerving, disappointing, agonizing, appalling, sickening, shocking, dispiriting, disquieting, devastating, depressing, discouraging, disheartening, alarming, sobering, worrisome, false, distorted, uncensored, unanalysed, official, local, regional, world, international, headline, front-page, telegraphic

newsletter, newsletters See also *newspaper* timely, hand-written, glossy, weekly, fortnightly, monthly, quarterly, community, religious, underground

newspaper, newspapers classy, respectable, well-respected, decorous, illustrious, prestigious, (high-)quality, distinguished, venerable, esteemed, (un)readable, independent, honest, thoughtful, vigorous, spirited, sprightly, breezy, racy, influential, kingpin, aggressive, combative, investigative, uncensored, uncontrolled, pro-government, leading, major, established, legendary, highbrow, widely-read, big, (in)accessible, (un)profitable, entertaining, stodgy, stolid, conventional, dull, serious, stuffy, staid, small, tiny, contemporary, fresh, scurrilous, intrusive, insensitive, vile, malicious, boring, worthless, sleazy, dishonest, yellow, newsy, saucy, salacious, down-market, raunchy, brassy, garish, sensational, lurid, (now-)defunct, ailing, money-losing, failing, dying, troubled, crumpled-up, short-lived, day-old, reformist, liberal, left-wing, subversive, underground, inflammatory, partisan, morning, afternoon, evening, local, suburban, regional, metropolitan, national, global, daily, weekly, tabloid, mass-circulation, community, opposition, cooperative, in-house, all-ad, free

nickname, nicknames See *name*

night, nights clear, serene, quiet, silent, tranquil, calm, soundless, still, soft, windless, balmy, peaceful, tender, (un)comfortable, splendid, languorous, moony, (half-)moonlit, shiny, starlit, starry, bright, lustrous, luminous, gaudy, enchanting, magic, velvety, cloudless, mistless, moonless, starless, scant-starred, (pitch-)dark, bad, awful, impenetrable, bleak, sable, (coal-)black, pitch-black, blustery, disturbed, doleful, bitter, chilly, parky, crisp(y), frigid, cold, freezing, frozen, frosty, icy, misty, damp, vile, rainy, rain-swept, squally, pouring, overcast, windy, blustery, stormy, steamy, clammy, sultry, blistering, muggy, restless, wakeful, sleepless, fitful, rough, wild, tempestuous, turbulent, unruly, boozy, frightening, murky, gloomy, watch, opening

nightlife, nightlives See also *life* swinging, gaudy, steamy, erotic, lustful

nightmare, nightmares frightening, racking, haunting, creeping, waking, recurrent, frequent, sharp, dreadful, horrific, terrible, violent, unrelenting, relentless, ruthless, pitiless, heartless, merciless, unreal, curious, bizarre, noisy, wakeful, vivid, living, modern-day, public, neurological, Sisyphean

nobility, nobilities aristocratic, courtly, distinguished, eminent, illustrious, highborn, imperial, lordly, genuine, unalloyed, privileged, (un)titled, well-acred, landholding, false, hard-pressed, parasitic, feudal

nobleman, noblemen See *nobility*

nod, nods curt, modest, silent, slight, vigorous, imperceptible

noise, noises piercing, deafening, grinding, murmuring, buzzing, grating, rustling, warbling, rumbling, thumping, rasping, prancing, snapping, groaning, swishing, sucking, threatening, annoying, nerve-racking, skull-splitting, compelling, distinct-sounding, distracting, gleeful, constant, sustained, incessant, unceasing, ceaseless, continuous, everlasting, discordant, queer, strange, loud, astounding, tremendous, throaty, hideous, loathsome, terrible, horrendous, awful, incredible, unbelievable, unrelenting, unbearable, barbaric, harsh, sharp, prodigious, shrill, abrupt, staccato, repetitive, hollow, low-frequency, extraordinary, infernal, thunderous, offensive, crude, uncouth, unwanted, untolerated, insidious, furtive, stupefying, indecipherable, slight, diurnal, white, background, surface, seismic, guttural, ambient

nomad, nomads See also *wanderer* roving, wandering, migrant, migratory, homeless, vagrant, footloose, restless, pastoral, desert, tribal

nomination, nominations uncontested, presumptive, unanimous

nominee, nominees See *candidate*

nonsense absurd, foolish, idiotic, amphigoric, capricious, fanciful, imbecilic, preposterous, ridiculous, senseless, silly, stupid, whimsical, simple-minded, mendacious, utter, perfect, total, sheer, pure, unadulterated, rank, stark, madcap

non-smoker, non-smokers adamant, sanctimonious, militant, unyielding

nook, nooks See *retreat* (2)

noon, noons heat-delirious, high

nose, noses perfect, dainty, fine, thin, aquiline, classical, Roman, haughty, puffed-up, turn-up, uplifted, bulbous, sharp, straight, snub, protuberant, prominent, bulging, stubby, pug, fleshy, cushiony, parrot-beak, broad, wide, square, flat, crooked, rounded, cocked, curved, chiselled, flat(tish), freckled, tapered, high-bridged, snout-like, sunburned, itchy, bloody, swollen, stuffy, drippy, runny, watery, shiny, knowing, twitching, inquisitive, keen, sensitive

nostalgia longing, yearning, easy, intense, acute, impassioned, vicarious, bizarre, hopeless, melancholic

notable, notables See *celebrity*

notation, notations numerical, decimal, musical

note, notes (1: melody; tone) pure, clear, simple, well-defined, melodious, sharp, vibrant, colourful, upbeat, ecstatic, haunting, dominant, sonorous, twittering, chirping, jarring, cacophonic, harsh, disconnected, disjointed, poor, sour, discordant, false, queer, macabre, fluffy, hooty, shrill, inexplicable, clipped, sombre, wistful, low, sustained, climbing, floating, beat, high-pitched, rasping, sneering, cynical, ominous, disquieting, specified, (double-)dotted, staccato, whole, passing, wood, half, pentatonic, musical

note, notes (2: short letter; written comment) conciliatory, courteous, (un)pleasant, memorable, (un)important, (il)legible, (in)decipherable, (un)ambiguous, (un)clear, (un)intelligible, (im)precise, jovial, flippant, hasty, little, detailed, comprehensive, voluminous, copious, terse, concise, meticulous, vagrant, urgent, prompt, obscure, handwritten, internal, bureaucratic, mental, personal, thank-you, confidential, ransom, suicide, advice, congratulatory; programme, marginal, textual, explanatory

note, notes (3: written promise to pay money) negotiable, promissory

notion, notions fond, (in)valid, (in)distinct, clear, self-evident, newfangled, simple, (un)conventional, singular, crucial, (un)traditional, complacent, general, common, old-fashioned, long-held, persistent, widespread, prevalent, prevailing, unformed, uneasy, strange, lunatic, absurd, idiotic, foolish, crazy, preposterous, outlandish, ridiculous, nutty, heretical, unthinkable, fallacious, fanciful, far-fetched, tantalizing, unthinkable, incredible, unbelievable, slippery, odd, queer, curious, eccentric, oppressive, unnerving, shocking, confused, hazy,

fuzzy, vague, dim, cloudy, foggy, addled, muzzy, faint, vaporous, misleading, false, mistaken, uninformed, wrong(-headed), (un)biased, distorted, freakish, empty, obsolete, antiquated, damnable, subversive, perverse, pernicious

notoriety See *fame*

noun, nouns concrete (material), abstract, proper, common, collective, singular, plural, masculine, feminine, neuter, anarthrous

nourishment rich, delicious, healthful, healthy, hearty, wholesome, attentive, (in)adequate, (im)proper, restorative, spiritual, intellectual

novel, novels fascinating, intriguing, absorbing, haunting, stirring, bracing, exciting, piercing, captivating, intellectually-appealing, stimulating, entrancing, enchanting, compelling, engaging, dazzling, exhilarating, satisfying, moving, touching, entertaining, amusing, prize-winning, award-winning, celebrated, fine, extraordinary, singular, exceptional, matchless, flawless, remarkable, original, unique, innovative, pioneer, groundbreaking, beautiful, spirited, vivid, lively, lifelike, truthful, crisp, powerful, forceful, vigorous, intense, provocative, evocative, timely, thought-provoking, issue-orient(at)ed, serious, expansive, terse, succinct, gritty, blockbuster, delightful, taut, schematic, shapely, polished, accomplished, finished, consummate, perfect, adroit, sensitive, superb, virtuoso, brilliant, masterful, masterly, imperishable, durable, timeless, (ever-)popular, successful, memorable, portentous, purple, ambitious, (un)conventional, (un)believable, rich, complex, intricate, convoluted, difficult, ambiguous, impenetrable, sophisticated, subtle, larky, sensational, suspenseful, mawkish, febrile, splashy, commercial, poignant, harrowing, apocalyptic, unfinished, massive, bulky, monumental, mammoth, three-volume, multi-volume, long-drawn-out, wistful, tawdry, unabridged, full-length, uncensored, libellous, blasphemous, controversial, fulsome, pungent, piquant, poignant, racy, irreverent, appalling, dreadful, shocking, revolting, tendentious, pornographic, obscene, salacious, indecent,

sexy, smutty, prurient, erotic,
adult-orient(at)ed, trashy, cheap, prosaic,
worthless, inferior, formless, shapeless,
sprawling, intractable, incoherent, strange,
odd, fragmentary, disjointed, flawed, wan,
youthful, boring, sombre, dark,
self-revealing, ruminative, contemplative,
introspective, funny, witty, farcical, ironic,
satiric(al), radical, poetic, gothic,
historical, epistolary, sociological,
science-fiction, time-dimension, spy,
suspense, crime, horror, whodunit,
graphic, visual, cinematic, classical,
Victorian, Edwardian, New (Nouveau),
(un)conventional, traditional,
old-fashioned, (post-)war, modern,
contemporary, philosophic(al), critical,
psychological, Freudian, linear, episodic,
dramatic, domestic, local, universal, dime,
picaresque, naturalistic, realistic,
stream-of-consciousness, experimental,
feminist, short, juvenile, pulp,
penny-dreadful, adventure, pseudonymous,
Aesthetic, Bildungsroman,
(semi-)autobiographical, outside, chronicle,
debut, serial, sequential, saga
(roman-fleuve), lyrical, poetic, romantic,
romance, sentimental, (anti-)Utopian,
problem, topical, escapist, symbolist,
allegorical, fantasy, impressionistic,
political, Catholic, religious, industrial,
proletarian, pastoral, regional, provincial,
colonial, meteorological, campus, literary,
paperback, soft-cover, hard-cover

novelist, novelists gifted, talented,
imaginative, premier, major, superlative,
(pre-)eminent, master, titanic, inveterate,
accomplished, famed, famous, noted,
notable, well-known, celebrated, renowned,
honoured, prominent, first-rate, popular,
canny, established, voluminous, prolific,
mass-market, embryo, budding, promising,
aspiring, first-time, struggling, would-be,
unknown, unbeknown, obscure, minor,
failed, living, dead, comic, satiric(al),
romance, spy, formula, proletarian,
regional, political, Marxist, inter-war,
post-war, imagist, feminist

nuisance, nuisances harassing, vexing,
stinging, aggravating, annoying,
distressing, provoking, cussed, cursed,
obstinate, hateful, pestiferous, loathsome,
tedious, intolerable, awful, pesky,
confounded, monumental, precious,
common, regular, occasional, complete,
utter, thorough, perfect, total, extreme;
public, private

number, numbers rising, growing,
(ever-)increasing, surging, swelling,
compelling, overwhelming, staggering,
stunning, mind-boggling, astonishing,
astounding, surprising, alarming, startling,
unsettling, record, unprecedented,
stupendous, incredible, unbelievable,
unusual, extraordinary, inordinate,
massive, gigantic, prodigious, excessive,
(in)significant, high, vast, siz(e)able,
substantial, respectable, large, endless,
incalculable, unimaginable, astronomical,
indefinite, (dis)proportionate, (un)realistic,
requisite, decisive, ominous, superior,
sheer, mass, imaginary, (un)lucky,
(un)favourable, (in)decipherable,
(im)precise, approximate, murky,
underlying, modest, paltry, low, tiny,
fallacious, undetermined, (un)counted,
(un)known, untold, unspecified,
(un)manageable, burdensome, absolute,
serial, (un)even, cardinal, ordinal, decimal,
fractional, rational, natural, compound,
mixed, octane, round, negative, real,
complex, square, whole, call, abstract,
concrete, figurate, polygonal, index,
irrational, (in)finite, neutron, odd,
oxidation, prime, composite, algebraic,
transcendent(al), identification, (multi-)digit,
magic, accession; atomic (proton)

nun, nuns meditative, contemplative,
remote, distant, otherworldly, solitary,
cloistered, secluded, mendicant, postulant,
ascetic, c(o)enobitic

nurse, nurses compassionate, humane,
vigilant, attendant, observant, hygienic,
conscientious, dedicated, saintly,
self-sacrificing, veteran, (in)competent,
(in)sensitive, (un)caring, (un)qualified,
(in)experienced, (un)sympathetic,
perfunctory, curt, impersonal, harsh,
dominant, practising, off-duty, on-duty,
night(-shift), practical, professional,
registered, student, graduate,
intensive-care, critical-care, acute-care,
scrub, emergency-room, clinical, hospital,
private-duty, geriatric, public-health,
obstetrics, paediatric, psychiatric,
home(-care), charge, district; dry, wet

nut, nuts (1: a piece of metal with a
threaded hole) soft hexagonal, slotted
hexagonal, lock, plain square, wing, acorn,
double-cupped, untapped joint, castle,
thumb, chamfered square
nut, nuts (2: hard-shelled fruit)
hard-shelled, thick-walled, two-lobed,
ridged, wrinkled, dry, crunchy, nutritious,
(in)edible, (un)popular, smooth, sweet,
delicious, flavourful, stale
nutrient, nutrients strengthening,
alimental, hearty, restorative, rich,
wholesome, healthful, healthy,
(in)adequate, (im)proper, poor, major,
crucial, essential, mineral
nutrition See *nutrient*

oasis, oases relaxing, secluded, far-flung, lonesome, removed, remote, sheltered, quiet, cool, unique, picture-book, paradisiacal, lush, verdant, meagre, man-made, date-palm, tropical

oath, oaths binding, restraining, solemn, sacred, devout, awe-inspiring, dignified, (un)equivocal, unbreakable, inviolable, dreadful, violent, verbal, ritualistic, formal, ceremonial, promissory, judicial, blood, civil, military, Stygian, Hippocratic

obedience strict, absolute, unreserved, subdued, unquestioning, blind, infallible, abject, servile, feather-brained, suicidal, resigned, submissive, passive, sheer, quiet, cheerful, willing, will-less, involuntary, filial

object, objects (1: material thing) concrete, visual, (in)tangible, (in)distinct, (in)visible, (in)animate, (im)mobile, (in)definable, (un)identifiable, collectible, stationary, strange, dim, faint, fuzzy, flying, dominant, unpromising

object, objects (2: part of speech) direct, indirect, cognate, reflexive

object, objects (3: objective) See *goal* and *aim*

objection, objections (in)discreet, strong, vigorous, strenuous, vehement, impassioned, invincible, insuperable, serious, dogged, vociferous, furious, (in)valid, unfounded, baseless, untenable, trifling, captious, petty, annoying, whimsical, frivolous, prudish, disingenuous, uncomprehending, muted, faint, central, cardinal, fundamental, primary, main, conscientious, formal

objective, objectives See *goal* and *aim*

objectivity calm, reasoned, mature, disquieting, detached, disinterested, fair, impartial, dispassionate, unallied, unbiased

objector, objectors raging, dissenting, violent, fierce, furious, strong, militant, well-intentioned, conscientious

objet d'art, objets d'art See *artefact*

obligation, obligations huge, monumental, extensive, heavy, great, nightmarish, absolute, solemn, unconditional, fixed, short-term, long-term, outstanding, indispensable, unique, simple, severable, (long-)overdue, twofold, reciprocal, unfulfilled, basic, primary, moral, ethical, sacred, pecuniary, financial, marital, sacramental, contractual, legal, social, religious, business, fiduciary, military, strategic, fundamental, statutory

oblivion thoughtless, heedless, neglectful, unmindful, eternal, everlasting, relative, self-imposed, inevitable, nirvanic, Lethean

obscurity deep, cryptic(al), dim, modest, enigmatic, relative, eternal, lifeless, self-imposed, affected, (in)evitable, (un)avoidable, oracular, Delphic (Delphian)

observance, observances strict, rigid, perfect, exacting, extreme, inflexible, puritanic(al), relentless, rigorous, scrupulous, unbending, uncompromising, unyielding, unswerving, excessive, militant, compulsory, ritual, religious; Sunday

observation, observations (1: remark) See also *remark* sensible, judicious, perceptive, trenchant, incisive, (in)appropriate, apt, felicitous, vivid, original, intelligent, acute, astute, shrewd, (un)sophisticated, genial, genuine, pungent, piercing, penetrating, incisive, potent, poignant, primal, withering, passing, mundane, small, common, trite, snide, scatological, impertinent, blatant

observation (2: the act of observing) acute, meticulous, close, subtle, careful, intelligent, vigilant, intensive, keen, impartial, unbiased, impersonal, dispassionate, calm, continuous, around-the-clock, casual, empirical

observer, observers subtle, acute, keen, precise, interested, shrewd, minute, astute, seasoned, piercing, discerning, correct, studious, careful, intelligent, vigilant, calm, silent, dedicated, dispassionate, neutral, detached, objective, subjective, (im)partial, (un)prejudiced, (im)personal, (un)sophisticated, casual, sceptical, superficial, naïve, first-time, first-hand, outside, scientific, latter-day; diplomatic; meteorological

obsession, obsessions, obsessiveness overwhelming, abiding, consuming, haunting, predominant, significant, fierce,

troublesome, harassing, besetting,
intrusive, weird, bizarre, active, fixed,
kooky, single-minded, dreamy,
off-the-wall, sexual, cloacal, scatological

obstacle, obstacles devastating,
mind-boggling, discouraging, disheartening,
formidable, serious, severe, solid,
substantial, tremendous, mammoth, big,
awesome, obdurate, difficult, prohibitive,
insidious, incredible, unbelievable,
outstanding, long-standing, impossible,
impassable, insurmountable, insuperable,
immovable, cumbrous, (in)significant,
major, chief, main, minor, partial,
temporary, (un)expected, unresolved,
man-made, artificial, arbitrary, physical,
bureaucratic

obstinacy, obstinacies mulish,
bull-headed, headstrong, inflexible,
intractable, obdurate, pedantic, pig-headed,
adamant(ive), tenacious, unyielding,
obstreperous, incredible, unbelievable,
conspiratorial

obstruction, obstructions See *obstacle*

obstructionist, obstructionists
implacable, unmitigated, inflexible,
inexorable, unappeasable

occasion, occasions gay, glad, joyous,
joyful, merry, happy, pleasurable,
enjoyable, exhilarating, glittering, fancy,
rumbustious, boisterous, special, certain,
unique, memorable, historic, outstanding,
rare, great, momentous, grand, opportune,
well-timed, timely, previous, handy,
(in)frequent, routine, (in)formal,
melancholy, sad, mournful, lamentable,
deplorable, grievous, unhappy, solemn,
festive, festal, ceremonial, ceremonious,
religious

occupation, occupations (1: vocation)
rewarding, prestigious, honoured,
honourable, noble, congenial, (un)pleasant,
placid, gainful, profitable, reputable,
proper, productive, indispensable, definite,
vital, lifelong, seasonal, sedentary, stressful,
nerve-racking, bookish, white-collar,
conventional, structured, high-risk,
hazardous, perilous, treacherous, low(ly),
humble, menial, shady

occupation (2: the control of an area, by
force) detestable, deplorable, hateful,
unpopular, abominable, lamentable,
reprehensible, heartless, pitiless, merciless,

ruthless, relentless, unrelenting, brutal,
murderous, bloody, tyrannical, illegal,
unlawful, unprovoked, naked, wretched,
continuous, protracted, permanent,
temporary, short-term, benign, military,
(neo)colonial

occurrence, occurrences revealing,
providential, commonplace, (un)common,
constant, (in)frequent, rare, unheard-of,
mysterious, random, sporadic, chance,
accidental, (un)expected, sparse,
simultaneous, lamentable, regrettable,
(un)fortunate, (un)interesting, cataclysmic,
disastrous, psychic, occult, spectral

ocean, oceans life-teeming, silent, still,
calm, restful, placid, (in)temperate,
massive, mighty, great, giant, infinite,
broad, vast, limitless, boundless, endless,
open, unbroken, uncharted, trackless,
featureless, choppy, stormy, tumultuous,
turbulent, raging, wild, furious,
tempestuous, freakish, hopeless,
implacable, unkind, rugged, lumpy,
sleepless, moonless, azure, cerulean,
turquoise, cobalt-vivid, cobalt-blue,
grey-green, misty, foggy, fog-shrouded,
sombre, rippling, sparkling, equatorial

ode, odes See also *poem* choral, Pindaric,
stanzaic, irregular

odour, odours (un)pleasant, (dis)pleasing,
(un)attractive, (dis)agreeable, seductive,
intriguing, irresistible, fine, subtle, flowery,
fruity, sweet, aromatic, pervasive, bracing,
sharp, rich, heavy, strong, telltale,
penetrative, penetrating, piercing,
searching, lingering, noticeable, distinctive,
distinct, curious, peculiar, intense, slight,
faint, odd, dry(ish), sour, astringent,
mysterious, nauseous, nauseating,
revolting, sickening, disgusting, sickly,
horrible, terrible, depressive, offensive,
foul, bad, repellent, repulsive, sickish,
oppressive, loathsome, vile, wicked, rank,
acrid, pungent, musky, noisome, earthy,
musty, mouldy, malty, fusty, resinous,
doggy, dank, warmish, steamy, greasy,
stale, deathly, primitive, natural, ageless,
personal

offence, offences minor, trivial, petty,
light, (un)pardonable, (un)intentional,
(non-)violent, grave, heavy, serious, major,
flagrant, egregious, deep, dreary, odious,
foul, hateful, heinous, outrageous,

monstrous, reprehensible, punishable, indictable, prosecutable, impeachable, sackable, arrestable, transportable, deportable, extraditable, bailable, penitentiary, mortal, penal, prison, hanging, political, alcohol-related, sex(ual), drug, terrorist, capital, criminal

offender, offenders serious, dangerous, vicious, cold-blooded, hardened, unfeeling, obdurate, flagrant, repeat, (non-)violent, first-time, second-time, natural-born, unrepentant, young, minor, juvenile, sex(ual), traffic

offensive, offensives See *attack*

offer, offers dazzling, tempting, enticing, alluring, inviting, seductive, (un)attractive, advantageous, generous, heaven-sent, unprecedented, gracious, handsome, remarkable, unbeatable, interesting, promising, lucrative, substantial, great, special, genuine, surprising, emphatic, (in)adequate, (un)reasonable, (un)satisfactory, (un)acceptable, innocuous, vague, solid, definitive, fresh, tentative, final, initial, long-standing, spontaneous, tawdry, unblushing, shameless, presumptuous, hollow, derisive, bold, free, unprompted, back-channel, (un)conditional, gentlemanly, standing, stand-by, peace, last-ditch, bona fide, promotional

offering, offerings generous, gracious, opulent, wondrous, irrepressible, meagre, humble, burnt, charitable, ceremonious, ceremonial, ritual, sacred, sacrificial, symbolic, votive, prayer, floral, propitiatory, expiatory, conciliatory, peace

office, offices (1: room used as a place for business) See also *room* luxurious, sumptuous, plush, stylish, (ultra)modern, spacious, adequate, suitable, well-run, book-lined, small, cubbyhole, outmoded, inadequate, modest, bare-bones, windowless, cavernous, congested, dismal, dingy, squalid

office, offices (2: duty) lofty, high(est), ultimate, (un)enviable, menial, elective, hereditary, public, political, ceremonial, honorary

officer, officers trusty, trustworthy, brilliant, natty, dapper, vigilant, strict, dictatorial, high-ranking, senior, chief, elder, superior, top, inferior, uniformed, retired, rebel(lious), renegade, career, commanding, field, warrant, (non-)commissioned, veteran, general, petty, reserve, peace, line, military, regular; probation, truant, returning, electoral, judicial, law-enforcement, executive, corporate

official, officials long-serving, (high-)ranking, senior, key, high(-profile), highly-paid, (high-)salaried, middle-ranking, ci-devant, junior, subordinate, low-salaried, low-profile, minor, able, dedicated, conscientious, (in)competent, (dis)honest, busy, above-board, (in)corruptible, corrupt, inept, hide-bound, obtrusive, pompous, gusty, petty, despicable, contemptible, negligent, bumptious, appropriate, elective, retired, out-of-work, public, law-enforcement, judicial

offspring, offsprings See *descendant*

oil, oils high-grade, first-press, (super-)light, virgin, synthetic, glutinous, sticky, viscous, thick, rich, fatty, essential, versatile, supernatant, aromatic, fragrant, (un)scented, (un)perfumed, rancid, pungent, murky, black, toxic, (un)refined, unadulterated, unfiltered, (un)saturated, monounsaturated, polyunsaturated, (home-)heating, (semi-)drying, fixed, volatile (essential), natural, animal, mineral, vegetable, cod-liver, sperm-whale, cosmetic, botanical; marine, crude, heavy; baptismal

old age secure, serene, ripe, unheralded, wispy, frail, pathetic, debilitating

old people See *old person*

old person, old persons comely, genial, mild, benign, gentle, benevolent, friendly, kindly, kind-hearted, grand, noble, fine, gracious, venerable, secure, spry, active, lively, nimble, dignified, unbowed, weathered, wrinkled, white-haired, hard-of-hearing, cold-susceptible, heat-susceptible, feeble, weak, rickety, frail, wiry, bent, stooped, senile, doddering, ailing, vulnerable, dysfunctional, helpless, forgetful, mumbling, ragged, ridiculous, crusty, dull, didactic, grumpy, surly, gruff, ill-humoured, bad-tempered, irascible, pok(e)y, stupid, peculiar, garrulous, grouchy, fussy, talkative, gossipy, flighty, tedious, cantankerous, arthritic

oligarchy, oligarchies incompetent, erratic, capricious, whimsical, oppressive, repressive, paranoid, bloody, overbearing, greedy, closed, pernicious, evil, wicked, hurtful, abhorrent, self-perpetuating

olive, olives See also *fruit* green, black, jumbo, ripe, fresh, hard, soft, mouldy, oily, wrinkled, (pimiento-)stuffed

omelette, omelettes savoury, fluffy, leathery, flat, soufflé (souffléed)

omen, omens propitious, auspicious, good, promising, encouraging, (un)lucky, ill, bad, evil, glaring, notable, inexplicable, unforgivable, ostentatious, fateful, menacing, inadvertent, (un)intentional, confirmed

omission, omissions shocking, conspicuous, curious, strange, extraordinary, odd, suspicious, (un)forgivable, (in)excusable, (in)explicable, (un)explainable, inadvertent, (un)intentional, deliberate, deplorable, unfortunate, major, minor

onion, onions See *vegetable*

onlooker, onlookers See *spectator*

onslaught, onslaughts See *attack*

opening, openings (the first performance) astounding, exciting, stunning, thrilling, sensational, emotional, extraordinary, impressive, splashy, spectacular, star-studded, grand, (un)official

opera, operas moving, emotional, eponymous, grand, serious, light (comic), ballad; soap

operation, operations (1: surgery) See also *surgery* painless, (partly-)successful, (un)feasible, major, delicate, critical, risky, hazardous, (un)necessary, (un)safe, (un)satisfactory, (in)adequate, drastic, gruelling, harrowing, distressing, painful, extraordinary, spectacular, dazzling, landmark, innovative, novel, experimental, radical, dramatic, controversial, minor, traditional, day-long, four-hour, routine, high-priority, multiple, medical, surgical, invasive, cosmetic, therapeutic, reconstructive, emergency, heart-implant, joint-replacement, prenatal, foetal, Caesarean

operation, operations (2: working; movement) large(-scale), vast, massive, substantial, marathon, elaborate, extensive, expansive, pervasive, flourishing, around-the-clock, (in)efficient, viable, expert, world-class, (il)legitimate, (il)legal, (un)lawful, (un)safe, trouble-free, innovative, sophisticated, high-tech, discreet, precise, quick, sensitive, autonomous, slow-and-steady, evolutionary, one-handed, shoestring, manual, small-potatoes, élitist, hidden, covert, secret, clandestine, secrecy-shrouded, mysterious, obscure, unknown, nefarious, evil, wicked, sloppy, shady, disreputable, (non-)violent, (un)profitable, marginal, small, low-tech, financial, military, naval, offensive, undercover, computer, day-to-day

opinion, opinions crisp, piquant, scrupulous, reliable, advisory, learned, considered, expert, informed, sensible, honest, frank, outspoken, thoughtful, unbiased, disinterested, humble, calm, temperate, right, genuine, sober, favourable, clear-eyed, discerning, fastidious, cogent, popular, determinate, emphatic, high, exalted, lofty, established, prevailing, current, widespread, rampant, common, authoritative, emphatic, decided, definite, blunt, advanced, adventurous, (un)orthodox, forward, vehement, contrary, opposing, conflicting, contradictory, reverse, opposite, discordant, dissenting, incongruous, received, pronounced, unvoiced, frequently-voiced, unsolicited, split, (un)alterable, fusty, old-fashioned, outmoded, antiquated, antediluvian, unchanging, set, caustic, pungent, irreligious, lowly, prejudiced, changeable, trite, wrong, mistaken, misleading, inflated, inimical, unfavourable, poor, low, light, ill-considered, outrageous, sordid, intemperate, spiky, aggregate, concurrent, private, personal, collective; public, professional, legal; golden

opponent, opponents peaceful, (un)worthy, (un)fair, (dis)honourable, powerful, formidable, implacable, irreconcilable, resolute, determined, obstinate, adamant, unpredictable, bitter, hostile, violent, fierce, vociferous, voracious, fearsome, staunch, unyielding, uncompromising, unrelenting, relentless, heartless, merciless, ruthless, pitiless, ardent, fervent, hard-line, militant, extreme, explicit, outspoken, vocal, tough, strenuous, avowed, competitive, doctrinaire, leading, feisty, worthless, contemptible, mean, foul, potential, seasoned, political

opportunism unabashed, shameless, brazen, barefaced, blatant, degrading, disgraceful, outrageous, unblushing, unscrupulous, wily, sly, crafty

opportunity, opportunities intriguing, dazzling, challenging, interesting, attractive, God-sent, God-given, heaven-sent, once-in-a-lifetime, unique, rare, extraordinary, unparalleled, unprecedented, fabulous, wonderful, excellent, admirable, remarkable, splendid, marvellous, magnificent, golden, precious, auspicious, advantageous, fit, superb, fine, terrific, favourable, real, positive, ample, substantial, rich, priceless, fitting, suitable, perfect, incredible, unbelievable, (un)limited, (un)restricted, unparalleled, unsurpassed, unusual, unexpected, undreamed-of, fiction-like, irresistible, watershed, obvious, vast, immense, tremendous, historic, spontaneous, transient, myriad, wasted, irrecoverable, new, novel, fresh, additional, meagre, unfolding, lagging, equal

opposer, opposers See *opposition*

opposite, opposites polar(ized), direct, exact, absolute, complete, diametrical

opposition, oppositions honest, frank, open, outspoken, vocal, friendly, peaceful, legitimate, healthy, credible, real, bitter, angry, downright, (in)visible, palpable, stubborn, obstinate, adamant, determined, formidable, obdurate, stout, implacable, irreversible, fierce, heated, fervent, passionate, insurmountable, savage, growing, long-standing, unrelenting, relentless, ruthless, merciless, heartless, pitiless, persistent, strenuous, strong, big, vociferous, vigorous, (non-)violent, stiff, intense, tough, vehement, resourceful, systematic, passionate, (un)successful, mindless, fractious, unspecified, sceptical, weak, mass, widespread, resurgent, diametrical, binary, internal, traditional, factious

oppression, oppressions besetting, crushing, distressing, domineering, exacting, overbearing, harassing, high-handed, brutal, relentless, ruthless, intellectual, educational

optimism sweeping, breathtaking, happy-go-lucky, sunny, jovial, wheezy, lavish, spirited, buoyant, considerable, high, profound, unreserved, unlimited, unbridled, runaway, untiring, tireless, eternal, blind, giddy, ebullient, unshak(e)able, gritty, intrepid, wild, bold, dogged, innate, forthright, surprising, impetuous, quiet, mild, credible, wary, cautious, sceptical, tempered, guarded, short-lived, officious, impractical, misguided, unfounded

optimist, optimists spirited, happy, enthusiastic, tough-minded, congenital, born

option, options thrilling, exciting, interesting, promising, unrivalled, (un)viable, (un)reasonable, (in)adequate, (un)acceptable, (un)attractive, (un)pleasant, (un)palatable, (un)desirable, constructive, live, straightforward, (in)expensive, open, obvious, (un)available, broad, endless, limitless, (un)limited, alternative, unavoidable, poor, only, first, second, third, soft, personal

orange, oranges (1: fruit) See also *fruit* green-rind, juicy, seedy, seedless, sweet, navel, bitter, Seville, marmalade, mandarin

orange (2: colour) deep, light, medium, feeble, pale, dark, brilliant, bright, dazzling, fiery, hot, cadmium, burned (burnt), lurid, rosy, purple

oration, orations See also *speech* funeral

orator, orators silver-tongued, convincing, persuasive, eloquent, brilliant, accomplished, mealy-mouthed, smooth-spoken, natural, gifted, skilled, inspired, fervid, passionate, colourful, pompous, windy, inflammatory, fiery

oratory inspirational, over-blown, hyperbolic(al), bombastic, inflated, pretentious, vague

orbit, orbits (un)safe, (un)stable, shifting, elongated, low, high, eccentric, elliptical, earth

orchard, orchards blossom-studded, fragrant, sweet-scented, dense, productive, prolific, fertile, fruitful, lush, picturesque, neglected

orchestra, orchestras fine, dynamic, fractious, full, 100-piece, huge, massive, world-class, world-renowned, notable, permanent, local, national, classical, philharmonic, string

ordeal, ordeals harrowing, distressing, devastating, agonizing, tormenting, terrible, long

order, orders (1: command) explicit, express, crisp, strict, vehement, specific, exact, imperative, authoritative, authoritarian, tyrannical, rasping, grating, gruff, harsh, stringent, open-ended, ambiguous, unexceptional, (il)legal, (il)legitimate, sudden, interim, temporary, restraining, back-to-work, shoot-on-sight, executive, court

order, orders (2: way; condition) dazzling, exacting, unimpeachable, meticulous, true, proper, neat, alphabetical, numerical, reverse(d), inverse, chronological, random, systematic, decorative, hierarchical

order, orders (3: request for goods) (ir)regular, seasonal, huge, mammoth, void, rush, standing, mail, market, money, advance, overseas, domestic, inland

order, orders (4: class; congregation) austere, strict, autonomous, knightly, monastic, lay, mendicant, holy, religious, fraternal, celibate, enclosed

organ, organs (1: bodily part) (un)healthy, essential, vital, internal, transplantable, enlarged, analogous, vestigial, visceral, human, vocal, digestive, sensory, vomeronasal, genital, reproductive, urinary, olfactory

organ, organs (2: wind instrument) mechanical, pipe, reed, electronic (electric), chamber; mouth

organism, organisms vital, tough, durable, minute, unidentified, unidentifiable, luminescent, social, microscopic, pathogenic, unicellular, two-celled, causative, larval, autopolyploid

organization, organizations solid, wonderful, significant, prestigious, huge, giant, influential, powerful, permanent, dedicated, canny, model, systematic, modern, (il)legitimate, (in)formal, secretive, subversive, invisible, shadowy, helter-skelter, haphazard, complex, anomalous, limp, sweeping, wide-ranging, mass(ive), fundamental; marginal,

extremist, activist, (neo-)anarchist, independent, representative, world-wide, international, front, umbrella, grass-roots, voluntary, non-profit, social, ethnic, (para)military, private, educational, major-league, civic, political, charitable, benevolent, humanitarian, philanthropic, aid, sectarian, non-partisan, cultural, patriotic, trading, corporate, public-interest, collective, fraternal, pluralistic, revanchist, criminal

orgy, orgies wild, unrestrained, untrammelled, unbridled, disgusting, frenzied, loose, riotous, uncivilized, hedonistic

origin, origins modest, humble, obscure, dubious, suspicious, questionable, (un)known, undocumented, distant, primordial, cultural, tribal, cataclysmic, evolutionary

originality, originalities remarkable, striking, resourceful, bold, disquieting, imaginative, unique, fresh, inventive, ingenious, unquestionable, visionary

ornament, ornaments astounding, fabulous, legendary, unbelievable, incredible, magnificent, elegant, elaborate, superb, exquisite, dainty, neat, modish, stylish, tasteful, imaginative, gay, fantastic, intricate, odd, quaint, catchpenny, coral, tasselled, tatty, tawdry, pectoral

ostentation garish, gaudy, showy, conspicuous, tasteless, vulgar, crude, disgusting, ill-mannered, rude, indecent

outbreak, outbreaks sporadic, occasional, (in)frequent, isolated, random, riotous

outburst, outbursts startling, sudden, spontaneous, (in)frequent, occasional, sporadic, intermittent, random, spasmodic, single, impassioned, fiery, violent, ferocious, rude, emotional

outcast, outcasts wretched, leprous, abject, social, tribal, virtual

outcome, outcomes See *result* and *effect*

outfit, outfits See *clothes*

outing, outings See *trip*

outline, outlines (un)clear, (in)distinct, well-defined, clear-cut, trenchant, sharp, broad, main, general, comprehensive, rough, bare, naked, dim, faint, vague, fuzzy, obscure, shadowy, spectral, rapid, fleeting

outlook, outlooks encouraging, promising,

bright, sanguine, rosy, sunny, optimistic, positive, hopeful, (im)mature, responsible, dreamy, woeful, clouded, cloudy, gloomy, saturnine, bleak, grim, negative, sceptical, pessimistic, murky, black, dark, blue, dismal, dire, malicious, mixed, tenuous, uncertain, extended, long-term, mundane, personal, global, meteorological

outpost, outposts unconquerable, impregnable, indomitable, insuperable, invincible, far-flung, vulnerable, assailable, assaultable, unguarded, unprotected

output, outputs See *production* (1)

outrage See *anger*

ovation, ovations stirring, rousing, resounding, roaring, deafening, exuberant, tremendous, thunderous, riotous, spontaneous, standing

oven, ovens glowing, moderate, slack, outdoor, portable, electric, gas, wood-burning, microwave, tandoori, Dutch, (under)ground, clay, earth, mud, brick, stone-lined, tile-faced, self-cleaning, revolving, communal, commercial

overcoat, overcoats See *coat*

overcrowding disheartening, despairing, hopeless, abject, desperate, forlorn, reckless, chronic

oversight, oversights (1: slip) serious, unfortunate, inadvertent, unintentional, regrettable, lamentable, understandable

oversight (2: supervision) See *supervision* and *management*

overtone, overtones See *tone* and *hint*

owl, owls blinking, hooting, too-whooing, noiseless, confident, wise, wild, elusive, enigmatic, secretive, reclusive, tawny (brown), great grey, barn (monkey-faced), typical, great horned, barred, snowy, long-eared, short-eared, pygmy, spotted, whiskered, wood

owner, owners rightful, putative, (il)legal, (il)legitimate, (un)lawful, exclusive, sole, wrongful, nominal, original, beneficial, hereditary, third-generation, joint, part

ownership See also *owner* clear, exclusive, dual, joint, limited, private, public, common(-share), total, partial, communal, collective, outside

pace, paces steady, measured, orderly, gentle, cautious, uniform, (un)even, (ir)regular, constant, unchanging, livable, (un)usual, sustained, easy, round, smart, lively, merry, active, deliberate, snappy, brisk, intense, feverish, energetic, frenetic, frenzied, vigorous, clipping, fast, hurried, furious, rapid, headlong, frantic, hectic, quick, inexhaustible, cracking, blistering, killing, dizzying, bewildering, reckless, breakneck, phenomenal, dramatic, tremendous, terrific, torrid, brutal, (world-)record, workaholic, manageable, urban, modest, slack, slow, snail(-like), languid, languorous, sluggish, anaemic, bovine, glacial, unhurried, leisurely, dreamy, lethargic, lacklustre, hypnotic, drowsy, set, stiff

package, packages light, fanciful, sanitary, (im)proper, recyclable, reusable, heavy, bulky, cumbersome, burdensome, unwieldy, enigmatic(al), suspicious, unlabelled, unmarked, surprise, aseptic

pact, pacts See *treaty*

page, pages brittle, fragile, grimy, musty, blank, (un)lined, (un)written, typewritten, double-sided, dog-eared, preceding, previous, preliminary, first, penultimate, last, final, next, inside, front, hand-written; Yellow

pageant, pageants See *show* and *display*

pain, pains harrowing, excruciating, agonizing, racking, scorching, searing, scalding, burning, splitting, cramping, consuming, sickening, distressing, frightening, punishing, nauseating, stabbing, throbbing, tearing, crushing, grinding, overpowering, debilitating, stunning, screaming, raging, unrelenting, piercing, sticking, catching, squeezing, shooting, lightning, haunting, growing, fleeting, tenacious, acute, torturous, intractable, (un)bearable, intolerable, insufferable, inconsolable, tough, keen, sharp, bitter, tight, fierce, deep, intense, severe, bad, violent, ferocious, vicious, savage, persistent, terrible, white-hot, incandescent, unpredictable, unforgettable, worrisome, depressive, incredible, unbelievable, inconceivable, unimaginable, undeserved, great, considerable, exquisite, monstrous, enormous, royal, tremendous, extreme, abnormal, extraordinary, unique, (un)usual, maximum, real, obtuse, dull, numb, helpless, indecisive, infinite, lasting, ceaseless, endless, unending, constant, lifetime, perpetual, chronic, terminal, sudden, spasmodic, occasional, recurrent, slight, minimal, small, indefinable, mild, secret, pleasurable, prideful, narrow, referred, feverish, physical, bodily, gristly, muscular, chest, internal, abdominal, teething, dental, sciatic, back, pelvic, (pre)menstrual, rectal, arthritic, anginal, haemorrhoidal, emotional, psychic, labour, sympathetic

paint, paints fresh, raw, flat, wet, dry, fading, glossy, water-soluble, oil, camouflage, outside, weather-proof, metal-protective, chemical-resistant, fire-retardant, heat-resistant, metallic, non-drip, thixotropic, acrylic

painter, painters See also *artist* brilliant, talented, exceptional, skilled, skilful, pioneering, notable, quintessential, unexceptional, versatile, second-rate, conventional, academic, still-life, figurative, impressionist, expressionist, abstract

painting, paintings valuable, priceless, pricey, costly, expensive, irreplaceable, sought-after, desirable, award-winning, coveted, charming, compelling, striking, magnificent, stupendous, superb, gorgeous, remarkable, splendid, masterful, marvellous, successful, powerful, opulent, elaborate, ambitious, grand, lush, handsome, glorious, genuine, real, authentic, original, spurious, (un)exhibitable, (un)sal(e)able, refulgent, luminous, vivid, vibrant, brilliant, intimate, sensuous, splashy, dynamic, peaceful, spritely, florid, misty, sombre, nostalgic, edgy, maudlin, life-size, gigantic, miniature, round, dense, busy, mysterious, controversial, pallid, innocuous, rude, rough, primitive, hack, worthless, boring, dull, uninspired, bizarre, whimsical, baffling, vulgar, awkward-looking, laboured, subjective, heroic, mural, watercolour, oil, brush, modernistic, encaustic, still-life, landscape, folk-art, minimalist, surrealistic, impressionist, expressionist, realistic, abstract, allegorical, action, Pre-Raphaelite, finger(tip), contemporary, pastoral, panoramic, baroque, mannerist, prize, pointillist, heirloom, sand, topographical, monochromatic, polychrome, electrostatic, acrylic, thin, linear, efflorescent, ink, antique, hieroglyphic, two-sided; yarn

pair, pairs (un)matching, (mis)matched, (un)likely, great, inseparable, curious, odd, eccentric, extraordinary, queer

palace, palaces dazzling, stunning, imposing, charming, luxurious, grand(iose), spectacular, stately, splendid, magnificent, glorious, fine, lordly, aristocratic, elegant, multistoreyed, elaborate, lavish, extravagant, opulent, sumptuous, dignified, ostentatious, voluptuous, huge, gaudy, sprawling, crumbly, decayed, hilltop, moated, imperial, royal, ducal, presidential, cultural, baroque, rococo, Romanesque, Gothic, Renaissance

paleness dead(ly), deathly, ominous, portentous, unhealthy, sickly, tired, anaemic, cheerless, dull, drab, ghastly, grim, lifeless, mousy

pallor See *paleness*

palm, palms (tropical tree) See *tree*

pamphlet, pamphlets informative, illustrated, elegant, many-coloured, glossy, four-page, free, inflammatory, seditious, illegal, hostile, polemical

pan, pans (non-)aluminium, (non-)metallic, shallow, deep, wide, large, round, rectangular, fluted, long-handled, heavy(-based), heavy-bottomed, copper-bottomed, non-stick, greasy

panel, panels See *jurist*

panic, panics rising, irrational, mindless, grisly, explosive, dreadful, nameless, indescribable, inexpressible, helpless, aimless, uncontrollable, (un)justifiable, unjustified, sick, endemic, sporadic, spontaneous, instant, exogenous, financial, environmental

pants See *trousers*

paper smooth, soft, fine, thin, glossy, marbled, quality, flowered, gilt(-edged), deckle-edged, blank, (un)lined, plain, loose, handmade, recyclable, sticky, carbonless, windblown, coarse, tough, durable, absorbent, waterproof, water-resistant, water-repellent, fine-textured, ribbed, opaque, brittle, rag, bark, heavy(-duty), scrap, note, waste, commercial, scratch, construction, filter, transfer, bond, rice, parchment, corrugated, test, sanding, touch, heat-sensitive, electrochemical, acid-free, linen, manila, tissue, toilet, white, wax, tar, India (Bible), Congo, crepe, carbon, litmus, glass, mercantile, graph, transparent, two-name, wove, matrix, ledger, computer

papers (documents) (ir)relevant, loose, fake, false, windblown, official, clearance, legal, second, personal

parade, parades dazzling, charming, dizzying, colourful, resplendent, splendid, vivid, fine, joyous, hour-long, endless, monster, huge, spectacular, seductive, shimmery, showy, ostentatious, gaudy, (il)legal, low-key, traditional, political, opening-day, inaugural, military, aerial, farewell

paradise, paradises appealing, delightful, pleasurable, nirvanic, pristine, untouched, unspoilt, pure, sheltered, lush, earthly, heavenly, recreational, tropical, photographic, fancied, external, Utopian, Elysian, Edenic

paradox, paradoxes baffling, astounding, puzzling, tantalizing, apparent, exasperating, inextricable, intractable, enigmatic, profound, impenetrable, obscure, abysmal, intricate, unsolved, unresolved, stupendous, ingenious, troublesome

paragraph, paragraphs brisk, pivotal, pithy, precise, stiff, first, opening, introductory, new, closing, last, second-last, ultimate, penultimate, preceding, succeeding, brief, long, lengthy, overlong

parallel, parallels striking, puzzling, perplexing, amazing, baffling, bewildering, astounding, astonishing, remarkable, close, instructive, ominous, frightening, startling, sinister, incomplete, inconclusive, coincidental

paralysis, paralyses total, partial, spastic, flaccid, facial; infantile

parasite, parasites fawning, freeloading,

sycophantic, microscopic, idle, bodily, social

parcel, parcels See *package*

parchment, parchments aged, fine, heavy, vegetable

pardon, pardons gracious, compassionate, clement, merciful, unvindictive, imminent, eventual, free, Royal

parent, parents doting, loving, understanding, (un)caring, dutiful, wise, supportive, tender, kind, fond, tolerant, concerned, anxious, solicitous, conscientious, devout, committed, responsive, beloved, benevolent, indulgent, perfect, sensitive, realistic, (im)partial, (un)just, punitive, lenient, permissive, (in)experienced, (ir)responsible, wishy-washy, hostile, alcoholic, heartless, merciless, ruthless, remorseless, relentless, unrelenting, cold, neglectful, unfit, absent, absentee, critical, awesome, harsh, rigid, authoritarian, restrictive, strict, severe, over-protective, over-indulgent, estranged, single-child, single, childless, expectant, natural, biological, genetic, surrogate, birth, adoptive, (non-)custodial, prospective, at-home

parentage distinguished, (pre-)eminent, illustrious, noble, unsure, dubious, uncertain, unknown, mixed

parenthood See also *parent* responsible, planned, surrogate, adoptive

park, parks lush, green, beautiful, pleasant, lovely, majestic, unique, impressive, spectacular, remarkable, wonderful, magnificent, splendid, extraordinary, premier, scenic, oceanfront, waterfront, seaside, lakeside, ravine, rain-forested, graceful, spacious, large, expansive, extensive, giant, enormous, square-block, sprawling, grassy, leafy, wooded, tree-shaded, tree-vaulted, secluded, remote, outlying, quiet, tranquil, serene, unsullied, inviolate, well-known, famous, central, prehistoric, drab, graceless, established, official, provincial, national, public, city, civic, urban, residential, suburban, bucolic, rustic, pastoral, ornamental, equestrian, zoological, marine, oceanic, water, cultural, hunting, imperial, memorial, historic, natural, wildlife

parking (im)proper, (in)adequate,

(ir)responsible, (un)available, ample, atrocious, clumsy, all-day, off-street, (un)restricted, long-term, special, plug-in, free, parallel, angle, diagonal, underground, roof-top, handicapped, multistorey, roadside

parliament, parliaments (in)effective, democratic, transitional, fragmented, multiparty, multiracial, new-style, rubber-stamp, bicameral, tricameral, long, rump, hung, federal

parole early, full, (un)conditional, imminent, impending, eventual

part, parts (1: portion) principal, integral, main, substantial, crucial, vital, essential, inescapable, indispensable, necessary, inseparable, permanent, proportional, proportionate, (un)equal, disparate, fractional, redundant, (ir)replaceable, interchangeable, constituent, automotive, organic, homogeneous, heterogeneous; private

part, parts (2: role) See *role*

partiality undisguised, unfair, unjust, one-sided

participant, participants active, full(-fledged), front-line, (in)appropriate, behind-the-scenes, eager, (un)willing, reluctant, unwitting, actual, volunteer

participation active, full, strong, tremendous, widespread, broad, whole-hearted, committed, eager, enthusiastic, vital, crucial, authentic, voluntary, compulsory, obligatory, mandatory, (un)willing, forced, reluctant, dubious, uncertain, risky, iffy, equal, joint, cynical

participle, participles present, past (passive), perfect, dangling

particle, particles invisible, unseen, microscopic, minuscule, fine, tiny, minute, indivisible; fundamental, elementary, (sub)atomic

particular, particulars See *detail*

parting, partings heartbreaking, disappointing, depressing, crushing, doleful, sad, sorrowful, dispirited, dejected, emotional, emotion-choked, difficult, bittersweet, irrevocable, final

partisanship, partisanships dogmatic, apoplectic, lusty, heinous, hideous, abominable, divisive

partner, partners steady, right, solid, (in)appropriate, (un)likely, (un)cooperative,

(un)easy, (in)compatible, unexpected,
(un)willing, reluctant, prospective,
(un)official, long-term, short-term, senior,
special, multiple, trilateral, dormant
(secret), silent (sleeping), associate, active,
nominal, managing, working, sparring;
marriage, marital, common-law, live-in,
domestic, sex(ual)

partnership, partnerships See also
partner solid, unlikely, general, particular,
limited, corporate, corporatist

party, parties (1: group of persons united in
policies) influential, (im)moderate, major,
main, established, grass-roots, (re)united,
unified, full-fledged, (all-)powerful,
(in)secure, populist, progressive, reform,
(ultra-)nationalist, authoritarian, hard-line,
unchallenged, middle-of-the-road,
right-leaning, left-leaning, right-wing,
left-wing, rightist, leftist, ultra-right,
ultra-left, far-right, far-left, old-line,
marginal, (brand-)new, small, tiny,
resurgent, (as-yet-)unformed,
inconsequential, (once-)dominant,
outgoing, overthrown, stagnant, dead,
defunct, weak, embattled, battered,
moribund, fractious, antagonistic,
leaderless, majority, minority,
narrow-interest, xenophobic, breakaway,
dissident, splinter, fringe, (il)legitimate,
legal(ised), illegal, clandestine, centrist,
centre-right, extremist, radical, reactionary,
political, progressive, conservative, liberal,
labour, ruling, opposition, national,
federalist, coalition, religious, secular,
regional, constitutional

party, parties (2: social gathering)
glittering, dazzling, elegant, chic,
glamorous, lavish, elaborate, big, huge,
gigantic, extravagant, spectacular,
pretentious, festive, lively, gay, merry,
jubilant, joyous, enjoyable, pleasant,
(un)interesting, crushed, beautiful, lovely,
magnificent, splendid, gorgeous,
incomparable, unequalled, hilarious,
labour-intensive, costly, correct, quiet,
noisy, loud, mad, boozy, hedonistic,
uproarious, razzle-dazzle, all-night, flat,
dull, listless, draggy, slow, lopsided,
formal, private, gala, fancy, stag, hen,
bachelor, farewell, launch, costume,
drinking, hunting, valedictory; surprise

party, parties (3: person; one who takes

part) disinterested, unwilling, reluctant;
third

passage, passages (1: a section of a
written work) See also *writing* (1) and *style*
(1) and (4) lively, charming, revealing,
rolling, powerful, rhetoric, circumstantial,
mawkish, homiletic

passage, passages (2: a voyage) See
journey

passenger, passengers tired, exhausted,
queasy, airsick, fearful, frightened,
white-knuckled, frustrated, unregistered,
inbound, long-distance, business, leisure,
economy-class, first-class

passion, passions enduring, abiding,
steadfast, lifelong, lifetime, exquisite,
tempered, refined, tart, inordinate,
unbridled, unruly, turbulent, disorderly,
(un)controllable, hectic, vehement,
intemperate, irrepressible, unrestrainable,
overwhelming, prevailing, towering,
sizzling, boiling, burning, overpowering,
consuming, writhing, all-embracing,
predominant, torrential, unfathomable,
frenzied, violent, fierce, destructive, fatal,
commonplace, vituperative, short-lived,
momentary, passing, lurking, secret,
shameful, dark(ling), morbid, lawless,
unlawful, lusty, lustful, fleshly, volatile,
unconsummated, demented, headlong,
mutual, unrequited, charitable, protective,
purple, elemental, mystical, sexual,
nationalist; animal

passport, passports (in)valid, false,
phon(e)y, fake, bogus, falsified,
temporary, internal, regional

past glorious, epic, remarkable,
magnificent, splendid, gracious, successful,
illustrious, golden, glittering, colourful,
flamboyant, vivid, chequered (checkered),
carefree, provocative, irreproachable,
tawdry, haunting, shameful, scandalous,
discreditable, disreputable, shady,
shadowy, cloudy, hideous, painful, bitter,
horrific, strange, controversial, turbulent,
tumultuous, stormy, troubled, violent,
irrevocable, immediate, recent, remote,
(not-too-)distant, not-so-distant, dead,
hidden, sporadic, primordial

pastime, pastimes exhilarating,
(un)exciting, stirring, thrilling, congenial,
pleasant, convivial, favourite, favoured,
fashionable, innocent, (un)wholesome,

(un)healthy, trivial, frivolous, laid-back,
low, national, childish, juvenile, adult

pastry (1: dough) sweet, savoury, tangy,
glorious, magnificent, plain, short, flaky,
crunchy, puff, feathery, light, soggy,
cruller-like, layered, frozen, home-made,
pre-made, choux

pastry, pastries (2: cake made with (1))
tempting, ravishing, captivating,
lip-smacking, mouthwatering, delicious,
tasty, delectable, honey-soaked, bite-sized,
vegetable, individual, fancy, Danish,
French, Swiss

pasture, pastures peaceful, sleepy,
nocturnal, lush, luxuriant, grassy, verdant,
green, emerald, fertile, fat, flowery,
(un)even, wide-open, high, (wide-)rolling,
hillside, stony, swampy, scrubby,
(thread)bare, thin, arid, parched, scorched,
chequered, (un)fenced, fenceless, terraced,
abandoned, permanent, tussocky

pastureland, pasturelands See *pasture*

path, paths (well-)beaten,
well-trod(den), well-travelled, well-marked,
discernible, conspicuous, correct,
unswerving, wide, straight, new, tidy, cool,
wistful, smooth, gentle, grassy, stony,
stone(-slabbed), dirt, weedy, rocky, gravel,
sylvan, riverside, mountain, shady,
umbrageous, shadowy, sycamore-shaded,
tree-lined, wooded, fenced, fenceless,
one-lane, circular, tortuous, anfractuous,
sinuous, circuitous, crooked, bent, curved,
twisting, winding, meandering, climbing,
snaky, twisted, devious, roundabout,
zigzag, squiggly, springy, resilient, elastic,
indirect, ragged, intricate, steep, arduous,
blind, tricky, hazardous, treacherous,
mossy, muddy, miry, offbeat, narrow,
crossed, unbeaten, untrod(den),
little-known, obscure, traceless, pedestrian,
mountain

patience angelic, saintly, saint-like, tender,
patriarchal, kingly, sublime, dreamy,
exemplary, proverbial, legendary, rare,
cooperative, unflagging, steadfast, tireless,
ageless, indefatigable, inexhaustible,
endless, (un)limited, infinite, never-ending,
enduring, immense, monumental,
immeasurable, incredible, unbelievable,
incomprehensible, troubled, servile, blind

patient, patients model, compliant,
(un)co-operative, yielding, (un)comfortable,

exhausted, restless, sleepy, suggestible,
reluctant, challenging, belligerent,
capricious, disgruntled, (un)complaining,
bitter, grievous, sore, desperate, irascible,
dysfunctional, frail, sallow, thin,
emaciated, sickly, convalescent,
(un)conscious, brain-dead, vegetative,
comatose, helpless, chronic, long-term,
(ir)regular, moribund, terminal, doomed,
mental, trauma, ambulatory,
(elective-)surgery, suicidal, day, private,
fee-paying, paediatric, geriatric,
psychiatric, obstetrical, high-risk,
transplant, respirator-dependent, in-home,
orthopaedic, antenatal, post-natal, medical,
(post-)surgical, maternity

patio, patios sunny, sunlit, moonlit,
stone-inlaid, flagstone, cement, brick,
spotless, shady, shaded, cool, breezy, wide,
expansive, spacious, grand, charming,
pretty, lovely, quaint, dainty, dandy,
flowered, cypress-spiked, (vine-)trellised,
colonnaded, hacienda-style, roofless,
sheltered, terraced, secluded, rickety,
streetside

patriot, patriots staunch, ardent, true,
loyal, faithful, steadfast, devout, devoted,
dedicated, zealous, chauvinistic, aggressive,
fanatical

patriotism unwavering, ardent, passionate,
unabashed, unalloyed, truculent,
aggressive, fanatical, strident, raucous,
jingoistic

patron, patrons generous, kind,
magnanimous, open-handed, prodigal,
devoted, zealous, enthusiastic, audacious,
conscientious, dutiful, private

pattern, patterns interesting, exciting,
exquisite, bright, imaginative, artful,
colourful, harmonious, graceful, delightful,
unique, distinctive, discernible, (in)distinct,
(un)identifiable, (im)perceptible,
(un)predictable, indeterminate, consistent,
steady, fixed, neat, orderly, uniform,
symmetrical, perfect, recurrent, running,
flamboyant, conventional, traditional,
age-old, (un)common, overriding,
dominant, implacable, mosaic, fantastic,
fanciful, ornate, decorative, floral, diverse,
varying, (ir)regular, haphazard, deficient,
erratic, random, busy, intricate, complex,
rigid, adaptive, strange, curious, bizarre,
eerie, sinister, garish, apparent,

undisturbed, detailed, characteristic,
incised, rectilinear, binary, spiral, circular,
zigzag, culture, herring-bone, abstract,
geometric(al), elliptical, futuristic,
climactic; behavioural

pause, pauses contemplative, thoughtful,
cogitative, pregnant, bewildered, dramatic,
(un)suitable, awkward, uneasy

pavement, pavements shady, smooth,
icy, ice-bound, slippery, snowy,
snow-covered, glassy, muddy, miry, slushy,
wet, pebbly, gravelly, greasy, stony, rocky,
dusty, littered, sloppy, rough, bumpy,
(un)even, rugged, hard-surfaced, cracked,
broken, pot-holed

paw, paws dext(e)rous, dainty, velvet,
fur-fringed, furry, hairy, webbed,
sharp-clawed, mammoth, huge, broad,
clumsy

pay See *payment*

payment, payments hefty, munificent,
generous, substantial, handsome, liberal,
lavish, high, exorbitant, punctual,
(un)steady, (in)adequate, (im)proper,
erratic, questionable, unauthorized,
modest, meagre, poor, paltry, scanty,
worthless, contemptible, (bi-)weekly,
monthly, quarterly, (semi-)annual,
short-term, long-term, (ir)regular,
(over)due, prospective, double, equal, half,
partial, final, standard, basic, minimal,
nominal, token, additional, extra,
proportional, lump-sum, differential,
retroactive, deferred, merit, incentive, side,
cash(less), severance, compensatory,
take-home, overtime, portal-to-portal,
down, advance, tributary, interest,
principal, back, retroactive, restitution,
ritual

peace enduring, (ever)lasting, stable,
permanent, uninterrupted, undiminished,
eternal, perpetual, long-term, profound,
wonderful, celestial, divine, heavenly,
blissful, generous, comprehensive,
new-found, workable, equitable, just,
partial, relative, nominal, uneasy, tense,
desultory, fragile, shaky, shattered, hasty,
temporary, tentative, so-called, delusive,
elusive, dubious, disappointing, fallacious,
hair-trigger, inward, inner, mental,
spiritual, global, universal, world

peacefulness unrelenting, amiable,
affable, genial, halcyon, harmonious,

nirvanic, restful, tranquil, undisturbed,
untroubled, Arcadian

peacock, peacocks majestic, proud, vain,
handsome, colourful, gaudy, showy,
finicky, screeching, tame

peak, peaks breathtaking, soaring,
sky-piercing, dizzy(ing), vertiginous,
precipitous, steep, (sky-)high, tall,
spectacular, dramatic, majestic, sacred,
glorious, mighty, splendid, magnificent,
gleaming, (un)climbable, (in)accessible,
trackless, hostile, (un)approachable,
nameless, wooded, forested,
snow-crowned, snow-spotted, snow-capped,
snow-covered, snowy, icy, glacial,
glacier-scarred, glacier-clad, gusty, sunlit,
misty, shadowy, bald, gaunt, jagged, tilted,
serrated, sharp, rough, rock-strewn, rocky,
craggy, sandstone, granite, volcanic,
black-lava, seething, symmetrical, twin,
serried, unnamed, mountain, alpine, aerial

pearl, pearls freshwater, mass-produced,
gritty, lustrous, gleaming, magnificent,
baroque, natural, cultured, imitation, false,
worthless, rough, seed

peasant, peasants hardworking,
(in)efficient, semi-literate, illiterate,
landless, hand-to-mouth, dirt-poor,
malnourished, stolid, brawny, stalwart,
hardy, indomitable, adaptable, easy-going,
simple, uncorrupted, landbound, grimy

peasantry See *peasant*

pebble, pebbles shifting, shimmery,
wave-rolled, foam-dappled, loose, coarse,
rounded, luminescent

peculiarity, peculiarities marked, genial,
quaint, temperamental, whimsical,
constitutional

pedestal, pedestals lofty, elevated

pedestrian, pedestrians careful,
(un)wary, careless, heedless, rapid, swift,
brisk, nimble, nervous, preoccupied

pen, pens (1: implement for writing) dry,
leaky, scratchy, quivering, quill, steel,
fountain, ball-point, cartridge, felt(-tip),
electronic, indelible, magic

pen, pens (2: style of writing) See *style* (1)

penalty, penalties easy, mild, nominal,
(un)just, (un)fair, (in)appropriate,
commensurate, tough, harsh, stiff, strict,
devastating, colossal, cumulative,
irrevocable, exemplary, punitive,
maximum, supreme, siz(e)able, dire,

controversial, death, cash, monetary, pecuniary, economic, financial

pencil, pencils sharp, blunt, pointless, stubby, lead, automatic (mechanical), propelling, slate, paper, wax, heavy-duty; eyebrow

penitence cringing, regretful, remorseful, sorrowful, scrupulous, repentant, rueful, verbal

pension, pensions big, fat, lavish, generous, cosy, (in)adequate, (in)sufficient, modest, frugal, meagre, hard-earned, (in)flexible, lifelong, joint, portable, military, private, contributory, non-contributory (free)

people, peoples See also Appendixes A and B and *person* thriving, peaceful, sturdy, vigorous, strong, free, refined, privileged, (un)sophisticated, moral, distinct, distinctive, friendly, elegant, lovely, invincible, neighbourly, fascinating, rugged, restive, varied, influential, subject, common, ordinary, regular, simple, plain, superstitious, unsuspecting, gullible, under-privileged, famine-stricken, homeless, displaced, stateless, defenceless, repressed, primitive, barbarous, uncivilized, nomadic, aboriginal, negroid, (partly-)native, (multi-)ethnic, rude, tribal, homogeneous, alien, (up)rooted, rootless, ostentatious, revolting, warlike, petty, retrograde; beautiful; chosen, boat

percentage, percentages whopping, staggering, shocking, large, siz(e)able, perilous, high, low, small, (in)significant, (un)just, right, (im)proper, balanced, (dis)proportionate, rough, wrong, debatable, infinitesimal, minimal, maximal

perfection, perfections absolute, complete, exemplary, spotless, stainless, faultless, immaculate, impeccable, infallible, incomparable, matchless, unparalleled, unsurpassed, inconceivable, chilling, utter, near

perfectionist, perfectionists compulsive, fierce, zealous

performance (1: the execution of an action) compelling, satisfying, felicitous, robust, impressive, masterly, perfect, spectacular, remarkable, strong, smooth, first-rate, world-class, (better-than-)expected, exceptional, artful, stellar, surreal, pivotal, rigid, puzzling,

negligent, slovenly, slipshod, disgraceful, delirious, dismal, poor, weak, wan, anaemic, flaggy, lacklustre, whirlwind, spotty, erratic, shameful, odious

performance, performances (2: performing of a play; public exhibition; concert) thrilling, stunning, outstanding, breathtaking, uplifting, exhilarating, moving, compelling, touching, loving, dazzling, soaring, (un)satisfying, unflagging, engaging, fascinating, competitive, star-studded, bravura, sterling, stupendous, creditable, superb, super, great, superlative, first-rate, flawless, faultless, unparalleled, definitive, electric, splendid, magnificent, spectacular, masterful, masterly, luminous, powerful, full-blooded, brilliant, impressive, inspired, spirited, sensitive, expressive, tremendous, taut, solid, elegant, graceful, beautiful, remarkable, memorable, unforgettable, historic, respectable, high-calibre, marvellous, finished, polished, perceptive, excellent, assured, irresistible, pyrotechnic, triumphant, glorious, tempestuous, animated, sensational, virtuoso, full-blown, fabulous, (in)competent, (un)balanced, (near-)perfect, (un)satisfactory, fine, good, (un)acceptable, (most-)popular, smooth, (un)convincing, buoyant, raucous, flamboyant, showy, hammy, continuous, repeated, straight, poor, lamentable, uneven, bad, ragged, inept, absurd, foolish, tepid, indifferent, pallid, dull, tedious, mechanical, soulless, lifeless, wooden, terrible, disgusting, abysmal, disastrous, abominable, flat, imperfect, defective, faulty, mediocre, inconsistent, shallow, artificial, disappointing, slipshod, rough-and-ready, terrible, odious, (un)affordable, nightly, (non-)scheduled, impromptu, sold-out, sell-out, command, preview, practice, première, private, public, orchestral, theatrical, dramatic, vaudeville, open-air, farewell, gala, live, interdisciplinary

performer, performers fine, accomplished, superb, exquisite, splendid, magnificent, outstanding, perfect, fastidious, (un)prepared, marvellous, (multi)talented, remarkable, distinguished, prominent, high-profile, big-name, renowned, well-known, celebrated, world-class, international, world-stage, glamorous, thrilling, enchanting, charismatic, veteran, avid, natural, versatile, solo, stand-up, mainstream, street, game, roving, on-site, amateur, professional

perfume, perfumes soothing, captivating, charming, enchanting, alluring, winning, haunting, insidious, assuasive, musky, balmy, pleasant, exquisite, sophisticated, fancy, sweet, saccharine, aromatic, fragrant, redolent, excessive, thick, potent, powerful, strong, pungent, piquant, drowsy, elusive, exotic, rare, pricey, cheap, animal, plant, synthetic

peril, perils See *danger*

period, periods fertile, memorable, idyllic, halcyon, delightful, all-important, crucial, critical, pivotal, momentous, substantial, brief, early, fleeting, cyclic, evolutionary, revolutionary, assimilative, (un)stable, (un)reasonable, (ir)regular, turbulent, heady, tempestuous, tumultuous, rough, (un)stimulating, (un)eventful, bizarre, cruel, awful, dismal, stressful, dark, hellish, chaotic, blue, peak, fallow, barren, lean, sterile, unprofitable, renewable, specific, (in)definite, (un)specified, go-slow, interim, transition(al), corresponding, trial, latent, dormant, sluggish, lethargic, refractory, convalescent, cooling-off, qualifying, colonial, baroque; base, climatic; (inter)glacial, geologic(al), Cretaceous, Jurassic, Pal(a)eolithic, Tertiary

periodical, periodicals See *magazine*

permission, permissions firm, constructive, unprecedented, unheard-of, rare, grudging, official, special

permit, permits (in)valid, proper, temporary, special, (un)limited, operating

persecution, persecutions intense, fierce, ruthless, pitiless, merciless, heartless, remorseless, relentless, unrelenting, murderous, bloody, unjust, intermittent, incessant, continued, religious

perseverance unyielding, untiring, stubborn, tenacious, obstinate, bull-headed, inflexible, dogged, sheer, resolute, unusual

persistence unyielding, unflagging, enduring, unfailing, untiring, unfeeling, unrelenting, relentless, callous, determined, indefatigable, indomitable, considerable, inexorable, dogged, obstinate, pertinacious,

tenacious, tireless, stubborn, legendary, courageous, uncommon, grim, deadly

person, persons See also Appendixes A and B distinguished, orderly, (un)stable, systematic, methodical, reliable, nice, affable, fine, mature, refined, polished, vital, prominent, saintly, sensible, impossible-to-categorize, wiry, intense, vocal, outspoken, misguided, unfortunate, average, reflective, private, solitary, sentimental, (in)consistent, unique, eccentric, impossible, ineffective, insecure, obnoxious, niggardly, colourless, negative, neurotic, mousy, (ir)replaceable, worthless, psychotic, immature, remorseless, unfeeling, ruffianly, worthless, feckless, wretched, miserable, superficial, shallow, troublesome, vile, vulgar, weedy, simple-minded, detestable, contemptible, unauthorized, unidentified, inadmissible, undesirable, objectionable, transient, displaced, stateless, self-employed, retired

personality, personalities See also Appendixes A and B appealing, pleasing, pleasant, graceful, amiable, striking, dynamic, inexhaustible, admirable, magnetic, charming, attractive, unique, galvanic, stimulating, impressive, lovable, singular, generous, outgoing, friendly, subtle, likeable, resplendent, hom(e)y, warm, genial, stable, temperate, no-nonsense, vivid, vibrant, bubbly, vivacious, effervescent, facile, yielding, expansive, distinguished, prominent, renowned, distinct, distinctive, leading, storied, phenomenal, memorable, ethereal, independent, powerful, strong, imposing, dominant, commanding, assertive, forceful, emphatic, competitive, electric, flamboyant, telegenic, insouciant, saccharine, fierce, overwhelming, undeveloped, quaint, strait-laced, self-directed, mobile, volatile, malleable, unstable, flawed, protean, quirky, ebullient, springy, presumptuous, rigid, dogmatic, flaring, complex, contradictory, deep, enigmatic, elusive, antithetical, reprehensible, ridiculous, brittle, abrasive, twisted, devious, aggressive, anti-social, mediocre, histrionic, megalomaniacal, schizoid, split, dual, complex, multiple, obsessive, compulsive, bisexual

perspective, perspectives proper, clear, unique, singular, well-rounded, balanced, new, fresh, personal, (un)limited, initial, skewed, aerial, linear, parallel (one-point), angular (two-point)

perspiration profuse, excessive, free, blocked, cold, smelly, clammy, (in)sensible, perceptible

persuasion, persuasiveness prevailing, stimulating, teasing, tempting, convincing, enticing, alluring, moving, beneficent, refined, gentle, friendly, charismatic, intense, forceful, powerful, vigorous, cynical

pessimism despairing, gloomy, husky, immense, brutal, undue, outlandish, congenital, well-founded

pest, pests See *nuisance* and *plague*

pet, pets endearing, darling, loving, lovable, adorable, winsome, companionable, benign, gentle, (un)popular, playful, cuddly, pliant, (un)friendly, devoted, fragile, hostile, repulsive, geriatric, exotic, grotesque, unusual, untrained, (well-)trained, underbred, home, farm

petition, petitions See *plea*

petrol clean, low-octane, high-octane, high-test, (un)leaded, regular, standard, premium (special)

phantom, phantoms See *apparition*

phase, phases passing, intensive, crucial, decisive, final, transitional, temporal, eternal, protracted, critical

phenomenon, phenomena staggering, puzzling, perplexing, bewildering, startling, amazing, baffling, intriguing, fabulous, remarkable, dramatic, curious, incongruous, extraordinary, paranormal, unusual, strange, paradoxical, unexplainable, inexplicable, (un)identifiable, (un)recognizable, unrecognized, unexamined, complex, controversial, troubling, specific, rare, fleeting, transient, out-of-this-world, unstoppable, huge, pervasive, widespread, worldwide, universal, daily, periodic, (super)natural, climatic, meteoric, solar, psychic, religious, astronomical, autokinetic

philosopher, philosophers wise, sophisticated, legendary, remarkable, controversial, self-styled, right-wing, left-wing, indigent, cracker-barrel, meditative, wandering, scholastic, positivist, transcendental

philosophy, philosophies sophisticated, frontier, aggressive, invasive, eclectic, esoteric, live-and-let-live, cracker-barrel, simple, false, erroneous, contrarian, pragmatic, mystic, synthetic, analytical, linguistic, monistic

phone, phones See *telephone*

phone call, phone calls See *call* (3)

phonetics articulatory, acoustic, auditory

photograph, photographs eye-startling, captivating, stunning, exciting, stirring, thrilling, vibrant, luscious, remarkable, wonderful, splendid, magnificent, superb, exquisite, impressive, spectacular, panoramic, high-quality, memorable, fantastic, sharp, clear, crisp, vivid, credible, candid, exclusive, rare, once-in-a-lifetime, first-of-a-kind, stodgy, evocative, alluring, revealing, naughty, lewd, (homo)erotic, smutty, sultry, surreptitious, damning, ghostly, gruesome, haunting, distressing, troubling, chilling, moody, instantaneous, fortuitous, old, (all-too-)familiar, up-to-date, unmarked, dog-eared, wrinkled, grainy, misty, murky, muddy, black-and-white, coloured, full-colour, brown-tone, candid-camera, fake, composite, static, still, three-dimensional, close-up, detailed, undated, confidential, documentary, archival, aerial, (spy-)satellite, weather-satellite, space, ultraviolet, nude, cover

photographer, photographers talented, (over-)zealous, enthusiastic, keen, eager, avid, sensitive, compulsive, persistent, intrepid, determined, resolute, inconspicuous, swarming, outstanding, front-line, expert, experienced, veteran, professional, amateur, self-employed, free-lance, transient, itinerant, commercial, underwater, newspaper, still, documentary, personal

photography See also *photographer* magnificent, superb, spectacular, lavish, creative, extraordinary, incomparable, trick, black-and-white, colour, stock, fashion, commercial, wet-plate, instant, high-resolution, high-speed, stereometric

phrase, phrases pithy, racy, pointed, polished, refined, well-chosen, deft, felicitous, apt, (in)accurate, exquisite, elaborate, handy, catch-all, well-turned, graceful, happy, measured, terse, laconic, (non-)committal, cheery, endearing, puzzling, chilly, unforgettable, euphonious, ringing, odd-sounding, high-sounding, sonorous, evocative, bridging, (un)conventional, (un)common, idiosyncratic, innocuous, pompous, gaudy, stiff, stilted, stodgy, wooden, worn-out, timeworn, stale, trite, hackneyed, obsolete, antiquated, (oft-)repeated, commonplace, stock, cant, ill-chosen, perfunctory, wry, pungent, caustic, biting, wounding, hurtful, uncouth, unnecessary, controversial, redundant, superfluous, flabby, slippery, pet, conjectural, catch, ritual, lyrical, proverbial, idiomatic, illustrative, (non-)restrictive, nominal, verbal, adjectival, adverbial, prepositional, interrogative

physician, physicians See *doctor*

physique, physiques See *constitution* (1)

pianist, pianists See *musician*

piano, pianos tinkling, tinkly, ornate, antique, old, thin, unrepaired, (ir)reparable, (un)tuned, poorly-tuned, out-of-tune, dumb, tinny, grand, upright, cottage, square, vertical, player, acoustic, electronic, electric, ragtime; thumb

pickle, pickles briny, salty, vinegary, garlicky, (half-)sour, boisterous, sweet, firm, crisp, thin-skinned, soft, mushy, soggy, mixed

picnic, picnics exhilarating, gratifying, satisfying, charming, cheerful, delightful, spirited, lively, nifty, pleasant, enjoyable, quiet, restful, intimate, elaborate, impromptu, nocturnal, group, community, school, farewell

picnicker, picnickers merry, jolly, joyous, mirthful, happy, playful, gay, cheerful

picture, pictures breathtaking, exciting, fascinating, striking, fabulous, genuine, pretty, beautiful, exceptional, magnificent, splendid, remarkable, intimate, effective, telling, meaningful, true, valuable, pleasant, memorable, emerging, loaded, rounded, unique, original, three-dimensional, clear, fuzzy, hazy, foggy, lurid, bleak, gloomy, dismal, satirical, slanting, salacious, obscene, pornographic, lascivious, racy, suggestive,

indecent, haunting, unsettling, unnerving, affronting, gruesome, mediocre, crude, awkward-looking, laboured, distorted, smudgy, pastoral, living, miniature, composite, talking, scriptural, word, verbal, mental, graphic, motion, file, library, video, high-resolution, polychrome, satellite, computer, stereo(scopic)

pie, pies See *cake* and *dessert*

piety purposeful, devoted, devout, zealous, amiable, genuine, intense, simple, (un)affected, ostentatious, superficial, meditative, private, conventional, (un)formalistic, hypochondriacal

pig, pigs grunting, squealing, shrieking, rooting, prostrate, suckling, fat, chunky, lean, rangy, bristly, squat, ugly, (half-)wild, domestic, potbellied, barnyard; chauvinist

pigeon, pigeons cooing, swooning, darting, dozing, tooth-billed, sea-going, fancy, tame, domestic, wild, homing, pouter, carrier, crowned, fruit, passenger

pile, piles neat, (un)tidy, siz(e)able, enormous, mighty, massive, mountainous, towering, lumpy-looking, tangled, twisted, crumpled, tattered, careless, messy, chaotic; voltaic (galvanic), atomic

pill, pills chewable, bitter, dissoluble, slow(ly)-dissolving, habit-forming, drowsy, pep, sleeping, enteric, contraceptive, abortion

pillar, pillars See *column*

pillow, pillows soft, gentle, (un)comfortable, comfort-shaped, cosy, fluffy, downy, puffed-up, refluffable, resilient, buoyant, contoured, curved, cylindrical, firm, plump, hard, goose-feather, tasselled, washable, odourless, mothproof, mildew-proof, non-allergenic, twin, standard, double, queen, king, inflatable, cervical

pilot, pilots accomplished, superb, capable, crack, (in)experienced, (un)skilful, (un)skilled, (un)licensed, error-prone, daring, stunt, (commuter-)airline, commercial, (non-)military, back-up, on-board, aerobatic; automatic, robot

pin, pins sharp, fresh, ornamental, small-headed, dull, rusty, straight (common), safety, bobby, hair, head, picket, Greek, Roman, Early French, Russian, Scandinavian, roundhead; cotter, belaying

pink deep, dusty, pale, livid, light,
washed-out, dusky, bright, throbbing,
(eye-)shocking, striking, electric, zesty,
modern, rosy, albino, flamingo, salmon,
fluorescent, greyish, brownish, yellowish,
puce, gold, chalky, frosty, clear,
picturesque, candy(-floss), bubbly,
bubble-gum, sunset, passionate, subdued,
Florentine

pioneer, pioneers authentic, intrepid,
fearless, brave, audacious, aweless,
courageous, daring, dauntless, hardy,
heroic, resolute, impavid, spirited,
indomitable, undaunted, unfearful,
unflinching, valiant, valorous, independent

pipe, pipes cylindrical, long-stemmed,
sharp-edged, curved, galvanized, insulated,
lead, copper, plastic, concrete, bamboo,
clay, brass(-lined), underground,
low-hanging; pneumatic, water, gas; pitch

pipeline, pipelines See *pipe*

pirate, pirates lawless, formidable,
dreadful, fearful, notorious

pistol, pistols horn-handled, ten-shot,
rapid-fire, automatic, muzzle-loading,
machine, pocket

pity acute, deep, ready, feigned, sham,
false, fake, pretended, phon(e)y, synthetic,
spurious, womanly

place, places sacred, holy, inviolable,
forbidding, rightful, silent, (im)proper,
(un)safe, secure, tranquil, peaceful, restful,
homely, popular, right, (un)suitable,
favoured, special, unique, prominent,
magical, pristine, (in)hospitable,
(in)accessible, opportune, strange, regular,
wonted, usual, habitual, conspicuous,
noticeable, varied, non-existent, crazy,
empty, forlorn, desolate, (un)likely, sinister,
secret, lonely, lonesome, mysterious, tight,
outlandish, faraway, out-of-the-way,
remote, withdrawn, secluded, messy, foul,
dreary, fearsome, inconspicuous

plagiarism outright, gross, shameless,
brazen, outrageous, blatant, flagrant,
careless

plagiarist, plagiarists inveterate, habitual,
unashamed, careless, unconscious,
inadvertent

plague, plagues troublesome, destructive,
fearsome, pernicious, calamitous, deadly,
virulent, brutal, worldwide, bubonic,
pneumonic, biblical

plain, plains (easy-)rolling, lush, fertile,
grassy, grass-covered, garden-striped,
mesquite-studded, green, ochre, savannah,
vast, broad, open, great, big, endless,
abyssal, unfathomable, high,
mountain-rimmed, ridged,
mountain-ringed, coastal, gentle, level, flat,
low, dusty, sandy, desert, rocky, stony,
gravel, brushy, marshy, soggy, swampy,
coastal, deltaic, featureless, treeless,
shadeless, dry, sere, (semi)arid, dissected,
desolate, bleak, bare, monotonous,
sun-beaten, windswept, windy, hot,
uncultivated, uninhabited, unpeopled,
flood, alluvial, fluvial

plan, plans See also *planning*
well-thought-out, well-worked-out,
well-laid, deep-laid, carefully-made,
in-depth, accurate, meticulous,
(over)ambitious, (un)realistic,
(un)workable, (im)practicable, (un)feasible,
(im)practical, (in)sensible, (in)coherent,
elaborate, welcome, unprecedented,
unique, revolutionary, novel, creative,
careful, fruitful, detailed, comprehensive,
grandiose, ambitious, big, extensive,
glowing, appealing, (un)successful, mature,
perfect, bold, audacious, daring, drastic,
radical, functional, (in)operable,
(in)flexible, (ir)reversible, precise, concrete,
serious, efficacious, mutable, foolproof,
definite, (un)certain, systematic, esoteric,
sinister, fanciful, airy, visionary, disparate,
confidential, broad, fluid, last-minute,
long-dormant, immediate, three-phase,
nine-point, stringent, threefold, foolhardy,
heady, impetuous, rash, suicidal, daunting,
footless, stupid, inept, fruitless, futile,
misbegotten, worthless, devious, wicked,
clandestine, dark, secret, evil, unsuccessful,
abortive, cumbersome, unwelcome,
controversial, senseless, short-lived,
unformed, unformulated, unratified,
tentative, interim, provisional, temporary,
alternative, ultimate, fundamental, first,
initial, preliminary, exclusive, rolling, final,
draft, master, long-range, long-term,
short-range, short-term, strategic

planet, planets (un)inhabitable, remote,
distant, (gas-)giant, gigantic, lifeless, cold,
blue(-hued), tempestuous, errant,
incomprehensible, hidden, shrouded,
unknown, nameless, terrestrial,

outer(most), superior, inferior, major, minor

planning See also *plan* innovative, prudent, careful, meticulous, reliable, cautious, inspired, judicious, sagacious, astute, shrewd, wise, ingenious, sensible, sophisticated, advance, tough-minded, detailed, extensive, forward, down-to-earth, (un)scientific, (un)orthodox, (in)effective, (im)practical, (in)adequate, hasty, botchy, poor, bad, cumbersome, ponderous, haphazard, careless, stagnant, sloppy, senseless, city, urban, regional, local, strategic, logistical

plant, plants flowering, fast-growing, slow-growing, climbing, (spring-)blooming, evil-smelling, low-growing, sprouting, ever-bearing, luxuriant, fecund, prolific, dense, hardy, tenacious, robust, coarse, tough, vigorous, healthy, colourful, fragrant, aromatic, viable, pest-resistant, drought-tolerant, drought-resistant, salt-tolerant, scraggly, delicate, tender, downy, succulent, weak, sickly, degenerate, effete, sapless, wispy, withered, barren, half-dead, decayed, unhealthy, scruffy, fragile, waterlogged, submerged, tall, giant, erect, spindly, trifoliate, viny, bushy, chubby, spiny, thorny, prickly, weedy, woody, rampant, tiny, dormant, bulbous, living, thrifty, exotic, unusual, rare, scarce, sparse, (non-)native, fleshy-leafed, tufted, rubiginous, fibrous, vascular, shrubby, woody-stemmed, degenerate, marsh, alpine, annual, biennial, perennial, (in)edible, culinary, terrestrial, aquatic, (sub)marine, (under)water, house, medicinal, agrarian, ferulaceous, ornamental, halophylic, urticaceous, asepalous, ericaceous, sapindaceous, balsaminaceous, ranunculaceous, chenopodiaceous, campanulaceous, musaceous, solanaceous, polygonaceous, caryophyllaceous, cyperaceous, cucurbitaceous, bulbiferous, asclepiadaceous, papaveraceous, carduaceous, euphorbiaceous, alliaceous, onagraceous, portulacaceous, cocciferous, cormous, iridaceous, piperaceous, tuberous, juncaceous, convolvulaceous, amaryllidaceous, disepalous, dispermous, caesalpiniaceous, apocynaceous, resedaceous, scrophulariaceous, anemophilous, entomophilous, cruciferous, zingiberaceous, malvaceous, bromeliaceous, herbaceous, deciduous, ligneous, leguminous, arenicolous, liliaceous, rosaceous, umbelliferous, papilionaceous, boraginaceous, one-celled, non-cellular, single-celled, unicellular, multicellular, diurnal, multitrunked, indigenous, sensitive, garden, evergreen, aroid, aphotic, antidromic, parasitic, hallucinogenic, seed-bearing, pollen-bearing, invasive, intrusive

plant, plants (2: factory) See *factory*

plastic, plastics hard, soft, transparent, decorative, (fire-)resistant, malleable, thermosetting, biodegradable

plate, plates elegant, hand-painted, gold-rimmed, ceramic, celadon, terracotta, porcelain, china, clay, stoneware, earthenware, cut-glass, polystyrene, disposable, large, shallow, octagonal-shaped, hexagonal, oblong, oval, microwavable, microwave-safe, ovenproof, side, serving

plateau, plateaus, plateaux high, lofty, low, rugged, rocky, treeless, scorching, uninhabitable, featureless

platform, platforms (declared aims, principles, etc.) (in)coherent, 40-point, narrow, lacklustre, political, campaign

platitude, platitudes prim, neat, dull, trite, stale, insipid, formal, impersonal

platter, platters See *plate*

plausibility placid, complacent, imperturbable, self-assured, smug, stolid

play, plays (1: stage representation of a story) compelling, intriguing, moving, bracing, stimulating, keen, stage-worthy, admirable, remarkable, masterful, superb, urbane, fine, polished, accomplished, finished, inimitable, shapely, powerful, mighty, effective, forceful, imperishable, timeless, durable, memorable, renowned, celebrated, noteworthy, esteemed, original, innovative, pioneer, timely, amusing, entertaining, sprightly, aesthetic, gritty, wry, gloomy, bittersweet, (un)playable, (un)actable, (un)stageable, (un)presentable, (un)popular, (un)convincing, static, quirky, crude, scandalous, risqué, bawdy, rubbishy, trashy, commonplace, miscast, flaccid, incoherent, digressive, diffuse, disjointed, shapeless, sketchy,

slow-moving, slow-paced, complex,
intricate, prosaic, apocryphal, goofy,
worthless, appalling, shocking, dreadful,
miserable, dense, dull, barren,
monotonous, clichéd, cliché-ridden,
characterless, crass, serious, funny,
uproarious, frenetic, straight,
full-scale, long, short, three-act, one-act,
contemporary, modern, old, repertory,
(un)conventional, sensational, maudlin,
mawkish, representational, humorous,
historical, chronicle, comic, farcical,
melodramatic, serio-comic, tragic,
tragi-comic, satirical, (un)realistic,
(anti)naturalistic, surrealistic, absurd(ist),
topical, dogmatic, doctrinaire, existential,
nihilistic, minimalistic, epic, folk,
eschatological, avant-garde, romantic,
classical, experimental, sentimental,
musical, psycho-dramatic,
(auto)biographical, personal, metaphorical,
well-made, anonymous, educational,
Nativity

play (2: recreation; fun; sport; game)
innocent, boisterous, rough-and-tumble,
motor, sensory, intellectual

player, players (1: one who plays in a
game) leading, star, key, pivotal,
outstanding, pre-eminent, prominent,
central, solid, reliable, practical,
bread-and-butter, dominant, veteran,
(un)skilful, capable, sound, careful, safe,
eager, great, consummate, dedicated,
valuable, expensive, indispensable,
top-level, world-class, cautious, prudent,
unbeaten, accomplished, all-round, crafty,
active, sly, shrewd, powerful, exceptional,
promising, (in)eligible, ardent, enthusiastic,
avid, feverish, eccentric, queer, erratic,
irregular, careless, rangy, hefty, muscular,
tough, exhausted, sweating, straining,
grunting, tricky, deceitful, losing, careless,
over-age, malicious, rival, full-time,
competitive, recreational, professional,
amateur

player, players (2: an actor) See *actor*

player, players (3: a performer on a
musical instrument) See *musician*

playground, playgrounds splashy,
(un)crowded, (un)safe, (un)suitable,
asphalt(ed), violent, adventure

playhouse, playhouses See *theatre*

playwright, playwrights See *dramatist*

plaza, plazas See *square*

plea, pleas sobbing, moving, rousing,
stirring, heartfelt, passionate, impassioned,
emotional, fervent, earnest, full-throated,
desperate, urgent, pressing, strident,
unabashed, prayerful, pathetic, last-ditch,
overt, explicit, ineffectual, ill-founded,
absurd, vain, unavailing, fruitless, useless,
humble, unheard

pleasure, pleasures enchanting,
satisfying, exquisite, heartfelt, genuine,
pure, signal, convivial, homely, lawful,
rightful, innocent, simple, small, frugal,
phlegmatic, hearty, unsurpassable, healthy,
healthful, (un)refined, (un)sophisticated,
infinite, enormous, tremendous, incredible,
unbelievable, inexorable, intimate, intense,
wonderful, terrific, rare, unexpected,
curious, special, unfeigned, uninhibited,
immediate, inexpressible, thorough,
smooth, sustained, enduring, perennial,
casual, passing, vicarious, nostalgic, hectic,
barren, wasteful, demoniac(al), empty,
idle, useless, worthless, malignant,
mischievous, malicious, frivolous,
unseemly, vain, seedy, lurid, cheap,
voluptuous, perverse, guilty, unlawful,
unrestrained, unfettered, unalloyed,
undiminished, sneaking, forbidden, illicit,
sinful, steamy, lustful, erotic, sensory,
sensual, sensuous, sexual, bodily, corporal,
physical, intellectual, worldly, material,
earthly, gustatory, outdoor, athletic,
childish, solitary, personal, family, social

pledge, pledges unequivocal, solemn,
sacred, serious, earnest, vague, profligate,
piddling, trifling, trivial, reiterated,
(un)qualified, honoured, unfulfilled,
military, financial

pledging See *pledge*

plight, plights devastating, rueful,
pitiable, deplorable, tragic, pathetic, sad,
sorry, despairing, dismal, lamentable,
pitiful, woeful, regretful, sorrowful,
doleful, wretched, unfortunate, terrible,
tearful, shocking, odious, mournful,
despicable, contemptible, disreputable,
calamitous, abominable

plot, plots (1: conspiracy; intrigue;
machination) meaty, subtle, clandestine,
secret, underhand, intricate, complicated,
sophisticated, intertwining, sly, devious,
deep, crafty, cunning, deceitful, hideous,

corrupt, infamous, bizarre, sinister, futile, evil, malevolent, vile, devilish, wicked, murderous, nefarious, audacious, preposterous, outlandish, ghastly, appalling, dreadful, frightful, awesome, gruesome, hateful, horrible, revolting, shocking, ugly, lurid, detestable, vicious, infernal, hellish, diabolic(al), fiendish, satanic, insidious, treacherous, jealous, murky, mucky, dirty, petty, stupid, (un)successful, elaborate, multi-tentacled, incomprehensible, labyrinthine, covert, overt, criminal, partisan, backroom

plot, plots (2: the plan or main story of a literary work) compelling, consuming, exciting, fascinating, thrilling, stirring, neatly-contrived, well-advanced, tidy, deft, rounded, careful, striking, original, (un)predictable, juicy, substantial, nifty, potent, formulary, ingenious, clockwork, elaborate, sensational, discernible, (in)coherent, (un)convincing, (im)plausible, (im)probable, (un)believable, (in)credible, absurd, tenuous, flimsy, poor, insubstantial, inconsistent, threadbare, hackneyed, trite, giddy, moth-eaten, clumsy, familiar, conventional, traditional, symmetrical, feathery, intricate, huddled, trumped-up, complicated, confused, contrived, (en)tangled, knotted, intertwining, complex, fragmented, devious, tortuous, labyrinthine, mazy, obscure, impenetrable, knotty, twisted, hurried, abstruse, central, fanciful, melodramatic, episodic, Gothic, Daedalian, Ibsenesque

plotting (conspiracy) See *plot* (1)

poacher, poachers greedy, ruthless, merciless, pitiless, relentless, unrelenting, wily, cunning, crafty, undaunted, bold, intrepid

poaching sly, slick, destructive, rampant, widespread

pocket, pockets bulging, (over-)stuffed, roomy, capacious, deep, secret, hand-stitched, lined, inset, upper, lower

poem, poems See also *poetry* and *poet* captivating, enchanting, fascinating, charming, (heart-)touching, moving, uplifting, compelling, haunting, pleasing, floating, marvellous, magnificent, splendid, exquisite, wonderful, brilliant, sublime, grand, noble, select, monumental, melodious, imperishable, pretty, delightful, tender, influential, popular, memorable, successful, graceful, original, idiosyncratic, imitative, derivative, discursive, complicated, laboured, intricate, confused, obscure, flimsy, lousy, scatological, little-known, stray, incongruous, maudlin, poignant, subdued, mournful, plaintive, serious, formal, ethic(al), occasional, inspirational, rhetorical, flirtatious, amatory, (mock-)heroic, narrative, lyric, epic, prose, blank-verse, symphonic (tone), erotic, anonymous, figurative, pastoral, idyllic, (non)dramatic, topographical, heroic-comical, didactic, symbolist, patriotic, satiric(al), descriptive, humorous, visual, personal

poet, poets See also *poem* and *poetry* consummate, veritable, compelling, articulate, full-fledged, major, premier, great, legendary, talented, born, significant, established, gifted, first-rate, superlative, distinguished, celebrated, notable, noted, prominent, famous, illustrious, luminous, sensitive, whimsical, eccentric, embryo, budding, aspiring, rising, struggling, promising, would-be, prospective, minor, obscure, failed, bad, unknown, poverty-stricken, ponderous, free-lance, moral, lyric, pastoral, narrative, dramatic, satirical (satirist), romantic, love, epic, tragic, vernacular, nomadic, modern(istic), neoclassical, pictorial

poetry See also *poem* and *poet* moving, spirited, vivid, vital, sublime, distinguished, imaginative, superior, essential, magnificent, splendid, exquisite, sleek, uncanny, well-ordered, rigorous, solid, sombre, tight, unified, good, simple, direct, (un)strained, (un)affected, (un)distinguished, trivial, inferior, mediocre, trite, bad, washy, trashy, loose, verbose, (un)translatable, formal, metric(al), syllabic, rhythmic(al), metaphorical, alliterative, visual, sensuous, subjective, imagist, mushy, concrete, sentimental, amorous, love, serious, didactic, heroic, pastoral, rustic, landscape, narrative, oral, written, bucolic, lyric(al), epic, ballad, dramatic, surrealist(ic), symbolic (symbolist), elegiac(al), (neo-)classical, romantic, melodramatic, structuralist, modern(ist), contemporary, topographical, descriptive, satirical, invective, sarcastic, ironic, witty, erotic, baroque, sibylline, rhetorical, metaphysical, post-structuralist, visual, haiku, (pre)Raphaelite, medieval, propaganda, iambic, trochaic, anapaestic, spondaic, metonymic, hyperbolic, hexameter, heptameter, emblematic, epigrammatic

point, points subtle, salient, cogent, intriguing, focal, central, prominent, noticeable, conspicuous, lofty, crucial, critical, decisive, key, (un)important, (in)consequential, major, debatable, (un)arguable, doubtful, moot, sticky, unimportant, (ir)relevant, striking, traumatic, climactic, midway, axial, strategic; cardinal; decimal; petit

point of view, points of view See *view*

poise unfaltering, imperturbable, calm, serene, cool, admirable, remarkable

poison, poisons virulent, deadly, fatal, lethal, subtle, strong, potent, powerful, malignant, malicious, hellish, insidious, treacherous, mysterious, tasteless, odourless, non-degradable, cumulative, unmanageable, systemic, agricultural, corrosive, anticoagulant

pole, poles soaring, straight, bent, warped, crooked, scraggy, extensible, wooden, metal, bamboo, clay-plastered, makeshift, netted, calib(e)red, weighed, forked, unsightly, totem, telephone, electrical, utility, hydro, telegraph, memorial, mortuary; intravenous (IV); magnetic, North, South, celestial, positive

police, policeman, policemen brilliant, diplomatic, lenient, taciturn, impassive, stone-faced, grim, alert, vigilant, watchful, solicitous, (all-)powerful, omnipresent, ubiquitous, (white-)helmeted, (un)armed, heavily-armed, burly, stocky, beefy, callous, unfeeling, aggressive, hard-boiled, heavy-handed, harsh, oppressive, raffish, brutal, ruthless, pitiless, merciless, heartless, relentless, unrelenting, riot-hardened, sceptical, wayward, rotten-apple, venal, disreputable, corrupt, powerless, ignorant, uniformed, plainclothes, undercover, secret, (internal-)security, special, riot,

(para)military, political, judicial, mounted, metropolitan, local, community

policy, policies (1: plan of action; statement of aims) impeccable, (in)consistent, (in)flexible, resilient, (im)moderate, lenient, unique, careful, (in)effective, (in)competent, (ir)responsible, fruitful, dedicated, vigorous, influential, (in)coherent, trenchant, articulated, liberal, reform-minded, explicit, stimulative, innovative, measured, restrained, calculated, decisive, prudent, rational, sensible, (in)sane, far-sighted, astute, pragmatic, (un)workable, cohesive, conciliatory, shrewd, firm, (in)correct, (un)acceptable, (in)appropriate, refined, benign, substantial, fresh, deliberate, aggressive, bold, fearless, tight, broad, stern, roll-up-the-sleeves, two-edged, fluid, (in)flexible, traditional, conservative, (long-)established, long-standing, prevailing, unchallenged, peculiar, hands-off, long-range, (ab)normal, (in)formal, sustainable, (in)valid, proletarian, bipartisan, naïve, erroneous, intemperate, deplorable, disorganized, neglectful, obstructive, flawed, retrograde, short-sighted, feckless, subversive, dangerous, disastrous, suicidal, erratic, pusillanimous, cowardly, fainthearted, poor, controversial, radical, crazy, reckless, screwy, inconsistent, dictatorial, discriminatory, ill-advised, imprudent, obsequious, conflicting, heavy-handed, (get-)tough, Draconian, hard-nosed, oppressive, repressive, restrictive, hard-line, stringent, rigorous, wobbly, intolerable, rigid, unbending, unyielding, stubborn, uncompromising, intractable, intransigent, pale, vague, willy-nilly, uncertain, ambiguous, outdated, battered, indecisive, senseless, mindless, misguided, schizoid, double, mandatory, (un)constitutional, economic, monetary, monetarist, fiscal, foreign, imperial, editorial, racist, isolationist, expansionist, corrective, interim, overall, protectionist

policy, policies (2: a written contract for insurance) small, large, renewable, convertible, expensive, lapsed, cash-value, whole-life, lifetime

politeness exquisite, ceremonious, studied, studious, honourable, painstaking, expansive, generous, genial, resilient, distant, barren, frigid, cold, false, morose, frightened

politician, politicians See also Appendixes A and B tough-minded, serious-minded, bold, smart, shrewd, canny, cautious, astute, maverick, noble, (dis)honest, (un)ethical, (un)trustworthy, (ir)responsible, credible, accommodating, accountable, consummate, (in)experienced, veteran, careful, skilful, prudent, pragmatic, practical, quintessential, outspoken, charismatic, demagogic, dynamic, visible, tireless, progressive, aggressive, radical, fundamentalist, ultimate, complete, big-name, powerful, (high-)ranking, high-powered, illustrious, distinguished, prominent, outstanding, popular, noted, busy, budding, aspiring, colourful, flamboyant, offbeat, mainstream, (un)conventional, eccentric, unusual, controversial, quirky, instinctive, middling, manipulative, acrimonious, subtle, sly, crafty, secretive, slippery, mercenary, crooked, unscrupulous, tortuous, tricky, deceitful, deceptive, venal, ambitious, greedy, power-hungry, partisan, self-serving, opportunist, treacherous, double-faced, two-faced, hypocritical, scandal-tainted, renegade, selfish, unpopular, opinionated, long-winded, snarling, picayunish, petty, generic, populist, professional, incumbent, civic, secular

politics audacious, courageous, creative, smart, astute, fractious, reckless, confrontational, heated, polarized, hard-line, pothouse, controversial, bitter, cautious, back-room, back-alley, secretive, hard-knuckle, dangerous, treacherous, crooked, unrelenting, relentless, ruthless, merciless, heartless, pitiless, brutal, internecine, apocalyptic, nightmarish, violent, tumultuous, turbulent, tangled, intricate, tortuous, inflexible, Byzantine, insignificant, petty, vulgar, low, profligate, perverse, divisive, traditional, conservative, mainstream, (non-)partisan, left-wing, right-wing, patrician, radical, armchair, sectarian, (big-)power, bloc, party, partisan, local, grass-roots, electoral, office

poll, polls, polling comprehensive, heavy, volatile, (in)accurate, misleading, recent, (non-)partisan, political

pollutant, pollutants noxious, deadly, deleterious, destructive, foul, evil, feculent, fetid, f(a)ecal, harmful, injurious, malodorous, offensive, venomous, virulent, putrid, pernicious, miasmic

pollution overwhelming, intense, heavy, massive, unrelenting, relentless, merciless, pitiless, ruthless, loathsome, hideous, irretrievable, unnecessary, residual, cumulative, man-made, chronic, industrial, (photo)chemical, air, environmental, atmospheric, marine, aesthetic, solid, liquid; visual, nasal

pond, ponds See also *lake* clear, serene, mirror-like, golden, blossom-strewn, marshy, rushy, inland, spacious, bottomless, shallow, peaceful, placid, silent, (un)friendly, freshwater, irregular, three-level, unruffled, smooth, stagnant, still, icy, glacial, frozen, dark, cold, rain-swollen, man-made, virgin, seasonal

pony, ponies See *horse*

pool, pools steaming, steamy, warm, clear, transparent, limpid, fabulous, ancient, flower-fringed, shallow, still, stagnant, muddy, mud-bottomed, mossy, sunken, inground, landlocked, indoor, outdoor, tiled, concrete, vast, spacious, gargantuan, Olympic-sized, freshwater, springwater, natural, curvaceous, healing, therapeutic, thermal, Venetian, tidal, rooftop

poor (un)deserving, (un)worthy, church-mouse, destitute, desperate, helpless, wretched, sorrowful, virtuous, new

popularity enduring, lasting, unwavering, burning, surprising, astounding, overwhelming, sweeping, soaring, tremendous, considerable, immense, enormous, unbounded, boundless, inexhaustible, broad, wide, extensive, genuine, solid, strong, die-hard, unrivalled, undisputed, undiminished, unprecedented, extraordinary, swift, immediate, momentary, precarious, cheap, new-found, universal, personal, mainstream

population, populations soaring, teeming, floating, bulging, swelling, (ever-)increasing, (fast-)growing, booming, siz(e)able, enormous, tremendous, large, huge, dense, (un)stable, static, stagnant,

217

sparse, small, scattered, undocumented, open, diverse, mixed, multicultural, disparate, heterogeneous, indigenous, thriving, viable, (under)privileged, somnolent, restive, original, aboriginal, native, ethnic, immigrant, permanent, transient, transplant, settler, cosmopolitan, inland, urban, agrarian, school-age, target

porcelain See also *china* fine, translucent, crazed, (high-)fired, salt-fired, hard-paste, soft-paste, traditional

porch, porches sweeping, wide, airy, breezy, shady, sunny, spotless, ornate, rickety, warped, colonnaded, sheltered, covered, shuttered, trellised, flowered, shaded, shadeless, wraparound, front, back, side

pornography hard-core, soft-core, (un)cut

porridge See *food*

port, ports See also *city* thriving, leading, large, great, vital, active, dense, exotic, historic, neutral, blocked, four-berth, (duty-)free, naval, strategic, deep-water, fishing, deep-sea, river

portfolio, portfolios (1: securities held by an investor) diverse, diversified, restricted, limited, tax-exempt, liquid, loan

portfolio, portfolios (2: role of the head of a government department) leading, high-ranking, intoxicating, challenging, lofty, influential, powerful, coveted, privileged, sensitive

portion, portions whopping, healthy, generous, ample, substantial, plentiful, goodly, hefty, siz(e)able, inordinate, major, (in)significant, (in)sufficient, (un)even, unused, modest, niggardly, meagre, minuscule, exiguous, scanty, token, undersized, individual, edible

portrait, portraits See also *painting* and *photograph* breathtaking, fascinating, striking, engaging, (un)flattering, less-than-flattering, baffling, (un)interesting, luminous, vivid, rare, sympathetic, perfect, masterly, (un)authentic, (in)accurate, incisive, powerful, up-to-date, candid, (un)recognizable, memorable, indelible, detailed, well-rounded, (un)balanced, one-sided, lifelike, realistic, natural, sensual, stiff, craggy, mediocre, perfunctory, distorted, composite,

unposed, life-size, full-length, head-and-shoulders, kaleidoscopic, ubiquitous, equestrian, biographical, ancestral, (anti-)mythic; spiritual, psychological

portrayal, portrayals fascinating, masterful, elegant, vivid, touching, frank, clear-eyed, rosy, (in)accurate, (un)fair, (un)convincing, unbiased, one-sided, raw, gross, blasphemous, chilling, razor-sharp, graphic, realistic

pose, poses natural, lifelike, habitual, (un)usual, hip, studied, model-like, provocative, idiotic, public

position, positions (1: job) intoxicating, challenging, exhilarating, leading, rewarding, lucrative, congenial, easy, splendid, stable, high(-ranking), high-level, lofty, influential, powerful, prominent, mainstream, responsible, respectable, (in)secure, tenurable, honoured, coveted, privileged, senior, sensitive, plush, salaried, full-time, part-time, ill-defined, low-level, menial, subordinate, ceremonial, (non-)executive, administrative, managerial, supervisory, clerical, academic, clinical, (quasi-)official, appointive, elective, fiduciary

position, positions (2: attitude) accommodating, conciliatory, pacifist, middle-of-the-road, firm, fixed, decisive, strong, powerful, commanding, favourable, advantageous, privileged, absolute, prominent, strategic, tenable, exalted, eminent, unique, (in)conspicuous, dignified, principled, subtle, courageous, dominant, clear(-cut), unassailable, realistic, exact, cautious, adversarial, (un)tenable, shaky, inescapable, desperate, ugly, unenviable, painful, pitiable, false, humiliating, disadvantageous, subservient, vulnerable, precarious, ambiguous, unclear, doubtful, uncertain, cynical, incongruous, unobtrusive, awkward, unknown, obscure, curious, unfavourable, awful, questionable, anomalous, delicate, intransigent, irreconcilable, uncompromising, rigid, relentless, hawkish, difficult, undignified, revealing, unaltered, (un)restrained, reversed, undercut, wait-and-see, offensive, defensive, bent-over, crouching, squatting, prostrate, oblique, erect, upright, foetal, prone, (semi-)recumbent, retracted, forward, rearward, sedentary, supine, centrist, personal

possession (1: the act of possessing) invincible, insuperable, compulsive, irregular, unreasonable, unauthorized, wrongful

possession, possessions (2: anything owned) precious, valuable, dear, fond, proud, prized, valued, unrivalled, indubitable, vast, incalculable, meagre, scant, poor, permanent, personal, worldly, earthly, material, spiritual, (extra)territorial, (il)legal, adverse, titular, fiduciary

possibility, possibilities intoxicating, intriguing, astonishing, amazing, stunning, astounding, interesting, promising, real, definite, distinct, clear, strong, serious, dramatic, wonderful, spacious, endless, limitless, unlimited, infinite, growing, (un)likely, (im)plausible, remote, faint, slight, slender, far-fetched, zero, fair, alternative, grim, unpleasant, disastrous, unimaginable

post, posts (1: pillar; column) ornamental, upright, vertical, perpendicular, skinny, erect, crooked

post, posts (2: job; position) See *job* (1) and *position* (1)

poster, posters eye-catching, striking, dazzling, glaring, glittering, sparkling, ornate, gaudy, lurid, flashy, colourful, bright, monochromatic, daring, aggressive, effective, vulgar, tattered, defaced, handwritten, big-character

postponement, postponements temporary, tentative, unforeseen, (un)expected, (un)avoidable, (in)evitable

posture, postures tranquil, good, normal, right, wrong, (un)balanced, bad, faulty, poor, awkward, obscene, erect, accumbent, recumbent, catatonic, stooped, static, seated, reclined, bipedal, sitting, moving, sleeping, testing, grotesque, self-effacing, antic

pot, pots See also *pottery* shiny, simple, earthen(ware), clay, ceramic, terracotta, copper, brass, cast-iron, aluminium, tapered, glazed, cylindrical, refractory

potato, potatoes See also *vegetable* mealy, dry, moist, firm, smooth, all-purpose, common, fondant, baked, puréed, hash brown, Irish, new, red, white; sweet

potential, potentiality staggering, tantalizing, promising, auspicious, unmatched, strong, enormous, considerable, vast, tremendous, phenomenal, boundless, endless, unlimited, limitless, (in)definite, remarkable, awesome, full, maximum, long-term, worldwide, likely, untapped, unfulfilled, revelatory, latent, inner, human, intellectual, mental, physical; chemical

pottery See also *pot* exquisite, fine, distinctive, finished, beautiful, flawless, rare, superb, magnificent, splendid, dainty, attractive, charming, elegant, elaborate, fascinating, graceful, impressive, prestigious, decorative, ornamental, ornate, utilitarian, (un)glazed, handmade, decorated, painted, sun-baked, crazed, primitive, redware, polychrome, terracotta

poultry See *chicken*

poverty snivelling, grinding, agonizing, struggling, disheartening, searing, suffocating, cramping, humiliating, appalling, squalid, dire, sordid, abject, miserable, wretched, dismal, bitter, unrelenting, relentless, merciless, heartless, ruthless, pitiless, painful, shameful, absolute, grim, blank, piteous, helpless, hopeless, desperate, unspeakable, (in)visible, total, utmost, extreme, exalted, widespread, vicious, needless, sharp, severe, chronic, endless, perennial, perpetual, essential, genteel; structural

powder, powders pure, smooth, fine, loose, subtile, translucent, crystalline, (in)soluble, (un)stable, impalpable, smokeless, tasteless, colourless, pungent, talcum, antimonial; black

power, powers soothing, matchless, incomparable, astounding, amazing, astonishing, dazzling, extraordinary, incredible, unbelievable, major, unknown, rare, massive, tremendous, enormous, vast, large, extensive, broad, phenomenal, legendary, gargantuan, colossal, immense, immeasurable, unfailing, limitless, (un)limited, unprecedented, absolute, optimal, uncontested, independent, pervasive, sweeping, extravagant, dominant, paramount, inexorable, ultimate, lasting, enduring, emerging, waning, shifting, shifty, unstable, unusable, imperturbable, awesome, frightening, terrible, uncontrollable, stimulative, binding, rapacious, coercive, tyrannical, dictatorial, brute, Draconian, demonic, belligerent, destructive, explosive, eerie, mysterious, raucous, corruptive, seductive, hidden, assumed, assured, untapped, unfettered, unrestrained, virtual, mortal, paper, monolithic, discretionary, (quasi-)legislative, executive, statutory, constitutional, regulatory, putative, latent, regal, feudalistic, military, marine, maritime, naval, mental, intellectual, temporal, spiritual, sacred, revelatory, political, motive, judiciary, judicial, royal, legal, sovereign, vocal, protective, redemptive, curative, healing, restorative, recuperative, plenipotentiary, creative, intuitive, monopoly, aerobic, corporal, emotive, regenerative, copulative, evil, industrial, earthly, signatory, occult, mysterious, supernatural, hypnotic, psychic, magical, talismanic, investigatory, investigative, colonial, home-rule, allied, unilateral, monopolistic, hegemonic, state-of-siege, graphic, advisory, erosive; motor, thermal, turbo, atomic, (hydro)electric, fossil-fuel, solar(-thermal), geothermal, propulsive

practice, practices discreet, laudable, lucrative, fruitful, sound, shrewd, pragmatic, resilient, artful, (il)legal, (dis)honest, (un)fair, (un)ethical, (un)acceptable, (un)healthy, ubiquitous, common, routine, standard, general, widespread, rampant, universal, habitual, (un)usual, (ir)regular, open, familiar, traditional, conventional, long-standing, age-old, centuries-old, time-honoured, ancient, venerable, hoary, limitless, unlimited, exorbitant, dicey, tricky, deceptive, restrictive, venal, corrupt, nefarious, pernicious, malevolent, wicked, iniquitous, sacrilegious, lax, discriminatory, demented, depraved, abnormal, hard, primitive, self-defeating, ignorant, short-sighted, fraudulent, sorry, lamentable, disgusting, sickening, deceitful, sleazy, controversial, heretical, dubious, questionable, amoral, peculiar, unlawful, fruitless, gruelling, reprehensible, outdated, outmoded, (long-)established, current, religious, ascetic, regulatory

prairie, prairies billowing, sparkling, gleaming, rolling, undulating, gentle, fragile, golden, bleak, harsh, arid, drought-stricken, bare, bald, desolate, lonesome, windy, windswept, sun-scorched, snow-covered, vast, boundless, infinite, unbounded, endless, wide, open, (griddle-)flat, upland, unscathed, broken, untamed

praise, praises graceful, (in)sincere, warm, well-earned, gentlemanly, expectable, enthusiastic, fervent, high, strong, absolute, generous, extravagant, effusive, lavish, unstinted, ample, profuse, excessive, unrestrained, exuberant, overflowing, thunderous, unending, unbounded, wide, overmuch, (in)frequent, overblown, magniloquent, superlative, unreserved, extraordinary, pretentious, high-sounding, hyperbolic, indiscriminate, boastful, fulsome, meretricious, false, preposterous, empty, indiscreet, oblique, faint, stilted, craven, spiritless, sugary, saccharine, honeyed, (un)qualified, unearned, due, unanimous

prank, pranks lively, frolicsome, merry, mirthful, playful, roguish, immature, adolescent, tiresome, youthful, boyish, childish, impish, mischievous, merry

prayer, prayers soul-stirring, exultant, deep, intense, active, devout, fervent, earnest, ardent, zealous, pious, reverent, respectful, sacred, sincere, serious, solemn, anguished, desperate, sorrowful, dolorous, appropriate, lonely, silent, tacit, languid, weak, humble, sensuous, melodic, optional, mandatory, central, unspoken, unanswered, repetitive, spontaneous, frequent, ceaseless, daily, bedtime, morning, usual, private, solitary, communal, group, benedictory, canonical, penitential, votive, supplicatory, Eucharistic, offertory, shamanistic, graveside

preacher, preachers fascinating, exciting, saintly, popular, populist, charismatic, fiery, persuasive, fervent, flamboyant, apocalyptic, inspirational, tireless, fallen, unfrocked, defrocked, fundamentalist, lay, itinerant, evangelical, hell-fire, television

preaching See also *preacher* dry, methodical, unaffecting, fatuous, soapbox

precaution, precautions (water)tight, ultra-tight, stringent, strict, extra, extreme, elaborate, (un)reasonable, (in)adequate, sensible, extraordinary, excessive, massive, special, standard, elementary, simple, obvious, painstaking, unprecedented, conceivable, imaginable, provident, lax, senseless, hygienic

precedent, precedents earthshattering, earthshaking, terrifying, long-standing, encouraging, (un)welcome, tremendous, dangerous, controversial, troublesome, ominous, set, legal

precious stone See *gem*

precipice, precipices hair-raising, frightening, frightful, abysmal, steep, giddy, dizzy, sheer, invisible, perpendicular, unexpected, deadly

preciseness engaging, exemplary, model, supreme, extraordinary, faultless, infallible, unerring, state-of-the-art, leading-edge, uncanny, exquisite, great, minute, mathematical, clockwork, cutting, studied, painstaking, luminous, incredible, unbelievable, gratuitous, finicky

precision See *preciseness*

predator, predators powerful, efficient, fearsome, deadly, dangerous, large

predicament, predicaments See *dilemma*

predictability See *prediction*

prediction, predictions (in)correct, (in)accurate, (in)valid, (un)realistic, confident, infallible, excited, rosy, sanguine, optimistic, gleeful, uncanny, perplexing, bewildering, puzzling, extravagant, weird, eerie, mysterious, merciless, ruthless, relentless, unrelenting, ominous, pessimistic, grim, gloomy, dire, alarming, depressing, blunt, awful, bitter, mistaken, unfounded, premature, myopic, widespread, long-term, long-range, astrological, psychic

predisposition, predispositions See *tendency*

preface, prefaces glowing, flattering, vibrant, vivid, brilliant, enthusiastic, lively, graceful, disarming, self-serving, dedicatory, biographical, explanatory

preference, preferences strong, definite, clear, marked, professed, avowed, identifiable, myopic, personal, congregational

pregnancy, pregnancies noticeable, (im)possible, full-term, first, blissful, (ab)normal, (un)successful, (un)healthy, trouble-free, problem-free, uneventful,

(un)safe, tense, risky, high-risk, dangerous, difficult, life-threatening, advanced, late, stormy, humiliating, complicated, unconfirmed, unwanted, unplanned, unwelcome, accidental, adolescent, tubal, test-tube, ectopic

prejudice, prejudices well-bred, ingrained, entrenched, long-held, (centuries-)old, inveterate, deep(-rooted), latent, hidden, pent-up, strong, significant, harsh, violent, vicious, blind, narrow, unaccountable, unjustified, unwarranted, ill-judged, heedless, illogical, unreasoning, irrational, unpardonable, invincible, insular, unattractive, shocking, appalling, petty, blatant, national, racial, ethnic, sectarian

première, premières See *performance* (2)

premises See *building*

preoccupation, preoccupations obsessive, absorbed, narcissistic, single-minded, fanatical, intense, relentless, tiresome, wasteful, tremulous, swooning, distracting, divisive, sophomoric, monumental, gross, self-conscious, fatalistic, mundane, earthly, mortal, secular, worldly

preparation, preparations elaborate, extravagant, extensive, detailed, studious, careful, scrupulous, meticulous, rigorous, needful, (un)necessary, (in)sufficient, (im)proper, (in)adequate, lengthy, hasty, last-minute, frantic, hectic, plodding, sloppy, substandard, careless, apparent, secret, covert

prerequisite, prerequisites See *requirement*

prerogative, prerogatives myriad, innumerable, multitudinous, lineal, royal

prescription, prescriptions prudent, (in)appropriate, simple, lengthy, fillable, refillable, unfillable, brand, generic

presence smiling, tranquil, fragrant, heavy, powerful, august, imperious, overbearing, overwhelming, imposing, commanding, domineering, haunting, pervasive, high-profile, continual, permanent, lasting, enduring, abiding, incredible, unbelievable, disturbing, (in)significant, ubiquitous, (in)visible, unseen, low-profile, collective, physical, military

present, presents See *gift* (2)

presentation, presentations graceful, elegant, (un)impressive, (un)persuasive, (un)convincing, succinct, rambling, confused

presenter, presenters high-profile, resourceful, flamboyant, star

President, Presidents See also *leader* and Appendixes A and B glamorous, youthful, hard-line, autocratic, authoritarian, lame-duck, feeble, weak, self-proclaimed, incoming, outgoing, current, provisional, interim, executive, ceremonial, honorary, federal

press (journalism) See also *newspaper* and *journalism* free, pervasive, independent, voluble, quality, (ir)responsible, (un)caring, daring, unrelenting, relentless, ruthless, heartless, merciless, pitiless, opinionated, uncontrolled, unshackled, unfettered, uncritical, vicious, prying, curious, inquisitive, nosy, intrusive, sensational, gutter, underground, national, foreign, yellow, tabloid, opposition, alternative

pressure, pressures enervating, staggering, crushing, serious, intense, great, tremendous, enormous, heavy, excessive, extreme, considerable, immense, rigorous, aggressive, untoward, phenomenal, awful, unbearable, intolerable, dramatic, terrible, heavy-handed, unrelenting, relentless, ruthless, merciless, pitiless, heartless, brutal, fierce, persistent, constant, pervasive, widespread, incredible, unbelievable, undue, hysterical, irresistible, inescapable, superincumbent, subtle, pent-up, steady, (in)effective, smouldering, continued, concerted, domestic, internal, external, inside, outside, ambient, daily, competitive, social, societal, cultural, moral, ideological, parental, partial, token, political, diplomatic, physical; barometric, atmospheric, air, radiation, vapour, hydraulic, static; systolic, diastolic, intracranial, nasal, facial; mental, psychological; monetary, economic, inflationary; military

prestige commanding, glaring, outstanding, striking, unique, eminent, notable, distinct, majestic, mighty, considerable, enviable

pretence, pretences mere, illusive, fraudulent, treacherous, sham, false, ridiculous, jocular, vapid, continued, defiant, impulsive, reflective

pretension, pretensions See *pretence*

pretext, pretexts persuasive, satisfying, (un)satisfactory, (im)plausible, (un)convincing, contrived, flimsy, feeble, frail, shallow, slender, slight, tenuous, thin, trivial, trifling, weak

prey, preys unsuspecting, unwitting, trusting, unwary, prostrate, innocent, helpless, hopeless, gullible, unintentional, easy, ready, cold-blooded, hapless, unfortunate, unlucky, accessible, yielding, favourite, potential, live

price, prices soaring, climbing, increasing, galloping, towering, rising, surging, flaring, thumping, gushing, shocking, dizzying, breathtaking, staggering, appalling, inordinate, exorbitant, sky-high, prohibitive, extortionate, awesome, fearful, ghastly, flyaway, astronomical, extravagant, high, lofty, heavy, large, substantial, colossal, gigantic, soggy, outrageous, painful, stiff(ish), excessive, unbelievable, ungodly, rapacious, fancy, upscale, runaway, inflated, stratospheric, bloated, unconscionable, steep, precious, hard, tidy, dear, heady, premium, spectacular, record, freakish, miserable, (un)affordable, (un)reasonable, (un)realistic, fair, regular, current, manageable, right, average, firm, unchanged, moderate, volatile, stable, equitable, appropriate, healthy, unprecedented, bewildering, fantastic, lucrative, profitable, keen, remunerative, fabulous, attractive, competitive, bargain, cut-throat, tempting, irresistible, unbeatable, popular, amazing, fabulous, exceptional, (lower-than-)prevailing, first-sale, cut-rate, floor, low(est), depressed, (rock-)bottom, below-market, paltry, nominal, modest, buoyant, uncertain, speculative, approximate, token, preferential, asking, selling, retail, wholesale, black-market, trade, flat, import, domestic, ceiling, base, equilibrium, fire-sale, (free-)market, untaxed, tax-free, overall, all-inclusive, all-in, resale, spot, bid, offer, break-even, closing, reserve

pride (im)modest, (il)legitimate, (un)justifiable, (un)rightful, defensive, new-found, becoming, glowing, opulent, grudging, defiant, punctilious, vicarious, fierce, insensate, hard, stubborn, prickly, testy, false, silly, abounding, overbearing, measureless, inordinate, excessive, immoderate, overweening, swelling, immense, enormous, intense, deep, unconcealed, evident, airy, intolerable, misguided, stiff-necked, imperial, civic, national, cultural, sectional, ethnic, patriotic, professional

priest, priests articulate, open-hearted, charitable, saintly, godly, perfect, infallible, sanctimonious, dedicated, tireless, inexhaustible, indefatigable, dynamic, energetic, fiery, (over-)zealous, visible, venerable, dreary, celibate, disaffected, (un)conventional, reform-minded, liberal, dissenting, renegade, hypocritical, fallible, perjured, unfrocked, defrocked, cassocked, beneficed, (white-)bearded, parish, resident, lay, secular, spiritual, senior, high, neophyte, chantry, Christian, voodoo, Hindu, Parsee, Buddhist, Shinto

prince, princes handsome, young, eligible, gold-crowned, crown, titular, dependent, subordinate, fairy-tale

principal, principals See *headteacher*

principle, principles inspirational, well-thought-out, deep-rooted, conventional, universal, profound, eternal, good, high, lofty, valued, legitimate, primary, basic, fundamental, rudimentary, seminal, cardinal, elemental, fixed, unbending, immutable, pliable, (in)flexible, firm, strict, ultimate, moving, recondite, underlying, guiding, lax, despotic, false, vague, abstruse, popular, moral, ethical, egalitarian, humanitarian

priority, priorities pressing, overriding, shifting, low, high(er), top, major, main, first, basic, urgent, long-term, short-term, ill-ordered

prison, prisons brutal, harsh, rough, unrelenting, relentless, ruthless, merciless, heartless, pitiless, formidable, infamous, grim, ghastly, gloomy, dismal, austere, depressing, cheerless, dingy, dull, frowzy, ugly, disorderly, joyless, glum, sombre, wretched, sordid, hideous, run-down, squalid, crude, scabrous,

dungeon-like, damp, (over)crowded, open, prototypical, remote, juvenile, escape-proof, maximum-security, medium-security, open

prisoner, prisoners trusty, hapless, wretched, unfortunate, harmless, unruly, intractable, violent, dangerous, unrepentant, rebellious, close, solitary, loose, free, secure, suicidal, virtual, wanted, condemned, extricable, long-term, long-serving, common, bona fide, criminal, political; virtual

privacy (in)violate, sacred, delightful, hermitical, reclusive, strict, intense, solid, obsessive, personal, individual, residential

privation, privations enduring, lasting, long-suffering, severe, miserable, ceaseless, endless, constant, physical

privilege, privileges intriguing, real, rare, glorious, singular, special, sacrosanct, inviolable, sacred, inestimable, (in)valuable, priceless, supreme, enormous, immense, mighty, full, partial, dubious, questionable, unheard-of, (ir)revocable, (un)equal, exclusive, reciprocal, diplomatic, ceremonial

prize, prizes prestigious, premier, grand, top, first, ultimate, glittering, gaudy, magnificent, rare, just, even-handed, equitable, fabulous, substantial, big, major, valuable, little, minor, annual, literary

probability, probabilities high, low, little, distant, (un)likely, (im)plausible, (un)convincing, posterior, prior, mathematical, conditional

probe See *inquiry* and *investigation*

problem, problems challenging, pressing, overriding, vexing, rankling, annoying, bewildering, baffling, puzzling, mind-boggling, burning, agonizing, heart-sickening, overwhelming, devastating, life-threatening, frightening, staggering, enduring, abiding, (long-)lasting, never-ending, (long-)smouldering, far-reaching, growing, (re-)emerging, acute, dire, grim, stark, serious, severe, crucial, critical, momentous, formidable, grave, horrendous, hard, knotty, intricate, ticklish, thorny, intractable, (in)surmountable, (un)preventable, (in)superable, (un)solvable, (in)soluble, (ir)remediable, (un)manageable, complicated, (un)tangled, unresolved, complex, many-sided, multidimensional, temporary, fleeting, paradigmatic, standing, urgent, immediate, troublesome, painful, profound, deep(-rooted), broad, sensitive, difficult, pernicious, catastrophic, tough, fearsome, awesome, ferocious, ghastly, weighty, unglamorous, volatile, sticky, tremendous, big, immense, massive, enormous, monumental, long-term, chronic, perennial, eternal, permanent, immemorial, murky, prickly, contentious, stubborn, abstruse, recondite, major, vital, fundamental, key, root, basic, core, number-one, fatal, deadly, lethal, costly, myriad, persistent, time-honoured, widespread, pervasive, ongoing, recurrent, age-old, endemic, unprecedented, progressive, universal, common, real-life, existential, day-to-day, latter-day, daily, topical, underlying, attendant, self-inflicted, incipient, potential, hidden, noticeable, conspicuous, unique, unusual, uncommon, needless, simple, moderate, inconsequential, insignificant, emotional, (non-)moral, behavioural, social, pecuniary, monetary, financial, health, technical, ethical, respiratory, professional, sectional, socioeconomic, arithmetic, mathematical, geometrical, operational, national, marital, domestic, personal; credibility, image; iatrogenic

procedure, procedures (im)proper, (un)safe, novel, elaborate, sophisticated, efficient, infallible, impeccable, stringent, special, invasive, rare, absolute, unvarying, (un)fair, traditional, (un)conventional, normal, standard, simple, sacred, needless, start-up, horrendous, costly, risky, dangerous, questionable, controversial, reprehensible, carefree, uninhibited, lengthy, time-consuming, futile, bureaucratic, cumbersome, burdensome, complex, intricate, complicated, confused, drawn-out, outdated, antiquated, flawed, well-defined, established, elective, parliamentary, legal, educatory, technical, biochemical, security, emergency, operating

proceeding, proceedings (in)formal, (ir)regular, lengthy, interlocutory, summary, judicial, criminal

proceeds See *profit*

process, processes thorough, comprehensive, elaborate, (in)efficient, workable, (life)long, never-ending, time-consuming, basic, fundamental, vital, irreversible, painful, painstaking, gruelling, excruciating, searing, agonizing, arduous, laborious, rigorous, complex, complicated, intricate, tangled, tortuous, tedious, baffling, mysterious, widespread, sweeping, intermittent, slow, risky, shoddy, costly, short-term, long-term, permanent, temporary, two-stage, two-step, reversal, backward, natural, physical, mental, electoral, transverse, cognitive, judicial, democratic, additive, subtractive, creative, reproductive, evolutionary, literary, political

procession, processions streaming, imposing, stately, majestic, dignified, impressive, exalted, ceremonious, grandiloquent, splendid, magnificent, palatial, regal, royal, courtly, fine, solemn, exuberant, candle-lit, torch-light, slow, endless, unbroken, vast, lengthy, zigzag, pompous, tawdry, strange, eerie, pious, religious, sacred, devotional, confirmatory, ceremonial, mayoral, funeral, Epiphany

proclamation, proclamations See *announcement*

produce (un)ripe, fresh, tasty, prime, choice, wholesome, disease-resistant, plentiful, inexhaustible, plenteous, (in)sufficient, bounteous, abundant, rich, bountiful, early-season, harvestable, marketable, exotic, withering, withered, poor, pale, tasteless, (un)conventional, organic, chemical-free, pesticide-laden, garden, farm, agricultural

product, products high-tech, high-quality, exceptional, exquisite, durable, (long-)lasting, established, proven, refined, prestigious, unbeatable, genuine, warrantable, exciting, unique, competitive, nutritious, (un)safe, (un)affordable, functional, (un)usable, (un)sal(e)able, (un)marketable, exportable, substandard, tawdry, shoddy, cheap, shabby, faulty, defective, fraudulent, crude, staple, disposable, perishable, waste, gross, unfinished, final, household, domestic, foreign, ready-made, home-made,

hand-made, brand-name, no-name,
copycat, secondary, incidental, speciality,
electronic, electrical, (non-)biodegradable,
energy-efficient

production (1: the act or process of
producing) intensive, prolific, prodigious,
monumental, frenetic, big-volume, peak,
continual, sustained, profitable,
exceptional, modest, single-handed,
unrealized, streamlined, (un)limited,
overall, mass, domestic, capitalistic,
automotive

production, productions (2: artistic
effort) stunning, outstanding, satisfying,
groundbreaking, thrilling, astounding,
breathtaking, uplifting, moving,
compelling, absorbing, touching, sensitive,
(un)successful, (un)imaginative, impressive,
spirited, hypnotic, energetic, polished,
splendid, first-rate, state-of-the-art,
exceptional, flawless, faultless, masterly,
masterful, spiffy, innovative, lavish,
glittery, ambitious, extravagant,
large-scale, remarkable, magnificent,
spectacular, spanking, grandiose,
mammoth, gigantic, huge, prolific,
abundant, opulent, major,
lavish(ly-detailed), eclectic, transatlantic,
celebrated, eccentric, unusual, offbeat,
staid, second-rate, tedious, dusty,
no-script, popular, theatrical, touring

productivity tenacious, enormous, high,
low, sluggish

profession, professions prestigious,
impressive, influential, high-status,
noble, honourable, learned, lucrative,
thriving, well-paid, dignified, glamorous,
grave, genteel, (un)satisfying, exacting,
demanding, tiring, bizarre, fraudulent,
independent, legal, low-status,
grubby

professionalism polished, refined, tactful,
suave, urbane, diplomatic, bland, smooth,
politic

professor, professors awe-inspiring,
studious, erudite, learned, knowledgeable,
extraordinary, exuberant, witty,
open-minded, absent-minded,
liberal-minded, conservative-minded,
(un)orthodox, (un)conventional, recluse,
reclusive, unflappable, imperturbable,
dogmatic, cold, heavy-handed, stuffy,
eccentric, dedicated, meticulous,

systematic, thorough, (in)competent,
(un)conscientious, full-fledged, former,
one-time, quondam, erstwhile, adjunct,
visiting, Regius, assistant, associate, full,
emeritus

profile, profiles clear, (in)accurate, low,
high, jagged, angular, literary, personality

profit, profits soaring, rising, huge,
substantial, lucrative, high, handsome,
fabulous, big, vast, healthy, record, peak,
plump, enormous, tidy, hefty, robust, neat,
fat, excessive, swollen, run-up, stunning,
astonishing, astounding, dramatic,
impressive, spectacular, easy, rich, heady,
windfall, lustrous, quick, excess, obscene,
steady, potential, prospective,
(im)probable, (un)due, (un)clear, incoming,
short-term, honest, untidy, filthy, (il)licit,
(il)legal, (il)legitimate, lacklustre,
minuscule, lean, poor, slim, anaemic, fair,
small, marginal, puny, modest, sliding,
plunging, tumbling, (un)expected,
undisclosed, unreported, untaxed,
pecuniary, overall, gross, net, paper,
operating, after-tax, pre-tax, corporate

profusion See *abundance*

prognosis, prognoses encouraging,
(in)auspicious, (un)propitious,
(un)favourable, grim, bleak, dismal

programme, programmes fascinating,
superb, magnificent, remarkable,
delightful, exemplary, ambitious, dynamic,
vigorous, worthy, vaunted, credible,
one-of-a-kind, unique, imaginative,
innovative, groundbreaking, radical,
unusual, inventive, creative, pioneer,
aggressive, (in)sensible, (un)reasonable,
informative, beneficial, flawless,
(in)coherent, (in)effective, (un)workable,
(un)realistic, progressive, graduated,
(in)flexible, (un)feasible, (in)accessible,
structured, steady, verifiable, well-rounded,
(un)traditional, indigenous, rigorous,
exorbitant, high-powered, heavy, rigid,
oppressive, ruthless, stringent, intensive,
extensive, massive, far-reaching,
comprehensive, sweeping, expensive,
hard-hit, bare-bones, low-cost, mandatory,
compulsory, optional, interchangeable,
top-secret, government-run, long-term,
short-term, versatile, multi-faceted,
ongoing, fast-moving, slow-moving,
top-flight, basic, eclectic, neglectful,

controversial, wasteful, pernicious, disjointed, crippled, half-baked, computerized, (well-)established, disorganized, (well-)funded, stopgap, pilot, crash, social, catch-up, anti-drug, experimental, trial, volunteer, rehabilitative, therapeutic, overall, interpretive, recreational; television, live, call-in, phone-in, prime-time

progress staggering, exciting, amazing, astonishing, astounding, striking, startling, incredible, unbelievable, epic, fantastic, substantial, great, tremendous, (in)significant, considerable, spectacular, big, deep, incremental, impressive, remarkable, solid, encouraging, meaningful, triumphal, revolutionary, cautious, steady, smooth, real, concrete, quantifiable, visible, tangible, noticeable, marked, major, undeniable, (un)satisfactory, hard-won, inexorable, brisk, rapid, speedy, meteoric, painful, slight, erratic, spotty, slow, sluggish, disappointing, discouraging, minimal, lacklustre, human, material, social, scientific, technological, medical

prohibition, prohibitions outright, complete, total, state-wide, official, paper

project, projects meritorious, impressive, innovative, unique, exciting, intriguing, marvellous, worthwhile, ambitious, high-profile, patrician, majestic, major, large, big, monumental, gigantic, giant, mammoth, colossal, vast, huge, massive, large-scale, far-flung, enormous, lavish, challenging, grand, spectacular, grandiose, stunning, dramatic, important, capital, indispensable, (un)feasible, risk-free, risky, labour-intensive, expensive, painstaking, rash, mad, dreamy, foolish, ill-conceived, misguided, ill-judged, wasteful, controversial, five-year, initial, short-term, long-term, sudden, ongoing, small-scale, (state-)funded, (super)secret, industrial, pilot, experimental, pet

promise, promises binding, disarming, bankable, reliable, dependable, bright, earnest, fervent, faithful, substantive, meaningful, solemn, sacred, inviolable, perennial, flat, obligatory, long-standing, unconditional, specific, null, quick-fire, glib, perfidious, hollow, worthless, silly, false, empty, absurd, fuzzy, outlandish,

alluring, specious, vain, meaningless, vague, evasive, mighty, (un)substantial, ludicrous, fair, bare, contradictory, hasty, rash, reckless, ruinous, airy, visionary, fanciful, reluctant, overblown, extravagant, contrite, unfounded, unkept, unfulfilled, unrealized, humble, modest, mutual, oral, verbal, written

promontory, promontories bold, steep, abrupt, rocky

promotion, promotions (1: advancement in rank) (well-)deserved, nice, rapid, imminent, (un)justifiable, undeserved, unexpected, automatic

promotion, promotions (2: encouragement of sale) See *advertising*

promptness compulsive, habitual, customary, (un)usual, methodical

pronoun, pronouns disjunctive, demonstrative, personal, possessive, relative (conjunctive), interrogative, indefinite, reflexive, intensive

pronouncement, pronouncements See *announcement*

pronunciation full, broad, baffling, lilting, (in)distinct, (im)proper, (in)correct, wrong, faulty, bad, standard, received, usual, local, variant, explanatory, spelling

proof, proofs solid, substantial, perfect, clear, incontestable, valid, positive, indisputable, unarguable, unquestionable, irrefutable, conclusive, concrete, incontrovertible, sure, definite, definitive, irrecusable, empirical, stupendous, spectacular, indubitable, eloquent, palpable, conspicuous, tangible, presumptive, firm, absolute, pregnant, abundant, (in)sufficient, vivid, hard, strong, solid, speaking, distinctive, dramatic, striking, rigorous, ultimate, contending, trifling, (un)convincing, visual, documentary, empirical, theistic, classic, scientific, clinical, direct, indirect; living

propaganda efficacious, sophisticated, subtle, (in)effective, masterful, (im)plausible, (un)biased, massive, widespread, all-pervasive, unrelenting, forceful, crude, crafty, boastful, scurrilous, malicious, venomous, baleful, harmful, menacing, vindictive, political, Orwellian

property, properties (1: possession; land; real estate) handsome, desirable, marketable, valuable, priceless, profitable, (un)usable, choice, (non-)strategic, exclusive, upscale, vast, hot, splendid, sacrosanct, portable, immovable, alien(able), landed, whole, tangible, rightful, riparian, fiduciary, personal, private, public, communal, common, corporal, real, rental

property, properties (2: feature; quality or attribute of a thing) (un)desirable, (un)usual, peculiar, mysterious, legendary, magical, remarkable, intensive, physical, chemical, biological, generic, medicinal, healing, curative, therapeutic, salubrious, aphrodisiac, phenomenological, structural, constituent (constitutive), ontological, magnetic, magical

prophecy, prophecies astounding, self-fulfilling, encouraging, optimistic, hopeful, sanguine, sunny, zealous, agreeable, beamish, eerie, grim, gloomy, doleful, pessimistic, ghastly, macabre, relentless, ruthless, merciless, sinister, threatening, frightening, apocalyptic, oblique, false, unfulfilled

prophet, prophets (in)fallible, false, fake, bogus, deceitful, sham, biblical, messianic, weather

proponent, proponents See *advocate*

proportion, proportions (relationship between things) perfect, just, right, proper, high, low, rare, rough, wrong, debatable

proportions (size; extent; dimensions) harmonious, balanced, realistic, lavish, ample, whopping, staggering, shocking, gargantuan, monumental, (un)manageable, incalculable, (in)significant, large, siz(e)able, awesome, prodigious, massive, significant, frenzied, hysterical, fearsome, frantic, panic, cataclysmic, staggering, alarming, shocking, epidemic, deadly, tragic, calamitous, catastrophic, crisis, psychotic, ludicrous, fantastic, superhuman, mythic(al), epic, legendary, historical, galactic, Utopian

proposal, proposals concrete, definite, clear-cut, specific, positive, constructive, solid, (un)acceptable, (un)reasonable, (in)appropriate, (in)adequate, imaginative, workable, conciliatory, encouraging, compromise, intermediary, pacific, starry-eyed, ambitious, provocative, bold, radical, heretical, (un)orthodox, detailed, long-term, grand, substantial, substantive, stunning, timely, roundabout, controversial, contentious, vague, lunatic, mad, foolish, rash, ridiculous, shocking, indecent, revolting, hazy, monstrous, hardheaded, uninspiring, unbelievable, objectionable, unpalatable, costly, harmful, draft, bottom-line, surprise, comprehensive, collective, marriage

proposition, propositions See also *proposal* pacific, conciliatory, profitable, particular, (ir)rational, (im)practical, practicable, viable, extraordinary, attractive, (un)acceptable, defensible, debatable, disputable, arguable, chanc(e)y, risky, dicey, hazy, expensive, contrary, negative, offensive

proprietor, proprietors See *owner* and *landlady*

propriety singular, exceptional, remarkable, peculiar, quaint, striking, unique

prose living, compelling, moving, unerring, chiselled, facile, light, flexible, elegant, effective, clean, tight, unrestrained, graceful, stylish, vivid, unexceptionable, simple, plain, clear, lucid, straightforward, concise, supple, vigorous, forceful, articulate, acute, smooth, readable, unadorned, bald, homespun, florid, measured, stately, sequined, alluring, eloquent, witty, jok(e)y, ornate, richly-textured, pyrotechnical, dense, fast, snappy, inimitable, (un-)self-conscious, structured, headlong, leaden, pin-drop, turgid, pedestrian, over-wrought, convoluted, tedious, dull, trite, commonplace, obscure, graceless, sloppy, bad, careless, stilted, pompous, bombastic, overblown, stiff, superficial, catty, bureaucratic, journalistic, polyphonic, poetic, heroic, evocative, (non-)fictional

prospect, prospects (un)promising, exciting, stirring, thrilling, gratifying, enticing, rosy, sunny, bright, auspicious, favourable, hopeful, good, excellent, strong, heady, secure, desirable, pleasant, realistic, clear, extensive, long-term, far, remote, distant, blank, uncomfortable, uncertain, dubious, unlikely, slim, unthinkable, black, bleak, ominous, formidable, disheartening, unnerving, alarming, frightening, grinding, dreary, dire, dim, grim, sombre, gloomy, depressing, dismal, joyless, meagre, slender, undesirable, catastrophic, nasty, awful, future, financial

prospector, prospectors eager, anxious, avaricious, earnest, greedy, fearful, impatient, restive

prospectus, prospectuses informative, easy-to-follow, explanatory, illustrated, preliminary, final, free, 50-page, glossy, sensual, elegant, free, full-colour

prosperity sound, unbounded, unprecedented, undreamed-of, carefree, calm, easy, unruffled, newfound, permanent, unheralded, modest, painless, risk-free, illusive, illusory, deceptive, fleeting, unctuous, circumstantial, general, relative, comparative, material

prostitute, prostitutes repentant, under-age, amiable, lecherous, lewd, sexy, seductive, alluring, enticing, tempting, expensive, high-priced, high-class, enterprising, ambitious, infamous, vile, slovenly, (AIDS-)infected, bisexual, transvestite, tough-looking, male, street, junkie, vulnerable, (un)paid

prostitution pestilent, pernicious, rampant, widespread, uncontrollable, endemic, unrestrained, unrestricted

protagonist, protagonists See *character* (2) and *champion*

protection, protections permanent, round-the-clock, long-lasting, extended, absolute, maximum, stringent, iron-clad, authoritative, effective, attentive, special, (in)secure, (un)equivocal, explicit, (in)significant, (in)adequate, (in)sufficient, (un)limited, frail, rudimentary, marginal, extra, additional, double, partial, minimum, routine, mutual, maternal, paternal, parental, moral, financial, legal, statutory, emergency; environmental, cathodic

protest, protests peaceful, mild, benign, (non-)violent, strong, vigorous, vehement, emotional, impassioned, anguished, persistent, brave, uninhibited, dramatic, sharp, intense, explosive, raucous, vocal, clamorous, loud, noisy, indignant, furious, angry, vociferous, heated, fiery, searing, bitter, acrimonious, confrontational, blasphemous, ground-swell, overwhelming, great, massive, huge, nationwide, mass, popular, widespread, ongoing, growing, sweeping, spontaneous, futile, indeterminate, small, weak, sporadic, implicit, organized, muffled, upheld, formal, written, solemn, sit-down, sit-in, street, campus

protester, protesters peaceful, well-intentioned, defiant, (un)armed, violent, militant, placard-waving, jeering, stone-tossing, anguished, pro-reform, anti-government, anti-abortion

proverb, proverbs priceless, timeless, apt, appropriate, relevant, pointed, poignant, off-the-cuff, common

providence kind(ly), charitable, clement, compassionate, merciful, pitiful

provider, providers sole, only, single, (un)reliable, (ir)responsible

province, provinces See *region*

provision (condition) See *condition*

provisions (supply or stock of food) abundant, plentiful, inexhaustible, plenteous, (in)adequate, (in)significant, (ir)regular, (in)sufficient, (un)wholesome, poor, household

provocation, provocations serious, deliberate, unnecessary, useless, blatant, rude, boisterous, brazen, clamorous, coarse, glib, loud, noisy, obtrusive, offensive, raucous, vulgar, vociferous, slight(est)

prudence sober, solemn, collected, dispassionate, rational, wise, fiscal

psychology educational, clinical, child, forensic, developmental, applied, social, abnormal, comparative, environmental, community, experimental, behavioural, analytic, biological, physiological, cognitive, constitutional, dynamic

pub, pubs See also *restaurant* cosy, lively, bouncy, cheerful, gay, (in)decent, paltry, boisterous, rough, raunchy

public indulgent, (un)restrained, (in)coherent, insatiable, indifferent, complacent, indignant, furious, abusive, lay, general

publication, publications respectable,

influential, profitable, popular, hot,
officious, dominant, pre-eminent, glossy,
vanguard, fugitive, small-scale, faddy,
impious, underground, samizdat, transient,
ephemeral, dormant, obscure, short-lived,
general-interest, intellectual, liberal,
periodical, all-ad, official, professional

publicity sophisticated, subtle, glitzy,
splashy, intense, wide, worldwide,
prejudicial, bad, negative, adverse,
advance, front-page

publisher, publishers distinguished,
prestigious, prominent, well-established,
venerable, respectable, leading, enterprising,
shoestring, small, obscure, (dis)reputable,
greedy, sensation-orient(at)ed, educational,
avant-garde

pull-out, pull-outs See *withdrawal*

pulse, pulses (ir)regular, (ab)normal,
disordered, heavy, strong, quick, rapid,
fast, slow, small, weak, thready, faint,
mild, discernible, palpable, febrile,
femoral; electromagnetic

pump, pumps powerful, communal, hand,
variable, volumetric, centrifugal,
centripetal, axial-flow, air(-lift), hydraulic,
electromagnetic, diesel-powered

pun, puns witty, ingenious, tiresome

punctuality (un)usual, fiendish, fastidious,
meticulous, fierce, sinister, frightful,
clock-like, scrupulous, conscientious, rigid,
undeviating

punctuation (in)correct, chaotic, close(d),
open

punishment, punishments condign, apt,
(well-)deserved, (un)fair, meaningful,
fit(ting), (un)just, lenient, negligible,
merciful, light, mild, (un)avoidable,
(in)evitable, swift, sure, (in)adequate,
(in)effectual, (in)appropriate, painful,
searing, harsh, stiff, stern, drastic,
excessive, extreme, severe, heavy,
exemplary, deterrent, dire, bitter,
appalling, revolting, abhorrent, ignorant,
meaningless, bizarre, cruel, unusual,
unfeeling, merciless, ruthless, pitiless,
remorseless, heartless, relentless,
unrelenting, inhuman, brutal, degrading,
debasing, disgraceful, basic, vicarious,
physical, corporal, collective, capital,
disciplinary

pupil, pupils attentive, eager, enthusiastic,
docile, proficient, diligent, apt, clever,

talented, distinguished, painstaking,
advanced, prize, slow, dull, backward,
learning-disabled, unprepared, stupid,
unwilling, reluctant

puppy, puppies See *dog*

purchase, purchases booming, expensive,
big, large, largest-ever, extravagant,
reckless, outlandish, bargain-priced, blind,
sight-unseen, compulsory, mail-order,
over-the-counter, regular, one-off

purchaser, purchasers See *buyer*

purge, purges sweeping, large-scale,
widespread, comprehensive, internecine,
cultural, internal; cathartic

purity absolute, spotless, unsullied,
unalloyed, immaculate, speckless,
unblemished, unspotted, wonderful,
impossible, (un)questionable, tainted,
lifelong, pristine, environmental, spiritual,
genetic, racial, cultural

purple light, medium, deep, dark, dusky,
muted, lurid, pale, royal, violet, florid,
bright, tawny, rosy, reddish, bluish,
brownish, pinkish, blackish, preposterous,
luscious, iridescent, Tyrian

purpose, purposes rational, lofty, noble,
divine, pacific, constructive, useful,
meaningful, worthwhile, worthy, credible,
earnest, primary, fundamental, ultimate,
central, overriding, changeless, firm,
steady, definite, determined, fixed,
resolute, practical, express, specific,
special, particular, major, chief, set,
apparent, ostensible, mundane, utilitarian,
demonstrative, identifiable, deliberate,
secret, hidden, obscure, esoteric,
incomprehensible, frivolous, awesome,
corrupt, lethal, unworthy, dark, sinister,
evil, pretended, professed, avowed,
single-minded, sole, dual, double, twofold

purse, purses bulging, sling, bead,
crocodile-skin, leather, plastic, plump, fat,
lean, thin, empty, housekeeping; public,
privy

pursuit, pursuits gracious, lucrative,
all-consuming, excessive, exceptional,
long-term, perpetual, eternal, enthusiastic,
ardent, hot, frenzied, vigorous, close,
tireless, relentless, persistent, dogged,
aggressive, single-minded, here-and-now,
hazardous, useless, mad, reckless, trivial,
furtive, elusive, esoteric, cerebral,
intellectual, literary, physical, worldly

puzzle, puzzles baffling, exasperating, fascinating, intriguing, intractable, uncrackable, incredible, unbelievable, intricate, complex, unsuspected, unsolved, unlocked, untangled, classic, mathematical, abstract

pyramid, pyramids imposing, spectacular, enormous, huge, gigantic, great, tall, lofty, awesome, distinctive, storied, famed, famous, terraced, step, flat-topped, truncated, inverted, regular, volcanic, Egyptian, (Meso-)American

qualification, qualifications exceptional, unique, outstanding, excellent, nonpareil, pre-eminent, remarkable, scarce, superior, unusual, extraordinary, unequalled, requisite, mandatory, essential, (un)required, (un)necessary, dubious, questionable, controversial, suspect, academic

quality, qualities outstanding, shining, sterling, compelling, winning, staying, meretricious, unique, exquisite, significant, pre-eminent, special, unusual, unequalled, nonpareil, admirable, exceptional, extraordinary, excellent, remarkable, scarce, superior, commendable, estimable, impeccable, durable, ageless, prevailing, extra, inexorable, yeasty, unnerving, uncertain, poor, second-rate, substandard, questionable, latent, basic, essential, distinctive, uniform, consistent, correlative, connate, cognate, natural, magical, mystical, positive, negative, alien, unfamiliar, strange

quantity, quantities staggering, vast, immense, prodigious, copious, substantial, notable, appreciable, massive, huge, incredible, unbelievable, inexhaustible, fabulous, (im)measurable, overflowing, supernumerary, (in)appropriate, (un)satisfactory, (un)even, (un)known, (un)equal, minute, tiny, microscopic, affirmative, specific, unspecified

quarrel, quarrels irreconcilable, sordid, acrimonious, bitter, furious, violent, serious, unholy, outrageous, disgraceful, humiliating, heated, incendiary, nasty, fierce, angry, malignant, wicked, petty, messy, stormy, noisy, boozy, deadly, unrestrained, incessant, endless, open, incipient, momentary, negotiable, nationalistic, factious, fratricidal, marital, ethnic

quarrelling See *quarrel*

quarter, quarters (district; area) See *district* and *area*

quarters (source of information) See *source* (2)

queen, queens See also *king* elegant, matronly, titular, ruling, regnant; uncrowned

query, queries See *question* and *inquiry*

quest, quests See *search*, *investigation* and *pursuit*

question, questions (1: interrogative sentence) penetrating, searching, tantalizing, intriguing, thought-provoking, haunting, plain, direct, specific, pointed, well-chosen, pregnant, (ir)relevant, pertinent, legitimate, fair, knowledgeable, appropriate, ingenious, provocative, clever, sensible, rapid-fire, subtle, (in)consequential, immediate, refined, simple, incisive, crisp, biting, cutting, clear-cut, trenchant, acute, leading, key, basic, age-old, eternal, crucial, central, vital, pivotal, core, fundamental, big, dominant, momentous, delicate, widespread, blunt, point-blank, bald, irresistible, obtrusive, startling, puzzling, perplexing, thorny, ticklish, complex, enigmatical, aggressive, explosive, lingering, inevitable, unavoidable, inescapable, tough, hard, loaded, burning, casual, offhand, haphazard, random, double-barrelled, moot, intimate, (un)usual, resonant, peculiar, routine, persistent, insistent, impatient, catchy, (un)answerable, (in)direct, flat, uninflected, bleak, (in)valid, pugnacious, hostile, vapid, carping, contentious, arcane, sly, irrelevant, offensive, prying, superfluous, irresponsible, illegitimate, inappropriate, controversial, off-putting, steamy, senseless, meaningless, pointless, inconsequential, innocuous, stupid, trivial, inane, insidious, awkward, thoughtless, silly, agonizing, nerve-racking, nasty, puerile, childish, captious, tricky, catchy, crafty, Machiavellian, deceptive, treacherous, artless, misleading, rude, unsettling, upsetting, worrisome, troublesome, annoying, (still-)unanswered, true/false, semantic, intrinsic, extrinsic, rhetorical, numinous, pragmatic, trick, hypothetical, sophistical, rhetorical, theoretical, academic, analytical, open-ended, direct, indirect, multiple-choice, yes/no, previous

question, questions (2: problem) See also *problem* searing, exciting, burning, disquieting, upsetting, vexing, overriding, leading, fundamental, big, major, crucial, urgent, weighty, key, critical, all-important, pivotal, pertinent, thorny, problematic, knotty, grave, vexed, ever-present, serious, intense, delicate, prickly, momentous, endless, dubious, contentious, troublesome, intractable, touchy, live, simplistic, controversial, (wide-)open, arbitrable, (un)researchable, doubtful, specific, debatable, unresolved, unsettled, undecided, cosmic, moral, procedural

questioning (un)justifiable, (un)warranted, (un)acceptable, ceaseless, incessant, unceasing, unending, endless, intense, intensive, hard, fierce, forceful, threatening, heartless, merciless, ruthless, pitiless, relentless, unrelenting, obdurate, persistent, insistent, stubborn, hectic, determined, dogged, obstinate, pressing, untiring, routine, pre-trial

questionnaire, questionnaires
extensive, detailed, comprehensive, (un)reliable, (un)dependable, (un)trustworthy, confidential, self-administered

queue, queues unending, unceasing, humiliating, debasing, degrading, staggering, crazy, frustrated, restless, endless, ceaseless, incessant, disgraceful, patient

quiet, quietness See *tranquillity* and *silence*

quota, quotas high, low, stringent, strict, established, set, fixed, (self-)determined, discriminatory

quotation, quotations apt, felicitous, appropriate, fitting, congruous, pertinent, poignant, pointed, proper, relevant, suitable, clever, stimulating, piquant, pungent, copious, classic, quotable, colourful, illustrative, (in)direct, well-worn, well-known, trite, stale, hackneyed, banal, common(place), jejune, platitudinous, worn-out, vapid, inappropriate, incongruous, impertinent, irrelevant, unsuitable, spurious, fake, garbled, unattributed, misattributed

rabbit, rabbits furry, fluffy, lop-eared, silky-haired, feisty, excitable, irritable, frightened, quiet, caged, wild, tame, domestic, cotton-tail, pet, marauding

race, races (1: a contest) challenging, legendary, fast, tight, close, endless, never-ending, neck-and-neck, gruelling, dizzying, tough, marathon, frantic, frenetic, hectic, feverish, zealous, fevered, desperate, ill-fated, (un)scheduled, flat, competitive, opening, closing, cross-country; Presidential, gubernatorial

race, races (2: a group of people with similar ancestry) chosen, superior, super, pure, (un)dignified, sturdy, dominant, feuding, shifting, shiftless, vague, mysterious, inferior, impure, human, ancestral, white, black, yellow, Negro

racer, racers See also *athlete* darting, enthusiastic, ardent, avid, excited, feverish, ecstatic, frantic, frenzied, zealous, zestful, active, novice

racing See *race* (1)

racism polite, subtle, blatant, obvious, apparent, real, hidden, (sub)conscious, implicit, explicit, latent, unquestionable, undeniable, deep, harsh, violent, brutal, callous, cruel, emotionless, insensitive, unfeeling, cold-hearted, snarling, poisonous, destructive, pernicious, divisive, rampant, widespread, systematic, endemic, institutional

racist, racists unequivocal, unfeeling, bull-necked, brutal, callous, cruel, emotionless, insensitive, cold-hearted, (im)polite

raconteur, raconteurs entertaining, amusing, charming, exuberant, enthusiastic, ecstatic, spontaneous, avid, natural, unrestrained, exquisite, accomplished, ingenious, brilliant, fluent, eloquent, animated, lively, delightful, tireless, irrepressible, inexhaustible, compulsive, versatile

radiation diffuse, intense, coherent, residual, harmful, lethal, low-level, high-level, high-energy, low-intensity, shortwave, thermal, visible, fossil, ultraviolet, infrared, solar, electromagnetic, natural, nuclear

radical, radicals See *extremist*

radio, radios (1: radio set) pocket-size, suitcase-size, (in)operative, crackly, old-fashioned, portable, digital, shortwave, all-wave, high-frequency, AM, FM, battery(-powered), transistor, two-way, stereophonic

radio, radios (2: radio transmitting station) brassy, noisy, state-run, amateur, ham, clandestine, commercial

rage, rages See also *anger* towering, overwhelming, consuming, passionate, (steam-)heated, intense, explosive, violent, furious, mad, maniacal, murderous, helpless, frantic, hysterical, frenzied, uncontrollable, ungovernable, inextinguishable, implacable, monumental, unceasing, unbounded, relentless, unrelenting, senseless, conclusive, pent-up, flaming, apoplectic, liverish, unheeding, unwarranted, blind, jealous, diabolical, stentorian, inarticulate, speechless, petty, infantile, cold, white, impotent, idle, bewildered, naked, silent, smouldering, momentary, drunken, Olympian; steroid

raid, raids roaring, lightning, wide-ranging, massive, broad, intense, heavy, flagrant, audacious, awful, ghastly, wicked, vicious, barbarous, barbaric, punitive, sporadic, abortive, impending, nocturnal, night, nightly, daybreak, pre-dawn, bombing, strafing, air, hit-and-run, suicide, commando, helicopter-borne, cross-border, amphibious, kamikaze

rail, rails elaborate, rusty, third, light

railing, railings See *rail*

railway, railroad transcontinental, inter-city, one-track, single-track, double-track, narrow-gauge, elevated, bankrupt, cable, funicular, underground, rack(-and-pinion); miniature, model

rain, rains hissing, rattling, whispering, hammering, pelting, pouring, slashing, soaking, raking, stinging, trickling, life-sustaining, nourishing, refreshing, (un)welcome, (un)timely, (un)favourable, (un)kindly, (in)temperate, well-spaced, gentle, fine, thin, slight, light, soft, warm, beady, feathery, heavy, hard, sharp, generous, copious, plump, teeming, mountainous, fertile, abundant, ample, plentiful, fruitful, wild, dreary, grey, persistent, continual, incessant, (un)steady, perpetual, periodic, occasional, intermittent, (in)frequent, scattered, tentative, freakish, chancy, uncertain, spotty, desultory, (un)predictable, thundery, thunderous, tempestuous, gusty, torrential, severe, vigorous, violent, intense, incredible, unbelievable, niggling, unrelenting, relentless, heartless, pitiless, ruthless, merciless, unmerciful, wind-swept, wind-driven, squally, chilly, cold, ice, frozen, freezing, chilling, icy, steamy, misty, drizzly, sparkling, humid, additional, imminent, impending, sudden, measurable, recordable, (ab)normal, above-normal, subnormal, below-normal, (below-)average, moderate, scant(y), minimum, brief, seasonal, summery, cyclonic, acid, primordial, monsoon; black

rainbow, rainbows imposing, striking, flashing, shining, glittering, glowing, gleaming, sparkling, glistening, twinkling, dazzling, resplendent, brilliant, magnificent, majestic, marvellous, spectacular, fantastic, splendid, beautiful, ephemeral, special, daytime, lunar, primary, secondary

raincoat, raincoats See also *coat*
waterproof, water-repellent, water-resistant, showerproof, plastic, dirty

rainfall See *rain*

rake, rakes (an immoral man) dissipated, dissolute, extravagant, debauched, degenerate, depraved, shameless

rally, rallies dazzling, imposing, peaceful, benign, massive, monster, huge, torch-light, colourful, splendid, spectacular, enthusiastic, noisy, bitter, clandestine, secret, (un)lawful, (il)legal, (well-)organized, open-air, adulatory, commemorative, protest

rambling, ramblings demented, mad, insane, deranged, crazed, crazy, idiotic, wild, daft

ramification, ramifications (consequence) See *consequence*

ranch, ranches ostentatious, showy, pretentious, large, cattle

rancour See *hate*

range (extent) (un)limited, endless, unending, wide, narrow, bewildering,

amazing, dazzling, astounding, baffling, unequalled, eclectic

rank, ranks exalted, high, first, queenly, subordinate, permanent, temporary, military, social, substantive; serried

ransom, ransoms enormous, large, huge, immense, staggering, substantial, unreasonable

rape, rapes cruel, barbaric, brutal, savage, gory, abhorrent, repugnant, inhuman, murderous, pitiless, heartless, merciless, remorseless, ruthless, relentless, unrelenting, vicious, violent, forcible, statutory, gang, multiple, serial, random, homosexual, alleged; ecological, economic

rapidity See *speed*

rapids foaming, turbulent, thunderous, tumultuous, stormy, violent, wild, dangerous, murderous, treacherous, impassable, mighty, nasty, white-water

rarity extreme, increasing, comparative

rascal, rascals wicked, mendacious, mendicant, uncaring, graceless, unprincipled, conscienceless, inveterate, confirmed, unmitigated, damned, thorough, absolute, out-and-out, grasping, covetous, avaricious, unscrupulous, unnatural, treacherous, deceitful, vicious, unconscionable, sly, vagrant, debauched, degenerate, depraved, shameless

rate, rates whopping, staggering, alarming, hair-raising, inflated, high(er-than-expected), record-high, sky-high, extortionate, flash-flood, exorbitant, prodigious, phenomenal, unimagined, striking, amazing, usurious, ruinous, significant, unprecedented, incredible, unbelievable, steep, floating, prevailing, fluctuating, varying, variable, volatile, current, effective, seasonal, long-term, short-term, adjustable, sustained, (un)stable, (in)consistent, flat, uniform, steady, constant, sedate, fixed, (near-)static, progressive, differential, (in)sufficient, remarkable, appealing, attractive, competitive, (un)favourable, (un)reasonable, (un)healthy, realistic, irresistible, cheap, concessionary, modest, low, negligible, puny, microscopic, anaemic, basic, discount, off-season, trendsetting, going, official, prime; metabolic

rating, ratings high, low, bottom-drawer, scholastic

ration, rations whopping, staggering, shocking, hefty, (in)adequate, (in)appropriate, (in)sufficient, (dis)proportionate, extra, (un)equal, (un)fair, (un)just, short, scanty, meagre, minimal, double, (un)due

rationale, rationalization elaborate, satisfying, sound, reasonable, (un)substantial, (im)plausible, (un)convincing, (un)satisfactory, (in)valid, convolute(d), flimsy, limp, sleazy, feeble, weak, fragile, puerile, shallow, shaky, superficial, ultimate, ideological

rationing See also *ration* stringent, voluntary, compulsory, partial, country-wide

ray, rays See also *light* fierce, harmful, harmless, warm, soft, mellow, luminous, blue, green, (ultra)violet, actinic, positive, incident, solar, cosmic; vascular

reaction, reactions reassuring, (un)enthusiastic, (un)sympathetic, (un)healthy, (in)appropriate, (un)predictable, restrained, mild, defensive, understandable, thoughtful, loud, extreme, strong, powerful, forceful, acute, intense, severe, overwhelming, violent, heated, fiery, fierce, harsh, ferocious, heavy-handed, excessive, quick, swift, immediate, instant, slow, growing, spontaneous, cautious, hesitant, unsure, sceptical, (un)common, universal, revealing, astonishing, astounding, unbelievable, incredible, unequivocal, undesirable, indignant, furious, angry, chilly, icy, cool, lukewarm, indifferent, blasé, debilitating, stinging, life-threatening, fatal, dangerous, explosive, adverse, runaway, hostile, muted, giddy, knee-jerk, reflex, initial, positive, negative, impulse, instinctive, nuclear, chemical, emotional, allergic, dark, light

reactionary, reactionaries extreme, odd, relentless, die-hard

reactor, reactors powerful, fast, (in)operable, mock-up, commercial, civilian, atomic, nuclear(-power)

reader, readers compulsive, avid, voracious, omnivorous, devouring, wide, insatiable, ravenous, eager, ardent, enthusiastic, zealous, incessant, constant, habitual, inveterate, indefatigable, untiring, diligent, devoted, absorbed, ruminant, knowledgeable, (un)informed, selective, eclectic(al), discerning, judicious, (in)discriminate, (in)discriminating, (un)critical, (in)attentive, alert, observant, (un)intelligent, unlettered, slow(ish), hasty, circumspect, tolerant, expressive, credulous, unilingual, bilingual, general, armchair

reading extensive, immense, wide, close, thorough, unceasing, ceaseless, endless, unending, constant, undisturbed, heavy, serious, solemn, glum, instructive, diligent, busy, assiduous, omnivorous, worthwhile, amusing, fascinating, curious, pleasant, agreeable, self-indulgent, compelling, quiet, out-of-the-way, esoteric, racy, miscellaneous, (un)methodical, (un)interesting, (un)systematic, (in)discriminate, cursory, superficial, hasty, desultory, dull, insipid, aimless, intermittent, light, leisurely, entertaining, recreational, compulsory, obligatory, study-type, collateral, remedial, developmental, public, silent, oral, bedtime; systolic, diastolic

realism profound, gritty, plucky, spirited, sabulous, vibrant, compelling, animated, vigorous, lively, oscillating, shivering, utter, stark, graphic

realist, realists sober(-minded), serious, solemn, devout

reality, realities sober(ing), solid, heady, stern, harsh, grim, inexorable, unrelenting, relentless, merciless, pitiless, heartless, ruthless, inflexible, sombre, inescapable, sordid, cold, stark, unvarnished, unmistakable, uncontestable, incontestable, dull, terrible, shocking, bleak, desolate, gritty, awful, ugly, unwelcome, unpleasant, unbearable, painful, cruel, brutal, brutish, grisly, sad, sham, new, shining, enduring, elusive, sleazy, overwhelming, overpowering, distorted, surface, thin, substantial, underlying, basic, fundamental, practical, tangible, familiar, mundane, fantastic, empirical, absolute, subjective, objective, transcendental, artistic

realization growing, sobering, stunning, crushing, devastating, startling, astounding, poignant, belated

realm, realms timeless, ageless, eternal, everlasting, far-flung, bizarre, fantastic, fictitious, mythical, allegorical, anecdotal, imaginary, visionary, legendary, parabolical, subterranean

reason, reasons (im)proper, (un)acceptable, sound, subtle, good, cogent, valid, airtight, (un)convincing, (im)plausible, (un)believable, (in)credible, substantial, solid, real, true, creditable, understandable, (ir)rational, powerful, (il)legitimate, perspicacious, (il)logical, sensible, competent, (in)adequate, (un)justifiable, compelling, pressing, provocative, (in)sufficient, discerning, ample, prevalent, far-reaching, fundamental, leading, classic, chief, main, basic, prime, primal, primary, foremost, special, specific, (un)specified, actual, exact, particular, practical, clear(-sighted), obvious, apparent, ostensible, tangible, objective, earthly, (un)identifiable, (un)clear, inexplicable, unaccountable, undisclosed, diverse, possible, underlying, big, built-in, sweet, altruistic, adverse, obscure, awkward, petty, ridiculous, outrageous, murky, cold, invalid, phon(e)y, zany, crazy, urgent, private, personal, tactical

reasoning solid, substantial, (un)sound, crisp, clear, acute, sharp, close, accurate, precise, (il)logical, keen, (in)correct, right, (un)convincing, (im)plausible, specious, sophistic, fallacious, erroneous, inconsequent, perverse, wrong, faulty, false, flawed, bad, tortuous, circular, roundabout, devious, convoluted, indirect, far-fetched, blind, vicious, abstruse, abstract, discursive, analytical, hypothetical, heuristic, inductive, deductive, judicial, syllogistic

rebel, rebels zealous, strident, authentic, dedicated, bona fide, indomitable, intransigent, hard-core, desperate, uncontrollable, out-and-out, unruly, tough, wild, intractable, irreconcilable, radical, persistent, menacing, unyielding, uncompromising, unrepentant, obstinate, stubborn, impetuous, violent, well-armed, retreating, arch, chief, principal, secessionist, anti-government

rebellion, rebellions glorious, fruitful, dramatic, bloodless, open, frank, undisguised, plain, downright, popular, widespread, mass, full-blown, full-scale, broad, perpetual, concerted, spontaneous, growing, failing, (un)controllable, tumultuous, bloody, (non-)violent, barren, futile, fruitless, abortive, (un)successful, armed, military, internal, counter-revolutionary, separatist, secessionist, ethnic, labour, tribal, Jacobite

rebuke, rebukes diplomatic, kindly, smart, mild, slight, staid, gratuitous, scathing, vigorous, severe, harsh, sharp, grave, caustic, hurtful, scalding, truculent, virulent, pungent, vitriolic, foul, vituperative, stinging, indignant, savage, resounding, scornful, contemptuous, (un)deserved, unjustified, (un)qualified

reception (1: the act of receiving) splendid, favourable, encouraging, enthusiastic, immense, hospitable, emotional, warm, cordial, flattering, tumultuous, delirious, festive, cautious, cool, cold, chilly, frigid, frosty, lukewarm, unfavourable, indifferent, restrained, sour, mixed, hostile, rowdy, rocky, angry

reception, receptions (2: social gathering) glittering, bubbly, elegant, beautiful, ceremonious, lavish, occasional, celebratory, (in)formal, full-dress, diplomatic, civic, invitation-only

recession, recessions shallow, mild, moderate, brief, short, temporary, minor, major, full-scale, full-fledged, intense, painful, persistent, (decade-)long, endless, unending, bad, severe, harsh, deep, far-reaching, biting, crushing, devastating, turbulent, costly, (un)avoidable, (in)evitable, outright, widespread, economy-wide, global, world(wide), current, recent, forecast, technical

recipe, recipes subtle, distinctive, original, detailed, stimulating, exciting, intriguing, favourite, tried, precious, antique, delicious, tasty, (taste-)tempting, lip-smacking, mouthwatering, stunning, straightforward, short-cut, simple(-and-quick), quick(-and-easy), easy, fail-safe, trouble-free, make-ahead, potent, versatile, (un)imaginative, (un)healthy, standard, different, exotic, tricky, complicated, untried, natural, nutritional, low-fat, fat-laden, gourmet, secret, indigenous, family

recipient, recipients (un)willing,
potential, (un)likely, needy, desperate,
destitute

reciprocity common, equal, instantaneous,
immediate

recital, recitals glorious, spirited,
vivacious, lively, rhapsodic, unique, dull,
insipid, vapid, spiritless, lifeless, jejune

recitation, recitations spirited, vivacious,
glorious, lively, spiritless, lifeless, jejune,
vapid, insipid, dull, monotonous,
singsong

recluse, recluses unsociable, confirmed,
determined, solitary, withdrawn, total,
virtual, cloistered, ascetic, hermitical,
monastic

recognition welcome, astute, shrewd,
substantial, wide, quick, instant,
immediate, outright, just, overdue,
conspicuous, implicit, explicit, grim,
belated, eventual, premature, undreamt-of,
reciprocal, public, formal, official, legal,
diplomatic, symbolic; character

recollection, recollections See *memory*
(1)

recommendation, recommendations
glowing, enthusiastic, warm, excellent,
significant, useful, constructive,
no-nonsense, dramatic, contentious,
cautious, (non-)binding, unmodified,
unaltered, unadopted, specific

reconciliation, reconciliations touching,
emotional, dramatic, impassioned, excited,
passionate, lasting, hopeful, brief,
short-lived, fragile, hasty, speedy, melting,
temporary, national

record, records (1: document; evidence)
unfailing, infallible, flawless, impeccable,
unblemished, spotless, exemplary, sterling,
clean, remarkable, insightful, intriguing,
splendid, respectable, honourable,
venerable, enviable, coveted, excellent,
terrific, brilliant, solid, impressive,
(un)distinguished, outstanding,
commendable, unbeaten, unbroken,
unmatched, unsurpassed, exceptional,
extraordinary, edifying, lucid, priceless,
minute, thorough, meticulous, authentic,
reliable, undisputed, creditable,
(in)accurate, (in)adequate, erroneous,
detailed, extensive, lengthy, comprehensive,
exacting, up-to-date, (un)known, surviving,
missing, fraudulent, bootleg, secret, hazy,

heady, fragmentary, spotty, patchy,
unexceptional, terrible, bad, atrocious,
disgraceful, tainted, oblique, grim, dismal,
bleak, reckless, grisly, abysmal, official,
documentary, photographic, pictorial,
mnemonic, archaeological, historical,
academic, court, congressional, criminal,
confidential, baptismal, burial, memorial;
all-time

record, records (2: disc) vinyl,
enterprising, (un)equivocal, (un)breakable,
(un)scratched, single, long-playing,
original, duplicate, bootleg, debut

recovery speedy, rapid, quick, full,
complete, vigorous, strong, robust,
powerful, solid, incredible, unbelievable,
fantastic, magnificent, wonderful, amazing,
surprising, astonishing, astounding,
remarkable, terrific, spectacular,
(un)eventful, true, (in)significant,
sustained, lasting, resilient, fortunate,
miraculous, providential, abrupt,
spontaneous, slow, sluggish, short-lived,
spotty, anaemic, lengthy, costly

recreation, recreations exhilarating,
congenial, convivial, healthy, healthful,
wholesome, salutary, pleasant, enjoyable,
exciting, stirring, thrilling, innocent,
favourite, favoured, popular, fashionable,
year-round, inexpensive, low-cost, active,
onerous, demanding, taxing, passive,
trivial, frivolous, laid-back, outdoor,
indoor

recruit, recruits (well-)trained, able,
accomplished, adept, capable,
(in)experienced, (highly-)skilled, unskilled,
untrained, raw, latest, military

rectitude model, exemplary, archetypal
(archetypical), paradigmatic, typical,
Victorian

recuperation See *recovery*

recurrence, recurrences active, constant,
periodic, fatalistic

red dazzling, gleaming, glaring, throbbing,
flaming, gay, lively, vivid, bold, brilliant,
lurid, furious, angry, hectic, solid, golden,
orangeish, scarlet, rose, floral, cherry,
pinkish, purplish, bluish, yellowish, bright,
deep, cardinal, racy, coppery, chrome,
pomegranate, cerise, raspberry, moderate,
brick(y), wine, molten, light, medium,
dark, dull, opaque, muted, pale, rusty,
smoky, sensuous, raunchy, blood,

fire-engine, Turkey, Venetian, Chinese, Indian, Congo, Pompeiian

reduction sensible, judicious, wise, fair, (in)tolerable, (in)appropriate, (un)reasonable, (un)acceptable, (in)sufficient, permissible, orderly, lasting, permanent, temporary, gradual, progressive, pre-emptive, massive, considerable, dramatic, appreciable, substantial, gigantic, slashing, drastic, harsh, radical, severe, devastating, marked, (in)significant, (in)visible, major, minor

reef, reefs teeming, soft, gentle, shallow(-water), small, massive, enormous, spectacular, jagged, hard, sharp, blunt, knobby, treacherous, dangerous, abrasive, long, narrow, unassailable, artificial, coral, sandstone, plunging, protective, productive, precious, fish-rich, surf-fringed, upthrust, hidden, subdued, submerged, sunken, bioluminescent, gorgonian, offshore, barrier

re-examination, re-examinations See *examination* (2)

reference, references (allusion) discerning, tantalizing, apt, laudatory, careful, sophisticated, (in)discreet, clear, apparent, unmistakable, obvious, overt, (in)direct, explicit, implicit, oblique, casual, passing, chance, random, incidental, scanty, scattered, innumerable, unpredictable, unthinking, vague, obscure, meaningless, furtive, sly, esoteric, ironic, facetious, gratuitous, unjustified, injurious, acid, catty, mean, callous, unfeeling, insensitive, spiteful, derogatory, derisive, sneering, imprudent, lukewarm, tongue-in-cheek, intended, unconcealed, veiled, cross, contemporary, topical, anecdotal, literary, historical, nostalgic

reference book, reference work See also *book* authoritative, definitive, comprehensive, exhaustive, respectable, valuable, useful, ultimate, impeccable, prized, (un)dependable, (un)reliable, standard, topical, genealogical

referendum, referendums (referenda) crucial, decisive, compulsory, optional, (non-)binding, statutory, constitutional, national

reflection, reflections (1: a serious thought; meditation) pleasant, melancholy, gloomy, sad, serious, sombre, silent, quiet, whimsical, naïve, mordant, caustic, biting, obscure, philosophical

reflection, reflections (2: an image of anything in a mirror or in water) vivid, visible, contorted, inverted, intorted, unsteady, pale, partial

reform, reforms promising, far-reaching, sweeping, extensive, meaningful, well-intentioned, genuine, real, salutary, beneficial, peaceful, bold, unstoppable, key, basic, fundamental, solid, radical, drastic, tough, permanent, total, revolutionary, (un)limited, (un)successful, (in)effective, (in)significant, moderate, innocuous, aggressive, incremental, unimaginable, speedy, rapid, gradual, progressive, piecemeal, cautious, impending, recent, (over)due, half-hearted, lagging, misguided, doomed, putative, puritanical, reorganizational, internal, social, legislative, agrarian, financial, economic, tax, parliamentary, religious, political, grass-roots

reformer, reformers innovative, inventive, creative, high-minded, starry-eyed, visionary, bright, determined, resolute, energetic, active, aggressive, dynamic, high-powered, vigorous, enthusiastic, industrious, zealous, keen, radical, (un)reasonable, fanatical, militant, rabid

refuge, refuges See *retreat* (2)

refugee, refugees bona fide, (non-)genuine, real, proven, undisputed, permanent, temporary, would-be, pouring, starving, starved, poverty-stricken, homeless, stateless, penniless, destitute, desperate, helpless, tired, bedraggled, unhappy, fake, phon(e)y, bogus, sham, dubious, (un)settled, unwanted, economic, religious, political

refusal, refusals understandable, clear-headed, polite, long-standing, steadfast, adamant, obdurate, stubborn, obstinate, unyielding, unbending, firm, consistent, unmistakable, inexorable, inflexible, staunch, mulish, stony, calculated, stolid, callous, flat, stern, tart, outspoken, blunt, passive, point-blank, outright, downright, absolute, overwhelming, obtuse, (un)qualified, indignant, puckish, haughty, vaunted, frigid, perverse

regard affectionate, respectful, special, courteous, exalted, high, low, precocious

regime, regimes (1: a government or social system) (un)stable, (in)secure, long-lived, unbroken, (il)legitimate, liberal, (un)democratic, tough, theocratic, autocratic, dictatorial, totalitarian, authoritarian, fascist, hard-line, repressive, hard-pressed, iron-fist, martial-law, spartan, ascetic, austere, non-democratic, restrictive, merciless, ruthless, bloody, brutal, murderous, rigid, secretive, dubious, corrupt, decadent, insecure, tottering, expiring, eccentric, radical, unsavoury, distasteful, sleazy, puppet, defunct, pluralistic, nationalistic, secular, military, one-party, centralist, fascist(-type), Marxist, communist, socialist, apartheid, racist, caretaker

regime, regimes (2: regimen; systematic course of therapy) punishing, unrelenting, ascetic, intense, intensive, extreme, strict, severe, tedious, boring, dreary, monotonous, tiresome, wearisome, comprehensive, long, temporary, daily, dietary

regimen, regimens See *regime* (2)

region, regions healthful, livable, peaceable, calm, (un)stable, vibrant, dynamic, confident, autonomous, exotic, fascinating, intriguing, expensive, prosperous, flourishing, fertile, privileged, temperate, vegetated, wooded, scenic, self-assured, developed, immense, vast, faraway, remote, far-flung, outlying, isolated, interior, internal, distinct, diverse, homogeneous, peripheral, rolling, highland, mountainous, mountain-girt, hilly, coastal, sandy, treeless, tundra, barren, arid, swampy, insurgent, secessionist, breakaway, embattled, contested, tumultuous, strife-prone, rebellious, troubled, riot-torn, strife-torn, restive, restless, unruly, troubling, volatile, fragile, famine-threatened, drought-stricken, drought-ridden, distressed, depressed, sullen, drab, bleak, dreary, gaunt, desolate, melancholy, forlorn, hopeless, unhealthful, unhealthy, forbidding, formidable, inaccessible, impenetrable, little-known, roadless, trackless, rugged, backward, primitive, sleepy, wild, uncivilized, unexplored, uninhabited, uncultivated, undeveloped, underdeveloped, underprivileged, disadvantaged, poor, rainy, cold, arctic, (peri)glacial, tropical, pelagic, natural, wild(erness), ecological, biological, zoographic, geographic(al), celestial, spatial (spacial), infernal, agricultural, industrial, metropolitan, economic, cultural, historical, political, administrative

regret, regrets genuine, honest, sincere, warm, undoubted, deep, sharp, poignant, moving, touching, pungent, profound, piercing, deepfelt, intense, petulant, sombre, angry, wistful, painful, vain, mild, lingering, eternal, infinite

regularity unfailing, clockwork, methodical, unbroken, smooth, uninterrupted, business-like, stern, strict, austere, harsh, inflexible, relentless, unrelenting, rigid, unyielding, sterile, bland, boring, monotonous, dizzying, mechanical

regulation, regulations progressive, (un)necessary, (in)effective, (in)adequate, (un)fair, unbending, unyielding, demanding, unrelenting, relentless, ruthless, stringent, rigid, severe, strict, austere, tight, tough, harsh, oppressive, onerous, (in)flexible, lax, feeble, obsolete, burdensome, suffocating, conflicting, (over-)zealous, petty, tangled, bureaucratic, comprehensive, standing, punitive, safety, environmental, emergency

rehabilitation See *recovery*

rehearsal, rehearsals conscientious, meticulous, scrupulous, fastidious, strict, painstaking, punctilious, careful, encouraging, first, final, dress, ceremonial, theatrical, dramatic, operatic, orchestral

reign, reigns splendid, lustrous, glorious, shining, radiant, brilliant, benevolent, peaceful, (un)distinguished, (un)successful, tenebrous, turbulent, bloody, genocidal, tyrannical, long, clouded, father-to-son

reinforcement, reinforcements heavy, bulky, massive, weighty, adequate, belated

rejection, rejections clear(-headed), understandable, massive, unanimous, overwhelming, strong, forceful, fundamental, stern, categorical, definitive, unequivocal, blunt, firm, inflexible, unqualified, inexorable, explicit, (point-)blank, outright, downright, flat, complete, unyielding, unbending, obdurate, adamant, stubborn, obstinate, defiant, persistent, callous, stinging, haughty, arrogant, contemptuous, harsh, curt, brusque, bluff, chill, initial, implicit, calculated, social

relapse, relapses See *setback*

relation, relations (1: connection) amiable, amicable, friendly, cordial, sympathetic, warm, good, excellent, close-knit, special, peaceful, harmonious, straightforward, (un)stable, uneasy, uneven, shaky, fragile, uncertain, stiff, tense, strained, testy, sour, hostile, chaotic, rocky, frosty, icy, chilly, frigid, frozen, cool, unnatural, ambiguous, abysmal, precarious, dubious, phon(e)y, (long-)troubled, complicated, tangled, confused, intricate, bilateral, parental, public, trade, industrial, diplomatic, labour, foreign, business; extramarital, sexual; spatial(spacial), spatiotemporal

relation, relations (2: relative) beloved, illustrious, distinguished, impressive, near, close, distant, remote, not-too-distant, (non-)blood, collateral, lineal, conjugal, biological, common-law

relationship, relationships rewarding, appealing, touching, loving, caring, satisfying, understanding, sustaining, enduring, long-standing, (long-)lasting, lifetime, long-term, idyllic, blissful, meaningful, beneficent, harmonious, unique, productive, fruitful, vibrant, successful, workable, real, proud, positive, easy, healthy, emotion-laden, unshak(e)able, powerful, firm, supportive, unrivalrous, civilized, cosy, warm, (un)friendly, good, viable, intense, special, direct, clear-cut, close, deep, (un)stable, delicate, intimate, tight, limited, short(-term), continuous, (ab)normal, (un)conventional, fledgling, budding, crucial, essential, pivotal, complex, intricate, enigmatic, puzzling, bewildering, perplexing, uncanny, mysterious, weird, strange, odd, uneasy, arm's-length, cool, chilly, dull, humourless, antagonistic, hostile, stagnant, prickly, tempestuous, stormy, rocky, obsessive, tumultuous, uneven, casual, superficial, fragile, kinky, frizzy, uninspired, unproductive, barren, painful, unhealthy, problematic, destructive, disastrous, distrustful, loveless, abusive, rivalrous, clandestine, illicit, unfulfilled, unconsummated, unresolved,

complicated, complex, convoluted, twisted, nominal, distant, converse, inverse, equal, one-sided, (inter)personal, bilateral, mutual, reciprocal, ritual, complementary, paternal, sibling, symbiotic, exclusive, marital, conjugal, spousal, monogamous, polygamous, bigamous, common-law, amoral, adulterous, consensual, same-sex, physical, sexual, emotional, platonic, mystical, financial, trading, working, long-distance, sado-masochistic; cause-and-effect, statistical

relative, relatives See *relation* (2)

relaxation fascinating, welcome, complete, total, easy, enjoyable, delightful, happy, pleasant, blissful, meditative, physical

release (un)conditional, imminent, immediate, eventual, impending, ultimate, (un)likely, (im)probable, (un)certain, controversial, doubtful, questionable

reliability utter, absolute, unqualified, complete, unequalled, unprecedented, questionable

reliance See *dependence*

relic, relics precious, (in)valuable, rare, priceless, momentous, important, significant, unparalleled, remarkable, splendid, magnificent, wonderful, surviving, identifiable, evocative, poignant, fusty, miraculous, sacred, shamanistic, prehistoric

relief beautiful, buoyant, sweet, quiet, welcome, blessed, inexpressible, deep, profound, appreciable, immense, enormous, big, vast, substantial, total, widespread, (un)qualified, effective, intense, fast, speedy, instant, on-the-spot, explosive, desperate, apparent, marked, (long-)lasting, permanent, short-lived, temporary, momentary, transient, little, high, charitable, secure; public, outdoor, indoor, pecuniary, financial; physical, symptomatic

religion, religions (in)tolerant, confident, natural, (pre)dominant, traditional, ancient, established, long-gone, prehistoric, major, new(-age), vital, vibrant, austere, exacting, demanding, rigid, complex, arcane, uncompromising, secretive, experimental, pagan, animist, ancestral, organized, state, Catholic, Protestant, Orthodox, Muslim, Hindu, Jewish,

Confucian, Buddhist, Shinto, Taoist
reluctance despondent, disheartened,
dejected, dispirited, cautious,
understandable, (in)comprehensible,
(un)usual, (ab)normal, much, considerable,
extraordinary, utmost, obvious, distinct,
feigned, stupid, obstinate, mulish, initial
remains sacred, multitudinous, intact,
fragmentary, tattered, shattered, tumbling,
mouldering, crumbly, rickety, fragile, frail,
feeble, unidentified, tangled, dilapidated,
tangible, earthly, ancestral, skeletal,
human, archaeological; siliceous
remark, remarks potent, salty, facetious,
sincere, tactful, relevant, judicious,
inoffensive, politic, considerate, significant,
penetrating, felicitous, clever, ingenuous,
artless, kind, trenchant, apropos,
(im)proper, (in)appropriate, fitting,
suitable, apt, germane, opportune,
well-timed, wise, self-revelatory,
interesting, pointed, perceptive, pithy,
witty, provocative, suggestive,
good-humoured, innocuous, sensible,
meaningful, discerning, knowing,
profound, piquant, stimulating, pertinent,
trustworthy, charitable, colourful,
complimentary, happy, discreet, wise,
(im)prudent, revealing, unpremeditated,
unstudied, premature, queer, strange, odd,
cryptic, puzzling, enigmatical, inaudible,
droll, (un)intentional, parenthetic(al),
humorous, teasing, jocular, staccato,
waggish, cryptic, ad-lib, (un)intelligible,
rueful, apposite, incidental, casual,
desultory, random, chatty, idle, critical,
impetuous, trite, stock, blunt, surly,
obnoxious, hurtful, disagreeable,
disobliging, stinging, biting, deprecating,
cutting, insulting, humiliating, scathing,
jeering, exasperating, aggressive, hostile,
truculent, belligerent, quarrelsome, bizarre,
snide, insincere, acid, caustic, banal,
obvious, artificial, sarcastic, tart, clumsy,
jejune, cynical, flippant, fatuous,
frivolous, irrelevant, injudicious, witless,
inept, misguided, indelicate, thoughtless,
inconsequent(ial), inconsiderate, wry,
impertinent, hurtful, offensive, impudent,
pungent, insolent, uncouth, vague, rude,
bland, puerile, sly, insinuating, tangent,
invidious, odious, playful, saucy,
contemptuous, disrespectful, unhappy,

infelicitous, cruel, unsolicited, uncalled-for,
unnecessary, improper, nasty, cheap,
inane, irresponsible, haphazard, ill-timed,
hurried, imbecile, foolish, stupid, inane,
silly, senseless, trivial, ignorant,
meaningless, pointless, inapt, indiscreet,
tactless, imprudent, unwise, indelicate,
testy, exasperated, ill-humoured, vapid,
flat, uninteresting, naïve, nonsensical,
obtuse, outrageous, platitudinous,
unfortunate, unkind, violent, careless,
ill-considered, unconsidered, bad-tempered,
grim, mean, crusty, crabbed, harsh,
extraneous, impersonal, indefensible,
inexcusable, inopportune, ambiguous,
double-barrelled, double-edged, slanderous,
libellous, derogatory, untrustworthy,
catastrophic, stereotyped, commonplace,
uncharitable, vacuous, catty, spiteful,
flattering, off-colour, scurrilous, shocking,
unprintable, irreverent, vulgar,
objectionable, lewd, unchaste, scatological,
salacious, racist, sexist, homophobic,
impromptu, off-the-cuff, extemporaneous,
interrogatory, quotable, preliminary,
personal, inaugural
remedy, remedies (un)safe, (in)effective,
(in)efficacious, (in)effectual, unfailing,
infallible, active, potent, powerful, drastic,
sure, magical, operative, sovereign,
traditional, ancient, (age-)old, old-time,
time-honoured, new, instant, immediate,
specific, internal, external, (in)expensive,
desperate, hurtful, dubious, inoperative,
superficial, temporary, secret, quack,
occult, local, topical, herbal, folk,
venereal, restorative, patent, hom(o)eopathic
reminder, reminders gentle, (un)pleasant,
pleasing, significant, tangible, ever-present,
constant, perpetual, once-in-a-while,
occasional, pointed, sharp, compelling,
stunning, uncomfortable, grim, startling,
chilling, sobering, poignant, painful,
pitiful, sore, dire, humbling, stark, stern,
bleak, ominous, blunt, powerful, forceful,
harsh, agonizing, distressing, excruciating,
unbearable, vexatious, scary, frightening,
ghastly, haunting, grotesque, eerie, strange,
well-timed, (in)direct, graphic, visible,
symbolic
reminiscences See *memory* (1)
remnant, remnants sole, single, only, one,
scattered

remorse agonizing, afflicting, excruciating, deep, genuine, apparent, conspicuous, ostensible, seeming, unmistakable, visible, painful, burdensome, insufferable, intolerable, unbearable, unwarranted

remoteness formidable, sequestered, secluded, withdrawn, Olympian

removal, removals forcible, voluntary

remuneration See *payment*

renovation, renovations See *repair*

renown See *fame*

rent, rents (un)reasonable, (un)affordable, considerable, exorbitant, outrageous, prohibitive, (sky-)high, soaring, (over)due, uncontrolled, long-frozen, modest, low, cheap, nominal, peppercorn, ground, economic

reorganization See *organization*

repair, repairs lasting, thorough, ingenious, (im)proper, extensive, major, rampant, extravagant, luxuriant, costly, multi-stage, large-scale, full-scale, minor, (over)due, hasty, structural, functional, cosmetic, running

repartee, repartees sparkling, crisp, lively, pithy, snazzy, piquant, caustic, acrimonious, sarcastic, biting, cutting, pungent, witty

repatriation, repatriations (in)voluntary, compulsory, forcible, forced

repercussion, repercussions See *effect*

repertoire, repertoires rich, copious, superb, unequalled, varied, diverse, extensive, habitual, standard, (un)traditional, (un)conventional, (un)characteristic, narrow

repertory, repertories See *repertoire*

repetition, repetitions maddening, annoying, exasperating, sickening, awful, useless, unnecessary, tedious, unbearable, hopeless, steady, unending, endless, ceaseless, continuous, constant, incessant, infinite, invariant, perpetual, persistent, unceasing, unchanging, uniform, unvarying, countless, periodic, spasmodic, intermittent, mantra-like, protracted, unbroken, uninterrupted, punctilious

replica, replicas perfect, exact, accurate, unequalled, life-size, pale, anaemic, dim, colourless, faint, lifeless

reply, replies placid, calm, (in)decisive, (in)effective, courteous, gracious, articulate, pertinent, relevant, spirited, candid, sage, respectful, determined, resolute, unmistakable, unequivocal, clear, plain, decided, tactful, apt, (un)suitable, (un)truthful, (in)appropriate, feeling, neat, concise, terse, pithy, laconic, crisp, frank, sharp, prompt, immediate, instantaneous, spontaneous, brief, laconic, emphatic, automatic, instinctive, bland, overwhelming, powerful, stern, harsh, authoritarian, firm, swift, immediate, (un)favourable, quick, obligatory, categorical, jocular, comic, humorous, stock, timeworn, encouraging, discouraging, cynical, complacent, indomitable, pungent, tough, wrong, curt, discourteous, bad-tempered, unhelpful, shifty, inarticulate, cutting, caustic, sarcastic, crushing, astounding, equivocal, elusive, evasive, dubious, tart, indignant, angry, churlish, rude, brittle, gruff, surly, cross, biting, hasty, hurried, insolent, disrespectful, rousing, insulting, impertinent, impudent, irreverent, cocky, offensive, tactless, ill-tempered, bitter, speechless, timid, meek, submissive, defiant, tardy, dilatory, neglectful, ambiguous, flippant, ignorant, cold, impatient, fretful, peevish, irritable, pettish, acrid, revengeful

report, reports authoritative, (in)conclusive, (dis)honest, (un)truthful, (in)accurate, thoughtful, insightful, incisive, clear-cut, (un)even, candid, circumstantial, revealing, trustworthy, credible, (in)coherent, up-to-date, factual, groundbreaking, meticulous, detailed, in-depth, compelling, veracious, (un)reliable, first-hand, substantial, weighty, inclusive, laconic, terse, lengthy, comprehensive, extensive, immense, massive, hefty, voluminous, blockbuster, uncensored, immediate, belated, recurrent, (ir)regular, weekly, premature, enthusiastic, optimistic, rosy, encouraging, upbeat, commendatory, (un)favourable, sensational, eulogistic, glowing, off-beat, unconventional, unusual, contradictory, dissenting, hard-to-confirm, critical, poignant, censorious, ten-page, downbeat, pessimistic, gloomy, grim, (un)available, resultant, persistent, tough, no-holds-barred, dismal, calamitous, astonishing, startling, alarming,

disquieting, discouraging, sobering,
shocking, frightening, spine-chilling,
depressing, devastating, misleading,
scathing, deceptive, worrisome, unshielded,
chummy, anecdotal, vague, one-sided,
slanted, prejudiced, partial, unfair,
careless, shoddy, unscrupulous,
tendentious, distorted, false, flawed,
fallacious, inflated, mendacious, libelious,
scandalous, disgraceful, stinging, lying,
disjointed, disconnected, unconnected,
adverse, idle, unfounded, groundless,
baseless, fragmentary, patchy, incomplete,
flatulent, scrappy, skimpy, sketchy,
unsubstantiated, unconfirmed, unverified,
unauthorized, secret, inside, internal,
exclusive, classified, news(paper), feature,
documentary, interim, preliminary, initial,
subsequent, follow-up, final, (semi-)annual,
draft, tabular, confidential, top-secret,
intelligence, (un)official, written, oral, live,
on-scene, news(-pool), pool, investigative,
eye-witness, audit, financial

reporter, reporters See also *journalist*
thorough, careful, superb, crack,
diplomatic, seasoned, (in)experienced,
trusty, (un)conscientious, (in)curious,
flamboyant, colourful, aggressive, intrepid,
adventurous, enterprising, swashbuckling,
(ir)regular, investigative, roving, on-the-air,
local, overseas, parliamentary

reporting enterprising, solid, first-hand,
careful, meticulous, exhaustive,
painstaking, detailed, vivid, objective,
impartial, even-handed, aggressive,
(in)accurate, (un)authoritative, (un)reliable,
(un)scrupulous, (un)conscientious,
(un)trustworthy, (un)balanced, (un)biased,
(un)fair, (im)partial, careless, dull, turgid,
pompous, bombastic, investigative

repose See *rest*

representation authentic, real,
(un)realistic, (un)proportional, (un)equal,
(in)equitable, (un)fair, (in)adequate,
(in)effective, (un)weighed

representative, representatives
distinguished, eminent, illustrious, noble,
splendid, sole, only, single, unique,
credible, (un)official, (il)legitimate,
alternate, itinerant, regional

repression increasing, systematic, harsh,
heavy, rigid, violent, absolute, monstrous,
brutal, vicious, savage, cruel, grim,
despotic, extreme, heartless, remorseless,
merciless, pitiless, ruthless, relentless,
unrelenting, tyrannical, uncivil, religious,
colonial

reprisal, reprisals See *retaliation*

reproach, reproaches See *rebuke*

reproduction, reproductions (1: copy)
perfect, exact, faithful, identical, accurate,
slavish, obsequious, cunning

reproduction (2: producing offspring)
(a)sexual, rapid

reproof, reproofs See *rebuke*

republic, republics (un)stable, restive,
precarious, clamorous, (un)equal, liberal,
sovereign, autonomous, independent,
democratic, federal, constituent,
self-proclaimed, breakaway, rebel,
rebellious, secessionist, socialist, secular

repudiation See *refusal*

reputation, repute unblemished, unsullied,
pure, stainless, flawless, sterling,
unspotted, spotless, solid, high, lofty,
good, decent, secure, strong, glittering,
sunny, unshak(e)able, distinguished, intact,
unequalled, unsurpassed, golden,
unrivalled, impressive, imperishable,
lasting, enduring, lingering, legendary,
immortal, overwheiming, formidable,
considerable, enormous, fine, enviable,
(un)favourable, budding, growing,
widespread, popular, world-wide,
international, glitzy, flashy, flaming,
notorious, once-sterling, fuzzy, fair, paltry,
naughty, nasty, lurid, bad, scandalous,
scandal-ridden, evil, specious, vile, rakish,
cloudy, ill, wicked, hideous, unsavoury,
dubious, doubtful, questionable, infamous,
untrustworthy, controversial, grim, muted,
boorish, (un)deserved, well-deserved,
thoroughly-deserved, well-earned,
(well-)established, long-established, spotted,
withered, posthumous, professional

request, requests earnest, courteous,
(im)proper, obliging, moderate, humble,
modest, pointed, seasonable,
(un)reasonable, straightforward, vague,
hesitant, extravagant, frivolous, trivial,
(un)timely, (in)opportune, startling, odd,
macabre, touching, pained, pathetic,
outlandish, outrageous, audacious,
presumptuous, insistent, pressing,
urgent, peremptory, incessant, persistent,
final, last-minute, (in)formal, special,

specific, (un)usual, tardy, written, pecuniary

requirement, requirements lenient, elastic, (in)flexible, (un)necessary, (in)appropriate, (un)reasonable, growing, complex, absolute, essential, urgent, peremptory, outrageous, prodigious, stiff, stringent, rigorous, rigid, tough, high, demanding, exacting, harsh, severe, arbitrary, uncompromising, punitive, quirky, insane, basic, minimum, regulatory, safety, financial, practical, legal, academic, dietary

rescue, rescues miraculous, providential, supernatural, heroic, sensational, emotional, astounding, phenomenal, dramatic, spectacular, stunning, stirring, thrilling, exciting, daring, bold, fearless, dangerous, instant, orderly, easy

research, researches brilliant, solid, sound, valuable, worthwhile, bewildering, amazing, fascinating, impressive, provocative, splendid, remarkable, authoritative, conclusive, breakthrough, groundbreaking, front-line, state-of-the-art, awe-inspiring, new, up-to-date, original, innovative, disparate, sophisticated, recondite, meaningful, encyclopaedic, empirical, extensive, prodigious, meticulous, thorough, intensive, exhaustive, faithful, laborious, determined, resolute, systematic, plodding, wide-ranging, unrecognized, painstaking, patient, unwearied, long-standing, long-term, recent, current, ongoing, expensive, peaceful, rewarding, skimpy, sterile, controversial, conflicting, spotty, undocumented, sloppy, curiosity-driven, close, primary, independent, basic (fundamental), motivation(al), operations (operational), laboratory, clinical, (non-)experimental, industrial, pure, archival, archaeological, multidisciplinary

researcher, researchers persevering, hardworking, painstaking, indefatigable, assiduous, industrious, diligent, meticulous, thorough, careful, scrupulous, conscientious, enthusiastic, objective, prolific, seasoned, tenacious, determined, pioneer, academic, independent

resemblance striking, amazing, astonishing, astounding, remarkable, extraordinary, uncommon, unusual, strong,

close, profound, noticeable, obvious, distinct, conspicuous, marked, definite, true, particular, formal, unwitting, eerie, uncanny, mysterious, faint, superficial, facial, physical, temperamental

resentment seething, boiling, (long-)smouldering, lingering, underlying, quiet, deep(-seated), profound, considerable, contemptuous, bitter, dark, fierce, stubborn, militant, explosive, pent-up, ethnic, racial, political

reservation, reservations (limitation; qualification) strong, serious, grave, considerable

reserve (1: restraint; caution; closeness) impenetrable, inscrutable, impervious, unfathomable, quiet, exquisite, maidenly

reserve, reserves (2: something stored for future use) huge, massive, enormous, standby, mysterious, unknown, proven, vestigial, gold, oil, bank, loan-loss, ecological

reshuffle, reshuffles See *organization*

residence, residences See also *home* and *house* palatial, stately, grand, gracious, superb, splendid, proud, sumptuous, costly, capacious, fortified, desirable, settled, fixed, official, habitual, permanent, temporary, short-term, country, suburban, summer

resident, residents urban, rural, uptown, local, area, low-income, high-income, scattered, lifelong, long-time, permanent, full-time, part-time, (il)legal, clandestine

resignation, resignations (1: giving up of a job) irrevocable, unalterable, firm, immutable, intractable, (un)likely, (im)probable, putative, immediate, surprise, dramatic, sudden, abrupt, imminent, inevitable, unavoidable, peaceful, graceful, dignified, embarrassed, reluctant, sad, regrettable, unfortunate, (un)expected, voluntary, mass

resignation (2: submission; passive acquiescence) yielding, truckling, fawning, cringing, humble, obsequious, servile, slavish, gloomy

resistance courageous, intense, vehement, energetic, staunch, stiff, tough, stout, determined, firm, sturdy, fierce, ferocious, terrific, (non-)violent, tenacious, stubborn, obstinate, suicidal, phobic, widespread, real, deadly, appreciable, indefinite, sullen, minimal, perfunctory, residual, moderate, light, faint, feeble, weak, crumbly, partial, nominal, token, initial, popular, collective, passive, armed, underground, physical

resister, resisters defiant, hard-line, die-hard, bold, fierce, fearless, audacious, rebellious, courageous

resolution (1: solemn commitment; determination) See *determination*

resolution, resolutions (2: formal proposal or statement) just, equitable, (im)proper, (un)favourable, oppressive, expeditious, (non-)binding, (non-)negotiable, compromise, mandatory, unilateral, bilateral, unanimous, joint, companion, draft

resolution (3: solving; determining) peaceful, happy, practised, bold, timid, arbitrary

resolve (resolution) See *resolution* (1)

resonance, resonances See *sound*

resort, resorts booming, thriving, enticing, enchanting, charming, tempting, alluring, fascinating, inviting, attractive, intimate, full-fledged, well-established, legendary, famous, renowned, well-known, sought-after, popular, first-rate, pretty, quaint, fine, lush, (ultra-)élite, ultimate, elegant, luxurious, luxury, posh, chic, ritzy, (un)fashionable, exclusive, up-market, pric(e)y, world-class, international, refined, glamorous, jet-set, unique, one-of-a-kind, ultra-touristy, glitzy, warm-climate, all-inclusive, self-contained, all-round, scenic, sleepy, drowsy, peaceful, quiet, relaxing, anxiety-free, remote, hideaway, hidden, undeveloped, unspoiled, undiscovered, major, third-rate, sleazy, seasonal, summer, winter, year-round, suburban, lakeside, seaside, beach, mountain, island, tourist, ski, spa, health, therapeutic, pleasure, vacation, holiday, honeymoon

resource, resources precious, priceless, rich, lucrative, profitable, valuable, considerable, never-failing, ample, (un)limited, enormous, extensive, copious, vast, abundant, vital, strong, formidable, (in)adequate, (un)balanced, durable, super-renewable, (non-)renewable, (ir)replaceable, (in)exhaustible, (un)perishable, expendable, cyclical, (un)available, (in)accessible, sal(e)able,

immediate, precarious, fragile, lean, tight, razor-thin, scant(y), stretched, threatened, unprotected, narrow, meagre, scarce, marginal, vanishing, uncertain, (un)known, (un)developed, untapped, uncommitted, raw, natural, physical, agricultural, industrial, environmental, human, marine, technical, mineral, economic, financial, moneyed, holistic

respect absorbing, deep, profound, unabated, unbounded, boundless, excessive, immense, enormous, tremendous, reverential, idolatrous, solemn, tenacious, attentive, impressive, fundamental, awesome, fearsome, sneaking, (be)grudging, wry, (in)sufficient, scant, instant, mutual, palpable, due, (un)deserved, filial, spiritual

respiration normal, (un)even, (un)easy, (un)restricted, deep, shallow, natural, artificial, wheezy, asthmatic, external, internal (tissue), cellular

respite, respites welcome, pleasant, blessed, blissful, enjoyable, delightful, well-deserved, all-important, momentary, brief

response, responses sound, thoughtful, gracious, laudatory, warm, positive, (in)effective, (in)adequate, (un)favourable, candid, (un)enthusiastic, (over-)zealous, (un)pleasant, pleasing, upbeat, generous, euphoric, overwhelming, massive, tremendous, remarkable, measurable, optimum, phenomenal, unprecedented, (un)sympathetic, loyal, astute, sagacious, shrewd, canny, heartfelt, encouraging, dramatic, intriguing, substantive, rousing, sensational, emotional, artful, deft, intelligent, meaningful, pragmatic, wary, cautious, non-committal, concrete, unequivocal, unmistakable, credible, understated, (in)flexible, firm, emphatic, sharp, harsh, vigorous, deep, powerful, lusty, vociferous, extreme, uncompromising, puzzling, evanescent, blunt, (in)voluntary, natural, normal, automatic, repetitive, traditional, ambivalent, complete, partial, limited, understandable, (in)coherent, heated, aggressive, stormy, indignant, visceral, (dis)proportionate, cryptic, jittery, frustrated, rancorous, acerbic, snorting, heavy-handed, awful, Draconian, crushing,

devastating, phon(e)y, angry, hostile,
vengeful, sour, half-hearted, uninteresting,
cool, tepid, frosty, discouraging, grudging,
disheartening, negative, cynical,
forthcoming, immediate, swift, prompt,
hasty, curt, lackadaisical, sluggish, limp,
lax, slow, mild, feeble, faint, poor,
restrained, subdued, measured, calculated,
muted, conditioned, unsolicited,
unjustifiable, (un)predictable,
(un)expected, withdrawn, sullen, glum,
evasive, objective, subjective, initial,
minimal, stock, popular, emotional,
protective, congratulatory, unified,
collective, symbolic, aesthetic

responsibility, responsibilities
demanding, crushing, (un)rewarding,
enormous, heavy, grave, weighty,
incredible, unbelievable, burdensome,
awesome, awful, sacred, onerous, arduous,
stressful, complex, diminished, irrevocable,
indispensable, exclusive, sole, full, prime,
primary, additional, inherent, specific,
direct, ultimate, joint, collective, moral,
legal, criminal, public, personal, tutelary,
financial, corporate, parental,
constitutional

rest welcome, well-deserved, blissful,
blessed, all-important, thorough, pleasant,
enjoyable, good, ample, daily, fitful,
(in)adequate, momentary, forgone,
(un)broken; parade

restaurant, restaurants palatial, posh,
glitzy, exclusive, soigné, modish, glittering,
elegant, regal, majestic, grand, lofty,
trendy, luxury, luxurious, magnificent,
superb, fancy, pric(e)y, unaffordable,
plush(y), up-market, classy, upper-crust,
glamorous, sophisticated, suave, clubby,
rich, prestige, prestigious, deluxe,
esteemed, famed, memorable, major,
legendary, creditable, distinguished,
venerable, reputable, meritorious, formal,
opulent, fashionable, top(-level),
chandeliered, snooty, decorous,
high-ceilinged, massive, spacious,
sumptuous, comfortable, pretty, charming,
attractive, delightful, delectable, smart,
urbane, nice, lovely, pleasant,
recommendable, top-value, well-appointed,
handsome, cheery, colourful, imaginative,
innovative, experimental, all-night,
neon-lit, ubiquitous, tourist, authentic,

hom(e)y, family-run, commendable, fine,
wonderful, swank, old-fashioned, lively,
busy, clamorous, boisterous, noisy,
favourite, rustic, rural, local, suburban,
provincial, regional, ethnic, tiny, little,
cavernous, mundane, gloomy, drab,
grubby, sleazy, humble, (dis)agreeable,
(un)hygienic, unpretentious, (un)licensed,
self-service, fast-food, single-dish, organic,
vegetarian, seafood, hotel, revolving,
floating, marina, outdoor,
open-fronted, open-air, garden, streetside,
roadside, highway, harbour-front,
waterfront, terrace

restlessness See *uneasiness*

restraint astounding, impressive, heroic,
clear-headed, thoughtful, perceptive,
sagacious, judicial, commendable,
remarkable, admirable, rational, wise,
sensible, wholesome, rigorous, severe,
maximum, unprecedented, rare, voluntary,
budget, fiscal, financial, monetary, price,
wage, sexual, emotional, physical

restriction, restrictions (il)legal,
(un)lawful, (un)justifiable, (in)excusable,
(il)legitimate, (un)reasonable, (un)official,
(un)warrantable, (un)necessary,
(im)permissible, (un)fair, stringent, tight,
tough, heavy, sharp, harsh, severe, drastic,
suffocating, excruciating, annoying,
irksome, acrimonious, elaborate,
long-standing, commonplace, mild,
self-imposed, temporal, dietary, physical,
travel, curfew

result, results intriguing, thrilling,
exciting, stirring, captivating, fascinating,
interesting, encouraging, gratifying,
startling, smashing, astounding,
astonishing, amazing, surprising, puzzling,
stunning, staggering, promising, dazzling,
glowing, soothing, optimistic,
(un)spectacular, (un)impressive,
(un)dramatic, landmark, undreamed-of,
incredible, unbelievable, (im)precise,
(in)accurate, (un)reliable, magnificent,
remarkable, superb, fruitful, welcome,
meaningful, beneficial, notable,
(in)significant, substantial, (un)satisfactory,
(in)conclusive, positive, decisive,
(un)certain, (un)confirmed, complete,
practical, actual, concrete, tangible,
demonstrable, observable, perceptible,
evident, apparent, (in)consistent, enduring,

(long-)lasting, (in)direct, (in)evitable, (un)avoidable, (un)escapable, inescapable, natural, immediate, initial, preliminary, (un)predictable, (im)probable, flat, (im)measurable, long-range, short-range, long-term, short-term, short-lived, potential, (un)likely, early, quick, ultimate, final, (un)intended, (un)deniable, presumable, (il)logical, undreamed-of, alternative, equivocal, (un)necessary, negative, grotesque, oblique, concomitant, varied, sole, unprecedented, (un)foreseen, (un)expected, mixed, overnight, bottom-line, lamentable, dubious, unsettling, devastating, alarming, horrible, bloody, fatal, tragic, dire, dreadful, dismal, disastrous, calamitous, unproven, ambiguous, (un)questionable, unconvincing, inconclusive, perverse, grim, poor, insignificant, meagre, fruitless, unhappy, conflicting, contradictory, messy, desultory, unfair, hurtful, heartbreaking, disappointing, ominous, cumulative, diagnostic

retailer, retailers See *merchant*

retaliation crushing, unflinching, overwhelming, measured, swift, immediate, straightforward, outright, decisive, massive, intensive, intense, severe, apparent, overt, (in)direct, unmistakable, tongue-in-cheek, indiscriminate, petty, ugly, venomous, brutal, vicious, unconcealed, unspecified, trade, pre-emptive

reticence See *reserve*

retirement dignified, graceful, peaceful, blissful, delightful, sweet, easy, quiet, welcome, enjoyable, contented, restful, worry-free, undisturbed, active, uneventful, (un)pleasant, (un)satisfactory, (un)happy, (un)comfortable, good, frugal, economical, obscure, (un)expected, impending, early, optional, (semi-)voluntary, compulsory, mandatory, flexible, full-time, statutory, (un)constitutional, migratory

retort, retorts See also *reply* vivid, pithy, crisp, terse, curt, epigrammatic, neat, pointed, polished, succinct, trenchant, spiteful, vicious, abusive, mean, vindictive, malicious, catty, acerbic, spontaneous

retreat, retreats (1: withdrawal) judicious, masterly, tactical, strategic, (dis)orderly, undisciplined, chaotic, forced,

ignominious, degrading, disgraceful, ignoble, dishonourable, humiliating, shameful, discreditable, bitter, forlorn, indifferent, last-minute, prompt, hasty, hurried, speedy, apparent, full-scale, partial, (un)conditional; religious; political

retreat, retreats (2: quiet place) paradisal, idyllic, ideal, balmy, posh, exclusive, ultimate, pleasant, popular, favourite, welcome, cosy, gentle, peaceful, quiet, tranquil, relaxing, stress-free, remote, removed, hidden, inaccessible, undiscovered, withdrawn, elusive, reclusive, lonely, lonesome, secluded, secret, obscure, safe, unfrequented, unspoiled, everlasting, temporary, momentary, extemporaneous, sheltered, one-of-a-kind, leafy, (palm-)shaded, (half-)cloistered, year-round, summer, winter, weekend, sylvan, mountain, alpine, hillside, rustic, rural, wilderness, wildlife, suburban, Spartan, tourist, family, private

return, returns (1: coming back) joyous, cheerful, delightful, festive, triumphant, emotional, nostalgic, safe, imminent, impending, prompt, (un)scheduled, pending, undecided, eventual, phoenix-like, sad, reluctant, forcible, forceful

return, returns (2: profit; yield) See also *interest* (2) and *profit* attractive, stable, respectable, diminishing, eventual, initial, annual

reunion, reunions dramatic, warm, emotional, tearful, touching, grim, joyful, glad, ecstatic, joyous, blissful, delightful, (un)happy, (un)pleasant, (un)enjoyable, halcyon, raucous, unplanned, family

revelation, revelations interesting, tantalizing, exciting, stirring, thrilling, astonishing, startling, astounding, stunning, glaring, shocking, earthshattering, damning, blistering, subtle, savoury, extraordinary, dramatic, sensational, provocative, remarkable, spectacular, explosive, bizarre, questionable, nasty, sordid, full, major, universal, sudden, gradual, early, emotional; divine

revelry See *celebration* and *festival*

revenge understandable, (in)comprehensible, effective, elaborate, rampant, wanton, swift, immediate, tardy, futile, petty, otiose, ferocious, crushing, devastating, destructive, brutal, spiteful, vicious, unappeasable, rancorous, splenetic, venomous, vindictive, calculated, misguided, bloody, summary, personal

reverence See *respect*

reversal, reversals drastic, rare, abrupt, sudden, unexpected, extraordinary, uncommon, dramatic, remarkable, astonishing, stunning, striking, amazing, surprising

review, reviews (1: critical evaluation) insightful, incisive, acute, perceptive, breezy, rave, raving, glowing, overwhelming, rhapsodical, (un)enthusiastic, ecstatic, positive, strong, passionate, generous, good, commendatory, laudatory, respectful, upbeat, mixed, ambivalent, negative, poor, mean, snide, scathing, rancorous, bad, savage, killer, bumpy, uneven, carping, dull, donnish

review, reviews (2: examination; survey) massive, comprehensive, lengthy, ongoing, independent, one-sided, objective, uncalled-for, (un)official, internal, external

reviewer, reviewers See *critic*

revision, revisions sweeping, total, complete, full(-scale), profound, extensive, incessant, major, substantial, fundamental, significant, drastic, scrupulous, conscientious, thorough, patient, last-minute, minor, marginal

revolt, revolts See *rebellion*

revolution, revolutions (1: overthrow of government; sudden change) authentic, (un)successful, overt, major, tremendous, far-reaching, unstoppable, turbulent, tempestuous, tumultuous, violent, relentless, ruthless, merciless, bloody, bloodless, red, chaotic, local, proletarian, industrial, social, cultural, sexual, technological, scientific, electronic, green

revolution, revolutions (2: rotation) See *rotation*

revolutionary, revolutionaries See *rebel*

revolver, revolvers ivory-handled, snub-nosed, ancient, antique, priceless, (un)loaded, single-action, double-action, (un)cocked

revue, revues See *show*

reward, rewards encouraging, tempting, sweet, subtle, prestigious, princely, solid, prime, munificent, lucrative, rich,

handsome, (un)generous, vast, tremendous, ample, immense, substantial, large, (im)measurable, quick, paltry, meagre, (un)fair, (un)just, esteemed, (un)deserved, well-deserved, (un)merited, (in)tangible, potential, unexpected, pecuniary, financial, monetary, material; heavenly

rhetoric appealing, stirring, impassioned, lofty, high, facile, upbeat, flamboyant, verbose, colourful, florid, prolix, overblown, extravagant, pompous, bombastic, windy, sonorous, unconvincing, transparent, hollow, empty, stale, tired, old-fashioned, artificial, diversionary, mushy, strident, defiant, harsh, tough, rough-and-tumble, feverish, heated, fiery, incendiary, explosive, apocalyptic, hard-line, militant, bellicose, bloodcurdling, bitter, deceitful, political, patriotic, electoral

rhinoceros, rhinoceroses aggressive, heavy, clumsy, lumbering, charging, elusive, unpredictable, curious, short-sighted, one-horned, two-horned, hairy, long-lipped, square-mouthed, black, white, Javan, Sumatran, Indian, African

rhyme, rhymes perfect, correct, faultless, brilliant, rich, complex, ragged, poor, female, feminine, masculine, internal, terminal, double, half (near, oblique, slant); popular, traditional, well-known, nursery

rhythm, rhythms subtle, leisurely, easy(-going), laid-back, unhurried, smooth, inexorable, stately, hypnotic, bewitching, charming, haunting, soothing, harmonious, (un)intelligible, resounding, percussive, syncopated, sinuous, interweaving, short, plangent, (un)steady, (un)even, (ir)regular, (ab)normal, cyclic, repetitive, light, airy, superficial, singsong, monotonous, tireless, (un)predictable, precise, deliberate, insistent, chugging, spooky, chaotic, vast, heady, wild, vigorous, powerful, muscular, ponderous, harsh, explosive, intricate, curious, eerie, strange, sextuple, broken, (un)sprung, modern, ancient, classical, mystic(al), conversational, circadian, biological, physiological, cardiac, double-dotted

rice crispy, fluffy, soggy, sticky, clumpy, moist, dry, glutinous, white, brown, saffron, fancy (choice), scented (aromatic),

short (pearl), medium, long(-grain),
lowland (swamp, wet), upland (hill, dry);
wild (Canada, Indian)

riches See *wealth*

richness See *wealth*

ride, rides (un)comfortable, smooth,
tranquil, scenic, exhilarating, wonderful,
glorious, enjoyable, (un)pleasant, precision,
thrilling, stirring, exciting, breathtaking,
unforgettable, breathless, spectacular,
quick, brisk, stealthy, slow, short,
two-hour, hour-long, interminable, endless,
reckless, jerky, bumpy, rough, scary,
wearisome, tortuous, backbreaking,
(bone-)jarring, tooth-jarring, daredevil,
whirling, harrowing, hair-raising,
nightmarish, joyless, boring; joy

rider, riders solitary, lone, only, single,
sole, companionless, graceful, magnificent,
superb, rough

ridicule eternal, thoughtless, unthoughtful,
cruel, inconsiderate, indifferent,
unmindful, disregardful, fierce, harsh,
heartless, malicious, relentless, ruthless,
unrestrained, wicked, vicious

rifle, rifles express, rapid-fire, light,
powerful, high-powered, high-velocity,
slung, old-fashioned, recoil-less,
take-down, sawn-off, shoulder,
(semi)automatic, single-shot,
muzzle-loading, breech-loading,
double-barrel(led), short-barrelled,
bayoneted, percussion-lock, revolving,
repeating, bolt-action, lever-action,
pump-action (slide-action), assault,
sporting, hunting, darting

rift, rifts complete, serious, deep, siz(e)able,
unfortunate, deplorable, wretched,
eventual, diplomatic

right, rights indisputable, incontestable,
undeniable, undisputed, unquestionable,
inalienable (unalienable), irrevocable,
indefeasible, (un)definable, elusive,
(un)equal, unprecedented, new-found,
precious, (im)prescriptible, prescriptive,
forfeitable, (un)restricted, partial, full,
absolute, ultimate, basic, fundamental,
essential, critical, necessary, important,
urgent, automatic, elementary, sole,
exclusive, special, personal, sacred,
privileged, inherent, natural, legal, lawful,
human, civil, divine, God-given, sovereign,
traditional, hereditary, civic, pre-emptive,

belligerent, moral, patent, political,
proprietary, riparian, mineral, water,
(extra)territorial, conjugal, marital,
contractual, incorporeal, constitutional,
statutory, individual, collective, societal,
social

rigidity inexorable, inflexible, obdurate,
unyielding, immovable, granitic, relentless,
unbending, unrelenting, unshak(e)able

ring, rings See also *jewel* fine, stone,
pearl, diamond, enamel, solitaire, plain,
fancy, sparkling, flashy, hefty, tight, loose,
eternity

riot, riots full-scale, large-scale,
widespread, massive, major, minor,
sporadic, periodic, deadly, bloody,
ferocious, savage, vicious, bitter, fiery,
tumultuous, drunken, inter-communal,
sectarian, ethnic, racial, race, street

rioting See *riot*

rise stunning, striking, astonishing,
astounding, dazzling, startling, stupefying,
surprising, alarming, headlong, meteoric,
phenomenal, spectacular, sharp, dramatic,
cyclic

risk, risks high, grave, serious,
higher-than-average, inordinate,
spectacular, siz(e)able, great, steep, huge,
substantial, enormous, significant, big,
considerable, incalculable, incredible,
maximum, alarming, fatal, catastrophic,
fearsome, terrible, good, inevitable,
(un)avoidable, long-term, exceptional,
unnatural, unnecessary, varied, imminent,
potential, (un)predictable, obvious,
apparent, evident, clear, possible, brave,
poor, lurking, receding, (un)acceptable,
(un)reasonable, relative, small, slight, tiny,
minuscule, infinitesimal, minimum, low,
negligible, minute, non-existent, remote,
(well-)calculated

rite, rites refreshing, amusing, lavish,
spectacular, elaborate, impressive,
glittering, proud, solemn, serious, intense,
dispiriting, disheartening, grim, gruesome,
(un)familiar, unique, curious, strange,
secret, mysterious, annual, daily, ancient,
(centuries-)old, time-worn, traditional,
ascetic, austere, severe, rigid, stringent,
careful, complex, complicated, intricate,
simple, benign, meaningless, menacing,
violent, foul, bloody, special, mandatory,
elemental, basic, standard, healing,

therapeutic, ceremonial, sacramental, sacrificial, mystic, hedonistic, orgiastic, superstitious, surrealistic, public, social, tribal, native, pagan, totemic, animistic, holy, religious, masochistic, cannibalistic, satanic, prenuptial, baptismal, burial, funeral, funerary; last

ritual, rituals See *rite*

rival, rivals (un)successful, powerful, serious, fierce, bitter, formidable, mortal, fatal, heartless, querulous, long-time, major, arch, foremost, chief, principal, minor, precocious, wary, unwitting

rivalry, rivalries amiable, constructive, (un)healthy, (un)friendly, lingering, long-time, endless, ceaseless, intense, petty, bitter, querulous, destructive, violent, fierce, serious, sibling, tribal, internal, intercommunity, ethnic, factional, national, political; binocular (retinal)

river, rivers murmuring, brawling, swishing, surging, hurrying, raging, gushing, plunging, thrusting, rolling, splashing, foaming, rippling, sparkling, twinkling, flashing, meandering, wandering, (free-)running, (fast-)flowing, fast-moving, free-flowing, winding, bending, swelling, overflowing, brimming, unceasing, slow-flowing, slow-moving, lazy-looping, boisterous, rambunctious, torrential, turbulent, wild, unpredictable, furious, angry, swift, fast, sluggish, sullen, principal, navigable, passable, hospitable, sustaining, high, huge, great, big, large, wide, broad, considerable, mighty, awesome, monster, majestic, spectacular, magnificent, splendid, interminable, scenic, glorious, noble, legendary, famed, fabled, ample, plenteous, bountiful, life-giving, glass-like, white-water, clear, clean, sweet, pure, still, calm, placid, quiet, tranquil, silent, peaceful, mysterious, smooth, orderly, lovely, (un)friendly, pristine, antediluvian, (in)accessible, undeveloped, uncharted, unmapped, undammed, sinuous, intricate, treacherous, circumfluent, confluent, braided, reef-strewn, (rain-)swollen, monsoon-swollen, bloated, fordless, earth-brown, isleted, tidal, silt-laden, mud-laden, mud-gorged, muddy, dirty, murky, putrid, bug-ridden, sedgy, turbid, upper, frigid, frozen, snow-fed, sludgy,

dry, (waist-)deep, shallow, low, snaggy, wan, puny, drought-stricken, open, recreational, (sub)tropical, coastal, pastoral, mountain, jungle, subterranean, estuarine, tributary, distributary

road, roads spectacular, first-class, (im)passable, (un)usable, (un)paved, smooth, plain, major, arterial, through, direct, scenic, (im)practicable, clear, wide, broad, open, spacious, unobstructed, safe, quiet, low-traffic, uncrowded, well-lit, straight, forest-lined, tree-lined, tree-shaded, hard-surfaced, rough-edged, single-tracked, pitted, lonely, lonesome, secluded, desolate, unused, unfrequented, unnamed, obscure, untravelled, forgotten, interdictable, remote, Tarmac, sand, stony, rocky, dirt, laterite, hilly, depressed, convergent, converging, forked, extended, corkscrew, uphill, downhill, serpentine, hairpin, time-consuming, snakelike, twisty, devious, roundabout, tortuous, crooked, sinuous, winding, steep, roller-coaster, flooded, washed-out, greasy, soggy, dusty, whirlwind, mushy, muddy, boggy, arduous, long, slippery, wet, sloppy, crude, uneven, bumpy, unfit, rough, jarring, snowy, snow-blocked, snowbound, snow-covered, ice-slick, moss-covered, treacherous, unsafe, hazardous, perilous, dangerous, harrowing, hair-raising, murderous, miry, wretched, (in)accessible, pot-holed, cracked, hummocky, abominable, abysmal, undulating, busy, heavy, fair, narrow, primitive, outback, single-lane, one-lane, two-lane, (un)divided, local, secondary, side, rural, ring, post, mountain, military, vicinal, wrong, ancillary, back, country, arterial, gravel, toll, access, provincial, boundary, residential, private, loop

roadway, roadways See *road*

roar, roars thundering, resounding, swelling, overpowering, deafening, ear-splitting, rumbling, thunderous, tumultuous, full-throated, explosive, mighty, hollow, continual, ominous, angry, wrathful, throaty, guttural

robber, robbers accomplished, lucrative, brutal, ruthless, heartless, pitiless, merciless, relentless, unrelenting, daring, bold, enterprising, energetic, astute, crafty, sly, stealthy, irresolute, uneasy, downright,

outright, notorious, common, habitual,
inveterate, unrepentant, masked,
(un)armed, self-confessed

robbery, robberies reckless, dauntless,
fearless, intrepid, venturesome,
adventurous, daring, daylight, brutal,
brazen, bold, armed, bare-faced, massive,
systematic, first-degree, second-degree

robe, robes flowing, loose-fitting,
flapping, wraparound, saffron,
brocaded, hooded, gold-trimmed,
ermine-trimmed, layered, flamboyant,
heavy, costly, distinctive, gorgeous,
unbecoming, tattered, traditional, regal,
ceremonial, royal, priestly, sacerdotal,
monastic, judicial, court, academic; terry

robot, robots productive, chip-smart,
self-conscious, ambitious, elaborate,
advanced, inscrutable, programmable,
insensate, unfeeling, mechanical

rock, rocks superjacent, stupendous,
monstrous, gigantic, mighty, frightful,
massive, immense, enormous, pendant,
immovable, firm, solid, flinty, steely,
steady, stationary, vertiginous,
spear-shaped, serpentine, angular, craggy,
projecting, ragged, serrate, jagged, sharp,
odd-shaped, contorted, deformed,
humped-up, double-headed,
double-humped, porous, spongy,
underwater, submerged, ocean-floor,
littoral, barren, bare, naked, torpid,
sunken, steep, dangerous, treacherous,
slick, slippery, exposed, shaded,
(pine-)topped, kelp-ringed, cacti-studded,
mossy, moss-covered, weed-covered,
lichen-covered, snow-covered,
snow-crusted, savage, barbaric, hostile,
(wind-)eroded, wind-swept, sun-beaten,
weather-beaten, (un)weathered, effusive,
molten, friable, scab, sheer, sound, light,
insensate, natural, (un)stratified,
saw-toothed, rough-cut, glassy, volcanic,
granitic, sialic, plutonic, vitreous, tabular,
cap, extraneous, fine-grained,
close-grained, coarse-grained, living,
(im)permeable, impervious, sandstone,
oil-bearing, gas-bearing, diamond-bearing,
coral, primal, ultrabasic, molten, mottled,
(non-)metalliferous, igneous, metamorphic,
sedimentary, extrusive, intrusive, basalt,
sulphurous, saliferous, eruptive,
xenomorphic, crystalline, allochthonous,

autochthonous, arenaceous, argillaceous,
argilliferous, auriferous

rocket, rockets interplanetary,
(un)manned, stubby-winged, instrumental,
experimental, solid-fuel, liquid-fuel,
multi-stage (multi-step), two-stage, electric,
sounding (meteorological),
ionic-propulsion, military

rod, rods stumpy, supple, flexible,
adjustable, pliant, stiff, traverse,
decorative, connecting (piston), telescopic

rogue, rogues unprincipled,
conscienceless, unscrupulous, unnatural,
treacherous, deceitful, vicious,
unconscionable, sly, subtle, cunning, wily,
idle, lazy, vagrant, knavish, out-and-out,
thorough, complete, unmitigated, utter,
absolute, lovable

role, roles challenging, peaceful, heroic,
beneficent, useful, constructive, protective,
meaningful, productive, lucrative, proper,
assertive, pervasive, dominant,
domineering, overbearing, powerful,
preponderant, (in)significant, central, key,
pre-eminent, prominent, important,
lead(ing), chief, pivotal, vital, big, large,
crucial, decisive, essential, influential,
major, profound, demanding, exacting,
indispensable, substantial, subtle, historic,
visible, (in)conspicuous, (in)appropriate,
odd, active, (un)sympathetic, (un)favourite,
special, animated, delicious, plum, juicy,
symbolic, (non)traditional, conventional,
classical, multiple, multi-faceted, divergent,
diverse, onerous, double, dual, full,
mythic, rare, precise, (in)direct,
behind-the-scenes, indeterminate,
mysterious, controversial, insidious,
thankless, superfluous, narrow, subsidiary,
auxiliary, support, walk-on, minimal,
junior, secondary, token, silent, speaking,
animated, solo, neutral, minor, murky,
vague, improper, useless, destructive,
clear-cut, unspecified, (un)limited, bardic,
star, starring, character, ingénue, title,
marital, parental, investigatory,
supervisory, managerial, strategic,
ceremonial, diplomatic, absentee,
hegemonic

romance, romances enduring, lasting,
idyllic, fairy-tale, tender, delicious,
luscious, (un)happy, (in)famous, minor,
major, soppy, giddy, whirlwind, lopsided,

lacklustre, sizzling, steamy, reluctant, fugitive, (il)licit, private, public, long-distance; epistolary, heroic

romantic, romantics sentimental, die-hard, dreamy, quixotic, Utopian, incurable

roof, roofs massive, (water)tight, steep, tumbling, leaky, fragile, sagging, flying, (sand)stone, concrete(-and-steel), (black-)tiled, red-tiled, slate(-covered), tin, (corrugated-)iron, leaden, metal, thin-shell, (burnished-)copper, timber, cedar, shake, sod, clay, bark, terracotta, lattice-work, thatch(ed), palm-thatch, palm-frond, stone-laden, tar-and-gravel, pyramidal, trapezoidal, paraboloid, pagoda-like, cathedral-like, gable(d), flat, saddle-shaped, low-slope, barrel-vaulted, double-curve, retractable, movable, (low-)pitched, high-pitched, (high-)peaked, pinnacled, lean-to, saw-toothed, imperial, conical

rook, rooks See *crow*

room, rooms cheerful, cheery, airy, spacious, huge, gigantic, large, colossal, bright, sound-proof, sunlit, sunny, pleasant, intimate, snug, comfortable, cosy, attractive, charming, relaxing, quiet, still, orderly, neat, tidy, immaculate, spick-and-span, splendid, handsome, elegant, imposing, prim, tastefully-furnished, ostentatious, germ-free, all-weather, lofty, high-ceiling(ed), oblong, cylindrical, canvas-covered, cork-lined, rough-hewn, sunken, cathedral-ceilinged, cavernous, balconied, bay-windowed, ingle-nooked, circular, tall, pastel, ground-floor, vacant, empty, separate, private, inner, outer, adjoining, adjacent, contiguous, outward, outside, side, middle, central, small, tiny, little, simple, sparsely-furnished, spartan, poorly-furnished, poky, cramped, untidy, frowzy, forbidding, airless, (over)crowded, disorderly, grim, messy, musty, dark, dim, dingy, sunless, cavernous, grubby, unfriendly, cheerless, sombre, gloomy, dreary, unpleasant, comfortless, squalid, wretched, tattered, mean, dirty, filthy, nasty, stuffy, close, viewless, windowless, drafty, obscure, shadowy, noisy, dim(ly-lit), smoky, shopworn, drab, desolate, clumsy, sultry, frowzily-curtained,

light, thermal, family, spare, intensive-care, memorial, ceremonial, common, communal

rooster, roosters See *cock*

root, roots deep, firm, hard, strong, intact, esculent, (in)edible, starchy, poisonous, aromatic, premorse, pungent, turnip-like, octopus-like, serpent-like, intertwining, tangled, thready, woody, rounded, fascicled, gnarled, shallow, fleshy, tender, primary, secondary, tertiary, fibrous, tuberous, adventitious, parasitic, buttress; (multi)ethnic, biological

rope, ropes restraining, tense, tight, taut, heavy, (fist-)thick, rough, coarse, foul, slippery, slender, thin, tenuous, slack, weak, handmade, braided, cable-laid, plain-laid, loose, right-hand, sisal, hemp, jute, coir, nylon, wire, steel, walrus-hide, straw, Manila, Henequen

rose, roses See also *flower* dewy, fresh, demure, fragrant, sweet-smelling, lovely, beautiful, fair, full-blown, overblown, velvety, crimson, red, bi-coloured, long-stemmed, single, double, perpetual, miniature, wild

rotation, rotations negative, yearly, annual, daily, diurnal; strict; agricultural, crop

route, routes (un)navigable, (im)passable, (in)accessible, (un)safe, main, classic, (un)likely, long, spectacular, scenic, easy, exact, same, alternative, subsidiary, (in)direct, odd, sinuous, circuitous, roundabout, hairpin, devious, tortuous, risky, treacherous, perilous, challenging, forbidding, strenuous, painful, arduous, clandestine, unpaved, eastern, northerly, south-easterly, south-eastward, (over)land, water, rural, supply, trade, transit, recreational, migratory, back-door

routine, routines placid, (dis)orderly, (ir)regular, (un)conventional, (un)official, (un)familiar, standard, normal, dull, uneventful, monotonous, mechanical, tedious, mindless, uninterrupted, out-of-date, intrepid, fearless, brave, dictatorial, staggering, gruelling, grinding, demanding, stressful, severe, unrelenting, relentless, ruthless, pitiless, merciless, heartless, deadly, staid, grim, dreary, gloomy, cheerless, daily, day-by-day, day-to-day, year-to-year

row, rows (1: series of things or persons in

a line) orderly, neat, precise, confused, solid, continuous, endless, soldierly

row, rows (2: noisy disturbance; brawl) See *quarrel*

rubbish sickening, nauseating, reeking, stinking, rank, rancid, putrid, putrescent, rotten, smelly, filthy, verminous, maggoty, slimy, harmful, deadly, dangerous, toxic, hazardous, nauseous, odious, foul, offensive, repulsive, repugnant, unsightly, ugly, knee-deep, shin-deep, voluminous, recyclable, (non-)biodegradable, odourless, odorous, raw, urban, household, residential, industrial, roadside

rudeness mortifying, humiliating, unexpected, untoward, shameful, shameless, aweless, surly, outspoken, audacious, brazen, crude, severe, heartless, devilish, arrogant, imperious, unbearable, insufferable, intolerable, inexcusable, unpardonable, unforgivable

rug, rugs See also *carpet* exquisite, beautiful, precious, expensive, rare, antique, flawless, plush, vivid, bright, multicoloured, wool(len), leopard-skin, bear-skin, fibre, velvet, cotton, machine-washable, hand-made, hand-woven, machine-woven, loom-made, flat-weave, hooked, braided, inexpensive, cheap, well-worn, threadbare, shaggy, rag, broadloom, alpaca, Oriental, Persian, Turkish, Turkmen, Caucasian, Chinese, Indian, Berber, Bukhara (Bokhara)

ruin, ruins (1: building in disrepair) fascinating, splendid, diverse, dramatic, famous, fabled, formidable, extensive, massive, haunted, awful, shapeless, desolate, shabby, ghostly, moss-covered, unexplored, tumbling, ancient, prehistoric, mythical, classical, funerary

ruin (2: collapse) total, utter, irretrievable, irrevocable, ecological, financial

rule, rules (1: government; authority) masterful, glorious, splendid, democratic, constitutional, impartial, (in)efficient, (in)competent, lenient, lax, violence-ridden, stodgy, paternalistic, chaotic, erratic, forceful, harsh, arbitrary, Draconian, oligarchical, totalitarian, dictatorial, heavy-handed, oppressive, despotic, autocratic, tyrannical, repressive, iron-fisted, murderous, genocidal, merciless, ruthless, remorseless, heartless,

pitiless, relentless, unrelenting, military(-backed), military-dominated, one-man, one-party, single-party, socialist, imperial, colonial, alien, foreign, white, local, legislative, direct

rule, rules (2: regulation) sacred, old, precise, (un)clear, infallible, (in)effective, high-minded, (un)fair, enforceable, (il)liberal, (in)flexible, unbending, demanding, crabbed, rigid, strict, hard-and-fast, fixed, firm, (in)adequate, (in)equitable, (un)alterable, inviolate, inviolable, iron(clad), rigorous, tough, stringent, tight, constrictive, restrictive, infrangible, irrefragable, unbreakable, (in)applicable, definite, no-nonsense, (un)written, unspoken, broad, outmoded, archaic, obsolete, (long-)standing, temporary, special, built-in, variable, recognizable, complex, obscure, arcane, secretive, deceptive, misleading, petty, effluvial, toothless, elastic, lenient, (well-)established, set, self-imposed, (un)written, basic, mandatory, (un)constitutional, environmental, procedural, canonical; golden, cardinal

ruler, rulers benign(ant), gracious, benevolent, (un)just, kindly, inclement, (in)experienced, incorruptible, unifying, (in)effectual, astute, wise, sagacious, high-minded, dynamic, (ir)responsible, conservative, pragmatic, princely, bold, powerful, strong, mighty, (omni)potent, absolute, severe, power-hungry, sanguinary, despotic, tyrannical, high-handed, autocratic, hard-line, arbitrary, oppressive, repressive, self-styled, inept, weak, feeble, lame-duck, cruel, figurehead, de facto, supreme, (il)legitimate, rightful, hereditary, titular, sovereign, nominal, holy, theocratic, temporal, secular, feudal

ruling, rulings sage, crucial, key, landmark, groundbreaking, novel, temporary, controversial, misguided, unchallenged, binding, unanimous, official, (un)constitutional, technical, court

rumour, rumours spreading, circulating, floating, rippling, recurrent, persistent, insistent, widespread, rampant, plentiful, rife, current, premature, speculative, credible, definite, (in)accurate, false, vague, faint, baseless, erroneous, conflicting, contradictory, hesitant, idle, unlikely, impossible, exhilarating, sensational, hot, sanctimonious, catty, unkind, dirty, scandalous, wild, prejudiced, ugly, derogatory, mischievous, virulent, acrimonious, venomous, malicious, vicious, sinister, panicky, alarming, disquieting, inflammatory, shameful, disgraceful, revolting, shocking, awful, terrible, ignoble, vile, despicable, slanderous, unkind, forbidding, unconfirmed, unsubstantiated, home-made

run, runs hard, brisk, vigorous, arduous, marathon, smooth, routine, straight, broken, downhill, uphill, (long-)distance, mid(dle)-distance

runner, runners limber, nimble, loose-jointed, long-winded, long-breathed, serious, ranking, front, avid, dedicated, confirmed, champion, élite, top, experienced, premier, all-around, efficient, swift, fast, quick, rapid, speedy, slow, exhausted, obsessive, compulsive, obligatory, professional, amateur, marathon, long-distance, mid(dle)-distance, cross-country

running See *run*

rush, rushes bewildering, annoying, maddening, hectic, feverish, restless, tremendous, unrestrained, unabashed, confused, disordered, chaotic, wild, frantic, mad, violent, sudden, inevitable, unavoidable, headlong, precipitous, reckless, clumsy, competitive

ruthlessness barbaric, hard-fisted, heartless, merciless, pitiless, relentless, unrelenting, unmerciful, unsparing, bumptious, obtrusive, legendary, revengeful, concealed

sabotage See *saboteur*

saboteur, saboteurs sophisticated, elaborate, crafty, sly, wily, criminal, wicked, vile, disgraceful, deplorable, unwitting, reprehensible, vicious, nefarious; hunt

sacrifice, sacrifices heroic, valiant, fine, noble, supreme, ultimate, final, tireless, endless, substantial, tremendous, stunning, stupefying, astounding, astonishing, wonderful, impressive, unexampled, unprecedented, incredible, unbelievable, bitter, painful, unnecessary, small, self-imposed, vicarious, substitutionary, personal, financial, votive, sacramental

sadness heart-rending, agonizing, disquieting, besetting, overwhelming, haunting, sharp, quiet, ineffable, unadulterated, awful, immeasurable, infinite, obsessive, irremediable, unutterable, indescribable, compassionate, heartfelt, reflective

safeguard, safeguards basic, essential, fundamental, true, first-rate, cast-iron, tight, stringent, standard, proper, indispensable, permanent, dubious

safety perfect, maximum, unbounded, measurable, appreciable, tight, relative, fragile, fleeting, personal, communal, national, industrial

saga, sagas See also *narrative* (centuries-)old, ancient, (time-)honoured, venerable, glorious, boastful, historical, family

sail, sails billowing, balloon-shaped, cotton, synthetic, Dacron, threadbare, tattered, patched, patchable, main, top, second, third, three-sided, square, lateen

sailing exciting, stirring, thrilling, challenging, smooth, circular, oblique, big-water, spherical

sailor, sailors ruddy, superb, fine, accomplished, (in)experienced, (un)enthusiastic, (in)competent, (un)able, (un)skilled, (un)skilful, daring, questing, drunk(en), weary, mutinous, salt-water; recreational; self-taught; lone, round-the-world, weekend

saint, saints exalted, infallible, gentle, kind, noble, tortured, local, ascetic, tutelary, patron, healing, wooden, plaster, secular

salad, salads crunchy, crisp, leafy, spicy, gritty, garlicky, savoury, zesty, flavourful, tasty, sweet, attractive, simple, side, limp, antipasto, Basque, Breton, composée (combination), Florentine, Greek, green, Harlequin, Italian, Japonaise, Lyonnaise, mixed, niçoise, Parisienne, plain, Provençale, Roman, royal, Waldorf

salary, salaries handsome, high, fat, lavish, princely, fantastic, magnificent, extravagant, excessive, substantial, heavy, outrageous, exorbitant, good, (in)sufficient, (in)adequate, (un)reasonable, regular, static, stagnant, uncertain, low, modest, meagre, skimpy, little, small, wretched, trifling, annual, yearly, monthly, base, starting, entering, entry-level, pre-retirement

sale, sales robust, solid, healthy, buoyant, big, immense, heavy, gigantic, spectacular, blockbuster, brisk, outright, instantaneous, potential, impending, conditional, restrictive, well-timed, ill-timed, irrevocable, under-the-counter, clandestine, (il)licit, (un)lawful, dubious, secret, mediocre, lacklustre, dreary, static, anaemic, depressed, sluggish, slow, flat, mid-year, (semi-)annual, special, overseas, domestic, retail, post-holiday, post-Christmas, end-of-season, close-down, advance

salesman, salesmen See *salesperson*

salesmanship See *salesperson*

salesperson, salespersons (fully-)trained, well-trained, knowledgeable, shrewd, astute, able, superb, energetic, aggressive, enterprising, natty, (dis)honest, (un)successful, (in)experienced, (im)plausible, (un)scrupulous, glib, slick, sleek, smooth-tongued, smooth-spoken, plausible, talkative, wordy, loquacious, suave, low-pressure, persevering, persistent, tenacious, stubborn, insistent, high-pressure, high-powered, demon, crooked, rude, travelling, door-to-door

salt, salts fine, coarse, loose, fossil, insoluble, crystalline, table, smelling, rock, volatile, microcosmic, physiological, normal, alkaline, acid, basic, common, Epsom

salute, salutes rousing, jubilant, snappy, thundery, stiff, loose, hand, stiff-armed, three-fingered

sameness dull, boring, eternal, hopeless, irksome, lacklustre, lifeless, monotonous, wearisome

sample, samples exquisite, splendid, finished, complete, good, true, typical, (un)representative, (un)scientific, working, made-up, random, indifferent, unusual, sorry, core

sanction, sanctions sweeping, wide-ranging, long-standing, working, complete, total, explicit, pragmatic, efficacious, (un)bearable, (in)effective, intrusive, harsh, stringent, stiff, tough, authoritarian, Draconian, tight, leaky, punitive, mandatory, compulsory, voluntary, selective, comprehensive, world-wide, international, global, (un)official, economic, naval, air, UN-imposed, criminal

sanctity blessed, pious, pure, reverential, inviolable, unassailable, vast, inexhaustible, thoroughgoing

sanctuary, sanctuaries venerable, inviolable, unassailable, vast, inexhaustible, permanent, temporary, verdant, floral, spiritual

sand, sands (sugar-)soft, powdery, fine, coarse, heavy, gritty, loose, silty, porous, lone, empty, level, countless, incalculable, pristine, foam-dappled, barren, arid, hot, fiery, torrid, scorched, scorching, seething, abrasive, gleaming, luminescent, (ivory-)white, yellow, dark, grey, coral, silver-powdered, volcanic

sandal, sandals open-toed, thonged, winged, jewelled, coloured, laced, low-heeled, heel-less, strappy, flip-flop, gold-lamé, simple, fanciful, modern, ancient, sturdy, rubber, leather, snakeskin, straw, Egyptian, Greek, Roman, Japanese

sandwich, sandwiches fresh(ly-cut), crusty, moist, plump, hefty, overstuffed, dainty, delightful, savoury, (un)satisfying, quick, clumsy, limp, (well-)trimmed, unbuttered, open(-face), finger, bite-size, three-decker

sap milky, juicy, succulent, vital, rising

sarcasm brilliant, polished, sophisticated,

obvious, playful, poignant, keen, mordant, caustic, barbed, sharp, biting, wounding, piercing, cutting, corrosive, cruel, bitter, pungent, racy, piquant, incisive, truculent, rueful, cold, unbearable, intolerable

satellite, satellites out-of-control, crippled, defunct, nuclear-powered, solar-powered, artificial, orbital; planetary

satire, satires good-natured, gentle, cheerful, brilliant, playful, hilarious, rollicking, diverting, sophisticated, obvious, (in)offensive, outrageous, mordant, piquant, vulgar, ill-natured, unsparing, pungent, poignant, keen, biting, cutting, piercing, wounding, incisive, abusive, scurrilous, rueful, truculent, harsh, caustic, barbed, sharp, corrosive, apocalyptic, cruel, savage, acerbic, bitter, unmerited, racy, denunciatory, partisan, political

satisfaction, satisfactions enduring, abiding, permanent, unabashed, unalloyed, perfect, genuine, real, true, solid, infinite, deep, full, total, tremendous, immense, intense, ineffable, indescribable, quiet, immediate, heartfelt, obvious, special, cocky, proud, smug, recurrent, short-lived, fleeting, perverse, childlike, tangible, intrinsic, inherent, private, personal, mutual, philosophical, emotional, sexual, aesthetic

sauce, sauces taste-tempting, delectable, flavourful, fabulous, gourmet, credible, special, subtle, rich, powerful, thick, heavy, creamy, milky, thin, light, smooth, sumptuous, delicate, lumpy, chunky, white, buttery, warm, mild, medium, hot, spicy, tangy, piquant, peppery, fat-free, sweet, foamy, Alabama, Bolognese, Bordelaise, Béarnaise, brown, chasseur, Provençale, supreme, sweet and sour, tartare, Venetian

saucepan, saucepans See *pan*

savage, savages berserk, frenzied, enraged, crazed, atrocious, bestial, brutish, ferocious, merciless, ruthless, pitiless, relentless, unrelenting

savagery See also *savage* wanton, unspeakable, appalling, malicious, merciless, ruthless, pitiless, heartless, relentless, unrelenting, exultant, unparalleled, unprecedented, boorish, primitive

saver, savers inveterate, habitual, chronic,

adamant, obstinate, persistent, reluctant, obsessive, thrifty

saving, savings considerable, enormous, large, (in)significant, vaunted, sensational, vanishing, precious, low-risk, dormant, modest, painless, hard-won, cooperative, private, personal, domestic, national

saviour, saviours God-sent, heaven-sent, last-minute, unexpected

saw, saws snarling, abrasive, (extra-)large, thin, narrow, fine-toothed, coarse-toothed, two-handed, two-handled, diamond-tipped, diamond-faced, power(-operated), fuel-powered, computer-assisted, computer-driven, tapering, circular, rotary

saying, sayings faithful, trustful, witty, pithy, snappy, proverbial, prophetic, famous, well-known, common(place), colloquial, deep, mysterious, secret, obscure, dark, trite, hackneyed, well-worn, stale

scale, scales (1: hierarchy; level) astonishing, grand, large, big, enormous, monumental, massive, gigantic, unprecedented, high, ingratiating, special, minute, small, (un)satisfactory, global, sliding

scale, scales (2: weighing machine) delicate, (in)sensitive, (in)accurate, (un)balanced, (dis)honest, portable, hanging, centesimal, main, auxiliary, electronic

scale, scales (3: sequence of musical notes) pentatonic, minor, major, chromatic

scandal, scandals stinking, disgusting, appalling, atrocious, disgraceful, disreputable, shameful, real, open, flagrant, (un)common, widespread, spectacular, odious, outrageous, notorious, nasty, racy, tawdry, unsavoury, unpardonable, wild, public, domestic, national, political, financial, sex

scar, scars lasting, permanent, deep, obvious, distinctive, (un)recognizable, (in)visible, (in)conspicuous, hidden, fading, (un)healing, temporary, indelible, sickle-shaped, unsightly, hideous, ugly, grievous, congenital, facial, physical; emotional, psychological, psychic

scarcity See *rarity*

scarf, scarves exquisite, fine, luxurious, elegant, fussy, dated, light, flimsy,

diaphanous, translucent, sheer, bright, multicoloured, colourful, floral, polka-dot, triangular, square, full-sized, flowing, tasselly, (hand)woven, warm, woollen, chiffon, silk(en), gossamer, cotton, batik, plaid, paisley, tartan

scene, scenes soothing, rewarding, commanding, compelling, intriguing, stunning, amazing, breathtaking, thrilling, startling, (soul-)staggering, haunting, fascinating, entrancing, bewitching, charming, enchanting, alluring, glittering, dazzling, sweeping, outstanding, fabulous, legendary, magical, spectacular, heady, colourful, glorious, grand, sublime, sumptuous, magnificent, splendid, wonderful, super, superb, exquisite, gorgeous, stately, majestic, gracious, dramatic, luxuriant, unsurpassed, matchless, unmatched, unequal, unaccustomed, unique, unforgettable, memorable, indescribable, (in)distinguishable, unbelievable, incredible, peaceful, restful, serene, quiet, intimate, secluded, (un)familiar, exotic, vivid, varied, lively, climactic, telling, variegated, euphoric, picturesque, panoramic, postcard-perfect, (picture-)perfect, picture-postcard, photogenic, quaint, pleasant, beautiful, attractive, fine, imaginary, visionary, evocative, outlandish, bizarre, unsettling, forbidding, awesome, grim, grisly, scary, weird, grotesque, phantasmal, wild, unearthly, uncanny, poignant, touching, heart-rending, agonizing, depressing, searing, harrowing, distressing, painful, melancholy, sad, grim, macabre, desolate, sickening, tense, rugged, savage, rowdy, steamy, lustful, erotic, chaotic, stark, banal, familiar, torpid, simple, eons-old, pristine, primitive, rural, sylvan, country, rustic, arcadian, pastoral, idyllic, mountain, Alpine (alpine), wilderness

scenery See *scene*

scent, scents cloying, overwhelming, lingering, fleeting, momentary, unexpected, subtle, delightful, exquisite, glorious, heavenly, pleasant, romantic, spirited, fresh, sweet, mellow, rich, air-borne, hot, warm, keen, cold, faint, weak, strong, heady, deep, (too-)thick, heavy, repugnant, detectable, (in)definable, (un)familiar, exotic, new, bitter, musty, fusty, musky, rural, chemical, aphrodisiac

sceptic, sceptics confirmed, inveterate, habitual, chronic

scepticism See *doubt*

schedule, schedules (un)reasonable, (un)feasible, optimistic, disciplined, punctual, (in)efficient, well-thought-out, typical, (ir)regular, set, (ab)normal, (in)flexible, elastic, ambitious, marathon, long, busy, heavy, active, full, fixed, strict, rigid, tight, (over)crowded, demanding, tiring, staggering, grinding, gruelling, taxing, optimum, fast, helter-skelter, complicated, complex, intricate, hectic, rigorous, tough, frantic, fierce, brutal, strenuous, disorderly, confused, chaotic, daily, weekly, monthly, year-round, formal, skeleton, social, domestic

scheme, schemes (in)effective, (un)feasible, (un)workable, prudent, subtle, simple, neat, substantial, clever, (in)sensible, sane, wise, ingenious, (in)flexible, (dis)honest, elaborate, sophisticated, (un)fruitful, (im)mature, revolutionary, model, massive, grand(iose), spectacular, long-range, (im)practicable, (un)practical, (im)practical, substantive, visionary, chimerical, romantic, fanciful, airy-fairy, (un)real, ambitious, audacious, giddy, sinister, barren, fruitless, cock-eyed, crude, tortuous, intricate, wild-eyed, (il)licit, abortive, absurd, impossible, mad, artful, dubious, half-baked, foolish, (im)prudent, sly, crafty, tricky, wild, rash, crazy, malicious, (in)(un)substantial, crackbrained, senseless, eccentric, strange, delusive, misleading, fraudulent, deceptive, insane, hare-brained, ill-advised, ill-judged, imprudent, (un)wise, (dis)honest, mean, rascally, base, (il)legal, devious, nefarious, (im)mature, get-rich-quick, infinite, pervasive, latent, regulatory, procedural, pilot

scholar, scholars erudite, accomplished, complete, exceptional, competent, well-known, noted, famous, eminent, established, ripe, distinguished, (much-)honoured, renowned, venerable, estimable, celebrated, first-rate, outstanding, once-in-a-millennium, notable, illustrious, successful, great, global, brilliant, superb, natural, assiduous, vigorous, persevering, hardworking, ever-toiling, diligent, industrious, weary, thorough, profound, true, meticulous, systematic, accurate, careful, dedicated, punctual, patient, conscientious, (un)orthodox, (un)conventional, open-minded, liberal, genial, absent-minded, eccentric, ungainly, sedentary, dull, gloomy, earnest, solemn, austere, ponderous, resident, visiting, vagrant, wandering, ideological, religious, literary

scholarship (1: learning) sound, accurate, precise, scrupulous, thorough, impressive, solid, profound, painstaking, amazing, striking, outstanding, original, fruitful, passionate, refined, (in)adequate, liberal, sterile, fruitless, sloppy

scholarship, scholarships (2: grant-in-aid) open, closed, athletic, academic

school, schools (institution for learning) illustrious, prestigious, fine, quality, renowned, reputable, blue-ribbon, exclusive, pricey, upper-crust, upper-class, superior, selective, élite, prized, thriving, ambitious, innovative, (un)accredited, (un)licensed, (over)crowded, congested, mediocre, dreadful, regular, common, traditional, alternative, national, special, compulsory, voluntary, free, paying, for-profit, single-sex, boys(only), (all-)girls, all-male, all-female, coeducational, (non-)sectarian, (de)segregated, mixed, multiracial, state-run, church-run, denominational, multicultural, rural, urban, diocesan, parochial, year-round, spare-time, maintained, opted-out, grant-maintained, voluntary-aided, spartan, continuation, elementary, preparatory, model, primary, secondary, high, boarding, residential, day, evening, night, independent, private, public, grammar, technical, industrial, academic, comprehensive, vocational, technological, normal, trade, commercial, secretarial, language, progressive, consolidated, charity, reform, reformatory, summer, Sunday

schooldays See *days*

schooling See *education*

schoolmaster, schoolmistress See *teacher*

science, sciences exact, rudimentary,
big, contentious, descriptive, explanatory,
experimental, cognitive, natural, social,
applied, physical, political, mathematical,
earth, pure, biological, zoological,
behavioural, forensic; occult, domestic
scientist, scientists credible, persevering,
hardworking, ever-toiling, (un)orthodox,
(un)conventional, senior, brilliant,
absent-minded, patient, cool, dedicated,
eminent, distinguished, famous, illustrious,
celebrated, renowned, well-known, notable,
reputed, prominent, leading, accomplished,
noted, established, honoured, venerable,
first-rate, outstanding, top-notch, great,
global, world-class, superb, successful,
earnest, thorough, meticulous, systematic,
innovative, productive,
once-in-a-millennium, budding, promising
scolding mild, smart, (un)qualified, good,
sharp, severe, harsh, stinging, indignant,
caustic, hurtful, truculent, virulent,
vitriolic, vituperative, (un)just,
(un)deserved, unearned, (un)warranted,
unjustified, (un)justifiable
scorn devastating, withering, stinging,
sonorous, robust, radiant, oblique, dry,
contemptuous, derisive, disdainful, snippy,
supercilious, critical, (un)warranted, bitter,
regal, righteous, unearned, (un)deserved,
(un)just, unjustified, (un)justifiable
scoundrel, scoundrels out-and-out,
thorough, complete, unmitigated, utter,
absolute, thoroughgoing, heavy, veritable,
great, outright, precious, deep-dyed,
dyed-in-the-wool, abominable, treacherous,
deceitful, unscrupulous, unconscionable,
vicious, barbarous, cunning, sly, crafty,
usurious
scream, screams (ear-)piercing,
ear-splitting, (blood-)chilling,
bloodcurdling, hair-raising, ecstatic,
exultant, jubilant, joyous, blissful,
victorious, triumphant, throaty, hoarse,
round, mighty, wild, metallic, shrill, long,
sustained, insistent, interminable,
incoherent, unforgettable, grotesque,
curious, eerie, ghostly, mysterious,
unearthly, delirious, blasphemous, tense,
stifled, (half-)suppressed, muffled,
repeated, primal, prim(a)eval
screaming See *scream*
screening thorough, astute, perceptive,

incisive, precise, intimate, detailed,
exhaustive, comprehensive, profound,
in-depth, mandatory, optional
scrutiny proper, careful, meticulous,
narrow, strict, rigid, close, intense,
thorough, minute, rigorous, severe,
exhaustive, considerable, extensive,
ceaseless, unremitting, unwinking, basic,
essential, fundamental, preliminary,
microscopic, extra, sceptical, curious
sculptor, sculptors See also *artist*
abstract, kinetic, minimalist
sculpture, sculptures dazzling,
spectacular, glorious, superb, exuberant,
delightful, genuine, authentic, spurious,
5-metre-high, monumental, gigantic,
alabaster, bronze, ebony, granite, iron,
steel, ivory, jade, lacquer, marble, plaster,
plasticine, porcelain, ceramic, terracotta,
clay, wooden, hand-carved, lonely,
moving, free-standing, (audio)kinetic,
dynamic, static, relief, abstract, heroic
sea, seas murmuring, foaming, glittering,
shining, seething, lapping, rollicking,
rippling, tossing, buoyant, enchanted,
quiet, calm, serene, peaceful, restful, still,
unruffled, plumy, inviolate, gentle,
majestic, splendid, magnificent,
unpolluted, sunny, moonlit,
morning-becalmed, mirror-smooth,
crystal(line), iridescent, amber, jade,
emerald-green, blue(-green), blue-grey,
too-blue-to-believe, azure, cerulean, indigo,
brownish, turquoise, aquamarine, copper,
black, dark, mottled, sullen, bountiful,
boundless, tideless, wind-blessed, open,
giant, steep, uncharted, sleepless,
sub-polar, high, territorial, frigid, chilly,
frozen, trackless, impassable, hostile, cruel,
inhospitable, unkind, wavy, billowy,
choppy, rough, stormy, heavy, confused,
tormented, agitated, turbulent, wild,
ferocious, furious, raging, towering,
mountainous, fretful, troubled, boisterous,
restless, changeable, volatile, unpredictable,
mysterious, fidgety, roaring, tempestuous,
tumultuous, violent, formidable, harsh,
storm-tossed, white-capped, windswept,
ice-covered, tide-driven, tide-ridden,
current-ridden, treacherous, lumpy, fair,
stratified, salty, unproductive,
trash-strewn, landlocked, inland
seal, seals squalling, snarling, roaring,

howling, bleating, snorting, sprawling, splashing, sluggish, harmless, ringed, spotted, true (hair), eared, hooded

seaman, seamen See *sailor*

search, searching useful, (un)fruitful, (un)productive, leisurely, (un)reasonable, careful, meticulous, (im)proper, serious, diligent, close, narrow, thorough, intensive, concerted, large-scale, full(-scale), massive, exhaustive, strenuous, painful, painstaking, rigorous, unyielding, determined, obstinate, obsessive, energetic, frenzied, feverish, frantic, fervid, tense, hazardous, time-consuming, long, lengthy, three-day, never-ending, endless, ceaseless, continual, sempiternal, quixotic, insatiable, exasperating, irritable, desperate, piteous, doleful, dubious, furtive, futile, bootless, fruitless, useless, vain, unavailing, inconclusive, needless, deliberate, surreptitious, elusive, unabashed, haphazard, perfunctory, impulsive, inept, instant, swift, random, initial, nationwide, house-to-house

season, seasons enchanting, vitalizing, auspicious, enchanted, festal, festive, gay, joyous, lustrous, exciting, stirring, thrilling, spectacular, sensational, glorious, magnificent, active, busy, vibrant, hectic, frenzied, intemperate, rush, crucial, distinct, early, late, slow, slack, off, stagnant, inactive, open, behindhand, current, peak, dull, backward, rutting

seat, seats deep, springlike, springy, cushiony, cushioned, decent, plush, luxuriant, soft, hard, rigid, fixed, immovable, flexible, straight-backed, squeaking, cramped, regular, customary, usual, habitual, inside, outside, rush, rustic, webbed, reeded, (un)reserved, unfilled, unoccupied, vacant, bookable, contested, back, rear, front(-row), sliding, folding; hot; parliamentary

seaweed, seaweeds See *weed*

seclusion peaceful, restful, delicious, aloof, inaccessible, unapproachable, monastic, hermitical, monkish, cloistered, withdrawn, solitary, detached, virtual, strange, sullen, deep

secrecy alert, deep, profound, impenetrable, unfathomable, dead, total, utter, complete, strict, tight, stunning, thrilling, curious, murky, notorious, pathological, golden

secret, secrets stunning, thrilling, threatening, tormenting, emerging, impenetrable, unfathomable, profound, deep, mysterious, obscure, top, dark, open, little, grisly, naughty, saucy, terrible, wretched, dirty, sensitive, shameful, innermost, dead, ancient, hidden, least-known, (better-)kept, best-kept, guarded, unfathomed, ill-begotten, forbidden

secretary, secretaries loyal, devoted, (in)experienced, (in)capable, (in)competent, (un)able, (un)qualified, (in)efficient, senior, junior, acting, confidential, personal, private, executive, administrative, principal, legal, medical

sect, sects tiny, secretive, perdurable, dissident, indigenous, native, religious

security (1: safety; protection) overwhelming, lasting, assured, (ultra-)tight, tough, inviolable (inviolate), (in)effective, (in)adequate, strict, rigorous, intense, intensive, stringent, real, genuine, cosy, (in)competent, flawed, leaky, lax, skimpy, flimsy, illusory, (in)conspicuous, unobtrusive, long-term, short-term, ultimate, collective, cooperative, internal, regional, national, social, personal, material, financial

security, securities (2: surety; evidence of property) gilt-edged, good, marketable, speculative, (un)safe, (un)reliable, high-risk, low-interest, high-interest, short-term, long-term, (ir)redeemable, registered, collateral

seed, seeds (im)mature, air-borne, wind-borne, aromatic, pungent, clean, dormant, fertile, viable, rare, beanlike, stony, woody, pulpy, oleaginous, oily, starchy, edible, hybrid, monocot, dicot; canary

segregation total, complete, compulsory, obligatory, mandatory, (in)voluntary, racial, residential, civic, de facto

selection, selections dazzling, astonishing, striking, intriguing, staggering, stunning, unrivalled, unequalled, judicious, wise, well-advised, superb, wonderful, fantastic, incisive, (un)limited, thorough, careful, careless, (un)fair, (un)worthy, vast, extensive, bountiful, wide(-ranging), eclectic, (un)representative, rigorous, skeletal, poor, ill-advised, random; natural

self-assurance exhilarating, graceful, bold, powerful, impregnable, airy, affected, feigned, high-handed, overbearing, overpowering, domineering, arrogant, haughty, vainglorious, brash, arbitrary, diminished

self-confidence See *self-assurance*

self-defence (il)legitimate, (il)legal, (un)lawful, (un)warranted

self-denial rigorous, Spartan, rigid, austere, drastic, harsh, inclement, relentless, restrained, ruthless, tough, vigorous, unyielding

self-esteem unblemished, (un)flawed, high, boundless, (in)sufficient, low, poor

selfishness infernal, atrocious, awful, terrible, incredible, unbelievable, rampant, abiding, unrestrained

self-satisfaction See *satisfaction*

seller, sellers See also *salesperson* shrewd, (un)scrupulous, (dis)honest, wily, crooked, (over-)anxious, wholesome

seminar, seminars arcane, esoteric, recondite, academic, advisory

send-off, send-offs warm, affectionate, cordial, enthusiastic, genial, emotional, excited, fervent

senility See *old age*

sensation, sensations refreshing, vivid, visceral, agreeable, wonderful, sweet, delicious, (un)pleasurable, unforgettable, incredible, unbelievable, curious, queer, eerie, inexplicable, inexpressible, uneasy, numb, dizzy, sick, cold, intense, intimate, sour, dull, tight, painful, prickly, hair-prickling, startling, tingling, burning, sickening, griping, suffocating, cramping, lurking, haunting, lingering, passing, momentary, short-lived, sudden

sensationalism sheer, cheap, popular, vulgar, worthless, coarse, clumsy, bizarre, sickly, mawkish, tasteless, unabashed

sense, senses (1: ability) sound, unerring, proper, practical, keen, acute, refined, exhilarating, fearful, shaky, wavering, defective, intuitive, illusory, special (exterior), general (interior), visceral, tactile, optical, visual, auditory, olfactory, artistic, commercial; sixth

sense, senses (2: meaning) See *meaning*

sense of guilt vague, dubious, indefinable, superstitious, fearful

sense of humour See also *humour* subtle, keen, trenchant, elaborate, great, strong, wonderful, quick, lively, bubbly, notable, exquisite, delightful, warm, fantastic, pawky, unfailing, unsleeping, exuberant, ebullient, built-in, irrepressible, saving, lambent, quiet, reserved, subdued, dry, mild, (un)healthy, offbeat, whimsical, clumsy, queer, peculiar, odd, weird, bizarre, wry, sardonic, mustardy, sly, wicked, impish, mischievous, sarcastic, transcendent, bitter, (self-)mocking, self-deprecating, off-colour

sensitiveness, sensitivity exquisite, delicate, finished, rare, discriminative, acute

sentence, sentences (1: complete thought expressed in words) shapely, balanced, careful, (in)coherent, effective, terse, expressive, punchy, commonplace, convoluted, complicated, laboured, confused, intricate, tortuous, tumid, ambiguous, unintelligible, cryptic, cumbersome, cumulous, awkward, clumsy, prolix, wordy, perfunctory, careless, disjointed, rambling, dangling, fragmented, run-on, sesquipedalian, redundant, spasmodic, choppy, verbose, false, flat, long-winded, shoddy, objectionable, assertive, interrogative, declarative, imperative, exclamatory, simple, compound, complex, causative, loose, periodic, closed, open

sentence, sentences (2: period of prison confinement) stiff, heavy, harsh, severe, Draconian, irreversible, irrevocable, maximum, perverse, inconceivable, (in)determinate, (in)definite, unusual, (in)adequate, (im)moderate, lenient, light

sentiment, sentiments high-minded, winged, elevated, lofty, fantastic, tender, heartfelt, pacifist, deep, plentiful, widespread, prevailing, ruling, genteel, (im)proper, (un)becoming, (un)suitable, misguided, hawkish, glum, washy, mushy, hollow, (in)sincere

sentimentalism, sentimentality cloying, whining, mawkish, insipid, unabashed, callow, sickly, cheap, vulgar, coarse, clumsy, bizarre, inexpressible, shallow

separation amicable, peaceable, peaceful,

(un)friendly, unimaginable, unfortunate, painful, wretched, acrimonious, indefinite, eventual, imminent, (un)avoidable, inevitable, (un)timely, (un)expected, absolute, total, complete, voluntary, judicial, legal, racial, emotional; surgical

sequence, sequences (im)proper, (il)logical, random, rapid(-fire), quick, endless, continuous, alphabetical, chronological, numeral, ordinal

serenade, serenades love-sick, yearning, wishful, nostalgic

serenity See *calm*

series intriguing, exciting, thrilling, stirring, interesting, great, (un)successful, popular, endless, unending, undying, unbroken, ongoing; asymptotic(al)

seriousness profound, deep, solemn, stern, grave, dead(ly), complete, absolute, mock

sermon, sermons stirring, moving, eloquent, aphoristic, ornate, fine, sober, sombre, dreary, boring, (un)interesting, dull, tedious, garrulous, never-ending, lay

serpent, serpents See *snake*

servant, servants trusty, devoted, dedicated, responsible, attentive, efficient, tasteful, dutiful, duteous, obsequious, fawning, humble, slavish, (dis)loyal, (dis)honest, clumsy, unwilling, (dis)obedient, (un)faithful, (un)grateful, (im)competent, (ir)responsible, (un)trustworthy, stolid, impassive, liveried, uniformed, indoor, outdoor, household, domestic, personal, public; civil

service, services (1: work performed; employment) caring, attentive, deferential, respectful, helpful, faithful, dedicated, genuine, golden, inestimable, meritorious, impeccable, exemplary, unsurpassed, peerless, incomparable, laudatory, noble, courtly, prompt, unselfish, superior, knowledgeable, commendable, distinguished, outstanding, exceptional, (pre-)eminent, singular, noteworthy, indefatigable, fastidious, state-of-the-art, perfect, (in)efficient, (in)competent, (ultra-)posh, excellent, friendly, lasting, (in)adequate, (un)reliable, (in)accessible, (in)frequent, (un)affordable, gracious, courteous, cheerful, fast, immediate, instinctive, noted, (un)obtrusive, resolute, viable, necessary, basic, essential, core,

indispensable, valuable, extensive, comprehensive, enormous, immeasurable, exhaustive, special, round-the-clock, all-day, gratuitous, thankful, discretionary, discreet, peculiar, bare-bone, skeleton, unusual, esoteric, casual, intermittent, intrusive, snobbish, rude, poor, slovenly, remiss, slow, inferior, menial, sullen, inefficient, indifferent, grudging, venal, awful, dismal, lamentable, chaotic, half-baked, shoddy, spotty, scant, meagre, non-existent, unnecessary, corrupt, dubious, clandestine, insouciant, surly, (now)defunct, experimental, elective, voluntary, compulsory, obligatory, (un)professional, actual, active, nominal, pensionable, wartime, consumer, secret, public, social, civil, personal, diplomatic, medical, therapeutic, divine, sacrificial, emergency, selective, recreational, community, ancillary, auxiliary, supplementary; military

service, services (2: religious ceremony) stirring, emotional, pious, dedicated, devout, solemn, sombre, mournful, joyful, joyous, elaborate, beautiful, impressive, formal, secular, religious, (multi-)denominational, non-denominational, public, choral, divine, holy, blessed, commemorative, remembrance, memorial, requiem, funeral, marriage, matrimonial, baptismal, religious, liturgical, ecumenical, Sunday, Thanksgiving, Passover, Christmas, Easter

serving, servings generous, ample, plentiful, large, big, sinful, individual, small, scanty, skimpy, stingy, measly, second, subsequent

servitude ignominious, degrading, debasing, disgraceful, dishonourable, humiliating, shameful, vile, low, contemptible, disgusting, repulsive, involuntary, political, intellectual; penal

session, sessions fruitful, lively, intimate, cosy, (un)productive, (un)successful, arduous, time-consuming, fruitless, miserable, testy, stormy, hectic, heated, fierce, tumultuous, marathon, hilarious, typical, (in)formal, unprecedented, morning, summer, five-hour, all-night, late-night, round-the-clock, follow-up, current, plenary, group, public, private, special,

open, closed(-door), extraordinary, joint,
emergency, working, legislative, surgical,
photo, memorial, parliamentary, tutorial,
remedial

set, sets (series; collection) dazzling,
coveted, priceless, one-of-a-kind, unusual,
unique, fine, irreplaceable, impressive,
antique, mathematical, (im)perfect,
(in)complete, whole, broken

setback, setbacks crushing, stunning,
debilitating, humiliating, painful, lethal,
decisive, serious, severe, major, huge,
significant, remarkable, sharp, sad,
sudden, temporary, slight, minor

setting, settings attractive, fine,
appropriate, colourful, pretty, picturesque,
picture-postcard, superb, exquisite,
remarkable, splendid, magnificent, quiet,
peaceful, tranquil, relaxing, enervating,
casual, congenial, quaint, cosy, intimate,
idyllic, unique, exotic, dramatic, majestic,
spectacular, harmonious, park-like,
circumspect, private, romantic, poetic,
nostalgic, opulent, elaborate, extravagant,
ornate, luxuriant, imperial, perfect, proper,
(in)appropriate, unlikely, artificial,
grandiose, visual, geographic(al), pristine,
natural, bosky, rural, pastoral, wooded,
sylvan, alpine, foreign, indigenous,
metropolitan, true-to-life, fairy-tale,
cerebral

settlement, settlements (agreement)
groundbreaking, amicable, peaceful,
(un)reasonable, hopeful, equitable,
(un)fair, (un)just, (un)satisfactory,
comprehensive, overall, high-wind, ample,
generous, speedy, imminent, permanent,
lasting, tentative, negotiable, compromise,
final, binding, voluntary, communal,
social, financial, strike-free, penal,
out-of-court

settler, settlers stout-hearted, brave,
courageous, undaunted, (un)satisfied,
early, original, pioneer, permanent,
temporary, homesteading

severity exacting, blistering, domineering,
overbearing, excruciating, gruelling,
scorching, trying, uncompromising,
unrelenting, harsh, stringent, puritanical,
rigid, rigorous, strict, narrow-minded,
prudish, priggish, austere, Victorian,
Draconian

sex, sexes (1: one of two groups into

which animals are divided) fair, gentle,
embattled, undetermined

sex (2: sexual intercourse; sexual
matters) (un)satisfactory, (un)safe,
(un)protected, (ab)normal, (un)restricted,
consensual, enjoyable, playful, guilt-free,
free, excessive, (in)frequent, repeated,
lusty, steamy, erotic, promiscuous,
orgiastic, immoral, perverse, explicit, prior,
premature, kinky, forcible, forced,
coercive, brutal, painful, disgraceful,
degrading, hazardous, high-risk, risky,
unwanted, uninhibited, unrestrained,
unscheduled, spontaneous, compulsive,
predatory, desultory, fleeting, random,
casual, penetrative, solitary, oral, anal,
vaginal, marital, extra-marital, pre-marital,
(il)licit, (un)lawful, anonymous, gay,
homosexual, lesbian, heterosexual, straight

sex appeal disarming, ingratiating,
charming, captivating, bewitching,
enchanting, entrancing, fascinating,
tempting, attractive, irresistible, magnetic,
mesmeric

sexism counter-productive, reverse,
historic, systemic

shack, shacks See *hut*

shade (1: shelter from the sun) cool,
plenteous, leafy, wispy, slight, faint,
subtle, momentary, fleeting, steamy,
(sun-)dappled, mottled, protective

shade, shades (2: variation of colour) See
colour

shade, shades (3: slight difference;
nuance) subtle, imperceptible

shade, shades (4: flexible screen for
windows) See *blind* and *curtain*

shadow, shadows fleeting, momentary,
darkling, morose, ominous, hanging,
dappled, giant, mournful, fantastic, odd,
grotesque, queer, mysterious,
indecipherable, ambiguous, obscure, faint,
indistinct, feeble, dim, subdued, unbroken,
gaunt, distorted

shake-up, shake-ups See *organization*

shaking severe, rigorous, terrible, violent,
persistent, ceaseless, unceasing, endless,
unending, rapid, convulsive

shame, shamelessness overwhelming,
everlasting, wounding, crying, burning,
degrading, debasing, fawning, cringing,
frightful, dirty, mortal, terrible,
confounded, abject, inglorious,

ignominious, infamous, vulgar, disgraceful, colossal, abysmal

shape, shapes elegant, graceful, impressive, wonderful, distinctive, final, simple, elementary, primitive, basic, rudimentary, embryonic, complex, bold, mobile, exact, precise, (un)certain, (in)definite, (un)usual, (un)familiar, (ir)regular, (in)distinct, vague, random, dim, faint, strange, awkward, uncanny, fantastic, odd, grotesque, eccentric, obscure, monstrous, ghostly, awful, disgraceful, weird, bizarre, exotic, distorted, inhuman, dark, bad, base, despicable, (un)faceted, multifaceted, diverse, rigid, persistent, boxy, round, square, oblong, triangular, rectangular, polygonal, quadrilateral, pentagonal, hexagonal, heptagonal, octagonal, nonagonal, decagonal, hendecagonal, nebular, spiral, angular, oblique, geometric(al), pyramidal, aerodynamic

share, shares (1: portion; allotment) (in)equitable, (dis)proportionate, inordinate, all-important, siz(e)able, good, large, big, considerable, huge, enormous, generous, immense, whopping, (in)significant, meagre, small, little, tiny, trifling, lump-sum

share, shares (2: each of the equal parts into which a business is divided) See also *stock* (1) (fast-)growing, soaring, good, worthless, deferred, preference, subordinate, convertible, common

shareholder, shareholders See also *investor* major, small, nervous, public, institutional, majority, minority

shark, sharks darting, twisting, circling, basking, fearsome, aggressive, remorseless, ferocious, predatory, docile, harmless, slim-bodied, smooth-skinned, six-gilled, deepwater, pelagic, viviparous, shale, white, blue, dusky

shawl, shawls fine, (extra-)luxurious, diaphanous, translucent, sheer, plaid, paisley, colourful, painted, hand-knit, (hand-)woven, tasselled, fringed, whimsical, full-sized, silk

shay, shays See *carriage*

shed, sheds wooden, slant-roofed, tin-roofed, rustic, rude, rudimentary, jerry-built, precarious, modest, lowly, humble, sordid, squalid, uncouth, damp,

weathered, weather-beaten, cramped

sheep bleating, snuffling, wandering, skittish, uncontrollable, stray, silly, gaunt, docile, friendly, fluffy, fat-tailed, horned, fleecy, curly-fleeced, fine-wool(l)ed, long-wool(l)ed, crossbred-wool(l)ed, medium-wool(l)ed, coarse-wool(l)ed, big-boned, domestic, wild

sheet, sheets (broad piece of cloth) soft, itchy, coloured, plain, snowy, starched, waterproof; winding

shelf, shelves top, bottom, high, low(er), deep, slant, sloping, adjustable, fixed, wall-mounted, crowded, (over-)crammed, bare, mantel

shell, shells (the outer protective covering) protective, smooth, delicate, graceful, (rock-)hard, impenetrable, unusual, perfect, (im)mature, spiral, conical, ellipsoidal, cordate, helmet-like, flaky, husky, spiny, ridged, cone-shaped, pointed, bevelled, cracked, spent, algae-bearded, whorled, calcareous, helical, molluscan (molluscous)

shellfish See *fish*

shelter, shelters (in)adequate, (un)comfortable, (un)affordable, (im)proper, (in)secure, (un)safe, rainproof, protective, shady, leafy, breezy, rudimentary, crude, meagre, idle, useless, temporary, permanent, extemporaneous, hardened, fortified, emergency, crisis, underground; divine

shepherd, shepherds wandering, roving, nomadic, migrant, migratory, itinerant, unwary, rustic, rural

shield, shields sheltering, protective, defensive, indestructible, round, oval, rectangular, oblong, decorated, canvas-covered; human

shift, shifts (1: change in place or position) subtle, commendable, remarkable, historic, baffling, bewildering, radical, dramatic, absolute, sudden, abrupt, far-reaching, major, tremendous, substantial, massive, broad, fundamental, marked, perceptible, noticeable, manifest, obvious, (un)predictable, gradual, downward, minor, cataclysmic, terrible, deadly, tectonic, temporal, spatial, demographic; paradigm(atic)

shift, shifts (2: group of people working at one time) (un)popular, (un)desirable,

(ir)regular, long, short, early, late, day, night, varying, swing, split, double, back
ship, ships wallowing, veering, passing, speeding, floating, sinking, saucy, smart, sleek, nimble, graceful, trim, leisurely, seaworthy, able, (un)steady, (un)stable, fine, luxurious, luxury, (ultra-)deluxe, staunch, unsinkable, state-of-the-art, vintage, doughty, snug, well-built, heavy-timbered, (well-)prepared, swift, sweet, proud, sophisticated, fabulous, majestic, magnificent, glamorous, legendary, sturdy, clean, sound, glittery, gleaming, (full-)rigged, square-rigged, bark-rigged, capacious, large, gargantuan, monster, tall, heavy, beamy, twin-hulled, steel-hulled, narrow-beamed, high-masted, high-funnelled, two-masted, three-masted, four-masted, high-bowed, sleep-aboard, deep-draught, sickle-shaped, stubby, leaky, sunken, lost, unseaworthy, crank, rusted, rusting, rust-streaked, stricken, grubby, derelict, stiff, ungainly, wobbly, obsolete, unusable, clumsy, irreparable, slender, seafaring, transatlantic, empty, unmanned, becalmed, well-appointed, well-found, weather-bound, fogbound, storm-battered, ice-bound, handy, (nuclear-)armed, nuclear-powered, ghostly, phantom, fighting, war, capital, naval, motor, sailing, passenger, rotor, merchant, commercial, whaling, oceanographic
shipment, shipments incoming, outgoing, big, secret, clandestine, illegal, unimpeded, humanitarian
shirt, shirts designer, tailor-made, fancy, dashing, exquisite, (un)comfortable, crisp, cool, slim, heavy, stiff, close-fitting, tight, loose, roomy, long-sleeved, shiny-fronted, French-cuffed, button-down, open-neck, turtleneck, spread-collar, collarless, slipover, lace-jabot, plaid, (pin-)striped, checked, flowered, oxford, print, stencilled, ruffled, long-john, bold, muted, see-through, plain-vanilla, flannel, cotton, silk, linen, chambray, muslin, batik, shrunken, threadbare, scruffy, tacky, flashy, dress, casual; hair
shock, shocks appalling, distressing, frightening, startling, stunning, humiliating, degrading, severe, terrible, nasty, (un)pleasant, rude, awful, traumatic, brutal, dreadful, deep, profound,

powerful, considerable, pervasive, nationwide, irreversible, genuine, curious, faint, initial, secondary, electric(al), economic, cataclysmic, psychological, seismic, thermal; anaphylactic
shoe, shoes elegant, dainty, trendy, sumptuous, fabulous, durable, sturdy, easy, snug, (un)comfortable, custom-made, superior, light, fanciful, unique, revolutionary, ready-made, machine-made, flat, upturned, (well-)polished, shining, gleaming, shiny, pointy, toeless, open-toed, cushion-soled, crepe-soled, rubber-soled, heavy-soled, rigid-soled, tough-soled, well-heeled, flat-heeled, spiked(-heel), low-heeled, heelless, low-cut, low-top, high-top, lace-up, wedged, heavy, sturdy, waterproof, water-repellent, non-skid, multicoloured, tight, ill-fitting, pinching, (un)laced, tightly-lace(d), laceless, ribboned, hobnailed, pomponed, covered, protective, delicate, suede, leather, canvas, corduroy, suede-bottom, patent-leather, crocodile, snakeskin, wooden, silver-sheathed, sedate, fantastical, extravagant, old-style, funny-looking, odd, clumsy, loose, floppy, slippy, slippery, slithery, scruffy, slipshod, shabby, sloppy, pathetic, (out)worn, well-worn, worn-out, shredded, broken, threadbare, sweaty, leaky, muddy, soil-dusty, grubby, noisy, squeaky, sodden, cast-off, missing, damp, inferior, dress, casual, athletic, orthotic, orthopaedic, corrective, platform, all-round
shooting, shootings rough, brutal, savage, wild, futile, unjustifiable, indiscriminate, wanton, random, sporadic, (un)systematic, controversial, unlawful, offhand, gang-related, terrorist, celebratory
shop, shops See also *store* fashionable, trendy, smart, elegant, reputable, stately, scrumptious, sumptuous, posh, up-market, expensive, dear, enticing, wonderful, off-beat, unusual, unconventional, sleek, busy, curio, well-stocked, sparkling, intriguing, tiny, pristine, thrift, mass-appeal, second-hand, tacky, shabby, dingy, dim, cramped, unkempt, unswept, shuttered, private, state-run, local, open, closed, preferential, rental, self-service, artisan, porno, duty-free; (non-)union
shopkeeper, shopkeepers See *merchant*
shopper, shoppers smart, shrewd,

(un)wise, hesitant, reluctant, cautious, careful, frugal, thrifty, recession-wary, price-conscious, bargain-conscious, bargain-crazy, aggressive, fastidious, demanding, eager, (dis)satisfied, last-minute, panicky, frantic, irascible, irritable, testy, weary, strolling, hurrying, gullible, cash-starved, disgruntled, impulsive, impulse, hard-core

shopping enticing, attractive, easy, (un)pleasant, prudent, irksome, strenuous, one-stop, impulse, cashless, cross-border, toll-free; armchair, window

shore, shores inviting, alluring, balmy, floral, palm-fringed, cactus-studded, playful, moonlit, sunlit, (in)visible, far-distant, dramatic, spectacular, majestic, endless, bare, virgin, interminable, muddy, sandy, marshy, swampy, craggy, gravelly, rocky, granite, pebbled, complex, steep, precipitous, sloping, twisting, curving, rambling, shallow, shelving, serrate, unknown, strange, exotic, vulnerable, forbidding, unforgiving, hostile, (in)hospitable, bleak, evil-looking, wild, lonely, primitive, untamed, exposed, unprotected, rugged, wave-eroded, scalloped, jagged, ragged, frigid, coastal, coral, lee

shortage, shortages agonizing, biting, alarming, pressing, recurrent, widespread, massive, dramatic, critical, crucial, drastic, acute, persistent, chronic, endemic, perpetual, temporary, unforeseen, sporadic, dangerous, painful, terrible, desperate, crisis-level, serious, dire

shortcoming, shortcomings See *defect*

shot, shots (1: a discharge of a firearm) easy, fluent, perfect, precise, sure, unerring, (in)correct, faulty, rash, scratch, bad, dead, return, simultaneous, parting, close, solitary, scattered, point-blank, warning, random

shot, shots (2: photograph; snapshot) See *photograph*

shoulder, shoulders sturdy, strong, powerful, muscular, broad, narrow, square, rounded, straight, huge, plump, massive, hulking, hulky, bull-like, firm, bent, scrawny, stooped, stooping, sloping, sagging, slouching, sore, aching, stiff

shout, shouts triumphant, exultant, ecstatic, jubilant, rejoiceful, blissful, mighty, stentorian, sustained, ragged, gruff, muted, muffled, eerie, mysterious, ghostly, unearthly, frantic, bloodcurdling, futile, uncontrollable

shouting See *shout*

shovel, shovels long-handled, short-handled, narrow-bladed, hooded, cumbersome, clumsy, heavy, pneumatic, hydraulic

show, shows exciting, breathtaking, thrilling, stirring, dazzling, glittering, fascinating, entertaining, enduring, premier, landmark, imaginative, glamorous, glitzy, fine, elaborate, spectacular, lavish, grand, polished, intelligent, hit, blockbuster, smash, fresh, authentic, slick, extraordinary, dramatic, superlative, terrific, lively, radiant, colourful, provocative, psychoactive, psychotropic, superb, brilliant, splendid, marvellous, magnificent, remarkable, wonderful, swell, choice, first-rate, prime-time, ambitious, high-profile, flashy, ostentatious, pretentious, splashy, dizzying, sputtering, hip, (un)successful, flawed, clumsy, boring, claustrophobic, disgusting, abominable, raunchy, indecent, risqué, off-colour, peep, girlie, jivey, slight, (un)affordable, (un)profitable, complex, imperturbable, homespun, huge, daring, late-night, all-night, (serio-)comic, one-man, solo, floor, side, travelling, dumb, retrospective, vaudeville, television, phone-in, call-in, open-line, gala, cultural, educational, vocal

shower, showers See *rain*

shred, shreds flimsy, delicate, feeble, fragile, slender, slight, thin, tenuous, weak

shriek, shrieks See *scream* and *cry*

shrine, shrines sacred, splendid, golden, pagoda-roofed, single-domed, wayside, roadside, national, Christian, Buddhist, Shinto

shrub, shrubs See also *plant* prostrate, procumbent, erect, low-growing, climbing, twining, flowering, many-branched, bushy, thorny, prickly, wiry, aromatic, ornamental, evergreen, herbaceous, ericaceous, berberidaceous, bignoniaceous, betulaceous, rutaceous, myrtaceous, capparidaceous, caprifoliaceous, euphorbiaceous, rhamnaceous, lythraceous

shrug, shrugs gentle, expressive,

indicative, meaningful, significant,
perceptible, noticeable, emphatic,
dismissive, hopeless
shudder, shudders conclusive,
convulsant, convulsionary, nervous,
spasmic, uncontrollable, rollicking,
laughing
shutters perforated, painted(-on), louvred,
slatted, roll-down, wooden, metal
shyness ghastly, dry, dismal, desperate,
awkward, uneasy, inarticulate,
unaggressive, embarrassed, confused,
humble, painful, inherent
sibling, siblings See *brother* and *sister*
sick See *patient*
sickness, sicknesses See *illness*
side, sides distant, yonder, farther,
reverse, opposite, other, inner, outer,
interior, exterior, right, wrong, affirmative,
dark, east, sunny, port, starboard,
larboard, decanal, cantorial; flip; distaff
side effect, side effects See also
effect beneficial, (ir)reversible, happy,
mild, minimal, (un)predictable, potential,
adverse, serious, harmful, bizarre,
undesirable, rare, common, permanent,
fatal
sidewalk, sidewalks See *pavement*
sigh, sighs, sighing deep, profound,
deep-seated, long, weighty, great, ecstatic,
exultant, ardent, amorous, contented,
expressive, expiratory, tender, slow,
indolent, languishing, short, sharp, weary,
tired, smothered, steamy, rueful, dreamy,
drowsy, wistful, exasperated, shuddering
sight, sights (1: spectacle; view)
impressive, lovely, noble, grand, lavish,
tremendous, stately, splendid, magnificent,
exquisite, stupendous, marvellous,
stunning, amazing, astonishing,
astounding, staggering, perplexing,
immense, wonderful, breathtaking,
glorious, heartwarming, gratifying,
pleasing, pleasant, fine, reassuring,
spectacular, fantastic, unique, showy,
unbelievable, incredible, rare, dazzling,
gallant, gay, (un)usual, (un)common,
(un)familiar, habitual, customary,
unaccustomed, unprecedented, strange,
curious, weird, incongruous, moving,
pitiful, sorry, pathetic, rueful, woeful,
sorrowful, sad, terrible, fearful, dreadful,
awesome, fearsome, frightful, unnerving,

appalling, staggering, unsettling, ghastly,
horrible, grisly, stark, nauseous, gruesome,
offensive, disgusting, obnoxious, eerie,
bizarre, macabre, primordial; rear
sight (2: the power of seeing; vision) See
vision (1)
sightseeing exciting, breathtaking,
stirring, thrilling, endless, energetic
sign, signs encouraging, promising,
conciliatory, welcome, inspirational, vital,
reliable, healthy, hopeful, positive, sure,
propitious, auspicious, unmistakable, true,
tangible, visible, conspicuous, prominent,
ubiquitous, abounding, flashing, sure,
obvious, unfailing, telling, telltale,
(un)common, (un)familiar, contrary,
nascent, first, cautionary, premonitory,
ominous, slight, grim, disquieting,
worrisome, headstrong, unhealthy, secret,
jaunty, flashy, showy, gaudy, garish, eerie,
grotesque, outward, sonorous, radical,
vulgar; cuneiform, (spray-)painted,
hand-painted, (hand-)lettered, calligraphic,
crooked, lopsided, (picto)graphic, electric,
commercial, neon
signal, signals conciliatory, (all-)clear,
go-ahead, distinctive, faint, sporadic,
discontinuous, (ab)normal, curious,
oblique, (un)ambiguous, misleading,
conflicting, contradictory, deceptive,
mixed, faulty, gloomy, ominous, warning,
cautionary, admonitory, worrisome,
formal, directional, visual, auditory,
digital, electronic, short-wave,
international, hand, marine, military,
seismic
signature, signatures (il)legal,
(un)authentic, (un)genuine, (in)valid,
counterfeit, fake, unmistakable, inimitable
significance real, apparent, obvious,
cardinal, weighty, tremendous, deep,
durable, enduring, (ever)lasting, ominous,
inauspicious, portentous, premonitory,
sinister, prophetic, unpropitious,
disproportionate, special, symbolic,
historical
silence, silences overpowering,
prevailing, embracing, resounding,
puzzling, unchanging, stifling, suffocating,
churchlike, tomblike, respectful, reverent,
solemn, dignified, blessed, discreet,
judicious, austere, wide, deep, profound,
complete, absolute, total, utter, perfect,

immense, illimitable, limitless, open-ended, significant, enormous, massive, rigid, stony, intense, stark, heavy, pin-drop, breathless, hushed, muffled, obdurate, dead(ly), deathly, death-like, ghostly, rapt, oppressive, incredible, unbelievable, pregnant, impregnable, deceptive, (un)comfortable, hateful, painful, awful, terrible, brutal, unbearable, intolerable, thick, leaden, stricken, impotent, blank, awesome, calculated, moody, dread, taut, tense, strained, strange, curious, sinister, eerie, awkward, embarrassed, confused, astonished, bewildered, drowsy, lethargic, sleepy, mysterious, stupefied, bleak, grim, guilty, glacial, dutiful, loud, ominous, unaccountable, unaccustomed, unusual, uncanny, hollow, monotonous, sullen, uneasy, stoic, wistful, ungrateful, electric, momentary, eternal, unbroken, suspended, instant, tentative, meditative, contemplative, rejective

silk fine, translucent, shimmery, diaphanous, smooth, splendid, rich, costly, lustrous, real, heavy, cool, figured, plain, golden, durable, colourful, shot, changeable, thin, delicate, fragile, flimsy, unbleached, washable, languid, natural, artificial, moiré, crosscut, wild, raw, ribbed, stencilled, spun, thrown, degummed, vegetable

silver glittering, gleaming, shiny, radiant, beaten, handwrought, scrolled, tarnished, sterling, pure, free, brittle

similarity, similarities compelling, striking, surprising, astonishing, astounding, intriguing, provocative, tremendous, strong, close, significant, remarkable, intrinsic, inherent, fundamental, key, real, true, genuine, marked, noticeable, rough, spooky, bizarre, passing, troubling, facial

simile, similes felicitous, fine, apt, fitting, suitable, appropriate, well-chosen, apposite, relevant, expressive, compact, fanciful, glittering, forced, strained, far-fetched, ridiculous, Homeric

simplicity witching, fascinating, charming, unassuming, easy, perfect, meticulous, elegant, clear-eyed, stark, guileless, unaffected, quaint, blundering, studied, artless, child-like, rustic, pastoral, natural, classical, Spartan, Homeric, deceptive

sin, sins besetting, searing, harassing, enticing, tempting, crying, flagrant, mortal, venial, heinous, unspeakable, ugly, grievous, evil, grave, (ir)remissible, (in)expiable, (un)pardonable, (un)forgivable, (un)forgiven, deadly, cardinal, capital, carnal, prime, original, actual

sincerity genuine, heartfelt, honest, pure, unaffected, whole-hearted, absolute, unfeigned, warm, down-to-earth, transparent, radiant

singer, singers fine, velvet-throated, accomplished, superb, exquisite, leading, world-class, award-winning, brilliant, gifted, talented, first-rate, superlative, unique, major, lead, popular, thrilling, glittering, flamboyant, colourful, sultry, renowned, famous, well-known, notable, prominent, aspiring, promising, budding, struggling, would-be, nameless, obscure, minor, little-known, unknown, terrible, brass-voiced, temperamental, highly-strung, excitable, country, hillbilly, bass, operatic, pop

singing moving, (un)inspired, radiant, wonderful, miraculous, passionate, (un)sentimental, spontaneous, continuous, open-throttle, resonant, vibrant, rapturous, frenzied, frenetic, wild, spasmodic, lusty, boozy, rhythmic, deep-throated, off-key, dull, mechanical, congregational, community, folk, ceremonial, choral, solo, antiphonal

sinner, sinners contrite, regretful, remorseful, rueful, tortured, (un)repentant, (im)penitent, (un)regenerate, flagrant, brazen, obdurate, stubborn, unfeeling, miserable, wretched, poor, benighted, hard(ened), reformed

siren, sirens (1: warning) wailing, screaming, shrieking, blasting, sounding

siren, sirens (2: alluring woman) sultry, seductive, fatal

sister, sisters foster, twin, full, whole, half, step, adoptive

site, sites peaceful, spectacular, breathtaking, impressive, magnificent, splendid, exquisite, superior, valuable, lucrative, original, unique, magical, mysterious, beachfront, strategic, dominant, critical, principal, prominent, (un)likely, (un)suitable, supposed, temporary, permanent, grand, giant, massive, sprawling, huge, remote, (in)appropriate, (un)interesting, (un)important, hazardous, (still-)controversial, eventual, prospective, potential, vacant, buildable, (yet-to-be-)chosen, unpopulated, abandoned, undisturbed, (pre)historic, archaeological, sacred, holy, ceremonial, sacrificial, burial, industrial, military, strategic; building, level, oblong, (pie-)shaped, resellable, (re)sal(e)able, x-foot-wide, residential, commercial

situation, situations rosy, hopeful, (un)promising, lucrative, profitable, (un)favourable, ideal, (un)pleasant, (un)stable, unfailing, wholesome, (un)comfortable, manageable, unique, windfall, humorous, convivial, ludicrous, touch-and-go, competitive, real-life, unprecedented, current, (ab)normal, (un)common, (un)usual, (un)familiar, (un)predictable, urgent, whimsical, lethal, confrontational, explosive, irreconcilable, turbulent, stressful, disagreeable, irksome, dismal, fragile, tough, rattling, perplexing, baffling, unexplainable, desperate, painful, forlorn, tight, impossible, perilous, gloomy, inescapable, irretrievable, acute, grave, lamentable, deplorable, pitiable, unsavoury, objectionable, distasteful, questionable, shameful, improper, risqué, indecent, outrageous, unfavourable, intolerable, bitter, ridiculous, risky, profitless, hostile, dicey, delicate, ticklish, tender, tricky, intimate, complex, tangled, intricate, confused, awkward, absurd, funny, sticky, critical, hopeless, nasty, wretched, unsettling, unpleasant, trying, despicable, disastrous, appalling, messy, tense, anxious, stressful, reprehensible, violent, no-hope, no-win, dead-end, chaotic, life-and-death, exasperating, (anxiety-)provoking, inflamed, inflammable, combustible, changeable, terrible, topsy-turvy, tenuous, volatile, shaky, unstable, precarious, fluid, troublesome, troubling, perilous, unbearable, atrocious, abusive, monstrous, bizarre, nightmare, frightening, scary, panicky, traumatic, unenviable, uncomfortable, murky, unexpected,

comparable, stereotypical, hypothetical, stock

size, sizes astonishing, imposing, weighty, large, gigantic, prodigious, impressive, unwieldy, immense, awesome, monstrous, alarming, ghastly, (un)equal, (un)manageable, stock, standard, uniform, (ab)normal, natural, (ir)regular, regulation, middle, medium, middling, small, petite, diminutive, puny, approximate

skater, skaters confident, nimble, flashy, gusty, avid, ardent, enthusiastic, daring, gold-medal, premier, (un)skilled, (un)graceful, graceless, ungainly, clumsy, stiff, awkward

sketch, sketches vivid, lively, crisp, sharp, pointed, spirited, colourful, vibrant, freehand, brief, thumbnail, concise, comprehensive, lightning, crude, clumsy, hasty, humorous, anatomical, literary, pencil, pen-and-ink; vaudeville

skier, skiers See also *athlete* speeding, flawless, skilled, skilful, expert, flashy, gusty, adventurous, champion, gold-medal, confident, out-of-control, multi-event, professional, amateur, avid, ardent, (un)graceful, awkward, stiff, ungainly, clumsy, alpine, Olympic

skiing all-terrain, deep-powder, amateur, professional, aerial, freestyle, mogul, recreational, competitive, alpine, Nordic, Olympic

skill, skills deft, dext(e)rous, nimble, unfailing, enduring, overwhelming, dazzling, consummate, quaint, high-level, masterly, exquisite, admirable, remarkable, sterling, acute, enormous, considerable, limitless, formidable, impressive, phenomenal, superlative, superb, magnificent, extraordinary, incomparable, unmatched, uncommon, uncanny, sophisticated, innovative, proper, crucial, specific, special, peculiar, adequate, unobtrusive, effortless, complex, hard-edged, hard-earned, centuries-old, invincible, undreamed-of, obsessive, tangible, useful, marketable, quirky, rusty, outdated, (un)limited, tenuous, trifling, humble, unemployed, practised, untaught, intuitive, experimental, eclectic, practical, basic, fundamental, vital, manual, pedagogical, academic, technical, literary, artistic, musical, narrative, linguistic,

communicative, dialectical, athletic,
physical, visual, imaginative, perceptual,
conceptual, cognitive, numerical,
computational, analytic(al), magical,
entrepreneurial, organizational,
administrative, interpersonal, diplomatic,
occupational, people
skin, skins comely, lubricious, delicate,
gentle, smooth, supple, soft, fine, clear,
glowing, clean, healthy, oil-free, taut,
tight, hairless, scaleless, flawless,
unbroken, unscarred, pure, alabaster,
sheer, iridescent, transparent, rosy, ruddy,
dusky, (sun-)sallow, magnolia, brunet,
tawny, yellowish, auburn, fair, dark,
swarthy, black, ebony, copper, bronze,
coffee-coloured, honey-coloured, ivory,
pink, flushed, pallid, pale, light, damp,
moist, parchment-like, downy, puddingy,
rough, coarse, thick, calloused, dry, flaky,
scaly, crusty, clammy, slimy, oily, greasy,
waxen, exposed, unprotected, ugly, itchy,
sore, numb, muddy, raw, slack, loose,
rubbery, resilient, sagging, floppy, wrinkly,
tired(-looking), tingling, pimply, crackly,
bristly, blotchy, blotched, mottled,
discoloured, burnt, inflamed, wrinkled,
cracked, chapped, allergic, (in)sensitive,
facial
skirt, skirts (softly-)belled, knit,
(hand-)woven, pleat, draped, ribbed,
(top)stitched, sheer, diaphanous, gauzy,
plaid, tube, voluminous, bouf(fant),
reversible, puffball, billowy, frilly, floral,
abstract-pattern, vestigial, flirty,
(too-)tight, skin-tight, tight-fitting, dumpy,
loose, skimpy, sexy, projecting,
expandable, high-waisted, air-blown,
flowing, balloon-shaped, lantern-shaped,
hopscotch, (well-)above-the-knee, circular,
full-circle, circular, kilt-like, awry, mini,
maxi, midi, ra-ra, full, straight, sheath,
wrap(around), ruffled, hobble, silk, tweed,
velvet, taffeta, alpaca, batik, sisal, grass
skull, skulls gracile, asymmetric(al),
fragmentary
sky, skies lowering, varying, sparkling,
dazzling, glowing, flaming, pearling,
raging, maddening, threatening, vaulting,
yawning, peerless, dappled, fleecy, mottled,
striate(d), seamless, sunny, big-clouded,
cloudy, cloudless, cloud-mottled, rainless,
windless, starry, star-studded,
(star-)spangled, starless, starlit, twilit,
enormous, immense, big, wide(-open),
spacious, unfathomable, remote, drowsy,
tranquil, peaceful, heady, dull, opaque,
turquoise, red, rose-coloured, colourful,
cerulean, livid, aquamarine, azure, cobalt,
bluish, blue-glazed, indigo, pastel-blue,
frost-blue, slate, slate-blue, grey(-blue),
silver-grey, lead, misty-grey, cinereous,
white, milky, black-sulphur, black(-satin),
velvet-black, inky, colourless,
heat-discoloured, veiled, clear, lambent,
bright, brilliant, serene, crystal(line), pure,
unpredictable, rueful, moody, angry,
chaotic, dour, ugly, gloomy, dismal, sullen,
overcast, Stygian, ponderous, heavy,
windy, stormy, rainy, dreary, pale, hazy,
sable, dusky, dull, inert, pewter, smok(e)y,
sooty, smoggy, grimy, dark(-bellied), lurid,
sombre, bleak, leaden, moisture-laden,
watery, soggy, snow-laden, wintry, lunar,
oceanic, mackerel
skyline, skylines dazzling, glittering,
imposing, eye-catching, striking, glorious,
spectacular, sleek, drab, congested,
gloomy, treeless, mountain, snow-capped,
jagged, high-rise, urban, rural
skyscraper, skyscrapers See *building*
slander, slanders degrading, insulting,
shocking, outrageous, atrocious,
monstrous, wicked, vicious, evil,
disgraceful, abusive, actionable
slaughter, slaughters See *killing*
slave, slaves trustworthy, fugitive,
unwitting, willing, runaway, domestic,
tributary; white
slavery monstrous, heinous, hideous,
shocking, painful, (il)legal, debt,
(un)lawful; white, sexual
sleep (un)sound, golden, placid, soft,
gentle, peaceful, serene, calm, intense,
restful, blissful, unbroken, uninterrupted,
undisturbed, secure, (un)easy, profound,
deep, heavy, snug, (un)comfortable,
(in)sufficient, refreshing, dewy, luxuriant,
good-quality, dead(ly), death-like, swinish,
excessive, complete, irresistible,
(well-)deserved, forgetful, lethargic,
grateful, (non-)dreaming, dreamless,
shallow, turbulent, wheezy, irregular,
troubled, fitful, dreary, light, restless,
brief, spasmodic, exhausted, fragmented,
semi-conscious, twilight, winter, beauty

sleeper, sleepers fast, sound, sensitive, light

sleeplessness See *insomnia*

sleeve, sleeves wide, long, short, plain, tight, loose(-cut), tapered, laced, stitched, (yellow-)trimmed, elbow-length, rustling, swirling, swirly, wingy, winged, bubble, puff(ed), bouffant, set-in, leg-of-mutton, unmounted, three-quarter, raglan, batwing, cap, bishop

slight, slights minor, inadvertent, (un)conscious, (un)intentional, thoughtless, unthoughtful, inconsiderate, careless, imprudent, gratuitous, uncalled-for, unwarranted, unnecessary, needless, (un)premeditated, spontaneous, voluntary

slipper, slippers elegant, comfortable, easy, light, quiet, tight, gleaming, shiny, multicoloured, (pink-)flowered, beaded, sequined, ribboned, crepe-soled, rubber-soled, heavy-soled, tough-soled, monogrammed

slogan, slogans pious, proud, popular, potent, viable, catchy, snappy, instructive, grandiloquent, pompous, nebulous, silly, trite, hackneyed, take-off, inflammatory, defamatory, derogatory, nasty, political, patriotic

slope, slopes soft, gentle, moderate, graceful, gradual, terraced, open, vertical, upward, (un)stable, jagged, quirky, steep, sharp, precipitous, vertiginous, plunging, dizzying, forbidding, towering, soaring, massive, abrupt, suspicious, tricky, dangerous, treacherous, tortuous, cracked, avalanche-prone, muddy, slippery, grassy, wooded, forested, logged, gullied, bleak, bare, volcanic, ravine-cut, rock-strewn, snow-muted, snow-bound, snow-covered, mist-shrouded, eroded; nursery

slowness crawling, creeping, lingering, procrastinating, tantalizing, teasing, tormenting, excruciating, disappointing, boring, deliberate, solemn, glacial, indolent, languid, leisurely, lethargic, phlegmatic, sluggish, snail-paced, weary, deceptive, purposeful

slum, slums dispiriting, disheartening, disgusting, teeming, bad-smelling, smoking, smok(e)y, noisome, offensive, poor, tough, feculent, dingy, dirty, filthy, foul, rancid, seedy, shabby, sordid, squalid, miserable, terrible, degraded, dilapidated, rickety, wretched, crime-ridden, dense, monstrous, tenemented, ghetto, urban, rural

slumber, slumbers See *sleep*

slump, slumps See *depression* (1)

smell, smells soothing, refreshing, appetising, intriguing, delicious, sweet(ish), mellow, soft, clean, agreeable, pungent, piquant, savoury, (un)pleasant, (un)friendly, fragrant, sappy, intriguing, overpowering, heavy, heady, sharp, thick, strong, powerful, faint, queer, unbelievable, unmistakable, identifiable, distinct(ive), elusive, indefinable, tarnished, sun-dried, woody, musty, humid, damp, mouldy, sweetish, salty, earthy, dusty, bitter, musky, sour(ish), winy, spicy, meaty, offensive, pungent, acrid, intolerable, nauseous, horrible, vile, nasty, loathsome, fleshy, swinish, doggy, objectionable, obnoxious, sickening, disagreeable, sickish, sickly, foul, f(o)etid, stale, revolting, rancid, putrid, disgusting, nauseating, evil, noxious

smile, smiles ingratiating, welcoming, blinding, beaming, flashing, dazzling, taking, captivating, tempting, inviting, disarming, enchanting, bewitching, alluring, enticing, engaging, endearing, winning, charming, fascinating, pleasing, flowery, sweet, saccharine, cordial, friendly, companionable, affectionate, intimate, tender, kindly, benevolent, felicitous, beatific, golden, delightful, amiable, angelic, genial, magnetic, pretty, winsome, attractive, vivacious, warm, luscious, seductive, saintly, cherubic, nice, lovely, benign, eager, intent, lively, joyful, animated, jovial, cheerful, cheery, optimistic, carefree, gay, happy(-go-lucky), perky, bright, radiant, lustrous, incandescent, serene, tranquil, suave, seraphic, glorious, triumphant, proud, stylish, sunny, sprightly, subtle, ethereal, imperious, courteous, gracious, forgiving, wise, knowing, superior, bacchanalian, contagious, infectious, encouraging, teasing, telling, provocative, coy, shy, bashful, demure, rapturous, prodigious, open, big, oceanic, fat, large, huge, enormous, broad, wide, megawatt, high-voltage, gritty, rapt, rare, expectant, proud, dignified, indulgent, placid, ungrudging, smug, sympathetic, (in)sincere, cocksure, understanding, faint, weak, strengthless, languid, short, sidelong, humourless, small, slight, tiny, thin, aggressive, self-reliant, self-deprecating, involuntary, tight-lipped, complacent, contented, defeatless, irrepressible, nostalgic, nervous, timid, apprehensive, cautious, expressive, indefatigable, constant, everlasting, (ever-)ready, (un)easy, habitual, persuasive, withdrawn, soft, slow, tentative, hesitant, uncertain, wobbly, vague, inscrutable, steely, groggy, dazed, glazed, fixed, inanimate, immovable, arched, inert, secretive, mysterious, enigmatic, sceptical, quizzical, questioning, searching, formidable, incredulous, dreamy, sleepy, deep, pixieish, Mona Lisa, rueful, toothy, white-toothed, impulsive, spontaneous, reflexive, patient, strobe-light, swift, fleeting, vapid, sardonic, inexpressive, indefinable, nonchalant, wooden, cardboard, automatic, derisive, arch, sly, crafty, cunning, wry, roguish, unkindly, embarrassed, forced, constrained, (re)strained, stiff, taut, twisting, unnatural, supercilious, impish, mischievous, conspiratorial, simpering, acid, sour, grim, wicked, strange, queer, odd, weird, insidious, saucy, hideous, bland, frozen, cold, frigid, wintry, chilling, artificial, affected, insincere, foolish, vacuous, infantile, contemptuous, factitious, inane, vacant, shamefaced, haughty, spiritless, dispirited, twisted, crooked, lopsided, acidulous, malicious, cynical, fatuous, wan, ironic, sickly, measly, wretched, covetous, confidential, insinuating, sibylline

smog, smogs See also *smoke* eye-stinging, suffocating, stifling, legendary, dreadful, opaque, thick, acrid, pungent, harmful, deadly, dangerous, noxious, sulphurous, photochemical, urban

smoke billowing, glowing, flashing, gushing, rising, thickening, smothering, blinding, vanishing, aromatic, fragrant, (sweet-)scented, reluctant, interminable, dense, thick, heavy, tremendous, turgid, impenetrable, thin, wreathed, swirly, wispy, pitchy, black, sooty, slaty, crimson, hot, acrid, foul, greasy, stinking, pungent, unbearable, undesirable, terrible,

toxic, sulphurous, combustible, second-hand, sidestream, volcanic, industrial

smoker, smokers mild, careful, (un)reformed, habitual, (ir)regular, confirmed, inveterate, adamant, recalcitrant, determined, chronic, addicted, compulsive, hard-core, die-hard, relentless, heavy, incessant, constant, unrepentant, long-time, desperate, careless, reckless, embattled, languid, secret, tobacco, chain, passive

smuggler, smugglers See *criminal*

smugness affected, bourgeois, complacent, contented, egocentric, (self-)inflated, self-satisfied, priggish, prim, sleek

snack, snacks See also *meal* and *food* nourishing, savoury, spicy, tasty, quick, light, dry, dental-smart, dentally-safe, dentally-wise, filling, fattening, caloric, junk-food, indigenous, after-theatre, mid-morning, midday

snake, snakes hissing, rustling, crawling, oscillating, twining, writhing, patch-nosed, spectacled, striped, slippery, slithery, wriggly, willowy, slender, long, giant, monstrous, (un)coiled, poised, inactive, sluggish, wary, torpid, dormant, aggressive, mighty, evil, harmful, vicious, deadly, ugly, (non-)venomous, (non-)poisonous, harmless, indigo, coral, smooth, grass

snare, snares See *trap*

sneer, sneers unthinking, contemptuous, cynical, derisive, disdainful, scoffing, sardonic, ironic(al), sarcastic

sneeze, sneezes, sneezing big, occasional, uncontrollable, irrepressible, suppressed

sniff, sniffs See *contempt*

snobbery, snobbishness sheer, downright, utter, complete, petty, outrageous, inverted, aristocratic, arrogant, haughty, supercilious, uppish

snore, snores rumbling, resounding, volcanic, tremulous, vigorous, loud, erratic, restless

snoring See *snore*

snow, snows hissing, dazzling, sparkling, glittering, blinding, unyielding, penetrating, tenacious, stubborn, hard, solid, thick, heavy, firm, crusty, frozen, compacted,

icy, deep, knee-deep, ankle-deep, light,
thin, soft, loose, powder(y), fine, dry, wet,
watery, soggy, sodden, mushy, slushy,
flaky, feathery, fluffy, crunchy, crackly,
brittle, sleety, granular, melting, alpine,
eternal, perpetual, occasional, pure,
undefiled, fresh(-fallen), virgin, new-fallen,
unbrushed, unmelted, clean, white, bright,
innocent, pristine, trackless, polluted,
dirty, bleak, fierce, (wind-)driven,
windblown, unexpected, sullen,
treacherous, artificial, man-made

snowfall, snowfalls blustery, squally,
heavy, light, record, four-day, large

snowflake, snowflakes See *snow*

snowstorm, snowstorms See *storm*

snub, snubs See *slight*

soap, soaps gentle, mild, soft, strong,
harsh, hard, smelly, frothy, sticky,
fragrance-free, liquid, metallic,
transparent, (un)scented, perfumed,
multicoloured, conventional, deodorant,
detergent, disinfectant, medicated,
granulated, carbolic, milled, hypoallergenic

sob, sobs heartfelt, dry, tearless, ecstatic,
fitful, spasmodic, convulsive, hysterical,
intermittent, ceaseless, endless, unending,
occasional, shuddering, uncontrollable,
irrepressible, audible, (body-)racking,
harsh, low

sobbing See *sob*

society, societies (1: all people
collectively) sound, coherent, cohesive,
free, civilized, just, fair, family-orient(at)ed,
decent, mannered, polite, refined, polished,
cultured, tolerant, dynamic, vigorous,
productive, purposeful, livable, peaceful,
ideal, utopian, stable, established, caring,
conformist, formal, civil, fashionable,
sophisticated, high-tech, perfectionist,
self-sufficient, self-reliant, determined,
distinct, developed, complex, exclusive,
aristocratic, class-conscious, structured,
classless, no-nonsense, fluid, open, inbred,
meritocratic, hardnosed, star-struck,
cowed, sedentary, leisurely, affluent,
prosperous, overfed, complacent,
materialistic, acquisitive, get-rich-quick,
success-orient(at)ed, (car-)crazed,
utilitarian, entrepreneurial, laissez-faire,
credit, consumer(-orient(at)ed), throwaway,
(un)thrifty, competitive, individualistic,
stingy, litigious, instant, fast, rootless,

mobile, laid-back, turbulent, defenceless,
unsuspecting, disjointed, shaky,
disconnected, disordered, ignorant,
bigoted, stratified, immutable,
unchangeable, unalterable, stagnant,
insular, static, rigid, closed, constrictive,
narrow, restrictive, prudish, polygamous,
permissive, tolerant, regenerate, dissolute,
decadent, imperfect, scandalous,
dissipated, degenerate, debased, flawed,
failed, sinful, self-destructive,
goal-orient(at)ed, directionless, uncaring,
unfeeling, cold, self-centred, repressive,
authoritarian, bilingual, bicultural,
multiracial, (non)racial, hierarchical,
pluralist(ic), diverse, various, multifaith,
multicultural, multiethnic, secular,
segmented, xenophobic, polyglot,
communal, nomadic, tribal, primitive,
phallocentric, matrilineal, maternal,
patrilineal, paternal, matriarchal,
patriarchal, ag(e)ing, egalitarian,
democratic, socialist, capitalist, feudal

society, societies (2: persons joined
together for a common aim) venerable,
distinguished, congenial, friendly, vibrant,
hierarchical, civil, bleak, cooperative,
scholarly, academic, learned, rigid, closed,
secret, underground, paramilitary, élite,
humane

sock, socks indestructible, woolly, cotton,
hand-knit, stretch, slouch, smelly, bobby,
pop

sofa, sofas easy, soft, puffy, roomy, deep,
posh, (un)comfortable, floral, flowered,
chintz (-covered), unwieldy, bulky,
cumbersome, sectional, three-cushion

soil, soils fertile, rich, lush, loamy, good,
unctuous, weed-free, hearty, arable,
(un)yielding, (un)productive, (un)fruitful,
(un)promising, sweet, generous, fat,
nutrient-rich, soft, mealy, friable, pervious,
permeable, benign, light, heavy, dense,
loose, dry, thirsty, moist, (dew-)damp, wet,
watery, soggy, mushy, flaky, crusty,
porous, open, rooty, sandy, rocky, stony,
chalky, powdery, clay, red-clay, black,
dusky, lime-rich, fallow, barren,
intractable, churlish, fragile, thin, meagre,
poor, sterile, shallow, hard, stiff, stubborn,
obstinate, sour, infertile, deficient,
untillable, erodible, (sub)marginal,
unresponsive, sinking, crumbly, withered,

eroded, tired, sparse, swampy, acidic, alkaline, alluvial, aggregate, saline, neutral, alkali, cohesionless (frictional), cohesive, calcareous, diamondiferous, virgin, holomorphic, hydromorphic, (im)mature, indurate, mellow, mineral, pyroclastic, volcanic, oven-dry, peat, plastic, saline–sodic, sodic, surface, (a)zonal, intrazonal, obsolete, solonetzic, volcanic(-ash), organic, black, brown, top

sojourn, sojourns See *stay*

soldier, soldiers See also *troop* tough, ferocious, trained, professional, capable, (dis)loyal, (un)faithful, patriotic, able-bodied, brave, courageous, stout-hearted, valiant, gallant, intrepid, bold, lion-hearted, devil-may-care, audacious, reckless, indomitable, spirited, decorated, veteran, heroic, hostile, battle-hardened, combat-hardened, war-hardened, obdurate, luckless, fallen, weary, bedraggled, disgruntled, mutinous, insurgent, rebel(lious), insurrectionist, treacherous, renegade, fugitive, nervous, fair-weather, boastful, braggart, swaggering, upstart, dashing, rifle-bearing, (steel-)helmeted, mounted, (un)armed, trench-coated, camouflage-uniformed, common, basic, green, simple, foot, volunteer, professional, career

solemnity imposing, awe-inspiring, august, dignified, elegant, elaborate, tragic, dreadful, fearful, horrible, oppressive, gloomy, measured, gaunt, grave, funereal, melancholy, parochial

solitude aloof, ivory-towered, reclusive, hermitic, splendid, glorious, welcome, profound, enormous, vast, overwhelming, unbroken, utter, total, complete, absolute, quiet, dead, speechless, germinative, unpretentious, boring, changeless, awful, dreadful, barren, bleak, desolate, dreary, cheerless, dejected, dispirited, depressing, morose, gloomy, ghostly, weird, inner, alpine

solution, solutions (1: solving; correct answer) (in)equitable, (un)just, (un)fair, novel, clear, full, meaningful, sensible, rational, shrewd, peaceful, right, (in)correct, expedient, ingenious, elegant, (in)effective, imaginative, revolutionary, innovative, unique, creative, comprehensive, permanent, (ever)lasting, orderly, (im)perfect, clear-cut, definite, dramatic, beneficial, harmonious, desirable, last-chance, (un)workable, pragmatic, feasible, practical, practicable, (in)conceivable, discernible, ready, affordable, (im)possible, (un)likely, (im)plausible, promising, concrete, aggressive, acquiescent, unhoped-for, (in)appropriate, (in)adequate, (un)satisfactory, (un)acceptable, (un)balanced, responsible, time-honoured, ancient, old-style, (un)conventional, (un)orthodox, outlandish, controversial, sweeping, obvious, middle-of-the-road, serious, drastic, radical, magic(al), miraculous, quick, surprising, costly, simplistic, simple, insignificant, inconsequential, fragile, elusive, cumbersome, problem-laden, flawed, muddy, careless, specious, face-saving, partial, bit-by-bit, compromise, specific, immediate, tentative, interim, temporary, stop-gap, short-term, long-range, long-term, ultimate, eventual, overnight, broad, joint, instinctive, alternative, conditional, diplomatic, political, military, Utopian, Solomonic

solution, solutions (2: liquid containing a dissolved substance) (un)saturated, dilute, basic, weak, strong, neutral, soap(y), saline, normal, gelatinous, colourless, viscous, sticky, pungent, cardioplegic, dichroic, therapeutic

son, sons perfect, devoted, duteous, obedient, helpful, paragon, favourite, dear, beloved, (un)mannerly, (in)considerate, (un)filial, (un)dutiful, reckless, prodigal, unruly, defiant, extravagant, estranged, putative, natural, adoptive, foster, posthumous, elder, eldest, adult, infant

song, songs bewitching, enchanting, charming, enticing, alluring, siren, wonderful, glorious, sweet, harmonious, melodious, tuneful, mellifluous, dulcet, liquid, irresistible, irrepressible, singable, rich, ample, musical, rhythmic, rhymed, radiant, lovely, exquisite, imperishable, sprightly, effervescent, spirited, soulful, airy, lively, joyful, gay, cheerful, cheery, exuberant, joyous, jubilant, droll, humorous, comic, music-hall, loud, stentorian, boisterous, rollicking, evocative, nostalgic, moving, haunting, rousing, stirring, thrilling, undulating, bellying, infectious, passionate, emotion-laden, inspirational, sentimental, spiritual, prayerful, dreamy, soft, soothing, introspective, plain, amorous, plaintive, sorrowful, mournful, wailing, sad, melancholy, melancholic, wistful, lonely, ghostly, tuneless, wordless, repetitive, scratchy, jocular, wild, ribald, risqué, indecent, raucous, bawdy, tireless, muted, old, traditional, familiar, popular, pop, epic, folk(loric), choral, lyrical, topical, sacred, polyphonic, patriotic, revolutionary, hit

sonnet, sonnets See also *poem* anguished, Petrarchan (Italian), Shakespearean (English; Elizabethan)

soot black, fuliginous, foul-smelling, pollutive, grimy, oily

sophistication unfathomable, immense, courtly, elegant, polished, exquisite, rare, subtle, refined, stately, stylish, superb, precocious, worldly, technological

sore, sores running, open, inflamed, angry, fiery, purulent, pus-filled, ulcerous

soreness severe, acute, blistering, gruelling, intense, piercing

sorrow, sorrows haunting, devouring, penetrating, piercing, touching, biting, genuine, frank, sincere, grievous, self-born, manifold, poignant, heavy, boundless, unbounded, endless, ineradicable, afflictive, inexpressible, bitter, distressful, irrecoverable, oppressive, profound, slow-brooded, unmitigated, unabated, unassuaged, unbearable, pent-up, acute, deep(-felt), keen, intense, painful, awful

soul, souls unsullied, untarnished, great, peaceable, immortal, rebellious, sorrowful, tormented, damned, blessed

sound, sounds hissing, (ear-)piercing, throbbing, crashing, cracking, warning, swashing, soaring, stirring, trembling, grunting, murmuring, sighing, tinkling, wailing, twittering, chirping, humming, buzzing, whispering, gasping, sparkling, rasping, swishing, warbling, rumbling, rolling, chugging, snapping, sweeping, brushing, penetrating, piercing, squeezing, roaring, fretting, sucking, squeaking, sobbing, whimpering, thumping, prancing, rustling, cooing, shuffling, thrashing, bleating, snorting, soothing, pleasing,

ingratiating, enticing, sultry, sensual, dulcet, sweet, harmonious, melodious, welcome, harmonic, gentle, soft, mellow, silky, high-fidelity, evocative, sonorous, resonant, crystal-clear, crystalline, visible, distinctive, (in)distinct, (in)articulate, (in)audible, (un)identifiable, unmistakable, crisp, brittle, sinuous, reverberate, reverberant, persistent, repeated, ubiquitous, swishy, windy, distant, remote, inchoate, low, dim, faint, muffled, ultralow, dead, small, obscure, hollow, tremulous, drowsy, lugubrious, mournful, normal, elusive, distorted, contorted, broad, ominous, eerie, nightmarish, weird, grotesque, strange, ghoulish, unearthly, unnatural, uncanny, ethereal, queer, crazy, wild, spooky, thunderous, raucous, harsh, rough, hoarse, shrill, sharp, strident, brassy, staccato, acute, high-pitch(ed), metallic, formidable, hideous, agitated, inharmonious, dissonant, unwanted, dull, flabby, fragmentary, discordant, cacophonous, dreadful, dismal, unwelcome, fundamental, elemental, white, high-decibel, electronic, ultrasonic, stereophonic, musical, sensuous, nasal, throaty, guttural, sibilant, labial, digital, high-frequency, low-frequency, abstract, ambient

soup, soups savoury, tasty, flavourful, delicious, appetizing, terrific, exquisite, splendid, remarkable, wholesome, nutritious, rich, hearty, spicy, tangy, aromatic, earthy, zesty, hot, steaming, scalding, lukewarm, smooth, thick, light, thin, jelly-like, watery, meatless, pungent, greasy, instant, green

source, sources (1: place from which something comes) unending, never-ending, everlasting, unfailing, sustaining, endless, boundless, inexhaustible, perennial, sustainable, incessant, (in)constant, dependable, ready, good, fruitful, solid, vital, major, important, colossal, fertile, ever-new, (un)renewable, (ir)replaceable, (in)accessible, (in)visible, pervasive, (in)adequate, primordial, primal, primary, secondary, first, original, potential, possible, precise, exact, infinite, ultimate, alternative, (un)conventional, sole, mysterious, surprising, unexpected, (un)likely, remote, obscure, elusive, trivial, cheap, (in)expensive, (un)determined, imperfect

source, sources (2: one that supplies information) qualified, knowledgeable, unimpeachable, (in)accurate, (un)trustworthy, (un)reliable, (un)dependable, last-resort, (un)informed, well-informed, well-placed, (dis)creditable, unmistakable, close, surprising, (un)official, (un)identifiable, anonymous, unnamed, confidential, diplomatic

souvenir, souvenirs perfect, useful, unique, selected, special, (ir)replaceable, eternal, (un)official, (un)authentic, tacky, ghastly, trashy, cheap, brash, plastic, take-home

sovereign, sovereigns gracious, kind, benign, righteous, unchallenged, (il)legitimate, absolute, aloof

sovereignty See also *sovereign* full, nominal, national, popular

spa, spas See *resort*

space, spaces vast, (wide-)open, (un)restricted, (un)limited, limitless, illimitable, ample, infinite, generous, extra, boundless, clear, blank, void, empty, vacant, untouched, tiny, tight, little, narrow, cramped, confined, oppressive, forlorn, (in)appropriate, (in)adequate, (un)usable, (un)rentable, (un)affordable, dead, dedicated, (un)reserved, (in)flexible, personal, private, storage, crawl, rentable; outer, galactic, intergalactic, interstellar, interplanetary, translunar, cislunar; inner

sparrow, sparrows See also *bird* twittering, chirping, darting, aggressive, quarrelsome, fragile, hedge, house (English), white-crowned, white-throated, Cockney

speaker, speakers exciting, engaging, convincing, compelling, sparkling, fluent, voluble, glib, articulate, extemporaneous, facile, smooth, forceful, forcible, effective, powerful, weighty, influential, motivational, impressive, masterful, charismatic, felicitous, delightful, informative, pithy, witty, emphatic, impassioned, (in)experienced, expert, plausible, persuasive, pre-eminent, first-rate, luminous, notable, stern-faced, poker-faced, dull, tedious, boring, long-winded, prosy, wordy, verbose, commonplace, fatuous, ironical, scurrilous,

inflammatory, rabble-rousing, platitudinous, windy, noisy, talkative, public, keynote

speaking See *speaker* and *speech*

spear, spears thin, fine, pointed, sharp, blunt, light, heavy, short, long, poison-tipped, flint-tipped, two-pronged, five-pronged, deadly, bronze, prehistoric, fish

speciality, specialities See *specialization*

specialization, specializations narrow, intriguing, arcane

species viable, glamorous, threatened, extinct, (now-)rare, scarce, (once-)abundant, little-known, distinct(ive), (un)identifiable, unusual, strange, unique, exotic, bizarre, (un)common, diversified, tough, precious, valuable, fine, (un)privileged, unsung, harmless, harmful, (in)edible, adverse, avian, migratory, primitive, indigenous, grasping, rapacious, (in)edible, hoofed, molecular, marine, pelagic, endemic, allopatric, sympatric, cryptic

specification, specifications exacting, precise, rigid, strict

specimen, specimens See *sample*

spectacle, spectacles See *sight* (1)

spectacles (eye-glasses) See *glasses*

spectator, spectators See also *audience* applauding, (un)discerning, shoulder-to-shoulder, tacit, silent, curious, astounded, surprised, shocked, startled, spellbound, breathless, (un)interested, high-spirited, delirious, unruly, nervous, fearful, bloodthirsty

spectre, spectres chilling, haunting, ominous, portentous, inauspicious, premonitory, unpropitious, disconsolate, fearful, ugly, grim, evil

spectrum, spectra (spectrums) broad, entire, full, colourful

speculation, speculations (un)informed, (un)safe, imaginative, fanciful, fascinating, fresh, voluminous, anxious, strong, intense, wild, growing, widespread, rampant, endless, unending, infinite, discursive, pure, bold, glum, grim, idle, wistful, shameless, vindictive, groundless, unfounded, ill-informed, public, abstract, metaphysical, academic, political; financial

speech, speeches inspirational, sensible, shrewd, conciliatory, splendid, suave, able, (un)refined, clever, polished, masterful, powerful, elegant, graceful, straight, candid, frank, honest, sincere, brilliant, apt, impressive, striking, commanding, effective, racy, dazzling, eloquent, fluent, mellifluous, meaty, lively, (in)coherent, (in)articulate, (un)intelligible, perspicuous, vigorous, strong, forceful, dispassionate, interesting, distinct, monumental, remarkable, core, pivotal, timely, opportune, memorable, measured, sententious, facetious, extemporaneous, unrehearsed, impromptu, offhand, off-the-cuff, ready-made, set, emotional, moving, demonstrative, provocative, fiery, impassioned, passionate, vehement, rhetorical, declamatory, windy, intoxicating, stirring, fulminating, raging, inflammatory, incendiary, seditious, subversive, warlike, uncompromising, (rabble-)rousing, unctuous, fervid, earnest, flattering, stern, poignant, thunderous, critical, controversial, theatrical, nationalistic, deliberative, commendatory, downright, frank, straightforward, blunt, candid, soaring, unpredictable, hesitant, revealing, grammatical, orotund, sonorous, bombastic, high-sounding, high-flown, inflated, turgid, verbose, dour, tumid, showy, pretentious, soporific, elliptical, rambling, chop-logic, jejune, empty, abrupt, brusque, jumpy, indistinct, equivocal, thick, salacious, reckless, rustic, trivial, vulgar, tiring, disconnected, disjointed, discursive, unconnected, unprepared, arid, foolish, tiresome, long-winded, stinging, flat, monotonous, uninteresting, mechanical, lifeless, halting, faltering, laboured, low-key, prolix, wordy, irreverent, sharp-tongued, grating, singsong, monotone, stilted, cliché-ridden, cliché-laden, tremulous, truculent, unguarded, wanton, unrestrained, ponderous, laborious, tedious, boring, dull, (pen)ultimate, uninterrupted, public, key(note), welcoming, visible, inaugural; slurred

speed, speeds dizzying, blistering, hair-raising, alarming, amazing, startling, surprising, astounding, stunning, astonishing, bewildering, mind-boggling, arrow-like, lightning, prodigious, vertiginous, breakneck, tremendous,

excessive, enormous, top, high, full, optimum, frantic, breathless, phenomenal, dangerous, deadly, furious, murderous, precipitant, heedless, unbridled, giddy, headlong, incredible, unbelievable, remarkable, extraordinary, terrific, appalling, awesome, significant, brisk, breezy, wrong, silly, unnecessary, free, singular, blurry, unaccustomed, unprecedented, customary, average, permissible, (in)appropriate, (un)reasonable, (im)moderate, (in)cautious, convenient, good, forward, steady, variable, fuel-efficient, supersonic, subsonic, ground, air, highway, synchronous

spell, spells (1: attraction) See *attraction*
spell, spells (2: an indeterminate period of time) See *period*
spelling, spellings right, wrong, (in)accurate, (in)correct, unverified, (un)certain, imaginative, creative, bad, poor, execrable, appalling, awful, deplorable, erratic, atrocious, anomalous, streamlined, standard, variant, archaic, phonetic
spender, spenders careful, sensible, thrifty, (im)prudent, (ir)responsible, (un)wise, (in)judicious, careless, senseless, foolish, reckless, loose, big, spur-of-the-moment
spending discretionary, sensible, cautious, aggressive, tight, stagnant, sluggish, flat, (un)wise, (ir)responsible, heedless, (in)effective, reckless, senseless, indiscriminate, foolish, frivolous, extravagant, heavy, lavish, wanton, profligate, impulsive, riotous, inflationary, runaway, massive, excessive, wasteful, uncontrolled, uninhibited, personal
spendthrift, spendthrifts imprudent, reckless, irresponsible, injudicious, heedless, senseless, careless, indifferent, indiscriminate, foolish, rash, thoughtless, wasteful
sphere, spheres hollow, smooth, narrow, imaginary, celestial, armillary
spice, spices rousing, fresh, fragrant, aromatic, mild, rich, hot, mouth-scorching, pungent, whole, basic, (un)common, rare, exotic, assorted
spider, spiders prowling, crawling, fast-moving, nimble, bold, laborious,

spill, spills

diligent, undisturbed, giant, dwarf, wily, venomous, predatory, carnivorous, deadly, drab, bony, bristly, hairy, furry, feathered, finned, long-legged, ogre-faced, spiny-backed, web-spinning, sedentary, hunting, jumping, fishing

spill, spills (un)controllable, uncontrolled, wasteful

spire, spires towering, high, lofty, tall, majestic, elegant, distinctive, slender, hexagonal, Gothic

spirit, spirits guiding, conciliatory, innovative, cooperative, uncomplaining, generous, noble, good-natured, high, blithe, gay, joyous, cheerful, cheery, happy, buoyant, (con)genial, omnipresent, lurking, exhilarating, serene, courageous, expiatory, indefatigable, implacable, indomitable, unconquerable, unbreakable, unquenchable, irrepressible, immortal, undying, undamped, resolute, moving, incomparable, strong, youthful, reverential, resilient, elastic, disembodied, fervent, restless, adventurous, venturous, venturesome, daring, insurgent, tumultuous, boisterous, reckless, fiery, unbridled, unrestrained, unruly, fierce, martial, warlike, fighting, revengeful, avenging, factious, clannish, malevolent, malignant, dastardly, spiteful, evil, forlorn, low, abject, sagging, ethereal, celestial, civic, public, kindred, nationalistic, entrepreneurial, competitive, athletic, ancestral, guardian; animal

spite envious, malicious, mean, poisonous, venomous, rancorous, splenetic, vengeful, vindictive, petty, ill-natured, sheer, covert, aforethought, intended, premeditated

splendour, splendours imposing, overpowering, rattling, screaming, startling, flashing, shining, lustrous, radiant, vivid, gorgeous, magnificent, luxurious, opulent, ornate, stately, sumptuous, unparalleled, unrivalled, awesome, feeble, regal, royal, (neo-)feudal, ceremonial, architectural, artistic

split, splits See *difference* (2)

spokesperson, spokespersons respectable, effective, fiery, oracular, eloquent, serious-faced, pugnacious, official, sole, only

sponge, sponges damp, moist, porous, absorbent, colourful, shapely, shapeless, synthetic, fresh-water, deep-sea, spherical

sponsor, sponsors kind, generous, good-hearted, philanthropic, open-handed, major, individual, corporate

spoon, spoons rounded, level, shiny, stained, rusty, greasy, decorative, apostle

sport, sports exciting, beloved, favourite, injury-free, clean, steroid-free, drug-free, lovely, tame, light, active, fast-moving, hardy, vigorous, rough, strenuous, high-intensity, high-performance, gruelling, punishing, rigorous, sweaty, rugged, risky, dangerous, violent, wild, barbaric, intricate, money-mad, profitable, youthful, manly, masculine, male, female, mainstream, quintessential, archaic, booming, unfamiliar, individual, competitive, casual, team, indoor, outdoor, year-round, spectator, rustic, field, water, aquatic, seaside, waterside, icy, winter, summer, (non-)aerobic, (non-)contact, professional, amateur, Olympic, equestrian, college, intramural, combat(ive), (inter)collegiate, international, national

sportsman, sportswoman See *athlete*

sportswear See *clothes*

spot, spots heavenly, beautiful, wondrous, idyllic, blissful, favourite, bright, convenient, strategic, scenic, historic, peaceful, retired, solitary, hidden, hard-to-reach, (in)visible, (un)usual, (un)likely, precise, identical, hot, cold, hazy, dark-coloured; tight, sore, weak, blind, black, slippery

spotlight, spotlights See *light*

spouse, spouses See also *husband* and *wife* supporting, supportive, (un)suitable, (un)faithful, (un)manageable, prospective, surviving, (in)dependent, abusive, vindictive, adulterous, delinquent, common-law, legal

spread, spreading alarming, frightening, appalling, frightful, relentless, unchecked, unabated, phenomenal, unprecedented

spring, springs (1: a season of the year) relaxing, soothing, enchanting, stirring, lovely, sweet, balmy, temperate, cool, benign, halcyon, sensational, serene, early, late, waning, wet(ter-than-usual), austral

spring, springs (2: a natural source of water that flows from the ground) unfailing, gushing, foaming, boiling, steaming, seething, flowing, soothing, relaxing, refreshing, healthful, freshwater, impenetrable, unfathomable, inexhaustible, fiery, bubbly, clear, crystal(-clear), effervescent, volcanic, natural, mineral, sulphur(ous), salt, artesian, chalybeate, hot (thermal), geothermal, therapeutic, healing, Pierian

spring, springs (3: a metal spiral) powerful, weak, volute, scroll-shaped, cylindrical, helical, spiral, interior

sprinter, sprinters See *runner*

spy, spies well-trained, master, first-class, greedy, intrepid, long-term, ill-disposed, disaffected, professed, suspected, undetected, disguised, retired, potential

squad, squads special, élite, firing, anti-narcotics, anti-terror, fraud

squalor contemptible, degraded, feculent, sordid, seedy, dingy, incredible, unbelievable, shocking, back-alley

square, squares (residential area) lordly, gracious, elegant, handsome, resplendent, picturesque, quaint, dainty, neat, dinky, rococo, enormous, huge, massive, spacious, open, stalwart, arcaded, tiled, cobblestone, main, central, (un)crowded, intimate, little, rambling, (un)tidy, littered, squalid, decayed, cacophonous, raucous, gaudy, town

squeak, squeaks shrill, piercing, high-pitched, sharp, frenzied

squirrel, squirrels creeping, graceful, frisky, lively, playful, high-spirited, quick, swift, active, secretive, striped, ground, red, grey, flying, tassel-eared, common

stability lasting, enduring, unchanging, permanent, long-term, constant, proverbial, welcome, remarkable, short-lived, lateral, political, economic, regional, emotional

stadium, stadiums See also *building* magnificent, modern, (un)safe, massive, deficient, derelict, decrepit, filthy, domed, retractable-roof, air-conditioned, indoor, outdoor, municipal, memorial, Olympic

staff, staffs accommodating, congenial, (un)friendly, (un)pleasant, (in)attentive, thoughtful, dedicated, committed, hardworking, diligent, industrious, (un)conscientious, (in)experienced, (in)efficient, (un)trained, (un)skilled, terse, surly, abundant, bloated, mammoth, low-paid, (low-)salaried, high-salaried, (non-)essential, temporary, permanent,

contract, full-time, part-time, casual, skeleton, general, professional, support, administrative, executive, academic, on-duty, round-the-clock

stage, stages (1: period; phase) meaningful, decisive, acute, vital, critical, crucial, dramatic, distinguishable, distinct, primitive, early, fledgling, preliminary, embryonic, transitory, (almost-)final, near-final, advanced, (im)perceptible, multiple, gradual, insensible, precarious, formative, exploratory, experimental, conceptual

stage, stages (2: raised platform on which the actors appear) bare, tiny, minuscule, sloping, old-style, gaudy, set, legitimate, outdoor, apron

stage-setting, stage-settings elaborate, extravagant, spectacular, ornate, minimal(ist)

stain, stains permanent, indelible, tough, obstinate, stubborn, impossible, (in)soluble, (un)removable, (un)noticeable, unsightly, characteristic, chemical, water

stair, stairs elegant, (un)sound, steep, slippery, menacing, life-threatening, footworn, creaky, rickety, squeaky, shaky, unprotected, uncarpeted, carpetless, wide, spiral, curving, front, rear, wooden, stone

staircase, staircases sweeping, dizzying, flying, winding, curving, circular, spiral, cylindrical, main, chief, principal, central, monumental, grand, spectacular, dramatic, bold, endless, ornate, metal, wrought-iron, marble, steep, narrow, wide, spacious, curved, warped, rickety, outdoor, Norman

stairway, stairways See *staircase*

stalemate, stalemates See *deadlock*

stamina See *strength* and *energy*

stammer, stammering See *stutter*

stamp, stamps rare, collectible, commemorative, definitive, surcharged, (in)expensive, mint, fine, foreign, postage, postal; trading

stance, stances See *attitude*

stand, stands conciliatory, laudable, gallant, courageous, bold, glorious, outspoken, staunch, magnanimous, moderate, independent, dramatic, (in)flexible, tough, strong, definite, unwavering, unshak(e)able, (un)equivocal, ambiguous, hard(-line), defiant, adamant, rigid, no-action, immoderate, controversial, hypocritical, obstructive, defensive, last-ditch

standard, standards demanding, exacting, relentless, stressful, stringent, rigorous, strict, tough, rigid, impossible, lofty, exalted, high, world-class, magnificent, (un)attainable, minimum, minimal, (un)acceptable, absolute, (un)reasonable, basic, equitable, uniform, common, variable, varying, changeable, shifting, definite, old-fashioned, traditional, conventional, mythical, local, worldly, new-fangled, suffocating, strange, appalling, insulting, derisory, modest, lax, sluggish, sordid, lamentable, deficient, sliding, faltering, objective, moral, ethical, aesthetic, double

standing long, high, full, good, legal, humble, low

star, stars (1: a heavenly body) shining, twinkling, glittering, bright, radiant, brilliant, effulgent, luminous, flashy, dark, subdued, glorious, huge, (super)giant, dwarf, untold, uncounted, countless, uncountable, innumerable, unnumbered, numerous, voluminous, clustering, myriad, lone, steady, fixed, distant, indifferent, dying, expiring, (in)visible, propitious, circumpolar, natal, supernal, celestial, fatal, binary (double), evening, morning, multiple, shooting, fallen, falling, polar, twin, exploding, variable

star, stars (2: a person distinguished in his/her field) super, top, outstanding, glamorous, bright, personable, legendary, breathtaking, flamboyant, unrivalled, high-priced, sought-after, sudden, instant, hot, (fast-)rising, budding, fading, retiring, romantic, reclusive, no-name, sports, screen, film, musical, sitcom

stardom See *star* (2)

stare, stares charming, appealing, all-embracing, penetrating, piercing, searching, exploring, glowing, liquid-burning, withering, unwinking, unwavering, unflinching, meaningful, eager, earnest, solemn, intense, deep, magnetic, fixed, steadfast, steady, straight, calculated, intent, dazed, liquid, misty, bland, blank, vacant, dull, vague, oblivious, drowsy, sleepy, inscrutable, enigmatic, incomprehensible, elongated, unhurried, restrained, unequivocal, stony,

steely, wooden, glassy, icy, frozen, frosty, glacial, leathery, speechless, silent, mute, tired, pinched, self-assured, curious, crystal, iridescent, overt, bold, unsympathetic, unfeeling, unfriendly, antagonistic, (un)hostile, resentful, fierce, indifferent, insane, fishy, furtive, stealthy, shocked, incredulous, morose, dark, bleak, vicious, lethal, frantic, startled, doe-eyed, protuberant, soft, narrow, spectral, accusative, judg(e)mental

start, starts See *beginning*

starvation deplorable, shocking, pitiable, calamitous, terrible, massive, mass, widespread, emotional

state, states (1: political community) sovereign, (semi)autonomous, independent, unified, unitary, democratic, moderate, viable, self-sufficient, neutral, exemplary, modern, emerging, nascent, hermit-like, borderless, unpredictable, minute, warring, self-proclaimed, bureaucratic, clerical, religious, theocratic, secular, welfare, socialist, jingoistic, corporate, federal, pluralist, multiparty, single-party, one-party, all-powerful, authoritarian, repressive, totalitarian, monolithic, fascist, feudal, tribal, vassal, police, supernational, buffer, garrison, satellite, puppet, nation, city, island, heterogeneous, indigenous, breakaway, rogue, hegemonic, Orwellian

state, states (2: condition) See also *condition* (1) blissful, cheerful, delightful, exalted, rosy, remarkable, nervous, abnormal, dream-like, trance-like, comatose, half-forgotten, fragmentary, distracted, agitated, confused, paradoxical, volatile, permanent, perpetual, chronic, vulnerable, quarrelsome, ruinous, sorry, wretched, intolerable, dirty, terrible, tattered, cataleptic, biological, psychological; trivalent

statement, statements conciliatory, clear-cut, categorical, conclusive, forthright, bald, plain, (un)diplomatic, blunt, empirical, lucid, laconic, curt, concise, terse, brief, detailed, sententious, emphatic, (in)consistent, meaningful, revealing, irrefutable, indisputable, definitive, (in)correct, (in)accurate, (un)true, (un)reasonable, explicit, simple, unequivocal, ingenuous, sincere, honest, precise, epigrammatic, proverbial,

veracious, candid, clean-cut, clear,
(ir)relevant, truthful, categorical,
unqualified, positive, unconditional,
emphatic, just, exact, strict, fair,
well-timed, momentous, express, abstruse,
emotional, impassioned, enthusiastic,
compelling, bewildering, astounding,
startling, bland, strong, tough, fiery,
flat-out, defensive, adamant, alarming,
eccentric, cautious, ominous, dissenting,
punishable, slanderous, libellous,
pejorative, defamatory, threatening,
inadmissible, disingenuous, vague,
ambiguous, (self-)contradictory,
irreconcilable, paradoxical, unproved,
unsubstantiated, meaningless, false,
fictitious, misleading, unfair, rash, hasty,
absurd, ill-advised, ridiculous,
preposterous, (dis)coloured, specious,
deceptive, ignorant, defiant, incendiary,
belligerent, bellicose, negative, embittered,
tendentious, wrong, incredible,
unbelievable, artless, conditional,
affirmative, casual, chance, surprise,
fundamental, blanket, public,
(semi-)official, formal, joint, prefatory,
(non-)binding, sweeping, wide-ranging,
financial, economic, assertive, apodeictic,
problematic

statesman, statesmen far-sighted,
foresighted, far-seeing, prescient, visionary,
intelligent, ingenious, accomplished,
skilful, shrewd, astute, crafty, diplomatic,
dignified, judicious, artful, prudent,
shrewd, sagacious, wily, wise, politic,
moderate, distinguished, celebrated,
eminent, illustrious, pre-eminent, elder

station, stations See also *building* swank,
spiffy, plush, posh, smart, elegant,
lush, luxurious, ostentatious, quiet,
(un)crowded, bustly, chaotic, main, local,
subsidiary, weather-worn, derelict, bleak,
cheerless, desolate, run-down, dreary,
dismal, abandoned, postal, electrical,
terminal

statistic, statistics overwhelming,
comprehensive, impressive, encouraging,
solid, vital, meaningful,
(in)comprehensible, (un)convincing,
(un)reliable, (in)accurate, tidy, unfounded,
(un)challengeable, inflated, swollen,
elusive, dubious, gloomy, grim,
frightening, sobering, alarming, startling,

staggering, chilling, troubling,
disappointing, worrying, galling, conflicting,
volatile, changeable, problematic, dull, dry,
raw, national, demographic

statue, statues See also *sculpture*
gleaming, striking, towering, imposing,
colossal, gargantuan, giant, gigantic,
magnificent, gilt, bronze, terracotta,
sandstone, brass(y), wooden, genuine,
authentic, spurious, ancient, famous,
intricate, enigmatic, absurd, lifeless,
motionless, ambulatory, grimy, fissured,
voluptuous, indecent, nude, unclothed,
life-size, equestrian, semi-recumbent,
three-headed, headless, abstract, memorial,
heroic, votive

stature, statures towering, great,
immense, considerable, colossal, gigantic,
full, international, unmistakable, average,
diminishing, diminished, emblematic

status, statuses privileged, preferential,
special, unique, nonpareil, particular,
distinct, lofty, elevated, high(-power),
superior, world-class, global, legendary,
élite, classy, mythic(al), (un)equal,
mainstream, present, former,
medium-power, second-class, second-string,
subordinate, uncertain, subservient,
inferior, humiliating, humble, low,
deplorable, fragile, precarious, tenuous,
undefined, short-lived, definitive, associate,
ceremonial, hereditary, putative,
(semi-)independent, (semi-)official, (il)legal,
social, economic, socioeconomic,
bureaucratic, political, diplomatic, double,
tax-exempt; alert

stay, stays lengthy, brief, short,
(un)eventful, (un)rewarding, (un)profitable,
(un)bearable, dull, extended,
(un)scheduled, unconstrained, curative,
therapeutic, restorative

steak, steaks See *meat*

steam hissing, billowing, scalding, live,
wispy, dense, wet, dry, hot, primary,
sulphurous, thermal

steamer, steamship See *ship* and *vessel*

steel hard, mild, flexible, rustproof,
stainless, tempered, austenitic, cast

steering same-side, right-hand, left-hand,
two-wheel, four-wheel, power; erratic

stem, stems gleaming, young, tough, stiff,
(in)flexible, woolly, long, slender, erect,
straight, swollen, twining, assurgent,

hollow, cylindrical, thorny, prickly, prickle-tipped, many-jointed, underground, ancipital

step, steps (1: movement, action) helpful, innovative, commendable, (im)proper, (in)appropriate, (il)logical, (un)safe, purposeful, positive, (in)effective, (in)effectual, concrete, firm, strong, constructive, liberating, active, careful, sensitive, intelligible, measured, steady, credible, dignified, bold, unhesitating, stunning, staggering, unprecedented, fantastic, natural, mincing, lithe, graceful, supple, rhythmic, nimble, brisk, quick, hurried, rapid, urgent, sudden, jerky, jaunty, fitful, youthful, manful, measurable, (in)sufficient, Draconian, major, monumental, giant, tremendous, substantive, vigorous, appreciable, (in)significant, momentous, crucial, dramatic, historic, revolutionary, key, big, (un)usual, radical, drastic, tiny, deliberate, belated, irretraceable, irreversible, pre-emptive, tangible, harsh, free, noiseless, plodding, tottering, springing, faltering, stumbling, fainting, dizzying, slouching, clumping, floppy, ponderous, timid, backward, retrograde, hazardous, faulty, false, elastic, springy, bouncy, jumpy, light, spiritless, awkward, clumsy, hesitant, leaden, dull, uncertain, precarious, careless, interim, intermediary, initial, tentative, introductory, (over)due, long-overdue, final, subsequent, preventive, retaliatory, separatist, symbolic

step, steps (2: tread in a stairway) graceful, (un)graduated, flinty, granite, stone, wooden, steep, narrow, squeaky, creaky, jagged, rickety, wobbly, shaky, slippery, hazardous, (un)safe, (time-)worn, well-worn, (half-)dark, straight, spiral

stick, sticks slender, thin, thick, stout, short, long, straight, crooked, rigid, pointed, hooked, forked

stigma, stigmas stinging, scorching, scathing, painful, disgraceful, shameful, social

stillness halcyon, hushed, dead, breathless, luscious, serene, peaceful, pacific, placid, exquisite, drowsy, eerie, terrible, deathly, profound, immense

stimulation, stimulations animating,

exotic, artificial, cheap, extraneous, sexual, physical, mental, electrical

sting, stings sharp, venomous, poisonous, baneful, virulent

stitch, stitches dext(e)rous, intricate, colourful, short, long, (un)even, strong, blind, interwoven, cross, diagonal, plaited

stock, stocks (1: a share in business) See also *share* (2) (un)safe, valuable, blue-chip, volatile, individual, worthless, wildcat, over-the-counter, joint, capital, common, preference, underlying, government

stock, stocks (2: a store or supply accumulated) See also *supply* open, surplus, household, domestic

stocking, stockings loose, (super)stretchy, durable, indestructible, elastic, hold-up, smooth, shining, flesh-coloured, sheer, fish-net, silk, nylon, woollen, lisle, mesh, seamless, glamorous, full(y)-fashioned, outmoded, crumpled, laddered, wrinkled, dowdy, support, surgical

stomach, stomachs rumbling, blundering, bulging, protruding, rapacious, greedy, tumid, taut, swollen, enlarged, bloated, queasy, gippy, roller-coaster, sensitive, well-fed, multichambered

stone, stones (semi-)precious, imperial, standing, transparent, clear, translucent, gleaming, immutable, pumice, jagged, ragged, smooth, clay, granite, serpentine, insensate, opaque, hard, flinty, abrasive, volcanic, gigantic, diorite, fibrous, porous, granular, waxy, rough, inanimate, lifeless, stationary, recumbent, conical, rectangular, mossy, fine-grained, close-grained, coarse-grained, weather-beaten, time-battered, foraminiferous, polychromatic, sepulchral, memorial, good-luck, granular, igneous, crystalline, monolithic, megalithic

stool, stools See also *chair* three-legged, four-legged, circular, revolving, milking, piano

stop, stops abrupt, sudden, requisite, final, overnight, jarring, screeching, apocalyptic, unexpected, (un)scheduled, emergency

storage temporary, cold, dead, archival, associative (content-addressable)

store, stores See also *shop* posh, fashionable, stylish, élite, chic, elegant,

trendy, exclusive, pricey, ritzy, fancy,
prestigious, snooty, glamorous, up-market,
major, ubiquitous, reputable,
well-run, eye-catching, quaint, swank(y),
tidy, smart, gargantuan, oversize,
conventional-size, jam-packed, crowded,
independent, small, dingy, dowdy,
unpretentious, drab, cheap, closed,
shuttered, cooperative, state-run, collective,
general, retail, self-service

storey, storeys See *floor*

storm, storms roaring, howling, raging,
hammering, cracking, passing, (on)coming,
impending, slow-moving, whirling,
swirling, blinding, devastating,
earthshattering, earthshaking, unexpected,
untimely, sudden, seasonal, (un)seasonable,
epochal, occasional, imminent, aberrant,
catastrophic, calamitous, destructive,
ruinous, harsh, vicious, gale-force,
cyclonic, deadly, lethal, murderous,
monstrous, monster, killer, severe,
unabated, all-night, dense, mighty, strong,
powerful, hard, vigorous, spectacular,
nasty, violent, awful, horrific, fearsome,
dreadful, horrendous, horrible, terrible,
frightening, wild, fierce, savage, brutal,
unrelenting, relentless, ruthless, merciless,
pitiless, rude, bad, uncontrollable,
tempestuous, rough, full-blown, massive,
tremendous, big, major, giant, serious,
furious, angry, gloomy, black-bellied,
frightful, freak, windy, torrential, winter,
electric, magnetic, equinoctial, solar

story, stories absorbing, engrossing,
touching, haunting, fascinating, intriguing,
compelling, moving, amusing, entertaining,
suspenseful, droll, juicy, substantial,
eventful, extraordinary, authentic, reliable,
trustworthy, decent, credible, effective,
imaginative, vivid, rich, spicy, colourful,
valid, remarkable, spectacular, original,
masterful, matchless, snappy, tremendous,
unique, schematic, coherent, well-rounded,
nice, great, accredited, affirmative,
tenacious, diversified, (un)familiar,
probable, plausible, special,
(un)conventional, (un)usual, ordinary,
popular, favourite, oft-told, best-loved,
facetious, funny, touchy, wry, mixed,
(un)likely, (un)true, incredible,
unbelievable, implausible, incongruous,
improbable, far-fetched, unconvincing,

overdrawn, laboured, contrived,
apocryphal, made-up, tall, false, fanciful,
inventive, complex, sinuous, domestic,
strange, untold, unqualified, inconclusive,
digressionary, disjointed, incoherent,
attenuated, plotless, ill-told, gaudy, absurd,
foolish, foggy, untrustworthy, dull, pallid,
repetitious, sordid, horrible, frightening,
agonizing, heart-rending, depressing, sad,
gloomy, grim, macabre, gruesome, ghastly,
horrible, shocking, grisly, hair-raising,
awkward, bawdy, broad, improper,
indecent, raw, vulgar, coarse, smutty,
smoking-room, obscene, rowdy, naughty,
unsavoury, disgusting, suggestive,
sensational, racy, off-colour, preposterous,
spicy, scandalous, ribald, robust, evocative,
meditative, illustrative, true-life,
(quasi-)supernatural, love, sentimental,
literary, comic, tragic, heroic, folk, epic,
allegorical, parabolic, mythic,
mythological, fantastic, picaresque,
romantic, classic, elegiac, didactic,
mystery, spy, detective, adventure, serial,
scriptural, biblical, epistolary, satirical,
anecdotal, suspense, cock-and-bull, inside,
eyewitness, feature, leading, front-page,
cover, investigative, shaggy-dog, pulp, sob,
bedtime, Rabelaisian

story-teller, story-tellers amusing,
charming, entertaining, natural, exquisite,
exuberant, enthusiastic, ecstatic,
spontaneous, unrestrained, brilliant, fluent,
eloquent, true, accomplished, ingenious,
avid, tireless, inexhaustible, clever,
delightful, versatile, compulsive,
innovative, plausible, itinerant

story-telling fascinating, charming,
absorbing, enchanting, enthralling,
thoughtful, inventive, good, old-fashioned

stove, stoves efficient, airtight, primitive,
squat(ty), wood, firewood, coal, cast-iron,
earthen, hand-cast, brick, tiled, open,
upright, potbelly (potbellied), portable

strain, strains heavy, severe, explosive,
excessive, considerable, persistent,
constant, incessant, ceaseless, unceasing,
lasting, endless, continuous, unaccustomed,
unusual, awesome, emotional, nervous,
financial, intellectual, mental; tensile

stranger, strangers mysterious, hostile,
untrustful, total, perfect, utter, entire,
virtual, relative, comparative

strategy, strategies (un)clear, (un)workable, well-thought-out, sensible, (un)reasonable, brilliant, smart, innovative, unique, aggressive, (in)effective, (un)dependable, impressive, elaborate, (in)appropriate, (un)acceptable, (in)valid, (in)coherent, superior, supreme, vigorous, masterful, skilful, crafty, shrewd, cunning, foxy, devious, daredevil, cruel, unforgivable, calculating, complex, confused, vague, obscure, murky, risky, single-minded, short-sighted, obstinate, outdated, long-term, short-term, unbreachable, alternative, political, tactical, organizational, procedural, joint

stream, streams See also *river* roaring, babbling, warbling, brawling, murmuring, prancing, splashing, (fast-)running, fast-moving, fast-flowing, swift-flowing, slow-flowing, clear-flowing, rippling, undulating, meandering, trickling, tumbling, sinking, winding, swelling, never-failing, drying, glowing, swollen, heavy, mighty, torrential, turbulent, irresistible, silt-coloured, translucent, transparent, clear, crystal(line), lucid, pellucid, bright, healthy, freshwater, alluring, gentle, placid, calm, quiet, silent, peaceful, subdued, alive, delightful, chattering, untouched, unspoiled, lonely, (sub)glacial, icy, chilly, freezing, cold, steady, endless, perennial, perpetual, constant, crooked, wayward, intricate, sullen, languid, sluggish, lazy, fast-paced, ankle-deep, steep-sided, shallow, turbid, broad, thick, thin, inconsequential, feathery, dappled, dimpled, sandy, rocky, muddy, silty, boggy, swampy, briny, sedgy, sedged, alder-shaded, willow-fringed, woodland, unhealthy, nameless, fishless, trout, spring-fed, snow-fed, glacier-fed, tidal, glacial, alpine, tributary, arterial, feeder, Stygian

street, streets tree-lined, leafy, shady, picturesque, wide, broad, spacious, gracious, quaint, elegant, handsome, enchanting, posh, (un)fashionable, (un)desirable, quiet, peaceful, (un)safe, majestic, clean, swept, major, legendary, historic, medi(a)eval, lively, vibrant, alive, shop-lined, busy, teeming, raucous, plangent, noisy, dead, ghostly, empty, traffic-free, straight,

right-angled, diagonal, undulating, branching, twisting, rambling, winding, meandering, twisted, tortuous, crooked, serpentine, labyrinthine, steep, narrow(-stepped), claustrophobic, constricted, oblique, short, long, flag-draped, sun-lit, light-dappled, treeless, marble-paved, stone(-paved), colonnaded, arcaded, walled, terraced, crescent-shaped, suburban, leafy, (rain-)flooded, windy, icy, ice-covered, hurried, crowded, congested, thronged, blocked, (traffic-)clogged, traffic-choked, chaotic, impassable, bumptious, filthy, grimy, sooty, dirty, cheap, seedy, mean, desolate, squalid, ramshackle, grubby, hideous, run-down, evil-smelling, dingy, dusty, dust-choked, muddy, rubble-strewn, litter-strewn, littered, drab, dowdy, tough, badly-lit, poorly-lit, dark, dim, grey, gloomy, mysterious, obscure, sodden, (semi-)desolate, war-weary, pitted, potholed, unpaved, cracked, main, prime, premier, principal, central, secondary, side, back, dead-end, blind, one-way, two-way, pedestrian, residential, suburban

strength See also *power* and *force* vigorous, phenomenal, superhuman, superior, prodigious, massive, Herculean, incredible, unbelievable, astonishing, enduring, unabated, tenacious, massive, tremendous, immense, formidable, rude, sinewy, masculine, smashing, crushing, ultimate, underlying, (in)sufficient, numerical, brute, physical, spiritual; tensile

stress, stresses overpowering, extreme, immense, excessive, intense, severe, acute, unbearable, unimaginable, unaccustomed, unusual, undue, apparent, awesome, explosive, persistent, tensile, ultimate, constant, endless, continuous, continual, incessant, unceasing, ceaseless, chronic, destructive, harmful, inner, daily, pent-up, job-related, grief-related, oxidative, physical, emotional, psychological, nervous, mental, intellectual, financial

stride, strides See *step* (1)

strife endless, perpetual, stubborn, wild, dishonourable, ignoble, violent, murderous, internecine, destructive, mental, racial, sectional, civil, sectarian, factional, regional, internal, (inter-)ethnic, local, intercommunal, political, marital, domestic

strike, strikes (1: a cessation of work) widespread, pervasive, persistent, large, massive, full-scale, all-out, total, country-wide, nation-wide, open-ended, two-day, short(-lived), long, sudden, (un)avoidable, (in)evitable, unprecedented, unpopular, militant, violent, devastating, disruptive, ugly, costly, bitter, rancorous, sporadic, rolling, (long-)threatened, unco-ordinated, (un)settled, national, constitutional, jurisdictional, (in)valid, (un)lawful, (il)legal, (un)official, unauthorized, general, wildcat, secondary, rolling

strike, strikes (2: an attack) See *attack*

striker, strikers militant, violent, adamant, obstinate, stubborn, tough, defiant, angry, undaunted, unyielding, dispirited

string, strings fragile, reticulate, straight, short, long, wiry, intricate, knotted, tangled, (un)broken

stroke, strokes (1: a single unbroken movement) single, bold, regular, continuous, backhanded

stroke, strokes (2: a sudden attack) devastating, full-blown, impending, paralytic

stroll, strolls, strolling See *walk*

stronghold, strongholds See *fort*

structure, structures forbidding, imposing, breathtaking, amazing, magnificent, wonderful, excellent, perfect, glamorous, amiable, lovely, handsome, comely, graceful, monumental, huge, massive, colossal, gigantic, impressive, awesome, grandiose, soaring, lofty, tall, ornate, monolithic, meretricious, innovative, sophisticated, (un)distinguished, durable, (un)safe, (un)stable, sound, gaudy, hulking, sprawling, tumbling, crumbly, shaky, crude, fragile, flimsy, dilapidated, tumbledown, ramshackle, rickety, derelict, ageless, archaic, rigid, complex, intricate, incomprehensible, temporary, movable, resilient, free-standing, tapering, recently-built, open-ended, symmetrical, crenulate, denticulate, geometric, conical, pyramidic (pyramidal), (neo)classical, futuristic, atomic, molecular, cellular, turn-of-the-century, historic, unitary, wrought-iron; fibrous, organic,

vertebrate, correlative, geological, deep

struggle, struggles just, heroic, epic, valiant, righteous, hopeful, magnificent, manful, effective, fruitful, (in)consequential, lively, interminable, perpetual, unending, never-ending, endless, incessant, ceaseless, unceasing, ongoing, (decade-)long, drawn-out, protracted, permanent, non-stop, lifelong, frequent, off-and-on, spasmodic, last-minute, big, major, titanic, monumental, gigantic, intense, vigorous, profound, hard, arduous, unabated, undiminished, determined, unflinching, hard-fought, harsh, fierce, (non-)violent, sharp, firm, tough, severe, unequal, (un)even, savage, ferocious, sanguinary, acrimonious, vicious, dog-eat-dog, internecine, unrelenting, relentless, ruthless, pitiless, merciless, remorseless, heartless, bitter, dreary, desperate, frantic, confused, odds-against, uphill, grim, dire, painful, traumatic, fateful, life-threatening, precarious, uncompromising, unavailing, fruitless, futile, pointless, gruelling, grinding, debilitating, impotent, ineffectual, ineffective, inconclusive, dreadful, turbulent, furious, bloody, hopeless, hand-to-hand, militant, armed, revolutionary, terrorist, electoral, internal, fratricidal, factional, political, earthly, ideological

stubbornness unyielding, unchanging, enduring, persevering, uncompromising, unmoving, unswerving, unwavering, unrelenting, relentless, ruthless, pitiless, heartless, merciless, devotional, incredible, unbelievable, immovable, firm, tenacious, pertinacious, determined, dogged, fixed, obdurate, pigheaded, mulish, inflexible, persistent, craggy, rigid, clumsy, destructive, defensive, go-it-alone

student, students diligent, proficient, outstanding, top, distinguished, attentive, bright, brilliant, apt, clever, smart, industrious, (un)methodical, ambitious, devoted, dedicated, all-round, model, keen, enthusiastic, zealous, earnest, serious, high-calibre, talented, careful, accurate, punctual, scrupulous, conscientious, precocious, gifted, curious, capable, fine, promising, striving, struggling, energetic, thoughtful, literate, advanced, adept, (un)popular, average, disadvantaged, mediocre, dull, pretentious, slow, spoon-fed, lazy, indolent, careless, slack, unprepared, incapable, immature, thoughtless, reckless, poverty-stricken, troubled, problem, apathetic, reluctant, semi-literate, militant, belligerent, restive, fitful, rebellious, violence-prone, radical, prospective, (un)qualified, (ir)regular, (post)graduate, doctoral, part-time, full-time, occasional, resident, mature, foreign, overseas, international

study, studies careful, exhaustive, deep, in-depth, detailed, lengthy, extensive, wide-ranging, comprehensive, large-scale, full-scale, massive, monumental, book-length, close, intensive, intense, thorough, meticulous, painstaking, authoritative, serious, fascinating, absorbing, solid, assiduous, meaningful, coherent, significant, remarkable, perceptive, recondite, seminal, erudite, learned, esoteric, reputable, revealing, first-hand, classic, effective, systematic, avid, provocative, ambitious, unconventional, landmark, unprecedented, substantial, up-to-date, amiable, persistent, dogged, unremitting, advanced, rigorous, prominent, notable, remarkable, splendid, magnificent, challenging, compelling, resolute, long-standing, long-term, month-long, conclusive, painstaking, objective, conventional, generalizable, nuanced, random, small-scale, superficial, desultory, casual, ponderous, dull, long-winded, obscure, ongoing, lateral, follow-up, preliminary, pilot, comparative, empirical, experimental, investigative, exploratory, diagnostic, scholarly, critical, interdisciplinary, clinical, laboratory, field, professional, collaborative, microscopic, behavioural, antiquarian, historical, scientific, social, divine, cultural, actuarial, strategic, demographic

stunt, stunts See *feat*

stupidity oafish, addle-brained, blockheaded, obstinate, idiotic, senseless, hopeless, crass, gross, monstrous, dreadful, outrageous, inexcusable, incredible, inconceivable, unbelievable, proverbial, sheer, stark, plain, downright, blank, pure, unalloyed, unqualified, unmitigated, vacuous, clumsy, blundering, colossal,

monumental, immeasurable, incalculable, abysmal, thick, impenetrable, invincible, blatant, obtrusive, conspicuous, obvious, apparent, smug, thoroughgoing, utter, complete, out-and-out, absolute, veriest, utmost, insensate, ineffable, child-like, surprising, amusing, unflattering

stupor, stupors torpid, lethargic, comatose, hypnotic, blind, drunken, narcotic, anaesthetic

stutter, stuttering severe, serious, slight, long-established, upsetting

style, styles (1: of writing) polished, racy, graphic, vivid, lively, spirited, passionate, expressive, crisp, concise, terse, clipped, compact, tight, lean, austere, spare, syncopated, graceful, earnest, lofty, sublime, lithe, magnificent, exquisite, chaste, harmonious, delicate, transparent, easy, simple, clear, plain, lucid, limpid, bare, bald, perspicuous, reasonable, rotund, delightful, sententious, pithy, vigorous, consummate, finished, matchless, perfect, alembicated, refined, elegant, lush, enchanting, unforced, natural, sinuous, flexible, fluent, flowing, copious, novel, innovative, laconic, identifiable, inimitable, agile, precious, forceful, weighty, exuberant, aggressive, volcanic, engaging, aesthetic, rapid, straightforward, mellow, detached, punchy, structured, antithetic, individual, dazzling, trenchant, expansive, archaic, old-fashioned, emphatic, chatty, artificial, euphuistic, omniscient, waspish, self-conscious, ornate, aureate, florid, unadorned, flowery, pulpy, tough, inflated, magniloquent, grandiloquent, grandiose, mannered, glib, solemn, deadpan, frothy, diffuse, industrious, turgid, laboured, laborious, verbose, wordy, sonorous, staccato, ponderous, high-sounding, stilted, pompous, stiff, bombastic, flatulent, pretentious, orotund, overwrought, forced, decadent, nervous, flat, muddy, flashy, catchy, grinding, spasmodic, plodding, disjointed, choppy, jerky, careless, elliptical, slovenly, slipshod, mandarin, intricate, convoluted, complicated, confused, obscure, inconsistent, earthy, flaccid, colourless, dull, pedestrian, monotonous, heavy, stodgy, stiff, weak, colloquial, epistolary, narrative, rhetorical, metaphorical, lyrical, oratorial, realistic, poetic(al), sentimental, satirical, sardonic, ironical, humorous, epigrammatic, sententious, biblical, Ciceronian

style, styles (2: manner; method; way) exemplary, singular, identifiable, lithe, graceful, inimitable, innovative, suave, lofty, sublime, exalted, dignified, noble, regal, grand, magnificent, (un)sophisticated, cerebral, tenacious, courteous, delightful, effective, eye-catching, striking, meticulous, precise, simple, rotund, divergent, familiar, murmurous, whiplash, cooperative, spartan, flamboyant, freewheeling, boisterous, pretentious, artificial, aggressive, confrontational, autocratic, hard-handed, uncompromising, abrasive, grating, authoritarian, opulent, rapid, lax, convoluted, slovenly, scrappy, worthless, slipshod, colourless, gruff, crude, waspish, adopted, classic, traditional, (un)conventional, old-fashioned, official, personal, individual, popular, folksy, youthful, mannish, masculine, idealist, pragmatic, analyst, synthesist, realist

style, styles (3: fashion) See also *fashion* sophisticated, luxurious, up-to-date, original, eye-catching, smashing, dignified, distinctive, lithe, graceful, magnificent, dependable, meretricious, elaborate, basic, simple, plain, formal, sedate, restrained, cool, severe, casual, transitional, frivolous, brash, showy, flashy, bland, shocking, hybrid, classic, conservative, modern, contemporary

style, styles (4: architectural; artistic) graceful, refined, lithe, lofty, sublime, magnificent, meretricious, unique, ambitious, novel, discernible, simple, unadorned, austere, ubiquitous, ornate, intricate, florid, elaborate, pretentious, showy, artificial, queer, odd, aberrant, garish, colourless, modernist, belle époque, baroque, neoclassical, Attic, Palladian, Doric, Ionic, Corinthian, Roman, Gothic, Decorated

subject, subjects (1: topic) fascinating, intriguing, exciting, stirring, thrilling, living, up-to-the-minute, topical, (un)favourite, (un)pleasant, (dis)agreeable, crucial, critical, ticklish, delicate, touchy, tender, sensitive, inexhaustible, old-time, universal, profound, specific, esoteric, arcane, exoteric, broad, staple,

(un)familiar, (un)usual, complicated, complex, intricate, confused, traumatic, manifold, controversial, contentious, elusive, unmentionable, disgusting, abominable, taboo, trite, mundane, hackneyed, well-worn, threadbare, narrow, grim, dry, sore, vexing, obsessive

subject, subjects (2: course of study) (un)popular, strong, weak, dry, required, compulsory, optional, elective, core, academic, vocational, technical

subject, subjects (3: a person owing loyalty to a sovereign) loyal, faithful, trustworthy, allegiant, honest, devoted, constant, patriotic, lowly

submarine, submarines lurking, diving, floating, moving, fast, midget, extra-large, watertight, nuclear(-powered), snorkel-equipped, steel-hulled, titanium-hulled

submission, submissions unblinking, quiet, tacit, mute, melancholy, selfless, abject, contemptible, voluntary, reluctant, mean, miserable, menial, obsequious, servile, fawning, truckling, yielding, cringing, degrading, pushing, supine, slavish, base, lowly, sheep-like, spaniel-like

subservience See *submission*

subsidy, subsidies heavy, massive, excessive, abundant, huge, ample, copious, bountiful, generous, lavish, plentiful, opportune, expensive, (un)restrained, (un)restricted, (un)limited, wasteful, scandalous, controversial, needless, paltry, implicit, (in)direct

substance, substances beneficial, (un)stable, innocuous, sticky, adhesive, gummy, glutinous, viscous, gelatinous, astringent, versatile, malleable, (in)elastic, oily, fatty, greasy, spongy, pulpy, airy, ethereal, wispy, flimsy, tinny, resinous, waxy, waxlike, crystalline, absorbent, absorbing, absorbative, springy, molten, compressed, (semi)solid, thick, coarse, tough, dense, aromatic, luminous, frangible, (water-)soluble, consolute, fireproof, (in)combustible, (non-)flammable, explosive, lethal, deadly, hazardous, toxic, poisonous, harmful, deleterious, nauseous, strong-smelling, corrosive, addictive, foreign, mysterious, mythical, arcane, opaline, odourless, colourless, edible, organic, natural, (bio)chemical, synthetic, living, dead, inert, alkaline, elementary, material, aseptic, anaesthetic, carcinogenic, radioactive, man-made, primary, paramagnetic, ferromagnetic, mucous, cupriferous, gonadotrop(h)ic, (extra)terrestrial, ectoplasmic (ectoplastic); controlled

substitute, substitutes voluntary, (un)willing, perfect, ample, (un)available, (un)satisfying, (un)acceptable, (un)workable, (un)equivalent, poor, temporary, permanent, retroactive

suburb, suburbs See also *district* difficult-to-reach, distant, neighbouring, new, sprawling, rich, wealthy, affluent, prosperous, elegant, fashionable, exclusive, (in)expensive, high-rise, verdant, slumbering, countrified, gritty, rugged, shabby, drab, inner, outer, industrial

success, successes resounding, telling, smashing, breathtaking, stunning, glittering, dazzling, dizzying, outstanding, rousing, roaring, overwhelming, whopping, exhilarating, startling, amazing, astonishing, astounding, surprising, striking, lasting, enduring, signal, incontestable, undeniable, brilliant, triumphant, unalloyed, (well-)deserved, unparalleled, unprecedented, unbroken, unequivocal, unequalled, unmatched, solid, noteworthy, story-book, decisive, decided, clear-cut, singular, exceptional, phenomenal, large-scale, spectacular, prodigious, tremendous, considerable, huge, wide, monumental, fabulous, major, worldwide, not-so-simple, thorough, blockbuster, enviable, emphatic, uproarious, thunderous, happy, raging, wild, splashy, admirable, precocious, remarkable, notable, noticeable, eminent, conspicuous, marked, discernible, surefire, mainstream, reportable, overnight, immediate, instant(aneous), near, ultimate, eventual, belated, potential, initial, meteoric, short-lived, partial, comparative, mixed, moderate, (un)limited, modest, marginal, middling, trifling, slight, ill, (un)qualified, discreditable, indifferent, proven, (un)expected, illusive, material, worldly, pecuniary, monetary, academic

succession (1: sequence; series) straight, (im)proper, continuous, quick, rapid(-fire), endless

succession (2: the taking over of office, title, or property) rightful, wrongful, (il)legitimate, (il)legal, apostolic, dynastic, smooth

successor, successors immediate, potential, worthy, credible, wrongful, rightful, (il)legal, (il)legitimate

suddenness shocking, frightening, startling, stunning, dramatic, unexpected, unforeseen, unprecedented, harsh, restless, brittle, (un)pleasant

sufferer, sufferers chronic, hardened, indomitable, stoic(al), imperturbable, unmoved, unmovable, (im)patient, resolute, impassive, dispassionate, indifferent, stolid, unfortunate, Spartan

suffering, sufferings acute, keen, intense, severe, deep, profound, horrible, indiscriminate, untold, unspeakable, indescribable, intolerable, insupportable, unendurable, unbearable, dire, poignant, piercing, painful, grievous, terrible, desperate, cureless, hopeless, needless, pointless, incomprehensible, unnecessary, hidden, unmerited, unrequited, unmitigated, vicarious, bodily, physical, emotional, mental

sufficiency fair, reasonable, adequate, appropriate, acceptable, moderate

sugar white, brown, soft, crude, raw, lump, cube, spun, (super)fine, powdered, granulated, (un)refined, (fine-)grained, castor (caster), Demerara, Barbados

suggestion, suggestions inviting, tempting, enticing, alluring, fascinating, attractive, positive, concrete, practical, workable, specific, definite, clear, strong, constructive, fertile, commonsense, commonsensical, insightful, sensible, perceptive, astute, shrewd, sound, useful, intriguing, exciting, stirring, thrilling, interesting, startling, astonishing, (im)mature, (in)appropriate, (un)fortunate, (un)worthy, noteworthy, improper, (dis)creditable, (un)palatable, (un)acceptable, (in)sane, radical, wild, sinister, oblique, half-hearted, bland, banal, marginal, absurd, puerile, silly, whimsical, fatuous, pointless, weak, fatal, prospective, tentative, overt, covert, implicit, explicit, post-hypnotic

suicide, suicides (un)common, (un)lawful, (physician-)assisted, attempted, premeditated, voluntary, collective, mass, ritual

suit, suits (1: costume) neat, smart, cool, natty, fancy, quintessential, smashing, tasteful, (super)fine, splendid, magnificent, off-the-peg, custom-made, made-to-order, bespoke, made-to-measure, tailor-made, ready-made, dress(y), full-dress, full-trimmed, two-piece, three-piece, single-breasted, double-breasted, streamlined, conservative, subdued, traditional, classic, professional, casual, lightweight, sporty, regular, plain, pin-striped, chalk-stripe(d), salt-and-pepper, herringbone, (loud-)checked, (mad-)plaid, low-slung, slope-shouldered, swallow-tailed, strapless, loose, close-fitting, stiff, flannel, velvet, satiny, tan, dark, blue-serge, buoyant, showy, garish, gaudy, glittering, flashy, loud, wrinkly, rumpless, rough, shabby, baggy, boxy, shiny, awful-looking, shapeless, tattered, torn, worn, rusty, business; protective, life-sustaining

suit, suits (2: lawsuit) See *case* (2)

suitcase, suitcases (un)fashionable, matchable, matched, large, massive, capacious, kayak-sized, heavy, bulky, cumbersome, unwieldy, weighty, lightweight, stout, tattered, dilapidated, crumpled, split

suite, suites See also *flat* lofty, luxury, viceregal, deluxe, executive, bridal

suitor, suitors bashful, shy, timid, blushing, diffident, hesitant, reluctant, boorish, clumsy, awkward, (un)satisfactory, jealous, persistent, clamorous, tireless, untiring, patient, embarrassed, unwanted, disappointed, (un)successful

sum, sums bountiful, vast, staggering, immense, enormous, astronomical, princely, prodigious, large, tidy, siz(e)able, considerable, goodly, infinite, monstrous, preposterous, huge, tremendous, substantial, decent, unimaginable, unprecedented, munificent, (in)significant, (in)adequate, exact, precise, correct, approximate, definite, specific, round, nominal, undisclosed, laughable, small, trifling, piddling, worthless, petty, paltry, derisory, lump, penal

summary, summaries detailed, succinct, concise, pithy, crisp, lively, quick, rapid, curt, snappy, straightforward, (in)complete, (too-)normal, slight, crude, cryptic

summer, summers blissful, green, lovely, vibrant, soft-edged, magical, cool, wet, damp, dry, (un)bearable, hot, steamy, close, stifling, sweltering, scorching, torrid, parched, miserable, sickly, stormy, languorous, oncoming, early, high, lingering, waning, late, austral, tropical; Indian

summit, summits See *peak*

sun caressing, scalding, scorching, burning, searing, blistering, blinding, dazzling, all-conquering, (late-)gleaming, rising, vanishing, dying, slanting, sinking, westering, rounding, beneficial, kindly, gentle, (un)friendly, (in)adequate, strong, (noon-)hot, torrid, ardent, fiery, vicious, savage, unrelenting, relentless, heartless, pitiless, merciless, ruthless, remorseless, callous, brutal, fierce, intense, white-hot, tropical, harmful, brilliant, radiant, resplendent, flamboyant, orient, garish, double-yolk, blood-red, orange, tangerine, brassy, pale, weary, weak, dim, vagrant, (early-)morning, high-altitude, scarce, unbroken, constant, permanent, eternal, year-round, (un)clouded, bloated, lopsided, westward, midday, midnight, mock, antipodean

sun-deck, sun-decks See *balcony*

sunlight life-giving, streaming, blinding, stabbing, piercing, diamond-dazzling, trickling, waning, lingering, slanting, perfect, brilliant, bright, shimmery, sharp, strong, harsh, hot, golden, hazy, mellow, soft, pale, cloudy, watery, wan, pallid, weak, faint, dappled, refracted, bristled, early

sunrise, sunrises stunning, dazzling, gleaming, glowing, breathtaking, refulgent, radiant, splendid, magnificent, brilliant, ecstatic, glorious, resplendent, golden, spectacular, powerful

sunset, sunsets glowing, flaming, breathtaking, dazzling, lurid, orange, blue-orange, mauve, violet, crimson, golden, incarnadine, rose-and-scarlet, roseate, colourful, fiery, brilliant, misty, fabulous, vernal, glorious, gorgeous, splendid, magnificent, beautiful, resplendent, spectacular, ecstatic, broken, intermittent, alpine

sunshine soothing, dazzling, searing, unrelenting, glaring, blinding, brilliant, bright, strong, harsh, iridescent, genial, mild, tender, soft, pleasant, warm, lambent, opulent, luxuriant, glorious, splendid, magnificent, prodigal, abundant, plentiful, profuse, pervasive, continuous, endless, intermittent, speckled, serene, clear, cloudless, scarce, wet, steamy, misty, fly-drowsy, stormy, (in)direct, meridian

superficiality fleeting, passing, incidental, casual, flimsy, skin-deep, tawdry, slick

superiority outstanding, surpassing, ruling, overwhelming, prevailing, shining, exceptional, paramount, predominant, evident, conscious, unequalled, unchallenged, undisputed, unquestioned, matchless, peerless, incomparable, (pre-)eminent, unsurpassable, unquestionable, passing, numerical, racial, cultural

superstition, superstitions popular, common, old, ancient, time-worn, antiquated, local, quaint, widespread, present-day, credulous, harmless, weird, destructive, baneful, pernicious, harmful, ruinous, medical

supervision careful, attentive, close, vigilant, strict, severe, rigid, rigorous, austere, active, direct, massive, around-the-clock, constant, unstinting, (in)adequate, (un)conscientious, inept, careless, weak, negligent, lethargic

supper, suppers See also *dinner* and *meal* late, midnight, potluck; Last

supplier, suppliers dominant, central, main, chief, principal

supply, supplies massive, ample, bottomless, limitless, endless, never-ending, unending, infinite, inexhaustible, unfailing, extensive, copious, plentiful, plenteous, liberal, bountiful, lavish, rich, (super)abundant, overgrown, non-stop, staggering, steady, (un)available, (in)accessible, fresh, good, judicious, crucial, dependable, (un)reliable, full, entire, complete, (ir)regular, (in)adequate, (un)predictable, (in)sufficient, (in)secure, (in)flexible, inelastic, desperate, low, scant(y), sparse, short, meagre, precarious, poor, tight, erratic, sporadic, intermittent, uneven, casual, doubtful, uncertain, vulnerable, necessary, needful, critical, floating, further, additional, surplus, back-up, basic, global, humanitarian, pecuniary

support loving, unflagging, unwavering, unfailing, unceasing, enduring, unquestioning, overwhelming, domineering, ringing, unqualified, unreserved, unfettered, (un)willing, (un)conditional, unequivocal, non-judg(e)mental, heartfelt, sympathetic, disinterested, thoughtful, wholehearted, loyal, sincere, genuine, pointed, unprecedented, unshaken, undiminished, open(-ended), solid, all-out, staunch, broad(-based), wide, widespread, massive, (near-)unanimous, nation-wide, popular, determined, forceful, fervent, effervescent, ardent, enthusiastic, feverish, generous, liberal, (in)valuable, gracious, proper, expert, crucial, vital, active, intensive, resolute, decisive, effective, efficient, capable, firm, strong, powerful, vociferous, considerable, tremendous, prompt, expedient, ongoing, intemperate, rigid, vital, unabashed, unquantifiable, (in)adequate, (in)sufficient, unwitting, grudging, knee-jerk, half-hearted, reluctant, hesitant, feeble, tepid, lukewarm, shallow, bedrock, minimal, untenable, infirm, uncertain, shaky, (un)limited, qualified, muted, transitory, tentative, clandestine, behind-the-scenes, tacit, implicit, explicit, covert, automatic, moral, emotional, professional, medical, promotional, financial, rhetorical, intellectual, visceral, logistical, mutual, public

supporter, supporters staunch, diehard, stalwart, rabid, aggressive, passionate, vocal, hawkish, enthusiastic, ardent, avid, fervent, exuberant, adamant, active, long-time, loyal, steadfast, faithful, strong, true, dedicated, uncompromising, unwavering, unflagging, disparate, venal, belligerent, sole

supposition, suppositions (un)reasonable, (ir)rational, (un)acceptable, (un)accountable, (in)appropriate, (im)proper, (un)justifiable, baseless

suppression crushing, devastating, overpowering, overwhelming, violent, vindictive, unfeeling, brutal, abominable, barbaric, beastly, bitter, cruel, ferocious, inhuman, bloody, unrelenting, relentless, ruthless, pitiless, merciless, remorseless, heartless, bland

supremacy indisputable, undeniable, incontestable, uncontestable, unchallengeable, unchallenged, undisputed, uncontested, assured, high-tech

surf See *wave*

surface, surfaces (un)even, level, flat, curved, slanting, sloping, oblique, plane, slick, sleek, smooth, glib, slippery, powdery, solid, hard, fixed, movable, resilient, durable, harsh, coarse, indurate, rough, nubby, brittle, free, limpid, tranquil-looking, gleaming, glistering, shiny, mirror-like, (heat-)resistant, mar-resistant, torrid, opaque, reflective, dead, dull, wearing, sleazy, pebbly, grainy, observable, intricate, incised, pockmarked, pockpitted, multifaceted, two-dimensional, geometric, outer, protective, hyperbolic, terrestrial, lunar, non-porous, elastomeric, anticlastic, synclastic, caustic, orthogonal, diacaustic

surgeon, surgeons deft, careful, (well-)trained, clever, able, capable, gifted, talented, celebrated, distinguished, illustrious, eminent, (un)skilled, (in)efficient, careless, (in)competent, (un)qualified, vascular, orthopaedic, paediatric, cardiac, thoracic, oral, urologic, colorectal, plastic, general

surgery effective, innovative, advanced, high-tech, radical, extensive, comprehensive, invasive, intricate, delicate, agonizing, major, minor, (un)conventional, controversial, frivolous, painful, painless, (un)affordable, (in)expensive, urgent, pointless, needless, (un)necessary, (un)avoidable, (in)evitable, (in)accessible, (un)safe, miraculous, miracle, life-saving, life-and-death, scarless, periodic, underside, out-of-hospital, out-patient, day, overnight, ambulatory, field, operative, exploratory, experimental, elective, reconstructive, corrective, plastic, cosmetic, aesthetic, orthopaedic, endoscopic, open-chest, open-heart, cardiac, by-pass, paediatric, cardiovascular, vascular, (cranio)facial, urologic, cutaneous, arthroscopic, abdominal, intestinal, pelvic, brain,

genetic, foetal, prenatal, traumatic, thoracic, stereotactic, transsexual

surplus, surpluses modest, vast, huge, ample, boundless, immense, lavish, colossal, massive, mammoth, enormous, mountainous, whopping

surprise, surprises delightful, enjoyable, (un)pleasant, salutary, (un)welcome, lovely, joyous, wonderful, sweet, agreeable, amused, serendipitous, rapturous, thrilling, stunning, passionate, gratifying, unexpected, unwanted, abrupt, great, big, deep, infinite, intense, tremendous, enormous, wide-eyed, shocked, shocking, painful, dumb, speechless, childish, complete, utter, total, sheer, unqualified, initial, last-minute, momentary, protracted, false, feigned, nasty, terrible, scant

surrender, surrenders absolute, total, complete, immediate, inevitable, unavoidable, graceful, orderly, peaceful, virtual, passive, (un)conditional, abject, shameless, submissive, meek, dishonourable, humiliating, demoralizing, formal

surrounding, surroundings cheerful, bright, propitious, peaceful, quiet, civilized, hygienic, secure, prosperous, sumptuous, (un)familiar, new, (un)favourable, (un)desirable, (un)pleasant, (un)comfortable, barren, spartan, miserable, deplorable, pitiable, gloomy, sordid, dingy, ghostly, immediate, natural, rural, urban, alien

surveillance See *supervision*

survey, surveys in-depth, exhaustive, comprehensive, extensive, full-scale, main, voluminous, systematic, inclusive, smooth, fast-moving, swift-moving, high-speed, reputable, recent, preliminary, pilot, formal, official, annual, nationwide, archaeological, scientific, seismic, aerial

survival basic, miraculous, providential, supernatural, superhuman, heroic, remarkable, wonderful, incredible, unbelievable, precarious, tenuous, cultural, linguistic

survivor, survivors nervous, distraught, dazed, tenacious, obstinate, stubborn, sole, only, lone, single, miracle

suspense twitching, exquisite, nervous, anxious, restless, tense, painful, stony, drowsy, profound, (un)bearable, (un)palatable, frozen

suspicion, suspicions lurking, sneaking, surreptitious, secret, underhand, just(ifiable), (un)justifiable, shrewd, well-founded, deep-seated, deep(-rooted), profound, growing, widespread, rampant, ever-present, long-standing, lasting, lingering, monstrous, serious, grave, glum, bitter, searing, deadly, cynical, heretical, groundless, unjust, unfounded, unconfirmed, vague, faint, dim, slight, unpleasant, uncomfortable, unnerving, stirring, degrading, uneasy, childish, instinctive, habitual, basic, mutual, reciprocal

swamp, swamps primordial, primeval, original, permanent, broad, vast, tidal, (un)reclaimable, stagnant, murky, damp, dark, gloomy, filthy, knee-deep, forbidding, (im)penetrable, (im)passable, reedy, miasmic, stygian; economic

swan, swans slow-moving, stately, graceful, majestic(-winged), gawky, pushy, ruby-eyed, fine-billed, waterlogged, migrant, black, black-necked, (un)pinioned, mute

sweat pouring, streaming, profuse, heavy, cold, beaded, gritty, pungent, stale, clammy, sticky, stinking, smelly, rotten, morbid, honest

sweater, sweaters exquisite, pricey, glittery, harlequin, multi-coloured, patterned, striped, jet-beaded, hand-knit, hand-made, home-made, cable-stitch, ribbed, fitted, close-fitting, loose, layered, hip-length, tunic-length, off-the-shoulder, hooded, unravelled, over-sized, thick, heavy, chunky, bulky, baggy, sloppy, tattered, shaggy, woollen, cashmere, angora, warm, scratchy, itchy, mothproof, cowl-necked, crew-necked, polo-neck, turtle-neck, roll-top, sporty

sweepstake, sweepstakes See *lottery*

sweets luxury, dainty, delicious, delectable, flavourful, tempting, mouthwatering, soft, hard, moist, gummy, sticky, crunchy, chewy, minty, sour, chocolate-covered, variegated, handmade, bagged, loose

swim refreshing, bracing, quick, impulsive, tough

swimmer, swimmers thrashing, splashing, frolicsome, avid, long-winded, superb, all-round, premier, remarkable, powerful, formidable, top, strong, fast, exhausted, amateur, professional, competitive, champion, world-class, serious, naked, long-distance

swimming brisk, graceful, clumsy, underwater, competitive, recreational, synchronized

swimsuit, swimsuits fashionable, (in)appropriate, snappy, stylish, attractive, shiny, expensive, skirted, long-line, high-cut, short-cut, one-piece, two-piece, bare-midriff, halter-neck, strapless, strappy, skimpy, scant(y), tiny, itsy-bitsy, sensuous, immodest, revealing, body-baring, provocative, daring

swimwear See *swimsuit*

sword, swords mighty, trusty, fierce, terrible, swift, blunt, bent, ornate, studded, fluted, gold-handled, brass-handled, one-hand, hand-and-a-half, two-hand, one-edged, single-edged, double-edged, two-edged, flat, broad(-bladed), untried, unused, unsheathed, naked, maiden, ceremonial, dress

syllable, syllables (half-)stifled, (ante)penultimate, long, short, meaningless, clipped, (un)stressed, unaccented, atonic, initial, closed, open, acute

symbol, symbols compelling, lasting, enduring, tenacious, powerful, potent, effective, quintessential, provocative, apt, appropriate, fitting, happy, ultimate, prime, visible, tangible, recognizable, unmistakable, (un)conventional, world-wide, universal, (un)familiar, (un)popular, complex, stagy, (in)decipherable, indelible, grotesque, arbitrary, living, abstract, graphic, primitive, mystic(al), mythological, phallic, heraldic, national, religious, ritual, scientific, verbal, numerical, algebraic, chemical, prosodic, pictographic, calendrical

sympathy yearning, warm, deep, real, profound, heartfelt, sincere, genial, great, considerable, total, (in)sufficient, tremulous, underhand, secret, sneaking, mawkish, sickly, counterfeit, deceitful, sham, feigned, pretended, condescending, sentimental, mutual, popular, public

symptom, symptoms (un)recognizable,

(in)distinguishable, distinctive, clear, overt, obvious, unmistakable, full-blown, classic, (a)typical, (un)common, (un)usual, (un)specific, outward, initial, immediate, early, mild, minor, major, significant, secondary, identical, grave, chronic, acute, serious, severe, ugly, ominous, menacing, debilitating, frightening, alarming, annoying, bothersome, unpleasant, adverse, vague, ambiguous, bizarre, intricate, complex, complicated, unexplained, baffling, mysterious, imaginary, physical, neurological, (psycho)pathological, toxic, physiological, scorbutic, diabetic, febrile, psychotic

syrup, syrups thin, light, heavy, thick, viscous, stick(y), (sticky-)sweet, fragrant, unflavoured; golden

system, systems fail-safe, (un)safe, (un)workable, (un)feasible, operational, manageable, functional, viable, productive, sustained, ingenious, flawless, infallible, (im)perfect, (in)efficient, (im)proper, (in)effective, superior, equitable, straightforward, sophisticated, innovative, ideal, elaborate, avant-garde, unique, (im)precise, (in)accurate, (in)adequate, (in)flexible, vigorous, unified, simple, (il)logical, (un)fair, mind-rocking, exclusive, multifarious, giant, incredible, unbelievable, unusual, competitive, progressive, (in)accessible, (un)available, (un)desirable, (un)balanced, universal, pervasive, prevalent, immiscible, pliant, capricious, second-wave, conformist, authoritarian, oppressive, discriminatory, restrictive, rudimentary, crude, rigid, patchwork, flawed, faulty, clumsy, cumbersome, sloppy, ailing, intractable, dilapidated, maddening, faltering, intricate, complicated, complex, shaky, rickety, fragile, decrepit, chaotic, bankrupt, rechargeable, insane, vulnerable, obscure, enigmatic, obsolete, haphazard, archaic, antiquated, outdated, strained, wasteful, corrupt, vile, auxiliary, disorganized, automatic, two-tiered, (inter)related, (re)structured, rebuilt; digestive, respiratory, nervous, urinary, circulatory, pulmonary, reproductive, skeletal, muscular, cardiovascular, limbic, ventricular, immune, immunological, vascular, musculo-skeletal, oxygen-delivery, lymphatic, pneumatic; monetary, metric, monandrous, water(-desalination), binary, tutorial, political, two-party, social, feudal, mercantile, postal, mail, astronomical, coordinate (rectangular coordinate), industrial, economic, immunological, educational, cultural, health, tricameral, neurochemical, ecological, territorial, electrical, mechanical, electronic, regulatory, administrative, electoral, short-wave, judicial, legal, sacramental, defensive, adversarial; allodial; Bertillon; Delsarte; Dewey, decimal; Ptolemaic, Copernican, solar, heliocentric; periodic; Cartesian

table, tables (1: piece of furniture) grand, huge, massive, spacious, luxurious, magnificent, superb, ornate, antique, food-laden, steady, (un)reserved, cloth-covered, makeshift, round, square, oval, oblong, long, narrow, bowed, horseshoe-shaped, kidney-shaped, free-form, revolving, compass-front, drop-leaf, built-in, spindle-legged, smoked-glass, inlaid, marble(-topped), baize-covered, wicker, wooden, cut-glass, baize, shaky, messy, rocky, sloppy, wobbly, unsteady, crude, occasional, side, night (bedside), umbrellaed, umbrella-topped, rotating, swivel, gateleg, Pembroke, Sheraton; head, high

table, tables (2: food served; persons sitting around a table) convivial, sumptuous, rich, opulent, generous, poor, bare, scanty, plain

table, tables (3: list) See also *list* clear, significant, informative, statistical, mortality (life), periodic, actuarial

tablecloth, tablecloths round, oval, square, oblong, lace, jacquard, linen, cotton, nylon, plastic, seersucker, damask, check, floral, colourful, lavish, plain, white, snowy, clean, dirty, grubby, stained, wrinkled

taboo, taboos strict, ghastly, unspoken, prevailing, irrational, (age-)old, deep-seated, ingrained, superstitious, religious

tact discriminating, soothing, rare, delicate, diplomatic, discreet, refined, thoughtful, perspicacious, fine, excellent, admirable, infinite

tactic, tactics shrewd, rational, clever, brilliant, masterful, inventive, aggressive, time-consuming, (il)legal, (un)ethical, (dis)honest, (un)fair, (un)successful, (in)effective, (im)practical, unenlightened, cautious, doctrinaire, theoretical, impractical, strong-arm, futile, soft, hard, tough, harsh, drastic, abrasive, militant, heavy-handed, brutal, repressive, bully(boy), despicable, provocative, dubious, nefarious, underhand(ed), shameful, evil, vicious, mean, deceptive, sly, unsavoury, (un)familiar, toothless, (un)justifiable, dilatory, diversionary, evasive, obstructive, obstructionist, secret, intimidation, pressure, campaign, scare, guerrilla, hit-and-run, battlefield, Fabian

tail, tails swishing, flapping, undulating, thumping, thrashing, waving, twitching, twisting, revolving, swaying, swinging, erect, upraised, hairless, spindly, bushy, furry, ponderous, rich, aristocratic, black-tipped, square-tipped, plumy, spiny, spiky, wiry, long(ish), broad, flat, heterocercal, homocercal, stubby, spear-shaped, lyre-shaped, arched, pointed, bowed, forked, tapered, barbed, knotted, curled, wiggly, wriggly, powerful, vibrant, gigantic, diminutive, vestigial, prehensile

tailoring masterful, elegant, sophisticated, flattering, soigné, bespoke

tale, tales See also *story* heartwarming, gratifying, pleasing, intriguing, stirring, captivating, charming, fascinating, winning, engaging, thrilling, exciting, striking, moving, inspirational, vivid, trenchant, witty, authentic, exotic, imaginative, taut, laconic, quaint, sensational, irresistible, dramatic, incredible, unbelievable, famous, celebrated, pointless, deadpan, quirky, (un)verifiable, (un)checkable, improbable, fanciful, insipid, dull, jejune, gruesome, troubling, lurid, sentimental, sad, melancholy, maudlin, tearful, woeful, sorrowful, mournful, frightening, agonizing, bloodcurdling, heart-rending, hair-raising, shocking, harrowing, distressing, unsettling, grisly, slender, sketchy, malicious, gossipy, wry, racy, rowdy, ribald, shaggy, scandalous, explicit, first-told, oft-told, cautionary, traditional, anecdotal, picaresque, classic, romantic, comic, tragic, heroic, folk, epic, cloak-and-dagger, fairy, fantastic, Gothic, subterranean, moral, didactic, autobiographical, (semi-)biographical, (quasi-)historical

talent, talents wasted, misapplied, glittering, shining, stunning, wonderful, splendid, remarkable, magnificent, eminent, marvellous, legendary, larger-than-life, divine, magic, high, brilliant, incisive, resplendent, dynamic, towering, monumental, phenomenal, immense, considerable, vast, enormous, uncommon, exceptional, unusual, extraordinary, genuine, congenial, distinctive, unequalled, incomparable, rare, unique, special, singular, incredible, unbelievable, unimaginable, precocious, prodigious, precious, deft, prolific, fertile, rich, multiple, protean, innovative, revolutionary, flamboyant, convivial, redoubtable, indisputable, undisputed, real, obvious, visible, respectable, employable, marketable, inborn, (super)natural, innate, native, raw, hidden, growing, budding, promising, little, marginal, mediocre, unappreciated, unrecognized, untrained, undetected, unschooled, uncultivated, untapped, creative, artistic, visionary, athletic, dramaturgic, histrionic, musical, literary

talk, talks uplifting, enchanting, charming, delightful, brilliant, eloquent, polished, (ir)rational, (in)decorous, conclusive, wide-ranging, serious, stern, substantive, reasonable, straight, healthy, plain, brave, frank, candid, spontaneous, extemporaneous, unpremeditated, unstudied, heart-to-heart, face-to-face, man-to-man, eyeball-to-eyeball, (in)audible, stammering, nice, persuasive, ponderous, reminiscent, fevered, feverish, impassioned, tearful, rosy, intense, smooth, fledgling, (in)conclusive, (in)complete, incessant, endless, unending, interminable, loose, rudderless, random, blundering, rambling, tiresome, giddy, vapid, boring, dull, lifeless, vague, pompous, windy, big, empty, distrustful, deceptive, rancorous, dire, ambiguous, shallow, boastful, extravagant, large, nonsensical, idle, frivolous, unreasonable, trifling, pedantic, vulgar, low, coarse, ribald, sloppy, despicable, careless, bawdy, boisterous, smutty, unsettling, argumentative, muffled, double, gossipy, baby, small, (in)formal, (in)direct, clandestine, secret(ive)

talker, talkers entertaining, amusing, glib, brilliant, great, tremendous, fluent, (in)effectual, (in)articulate, voluble, enthusiastic, avid, indefatigable, tireless, inexhaustible, relentless, incessant, compulsive, smooth, big, pompous,

haughty, boastful, reluctant, boring, poor

talking See *talk*

talks (negotiations) See *negotiations*

talon, talons See *claw*

tan, tans deep, nice, charming, attractive, fresh, youthful, golden, bronzed, perfect, (un)even, fabulous, artificial, indoor, sun-free

tank, tanks (armoured vehicle) thundering, roaring, rattling, rumbling, fast-moving, ferocious, state-of-the-art, disabled, cumbersome, obsolete, heavy, light, medium, armoured, Caterpillar-wheeled, amphibious, Panzer

tape, tapes transparent, sticky, adhesive, magnetic, quarter-inch, half-inch, one-inch (instrumentation), two-inch, insulating, surgical

tardiness See *delay*

target, targets inviting, enticing, alluring, tempting, attractive, favourable, popular, desirable, respectable, subtle, easy, defenceless, explicit, obvious, prime, primary, main, major, key, central, vital, frequent, ambitious, (un)identifiable, (in)accessible, deliberate, (il)legitimate, prominent, constant, siz(e)able, inevitable, unavoidable, surprising, new, fixed, flexible, meetable, (im)possible, (un)likely, demanding, potential, distant, movable, intact, unidentified, undefined, well-guarded, elusive, impersonal, abstract, sitting, (non-)military, strategic, terrorist

tariff, tariffs See *tax*

task, tasks heroic, noble, (un)rewarding, agreeable, (un)pleasant, challenging, vital, simple, easy, facile, ordinary, straightforward, mundane, delicate, sensitive, diurnal, specific, special, immediate, central, ambitious, paramount, big, massive, titanic, Herculean, mammoth, colossal, monumental, enormous, prodigious, awful, tough, heavy, hard, serious, rugged, formidable, (un)arduous, laborious, uphill, painful, gruesome, taxing, demanding, exacting, staggering, excruciating, agonizing, harrowing, sobering, grinding, gruelling, backbreaking, tiresome, wearisome, vigorous, complex, visionary, (near-)impossible, awesome, oppressive, difficult, tortuous, ticklish, onerous, unenviable, horrendous, insuperable, insurmountable, hellish, time-consuming, hopeless, grim, dreary, repetitive, soul-destroying, tedious, monotonous, dull, ungrateful, thankless, fruitless, vain, maddening, annoying, offensive, ugly, disagreeable, unsuitable, menial, manual, mindless, pointless, trivial, dirty, irksome, lowly, servile, degrading, repugnant, grisly, dangerous, perilous, fatal, traumatic, clear-cut, well-defined, routine, weekly, daily, sedentary, confidential, undercover, covert, proportional

taste, tastes (1: flavour) refreshing, fascinating, mouthwatering, tantalizing, intriguing, satisfying, enticing, appealing, ethereal, sublime, delightful, (un)pleasant, superb, delicate, rich, excellent, fabulous, sweet, great, lively, sunny, distinct, unique, sensational, perfumed, fruity, saccharine, spicy, smok(e)y, vinegary, lemony, medicinal, astringent, full-bodied, sharp, strong, keen, tangy, pungent, biting, acid, sour, forward, bitter, salt(y), briny, soapy, saline, brackish, flat, bland, dull, outrageous, odious, revolting, execrable, lingering, disguised

taste, tastes (2: liking) discerning, discriminating, subtle, good, nice, impeccable, exquisite, (un)sophisticated, elegant, exotic, admirable, refined, recherché, champagne, expensive, distinguished, luxurious, patrician, infallible, superb, exceptional, flawless, pure, fabulous, fastidious, fussy, squeamish, assured, informed, studious, extravagant, flamboyant, (ad)venturous, voluptuary, chaste, simple, (un)common, uniform, individual, personal, catholic, ruling, prevailing, popular, conventional, idiosyncratic, peculiar, special(ized), narcissistic, atavistic, bucolic, unsettled, wandering, changeable, questionable, fickle, morbid, philistine, gaudy, wild, vulgar, low, bad, preposterous, ghastly, indiscriminate, gross, plebeian, kitsch, abominable, corrupt, perverse, ingrained, acquired, newfangled, aesthetic, artistic, personal

tavern, taverns See *inn*

tax, taxes, taxation light, (in)tolerable, (un)fair, (in)(un)equitable, equal, uniform, minimum, old, new, extra, additional, existent, delinquent, refundable, (un)avoidable, (in)evitable, simple, complex, complicated, cumbersome, (in)visible, hidden, insidious, punitive, discriminatory, retaliatory, odious, annoying, unpopular, unpalatable, inefficient, anachronistic, big, massive, high, hefty, steep, heavy, tough, vexatious, burdensome, oppressive, onerous, exorbitant, legal, (un)constitutional, inflationary, retroactive, comprehensive, flat, across-the-board, automatic, universal, variable, differential, multi-stage, horizontal, protective, sumptuary, local, provincial, federal, state, unitary, progressive, regressive, (in)direct, domestic, personal, corporate, municipal, single, confiscatory, proportional

taxi, taxis See also *car* vacant, idle, collective

taxpayer, taxpayers indignant, angry, reluctant

tea, teas refreshing, high-grade, fine, subtle, delicate, weak(ish), thin, strong, hearty, full-bodied, thick, potent, heavy, heady, (high-)fired, over-fired, astringent, sweet, sugary, syrupy, clear, milkless, milky, mushy, scalding, steaming, savoury, delicious, flavourful, fragrant, aromatic, hot, bright, ruddy, dark, loose, one-leaf, pale, brisk, tangy, smok(e)y, spicy, musty, bitter, exotic, gourmet, green, medicinal, tonic, (loose-)leaf, black, (mid-)morning, afternoon, breakfast, high, common, ceremonial, Russian, Chinese, Indian; cream; Paraguayan, herbal, (pepper)mint

teacher, teachers (in)capable, (un)able, (in)efficient, (in)effectual, (in)effective, (in)competent, (in)experienced, (un)trained, (un)qualified, (un)satisfactory, devoted, dedicated, conscientious, caring, organized, professional, industrious, hardworking, diligent, open-minded, enthusiastic, inspiring, inspired, creative, interesting, natural, born, talented, entrancing, communicative, well-read, ideal, model, master, superlative, star, legendary, veteran, unforgettable, outstanding, vivid, magnificent, shining, friendly, loving, humorous, demure, naïve, easy, exact, busy, independent, determined, careful, clever, liberal, (un)orthodox, (un)conventional, (in)flexible, (un)popular, charismatic, influential, salty-tongued, cruel, dull, rigid, lax, negligent, careless, no-nonsense, demanding, exacting, disciplinarian, dogmatic, pedantic, stern, arbitrary, peremptory, imperious, probationary

teaching (1: act of teaching) See also *teacher* rewarding, conscientious, innovative, authentic, (in)effective, (in)adequate, (in)formal, tutorial

teaching, teachings (2: what is taught) beneficial, effective, valuable, useful, helpful, profitable, infallible, traditional, fundamental, (un)healthful, (un)wholesome, ruinous, pernicious, hurtful, destructive, injurious, deadly, baneful, detrimental, harmful, poisonous

team, teams (1: a group on one side in a match) top, devoted, dedicated, well-run, cohesive, crackerjack, excellent, outstanding, talented, selected, unified, (specially-)picked, fabled, legendary, matchless, peerless, powerful, high-powered, strong, mighty, tough, exciting, stirring, thrilling, bona fide, supreme, superior, invincible, unbeatable, high-goal, (cup-)winning, proven, cocky, unbeaten, undefeated, inspired, erratic, (un)even, (un)equal, offensive, woeful, inept, poor, downcast, sad, mediocre, sluggish, dispirited, dejected, rival, co-ed, mixed, (all-)male, (all-)female, all-girls, all-boys, girls-only, boys-only, integrated, juvenile, brand-new, local, provincial, national, international, home, visiting, scratch, haphazard, champion, all-star, all-time, part-time, Olympic, minor-league, major-league, varsity

team, teams (2: a number of persons associated together in work or activity) heroic, dedicated, devoted, smart, sophisticated, crackerjack, excellent, outstanding, top, matchless, peerless, bona fide, supreme, superior, six-member, small, (specially-)picked, close-knit, investigative, fact-finding, medical, paramedic, archaeological, tactical, multidisciplinary, joint, husband-and-wife

tear, tears rolling, trickling, flowing, burning, scalding, despairing, stinging, joyful, hot, bitter, acid, difficult, copious, fertile, deep, slow, sudden, dewy, eloquent, uncontrollable, unrestrainable, unexplainable, inexplicable, unabashed,

maudlin, emotional, repentant, sympathetic, contrite, obsequious, elongated, bottled-up, holy, frightened, irritant, puerile, womanish, unconsoled, unshed, unwept, unfallen, wasted, spiteful, false, sham, artificial; crocodile

technique, techniques inspired, innovative, modern, up-to-date, advanced, up-to-the-minute, aggressive, (un)sophisticated, (in)effective, (in)accurate, state-of-the-art, leading-edge, revolutionary, unique, ingenious, remarkable, superb, venerable, flawless, infallible, unfailing, refined, solid, mature, fascinating, straightforward, simple, invaluable, radical, promising, (in)valid, (in)flexible, structured, linear, (in)correct, (in)adequate, (im)proper, poor, controversial, expensive, slipshod, basic, (age-)old, new, space-age, standard, (un)traditional, (un)conventional, old-fashioned, ancient, experimental, avant-garde

technology, technologies exciting, dazzling, amazing, astounding, stunning, perplexing, fascinating, puzzling, (far-)advanced, unprecedented, innovative, breakthrough, revolutionary, new, latest, (ultra)modern, futuristic, superior, superlative, up-to-date, high, world-class, state-of-the-art, leading-edge, (un)sophisticated, complex, refined, prized, exact, (in)effective, (in)adequate, impressive, powerful, spectacular, remarkable, radical, unbelievable, incredible, unbridled, uncontrolled, unrestrained, unmanageable, runaway, ungovernable, (un)available, expedient, expensive, second-wave, primitive, rudimentary, crude, impractical, inferior, outdated, obsolete

tedium See *boredom*

teenager, teenagers earnest, enthusiastic, unspoiled, lively, experimental, studious, venturesome, scheming, crafty, wild, uncommunicative, capricious, modern, impressionable, socially-conscious, style-conscious, fashion-conscious, spunky, self-conscious, withdrawn, troubled, confused, mixed-up, materialistic, unfeeling, hard-hearted, promiscuous, defiant, rebellious, stubborn, wayward, truant, bull-headed, suicidal, runaway, uncomprehending, selfish, scruffy, skinny, gangling, lanky, awkward

teeth See *tooth*

telegraph cable, wireless, electric, bush

telephone, telephones ringing, dead, dysfunctional, (in)accessible, temperamental, busy, engaged, multiline, hand-held, transportable, underwater, hard-wired, battery-run, multifunction, mobile, wireless, cordless, digital, push-button, rotary, high-tech, portable, cellular, in-flight, in-car, video, pocket(-sized)

telescope, telescopes high-powered, powerful, refracting, reflecting, astronomical, equatorial, Newtonian, Cassegrainian

television, televisions ubiquitous, pervasive, blurry, (in)operative, (ir)reparable, 20-inch, black-and-white, colour(ed), large-screen, jumbo-screen, flat-screen, high-definition, surround-sound, state-run, unregulated, double-image, cable, commercial, satellite

temper, tempers clement, good, placid, calm, smooth, imperturbable, sanguine, (un)accountable, (un)steady, (un)even, (un)settled, (in)tolerant, warm, hot, (ultra-)sensitive, ardent, hasty, quick, irritable, unyielding, irascible, violent, vitriolic, intense, impetuous, fiery, rash, odd, nasty, inconsiderate, rebellious, short, sultry, bad, weak, ungovernable, uncontrollable, explosive, unruly, combustible, excitable, fierce, hair-trigger, inflammable, rough, wild, intractable, restless, uncertain, flaring, rising, variable, brittle, diabolic(al), perverse, savage, volcanic, sophomoric, passionate, overbearing, imperious, domineering, dictatorial, ungenerous

temperament, temperaments sweet, quiet, gentle, easy-going, bantering, buoyant, tenacious, sanguine, unflappable, stolid, phlegmatic, impassive, (un)conventional, (un)even, (un)steady, (un)stable, impetuous, (un)excitable, irritable, passionate, (un)argumentative, gusty, volatile, changeable, quick-witted, mercurial, quicksilver, elusive, capricious, nervous, touchy, (non-)aggressive, quarrelsome, tactless, roving, infectious, elastic, resilient, laconic, coarse, ebullient,

sensual, sensuous, orgiastic, servile; poetic, artistic

temperature, temperatures balmy, (un)pleasant, (un)comfortable, mild, average, mean, steady, even, uniform, equable, ambient, constant, (in)variable, unchangeable, persistent, varying, normal, above-normal, below-normal, extreme, record, record-high, near-record, subnormal, abnormal, maximum, minimum, optimum, rising, fluctuating, tepid, warm, hot, steaming, sweltering, blistering, searing, frying, infernal, brick-oven, lethal, intolerable, cool, frigid, (near-)freezing, sub-freezing, sub-zero, arctic, thermodynamic (absolute)

tempest, tempests See *storm*

temple, temples soaring, forbidding, imposing, impressive, awesome, scintillant, vast, spacious, massive, colossal, immense, huge, exquisite, splendid, remarkable, magnificent, elaborate, stupendous, grand, majestic, ostentatious, ponderous, mysterious, remote, renowned, fabled, columned, ornate, (well-)preserved, ruined, well-trodden, sacred, profane, funerary, mortuary, pagan

tempo See *pace*

temptation, temptations overwhelming, powerful, strong, terrible, enormous, great, constant, irresistible, insidious, subtle, smooth, dangerous, earthly, evil, ubiquitous, improvident, deliberate, lurking, fleeting, temporary, sexual

tenacity obstinate, stubborn, persistent, ferocious, viscous, blind, high

tenant, tenants incoming, outgoing, prospective, long-time, (ir)responsible, low-paying, low-income, vulnerable

tendency, tendencies reassuring, liberal, (un)healthy, (un)orthodox, maverick, sinister, curious, peculiar, intentional, growing, obsessive, chronic, violent, painful, annoying, troubling, worrisome, destructive, divisive, wicked, sinful, perverse, cerebral, religious, ingrained, natural, inborn, innate, homicidal, suicidal, genetic, biochemical, central, centralist

tenet, tenets See *doctrine*

tense, tenses present, past, future, perfect, indefinite, continuous (imperfect), habitual, conditional

tension, tensions long-standing,

high(-strung), deep, intractable,
considerable, enormous, excessive,
palpable, constant, unbreakable, explosive,
pent-up, brittle, nervous, anxious,
indecisive, curious, dreadful, intolerable,
unendurable, unbearable, unrelenting,
relentless, ruthless, merciless, heartless,
pitiless, painful, pained, abrupt, spastic,
undue, unreasonable, petty, curious,
potential, underground, subterranean,
ethnic, communal, regional, sectarian,
factional, racial, linguistic, marital,
political, physical, psychological, muscular,
emotional, sexual

tent, tents round, conical, cone-shaped,
pyramid-shaped, dome-shaped, domed,
multicoloured, double-layered, rain-slick,
voluminous, portable, makeshift, tattered,
leaky, leak-proof, dirt-floored, airless,
family, military, pop-up

tenure (in)secure, long-held

term, terms, terminology (1: word)
meaningful, (in)appropriate, (in)accurate,
(in)correct, (un)common, (un)printable,
esoteric, enigmatic, obsolete, restrictive,
abstruse, arcane, innocuous, meaningless,
tongue-in-cheek, scathing, derisive,
pejorative, derogatory, discriminatory,
loathsome, contradictory, loaded, absolute,
descriptive, technical, scientific, literary,
medical, legal

term, terms (2: period) short, long,
lengthy, substantial, (un)broken,
(un)renewable, half

terms (3: conditions) advantageous,
exclusive, (un)easy, friendly, (im)moderate,
generous, (un)favourable, preferential,
(un)familiar, (in)flexible, stiff, hard, rigid,
severe, harsh, burdensome, strident,
vindictive, defeatist

terrace, terraces shaded, shady, breezy,
cool, flowered, cypress-spiked, spotless,
pretty, lovely, quaint, ornate, simple,
wrought-iron, wooden, glass-verandahed,
semi-circular, projecting, wrap(a)round,
horseshoe, balustraded, cantilevered,
sheltered, secluded, moonlit, sunlit,
expansive, wide, spacious

terrain breathtaking, majestic, spectacular,
pretty, beautiful, (in)hospitable,
(un)inviting, welcoming, alluring,
attractive, open, vast, (un)familiar,
unusual, peculiar, soft, gentle, shifting,

dry-season, (drought-)parched,
mountainous, hilly, sandy, rocky, boggy,
marshy, scrubby, billowing, rolling, steep,
downhill, precipitous, treacherous,
insidious, unrewarding, forbidding, tough,
jagged, rough, harsh, stiff, firm, bouncy,
bleak, worn, rugged, broken, arduous,
difficult, inhospitable, hostile, unforgiving,
awesome, brutal, stark, desolate, barren,
bare, poor, hot, frozen, arctic, virginal,
featureless, dull, irregular, intricate,
abandoned, uncharted, eroded,
(well-)watered, varied, ample, marginal

territory, territories See also *land*
(in)hospitable, fertile, virgin,
(well-)travelled, immense, open, vast, huge,
substantial, sprawling, sacred, forbidden,
remote, definite, (un)familiar, minuscule,
dangerous, hostile, uncharted, unexplored,
government-established, rebel-held,
sovereign, neutral, alien, enemy, home,
ancestral

terror, terrors See *fear*

terrorism unrelenting, relentless, ruthless,
heartless, remorseless, merciless, pitiless,
grisly, outrageous, irrational, senseless,
mindless, unpredictable, unacceptable,
soaring, rampant, widespread, calculated,
state, international

terrorist, terrorists calculating, scheming,
audacious, bold, brazen(-faced), crazed,
lethal, bloody, nihilistic, cruel, dangerous,
murderous, heartless, merciless, ruthless,
pitiless, relentless, unrelenting, barbaric,
unrepentant, notorious, elusive,
unreasonable, potential, resolute,
determined, wanted, unidentified

test, tests (1: critical examination,
observation or evaluation) severe, tough,
rigorous, demanding, hard, difficult, stiff,
rugged, searching, competitive, crucial,
decisive, major, end-of-term, mid-term,
regular, occasional, intermittent,
subjective, objective, multiple-choice,
pencil-and-paper, compulsory, mandatory,
optional, standard

test, tests (2: experiment) sophisticated,
high-tech, state-of-the-art, searching,
empirical, thorough, infallible,
(in)accurate, precise, (un)reliable, unerring,
complaisant, definitive, (in)conclusive,
decisive, critical, crucial, advanced,
complex, arduous, strenuous, exhaustive,

preliminary, initial, routine, random, compulsory, mandatory, optional, voluntary, extensive, large-scale, mass, ultimate, unnecessary, needless, negative, positive, diagnostic, forensic, clinical, serological, projective, genetic, follow-up, ballistic, scratch, cardiovascular, pulmonary, pathological, mental, neurological, cognitive, modular

testimonial, testimonials high, excellent, glowing, significant, constructive, no-nonsense, contentious, cautious, non-binding, ambivalent

testimony, testimonies (in)credible, (un)convincing, (in)consistent, worthwhile, unbiased, objective, (ir)relevant, strong, compelling, admissible, revealing, eloquent, vivid, expert, poignant, explicit, extensive, decisive, key, crucial, sordid, emotional, tearful, bruising, dramatic, grim, grisly, unsolicited, self-serving, mischievous, false, (un)qualified, precarious, uncertain, dubious, disputable, contradictory, conflicting, oft-repeated, direct, closed-door, ocular, mute, oral, material, personal, public, graphological, graphic, eyewitness, anecdotal

testing (experiment) See *test* (2)

text, texts engaging, substantial, final, plain, understandable, limiting, hybrid, obscure, inscrutable, inexplicable, corrupt, outdated, rare, basic, canonical, original, authentic, definitive, lexical, sacred; optional, compulsory, set

textbook, textbooks See *text* and *book*

texture, textures smooth, fine, silken, loose, friable, close, firm, rough, coarse, medium, spongy, rubbery, dense, crisp

thanks warm, sincere, grateful, heartfelt, profuse, effusive, tardy, belated, automatic, due

theatre, theatres (of entertainment) vibrant, spirited, animated, exciting, challenging, entertaining, splendid, state-of-the-art, plushy, lavish, opulent, stately, magnificent, long-established, leading, celebrated, distinguished, famous, intimate, tiny, small, middle-sized, 800-seat, large-scale, vast, semicircular, domed, cockle-shaped, makeshift, ornate, outdoor, open-air, contemporary, amateur, (un)affordable, (un)fashionable, regional, national, live, slice-of-life, unsubsidized, professional, commercial, not-for-profit, legitimate, patent, alternative, fringe, experimental, little, repertory, flagship, epic, dramatic, resident, travelling, drive-in, musical, arts

theft, thefts lucrative, grand, major, petty, contemptible, brazen, abject, despicable, frivolous, slight

theme, themes epic, provocative, stimulating, uplifting, edifying, subliminal, coherent, unifying, favourite, popular, leading, central, chief, overriding, dominant, pervasive, general, universal, age-old, permanent, recurrent, challenging, innovative, (un)original, (un)familiar, (un)usual, well-worn, trite, common(place), banal, stale, hackneyed, established, stock, topical, crazy

theologian, theologians liberal, progressive, influential, powerful, authoritative, radical, dissenting, dissident, lay

theory, theories revolutionary, profound, cogent, stable, fruitful, well-defined, fascinating, intriguing, provocative, impressive, seminal, sound, elaborate, intrinsic, feasible, (in)correct, (un)popular, (un)tenable, likely, probable, (im)plausible, (un)convincing, fresh, novel, nascent, latest, up-to-date, ancient, well-established, predominant, prevalent, impenetrable, irreconcilable, incompatible, mutable, rigid, doctrinaire, intricate, complicated, complex, conflicting, contradictory, controversial, inconsistent, dubious, pernicious, antiquated, far-fetched, half-baked, untried, empty, abstract, monistic, fanciful, experimental, attributive, speculative, classical, militant, basic, pet

therapy, therapies See *treatment* (1)

thermometer, thermometers glass, oral, digital, electrical, clinical, rectal, personal, wet-and-dry, sugar

thief, thieves See *robber*

thigh, thighs bulging, big, thick, heavy, flabby, sloppy, flaccid, soft, limp, fleshy, plump, round, slender

thinker, thinkers perceptive, seminal, solid, profound, exact, sound, wise, deep, seamless, mature, provocative, acute, bold, creative, advanced, (un)original, stodgy, shallow, errant, linear, liberal, concrete, ideological

thinking logical, sequent(ial), shrewd, precise, sound, perceptive, original, creative, independent, straight, clear, exact, positive, sharp, awesome, innovative, traditional, fundamental, (un)conventional, (un)orthodox, old-fashioned, outdated, stereotyped, quick, hasty, loose, wrongful, narrow, fuzzy, cloudy, obscure, vague, confused, disordered, warped, heretical, woolly, murky, self-defeatist, compulsive, obsessive, polyphasic, wishful, critical, strategic, convergent, divergent, lateral

thirst consuming, devouring, raging, unrelenting, unremitting, irrepressible, unquenchable, intolerable, frightful, horrible, fearful, bitter, excessive, abnormal, violent, ghastly, ravenous, savage, constant

thorn, thorns long, short, hard, sharp-pointed, troublesome, vexatious, bothersome, poisonous

thoroughfare, thoroughfares See *street*

thoroughness enormous, unequalled, unprecedented, uncommon, remarkable, extraordinary, discernible, noticeable, significant

thought, thoughts loving, tender, fond, kindly, lofty, pleasant, genial, gentle, amusing, noble, nice, germinal, productive, pregnant, profound, fluent, nimble, appropriate, important, (in)coherent, rational, pithy, trenchant, innovative, provocative, bright, stupendous, great, systematic, colourful, free, serious, heavy, uneasy, chilly, frightening, chilling, oppressive, grave, solemn, polyphasic, inner(most), inmost, uppermost, reminiscent, obsessive, (all-)absorbing, recurrent, quick, swift, passing, fleeting, transient, casual, vagrant, erratic, chaotic, random, desultory, haphazard, jerky, spasmodic, impromptu, intrusive, malleable, shapeless, wandering, revolutionary, strange, private, intimate, wishful, malign, terrible, awful, unbearable, diabolic(al), heretical, evil, sick, morbid, melancholy, depressive, dreary, cheerless, gloomy, vacuous, unkind, mean, vile, ignoble, small-minded, selfish, vapid, painful, bitter, subversive, inappropriate, suicidal, destructive, tempting, lustful, forbidden, unseemly, capricious, angry, turbid, incongruous, confused, unfinished, imaginative, introspective, investigative, confessional, humanistic

thoughtlessness frivolous, reckless, heedless, inconsiderate, incorrigible, ineradicable

thread, threads filmy, cobweb(by), fine, tenuous, fragile, slender, delicate, gauzy, heavy, strong, tangled, two-ply, metallic, gold, silver, silk(en), cotton, nylon, woollen, byssal, linen, hempen, flaxen, homespun

threat, threats valid, peremptory, unmistakable, manifest, clear, explicit, implicit, deterrent, (thinly-)veiled, vague, (in)direct, salty, imperceptible, futile, (in)effective, fruitless, empty, idle, low, peripheral, prime, primary, vain, potential, new, long-range, constant, incessant, ceaseless, endless, unending, unremitting, enduring, ultimate, imminent, immediate, (un)verifiable, (un)predictable, explosive, bellicose, violent, petulant, mortal, deadly, brutal, destructive, formidable, impatient, blunt, drastic, powerful, brawny, substantial, great, major, serious, grave, dire, tough, alarming, chilling, agonizing, unsettling, intolerable, unbearable, grisly, insidious, vicious, dangerous, insurmountable, sinister, all-pervasive, rampant, credible, convincing, genuine, real, bogus, intrusive, terrible, wild, unconditional, mutual, anonymous, verbal, physical, internal, external, environmental

thrill, thrills exhilarating, throbbing, moving, breathtaking, breathless, intense, transcendent, intimate, galvanic, never-to-be-forgotten, tremendous, curious, uncommon, unusual, sudden, anticipatory, visceral, sensuous

throat, throats shapely, smooth, tight, dry, sore, swollen, inflamed, parched, raw, raspy, scratchy, skinny, slender, catarrhal

throne, thrones golden, superb, ornate, elaborate, magnificent, lofty, vacant, unsteady, tottering, papal, imperial

throng, throngs See *crowd*

thumb, thumbs See *finger*

thunder resounding, rattling, ground-shaking, roaring, grinding, rumbling, cracking, swelling, rolling, ominous, awful, visceral, loud, reverberant, growling, distant, muffled, muted, inexhaustible, prim(a)eval

thunderstorm See *storm*

ticket, tickets free, complimentary, full-fare, half-fare, overpriced, cut-rate, unsold, unused, unnumbered, (un)reserved, (un)available, (non-)transferable, counterfeit, first-class, second-class, single, one-way, return, round-trip, season, (general-)admission, black-market, advance; straight

tide, tides fluctuating, swelling, (swiftly-)flowing, receding, rising, incoming, outgoing, strong, slack, reversed, lee, convulsive, circumfluous, swirly, inexorable, variable, semi-diurnal, low, high, (un)certain, flood, ebb, neap, spring, daily, mixed, geologic(al)

tidings See *news*

tie, ties (1: bond; connection) beneficial, indissoluble, inextricable, close, permanent, (long-)standing, strict, tenuous, murky, shadowy, virtual, direct, traditional, cultural, mystical, diplomatic, ancestral

tie, ties (2: necktie) See *necktie*

tiger, tigers snarling, roaring, hissing, panting, prowling, running, bounding, yawning, graceful, magnificent, mighty, powerful, ferocious, fierce, angry, growling, fearsome, aggressive, wily, sabre-toothed; paper

tights See *stocking*

tile, tiles round, curved, (half-)cylindrical, hollow, flat, lightweight, utilitarian, beautiful, attractive, vivid, decorative, patterned, glazed, stencilled, slate, mosaic, arabesque, ceramic, pottery, clay, porcelain, wooden, terracotta, split-stone, mirror, lichen-covered, porous, stodgy, acoustic, thermal

timber See *wood* (1)

time, times ecstatic, euphoric, edifying, delightful, blissful, grand, seasonable, prosperous, affluent, plushy, enjoyable, great, lovely, glorious, lively, exciting, stirring, thrilling, spanking, perceptible, lucrative, precious, remarkable, splendid, admirable, marvellous, challenging, favourable, good, convenient, (im)proper, (in)adequate, (in)opportune, (in)appropriate, propitious, auspicious, expeditious, fortuitous, unique, jolly, gay,

rip-roaring, rollicking, (un)pleasant, (un)happy, enchanting, promising, inviolable, momentous, orderly, easy, calm, romantic, reminiscent, ample, handsome, (in)sufficient, lost, enough, (un)limited, unconscionable, (un)reasonable, (in)definite, specific, particular, actual, normal, old, ancient, bygone, former, elder, early, earlier, immemorial, changeful, volatile, modern, formative, crucial, unreturning, peak, rare, unusual, expansive, inconvenient, vacant, devastating, hard, trying, lean, austere, slack, frugal, worrying, bad, dull, unfavourable, degenerate, difficult, tough, tense, testing, taxing, rugged, anxious, distressing, harrowing, worrisome, parlous, bumpy, rocky, troubled, troublous, stirring, unsettling, unsettled, turbulent, tumultuous, heady, stressful, rough(-hewn), strained, prickly, uncertain, excessive, dangerous, lawless, dire, grim, dreary, traumatic, lonely, sad, stern, evil, spare, standard, sidereal, equinoctial, astronomical (mean, true), daylight-saving, civil, half, high, quick, (pre)historic, geologic(al), prime, colonial, biblical, predynastic, inflationary, recessionary; double

timetable, timetables exact, rigid, fixed, elastic, (in)flexible, (un)adaptable, slow, set, seasonal

timing uncanny, crisp, perfect, right, accurate, precise, excellent, impressive, astute, clever, sensible, fortuitous, propitious, (in)auspicious, (un)favourable, wonderful, remarkable, impeccable, (in)appropriate, (un)lucky, (un)fortunate, dramatic, split-second, coincidental, curious, odd, strange, ironic, questionable, suspicious, suspect, wrong, bad, terrible, synchronous

tip, tips generous, lavish, small, measly, (un)justifiable, (un)expected, (non-)traditional

tipping See *tip*

tiredness See *fatigue*

tissue, tissues fleshy, fat(ty), lean, tough, thick, rigid, porous, corky, elastic, gelatinous, translucent, inner, tight, taut, adipose, oxygen-starved, necrotic, human, foetal, ligamentous, vascular, epithelial, muscular, subcutaneous, connective (supporting), nervous (nerve), fibrous, cancerous, endometrial

title, titles (1: name of book, film, etc.) provocative, laconic, concise, terse, sharp, inventive, (in)significant, (un)dignified, (in)appropriate, pithy, felicitous, elegant, breezy, catchy, capital, strange-sounding, flippant, curious, lurid, prosaic, awkward, cumbersome, bulky, deceptive, misleading, tentative, half, running, descriptive, indicative, collective

title, titles (2: rank) honorific, prestigious, high-sounding, larger-than-life, myriad, irrevocable, automatic, extinct, unnecessary, presumptive, (in)appropriate, lordly, princely, honorary, prescriptive, hereditary, academic

title, titles (3: legal right) sound, valid, clean, clear, fake, sham, clouded

toast, toasts See also *bread* warm, crisp(y), burnt, blackened, buttered, garlic-rubbed, dry, French

tobacco smokeless, fine-cut, aged, flue-cured (bright), fire-cured (Virginia), air-cured

toe, toes See *finger*

togetherness See *unity*

toil See *work*

tolerance forbearing, enduring, untiring, long-standing, long-suffering, all-embracing, tense, (un)usual, comprehensive, (un)limited, meek, zero, scant, low, high, broad-minded, warm-hearted, indulgent, magnanimous, patient, officious, bored, religious, cultural, racial

toleration See *tolerance*

tomato, tomatoes See *vegetable*

tomb, tombs imposing, forbidding, grandiose, spectacular, elaborate, monumental, chambered, domed, dome-shaped, beehive, ornate, marble, concrete, mud-brick, subterranean, underground, above-ground, cliff-cut, simple, silent, undisturbed, untouched, unearthed, unopened, intact, tumbling, supposed, megalithic

tome, tomes See *volume*

tone, tones (1: sound) caring, soothing, rising, encouraging, prevailing, ringing, grating, piercing, commanding, overbearing, threatening, menacing, wavering, jeering, unaltering, murmuring, gentle, soft, silvery, mellow, level, calm,

hushed, mild, mellifluous, sweet, honeyed, dulcet, tasteful, light, playful, raptured, natural, peerless, genuine, proper, liquid, liquescent, pure, crisp, clear, hopeful, confident, conciliatory, matter-of-fact, confidential, interrogative, interrogatory, artificial, facetious, steady, insistent, partial, detached, phlegmatic, unmoved, drowsy, round, well-balanced, mournful, doleful, bleak, grim, despairing, lugubrious, regretful, deliberate, serious, grave, bass, harsh, virulent, gruff, high, shrill, sharp, resonant, hoarse, husky, incisive, loud, wiry, throaty, broken, stentorian, strident, high-pitched, staccato, brilliant, thunderous, superior, aggressive, arrogant, uncompromising, assertive, peremptory, (self-)assured, authoritative, imperious, dictatorial, magisterial, dominant, imperative, boastful, businesslike, warlike, sepulchral, ominous, hollow, dismal, affected, measured, false, languid, dull, eerie, contemptuous, argumentative, belligerent, combative, confrontational, angry, irate, indignant, scolding, peevish, querulous, passing; half (minor), whole (full, major), quarter

tone, tones (2: colour) See *colour*

tongue, tongues (1: language; speech) valorous, sweet, glib, fluent, natural, eloquent, silver, persuasive, subtle, ready, nimble, facile, limber, boundless, indefatigable, witty, dominant, unbridled, loose, unrestrained, soft, smooth, honeyed, rattling, flattering, whispering, gossiping, gossipy, vulgar, barbed, envenomed, poisonous, vitriolic, slanderous, venomous, tart, sharp, satirical, acid, raspish, malignant, evil, libellous, intolerant, salty, complex, native, ancestral

tongue, tongues (2: organ) thrusting, lapping, darting, forked, textured, furry, sticky, slobbery, slabbery, waggly, thick, parched, bloated, swollen, pink, prehensile

tool, tools useful, utilitarian, powerful, versatile, all-round, perfect, (im)proper, right, convenient, (un)suitable, (un)handy, (un)dependable, (un)reliable, (in)effective, (in)efficient, durable, indispensable, high-tech, arcane, crude, coarse, rude, clumsy, unwieldy, blunt, rusty, ill-made, useless, cumbersome, hazardous, dangerous, notched, basic, necessary, (un)common, (un)familiar, traditional, simple, archaic, primitive, rudimentary, prehistoric, bifacial, double-headed, pronged, cordless, manual, industrial

tooth, teeth gleaming, glittering, shining, flashing, brilliant, snow-white, pearly, flawless, perfect, efficient, sound, charming, (un)pleasant, straight, tight, (ir)regular, (un)even, well-kept, incisive, molar, sensitive, close, prominent, protuberant, elongated, fang-like, conical, angular, triangular, spade-shaped, pointed, spiked, inward-curving, razor-sharp, dagger-sharp, missing, snaggle, loose, bad, livid, yellow, (betel-)stained, lopsided, rotten, worn, cutting, crushing, forward, upper, lower, artificial, false, deciduous, permanent, intermaxillary, canine, wisdom; sweet

toothache, toothaches See *pain*

topic, topics profound, heavy, meaty, congenial, hot, explosive, prime, prominent, dominant, pressing, resonant, habitual, stock, standing, staple, (un)familiar, (un)usual, (ir)regular, diverse, (un)remarkable, (in)significant, (un)fit, untouched, marginal, narrow, unmentionable, taboo, sensitive, delicate, contentious, controversial, labyrinthine, thematic, conceptual

torch, torches flaming, glaring, dazzling, slow-burning, acetylene, electric, pocket

torment, torments See *torture*

tornado, tornadoes See *storm*

torrent, torrents See *flood*

torture, tortures sickening, shocking, devastating, appalling, excruciating, racking, searing, agonizing, unrelenting, relentless, pitiless, ruthless, merciless, remorseless, heartless, cruel, painful, intense, extensive, heavy, systematic, repetitious, protracted, persistent, unspeakable, indescribable, grievous, terrible, heinous, dreadful, ghastly, gruesome, savage, wicked, raw, pointless, senseless, physical, mental, psychological, moral

total, totals grand, cumulative

touch, touches tender, delicate, gentle, light, dainty, satiny, masterly, deft, sure, sensitive, affectionate, well-intentioned, magical, therapeutic, momentary, fleeting, incidental, casual, reciprocal finishing

touchdown, touchdowns See *landing*

tour, tours See also *journey* relaxing, enervating, leisurely, informative, successful, active, triumphant, festive, extensive, lengthy, month-long, grand, package(d), world(-wide), round-the-world, five-city, cross-country, circular, round, whirlwind, whistle-stop, solitary, out-of-the-way, walking, roving, on-shore, (motor-)coach, aerial, fact-finding, promotional

tourism booming, flourishing, thriving, rising, excessive, mass, herd-like, unbridled, (over-)organized, well-ordered, well-regulated, unregulated, unrestricted, wildlife-orient(at)ed, international, commercial

tourist, tourists avid, adventurous, (ad)venturesome, intrepid, curious, sluggish, unsuspecting, unwary, heedless, vulnerable, purblind, gawky, (foot-)weary, group-packaged, package, cash-bearing, budget-conscious, (low-)budget, lower-income, middle-income, well-heeled, value-conscious, picky, (un)cultured, (un)intelligent, casual, ubiquitous

tournament, tournaments See *game*

towel, towels lush, velvety, starchy, wrinkled, soiled, thick, absorbent, linen, cotton, huckaback, terry(-cloth), Turkish

tower, towers soaring, giant, mighty, massive, tall, high, lofty, stately, elegant, graceful, splendid, magnificent, 40-storey, thin, well-preserved, landmark, eminent, distinctive, panoramic, striking, gleaming, shiny, glassy, wrought-iron, dry-stone, mosaic-draped, monolithic, steel-supporting, flat-topped, obelisk-shaped, conical, round, rectangular, octagonal, circular, spiral, surrealistic, grim, solitary, unstable, crumbly, tottering, precarious, dilapidated, ruined, weather-eroded, twin, cooling, martello; ivory

town, towns refined, picturesque, scenic, (postcard-)pretty, quaint, handsome, (un)friendly, funky, carefree, populous, remote, quiet, tranquil, sleepy, dormant, drowsy, somnolent, lethargic, torpid, slow(-moving), laid-back, sedate, staid, dull, tiny, small, little, wide-open, one-horse, unpretentious, obscure, backwater, struggling, nondescript, destitute, stricken, ghost(ly), dirt-poor, shanty, seedy, backward, dingy, grimy, dusty, dowdy, redneck,

rough-and-ready, gossipy, medieval, old,
historic, biblical, walled, lakeside, seaside,
coastal, inland, mountain, hill(side), rural,
frontier, border, neighbouring, spread-out,
two-streets-deep, wet, dry, quintessential,
tourist-tawdry, upstate, provincial, county,
country, presidial, home, industrial,
one-industry, one-company, market,
garrison

toy, toys stimulating, satisfying, simple,
complex, sophisticated, imaginative,
creative, useful, colourful, harmless,
popular, favourite, marvellous, solid,
untested, (un)safe, little-used, abandoned,
worthless, useless, harmful, outlandish,
expensive, pricey, cheap, cuddly, soft,
woolly, plastic, (un)broken, fragile,
blockbuster, basic, primitive, classic,
traditional, home-made, hand-made,
mass-produced, one-dimensional,
(fast-)talking, mechanical, educational,
instructional, computer-driven, electronic,
clockwork, wind-up, inflatable, wheeled

trace, traces deep, indelible, permanent,
(in)visible, conspicuous, unmistakable,
authentic, faint, minute, slight, haunting,
fragmentary, provocative; seismic

track, tracks fresh, soft, deep, steep,
narrow, sinuous, faint, vague, dusty,
muddy, bumpy, stone-strewn, winding,
unprecedented, (un)beaten, untrodden,
little-known, little-used, abandoned,
impassable, desolate, rough, difficult,
arduous, tortuous, inside, outside, indoor,
outdoor, gravel, dirt, mountain; fast, right

trade (1: commerce) booming, teeming,
thriving, rousing, brisk, vigorous, active,
lucrative, (un)profitable, excessive,
pervasive, far-flung, frantic, cut-throat,
flat, unfettered, unrestricted, unregulated,
(un)free, open-market, (il)licit, (il)legal,
dubious, elusive, resilient, contraband,
fraudulent, staple, (in)direct, cross-border,
sea-borne, ocean-going, maritime, coastal,
import, export, retail, wholesale,
community, domestic, inland, internal,
inward, outward, external, foreign,
overseas, international (world), transatlantic,
intercontinental, reciprocal, bilateral

trade, trades (2: craft) See *craft*
trader, traders See *merchant*
trading See also *market* (1) brisk,
enthusiastic, heavy, hectic, frenzied,

frantic, roller-coaster, volatile, nervous,
erratic, choppy, bumpy, uncertain,
moderate, light, thin, quiet, lacklustre,
shady, illicit, unlawful, unauthorized,
fraudulent

tradition, traditions venerable, sacred,
noble, glorious, proud, sensitive, hoary,
unique, lavish, great, rich, expressive,
strong, old(est), age-old, centuries-old,
ancient, timeless, long-standing, enduring,
surviving, living, unshakable, unstoppable,
unquenchable, deep-seated, deep-rooted,
(long-)established, time-honoured,
(long-)unquestioned, unbroken, unfaded,
(in)formal, (in)tolerant, ruthless, follow-
the-leader, old-boy, clubby, odd, shaky,
fusty, long-abandoned, archaic, obsolete,
moribund, well-worn, learned, muddled,
embattled, verbal, oral, cultural, local,
fundamental, indigenous, ancestral, legal

traffic sluggish, slow, smooth, little, light,
(un)manageable, abundant, continuous,
fast, hurry-up, high-speed, heavy,
excessive, massive, drab, roaring,
horn-blasting, unforgiving, nerve-racking,
dizzying, annoying, snarled-up, congested,
frenzied, frenetic, frantic, chaotic, nasty,
noisy, torturous, horrendous, dreadful,
formidable, terrible, relentless, insane,
hellish, deadly, unusual, unaccustomed,
stationary, opposing, oncoming, outgoing,
outbound, eastbound, westbound, wheeled,
vehicular, one-way, rush-hour, pedestrian,
commercial

tragedy, tragedies (1: catastrophe)
haunting, howling, agonizing, unrelenting,
relentless, merciless, ruthless, pitiless,
heartless, cruel, inexorable, (un)avoidable,
(in)evitable, (un)preventable, senseless,
insufferable, intolerable, unbearable,
gruesome, grim, horrible, ghastly, bizarre,
repulsive, terrible, incomprehensible,
unthinkable, persistent, recurrent, high,
enormous, potential, impending, near,
utter, man-made, personal, ecological

tragedy, tragedies (2: serious play) See
also *play* touching, penetrating, poignant,
profound, tearful, insufferable, turgid,
bombastic, effusive, maudlin, haunting,
high-flown, ritualistic, realistic, heroic,
lyric

trail, trails easy, visible, (in)accessible,
(un)usable, well-trodden, well-worn,

much-used, regular, shaded, scenic, spectacular, panoramic, fascinating, quiet, narrow, clear, (in)distinct, (un)marked, well-marked, (in)discernible, land-scarring, hurried, faint, spongy, warm, parched, demanding, challenging, backbreaking, dizzying, vertiginous, steep, deep, rough, rugged, rubble-strewn, dusty, impassable, dangerous, precipitous, tortuous, circuit, twisted, winding, meandering, ambling, undulating, remote, lonely, primitive, mountain, alpine, coastal, cliffside, rock(y), geological, wooded, woodland, forest, jungle, desert, dirt, shale, bog, marsh

train, trains rumbling, chugging, roaring, rattling, grinding, passing, veering, staggering, rocking, steaming, super, powerful, august, luxurious, luxury, plush, efficient, frequent, punctual, comfortable, monumental, non-stop, through, high-speed, (super)swift, fast, quiet, ecology-friendly, right, wrong, (over)due, next, last, stationary, four-coach, northbound, inefficient, slow, fitful, runaway, rickety, noisy, creaky, rackety, dusty, long-distance, special, mainline, stock, night, commuter, suburban, local, steam(-powered), electric(-powered), diesel(-electric), epicyclic, narrow-gauge, miniature, model, toy, elevated, overhead, underground, passenger, freight, goods

training proper, meticulous, impeccable, incomparable, serious, consistent, intensive, intense, comprehensive, well-rounded, extensive, vigorous, rigid, rigorous, arduous, hard, gruelling, valuable, advanced, (in)adequate, (in)appropriate, poor, patchy, dull, (in)formal, (un)conventional, special, mandatory, compulsory, optional, refresher, universal, massive, preparatory, preliminary, elementary, basic, corrective, early, live-in, hands-on, on-the-job, interminable, five-hours-a-day, ongoing, vocational, educational

trait, traits See *characteristic*

traitor, traitors infamous, worthless, faithless, disloyal, perfidious, odious, vicious, notorious, wretched, wicked, degenerate, ignominious, Iscariotic

tramp, tramps (vagrant, vagabond) See *vagabond*

tranquillity embracing, pervasive, majestic, sublime, exalted, dignified, calm, undisturbed, sleepy, drowsy, incredible, unbelievable, easy-going, uneasy, strange, mesmeric, uncanny, preternatural, self-effacing, comparative, pure, absolute, utter, complete, deep, immeasurable, great, rapt, withdrawn, cool, deathly, meditative, solitary, domestic

transaction, transactions See *deal*

transcript, transcripts original, authentic, exact, (in)accurate, fraudulent, counterfeit, fake

transformation, transformations See *change* (1)

transition, transitions See also *change* (1) peaceful, amicable, (un)easy, neat, smooth, steady, quiet, enormous, historic, dramatic, fundamental, momentous, crucial, sharp, uneven, abrupt, awkward, turbulent, troubled, tempestuous, tumultuous, convulsive, painful, bumpy, rocky, rapid, slow

translation, translations careful, faithful, exact, (in)accurate, (in)competent, (in)adequate, vulgar, clumsy, close, literal, slavish, verbal, verbatim, liberal, free, loose, scholarly, interlinear, vernacular, simultaneous, extempore (extemporaneous), metrical

transmission, transmissions three-speed, manual-control, constant-mesh, synchromesh, automatic gear, fluid, radio, telephonic, telegraphic, televisual, mechanical

transport, transportation (un)reliable, (un)safe, (in)efficient, difficult, chaotic, free, low-cost, cheap, costly, direct, land, sea, air, automotive, wheeled, underground, coastal, marine, public

trap, traps humane, (il)legal, (in)discriminate, hideous, devilish, unyielding, invisible, deadly, fatal, (in)effective, leg-hold, iron-jawed, steel-jawed, quick-kill, live, double-spring, single-spring

trapping See *trap*

trauma, traumas lasting, emotional, mental, physical, post-operative

travel, travels exciting, thrilling, stirring, prodigious, trouble-free, carefree, merry, enjoyable, convenient, plush, lavish, prestigious, (un)affordable, (un)punctual, (un)safe, risky, vexatious, wearisome, tiresome, tiring, trying, gruelling, exhausting, hard, tough, arduous, tortuous, tedious, restless, wide-ranging, extensive, extended, wide, epic, endless, ceaseless, unceasing, (un)structured, (un)limited, undisrupted, (un)restricted, interplanetary, foreign, overseas, cross-border, transpacific, transatlantic, overland, supersonic, business, nomadic

traveller, travellers shrewd, well-informed, (in)experienced, (well-)seasoned, discriminating, fastidious, observant, meditative, romantic, wandering, independent, avid, duplicitous, inveterate, venturesome, adventurous, obdurate, hardened, intrepid, resolute, determined, (in)frequent, belated, benighted, stormbound, stranded, impulsive, compulsive, lone, solitary, lonely, fearful, nervous, unwary, vulnerable, naïve, luckless, hapless, jittery, exhausted, frustrated, disgruntled, weary, jet-lagged, jaded, footsore, trudging, well-heeled, wealthy, penniless, luggage-laden, unaccompanied, long-distance, international, overseas, commercial, casual, local

travelling See *travel*

tray, trays elegant, ornate, rattan, wicker, silver, brass, copper, lucite, teak, mahogany, plastic, circular, rectangular, hefty, ceremonial

treachery perfidious, rascally, seditious, unscrupulous, venomous, viperish, foul, repugnant, rank, abhorrent, hateful, detestable, loathsome, unspeakable, dishonourable, infamous, contrived, Iscariotic, Punic

treason, treasons See *treachery*

treasure, treasures exquisite, superb, magnificent, splendid, fantastic, prized, unique, peerless, exceptional, singular, precious, (in)valuable, inestimable, priceless, rare, irreplaceable, important, vast, incredible, unbelievable, fine, awesome, enormous, absolute, glittering, lavish, true, genuine, portable, movable, little-known, unreported, unclaimed, elusive, irrecoverable, earthly, national, ecological, environmental, archaeological, historic

treasury, treasuries bulging, siz(e)able, exhausted, cash-starved

treat, treats rare, privileged, special, unparalleled, unprecedented, refreshing, delightful, pleasant, gastronomic

treatise, treatises recondite, seminal, erudite, esoteric, learned, ponderous, dull, obscure, wordy, lengthy, long-winded

treatment, treatments (1: medical or surgical care) soothing, life-saving, prompt, immediate, sure-fire, dependable, premier, advanced, sophisticated, state-of-the-art, leading-edge, innovative, unheard-of, drastic, intelligent, fruitful, promising, exciting, empirical, (im)proper, painless, (in)appropriate, (in)adequate, (in)judicious, (un)acceptable, (un)proven, centuries-old, (un)conventional, traditional, standard, (in)efficient, (in)effective, (un)successful, intensive, extensive, complex, manipulative, (in)sufficient, helpful, (un)popular, long-lasting, permanent, lengthy, costly, controversial, negligent, neglectful, poor, quack, so-called, irrational, painful, fruitless, risky, short-term, long-term, problematic, stop-gap, alternative, holistic, dietary, nutritional, herbal, natural, primal, curative, supplemental, mandatory, compulsory, obligatory, optional, follow-up, medical, medicinal, (non-)surgical, operative, incisionless, intravenous, experimental, symptomatic, chemical-dependence, (non-)pharmacological, therapeutic, psychiatric, facial, palliative, hormonal, life-sustaining, prenatal, photodynamic, electroconvulsive, electromagnetic, cognitive, thrombolytic, radioactive, reconstructive

treatment (2: the act or manner of dealing with someone or something) red-carpet, star, royal, imperial, dignified, special, lenient, (un)favourable, (un)fair, (in)equitable, (un)equal, standard, differential, preferential, (un)discriminating, (in)appropriate, (in)sensitive, (un)informed, (un)pleasant, (un)civil, (un)gentle, (in)human, (in)humane, (un)sympathetic, curious, unheard-of, infamous, obsequious, (ir)rational, oppressive, cruel, remorseless, heartless, merciless, ruthless, pitiless, relentless, unrelenting, severe, barbarous,

harsh, hard, rough, brutal, dreadful,
rigorous, callous, rigid, (im)personal,
neglectful, perfunctory, shoddy, shabby,
disgraceful, shameful, cool, abusive,
arrogant, cavalier, patronizing, reciprocal,
orthodox, comprehensive, uniform,
computational, mathematical

treaty, treaties neat, simple, beneficial,
cohesive, toothless, collusive, patchwork,
comprehensive, verifiable, historic,
(un)precedented, self-executing, legal,
(in)valid, (in)formal, (un)official, bilateral,
trilateral, tripartite, triangular, three-way,
preliminary, political, strategic,
commercial, ecclesiastical; nude

tree, trees swaying, low-hanging,
low-spreading, fast-growing, slow-growing,
evening-scented, fragrant, shady, leafy,
fruitful, lush, sturdy, verdant, hardy,
spiny, spindly, scraggly, straight, erect,
tall, lofty, royal, majestic, stately, graceful,
huge, mighty, enormous, mammoth,
gigantic, giant, monstrous, overgrown,
flamboyant, dense, bushy, (im)mature,
gauzy, (centuries-)old, old-growth, ancient,
aged, long-lived, superannuated, scraggy,
shaggy, limber, pliant, twisty, flexible,
supple, waterside, solitary, lonely,
lonesome, young, skinny, short, low,
dwarfed, stunted, hollow, stark, leafless,
(half-)bare, (winter-)bare, sparse,
climbable, pop-up, tinder-dry, scrubby,
snaggy, sallow, thorny, scruffy, spunky,
mossy, moss-draped, frost-rimmed,
cone-bearing, motionless, barren, sterile,
sickly, dead, spectral, ghostly, skeletal,
still, scabby, broken-topped, spotted, split,
shredded, (long-)fallen, weather-beaten,
withered, dried-up, hollowed-out, stressed,
decayed, gnarled, tangled, twisted,
gum-stained, submerged, leguminous,
bombacaceous, rutaceous, rosaceous,
moraceous, betulaceous, sterculiaceous,
dipterocarpaceous, caesalpiniaceous,
anacardiaceous, bignoniaceous, fagaceous,
euphorbiaceous, thymelaeaceous,
sapindaceous, myrtaceous, araliaceous,
leguminous, oleaceous, lauraceous,
mimosaceous, sapotaceous, cornaceous,
coniferous, deciduous, needle-leaf,
broad-leaf, miniature, boot, cabbage,
calabash, camphor, silk-cotton,
ornamental, evergreen; genealogical, family

trek, treks See *journey*

tremor, tremors quavering, quivering,
wavering, rocking, shaking, giant,
harmonic, nervous, agitated, convulsive,
spasmodic

trend, trends welcome, encouraging, clear,
strong, unusual, current, new, modern,
recent, contemporary, going, budding,
growing, prevailing, prevalent, underlying,
lingering, fundamental, unmistakable,
upward, downward, broad, general,
(ir)reversible, (un)alterable, self-correcting,
silly, conflicting, troubling, alarming,
disquieting, depressing, discouraging,
distressing, ominous, worrisome, injurious,
dangerous, demographic, climatic

trial, trials (1: an examination in a law
court before a judge) (un)fair,
(in)adequate, high-security, new, pending,
four-day, two-month-old, famous,
celebrated, high-profile, unusual,
sensational, dramatic, bizarre, murky,
drawn-out, tardy, hasty, speedy, open,
mock, civil, criminal, summary

trial, trials (2: experiment) See *experiment*

triangle, triangles similar, congruent,
plane, spherical, scalene, isosceles,
equilateral, acute(-angled), right(-angled),
obtuse(-angled)

tribe, tribes peaceful, (un)friendly,
modern, exotic, kindred, local, prominent,
obscure, illiterate, uncivilized,
(still-)primitive, savage, barbarian, wild,
cannibal, hostile, warlike, rival, populous,
remote, lost, scattered, undiscovered,
unchanged, extended, vagrant,
(semi-)nomadic, wandering, roving,
sedentary, indigenous, aboriginal, venatic,
predatory, pastoral, animistic, prehistoric

tribunal, tribunals See *court* (1)

tribute, tributes lasting, enduring, fitting,
engaging, glowing, moving, elegant,
graceful, handsome, affectionate, tender,
fine, lovely, hearty, true, appropriate,
ecstatic, fervent, cordial, warm, apposite,
effusive, prodigious, generous, florid,
eloquent, unabashed, memorable,
extraordinary, magnificent, wonderful,
special, belated, indirect, grudging,
oblique, public, editorial; living

trick, tricks dazzling, entertaining, helpful,
neat, subtle, ingenious, clever, smart,
dext(e)rous, deft, nifty, artful, mesmeric,

crafty, sly, underhand, cunning, foxy, daring, dynamic, treacherous, dastardly, snide, dishonest, devilish, ghastly, scurvy, despicable, rotten, dishonourable, low(-down), mischievous, base, abject, grovelling, rascally, knavish, mean, cheap, ugly, unpleasant, objectionable, unscrupulous, dirty, deceitful, illusory, heartless, corny, dangerous, madcap, apish, pompous, weird, childish, infantile, silly, stupid, simple, theatrical, magic, semantic(al), rhetorical

trip, trips rewarding, relaxing, quiet, blissful, idyllic, dream, trouble-free, hassle-free, worry-free, jolly, memorable, superb, luxurious, luxury, extravagant, exclusive, exotic, legendary, epic, fabulous, romantic, (un)eventful, (dis)agreeable, (un)pleasant, (dis)organized, spectacular, scenic, busy, active, demanding, tiring, punishing, hair-raising, spine-jarring, bone-jarring, harrowing, hazardous, perilous, whirlwind, hectic, tedious, hard, dusty, dismal, disappointing, grim, clandestine, secret, expensive, costly, disastrous, fateful, forthcoming, unexpected, sudden, fleeting, annual, yearly, last(-ever), ultimate, long-scheduled, (in)frequent, all-day, same-day, huge, lengthy, circuitous, brief, overnight, continual, (un)necessary, trial, five-country, cross-country, overseas, island-hopping, day, night, nocturnal, moonlight, side, return, circular, round(about), business, corporate, all-expenses-paid, personalized, solo, private, educational, sabbatical, reporting, operational

triumph, triumphs See *victory*

triviality, trivialities seeming, apparent, ostensible, pompous, worthless, inconsequential, petty, empty, idiotic, abysmal

troop, troops trusty, loyal(ist), powerful, significant, multitudinous, (un)trained, well-trained, well-organized, (in)experienced, combat-ready, (in)effective, seasoned, veteran, heavily-armed, (battle-)ready, diehard, proud, victorious, deployable, expendable, uniformed, mobile, skyborne, airborne, irritable, flabby, exhausted, worn, blooded, dispirited, dejected, raw, crude,

unpractised, ill-armed, trigger-happy, unruly, undisciplined, insurgent, mutinous, rebellious, renegade, seditious, riotous, untrustful, thuggish, additional, extra, dug-in, auxiliary, expeditionary, allied, enemy, combat, frontline, support, assault, (ir)regular, reserve, special, regional, household, élite, parachute, paramilitary, peace-keeping, multinational, border

trophy, trophies prestigious, coveted, first-place, second-place, silver, gold, consolation

trouble, troubles deep, big, grave, serious, acute, tiresome, considerable, great, significant, much, dire, endless, abiding, chronic, permanent, potential, needless, fresh, insignificant, trifling, petty, small, paltry, trivial, slight, unexpected, unlooked-for, teething

troublemaker, troublemakers nasty, mischievous, spiteful, wicked, venomous, potential

troupe, troupes See *company* (2)

trousers neat, smart, snug, creaseless, corduroy, flannel, canvas, stretch, leather, fawn, billowy, twill, frieze, stretchy, tight, skin-tight, narrow, baggy, roomy, wide, shapeless, loose(-fitting), voluminous, well-worn, sloppy, crumpled, sodden, scruffy, striped, high-waisted, low-waisted, calf-length, cuffed, tailor-made, casual, work

truce, truces See *ceasefire*

truck, trucks See *lorry*

trunk, trunks (of a tree) smooth, bare, massive, huge, stubby, rough, gnarly, gnarled, twisted, pitted, perforate

trust (1: confidence) See *confidence*

trust (2: company; property interest) donative, testamentary, (ir)revocable, spousal, spendthrift, discretionary, secret

truth, truths startling, sober, comprehensible, honest, exact, precise, scrupulous, plain, naked, bare, stark, bald, unadorned, unvarnished, undeniable, indisputable, incontrovertible, unchangeable, unalterable, apparent, salient, conspicuous, obvious, (self-)evident, basic, fundamental, (well-)ascertained, ultimate, absolute, categorical, abstract, concrete, objective, solid, ancient, age-old, established, eternal, (ever)lasting, universal, profound, glorious, unpretentious, strict, rigid, relative, possible, whole, complete, demonstrable, homely, crude, hard, cold, inconvenient, unpopular, uncomfortable, bitter, brutal, dismal, grim, sad, dispiriting, disheartening, sobering, appalling, grisly, scaly, bleak, ghastly, prosaic, marrowless, incomprehensible, remote, unattainable, elusive, bracing, distorted, hidden, esoteric, literal, scientific, analytic, poetic, imaginative, empirical

tube, tubes open(-ended), hollow, minute, narrow, slender, long, vertical, (in)flexible, gas-filled, tracheal (tracheate), Venturi, bronchial, fallopian, tracheo(s)tomy, feeding, uterine, speaking, capillary, endotracheal, intravenous, nasogastric

tuition See *instruction* and *teaching* (1)

tumour, tumours advanced, massive, suspicious, aggressive, anarchic, malignant, benign, palpable, solid, soft, spongy, shallow, deep-seated, (in)accessible, (in)operable, primary, basal, histoid, spinal, pituitary, squamous, pleural, cancerous

tumult, tumults rumbling, boisterous, chaotic, distraught, unrestrained, utter, absolute, total, ugly, muted, emotional

tune, tunes lively, jaunty, sprightly, dance(-like), jig(-like), high, swaggering, rollicking, boisterous, merry, breezy, memorable, memory-laden, catchy, whistleable, pretty, ravishing, haunting, rousing, stirring, melting, well-known, old-time, (un)popular, soft, genteel, slow, simple, reedy, folk(sy), (un)familiar, ghostly, ghastly, doleful, melancholy, stately, metallic, off-key, mechanical

tunnel, tunnels yawning, gaping, winding, spiral, serpentine, convolute(d), spacious, underground, dank, dark, pitch-black, ghostly, gloomy, natural, man-made, wide, narrow, cavernous

turbulence, turbulences wild, violent, implacable, stormy, tempestuous, horrendous, dreadful, terrible, horrible, financial, emotional, atmospheric

turkey, turkeys mumbling, strutting, wandering, prostrate, plump, self-basting, wild, fierce, ocellated, tame, domestic(ated), brush; cold

turmoil, turmoils See *tumult*

turn, turns abrupt, sharp, sudden, quick, high-speed, three-point, ominous, mysterious, momentous, (un)expected, clockwise, anti-clockwise, counter-clockwise

turning-point, turning-points See *point*

turnout, turnouts encouraging, impressive, heavy, heavier-than-usual, (un)expected, unprecedented, record

turtle, turtles snapping, basking, slow, giant, freshwater, marine, aquatic, spotted, painted, yellow-bellied, red-bellied, snake-necked, leatherback, soft-shell(ed), hawksbill; mutant

twig, twigs See *branch*

twilight, twilights See also *light* shining, fading, soft, rosy, lilac-grey, frosty, yellow, short, false, civil, nautical, astronomical

twin, twins monovular, identical, dissimilar, fraternal, Siamese

twist, twists (unexpected turn or development) unpredictable, violent, tortuous, freakish, erratic, whimsical, capricious, bizarre

type, types See also *kind* main, exotic, distinct(ive), (extra)ordinary, (un)usual, blood, character

typewriter, typewriters noiseless, lightweight, high-speed, (ir)reparable, antiquated, ancient, battered, self-correcting, automatic, portable, manual, electric, electronic, Braille

tyranny, tyrannies See *despot*

tyrant, tyrants See *despot*

tyre, tyres squealing, resilient, deflatable, pneumatic, flat, chunky, heavy-duty, indestructible, recyclable, oversize, front, rear, heavy-treaded, treadless, bald, bias-ply, (steel-)belted, radial, all-season, tubeless, whitewall

ugliness preponderating, displeasing, frightening, hideous, grisly, repugnant, repulsive, unrelieved, undeniable, sloppy, grotesque, physical

ulcer, ulcers gnawing, rodent, skin, gastric, peptic, digestive, duodenal

umbrella, umbrellas dripping, colourful, untidy, stumpy, tight, crumpled, floppy, rolled, folding, collapsible, telescopic, see-through

unanimity See *agreement* and *consensus*

uncertainty haunting, harassing, frightening, lingering, obsessive, dark, troublesome, terrible

uncle, uncles See also *relation* (2) favourite, distant, maternal, paternal; Dutch

unconcern apathetic, blatant, obvious, apparent, vulgar, offensive

understanding sympathetic, friendly, intelligent, rational, balanced, sophisticated, deep, profound, acute, thorough, perfect, mature, practical, mighty, unpliable, fundamental, basic, rudimentary, crucial, clear, instant, sudden, uncommon, foggy, tacit, unspoken, limited, narrow, mutual, instinctive, intuitive

understatement, understatements gross, slight

undertaking, undertakings noble, worthwhile, profitable, subtle, huge, major, gigantic, massive, mammoth, heavyweight, formidable, titanosaurian, ambitious, long-standing, expensive, costly, laborious, risky, bold, rash, adventurous, complex, difficult, unlikely, ancillary, feasible, pleasurable, lighthearted, easy, small, abortive

underwear See also *clothes* tantalizing, daring, revealing, scanty, skimpy, sexy, see-through, transparent, sensuous, sensual, provocative, immodest, erotic, silky, nylon, woolly, lacy, shimmery, soft, frilly, pretty, floppy, modern, sensible, warm, thermal

unease, uneasiness understandable, vague, queer, extreme, growing, pervasive, persistent, acute, chronic, haunting, wandering, annoying, compelling, molten, incurable, neurotic, nervous, physical

unemployed destitute, impecunious, needy, helpless, powerless

unemployment rampant, rife, widespread, excessive, massive, record, protracted, long-term, endemic, chronic, hidden, high, low, negligible, structural, urban, rural, normal, seasonal, technological, cyclical

uniform, uniforms glittering, spanking, striking, elegant, dapper, spick-and-span, spiffy, natty, snappy, neat, smart, immaculate, resplendent, expensive, gold-buttoned, festive, colourful, distinctive, effective, ubiquitous, characteristic, pseudo, camouflage, khaki, olive-coloured, gold-braided, outsize, cumbersome, wrinkled, tattered, drab, ragged, grimy, desolate, unkempt, (un)comfortable, makeshift, mandatory, obligatory, special, (in)formal, official, full, standard, traditional, dress

uniformity See *regularity*

union, unions loving, (un)satisfying, enduring, lasting, permanent, perpetual, solid, close, meaningful, astute, indispensable, intact, perfect, viable, assertive, mighty, powerful, strong, full-fledged, high-profile, broad, diverse, (un)natural, (un)acceptable, (in)adequate, (un)breakable, (un)conditional, (un)workable, (in)effective, unwieldy, unthinkable, uneasy, superficial, whimsical, sham, loose, delicate, rickety, tenuous, fragile, fractious, meaningless, unusual, (un)likely, (im)probable, outrageous, unholy, (un)official, independent, separate, craft (horizontal), industrial (vertical), hypostatic, social, economic, monetary, political, strategic, military, matrimonial, monogamous, polygamous, multinational, ad hoc

unit, units standard, fractional, (un)adopted, metric, SI, imperial, monetary, thermal, astronomical

unity harmonious, (rock-)solid, cohesive, fruitful, unstinted, startling, astonishing, astounding, remarkable, unprecedented, strange, diverse, elusive, fragile, combative, organic, natural, national, universal

universe orderly, sensible, steady-state,

chanc(e)y, mechanistic, heliocentric,
egocentric, starry, alternative

university, universities prestigious,
venerable, august, illustrious, selective,
élite, élitist, distinguished, outstanding,
top-flight, esteemed, famed, renowned,
famous, prominent, high-profile,
innovative, demanding, isolated, pricey,
(ir)relevant, full-fledged, autonomous,
independent, Ivy-League, Oxbridge,
polytechnic, technological, red-brick,
instant, upstart, low-profile, obscure,
crowded, teeming, sprawling, turbulent,
state, state-run, private, public, religious,
(non-)residential

unkindness See *cruelty*

unpredictability refreshing, whimsical,
capricious, erratic, ambivalent, utter,
chameleonic

unrest unceasing, unending, wide-ranging,
widespread, endless, constant, ceaseless,
scattered, chronic, dull, bloody, popular,
fundamentalist, social, racial, ethnic,
sectarian, native, nationalist, civil, political

unveiling thrilling, stirring, exciting,
historic, dramatic, (over)due,
(un)scheduled, gradual

upbringing (im)proper, (in)correct,
(in)decent, (un)principled, (in)appropriate,
moral, religious, conservative, genteel,
strict, narrow, haphazard, (un)comfortable,
modest, poor

upheaval, upheavals See *disturbance*

upholstery elegant, stylish, tasteful,
exquisite, luxurious, (well-)sprung,
(un)comfortable, chintzy, cheap, gaudy,
threadbare, shabby, dull, fading, soiled,
worn

uprising, uprisings See *rebellion*

uproar, uproars See *disturbance*

upsurge, upsurges See *rise*

urge overwhelming, overpowering,
excessive, tremendous, strong, powerful,
desperate, resistless, irresistible,
uncontrollable, insatiable, recurrent,
sudden, faint, fundamental, intrinsic,
innate, basal, sexual, atavistic

urgency unmistakable, obvious,
undisguised, special, frantic, hectic,
desperate, awesome, zealous

urn, urns See *vase*

usage, usages See *use*

use, uses constructive, purposeful,
inestimable, (in)effective, peaceful,
(in)appropriate, (in)judicious, (in)sensible,
(in)temperate, (im)proper, (in)discriminate,
(un)profitable, unique, precise,
(in)efficient, (un)common, normal,
standard, (long-)rampant, widespread,
constant, ample, heavy, illimitable,
excessive, intensive, profligate,
(in)frequent, scant, marginal, current,
possible, conceivable, (non-)essential,
practical, successive, internal, external,
sustainable, private, public, exclusive,
multiple, intricate, obsessive, reprehensible,
ill-advised, ill-judged, imprudent,
questionable, controversial, offensive,
contemptuous, rough, neglectful, profitless,
senseless, clandestine, insidious,
unquestioned, unauthorized, devastating

user, users first-time, one-time, heavy,
habitual, frequent, (ir)regular, chronic,
sensible, senseless, careful, careless

usurpation, usurpations unjust, unfair,
inappropriate, total, virtual

utterance, utterances (in)significant,
(in)coherent, meaningful, pregnant,
emphatic, abrupt, tiresome, continued,
uninterrupted, unceasing, ironical,
scornful, craven, obscure, crass, glib,
platitudinous, sanctimonious, hollow,
empty, vacuous, meaningless, public,
oracular, cryptic

vacancy, vacancies immediate,
(un)expected, potential, temporary,
permanent, housing, industrial, holiday
vacation, vacations See *holiday*
vacationer, vocationers See *traveller*
vacuum deep, eerie, yawning, dangerous
vagabond, vagabonds (un)lovable,
incorrigible, unreformable, unruly, nasty,
truant, roofless, homeless, aimless,
philosophic
vagueness sheer, cloudy, confused, fuzzy,
foggy, misty, dim, cryptic, elusive
vainglory See *vanity*
valley, valleys compelling, enchanting,
lush, verdant, green, meadowy, grassy,
(densely-)wooded, forested, rural,
(un)productive, fertile, (wild)flowered,
flower-dappled, tree-studded,
cone-studded, magnificent, splendid,
spectacular, dramatic, pleasant, pretty,
tight, peaceful, serene, tranquil, placid,
quiet, secluded, sequestered, shadowy,
remote, solitary, lonely, lonesome, hidden,
uninhabited, roadless, broad, long, deep,
cliff-sided, steep-sided, hill-ringed, narrow,
high, lofty, shallow, wide, vast, winding,
hazy, misty, steamy, parched, scorched,
(un)sheltered, terraced, chambered,
sun-dappled, sun-beaten, snow-mantled,
ice-ridden, rain-graced, nameless, famed,
senile, scabrous, barren, arid, dry,
waterless, jagged, ragged, craggy, marshy,
desolate, drab, precipitous, dangerous,
interdunal, intermontane, longitudinal,
transverse, drowned, hanging, trunk,
pristine, pastoral, highland, mountainous,
alpine, rustic, bucolic, glacial, alluvial,
tributary
valour See *courage*
value, values meaningful, incalculable,
immeasurable, inestimable, deep,
tremendous, terrific, exceptional,
unbeatable, unique, priceless, irreplaceable,
(ever)lasting, enduring, substantial,
outstanding, eternal, undeniable, positive,
constrictive, rigid, stern, strong, sound,
solid, prevailing, universal, traditional,
hereditary, old-world, centuries-old,
apparent, fundamental, essential, extra,
plus, (in)valid, practical, full, core,
ultimate, fair, unattainable, inappreciable,
negligible, small, poor, negative, factitious,
dubious, shallow, questionable, distasteful,
corrupt, empty, sentimental, monetary,
pecuniary, numerical, commercial, alien,
inflationary, inherent, intrinsic, absolute,
relative, potential, individual, collective,
common, variable, going, current,
nominal, cultural, aesthetic, symbolic,
historical, strategic, religious, ethical,
moral, spiritual, practical, rat(e)able,
nutritional, calorific, numismatic
van, vans See also *vehicle* compact,
versatile, psychedelic, armoured,
four-wheel-drive, customized, transit
vandal, vandals See *vandalism*
vandalism malicious, vicious, wicked,
destructive, mindless, senseless,
devastating, deliberate, anonymous,
sporadic
vanity, vanities vaulting, overweening,
puffed, egregious, outrageous,
preposterous, abnormal, colossal,
inordinate, excessive, extravagant,
insatiable, intolerable, deeply-ingrained,
morbid, perverse, eccentric, unpardonable,
unwarrantable, playful, childish, naïve, small
vapour, vapours floating, rising, steaming,
saturated, misty, steamy, watery, muggy,
explosive, stifling, poisonous, noxious,
harmless, (un)pleasant, thin, thick
variation, variations See *change* (1)
variety, varieties mind-boggling,
overwhelming, bewildering, dizzying,
amazing, stunning, astonishing,
astounding, captivating, fascinating,
dazzling, staggering, incomprehensible,
remarkable, marvellous, wondrous,
impressive, exquisite, basic, wide,
abundant, lavish, rich, infinite, unlimited,
limitless, endless, countless, infinite,
immense, enormous, great, unbelievable,
incredible, unequalled, unparalleled,
exceptional, unknowable, extraordinary,
irreconcilable; rare, exotic, unusual
vase, vases hideous, elaborate, graceful,
fine, slender, delicate, beautiful, exquisite,
antique, valuable, precious, priceless,
ornate, hand-blown, wide-mouthed, eared,
globular, cylindrical, verdigris, enamel,

ceramic, porcelain, pottery, clay,
earthenware, stone(ware), metal,
(cut-)glass, crystal, pedestal, funerary,
modern, classical, Greek, Canopic

vegetable, vegetables (garden-)fresh,
green(house), home-grown, organic,
pesticide-free, ripe, crunchy, crisp, hard,
sturdy, delectable, flavourful, savoury,
tasty, tangy, colourful, saccharine, leafy,
starchy, meaty, unusual, exotic, scarce,
rare, raw, mixed, low-calorie, high-calorie,
day-old, stale, soggy, mealy, soft, gooey,
blotchy, clammy, mouldy, insipid,
tasteless, flavourless, rotten,
pesticide-laden, frozen, out-of-season,
seasonal, culinary, (in)edible, ornamental,
root, inflorescent, cruciferous,
umbelliferous

vegetation See also *plant* exuberant,
luxurious, luxuriant, (super)abundant, lush,
thick, dense, profuse, fresh, new, gross,
sprouting, vanishing, rank, sparse, fragile,
thin, scrawny, spiny, scragg(l)y, spongy,
thorny, tangled, tangly, riparian

vehicle, vehicles (un)safe, (un)reliable,
(un)comfortable, cosy, (un)stable,
(un)certified, (un)registered, (un)licensed,
rickety, decrepit, derelict, battered,
glass-shattered, elderly, old-fashioned,
odd-looking, pedal-powered, horse-drawn,
one-horse, wheeled, three-wheel,
two-wheeled, four-wheel-drive, all-terrain,
over-snow, no-frills, inexpensive, antique,
light, off-road, spare, motor(-driven),
utility, sport-utility, farm, commuter,
recreational, self-contained,
electric(-powered), solar-powered, robotic

veil, veils discreet, impenetrable, thick,
thin, filmy, gauzy, transparent, traditional,
bridal, mourning, religious

vein, veins (blood vessel) tight, bulbous,
tremulous, enlarged, swollen, constricted,
rubbery, purplish, livid, blue,
slate-coloured, slaty, synthetic, external,
varicose, jugular, femoral, basilic,
pulmonary

vendor, vendors eager, anxious, persistent,
tenacious, stubborn, pushy, aggressive,
bugle-throated, illegal, roving, mobile,
itinerant

veneration See *respect*

vengeance understandable, rampant,
swift, summary, immediate, unquenchable,
disproportionate, unappeasable, futile,
spiteful, devastating, brutal, petty, wanton,
unfocused, primal

venture, ventures viable, innovative,
special, ambitious, daring, extravagant,
(un)lucky, (un)fortunate, (un)wise, risky,
high-risk, hazardous, costly, controversial,
dubious, upstart, marginal, half-baked,
doomed(-to-fail), ill-starred, speculative,
joint, cooperative, operating, scientific,
industrial, commercial, business,
mercantile, military

verandah, verandahs See *porch*

verb, verbs finite, infinite (non-finite),
transitive, intransitive, regular, irregular,
weak, strong, defective, auxiliary,
copulative, principal, substantive,
athematic, deponent, reflexive

verdict, verdicts final, inescapable,
(un)welcome, (un)favourable,
(un)equivocal, harsh, perverse, (un)safe,
(un)appealable, (un)assailable, iffy, mixed,
unanimous, majority, special, open

verse, verses flowing, harmonious,
accomplished, masterly, tender, dainty,
delightful, graceful, elegant, smooth, terse,
bright, airy, facile, well-rhymed,
incandescent, heated, hectic, forthright,
dense, (over-)colourful, droll, taut,
(un)laboured, (un)pleasant, rigorous,
sonorous, cacophonous, (un)imaginative,
spiritless, soulless, tuneless, flabby, careless,
dull, clumsy, (un)ambiguous, artificial,
sterile, rough, ribald, trumped-up,
execrable, light, facetious, playful,
convivial, amatory, hortatory, impromptu,
occasional, (un)rhymed, free, blank,
end-stopped, run-on, rove-over, bound,
alliterative, dactylic, iambic, accentual,
comic, humorous, satiric(al), ironic,
elegiac, free, heroic, romantic, nostalgic,
evocative, reflective, narrative, artificial,
conventional, amoeb(a)ean, lapidary

version, versions elegant, succinct,
(in)correct, (un)reliable, faithful,
(in)accurate, inspired, extant, modern,
liberal, popular, (un)satisfactory,
indistinguishable, one-sided, second-rate,
distorted, misleading, dishonest, unfaithful,
watered-down, rudimentary, alternative,
authoritative, definitive, standard,
(un)official, original, final, miniature,
foreign, international

vessel, vessels See also *ship* and *boat* seaworthy, sea-going, ocean-going, sturdy, fast, swift, majestic, ornate, submersible, sloop-rigged, schooner-rigged, square-rigged, clinker-built, carvel-built, twin-hulled, fore-and-aft, engine-driven, nuclear-powered, nuclear-armed, two-masted, three-masted, oared, tidal, deep-draft, elemental, tight, leaky, rusty, frail, rickety, (over)crowded, waterlogged, auxiliary, merchant, naval, commercial

vest, vests (1: undergarment) lightweight, multipurpose, conservative, fancy, bulletproof, thermal, lacy, woollen, silky

vest, vests (2: waistcoat) See *waistcoat*

veteran, veterans See also *soldier* battle-hardened, decorated, disabled, one-legged, embittered

veto, vetoes absolute, limited, suspensory, pocket

vibration, vibrations sonic, harmonic, weak, strong, severe, deep(-toned), constant, natural, artificial

vice, vices unnatural, detestable, unspeakable, nameless, carnal, constitutional, ingrown, innate, hidden

victim, victims unwitting, unsuspecting, trusting, unwary, prostrate, innocent, helpless, easy, ready, hopeless, gullible, unintentional, (more-than-)willing, hapless, unfortunate, unlucky, (long-)suffering, anguished, pathetic, unarmed, unintended, doomed, distraught, aggrieved, potential, sacrificial

victory, victories crushing, grinding, smashing, overwhelming, sweeping, resounding, stunning, thrilling, startling, astonishing, astounding, amazing, lightning, convincing, enduring, lasting, elated, exultant, glorious, bright, sweet, welcome, sensational, decisive, conclusive, definitive, assured, clear(-cut), certain, indisputable, unquestionable, indubitable, undeniable, unopposed, absolute, outright, landslide, unprecedented, unparalleled, unequalled, unmatched, exceptional, extraordinary, signal, incredible, unbelievable, magnificent, remarkable, splendid, marvellous, spectacular, momentous, significant, story-book, substantial, tremendous, mighty, massive, immense, huge, total, unmitigated, broad, great, secure, notable, famous, landmark,

renowned, well-known, real, veritable, apparent, important, major, slow, ultimate, bloodless, easy, facile, swift, runaway, narrow, partial, lopsided, bloody, costly, hollow, empty, cheap, elusive, controversial, dubious, joyless, minor, little, meagre, marginal, trivial, easy; unexpected, (much-)deserved, short-lived, moral, technical, strategic, battlefield, tactical, diplomatic, personal, territorial, psychological, Cadmean, Pyrrhic; wingless

view, views (1: scene) See also *scene* knock-out, priceless, scenic, panoramic, distinct, distinctive, eloquent, clear, open, spacious, full-face, comprehensive, extravagant, wide, broad-windowed, heady, hazy, lateral, obscure, unlimited, unobstructed, uninterrupted, unimpeded, telescopic, aerial

view, views (2: viewpoint) compelling, realistic, understanding, tolerant, thoughtful, pacifistic, optimistic, rosy, cheery, messianic, sunny, sanguine, (un)balanced, sound, (im)mature, detached, impartial, unbiased, disinterested, objective, fresh, interesting, moderate, coherent, accurate, well-formed, lenient, unique, original, valuable, no-nonsense, (un)clear, (in)distinct, (in)definite, firm, strong, daring, luminous, (pre)dominant, prevailing, favourable, fashionable, convenient, advanced, radical, (un)orthodox, conventional, traditional, parochial, conservative, stereotypical, long-held, unaltered, unchanged, unhedged, (un)committed, shifting, outworn, out-of-date, narrow, smug, limited, one-sided, distorted, polemical, outspoken, forward, subjective, incompatible, opposing, dissenting, conflicting, discordant, contrarian, disparate, diverging, divergent, diverse, controversial, startling, renegade, unchallenged, incomprehensible, obscure, dim, unflattering, unfavourable, unsavoury, alarming, eccentric, heretical, prejudicial, opinionated, dogmatic, partial, self-centred, self-involved, negative, melancholy, gloomy, pessimistic, cynical, stern, anarchistic, indefensible, erroneous, jaundiced, embittered, slanted, repugnant, adverse, contemptuous, belittling, surface, mistaken, naïve, withering, essentialist, sceptical, philosophical, personal, inside, simplistic, intuitive, holistic, contemporary, revisionist, utilitarian, patrician, minority

viewer, viewers discriminating, attentive, eager, absorbed, credulous, docile, moderate, heavy, light, indiscriminate

vigilance alert, wary, wakeful, careful, watchful, persevering, eternal, undiminished, unremitting, constant, unceasing, ceaseless, unfailing, uninterrupted, perpetual

vigour See *vitality*

villa, villas See *house* and *home*

village, villages exurban, picturesque, postcard, quaint, pretty, lovely, fascinating, charming, beautiful, colourful, legendary, neat, immaculate, tidy, self-sufficient, booming, carefree, cheery, friendly, hospitable, medieval, historic, neolithic, unspoiled, peaceful, quiet, tranquil, serene, calm, somnolent, drowsy, sleepy, lethargic, lifeless, placid, silent, retired, solitary, lonely, far-flung, remote, outlying, distant, inaccessible, secluded, cloistered, sequestered, out-of-the-way, unknown, obscure, unchanging, tiny, little, miniature, small, diminutive, huddled, cramped, congested, populous, sprawling, spread-out, neighbouring, border, crossroads, upcountry, coastal, seaside, riverside, stilted, water-girt, mountain(-bound), upland, alpine, rural, nearby, flat, land-locked, shaggy, dispirited, rude, desolate, dusty, humble, primitive, wretched, ramshackle, scrubby, squalid, stark, dead-(and-)alive, dirt-poor, poverty-stricken, ancestral, native, peasant, rural; Olympic

villain, villains utter, proper, absolute, primary, arch, chief, principal, unmitigated, thoroughgoing, stony-hearted, veritable, shrewd, cunning, crafty, tricky, sly, motiveless, repulsive, condemnable, deep-dyed, double-dyed, confirmed, inveterate, raffish, rakish, perfidious, unscrupulous, unconscionable, evil, vicious, wretched, scheming, murderous-looking, omnipotent, fallen, lik(e)able

villainy See *villain*

vindication, vindications See *defence*

violation, violations trivial, minor, petty, unconfirmed, alleged, (un)common, (un)justifiable, (un)acceptable, clear, direct, serious, grave, gross, flagrant, extravagant, blatant, shocking, crude, nonsensical, mindless, senseless, repeated, scattered, fundamental, (un)ethical

violence unrelenting, relentless, pitiless, heartless, ruthless, remorseless, merciless, unpleasant, vicious, savage, outrageous, nightmarish, lawless, blind, bigoted, profane, insane, mindless, senseless, meaningless, inexplicable, gratuitous, (un)justified, (un)necessary, wanton, unrestrained, random, unruly, chaotic, uncontrollable, unnatural, grisly, indiscriminate, insidious, awesome, terrible, cruel, bloody, knock-down, repressive, widespread, rampant, endemic, mass(ive), excessive, unprecedented, large-scale, full-scale, unresolvable, inevitable, unavoidable, incredible, unbelievable, explosive, apocalyptic, cold-blooded, outright, persistent, recurrent, systematic, sudden, sporadic, scattered, random, potential, visible, civil, domestic, communal, ethnic, racial, tribal, factional, sectarian, religious, political, psychological, physical, sexual, verbal, drug-related, election-related, mob, ritual(ized)

violet (colour) See *purple* and *colour*

violinist, violinists See *musician*

virtue, virtues austere, strait-laced, untarnished, unsullied, speckless, unblemished, unspotted, spotless, glorious, unwavering, impregnable, rigid, prudish, long-lasting, eternal, old(-fashioned), traditional, cloistered, humane, heroic, sovereign, supreme, chief, cardinal, moral, theological; easy

virus, viruses stubborn, (un)common, ubiquitous, unidentified, mysterious, as-yet-unknown, lethal, (near-)fatal, deadly, mutant, mutated, virulent, infectious, contagious, malignant, pernicious, filtrable, harmless

visa, visas essential, compulsory, valid, temporary, short-term, long-term, (un)conditional, restrictive, transit

visage See *face* and *appearance*

visibility perfect, clear, excellent, decent, unobstructed, impaired, reduced, poor, (near-)zero

vision (1: ability to see) piercing, (in)distinct, clear, keen, sharp, acute, good, excellent, great, (in)substantial, (im)perfect, normal, functional, small, partial, defective, minimal, rudimentary, fuzzy, bleary, hazy, misty, dim, feeble, failing, poor, (un)limited, clouded, bleared, restricted, restorable, double, dual, split, peripheral, binocular, dichromic, myopic, near

vision (2: foresight; imagination; mental image) uplifting, fascinating, tantalizing, beatific, divine, heavenly, immortal, prophetic, apocalyptic, sympathetic, halcyon, unique, lambent, vibrant, distant, far-sighted, far-reaching, expansive, ambitious, commanding, grandiose, rosy, idyllic, imaginative, floating, fleeting, preposterous, unaccountable, hallucinatory, eccentric, comic, staggering, grim, purblind, pitiless, simplistic, detailed, unfulfilled, distorted, momentary, personal, popular, telepathic, heavenly, supernatural, strategic, global, heroic, religious, poetic, imaginative, psychedelic, Utopian

visit, visits stimulating, enjoyable, (un)pleasant, (un)satisfactory, goodwill, conciliatory, fence-mending, informative, eventful, (un)comfortable, nice, timely, recurrent, (in)frequent, (ir)regular, (un)seasonable, (in)opportune, rare, impromptu, spontaneous, lightning, hasty, flying, fleeting, swift, quick, brief, hurried, long, lingering, overnight, nocturnal, five-country, crowded, (un)eventful, (in)discreet, mysterious, furtive, illicit, exhaustive, wearing, consuming, irksome, fateful, nostalgic, tense, stiff, stilted, awkward, dull, fawning, obligatory, unnecessary, unceremonious, well-timed, ill-timed, (un)premeditated, (un)scheduled, rescheduled, unannounced, uninterrupted, (dis)continued, extended, long-drawn-out, protracted, intended, (in)formal, (un)official, state, personal, conjugal, casual, occasional, surprise, to-and-fro, reciprocal, subsequent, follow-up, working, valedictory, return

visiting See *visit*

visitor, visitors (un)welcome, (ir)regular, (in)frequent, (un)likely, unidentified, constant, habitual, repeat, daily, casual,

intermittent, transient, short-time, first-time, occasional, surprise, mysterious, anonymous, persistent, eminent, high-level, talkative, boring, curious, bogus

vitality living, overflowing, overwhelming, abounding, exuberant, impetuous, vehement, ardent, fervent, feverish, impassioned, passionate, fond, rushing, tremendous, terrific, voracious, indomitable, unquenchable, inextinguishable, radiant, contagious, youthful, restless, ox-like, dizzying, remarkable, surprising, astonishing, amazing, astounding, spiritual, physical, sexual

vitamin, vitamins essential, vital, fat-soluble, water-soluble

vivacity See *vitality*

vocabulary rich, extensive, enormous, standard, archaic, flabby, exotic, specialist, (in)formal, (un)limited, technical, foreign, classical; active (use), passive (recognition)

vocation, vocations See *profession* and *occupation* (1)

vodka, vodkas See *liquor*

vogue, vogues See *fashion*

voice, voices soothing, faltering, dying, appealing, yearning, alluring, ringing, rattling, melting, piping, piercing, commanding, grating, rasping, wailing, wavering, thundering, piping, quavering, trembling, rumbling, resounding, reassuring, simpering, ravishing, enchanting, engaging, bewitching, captivating, charming, haunting, sweet-sounding, deep-sounding, hollow-sounding, squealing, dissenting, ingratiating, breaking, melodious, cadenced, rhythmic(al), mellifluous, dulcet, sweet, honeyed, beautiful, delightful, rich, lush, gifted, remarkable, racy, (un)pleasant, agreeable, melodic, musical, beauteous, tuneful, harmonious, magical, hypnotic, voluble, wistful, suave, loving, blithe, cheery, cheerful, gay, thoughtful, soulful, solicitous, hearty, friendly, breezy, (un)sympathetic, affable, warm, limpid, fluid, crystalline, clear, bright, (in)audible, candid, distinct(ive), whispery, mellow, smooth, tender, languid, calm, quiet, laconic, fluty, resonant, fear-struck, bass, (un)familiar, (un)recognizable, confident,

hollow, weary, restrained, deep, raggedy,
slushy, persuasive, argumentative, light,
querulous, fretful, taut, tinny, tinned,
crisp, thready, treble, tentative, trembly,
shaky, silky, soft, firm, soapy, bubbly,
plaintive, supplicating, (un)even, big,
cavernous, dim, steady, flexible,
inexorable, peremptory, cold, neutral,
strong, full, guttural, frail, feeble,
effeminate, haughty, aristocratic, cultured,
deferential, strained, ragged, muted, thin,
dry, reedy, small, still, thick, squeaky,
scratchy, fluty, flat, toneless, patrician,
weepy, lugubrious, tearful, timid,
breathless, thready, throaty, crusty, giggly,
sombre, sepulchral, natural, sensual,
voluptuous, sultry, masculine, feminine,
little, no-nonsense, tremulous, vibrant,
harsh, leathery, cracked, distorted, croaky,
raucous, bass, hoarse, plangent, brittle,
husky, sonorous, abrasive, brazen, loud,
stentorian, high-toned, high-pitched,
bell-like, dominant, imperious,
authoritative, derisive, abusive, shrill,
sharp, metallic, powerhouse, powerful,
dramatic, (o)rotund, screechy, queer,
constrained, eerie, discordant, dull, rough,
grim, lifeless, monotonous, toneless, acrid,
inharmonious, sour, bitter, sceptical,
strident, twangy, singsong, gruff, gravelly,
raspy, unctuous, uncouth, suppressed,
slurred, falsetto, nasal

volcano, volcanoes rumbling, groaning,
seething, trembling, towering,
breathtaking, jutting, glowing, smoking,
solitary, lofty, majestic, mighty, gigantic,
massive, immense, eruptive, explosive,
angry, intermittent, dangerous, (in)active,
still-active, quiescent, (now-)dormant,
long-dormant, (long-)dead, (long-)extinct,
blown-out, sunken, underwater, subsea,
snow-mantled

volume, volumes See also *book*
sumptuous, elegant, handsome,
complementary, miscellaneous, massive,
stout, weighty, heavy, mammoth, hefty,
ponderous, average-size, well-worn,
weathered, much-read, handy, pocket,
octavo, duodecimo, miniature, omnibus,
companion

volunteer, volunteers energetic, dedicated,
enthusiastic, eager, conscientious,
(in)active, (un)willing, reluctant

vote, votes solid, (in)valid, (il)legal,
unanimous, overwhelming, honest,
(un)conscientious, fair, free, light, heavy,
lopsided, historic, crucial, (in)decisive,
highest, lowest, clear-cut, (un)decided,
positive, negative, dissent-free, dissenting,
unbiased, swing, fraudulent, blank, key,
snap, casting, proxy, postal, straw,
popular, public, electoral, multicandidate,
(non-)confidence, first-round, preliminary,
procedural

voter, voters independent, disinterested,
affirmative, (in)eligible, fictitious,
phantom, dummy, illiterate, swing, ethnic,
anonymous

voting See also *vote* reluctant, strategic,
democratic, cumulative, preferential,
multiple

vow, vows (in)effective, lofty, broken,
ardent, earnest, passionate, solemn,
fervent, defiant, grudging, reciprocal,
religious, monastic, nuptial

vowel, vowels rising, intervening, sombre,
short, long, sloshy, strident, well-rounded,
flat, atonic, close, slurred, acute, pure

voyage, voyages See *journey*

vulgarity unbelievable, cheap, boisterous,
crude, disgusting, ill-bred, ill-mannered,
odious, raffish, rakish, sordid, uncouth,
earthy, gross, coarse, sordid, low, mean,
Falstaffian, Hogarthian, Rabelaisian

wage, wages decent, honest,
high(er-than-average), steep, superior,
substantial, inflated, solid, (in)adequate,
(un)reasonable, (un)fair, stagnant, average,
low, skimpy, scant(y), meagre, pitiful,
sweated, daily, hourly, weekly, minimum,
base, basic, nominal, living, back,
retroactive, real, windfall

waist, waists high, low, ample, bulging,
slender, slim, thin, trim, wasp, non-existent

waistcoat, waistcoats fancy, plaited,
plicated, shirred

wait, waiting (im)patient, keen, eager,
anxious, watchful, empty, resigned,
lengthy, protracted, long, endless,
interminable, fruitless, (un)reasonable,
(un)bearable, weary, irksome, tedious,
boring, tiring, exasperating, agonizing,
needless, unnecessary, unexpected, tense,
nervous, desperate, wearisome, torturous

waiter, waiters accommodating, obliging,
courteous, solicitous, helpful, informed,
decorous, polite, smart, cheerful,
(in)attentive, affable, (un)pleasant,
(un)friendly, obsequious, fawning,
white-coated, starched, uniformed,
overwrought, rude, surly, snotty, sloppy,
uninterested, (non-)English-speaking,
elusive, dumb, uncommunicative, slow,
(ir)regular, head

waitress, waitresses See also *waiter*
pretty, charming, attractive, enchanting,
lively, pert, tart, motherly, slatternly

walk, walking (1: the act of walking)
soothing, relaxing, delightful, leisurely,
quiet, slow, unhurried, brisk, swift, quick,
fast, vigorous, energetic, toilsome,
laborious, sharp, goodish, marathon,
constitutional, daily, sunrise, moonlight,
noctambulous, 45-minute, confident, easy,
aggressive, springy, jerky, ape-like, clumsy,
unsteady, stumbling, wary, aristocratic,
effeminate, uphill, solitary, solo, lonely,
aimless, casual, recreational, guided

walk, walks (2: path) See *path*

walker, walkers rapid, swift, brisk,
nimble, active, energetic, hearty, avid,
seasoned, hardy, dedicated, enthusiastic,
weary, ordinary, recreational, competitive,
race

walkout, walkouts See *strike* (1)

walkway, walkways See *path*

wall, walls solid, stout, strong, sturdy,
thick, massive, gigantic, mighty, expansive,
towering, forbidding, impregnable,
impenetrable, invincible, climbable,
opaque, cyclopean, concrete, granite,
masonry, brick, stucco, earth, mud-brick,
clapboard, (dry)stone, squared-stone,
cinder-block, modular, marbled,
marble-lined, tapered, stencilled,
crenellated, frescoed, fabric-covered,
mosaic-covered, plaster(ed), tiled, textured,
mottled, recessed, ivied, ivy-covered,
concentric, porous, rubble-cored,
metre-thick, vertical, slanting, soundproof,
resonant, blind, blank, bare, uncluttered,
windowless, bullet-pocked, cracked,
weather-worn, flaky, scaly, slimy, dusky,
grimy, shabby, fragile, tumbling, adjacent,
adjoining, inner, outer, interior, exterior,
internal, external, retaining, dividing,
sheltering, (accordion-)folding, movable,
defensive; intestinal, abdominal

wallet, wallets See *purse*

wallpaper, wallpapers washable,
psychedelic, hideous, floral, flowered,
figured, sprigged, textured, gold-flecked,
Regency-striped, stencilled, silk, flock

wanderer, wanderers roofless, homeless,
penniless, aimless, truant, incorrigible,
unreformable, unruly, tough, stricken,
pedestrian

wandering, wanderings aimless,
unaimed, vagabond, footloose, erratic,
goalless, unpurposeful, futile, lonely,
endless, romantic

want, wants See *need*

war, wars gritty, heroic, courageous,
hardy, resolute, just, static, continuous,
intermittent, drawn-out, protracted,
ongoing, perpetual, unending, endless,
ceaseless, unceasing, interminable, long-
range, on-again-off-again, imminent,
impending, chronic, unprecedented,
avertible, (in)evitable, (un)avoidable,
unnecessary, misguided, complex,
(un)limited, (in)conclusive, unwinnable,
unpredictable, unprovoked, active, close,
chimerical, messy, desperate, ugly,

immoral, large-scale, full-scale, full-fledged, all-out, widespread, covert, unforgettable, intractable, deadly, genocidal, fratricidal, implacable, gruesome, ghastly, nightmarish, grisly, devilish, diabolic, fiendish, vindictive, hot, stupid, insane, senseless, mindless, petty, futile, bitter, internecine, fierce, savage, vicious, brutal, terrible, dreadful, heartless, remorseless, pitiless, ruthless, merciless, relentless, unrelenting, cruel, appalling, debilitating, devastating, catastrophic, disastrous, destructive, costly, calamitous, ruinous, tough, vigorous, bloody, intense, vengeful, vitriolic, dirty, cut-throat, cushy, unexposed, (as-yet-)undeclared, forgotten, invasive, no-win, two-front, total, preventive, strategic, tactical, offensive, defensive, (un)conventional, (un)orthodox, aerial, atomic, bacteriological, chemical, biological, (thermo)nuclear, revolutionary, underground, guer(r)illa, secessionist, anti-colonial, naval, marine, submarine, cold, diplomatic, mock, mimic, proxy, economic, religious, holy, civil, regional, brush-fire, psychological, verbal, paper, wordy, (anti-)drug, feudal, tribal, ethnic, racial, technological, high-tech, electronic

ward, wards (of hospital) many-bedded, communal, private, side, isolation, surgical, cardiac, neurological, geriatric, paediatric, chronic, acute, orthopaedic, neurosurgical, mental, psychiatric, paraplegic

wardrobe, wardrobes (1: clothes cupboard) capacious, large, roomy, spacious, fusty, mouldy, musty, stuffy, double, walk-in

wardrobe, wardrobes (2: clothes) See *clothes*

warehouse, warehouses See *building*

warfare, warfares See *war*

warning, warnings salutary, timely, opportune, clear, explicit, apt, unmistakable, blunt, terse, tongue-in-cheek, red-lettered, strong, tough(ly-worded), strongly-worded, stern, solemn, nervous, tense, angry, drastic, strident, poignant, ominous, apocalyptic, chilling, frantic, prescient, dire, dark, grim, blasphemous, abrupt, sufficient, final, previous, early, little, minimal, unnoticed, unjustified, veiled, fake, false, advance

warranty, warranties See *guarantee*

warrior, warriors chivalrous, gallant, intrepid, dauntless, fearless, stalwart, resolute, heroic, brave, valiant, doughty, audacious, daring, bold, steely, tenacious, invincible, stout, virile, formidable, fearsome, fierce, brutal, savage, truculent, ferocious, belligerent, cruel, crafty, resplendent, grim, compulsive, braggart, renegade, fallen, frontline, paramilitary, unknown

warship, warships See also *ship* powerful, nuclear-capable, nuclear-powered, nuclear-armed, lame-duck, obsolete, antiquated, outmoded, amphibious

wasp, wasps See also *insect* rasping, buzzing, irritable, frisky, lively, feisty, social, solitary

waste, wastes (1: failure to make proper use of something) sheer, substantial, tremendous, gargantuan, phenomenal, fantastic, (in)evitable, (un)avoidable, unnecessary, needless, senseless, mindless, sinful, incredible, unbelievable, inexcusable, unregulated, terrible, bleak, shocking, ghastly, deplorable, hopeless, futile

waste, wastes (2: discarded material) persistent, hazardous, dangerous, destructive, deadly, toxic, infectious, corrosive, ignitable, reactive, intermediate-level, high-level, low-level, solid, liquid, mushy, recyclable, (petro)chemical, industrial, urban, domestic, household, gaseous, organic, biological, intestinal, (bio)medical, radioactive, atomic, nuclear, synthetic, transuranic, cotton

wasteland arid, barren, sterile, uninhabitable, inhospitable, dreary, bleak, ghastly, forbidding, uninviting, trackless, windblown, scrubby, soggy, sprawling, scorching, stone, gravel, pebbled, icy, polar

watch, watches (1: a portable timepiece) precise, perfect, accurate, expensive, quality, valuable, brand-new, fine, elegant, trendy, (un)dependable, (un)reliable, (ir)reparable, trouble-free, poor, run-down, cheap, shoddy, gaudy, tawdry, garish, flashy, counterfeit, ticking, (un)wound, overwound, fast, slow, faulty, irregular, erratic, unregulated, unset, self-winding, analogue, digital, mechanical, quartz, antique, waterproof, shockproof,

antimagnetic, electric, automatic,
stainless-steel, silver, gold,
diamond(-studded), faceted, designer,
solar, electronic, wind-up, disposable

watch, watching, watchfulness
(2: close observation) discerning, acute,
intent, close, avid, careful, sharp,
wide-awake, open-eyed, diligent, vigilant,
devotional, constant, continuous,
incessant, steady, sphinx-like, intrepid,
intermittent

watchdog, watchdogs alert, attentive,
observant, vigilant, (wide-)awake, zealous

water, waters brawling, murmuring,
purling, swashing, swishing, rumbling,
running, receding, seething, gushing,
rippling, (free-)flowing, fast-flowing,
whirling, pouring, trickling, surging,
tumbling, splashing, bracing, refreshing,
fresh, limpid, (glass-)clear, transparent,
lucid, crystal(-clear), plain, pure, pristine,
potable, drinkable, suitable, sanitary,
healthy, (un)safe, sweet, clean,
uncontaminated, mineral-rich,
mineral-laden, sediment-laden, oxygen-rich,
calm, pacific, tranquil, silent, quiet, still,
motionless, placid, slick, limpid,
undisturbed, stagnant, standing, confined,
captive, moody, mysterious, scenic,
moonlit, sun-spangled, sun-dappled,
glittering, sparkling, glassy, stratified,
shallow, deep, abyssal, fathomless,
unfathomed, thermal, steaming, scalding,
boiling, hot, cold, tepid, frigid, gelid,
freezing, glacial, ice-cold, ice-covered,
ice-free, heavy, dead, soapy, solid, inky,
black, opaque, silt-brown, blue-green,
jade-green, indigo, moon-streaked, sunless,
low, high, slack, sluggish, fast, roily,
(un)navigable, unpredictable, chest-deep,
hip-deep, troubled, agitated, mist-draped,
lumpy, rough, sudsy, murmurous,
turbulent, copious, bubbly, foaming,
foamy, frothy, choppy, swollen, muddy,
murky, slimy, turbid, mucky, impure,
questionable, suspect, foul, deadly, fetid,
putrid, stinking, untreated, untested,
(oil-)polluted, tainted, insanitary,
dangerous, tricky, briny, salt(y), saltish,
brackish, saline, corrosive, soft, hard,
acidic, alkaline, mineral, fizzy, bottled,
piped(-in), uncharted, coastal, inland,
territorial, international, tidal, arctic, open,

heavy, white, gravitational, primordial,
holy, subterranean

waterfall, waterfalls roaring, thundering,
murmuring, raging, foaming, trickling,
billowing, tumbling, pouring, seething,
unremitting, sparkling, gleaming,
diaphanous, legendary, dramatic,
spectacular, thunderous, awesome,
unrelenting, relentless, ruthless, merciless,
feathery, slender, bridal-veil, secluded,
man-made

waterfront, waterfronts lively, scenic,
colourful

waterway, waterways safe, neutral,
(un)navigable, (un)safe, (in)secure,
(in)accessible, open, closed, slow, tranquil,
busy, meandering, man-made

wave, waves rumbling, thundering,
hissing, rattling, rustling, lapping,
smashing, swashing, swishing, receding,
breaking, billowing, struggling, quartering,
hammering, hurrying, rippling, rising,
surging, gentle, lazy, little, soundless,
rhythmic, (ir)regular, uniform, iridescent,
successive, incessant, ceaseless, endless,
unbroken, recurrent, frothy, foamy,
foaming, spumy, white-tipped, incoming,
tide-powered, swift, lateral, caterpillar-like,
scalloped, steep(-fronted), high,
three-metre, heavy, mighty, enormous,
siz(e)able, extensive, huge, giant, gigantic,
mammoth, monstrous, powerful,
mountainous, towering, gale-driven,
turbulent, restless, freak(ish), disorderly,
yeasty, choppy, tangled, rough, concussive,
violent, wild, vicious, ferocious, perilous,
(life-)threatening, destructive, terrible,
awesome, cruel, tricky, uncontrolled,
unstoppable, (un)negotiable, cold, tidal,
short, silver, light, continuous, transverse;
seismic, electromagnetic, acoustical,
ultrasonic; permanent

wax, waxes solid, soft, pliant, yielding,
carven, paste, commercial, white, mineral,
palm, wool, paraffin, vegetable, Canauba,
Chinese

way, ways (1: manner; method) See also
manner and *method* proper, right,
acceptable, confident, enthusiastic,
winsome, logical, graceful, sensitive,
marvellous, unique, civil, persuasive,
rational, polite, viable, practicable,
creative, equitable, efficient, imaginative,

telling, effective, frugal, ponderous,
backhand, decided, pronounced, marked,
humble, ceremonial, authoritarian,
haughty, deliberate, overwhelming,
traditional, old-fashioned, ancient,
hidebound, mischievous, unacceptable,
vague, inefficient, inscrutable, radical,
forward, adventurous, peculiar, erratic,
mutable, inconstant, unpredictable,
stealthy, roundabout, ill-natured,
cantankerous, awkward, gauche, clumsy,
boorish, negligent, treacherous, irrational,
devilish, wanton, unbecoming, crazy,
outlandish, childish

way, ways (2: path; road; course;
route) See *path* and *road*

weakness, weaknesses glaring, besetting,
anaemic, wearisome, profound, extreme,
shameful, lamentable, pitiful, deplorable,
despicable, woeful, inherent, human,
physical, constitutional

wealth staggering, colossal, vast, fabulous,
great, substantial, tremendous, spectacular,
enormous, unending, inexhaustible,
boundless, limitless, unlimited, eternal,
explosive, heady, undreamed-of,
unheard-of, untold, unprecedented, fabled,
mythical, amazing, remarkable,
unimaginable, unbelievable, incredible,
wild, undeniable, imaginary, conspicuous,
evident, (in)visible, hidden, untapped,
instant, sudden, new-found, potential,
unattainable, inaccessible, unreachable,
precarious, little, ill-gotten, unexplained,
wanton, sinful, comparative, relative,
taxable, natural, material, earthly, worldly,
paper

weapon, weapons sophisticated, modern,
up-to-date, advanced, high-tech,
(in)effective, telling, large-calibre,
muscular, powerful, high-powered, potent,
durable, costly, high-priced, high-cost,
enormous, first-strike, rapid-fire, (il)legal,
(un)concealable, aggressive, vicious,
indiscriminate, (non-)lethal, deadly, fatal,
doomsday, devastating, catastrophic,
dreadful, fearful, fearsome, horrendous,
horrific, evil, wicked, contemptible, cruel,
dubious, controversial, primitive, crude,
antiquated, outmoded, out-of-date,
obsolete, vintage, inadequate, worthless,
paltry, defective, fake, (un)serviceable,
explosive, (un)loaded, heavy, light,

portable, small, side, bloodstained, bladed,
pole, (un)conventional, non-conventional,
chemical, biological, bacteriological,
tactical, offensive, defensive, protective,
anti-personnel, infrared, (thermo)nuclear,
(semi-)automatic, anti-tank, long-range,
medium-range, short-range, battlefield,
infantry, ground, (anti-)aircraft,
(sub)marine, binary, dummy, psychotronic,
medieval, strategic, heraldic

weaponry See *weapon*

weather smiling, entrancing, relaxing,
enervating, soothing, conciliatory, idyllic,
fine, beautiful, nice, gorgeous, delightful,
marvellous, wonderful, splendid,
magnificent, perfect, ideal, mild,
(in)temperate, brisk, crisp, fresh,
refreshing, inspiriting, salubrious,
(dis)agreeable, pleasant, balmy, lovely,
stable, equable, (un)settled, clear,
seasonable, reliable, promising,
(in)clement, (un)merciful, serene, bland,
bright, prosperous, calm, quiet, tranquil,
incredible, unbelievable, exceptional,
extraordinary, abnormal, unusual,
appropriate, (un)cooperative, suitable,
helpful, (un)favourable, propitious, good,
right, benign, improving, normal, sunny,
windy, breezy, draughty, gusty, squally,
stormy, thundery, snowy, frosty, foggy,
misty, hazy, muggy, thick, bitter,
(bitter-)cold, icy, arctic, cool, severe,
extreme, sub-zero, frigid, raw, chilly,
snappy, sharp, wintry, warm(ish), hot,
sweltering, sultry, steamy, steam-bath,
humid, sticky, damp, soggy, clammy,
close, breathless, sleepy, wet, sloppy, rainy,
showery, drizzly, imponderable,
changeable, unstable, unsettled, moody,
erratic, crazy, weird, capricious, freak(ish),
funny, fickle, variable, inconstant,
uncertain, unreliable, dodgy, turbulent,
treacherous, unpredictable, doubtful,
adverse, hostile, gleamy, sulky, dismal,
grim, gloomy, unspeakable, terrible, filthy,
dirty, foul, ugly, tempestuous, wretched,
atrocious, pestiferous, blue, dark,
depressing, dispiriting, disheartening,
appalling, nasty, rugged, insalubrious,
villainous, wild, brutal, beastly, savage,
disagreeable, unpleasant, fair, heavy, dull,
dreary, awful, vile, sour, abominable,
damnable, gloomy, ill, violent, oppressive,

miserable, bad, ghastly, cruel, vicious, wicked, harsh, stark, rough, choppy, pitiless, merciless, ruthless, heartless, relentless, unrelenting, devastating

weave, weaving fancy, plain, loose, tight, close, knotty, intricate, rough

web, webs symmetrical, (un)tidy, (ir)regular, intricate, elaborate, complex, flimsy, delicate, dew-hung

wedding, weddings charming, imposing, impressive, glamorous, elaborate, extravagant, lavish, luxurious, elegant, magnificent, majestic, splendid, perfect, grand, colourful, lovely, pompous, showy, expensive, boozy, brawling, old-fashioned, (un)traditional, no-frills, (in)formal, mock, society, church, shotgun, golden, silver, pearl, ruby, diamond

weed, weeds (un)common, waist-high, dry-weather, edible, succulent, harmless, troublesome, harmful, pestilential, pernicious, devastating, rank, unsightly, ragged, sharp, leafy, broad(-leaved), coarse(-leaved), unidentified, uncontrolled, (un)controllable, (in)destructible, annual, biennial, perennial; aquatic

week, weeks See also *day* busy, hectic, solid, (un)eventful, memorable, consecutive, four-day, work, Holy, Passion

weekend, weekends See also *day* and *holiday* refreshing, satisfying, gratifying, relaxing, fascinating, enchanting, amusing, delightful, enjoyable, agreeable, wonderful, blissful, dreamy, happy, festive, jolly, joyful, merry, fine, nice, unforgettable, good, great, work-free, busy, hectic, (un)eventful, dismal, dreary

weeping hysterical, convulsive, fitful, uncontrolled, unrestrained, emotional, inconsolable, manipulative, copious, continuous, continual, incessant

weight, weights (1: the amount that a thing weighs; a unit of weight) ideal, appreciable, formidable, insuperable, (ab)normal, (extra)ordinary, unimaginable, honest, proportionate, (un)even, fluctuating, sagging, current, commensurable, invariable, intrinsic, false, total, gross, net, additional, excess, avoirdupois, metric, dead, atomic, troy, molecular

weight (2: importance; value; influence) See *importance*, *value* and *influence*

welcome, welcomes overwhelming, rousing, stirring, roaring, deep, mighty, big, grand, fantastic, elaborate, loud, uproarious, boisterous, unreserved, memorable, hysterical, rapturous, spectacular, frenzied, delirious, jubilant, extraordinary, exuberant, hearty, tumultuous, lavish, genial, charming, enthusiastic, cheerful, (un)friendly, kindly, warm, loving, genuine, sincere, emotional, grateful, cordial, ready, ecstatic, splendid, high-profile, royal, (in)hospitable, chill(y), icy, cold, cool, brusque, hostile, cautious, mixed, spontaneous, ceremonial

welfare common, public, social, material, spiritual, emotional, moral, physical, mental

well, wells gushing, deep(-bore), ultra-deep, bottomless, shallow, hand-dug, (un)productive, saline, (bone-)dry, offshore, oil, empty, octagonal, artesian, mineral, communal

well-being See *welfare*

whale, whales squealing, snorting, grunting, rumbling, sounding, spluttering, swarming, (free-)swimming, floating, diving, loafing, playful, frolicsome, wheezy, tame, gentle, docile, benign, placid, unflappable, swift, agile, flexible, manoeuvrable, graceful, magnificent, majestic, sleek, pygmy, powerful, ferocious, fearless, formidable, bloodthirsty, predatory, rapacious, carnivorous, beaked, shallow-water, deep-water, cold-adapted, right, circumpolar, humpback(ed), bowhead, toothed, baleen, killer, pilot (black), sperm, blue, grey, white (beluga), black-and-white

wheat seed-laden, (high-)quality, rippling, ripe, whole, short, lanky, beardless, bearded, winter, spring, hybrid

wheel, wheels rattling, whirling, moving, idle, creaky, toothed, spiked, grooved, (wooden-)spoked, three-spoke, iron-rimmed, notched, dished, spun, (hand-)powered, foot-powered, pneumatic-tyred, front, hind, massive, crown, disk, epicycloidal, eccentric, overshot, undershot, steering, grinding, spinning, Persian

whim, whims capricious, captious, crotchety, erratic, fanciful, desperate,

323

amusing, surprising, passing, slight,
personal

whimsy, whimsies See *whim*

whipping, whippings sound, thorough

whisky (whiskey) See also *liquor*
smooth(-tasting), nice, neat, proof,
straight, bootleg, bonded, bourbon, rye,
sour-mash, malt, Canadian, Scotch, Irish

whisper, whispers tiny, low, soft, quiet,
subdued, hushed, discernible, (in)audible,
(in)articulate, loud, leaf-like, husky,
hoarse, rasping, raspy, hollow, grim,
fretful, sepulchral, discreet, (im)polite,
furious, desperate, ominous, sly,
conspiratorial, confidential, stage

whistle, whistles (ear-)piercing, blasting,
screaming, high-pitched, sharp, shrill,
high-frequency, cheery, cheerful, merry,
musical, aerodynamic, steam; wolf

white dazzling, gleaming, blinding,
yellowish, greenish, greyish, pinkish,
bluish, pristine, pure, stark, gauzy,
unsullied, oyster, creamy, milky, icy,
antique, powdered, pasty, dirty, opaque,
sepulchral, Chinese

whiteness See *white*

whole, wholes indivisible, integral,
integrate, unified, coherent, continuous,
complete, organic

wickedness outright, enormous,
outrageous, abhorrent, depraved,
disgraceful, heinous, malicious,
mischievous, atrocious, shameful, hateful,
execrable, abominable, ingenious,
villainous, hellish, diabolical, devilish,
fiendish, ghoulish, insane, Babylonian,
Machiavellian, Mephistophelian

widow, widower unprepared, bereaved,
disconsolate, inconsolable, grief-stricken,
cheerless, dejected, vulnerable, needy,
poor, impecunious, indigent, celibate,
merry

wife, wives good, prodigious, wonderful,
faithful, virtuous, devoted, (ir)responsible,
perfect, model, ideal, quintessential,
adoring, affectionate, well-beloved, loving,
attentive, supportive, docile, tolerant,
tactful, suitable, staid, (in)dependent,
subordinate, submissive, subservient,
passive, obedient, (un)manageable,
satisfied, complacent, uncomplaining,
self-effacing, uncritical, questionless,
long-suffering, ill-used, formidable,

shrewish, abusive, ill-tempered,
bad-tempered, crabby, imperious, arrogant,
argumentative, domineering, exacting,
tactless, indiscreet, manipulative, spiteful,
sparing, frugal, thrifty, skimpy, stingy,
heedless, spendthrift, extravagant,
expensive, erring, errant, unfaithful,
flighty, runaway, negligent,
undomesticated, barren, frigid, dull, plain,
prosaic, uninteresting, commonplace,
unsuitable, plural, intended, prospective,
working, stay-at-home; common-law,
morganatic; corporate

wig, wigs trim, glamorous, towering,
obvious, awry, full, three-tailed,
professional, full-bottomed

wilderness, wildernesses breathtaking,
scenic, vivid, glorious, sublime, high,
marvellous, magnificent, splendid, fine,
gentle, priceless, rampant, vast, infinite,
boundless, unending, endless, limitless,
absolute, remote, roadless, trackless,
untracked, unscarred, uncharted,
untouched, unspoiled, uninhabited,
unpeopled, untamed, unruly, savage,
unknown, desolate, shabby, barren, sterile,
naked, bare, unprotected, raw, pure,
implacable, eternal, unconquerable,
impenetrable, rugged, silent, howling,
vicarious, diminishing, threatened,
vanishing, primitive, primeval, natural,
pristine, thorny, marshy, swampy,
forest-armoured, wooded, treeless,
mountainous, sea-girt, glacial, (sub)arctic,
(semi-)tropical

wildlife abundant, extinct, threatened,
protected

will, wills (1: statement of how property is
to be disposed of after death) basic,
current, (in)valid, (il)legal, (un)authentic,
(in)equitable, (ir)revocable, implicit,
explicit, (in)officious, (un)alterable,
(un)contested, unpublished, fake,
ambulatory, notarial, eccentric

will (2: willpower) resolute, indomitable,
adamantine, unyielding, unbending,
uncompromising, relentless, implacable,
inflexible, invincible, unshakable,
undaunted, (cast-)iron, steel, stubborn,
strong, powerful, firm, determined,
tenacious, indisputable, tough, immense,
sincere, weak, flabby, vacillating, ill,
spiteful, bitter, free, conscious, collective

willingness unconditional, real, consistent, unprecedented, feigned

willpower See *will* (2)

win crushing, devastating, decisive, quick, easy, clear, indisputable, satisfactory, emotional, tearful, (un)fair, (il)legitimate

wind, winds sighing, booming, shrieking, howling, blustering, rustling, piping, (ever-)shifting, quick-shifting, veering, circulating, whirling, swinging, billowing, tossing, taunting, raking, favourable, brisk, balmy, fresh, friendly, merciful, clement, relenting, Saturnian, fair, lively, slight, small, soft, light, gentle, thin, sleepy, soothing, bracing, invigorating, strengthening, dying, (un)faltering, tranquil, calm, mellow, (im)moderate, (in)temperate, (un)stable, (un)steady, (in)constant, restless, changeable, variable, fluky, fitful, catchy, capricious, unruly, uncontrollable, errant, frolicsome, boisterous, choppy, unpredictable, erratic, freak, whimsical, fickle, rising, swelling, following, prevailing, sweeping, persistent, sustained, incessant, ceaseless, unceasing, perpetual, tireless, outlying, adverse, contrary, contrarious, untoward, unfavourable, futile, frigid, bitter, (bone-)chilling, freezing, bleak, wintry, raw, icy, sleety, cutting, biting, searching, piercing, penetrating, (clawing-)cold, cool, glacial, chilly, nippy, arctic, polar, damp, misty, rain-bearing, rainy, rainless, snowy, snowless, dry, warm, salty, shrewd, snell, keen, arid, amazing, surprising, unexpected, unusual, frolicsome, swift, gritty, harsh, squally, vigorous, explosive, high, forcible, fierce, mighty, stiff, intense, raging, threatening, violent, angry, furious, mountainous, strong(ish), stout, rough, gusty, fretful, impetuous, tempestuous, blustery, torrid, scorching, searing, blistering, stinging, vehement, storm-force, gale(-force), hurricane-strength, upper-level, shrill, awesome, devastating, vicious, wicked, treacherous, foul, venomous, sharp, formidable, calamitous, grim, hellish, barbarous, barbaric, brutal, savage, tremendous, wild, devilish, demonic, inclement, heartless, pitiless, merciless, ruthless, relentless, unrelenting, crazy, ill, ferocious, destructive, catastrophic, deadly, unprecedented, pollen-laden, dusty, sandy, sand-blasting, indifferent, malign, turbulent, boisterous, stormy, noisy, preposterous, horrendous, tumultuous, cyclonic, horizontal, inshore, onshore, offshore, tramontane, transalpine, katabatic, anabatic, head, tail, side, cross, austral, western, solar, trade, subalpine, tropical, equatorial, equinoctial, seasonal, maritime, sea, stratospheric, leeward, berg

window, windows arched, angled, angular, slanting, sloping, curved, curving, vaulted, gabled, cathedral-style, plate-glass, stained-glass, tinted-glass, tilt-in, leaded-glass, ersatz, wire-mesh, (double-)glazed, small-paned, mullioned, latticed, frosted, opaque, one-way, sound-proof, bullet-proof, blast-proof, paneless, double, full-length, soaring, ceiling-high, floor-to-ceiling, ground-level, expansive, multi-paned, diamond-paned, shuttered, sealed, double-hung, grilled, half-open, shrouded, shaded, uncurtained, panoramic, rain-streaked, steam-covered, frost-ridden, grimy, sordid, shattered, dirt-streaked, loose, smudgy, clouded, frugal, sectional, inset, recessed, expansive, horizontal, winking, sliding, accordion, vertical, double-hung, drive-through, clerestoried, oriel, French, Gothic

wine, wines exhilarating, refreshing, cool, heavenly, suave, magnificent, splendid, great, superb, top-quality, famed, vaunted, racy, (un)distinguished, unique, premium, prized, noble, mellow, mature, (pine-barrel-)aged, heavy, ancient, old, fine, delicate, soft, smooth, rich, majestic, luscious, tasty, mouthwatering, delicious, frisky, generous, subtle, full-bodied, delightful, pleasant, sought-after, sincere, pure, elegant, attractive, lush, boutique, snob, mouth-filling, delectable, awesome, fragrant, aromatic, pricey, rare, cabinet, sweet, lively, cloying, intense, strong, potent, robust, fiery, durable, heady, sharp, conquering, forward, dry, brut, corky, nutty, fruity, raisiny, smok(e)y, grassy, effervescent, structured, eccentric, traditional, young, fresh, unusual, unattainable, unsung, pale, gold(-coloured), amber(-coloured), out-of-stock, sour, watery, neutral-base, mild, feeble, weak, foxy, flinty, insipid, bland, uninspired, dull, dubious, poor, cheap, ordinary, standard-quality, rough-edged, brambly, watered-down, low-alcohol, clear, sacramental, holy, bootleg, light, still, sparkling, organic, table, red, white, rosé, private-stock, house, all-purpose, local, domestic, varietal

wing, wings sheltering, flapping, twitching, (half-)open, graceful, swift, fast aggressive, motionless, functional, protective, long, stubby, horny, feathery, leathery, heavy, translucent, iridescent, gauzy, lacy, vibrant, flipperlike, (non)rigid, fragile, thin, weak, strong, tough, large, immense, slender, tiny, stunted, broad, pointed, curved, banded, vestigial, venous, membranous, gossamer

wink, winks knowing, designing, scheming, droll, sly, perceptible, responsive, conspiratorial

winner, winners clear(-cut), outright, sure(-fire), indisputable, big, perennial, exultant, exuberant, unexpected, (im)probable, potential, ultimate, final, overall, medal, bronze-medal, silver-medal, gold-medal

winter, winters mild, (im)moderate, (in)temperate, snowless, cruel, hard, harsh, tough, severe, bitter, fierce, arduous, terrible, rough, (bone-)chilling, cold, frigid, frosty, bland, white, devastating, snow-bound, snowy, stormy, blustery, vicious, brutal, rugged, grey, desolate, grim, bleak, sunless, squaw, record-breaking, record-setting, interminable, long, short, oncoming, waning, open, antipodean

wire, wires fine, thin, (in)flexible, tight, taut, live, hot, cylindrical, rusty, broken, tangled, cross, high-tension, electric(al), barbed, razor(-edge)

wisdom acute, guileless, infallible, mature, supreme, supernal, superlative, innate, penetrative, proverbial, conventional, traditional, folk, worldly, practical, enduring, lasting, infinite, unbounded, deep, quiet, acid, sly, craft, cunning, hard-hearted, diabolic(al), serpentine, spurious

wish, wishes warm, dearest, fervent, fond, good, express, clear, prevailing, long-standing, simple, naïve, childlike, eccentric, useless, hasty, unconscious, subliminal, subconscious, mutual

wit, wits dazzling, flashing, sparkling, twinkling, coruscating, bantering, enduring, polished, refined, nimble, lively, playful, comic, lambent, innocuous, sterling, incisive, subtle, epigrammatic, pregnant, piquant, racy, pungent, shrewd, clever, sharp, razor-like, keen, precocious, sunny, unique, inimitable, unrivalled, strong, quick, easy, ready, pointed, sugar-coated, volatile, prodigious, mercurial, peppery, self-conscious, self-assured, airy, whimsical, allusive, aggressive, pugnacious, edgy, arrogant, sharp-tongued, unmerciful, merciless, ruthless, pitiless, heartless, relentless, unrelenting, acid, ribald, vinegary, acerbic, incisive, slashing, devastating, penetrating, biting, piercing, stinging, crushing, cutting, cauterizing, unsparing, razor, tainted, malicious, mischievous, impish, poignant, trenchant, dour, sardonic, corrosive, mordant, sarcastic, caustic, satiric(al), wry, coarse, thin, forceful, forced, false, (bone-)dry, blunt, wooden, dull, perfunctory, stupid, feeble, dandiacal, earthy, mother, Attic

witch, witches wicked, evil, malicious, malign, villainous, cursed, white, grey, maligned

withdrawal, withdrawals dignified, peaceful, honourable, prudent, careful, safe, clean, speedy, rapid, hasty, prompt, stealthy, slow, imminent, belated, eventual, (over)due, (long-)overdue, massive, total, full, (in)complete, partial, limited, modest, voluntary, (un)conditional, forced, (well-)phased, systematic, tactical

witness, witnesses impeccable, credible, dependable, veracious, trustful, faithful, truthful, competent, independent, effective, expert, unflappable, (un)reliable, (un)trustworthy, (dis)honest, (un)prejudiced, interested, sufficient, perjured, false, (un)willing, (un)likely, reluctant, silent, mute, eye, key, star, Crown

witticism, witticisms See *wit*

woe, woes See *sorrow*

wolf, wolves howling, wailing, swift, cunning, dire, wild, bloodthirsty, vicious, unrelenting, ravenous, greedy, hungry, arctic, timber, grey, red

woman, women See also Appendixes A and B charming, fascinating, bewitching,

stunning, good-looking, magnetic,
attractive, beautiful, handsome,
well-formed, well-built, leggy,
well-preserved, statuesque, curvaceous,
well-groomed, well-dressed, spruce,
elegant, stylish, glamorous,
fashion-conscious, feminine, bejewelled,
fur-clad, classy, pleasant, gentle, decent,
delicate, affable, desirable, lovely, veiled,
shrouded, demure, coy, noble,
accomplished, magnificent, loving,
maternal, matronly, elderly, motherly,
modest, chaste, virtuous, impeccable,
dignified, (un)marriageable, broody,
fecund, sterile, barren, (in)fertile,
(post)menopausal, childless, pregnant,
single, (un)married, (un)attached, free,
feminist, outspoken, active, sedentary,
strong-minded, contemporary, modern,
New, high-powered, rebellious,
revolutionary, extraordinary, malleable,
trail-blazing, self-reliant, independent,
liberal-minded, macho, professional,
career, helpless, subordinate, submissive,
subservient, acquiescent, plain, mannish,
unfeminine, wrinkled, frigid, matronly,
gutsy, bitchy, catty, cantankerous,
ill-natured, termagant, quarrelling,
quarrelsome, domineering, ebullient,
redoubtable, formidable, turbulent,
ill-tempered, sharp-tempered, vixenish,
whimpering, shrewish, gossipy, spiteful,
blowzy, affected, flighty, brazen, dowdy,
buxom, full-bosomed, bosomy,
coquettish, sexy, alluring, enticing,
tempting, seductive, provocative, receptive,
lewd, lecherous, voluptuous, sensual,
sensuous, approachable, beddable, loose,
frail, wanton, immoral, abandoned,
debauched, fallen, scandalous,
disreputable, ill-behaved, slatternly,
skittish, obscene, fickle, promiscuous,
unchaste, hoydenish, leering,
nymphomaniac; scarlet, honest

womanizer, womanizers determined,
inveterate, addicted, confirmed, habitual,
incorrigible

wonder (1: astonishment) See *astonishment*

wonder, wonders (2: marvel; wonderful
deed or event) unprecedented,
unbelievable, incredible, nine-days'

wood (1: timber; lumber) high-grade,
flawless, merchantable, clear, brittle,
brashy, knotty, soft, hard, bent, smooth,
rough, dense, sound, durable, heavy,
compact, laminate(d), cross-grained,
close-grained, fine-grained, curly-grained,
mottled, resinous, swollen, warped, rotten,
decayed, petrified, (rough-)sawn,
(hand-)inlaid, untreated

wood, woods (2: forest; woodland) verdant,
green, luxuriant, leafy, colourful,
enchanted, (sun-)dappled, tangled,
pathless, dense, thick, bushy, downy, deep,
impenetrable, shadowy, dark, gloomy,
houseless, primeval, wild, rooky,
coniferous, truncated, terraced, oozy, slimy

wool pure, virgin, resilient, soft, fine,
thick, scratchy, kinky, (fine-)textured,
bulky, clean, (machine-)washable,
homespun, bainin, berlin, cashmere, Aran,
Shetland, Angora, Merino, Botany;
mineral (rock)

word, words choice, sober, well-spoken,
well-chosen, discreet, measured,
appropriate, elegant, simple, precise, exact,
incisive, direct, significant, wise, courteous,
fair, civil, sympathetic, kind, merciful,
loving, tender, affectionate, pleasant,
gracious, magnificent, impressive,
passionate, peaceable, pacific, courageous,
brave, daring, moving, heart-warming,
gratifying, hopeful, audible, explicit,
confident, coherent, evocative, loaded,
magic, gushy, flowing, fine-sounding,
cadenced, rhythmical, resonant, brassy,
stentorian, baffling, earnest, satisfying,
apologetic, excusatory, hot, heated,
inflammatory, memorable, all-embracing,
operative, favoured, winged,
namby-pamby, honeyed, sweet, sugary,
hollow, insincere, superfluous, empty,
senseless, meaningless, futile, ill-chosen,
inappropriate, idiotic, unintelligible,
inaudible, stark, impetuous, poignant,
sharp, quizzical, facetious, jocular, witty,
sarcastic, derisive, wrathful, spiteful,
vicious, malicious, twisted, ambiguous,
belligerent, unkind, nasty, filthy, obscene,
naughty, objectionable, offensive, taboo,
hurtful, unprintable, indiscreet, pungent,
defamatory, hideous, libellous, incoherent,
venomous, scathing, virulent, angry, biting,
deceitful, bitter, searing, harsh, tough,
severe, vitriolic, black, heartless, merciless,
unfeeling, cruel, comfortless, moronic,

(un)genial, (un)translatable, coruscating,
elusive, cryptic, imitative, redundant,
made-up, sexist, dying, archaic,
obsolescent, obsolete, antiquated,
outmoded, colloquial, dialect,
interchangeable, technical, derivative,
distributive, atonic, trisyllabic,
monosyllabic, polysyllabic, multisyllabic,
portmanteau, demonstrative, interrogative,
echoic, poetic, rhetorical, onomatopoeic,
key, sight(-vocabulary), last, weasel,
scatological, nonce, household,
gender-specific, circumlocutory,
interlocutory, visceral, taboo,
augmentative, euphemistic, synonymous,
clitic, proclitic, enclitic, deictic, elative,
illative
wording careful, precise, (un)clear,
(un)intelligible, (un)ambiguous, sloppy,
careless, loose, obscure, intricate,
confused, complicated, random, rambling,
vague, legal, poetic
work careful, conscientious, congenial,
meaningful, seminal, honourable,
(un)productive, (in)efficient, exact(ing),
fastidious, exemplary, perfect, outstanding,
sterling, diligent, splendid, agreeable,
pleasant, challenging, promising, exciting,
skilled, expert, worthwhile, honest,
groundbreaking, superior, definitive,
active, all-consuming, absorbing, suitable,
satisfying, (un)rewarding, (un)productive,
non-routine, independent, uplifting,
monumental, voluminous, Herculean,
never-ending, unremitting, continuous,
perpetual, endless, burdensome, stressful,
hectic, feverish, wearisome, grinding,
backbreaking, painstaking, sweating,
sweated, irksome, concentrated, intense,
intensive, vigorous, arduous, hard,
unrelenting, relentless, ruthless, merciless,
pitiless, heartless, unstinted, unendurable,
harrowing, gruelling, strenuous, grinding,
tiring, heavy, toilsome, tiresome, harsh,
laborious, tenacious, unpleasant,
disagreeable, (hand-)blistering, punishing,
tough, delicate, time-consuming, risky,
dangerous, tedious, monotonous, boring,
humdrum, dreary, depressing, barren,
repetitive, routine, killing, brutal, servile,
menial, penal, cheap, inexpensive, costly,
low-paying, low-paid, unpaid, mucky,
unworthy, dirty, grimy, sweaty, careless,

slipshod, shoddy, sloppy, messy, spotty,
hasty, indifferent, mediocre, slovenly,
unprofessional, forced, controversial, raw,
complete, finished, ongoing, unstinting,
vicarious, facile, easy, sheer, timeless,
indoor, outdoor, collaborative, temporary,
casual, steady, permanent, seasonal,
regular, hack, voluntary, low-skill(ed),
(un)skilled, (un)organized, (non-)union,
intellectual, clerical, manual, physical,
paper, head, social, investigative,
restorative, insurable, promotional
work of art, works of art See *artefact*
worker, workers indispensable,
methodical, thorough, cheerful, careful,
dedicated, serious, earnest, zealous,
persistent, patient, stoic, strenuous, rapid,
speedy, industrious, untiring, tireless,
indefatigable, diligent, hardworking,
sedulous, assiduous, persevering,
top-quality, competent, dext(e)rous, smart,
(in)experienced, versatile, adaptable,
master, well-trained, high-wage, voluntary,
unsung, unrelenting, husky, well-built,
brawny, (un)productive, (in)capable,
(un)conscientious, (dis)loyal, (un)reliable,
(un)willing, (in)efficient, (un)qualified,
(un)skilful, (semi-)skilled, (un)handy,
ordinary, common, idle, gruff, slapdash,
careless, slow, indolent, unmotivated,
inferior, bungling, clumsy, awkward,
truant, errant, sluggish, desperate,
grim-faced, grimy, (il)legal, striking,
militant, (non-)union, redundant,
disgruntled, embittered, (un)organized,
low(er)-paid, (un)employed,
underemployed, soon-to-be-employed,
exploited, retired, steady, longtime, stable,
full-time, part-time, hourly, shift, day,
night, permanent, seasonal, temporary,
casual, essential, contingent, contract,
informal, immigrant, migrant, migratory,
transient, itinerant, expatriate,
replacement, scab, assembly-line, manual,
blue-collar, white-collar, industrial,
agricultural, social
workforce See also *worker* growing,
productive, cohesive, regular, casual
workload, workloads staggering, harsh,
heavy, horrendous, (un)manageable, light
workmanship delicate, exquisite, intricate,
nice, skilful, expert, fine, superior,
superlative, magnificent, astonishing,

astounding, unequalled, matchless, peerless, flawless, ingenious, perfect, solid, accomplished, dainty, finished, (in)accurate, cunning, rude, inferior, bad, abominable, crude, shoddy, faulty

works See *writing* (4)

workshop, workshops (1: a group of people working on a project) special, intimate, one-day, intensive, compulsory, mandatory, optional, live-in

workshop, workshops (2: a room where work is done) (un)tidy, busy, ramshackle, noisy

world, worlds perfect, stupendous, marvellous, problem-free, (un)civilized, weapon-free, mysterious, awesome, make-believe, possible, alternative, fast-paced, troubled, complicated, (war-)crazy, hectic, stressful, weird, topsy-turvy, complex, cold, cruel, imperfect, tough, incomprehensible, unintelligible, unfathomable, private, fantasy, dream, everyday, infernal, undersea, nether, physical, outside, mortal, future, other, prehistoric; Old, New; Third

worm, worms squirmy, curly, wriggly, wiggly, sluggish, slothful, parasitic, carnivorous, predatory, revolting, lowly, (in)active, tiny, microscopic, segmented, subterranean, marine, nematode, trematode, anaerobic

worrier, worriers chronic, habitual, born

worry, worries growing, pressing, tormenting, distressing, terrible, excessive, deep, vague, groundless, (un)necessary, (un)justifiable, (il)legitimate, chronic, persistent, (in)evitable, (un)avoidable, (un)manageable, (un)reasonable, vestigial, (un)founded, unjustified, latent, mental

worship consuming, engrossing, absorbing, inexpressible, mute, silent, calm, quiet, solemn, pure, tender, timid, timorous, bashful, childlike, faithful, servile, responsive, elemental, aphonic, divine, mystical, religious

worshipper, worshippers meditative, persevering, fervent, impassioned, earnest, serious, solemn-faced, self-possessed, devoted, devout, prayerful, sincere, ardent, silent, solitary, sole, pagan, devil

worth incalculable, sterling, genuine, true, intrinsic, fundamental, actual, essential, relative, net

wound, wounds gaping, bleeding, life-threatening, healing, slight, minor, superficial, surface, external, bloodless, new, fresh, recent, green, raw, severe, sharp, bitter, serious, grave, deep, nasty, bloody, oozy, old, permanent, irritable, ragged, tender, sore, painful, ugly, dangerous, angry, grievous, vital, massive, traumatic, dirty, fatal, lethal, mortal, deadly, incurable, immedicable, unhealed, self-inflicted, unexplained, septic, internal, open, closed, emotional, psychological, mental, physical

wrath See also *anger* divine, Achillean

wreck, wreckage smoking, burning, flaming, smouldering, rustling, writhing, tangled, ghastly, horrible, terrible, fatal, (un)identifiable, untowable

wrestler, wrestlers burly, massive, strong, grunting, brawny, muscular, amateur, professional, flyweight, bantamweight, featherweight, lightweight, welter-weight, middle-weight, light heavyweight, heavyweight, Greco-Roman, Catch-as-Catch-Can, sumo

wretch, wretches destitute, wicked, abandoned, profligate, shameless, besotted, poor

wrinkle, wrinkles fine, deep, aged, premature, facial

wrist, wrists powerful, thick, thin, slender, weak, floppy, bony, needle-scarred, mottled, swollen, twisted, turgid

writer, writers exquisite, magnificent, superb, unique, accomplished, careful, fastidious, diligent, brilliant, spirited, graceful, busy, fertile, (hyper)prolific, many-sided, versatile, protean, all-round, extensive, skilled, gifted, talented, able, felicitous, adept, delightful, volatile, tireless, indefatigable, inimitable, original, innovative, stunning, major, premier, prominent, renowned, celebrated, well-known, famous, notable, noted, (pre-)eminent, high-profile, foremost, illustrious, distinguished, revered, honoured, esteemed, veteran, sophisticated, superlative, powerful, expressive, outspoken, first-rate, big, breakthrough, recondite, knowledgeable, interesting, readable, novice, apprentice, would-be, budding, aspiring, struggling, promising, unread, hard-driven, anonymous, nameless, minor, little-known, un(be)known, unheard-of, obscure, misunderstood, frustrated, despondent, disaffected, radical, solitary, reclusive, self-centred, impressionable, preachy, failed, wordy, diffuse, verbose, prolix, crabbed, abusive, superficial, perceptive, intuitive, fanciful, logical, intellectual, sensational, passionate, evocative, populist, ethnic, expatriate, totemic, miscellaneous, hack, freelance, creative, comic, satirical, peripatetic, modernist, contemporary, antinomian

writing (1: style) See also *style* (1) crisp, concise, masterly, fine, (in)distinct, clear, plain, perspicuous, austere, tight, amiable, terse, virtuoso, erudite, discerning, perceptive, simple, straightforward, compulsive, (un)self-conscious, evocative, colloquial, colourful, sarcastic, sardonic, pungent, racy, arch, pedestrian, seditious, awkward, perplexing, intricate, puerile, salacious, spasmodic, choppy, waspish, watery, laboured, vituperative, vindictive, sloppy, hasty, truculent, vitriolic, disjointed, incoherent, abrupt, mediocre, banal, unoriginal, effeminate

writing (2: handwriting) See also *handwriting* backhanded, (in)distinct, clear, plain, crabbed, enchorial, (il)legible, minute, cursive, sloppy, cuneiform, phonetic, pictographic, italic, calligraphic, hieroglyphic, Kufic

writing (3: occupation of a writer) See *writer*

writing, writings (4: works) first-rate, high-calibre, avant-garde, landmark, prominent, lasting, enduring, permanent, voluminous, prolific, numerous, multifarious, extensive, monumental, erudite, abstruse, esoteric, exoteric, popular, (un)readable, lucid, occasional, sacred, extracanonical, prophetic, puerile, trivial, salacious, second-rate, desultory, creative, expository, pictorial, critical, scholarly, (semi-)fictitious, (auto)biographical, collected

wrong, wrongs grievous, flagrant, atrocious, severe, unpardonable, (un)correctable

wrongdoing serious, wicked, wilful, disgraceful, shameful, delinquent, beastly, bestial, felonious, alleged, (un)intentional, professional

yacht, yachts palatial, imperial, luxury, elegant, sleek, well-appointed, 21-metre, seagoing, sailing, pleasure, royal, toy, steam, motor

yard, yards (garden) See also *garden* front, back, rear

yarn three-ply, (un)tangled, man-made, natural, warp (vertical), weft (horizontal)

yawn, yawns tiny, deep, profuse, ostentatious, vulgar, ill-mannered, unrefined, stifled, suppressed

yawning See *yawn*

year, years peaceful, fruitful, triumphant, golden, abundant, crucial, momentous, dramatic, illustrious, early, next, recent, consecutive, passing, following, (in)coming, intervening, current, tumultuous, turbulent, hectic, weary, (un)eventful, dominant, traumatic, grim, drab, (un)successful, (un)prosperous, fruitless, lean, difficult, miserable, threadbare, penniless, waning, wasted, awful, bleak, lacklustre, adolescent, tender, young, immature, itinerant, reproductive, formative, watershed, war, financial, fiscal, college, school, academic, sabbatical, calendar (civil, legal), lean, liturgical, (bi)centennial, anniversary; leap, astronomical (natural), Platonic, lunar, round, equinoctial, tropical, sidereal

yearning, yearnings See *longing*

yell, yells See *scream*

yellow dazzling, gleaming, glaring, bold, sickly, rusty, smok(e)y, drab, lambent, dingy, dull, pale(ish), bright, vivid, brilliant, lustrous, cheery, sunny, pollen, pinkish, brownish, greenish, greyish, tawny, chrome, brassy, gold(en), metallic, lurid, buff, light, medium, dark, deep, canary, cream(y), splendid, cadmium, marigold, lemon, soft, clear, impassive, buttercup, sulphur, mustard, custard, Chinese

yield See *crop*

young man See *youth* and *boy*

young woman See *youth* and *girl*

youngster See *youth*

youth (1: young person) See also *teenager* and Appendixes A and B steady, reliable, vital, studious, obliging, suave, smug, mature, well-educated, fashion-conscious, stainless, clean-cut, neat, upright, promising, handsome, sweet-faced, personable, amiable, proper, fine, earnest, precocious, patrician, blithe, carefree, strong, muscular, sturdy, vigorous, well-set, athletic-looking, tall, gangling, lanky, weedy, bony, frail, awkward, gawky, clumsy, ungainly, angular, sedate, unruly, rowdy, crazy, ebullient, heady, disaffected, ill-disposed, wilful, rash, boisterous, rebellious, reckless, violence-prone, errant, wayward, troubled, wild, heedless, stubborn, spendthrift, impetuous, delinquent, heartless, unfeeling, immature, callow, dissolute, unemployable, fatuous, scruffy, inexperienced, superficial, trivial, materialistic, selfish, unsophisticated, naïve, conceited, ebullient, headstrong, hot-blooded, marriageable, eligible, nomadic, gilded

youth (2: young age) happy-go-lucky, carefree, blithe, profligate, wayward, presumptuous, eternal, fleeting, vanishing, misspent, misbegotten, long-gone, lost, jaded

zeal unflagging, rigid, single-minded, excessive, tremendous, boundless, extravagant, unbridled, fiery, ardent, animated, flaming, burning, fervent, feverish, fervid, intense, vigorous, vehement, (near-)fanatical, spirited, charismatic, bigoted, revolutionary, patriotic, religious

zealot, zealots intolerant, bigoted, dedicated, fanatical, blind, narrow-minded, opinionated, prejudiced, stubborn, religious, (neo-)Puritan

zest See *enthusiasm*

zone, zones (un)safe, exclusive, special, twilight, dead, autonomous, free, neutral, restricted, forbidden, controversial, disputable, self-proclaimed, military, combat, nuclear-free, frontier, time, free-trade, economic, climatic, seismic, demographic, tax-free, postal, fishing, archaeological, pedestrian, residential, school, riparian; temperate, torrid, frigid; Benioff (subduction)

zoo, zoos modern, progressive, humane, private, national

GOOD PERSONAL QUALITIES

able, above-board, abstemious, abstinent, accommodating, accurate, active, acute, adaptable, adept, affable, affectionate, agreeable, alert, ambitious, amiable, appreciative, approachable, articulate, aspiring, assiduous, astute, attentive, authoritative, avuncular

balanced, benevolent, benignant, big-hearted, bonhomous, bountiful, brainy, brave, breezy, bright, broad-minded

calm, candid, canny, capable, caring, cautious, charismatic, charming, cheerful, civic-minded, civilized, clear-eyed, clear-headed, clear-minded, clear-sighted, clever, close-lipped, close-mouthed, clubbable, cogent, collected, collegial, comely, companionable, compassionate, competent, compliant, composed, conciliatory, confident, conscientious, conservation-minded, considerate, contented, convivial, cool-headed, cooperative, correct, courageous, courteous, creative, credible, cultured

dapper, dauntless, debonair, decent, decided, dedicated, deferential, deft, delightful, demonstrative, dependable, determined, dexterous, diligent, direct, discerning, discreet, discriminating, disinterested, distinguished, distinguished-looking, dynamic

earnest, easy-going, effervescent, efficient, effusive, elegant, eloquent, eminent, emulous, energetic, enterprising, equable, equanimous, even-minded, even-tempered, expansive, experienced, extravert (extrovert)

fabulous, fair-minded, faithful, fascinating, fearless, fine, flexible, fluent, foresighted, forgiving, forthright, frank, friendly

generous, genial, gentle, gentlemanly, genuine, gingerly, giving, goal-orient(at)ed, good, good-hearted, good-humoured, good-natured, good-tempered, graceful, grateful, great-hearted, gregarious, guileless

handsome, handy, happy, hardworking, harmonious, health-conscious, healthy, heedful, helpful, high-minded, high-principled, high-spirited, holy, honest, honourable, hospitable, humane, humanitarian, humble, humorous

imaginative, impartial, impeccable, imperturbable, incisive, incorrupt, incorruptible, independent, indispensable, indulgent, industrious, ingenuous, intelligent, intent, interesting, intrepid, inventive

jaunty, jolly, judicious, just

keen, kind, kind-hearted, kindly, knowledgeable

large-hearted, large-minded, law-abiding, learned, liberal, likeable, literate, lively, lovable, lovely, loving, loyal

magnanimous, magnificent, mannerly, mature, merciful, methodical, meticulous, moderate, modest, moral

nationalistic, natty, natural, neighbourly, nice, noble-minded

obliging, observant, open, open-faced, open-minded, orderly, organized, original, outgoing

patient, peaceable, peaceful, peace-loving, penny-wise, perky, persevering, personable, perspicacious, placable, placid, plain-dealing, plain-spoken, pleasant,

pliable, plucky, poised, polished, polite,
precise, presentable, principled, productive,
proficient, progressive, prompt, prudent,
punctilious, punctual, purposeful

qualified, quick-witted

rational, realistic, reasonable, receptive,
redoubtable, refined, reform-minded,
regardful, reliable, remarkable, resilient,
resolute, resolved, resourceful, respectable,
respectful, responsible, righteous,
right-hand, right-thinking

sagacious, saintly, saving, scrupulous,
sedate, self-assured, self-confident,
self-made, self-possessed, self-reliant,
self-sacrificing, self-satisfied, self-sufficient,
sensible, sensitive, serious-minded, sharp,
sharp-witted, shrewd, silver-tongued,
sincere, single-hearted, skilled, skilful, slick,
smart, sober-minded, solid, spirited,
splendid, sprightly, spruce, spunky, stable,
staunch, steadfast, steady, sterling, stolid,
stout-hearted, straight(forward), strong,
strong-minded, strong-willed, suave,

substantial, subtle, supportive,
sweet(-tempered), sympathetic

tactful, talented, temperate, tender-hearted,
thoughtful, thrifty, tidy, tolerant, tractable,
trained, true, trustful, trusting, trustworthy,
trusty, truthful

unassuming, uncensorious, understanding,
unexceptionable, unprejudiced,
unpretending, unpretentious,
unquarrelsome, unruffled, unselfish,
unwavering, upright, upstanding, urbane

valiant, valorous, venerable, versatile,
vibrant, virtuous, vivacious

warm, warm-hearted, well-advised,
well-behaved, well-born, well-bred,
well-clad, well-conducted, well-disposed,
well-dressed, well-educated, well-groomed,
well-informed, well-mannered,
well-meaning, well-read, well-rounded,
well-spoken, well-trained, whole-souled,
wise, witty, wonderful, worthwhile, worthy

Appendix B
BAD PERSONAL QUALITIES

abandoned, abrasive, absurd, abusive, acerbic, acquisitive, acrimonious, adamant, addle-brained, addle-headed, addled, adulterous, aggressive, aimless, alcoholic, amoral, animalistic, annoying, anomalous, anti-social, apostate, arbitrary, arrogant, ashamed, assertive, avaricious, awkward

backward, bad, bad-tempered, barbarous, base, base-born, bellicose, belligerent, bibulous, bigamous, bigoted, bilious, bitter, blatant, blowzy, blundering, blunt, blustering, boastful, boisterous, boorish, boring, bossy, bovine, brainless, brassy, brazen(-faced), brutal, brutish, bull-headed, bumptious, bungling

cacophonous, calculating, callous, cantankerous, captious, careless, carping, changeable, cheap, chicken-hearted, chicken-livered, chilly, choleric, choosy, churlish, close, close-fisted, clumsy, coarse, cocksure, cocky, cold, cold-blooded, cold-hearted, combative, complaining, conceited, condescending, confused, conscienceless, contemptible, contentious, contradictory, contrary, contumacious, corrupt, covetous, cowardly, crabbed, crabby, crack-brained, crafty, cranky, craven, crazy, crooked, cross-grained, crotchety, cruel, cunning

daft, dangerous, dastardly, debauched, decadent, deceitful, deceptive, defiant, degenerate, degraded, delirious, demanding, dense, depraved, derelict, designing, despicable, despondent, despotic, destructive, detestable, devious, dictatorial, difficult, diffident, dilatory, dim-witted, dirty, disagreeable, discontented, discourteous, discriminatory, disdainful, dishonest, dishonourable, disingenuous, disloyal, disobedient, disorderly, disorganized, disparaging, displeasing,

disputatious, disregardful, disreputable, disrespectable, disrespectful, dissatisfied, dissentious, dissipated, dissolute, distrustful, divisive, dogged, dogmatic, doltish, domineering, dotty, double-dealing, double-faced, double-tongued, dour, drunk(en), dubious, dull, dull-witted, dumb, duplicitous, dyspeptic

edgy, egoistic, egotistic, envious, erotic, evasive, evil, evil-minded, excitable, explosive, extravagant, extremist

faint-hearted, faithless, fair-weather, false, false-hearted, fanatic, fanatical, fastidious, fault-finding, feckless, feeble, fickle, fiendish, filthy, finical, finicky, flaccid, flighty, flippant, foolhardy, foolish, forgetful, foul(-mouthed), foul-tongued, foxy, fractious, frenzied, fretful, frivolous, frothy, furious, fussy

garrulous, gawky, giddy, gloomy, gluttonous, gossipy, grasping, greedy, green-eyed, grey, grouchy, grovelling, gruff, grumpy, guileful, gullible, gusty

hard-headed, hard-hearted, hare-brained, harsh, hasty, haughty, headstrong, heady, heavy-handed, heedless, helpless, hesitant, hidebound, high-handed, high(ly)-strung, hoggish, hoity-toity, hollow-hearted, horrible, hostile, hot-blooded, hot-headed, hot-tempered, hypercritical, hypochondriac, hypocritical, hysterical

ignorant, ill-advised, ill-behaved, ill-bred, ill-conditioned, ill-disposed, ill-humoured, illiberal, illiterate, ill-mannered, ill-natured, ill-tempered, immature, immoderate, immoral, impassive, impatient, impertinent, impetuous, impious, impish, impolite, impolitic, impossible, impractical, improvident, imprudent, impudent, impulsive, inactive, inane, inappreciative, inattentive, incautious, incompetent, inconsiderate, inconsistent, incorrigible, indecisive, indifferent, indiscreet, indolent, ineffective, ineffectual, inefficient, inept, inflexible, iniquitous, injudicious, insecure, insensitive, insignificant, insincere, insipid, insolent, insubordinate, insulting, insupportable, intemperate, intolerable, intolerant, intractable, introvert, irascible, irrational, irregular, irresolute, irreverent, irritable

jealous

knavish

lackadaisical, laggard, languid, lascivious, lawless, lazy, leering, lethargic, lewd, libertine, licentious, light-fingered, light-headed, light-minded, lily-livered, listless, long-winded, loose, loud-mouthed, low-minded, lubricious, lustful

magniloquent, maladroit, malicious, manipulative, mannerless, marginal, mawkish, mealy-mouthed, mean, mean-spirited, meddlesome, mendacious, merciless, messy, mincing, mischievous, miscreant, miserly, misogynous, money-grubbing, moody, mousy, mouthy, murderous, mutable

narrow-minded, nasty, naughty, nefarious, negative, neglectful, negligent, nervous, niggardly, niggling, noisy

oafish, obdurate, objectionable, obnoxious, obsequious, obstinate, obstreperous, obstructionist, obtrusive, obtuse, odious, offensive, officious, open-mouthed, opinionated, oppressive, oppugnant, ostentatious, out-of-shape, overbearing, over-exacting, overweening

parsimonious, partial, peevish, penurious, perfidious, pert, perverse, pestiferous, pestilent, pettish, petty, petulant, phlegmatic, pigeon-hearted, pigeon-livered, piggish, pig-headed, pitiless, pompous, poor-spirited, pound-foolish, prejudiced, prejudicial, presumptuous, pretentious, prickly, prodigal, profligate, prurient,

prying, puckish, puerile, pugnacious, purchasable, purse-proud, pushing, pushy, pusillanimous

quarrelsome, queer, querulous, quick-tempered, quixotic

racist, rakish, rapacious, rascally, rash, rattle-brained, raucous, raving, raw, recalcitrant, reckless, refractory, remiss, remorseless, repetitious, reprehensible, reptilian, resentful, revengeful, ridiculous, rigid, roguish, rude, ruffianly, ruthless

sacrilegious, salacious, sanctimonious, sardonic, saturnine, saucy, scatterbrained, scheming, scoundrelly, scrappy, screwy, scruffy, scummy, scurrilous, self-absorbed, self-centred, self-important, selfish, self-serving, self-styled, self-willed, servile, shallow, shameless, sharp-tempered, sharp-tongued, sheepish, shiftless, shifty, short-tempered, shrewish, show-off, silly, sinful, sinister, sleazy, slipshod, slothful, slovenly, sluggish, sluttish, sly, small-minded, smarmy, snappish, snarling, sneaky, snide, snippy, snobbish, snobby, snotty, sottish, sour, sour-tempered, spineless, spiny, spiritless, spiteful, squeamish, squint-eyed, stingy, stodgy, stolid, stony-hearted, stubborn, stupid, subservient, suicidal, supercilious, superficial, surly

tactless, tart, temperamental, tenacious, tense, terrible, testy, tetchy, thankless, Thersitic, thick-skinned, thieving, thin-skinned, thoughtless, thriftless, tight, time-serving, timid, timorous, tiresome, toadyish, toplofty, tortuous, touchy, tough-minded, traitorous, treacherous, tricky, trifling, troublesome, truculent, two-faced, tyrannical

ugly, umbrageous, unadvised, unambitious, unappreciative, uncaring, unceremonious, uncivilized, uncommunicative, uncouth, uncreative, uncultured, undecided, undependable, undesirable, uneasy, uneducated, unemployable, unethical, unfair, unfaithful, unfeeling, unforgiving, unfriendly, ungenerous, ungrateful, unhandy, unhappy, unimaginative,

unintelligent, uninteresting, unjust,
unkempt, unkind, unlearned, unlettered,
unmanageable, unmannerly, unmindful,
unpleasant, unpolished, unprincipled,
unproductive, unread, unreliable,
unrighteous, unruly, unscrupulous,
unskilful, unsociable, unsophisticated,
unstable, unsteady, unsubtle, unthankful,
untidy, untrained, untruthful, untutored,
unwise, unworthy, unyielding, upstart,
useless, uxorious

vain, vainglorious, venal, vengeful, vicious,
vile, villainous, vindictive, violent,

visionless, vixenish, vociferous, volatile,
voracious, vulgar

wanton, wasteful, wavering, wayward,
weak, weak-minded, weak-spirited,
weak-willed, whimsical, whiny,
white-livered, wicked, wilful, wily,
wishy-washy, withdrawn, witless,
wooden-headed, worthless, wretched,
wrongful, wrong-headed, wrong-minded

yellow

SIMILES WITH ADJECTIVES

as *adroit* as a rhinoceros [jocular]

as *agile* as a cat

as *airy* as a bird-cage

as *ancient* as civilization (or as the Pyramids)

as *angry* as a tiger (or as a hornet)

as *antediluvian* as dinosaurs

as *arid* as a desert

as *artful* as a cart-(or waggon-)load of monkeys

as *bald* as a coot (or as an egg, or an orange)

as *bare* as a baby's bottom

as *beautiful* as a butterfly

as *big* as a house

as *bitter* as gall (or as aloes)

as *black* as coal (or as pitch, or the Pit, or soot, or a crock, or ebony, or your hat, or midnight, or jet, or ink)

as *blind* as a bat (or as a beetle, or a mole)

as *blithe* as a lark

as *blue* as the sky

as *bold* as brass (or as a lion)

as *bouncy* as a ball

as *boundless* as hope (or as the ocean)

as *brave* as a lion (or as a hawk)

as *bright* as a new pin (or as a button, or a spring morning, or day, or noonday, or the light, or silver)

as *brittle* as glass

as *broad* as a beam

as *brown* as a berry (or as fallen pine-needles in October)

as *busy* as a bee (or as Piccadilly Circus)

as *changeable* as the moon (or as a weathercock, or the barometer)

as *chaotic* as a rag-bag

as *chaste* as ice

as *cheap* as dirt

as *cheerful* as a lark

as *cheerless* as a prison

as *clean* as a whistle (or as a ball-room floor, or a sound sheep's heart)

as *clear* as crystal (or as glass, or the day, or the sun, or a tide-mark) [jocularly, as *clear* as mud]

as *clever* (*artful; crafty*) as a cart-(or waggon-) load of monkeys

as *cold* as charity (or as a well, or a fish, or a frog, or a stone, or marble, or impalpable ice, or icicles, or winter)

as *constant* as the northern star

as *cool* [i.e. calm] as a cucumber (or as ice, or a flea)

as *crafty* as the devil

as *cross* as a bear with a sore head (or as two sticks, or a tiger)

as *crowded* as Piccadilly Circus

as *cunning* as a fox

as *curious* as a cat

as *daft* as a brush

as *damp* as a swamp (or as a squib)

as *dangerous* as a dynamite bomb (or as sunstroke)

as *dark* as night (or as midnight, or pitch, or the inside of a whale)

as *dead* as a door-nail (or as a dodo, or mutton, or a herring, or Mars, or Queen Anne)

as *deaf* as a post (or as an adder, or as a tradesman's dummy)

as *deep* as the ocean (or as a well, or the sea)

as *delicate* as an eggshell

as *demure* as a nun

as *dewy* as a garden at dawn

as *different* as chalk from cheese (or as the poles)

as *distant* as the Alps

as *distinct* as white lace on velvet

as *dormant* as a winter field

as *dreamless* as the sleep of death

as *drowsy* (*sleepy*) as a doormouse

as *drunk* as a lord (or as a newt, or as Chloë)

as *dry* as a bone (or as summer dust, or a stick, or a mummy, or a biscuit, or parchment, or a lime kiln)
as *dull* as ditch-water (or as a bat)
as *dumb* as a statue (or as an image of stone)

as *eager* as a greyhound on his game
as *easy* as kiss (or as kissing) your hand (or as falling off a log, or ABC)
as *elusive* as a shadow
as *empty* as an echo
as *entrancing* as mystery
as *envious* as Satan
as *ephemeral* as a rainbow (or as the dawn)

as *fair* as a rose (or as a lily)
as *fast* as a hare
as *fat* as aldermen (or as butter, or a pig)
as *feeble* as a kitten
as *fickle* as a changeful dream
as *fierce* as a tiger (or as a famished wolf, or the winter wind on an open sea)
as *fine* as a lily
as *firm* as a rock (or as the oak on rocky heights)
as *fit* as a fiddle
as *fitful* as a bat
as *flat* as a pancake (or as a board)
as *fleet* as a deer
as *fleeting* as a cloud
as *fragile* as a sparrow (or as china, or a dream)
as *fragrant* as lilacs
as *frail* as a lily
as *free* as a bird (or as the air, or the four winds)
as *fresh* as a daisy (or as a rose, or a garden at dawn, or paint)
as *friendly* as a squirrel
as *full* of holes as a net
as *full* of notes as a bird

as *gaudy* as a butterfly (or as a peacock)
as *gay* as a lark (or as a spring morning, or the spring)
as *gentle* as a lamb (or as the dawning of light)
as *gloomy* as a thunderstorm (or as a gaol, or the Labrador coasts)
as *glum* as an undertaker
as *good* as a play [i.e., very delightful, or amusing]

as *good* as gold [i.e., valuable, or very well-behaved]
as *gorgeous* as the sunset
as *graceful* as a bird (or as a swan)
as *gracious* as a fairy
as *grasping* as a miser
as *grave* as a judge (or as an organ, or the song of the nightingale)
as *greedy* as a dog (or as a wolf)
as *green* as grass
as *grey* as sea fog (or as a whale)
as *gruff* as a bear

as *happy* (or *jolly*) as a sandboy (or as a lark, or the day is long, or a king, or a rose-tree in sunshine)
as *hard* as a brick (or as a rock, or iron, or marble, or flint, or stone, or adamant, or nails)
as *hardy* as a wolf
as *harmless* as a dove
as *harsh* as truth
as *hateful* as ugly
as *haunting* as a ghost
as *healthy* as a May-hedge in flower
as *heavy* as lead
as *high* as the sky (or as a mountain)
as *high* as a kite [i.e. intoxicated]
as *hoarse* as a crow
as *honest* as the day (or as the day is long)
as *hot* as hell (or as fire, or pepper, or pitch, or Hades, or dog-days)
as *hungry* as a hunter (or as a bear, or a pack of wolves)
as *hushed* as a desert

as *immeasurable* as the sea
as *immovable* as granite
as *impartial* as sunshine
as *impassive* as a toad
as *impenetrable* as granite
as *impersonal* as stars
as *impervious* as adamant
as *impressionless* as adamant
as *inaccessible* as a god
as *inanimate* as stone
as *inarticulate* as the bubbling of the rivers
as *incessant* as the sea-birds wheeling on the wind
as *ineluctable* as gravitation
as *inflexible* as an oak
as *inhospitable* as a snow bank
as *innocent* as a babe unborn (or as a

new-born babe, or a dove, or the young
moon, or a flower on the altar of the
Madonna)
as *insecure* as card castles
as *insensible* as bronze
as *intangible* as the ether (or as
sunlight)
as *invigorating* as a sea breeze

as *joyous* as the cadence of the sea
as *jumpy* as a goat (or as a kitten)

as *keen* as mustard

as *large* as life [jocularly: large as life and
twice as natural]
as *lean* as a greyhound (or as a rasher)
as *light* as a feather (or as thistledown, or
air, or a zephyr, or the sweep of a cloud)
[*light* being here opposed to *heavy*]
as *light* as a butterfly [*light* being here
opposed to *grave*]
as *like* as two peas (or as eggs, or daisies, or
lilies, or two brothers, or two beans, or
two drops of water)
as *limp* as a rag doll
as *lively* as a cricket
as *lonely* as the dawn
as *loose* as a rope of sand [*loose* here means
incoherent]
as *loud* as thunder
as *lovely* as a landscape in a dream
as *luminous* as stars
as *luscious* as the bloom on a peach

as *mad* as a March hare (or as a hatter)
as *mean* (*miserly*) as Shylock
as *meek* as a lamb
as *melancholy* as a gib cat (or as a bugged
bear)
as *mellow* as a golden flute (or the note of a
thrush in springtime)
as *merciless* as death
as *merry* as crickets (or as the month of
May, or monkeys, or blackbirds, or
clowns)
as *mighty* as the sword
as *mild* as a heifer
as *mischievous* as a monkey
as *modest* as a violet
as *motionless* as a statue (or as the summer
night, or a cypress shadow in the
moonlight)

as *musical* as a bird's song (or as purling
water)
as *mute* as a fish (or as mice)
as *mysterious* as death
as *mystic* as the wind

as *naked* as a jaybird
as *neat* as a pin
as *nervous* as a cat (or as a kitten, or a
squirrel's tail)

as *obstinate* as a mule
as *obvious* as the sea
as *old* as Methuselah (or as the hills, or
Adam, or man, or the sea, or the
stars)
as *opaque* as a wall
as *open* as daylight

as *pale* (or *pallid*) as marble (or as a ghost,
or death, or wax, or ashes, or a pearl)
as *patient* as Job (or as an ox)
as *pensive* as a forest
as *pervasive* as sunshine
as *piercing* as a gimlet
as *plain* as a pikestaff (or as the nose on
your face, or print, or day, or the sun in
the sky)
as *playful* as a kitten
as *pleased* as a dog with two tails (or as
Punch)
as *plentiful* as blackberries
as *plump* as a partridge (or as a quail)
as *poor* as a church mouse (or as Lazarus)
as *portly* as a seal
as *powerful* as a blacksmith's bellows
as *pretty* as a picture
as *prompt* as an echo
as *prosaic* as an auction catalogue
as *proud* as a peacock (or as Punch, or
Lucifer)
as *puffy* as cotton
as *pulseless* as a corpse
as *pure* as (the driven) snow (or as a drop of
dew, or an opal)
as *purposeless* as dreams

as *quick* as a flash (or as lightning, or
thought, or a swallow's turn in
flight)
as *quiet* as a mouse (or as mice, or a lamb,
or the grave, or a sepulchre, or a shadow,
or death)

as *radiant* as a spring morning (or as summer sunshine)

as *rapid* as lightning

as *rare* as a diamond

as *red* as a rose (or as a turkey-cock, or a beetroot, or blood, or coral, or fire, or a cherry, or a soldier's coat, or a cardinal's hat)

as *red-cheeked* as a winter apple

as *refreshing* as a draft from a cool spring

as *regal* as a king

as *regular* as clockwork

as *remote* as the Pole

as *restless* as a swallow (or as the sea)

as *rich* as Croesus

as *right* as a trivet (or as rain)

as *rigid* as quills (or as iron) [jocularly: as *rigid* as a concertina]

as *ripe* as a cherry

as *round* as a barrel (or as an orange, or an apple, or a ball, or a globe)

as *safe* as houses (or as the Bank of England)

as *salt* as the sea (or as brine, or a herring)

as *secret* as a grave (or as the grave)

as *secure* as sleep

as *serene* as a happy dream

as *shallow* as a looking-glass (or as a tin pan)

as *sharp* as a razor (or as a needle, or a two-edged sword)

as *shining* as moonlight

as *shy* as a girl (or as a mouse)

as *sick* as a dog (or as a pig, or a parrot, or a cat)

as *silent* as the grave (or as death, or the dead, or the stars, or the hush of evening, or the tender hush of twilight)

as *silly* as a goose (or as a sheep)

as *skinny* as a reed (or as a scraped shinbone) as *slender* as gossamer

as *slim* as a mannequin

as *slippery* as an eel

as *slow* as a snail (or as a turtle, or a tortoise)

as *sly* as a fox

as *smooth* as silk (or as velvet, or butter, or oil)

as *sober* as a judge [i.e. *solemn*]

as *soft* as butter (or as down, or wax, or a rose-leaf, or a snowflake, or moonlight)

as *solemn* as a requiem (or as temples)

as *solid* as the Rock of Gibraltar (or as rock)

as *solitary* as an eagle in the sky above the hills

as *sound* as a bell

as *sour* as vinegar (or as a crab [i.e. the wild apple])

as *spacious* as the skies

as *sparkling* as the dewy grass

as *startled* as a deer

as *stationary* as a stone

as *steady* as a rock (or as steel)

as *sticky* as glue

as *stiff* as a poker (or as a post, or a ramrod, or bristles)

as *still* as death (or as the grave, or a corpse, or a stone, or a statue, or a forest path, or a crouched tigress, or the night)

as *straight* as a ruler (or as an arrow, or a die, or sunflower stalks, or a candle) [i.e. uncurved]

as *straight* as a homing dove [i.e. direct]

as *straight-faced* as an owl

as *strong* as a horse (or as a lion, or an ox)

as *stubborn* as a mule

as *stupid* as a donkey

as *suave* as a Roman prelate

as *sudden* as lightning

as *supple* as a panther (or as an eel, or a serpent)

as *sure* as death (or as bloom follows bud, or a gun, or Sunday)

as *surly* as a bear

as *sweet* as a nut (or as sugar, or honey, or the fragrance from a rose)

as *swift* as an arrow (or as lightning, or thought, or the wind, or the flash of a sunbeam)

as *taciturn* as an Indian

as *tall* as a giant (or as a maypole, or a steeple, or a beanstalk)

as *tame* as a cat

as *tenacious* as a bulldog

as *tender* as a chicken (or as a baby's finger-tips)

as *thick* as a cable (or as hailstones, or hail)

as *thick* as blackberries [i.e. plentiful]

as *thick* as thieves [i.e. closely bound]

as *thick* as two short planks [i.e. stupid]

as *thin* as a lath (or as a wafer, or a rake, or a post, or a reed, or a shadow, or the gash of a razor, or a thread of a spider's web)

as *tight* as a drum

as *tight* as a tick [i.e. drunk]

as *timeless* as clouds

as *timid* as a hare

as *tough* as leather (or as old boots)

as *transient* as a breath upon a mirror (or as the dew, or a dewdrop)

as *trenchant* as an axe

as *tricky* as a monkey

as *true* as steel (or as grit, or the dial to the sun)

as *ugly* as sin (or as a scarecrow, or a toad, or an old hack)

as *uncomplaining* as a lamb

as *uncompromising* as justice (or as a straight line)

as *ungraspable* as a butterfly

as *unintentional* as the birth of a thought in the mind

as *unstable* as water

as *unvaried* as the note of the cuckoo

as *unyielding* as a trap

as *vacant* as an untenanted house

as *vain* as a peacock

as *valiant* as a lion

as *vast* as eternity

as *warm* as toast (or as wool, or a kitten)

as *watchful* as a hawk

as *watertight* as submarines

as *weak* as water (or as a baby, or a cat, or a kitten)

as *weightless* as a feather

as *welcome* as ice in summer

as *wet* as a drowned rat

as *white* as a sheet (or as snow, or death, or a lily, or wool, or a tallow candle)

as *whiteheaded* as a mountain

as *wicked* as the devil

as *wild* as a spark (or as a young colt)

as *wise* as Solomon (or as an owl, or a judge, or a serpent)

as *yellow* as mustard (or as a guinea, or a quince)

as *yielding* as wax